A Library of Universal Literature

IN FOUR PARTS

Comprising Science, Biography, Fiction and the Great Orations

PART TWO—BIOGRAPHY

Memoirs of Napoleon Bonaparte

FROM THE FRENCH OF

M. FAUVELET DE BOURRIENNE

BY

JOHN S. MEMES, LL.D.

NEW YORK

P. F. COLLIER AND SON

· M C M I ·

31

**PRESS OF
P. F. COLLIER & SON**

51160

A LIBRARY OF

UNIVERSAL LITERATURE

BIOGRAPHY

VOLUME THIRTY-ONE

MEMOIRS OF NAPOLEON BONAPARTE

CHAPTER I

This Biography's Claim to Authenticity — Birth and Parentage of Napoleon Bonaparte — His Education and Early Character — First Military Appointment

THE desire of commercial profit could alone have given birth to the torrent of publications which have appeared about NAPOLEON. While perusing these works —whether they assume the guise of historical narratives, or secret memoirs—one knows not which most to admire: the audacity of some compilers, or the easy faith of certain readers. These gross and undigested collections of ridiculous anecdotes and absurd disquisitions, of fictitious crimes and imaginary virtues, heaped together in daring disregard of date or order, instead of being consigned to merited contempt or speedy oblivion, find, in these our days, speculators ready to turn them to account, and, more wonderful still, obtain zealous partisans—enthusiastic apologists. Once, for a moment, I entertained the thought of exposing the numerous errors which thus abound on my present subject. But the idea was quickly renounced. The task would have proved too laborious in my case, and its results far too tedious for the reader.

Concerning that extraordinary man, whose name alone constituted a power to which we can with difficulty find a parallel, I am about to state all I know—all that I am confident I know well, and in my own belief, more perfectly than any one else—that which I have seen and heard, and on which I have retained copious notes. The intimate relations I enjoyed at all hours, and for so long a period, with

(8)

the General, the Consul, the Emperor, placed me in a situation to observe and to appreciate whatever was transacted—whatever was even projected—during that space. Not only was I admitted to unreserved confidence, while so many important events were planned, and their issues decided, but every day, notwithstanding the absorbing labor of almost continual occupation in those very affairs I now narrate, I found means to employ the brief leisure left me, in amassing the important documents exclusively in my possession; in taking notes; in registering for history the truth of facts so difficult to ascertain; and, above all, in preserving those profound, brilliant, pointed, and almost always remarkable sayings which burst from the ardent mind of Bonaparte, during the unrestrained flow of unstudied converse.

If, then, it be asked, why should we repose more confidence in you than in others who have written before you? my answer is a plain one. I enter upon my task now, at the eleventh hour; I have read ALL that my predecessors have published; I have an inward consciousness that all I state is true; I have no interest in deceiving, no disgrace to fear, no reward to expect; I have no desire either to obscure or to embellish the glory of Napoleon. I speak of him as I have seen, known, often admired, sometimes blamed him: in every circumstance, I relate what I have witnessed, heard, written, thought. I allow myself to be swayed by no illusions of imagination—neither by love nor by hatred. I shall not insert even a reflection which did not arise on the occurrence of the event that called it forth. Alas! how much awaits me to disclose, foreign to my character, feelings and principles, over which I can but grieve!

The assurance, also, that my intention always was to write and publish these Memoirs, ought to conciliate confidence; since, at the same time, I ever adhered to an unalterable resolution not to give them to the world, until it should be possible for me to speak the truth—the whole truth. For this reason, while Napoleon reigned in the plenitude of power, I withstood his pressing commands, and the entreaties of the greatest personages of the times. Truth would then sometimes have seemed flattery, and not infrequently, too, there would have been danger in its avowal. When, at a later period, the progress of events had relegated Bonaparte to a distant isle of the ocean, other considerations imposed upon me silence—considerations of propriety and of feeling. When death had removed these, other causes retarded the accomplishment of my design. The tranquillity of a retreat was requisite, to enable me to collect, compare and arrange the voluminous materials at my disposal. I had need, also, of a long course of reading, in order to rectify important errors, stated by some writers, through deficiency of authentic documents. The wished-for leisure I have now found.

Finally, it is not the entire life of Napoleon that I write. The reader, therefore, ought not to expect to find in these Memoirs the uninterrupted series of all his battles and his sixty victories. I shall speak but seldom of those events which I have not witnessed, of what I have not heard, or of any fact unsupported by official documents. Let every one do as much. To proceed:

NAPOLEON BONAPARTE was born at Ajaccio, in Corsica, on the 15th of August, 1769. The name had formerly been written *Buonaparte;* but, during his first campaign in Italy, he dropped the *u.* In this change he had no other motives than to assimilate the orthography to the pronunciation, and to abbreviate his signature. Some pretend that he gave himself out for a year younger than his real age, having been born in 1768. For this assertion there is no ground. To me, he always represented the 15th August, 1769, as his birthday; and, as I first saw the light on the 9th July of the same year, we loved to find, while at the Military School of Brienne, in this fortuitous concurrence of dates, an additional reason for our union and our friendship. The following extract from the register of M. Berton, sub-principal of the college, supports my reply to the above causeless supposition:

"Napoleon Buonaparte entered the Royal Military School of Brienne-la-Château, at the age of nine years, eight months, and four days. He remained there five years, five months, twenty-seven days, and removed, at the age of fifteen years, two months, two days, to enter the Military Academy of Paris, as appears from the register of the King's scholars, thus: '17th October, 1784, Passed from the Royal Military School of Brienne, M. Napoleon de Buonaparte, *Gentleman*, born in the city of Ajaccio, in the island of Corsica, 15th August, 1769, son of Charles-Marie de Buonaparte, *Noble*, Deputy of the Nobles of Corsica, inhabitant of the city of Ajaccio, and of Dame Lætitia Ramolyno, his wife, according to the certificate transcribed into the register of matriculation here, folio 31. He was received into this establishment 23d April, 1779.'"

This document, while it removes all doubts regarding Bonaparte's true age, also discredits those false aspersions which have been disseminated, touching the lowness of his extraction. His family certainly possessed no fortune: so far, remarks on this subject have been just. Not only was Bonaparte educated at the expense of the state—a royal benevolence extended to many youths of honorable parentage—but we likewise perceive, from the following petition, presented by his father to M. de Ségur, then minister at war, what circumstances obliged him again to solicit the same bounty in favor of one of Napoleon's brothers:

"MY LORD—Charles Buonaparte, of Ajaccio, in Corsica, reduced to indigence by an attempt to drain the salt marshes, and by the injustice of the Jesuits, who deprived him of the estate of Odonne, which had devolved to him, and which is now attached to the fund for public instruction, has the honor to inform you that his younger son has attended, during six years, at the Royal Military School at Brienne, and has always comported himself in a distinguished manner, as you may easily know, my lord, by referring to his certificates: that, according to the advice of M. le Comte Marbœuf, he has directed his studies to the naval service. His success has been such, that he was destined, by M. de Keralio, for the school at Paris, and afterward for the department of Toulon. The resignation of the former inspector, my lord, has changed the prospects of my son, who has now no longer any classes at college, except the mathematical, and is at the head of his division, with the suffrage of all his masters. The petitioner has boarded his third son at the same college of Brienne, in order that he may succeed to his brother's place. He has the honor to inclose the professor's certificate, and the extract of baptism, supplicating you, my lord, on giving a commission to his second son, to admit, as King's scholar, his third son, now nine years old, and supported at the expense of the petitioner, who has no longer the means of paying his salary and board. You cannot, my lord, perform an act of greater charity, than by thus assisting a family who find themselves without means, who have always faithfully served the King, and who will redouble their efforts for the good of the service.

"And the petitioner, etc., etc.   BUONAPARTE."

The minister has written on the top of this letter, "Return the usual answer, if a vacancy." On the margin is to be read, "This gentleman has been informed that his request cannot be granted while his second son shall be at the Military School of Brienne, two brothers not being admitted King's scholars at the same time in the military colleges."

At this era, the young Napoleon had not yet completed his fourteenth year. His father petitioned that he might be placed, as probably were all the youthful pensioners of from fourteen to sixteen years of age, who could command a slight degree of interest and favor, that is to say, as sublieutenant in a regiment. When Napoleon had attained the age of fifteen, he was sent to Paris till the proper period for entering the army. It appears that Lucien was not immediately named King's scholar; at least, that he did not receive his appointment before Napoleon had quitted the Military School of Paris.

I shall quote hereafter another document, likewise proving the unfortunate situation and the honorable connections

of this family in Corsica. Bonaparte, then, claimed to be
what is termed *well-born*. I have seen his genealogy, which
he caused to be sent from Tuscany to Milan, and which is
quite authentic. In several works mention is made of certain civil dissensions which had forced his family to leave
Italy and seek refuge in Sicily. Of these transactions I
know nothing.

Much, and in a very opposite spirit, has been said of
Napoleon's boyhood. Enthusiasm and ridiculous exaggeration have been alike at work. Writers have painted the boy
in the blackest colors, in order to have the pleasure afterward of making a monster of the man. It will ever be thus
with those whom their own genius or circumstances elevate
above their compeers. Why constantly endeavor to discover
in the first acts of infancy the germ of great crimes or of
shining virtues? This is to view too abstractedly those
circumstances—sports of fortune, and trains of events—
which often, as if in spite of himself, urge on the individual
to the highest renown. Men absolutely will have it, that he
who has distinguished his manhood should likewise have
exhibited an extraordinary infancy; yet, does not experience
show, that in truth one child can differ little from the
ordinary run? and how often do we find precocious talent,
promising the most brilliant future, pass through life in
a manner truly insignificant? Bonaparte himself laughed
heartily at all such fables, and at all those fooleries with
which writings, dictated by admiration or hatred, have em-
bellished or blackened his early years. I may here recall
a simple anecdote, which will be immediately recognized as
the original of numberless inventions and misrepresentations.

During the winter of 1788-84, so memorable for heavy
falls of snow, which everywhere lay to the depth of six or
eight feet, young Napoleon showed himself singularly out
of sorts. No more little gardens—none of the delightful
seclusion he so much courted. During his play hours, he
was constrained to mingle with the crowd of his companions,
and to walk with them backward and forward in a large

hall. In order to escape from this tiresome exercise, Napoleon contrived to stir up the whole school, by the proposal of a different amusement. This was to clear various passages through the snow in the great court, and with shovels to erect horn-works, dig trenches, raise parapets, construct platforms, etc. "The first labor finished," said he, "we can divide into parties, and form a kind of siege; and, as inventor of this new sport, I undertake to direct the attacks." Our joyous troop entered into this project with enthusiasm: it was executed, and the mimic combat maintained for the space of fifteen days. Indeed, our warfare ceased not, till, by gravel and small stones mixing with the snow, of which we made our balls, many of the students, besiegers as well as besieged, had been pretty seriously wounded. I remember well that, of all the scholars, none was more severely pelted than myself with these missiles.

It would be useless here to disprove various unfounded incidents of early life, such as the foolhardy adventure of Blanchard's balloon, falsely attributed to young Bonaparte. His thoughts were, in fact, soon directed to far other objects: he was occupied with the political sciences. A letter from the principal of the school of Brienne, since communicated to me, states that, of his vacations, one was passed there, while the preceding had been devoted to the society of the famous Abbé Raynal, who was good enough to receive and converse with the young student upon government, legislation, commerce and other similar subjects.

At our holiday fêtes, to which all the inhabitants of the place received invitations, guards were established for the maintenance of order, no one being permitted to pass to the inner hall without a ticket signed by the principal or sub-principal. The dignities of officer and subaltern were conferred only on the most distinguished; and, as ranking among these, there happened to Bonaparte, who commanded a station, a little adventure, which I cannot pass over in silence, because it afforded an opportunity of displaying his firmness of character. Upon one of the fêtes of St. Louis, the janitor's wife, who was, of course, perfectly well known, presented herself for admittance to the performance of the "Death of Cæsar," *corrected*, in which I played the part of *Brutus*. As she had no ticket, and persisted, raising a clamor, in the hope of passing, the sergeant of the post reported to his officer, Napoleon: he, learning the circumstances of the case, with an imperative tone exclaimed— "Let that woman be removed; she brings into this place the license of a camp."

Bonaparte and myself were little more than eight years old when our intercourse commenced. We soon became most attached. There appeared to exist between us one of those natural sympathies which quickly ripen. This intimacy and friendship I enjoyed without interruption, till 1784, when he quitted the seminary at Brienne, for that of Paris. Of all our schoolfellows, I best understood how to accommodate myself to his character, melancholy as it was, and severe. His habits of seclusion, his reflections on the conquest of his country, and the impressions graven on his young spirit of evils suffered by Corsica and by his own family, made him seek solitude, and rendered his address, though in appearance only, very forbidding. Age placed us together, in the classes of languages and mathematics. From his first entrance to school, he manifested an eager desire of acquiring knowledge. At this period, as he spoke only the Corsican dialect, and, on that account, already excited a very lively interest, the Sieur Dupuis, then sub-principal—a young man no less amiable than distinguished as a grammarian—undertook to give him private lessons in French. His pupil so well repaid this care, that in a very short space of time it was judged proper to commence the study of Latin. The youthful aspirant evinced to this language such unconquerable aversion, that in his fifteenth year he was still low in the fourth form. I had here easily left him behind, but remained throughout in the same mathematical class, where, unquestionably, he was the ablest of the whole school. I sometimes exchanged with him the solution of the problems given out—and which he demonstrated off-hand, with a readiness that always astonished me—for language exercises, of which he detested the very mention.

I have read the veriest nonsense about his being the hermit of the school, with no equals, and his schoolfellows all friends or flatterers. How sadly is the illusion of descriptions and pictures destroyed by a near view of objects! For, during nearly seven years of companionship, I can recollect nothing to justify such pitiful play of words. At Brienne, Bonaparte was remarkable for the color of his complexion, afterward so much changed by the climate of France; a quick and searching look; and for the tone of his conversation, with both masters and companions. There appeared always something of bitterness in his remarks; and he certainly seemed little inclined to cultivate the softer moods. He was, in fact, averse to forming particular attachments. This I have already attributed to the misfortunes of his early years: and the following is an instance how deeply he felt the subjection of his country. The students received invitations in turn to dine with Father Berton, principal of the seminary. Bonaparte's day having arrived, some of the professors, who knew his admiration of Paoli, affected to speak slightingly of that patriot. "Paoli," warmly replied Bonaparte, "was a great man— he loved his country; and I cannot forgive my father, formerly his adjutant, for having consented to the union of Corsica with France. He ought never to have forsaken the fortunes of such a leader, but to have fallen with him."

Generally speaking, Bonaparte was no favorite with his comrades, who, truly, were far from being his flatterers. He associated very little with them, and rarely joined in their sports. The painful remembrances already noticed weighed upon his young heart, and held him aloof from the boisterous enjoyments of others. But I was almost constantly in his company. On the arrival of our play hour, he flew to the library, where he devoured books on history, especially

Polybius and Plutarch. He liked Arrian also very much, but had little regard for Quintus Curtius. Often did I leave him thus quite alone, to mingle in the exercises of our companions.

The temper of the youthful Corsican was yet further soured by the railleries of the students, who often made game of his country and his name Napoleon. Repeatedly did he say to me, in the bitterness of the moment—"I will do these Frenchmen of thine all the mischief in my power"; and, upon my endeavoring to soothe his irritation, he would add—"But you, Bourrienne, you never insult me—you love me."

Our principal was named Louis. On one occasion, we had made some crackers in order to celebrate his birthday; and having ranged them on a bench in the court, they were somehow fired accidentally. Bonaparte standing hard by, sustained no injury; but a young scholar, who happened to be at his side, remained quite black from the effects of the explosion.

Father Patrauld, our professor of mathematics, though a very ordinary man, was much attached to Bonaparte, made a boast of his young friend's acquirements, and cherished a pride in having been his instructor. He had reason to do so. The other professors, in whose classes he did not shine, troubled themselves very little about him. He had no taste for polite literature, the study of languages, or any of the lighter accomplishments. As nothing announced that he would ever figure in the capacity of a learned Theban, the pedants of the establishment would charitably have put him down for a dunce. Yet across his pensive and reserved character were to be perceived indications of brightest intelligence. If the monks, good, easy men, to whom was confided the instruction of our youth, had possessed tact to appreciate his temperament, had their professors of mathematics been more able, and could they efficiently have turned our attention to chemistry, natural philosophy, and astronomy, I am convinced Bonaparte would have carried into studies of this nature those powers of research and of genius which shone forth in a career far more *brilliant, indeed, but much less useful to mankind. Unfortunately for us, these monks knew nothing, while they were too poor to procure good masters elsewhere. Nevertheless, they were obliged, after Bonaparte's departure, to bring two professors from Paris, under whom I studied, and without whose aid the school must have gone to ruin. The assertion, therefore, so often repeated, that Napoleon received at Brienne an accomplished education, is false; our good minims were incapable of conferring such a gift; and I avow, for my part, the instruction of the present age throws a disagreeable light on that which I received among those blockheads in cowls. It is difficult to conceive how even one man of talent could have come out of their institution.

Though Bonaparte had little cause to praise his fellow-students, as respected their conduct toward himself, he disdained to prefer complaints against them; and even when it came to his turn to see that the rules were not transgressed, he chose rather to submit to confinement than denounce the young culprits. Once I found myself an accomplice in this non-performance of monitorship: he persuaded me to follow him to prison, where we remained three days. This had oftener than once happened to him before; but punishment had been inflicted with less severity.

In 1783, the Duke of Orleans and Madame de Montesson came to Brienne. The magnificent residence of the count, for upward of a month, resembled a small Versailles, where variety of delightful amusements permitted not the illustrious travellers to regret the palace and the capital. During this period, the prince and his fair companion expressed a desire to preside at the distribution of honors in the royal college. Upon this occasion, Bonaparte and I carried off the prizes for mathematics, a department to which he had chiefly directed his studies, and wherein he excelled.

Napoleon, in the course of his life, performed a sufficiency of great actions, which render unnecessary here further explanation of the pretended marvels of his boyhood. I should be unjust were I to describe him as an ordinary boy; I never thought him so; but must on the contrary declare that, for various reasons, he was a most distinguished scholar in the seminary whence he was now to remove.

Over all the military schools an inspector presided, whose duty it was to transmit an annual report on the progress of each pupil, whether pensioned by the State, or educated at the charge of his family. I copied the certificate that follows from the report for 1784. I intended also to purchase the original manuscript, which had probably been stolen from the war-office, but Louis Bonaparte obtained this document. I did not transcribe the note concerning myself, because modesty would always have prevented my using it. It would have served, however, to show how great a distance chance and circumstances, in the course of life, may interpose between those whose situations on the forms of a school were very different. I affirm, without fear of contradiction, that not upon little Bonaparte would he, who should then have read the certificates of the students at Brienne, in 1784, have rested his predictions of greatness and renown, but upon several others, much more favorably noticed, who, notwithstanding, were left far behind.

"*1784—Report presented to the King, by M. de Keralio (inspector of the college at Brienne).*

"M. de Buonaparte (Napoleon), born 15th August, 1769, height four feet, ten inches, ten lines, has finished his fourth course; of good constitution, excellent health, of submissive disposition, upright, grateful, and strictly regular in conduct; has always been distinguished for application to the mathematics. He is tolerably well acquainted with history and geography. He is rather deficient in the ornamental branches, and in Latin, in which he has barely completed the fourth course. He will make an excellent seaman. He is fit to pass to the Military School at Paris."

Notwithstanding this, Father Berton opposed the removal of Bonaparte, because he had not finished the studies of the fourth division, whereas, by the rules, he ought to have been in the third. I have been positively informed by the sub-principal that a note touching Napoleon, despatched from the school at Brienne to Paris, designated him—"Character domineering, imperious, obstinate." I knew Bonaparte well, and, on the whole, approve the certificate of the inspector. I believe, however, it ought to have run thus: "He is *very well* acquainted with history, and especially geography. He is *very* deficient in the ornamental branches, and in Latin." There could be no grounds for saying that he would prove an excellent seaman: he never once entertained a thought of the naval service.

In consequence of the report of M. de Keralio, Bonaparte, with four others, passed to the Military Academy at Paris. His companions were also King's scholars, with certificates at-least equally good; indeed, cadets of this class only had the privilege of nomination to the Military College: there was no competition; age, and the certificates of the monks, determined the choice of the inspector in the twelve provincial seminaries. What then has induced writers to attribute this promotion to Napoleon's previous superiority at Brienne? The facts stated above, and the report of the. inspector, attest his slender progress in most of the ordinary branches except mathematics. Neither in these, as has been advanced, was great proficiency the cause of any premature removal to Paris. He had attained the proper age, could produce certificates sufficiently favorable, and was quite naturally one of the five selected in 1784, according to ordinary custom.

Bonaparte was fifteen years and two months old on his promotion to the Military College at Paris. I accompanied him in a gig to the stage at *Nogent-sur-Seine*. We separated with unfeigned regret, not to meet again till 1792. During these eight years, both maintained an active correspondence; but, so little did I foresee those high destinies announced by the pretended miracles of his boyhood (discovered, by the way, *after* his elevation). that I have preserved not a single letter of this period.

Upon entering the Military College, Napoleon found himself on a footing so brilliant and expensive, considering the professional and mental education there received, that he deemed it incumbent to draw up a memoir, addressed directly to the sub-principal Berton. The youthful reformer here insisted that the plan of education was really hurtful, and could never accomplish the end proposed by every wise government. He dwelt forcibly upon the effects of such a system affirming, "that the royal pensioners, being all gentlemen in reduced circumstances, instead of having their minds improved, could derive nothing therefrom save a love of ostentation, and sentiments of conceit and vanity; so that, on rejoining the domestic circle, far from relishing the frugal gentility of their home, they will feel inclined to blush for the very authors of their being, and to despise their modest mansion. In place," continued the memorialist, "of retaining a numerous crowd of domestics about these youths, setting before them meals of two courses daily, making a parade with a very expensive establishment of horses and grooms, would it not be better, without in the least interrupting the course of their studies, to oblige them to do everything for themselves, that is to say, with the exception of a little cooking, which should be done for them; to set before them regulation bread, or a quality approaching to it; accustom them to the business of the field; make them brush their own clothes, clean their boots and shoes, etc. Since they are far from rich, and since all are destined for the military service, is not the duty of that service the only and true education which they should receive? Habituated to a life of sobriety, to maintain with steadiness the bearing of a soldier, they would at the same time grow up more robust; would be able to brave the inclemencies of seasons; to support with courage the fatigues of war; and inspire the men under their command with respect and devoted attachment." Thus reasoned Napoleon at the age of sixteen; time and his subsequent doings show that he never departed from these early views of military education.

But, thus active, a keen observer, and speaking freely what he thought with energy, Napoleon remained not long at college. His superiors, tired of so decided a character, hastened the period of his examination, that he might be provided for elsewhere, as second lieutenant, on the first vacancy in a regiment of artillery. This regiment was then at Valence (1785), where he remained several years, in the usual obscurity of country quarters.

As for myself, having left Brienne in 1787, and been denied a commission in the same service, I repaired the following year to Vienna, in the hope of being attached to the French embassy at that court. But, after two months' stay, our minister, M. de Noailles, giving me some general instructions on diplomacy, recommended a course of national law, and of foreign languages, in one of the German universities. I entered at Leipsic.

Here I had scarcely settled when the Revolution broke out. Mighty was the interval between those reasonable meliorations, which time had rendered necessary, which men also of the most staid characters desired, and that total oversetting of all things—that destruction of the state, condemnation of the best of kings, and lengthened series of crime, with which France has sullied the pages of her history! In these remodellings of institutions, which time necessarily brings round, we may remark, that all the evil originates in a blind and presumptuous opposition on the one side, and in mad precipitation on the other. Time would have given to France what only terror and slaughter gave. Nothing proves that one generation ought to suffer for the happiness of its successors.

Having finished my diplomatic studies, and acquired the German and English languages, traversing Prussia and Poland, and passing through Vienna, I arrived in Paris, April, 1792. Here I found Bonaparte. Our friendship of boyhood, and of college days, yet remained undiminished. I had not been very prosperous; upon him adversity pressed heavily. He was often in absolute want of resources. We passed our time as may be imagined of two young men of twenty-three, with no occupation, and hardly more money. His finances were yet at a lower ebb than mine. Every day we projected some new scheme; having all eyes about us for some profitable speculation. At one time he proposed our jointly renting several houses then building in Montholon Street, in order to sublet them afterward. We found the terms would not suit. Everything failed us. Meanwhile, he was soliciting employment from the war office, and I from the secretariat for foreign affairs. For the moment, as will appear, I proved the luckier of the two.

While we were thus leading a somewhat vagabond life, the 20th June arrived—unhappy prelude to darker scenes. We had met on that morning as usual, preparatory to our daily lounge, in a coffee-room, Rue Saint Honoré, near the Palais Royal. On going out, we saw a mob approaching, which Bonaparte computed at five or six thousand men, all in rags, and armed with every sort of weapon, clamoring, vociferating in grossest abuse, and proceeding with rapid pace toward the Tuileries. This rout assuredly consisted of the vilest and most abject populace of the suburbs. "Let us follow that rabble," said Bonaparte to me. We got the start, and went to walk in the gardens, on the terrace overlooking the water. From this station, he beheld the disgraceful occurrences that ensued. I should fail in attempting to depict the surprise and resentment which these scandalous scenes aroused within him. He could not comprehend such weakness and forbearance. But, when the King showed himself at one of the windows fronting the garden, with the red cap which one of the crowd had just placed upon his head, Bonaparte's indignation burst forth uncontrolled. "What madness!" exclaimed he aloud, and in his *patois;* "how could they allow these scoundrels to enter? They ought to have blown four or five hundred of them into the air with cannon; the rest would then have taken to their heels!"

CHAPTER II

Bonaparte's Mission to Genoa—Retirement—Reinstalled, helps to suppress a Political Riot—Marriage with Josephine—Italian Campaign—Bourrienne joins Napoleon in Italy as Private Secretary—Napoleon's relation to the Directory

BONAPARTE, after the fatal 10th of August, retired to Corsica, whence he did not return till the following year, 1793. For my part, having been appointed Secretary of Legation at Stuttgart some days after the 20th of June, I set out on the 2d of August, and saw not again my young and ardent friend till 1794. "Your departure," said he, "will hasten mine"; and we took leave of each other, with feeble hope, as then seemed, of ever meeting more.

A decree of the 28th March, 1793, directed all French agents abroad to return to France within three months under pain of being treated as emigrants. What I had previously witnessed, and the exasperated state of all minds at home, make me shrink from being possibly forced either to take part in these afflicting scenes, or to become their victim. My disobedience inscribed me on the emigration list, from which my name was not erased till November, 1797.

, During our separation, Bonaparte, as chief of battalion, took part in his first campaign, in which he contributed so powerfully to the recapture of Toulon. With this period of his life I am unacquainted—at least I do not speak of it as an eyewitness; I only mention some particulars, and cite documents which filled up the time from 1793 to 1795, the date when he placed them in my hands. ·

On the 13th July, 1794 (25 Messidor, year II.), the representatives of the people attached to the army of Italy, passed the following resolution: "General Buonaparte will repair to Genoa, in order, conjointly with the ambassador

of the French republic, to confèr with the government of
Genoa, as his instructions bear.   The ambassador of the
French republic will acknowledge him, and cause him to
be acknowledged by the government of Genoa."   To these
public credentials were added secret instructions, "That he
should observe the state of the works and military stores of
the fortresses of Genoa and Savona, and the condition of the
surrounding country in both places."   He was directed,
also, "as far as possible, to unravel the conduct of the
French minister, Tilly, and the intentions of the Genoese
respecting the coalition."

This mission, and the secret instructions, prove the confidence with which Bonaparte, not yet twenty-five, had
inspired men determined on not being deceived as to the
choice of their agents.   Thus accredited, Bonaparte repaired
to Genoa, and there fulfilled his commission.   The 9th
Thermidor arrived: the terrorist deputies were replaced by
Albitte and Salicetti.   Whether the latter functionaries, in
the confusion then existing, were not informed of the orders
given to General Bonaparte; or whether some, jealous of the
rising fame of the young general of artillery, had prejudiced
Salicetti and his colleague against him, certain it is that
these representatives caused Bonaparte to be arrested and
his papers sealed; directing both him and them to be delivered up to the Committee of Public Safety at Paris.
Their resolution, dated 19th Thermidor (6th August), singular as it may appear, purports to be principally grounded
on the late journey made by General Bonaparte to Genoa—
a mission which, as we have just seen, he had undertaken
by the express orders of the representatives of the people.

Napoleon, at St. Helena, states that he was put under
arrest for some *minutes* by the representative Laporte: the
resolution, however, is signed by three persons, of whom
Laporte was probably the least influential, since he is not
even addressed in Bonaparte's appeal.   He continued under
arrest fifteen days.

If a similar decree had been passed three weeks sooner,

if Bonaparte had been denounced to the Committee of
Public Safety *before* the 9th Thermidor, his fate, in all likelihood, would have been sealed; and we should have beheld
perish on the scaffold, at the age of twenty-five, the man
who, for the next quarter of a century, was to astonish the
world by his vast conceptions, his gigantic designs, his grand
military genius, his prodigious fortune, his errors, his reverses, and his final abasement!

It is to be remarked that, in this *post-thermidorian* decree,
issued "after the death of the tyrant," not the slightest mention is made of any connection between Bonaparte and the
younger Robespierre. The severity of the decree, too, will
surprise the more now that the mission to Genoa is explained. Did there, then, exist anything against him? or
had calumny been able to efface the services he had just
rendered to his country? Often have I conversed with him
on this adventure; he constantly assured me he had nothing
wherewith to reproach himself, and that his defence expressed his real sentiments, and the exact truth.

Bonaparte was not yet inclined to view his situation as
desperate. He addressed a vigorous letter to Albitte and
Salicetti.

His defence, so remarkable for energetic simplicity, appears to have made an impression upon the representatives.
Particulars more precise were probably also more favorable
to the General; for on 3d Fructidor (20th August), 1794, a
resolution was passed, setting him provisionally at liberty,
but directing that he should remain at headquarters. Salicetti subsequently became the friend and even confidant of
young Bonaparte—a connection which did not survive his
elevation. We have thus seen that there was no question
about the impossibility in which the representatives found
themselves of dispensing with the General's talents. But
what are we to think both of the motives for the arrest, and
of the setting at liberty *provisionally*, when they knew
fully the error they had committed, and the innocence of
Bonaparte?

Another circumstance which has been connected with this period is the friendship of Duroc. It is said that this intimacy commenced at the siege of Toulon, when the General took Duroc as his aide-de-camp from the ranks of the artillery. It was much later, while in Italy, that Bonaparte attached to himself this subordinate. On hearing his praises, he requested the transference of his services from General L'Espinasse, commandant of the artillery, under whom Duroc had already served in one campaign, as captain of artillery. His character, cold and repellent, suited Napoleon, whose confidence, from the expedition to Egypt, during the consulate, and to his death, he continued to enjoy. Appointments were bestowed upon him, perhaps, somewhat beyond his abilities. Bonaparte often said at St. Helena, that he loved him much. I believe it; but have proof that Duroc did not return the sentiment. There are so many princes void of generosity, why should we not sometimes find courtiers ungrateful?

General Bonaparte returned to Paris, where soon after I also arrived from Germany. Our intimacy resumed its ancient footing. He gave me all the details of his campaign of the south. He liked to repeat and dwell upon his warlike achievements at Toulon, and in the Italian army; speaking of his first successes with the feeling of pleasure and satisfaction they had inspired.

At this period the government desired to send him to La Vendée as brigadier-general of infantry. Two motives determined the youthful general of artillery in his refusal to accede to the proposition. He looked upon this as by no means a field worthy of his talents; and the change to another branch of the service as a species of injustice. The second was the stronger, and the only reason officially assigned for his refusal—the change of service. On this was declared the following resolution, of the 15th September, 1794: "The Committee of Public Safety decrees, that General of Brigade Bonaparte shall be erased from the list of general officers employed, in consequence of his refusing to repair to the station tó which he had been appointed.'' Napoleon has told us from St. Helena that he sent in his resignation: this resolution proves the contrary. He was unwilling to acknowledge a dismissal.

Upon this unexpected blow Bonaparte retired into private life, constrained to an inaction most irksome to his ardent character, heightened yet more by youth. He then lodged, Rue de Mail, in a house near the Place des Victoires. We began again the course of life we had led before his departure for Corsica in 1792. He had no little difficulty in forming the resolution to abide the termination of the prejudices against him which those in power entertained. In the perpetual mutations of this same power, he hoped that it might pass to others more favorably disposed. He very frequently came to dine and pass the evening with myself and my elder brother, never failing to render these hours agreeable by his engaging manners and the charm of his conversation.

Women appreciate, more justly than men, the characters of young people on their entering the world. I shall, therefore, here transcribe, without changing a single syllable, the notes of Madame de Bourrienne, respecting this period in the life of my young companion, whom, from his intimacy with me, she had closely studied. All the facts are yet present to my recollection. I confirm the minutest particulars, though perhaps then viewing them with a different eye. Friendship probably blinded me to faults.

''The day after our second return from Germany, in May, 1795, we met Bonaparte in the Palais Royal. He embraced Bourrienne, as one would a comrade one loves and sees again with pleasure. We went to the Théâtre Français, where a tragedy was performed; but the afterpiece convulsed the house. The actor was often forced to stop till the bursts of laughter had subsided. Bonaparte alone—a circumstance which struck me very forcibly—maintained an icy silence. I remarked at this period of life, that his disposition exhibited coldness, and frequently gloom; his smile was false, and often exceedingly misplaced. As an illustration of this, I recollect, a few days after our meeting, he had one of his fits of ferocious hilarity, which shocked my feelings, and little disposed me to like him. He recounted to us, with the greatest gayety, an adventure before Toulon, where he commanded the artillery. An officer in this service, and under the General's own orders, had received a visit from his wife, to whom he had been recently united, and whom he tenderly loved. A few days after her arrival, directions were issued for a fresh attack upon the town, and the officer got orders to be on duty. His wife went to General Bonaparte, entreating him, with tears, to dispense with the presence of her husband for that day only. The General was inexorable, as he himself told us, with a gayety which amused, while it made one shudder. The moment of attack arrived, and this officer, who had always displayed extraordinary bravery, felt a presentiment of his approaching end: he became pale, and trembled. His station was by the General's side; and, at the moment of the hottest fire from the ramparts, Bonaparte cried out to him—'Beware! a shell! The officer,' added he, 'instead of throwing himself on the ground, only stooped, and was cut in two!' Bonaparte broke into shouts of laughter, while describing to us what part of the body was carried off!

"At this time, during a stay in Paris of six weeks, we saw him almost every day. He often dined with us; and, as there was a scarcity of bread—two ounces being the daily allowance in each section—it was the practice to ask the guests to bring their own bread, since it could not be procured for money. On these occasions, he and his brother Louis, then his aide-de-camp, an amiable and engaging youth, brought their rations, black and full of bran. It is with regret I say it, the aide-de-camp alone made use of this, and we procured for the General the finest white bread, of flour brought secretly from Sens, where my husband had a farm. It was baked in a case, at a pastry-cook's. Had we been discovered, there was quite enough to have sent

us to the scaffold. We very often went in company with
Bonaparte to the opera and Garat's charming concerts, the
first brilliant assemblies since the death of Robespierre.
There was always something singular in the habits of our
friend; for he would often disappear from beside us, without a single word; and, while under the impression that he
had left the theatre, we would discover him in a box of the
second or third tier, all alone, and looking quite gruff, like
one in a pet. We had come to town preparatory to my first
confinement, and, wishing to exchange our lodging for one
larger and more cheerful, Bonaparte accompanied us in our
search. We engaged a first floor, Rue des Marais, No. 19,
in a handsome new house. He wished to live in Paris, and
went to look at a dwelling opposite ours, which he proposed
renting with his uncle Fesch, afterward cardinal, and a person named Patrauld, one of his old masters at the Military
Academy. 'That residence,' said he to us one day, 'you,
my friends, over the way—a cabriolet—and I shall be the
happiest of mortals!' We departed for Sens, some days
after. The house remained unoccupied for him—other and
more important business was forthcoming. On our return
in November of the same year, all was changed.''

Madame de Bourrienne here alludes to the 13th Vendemiaire (5th October, 1795), now fast approaching. The
National Convention had been painfully delivered of a new
marvel—namely, the Constitution, so named, of the year
III., the era of its birth. It was adopted on the 22d August,
1795. These provident legislators did not forget their own
interests. They stipulated that two-thirds of their body
should compose a proportion of the new administration.
The party opposed to the Convention, on the contrary, .
looked forward, in a total renewal and by general elections,
to the introduction of a majority of their own opinion—that
power ought not to remain in the hands of men by whom
it had been so grossly abused. To this sentiment inclined
the greater part of the sections of Paris possessing the most
influence in respect of wealth and intelligence. These sec-

tions declared that, accepting the new constitution, they rejected the decree of the 30th August, touching the obligatory re-election of the two-thirds. The Convention thus saw itself menaced in its most cherished possession—power. The members took measures for their own security, declaring that, if attacked, they would retire to Châlons, on the Marne; and, as a preparatory step, issued orders to the representatives commanding the armed force to stand to their defence.

From the 25th September, disturbance began to manifest itself: the thunder commenced its distant growl. This agitation continued till the 5th October, when the storm burst. From that memorable day, on which the Sections of Paris attacked the Convention, is to be dated the rise of the incomprehensible destinies of Bonaparte. The events of that day became the unforeseen causes of great changes throughout Europe. The blood which then flowed fed the germs of his young ambition; and the history of past times affords few eras embracing events so wonderful as those which crowd the years between 1795 and 1815. The recital of that day, which I now give, is entirely his own, with all his peculiarities of style. The letter, written with his own hand, and now printed from the autograph, he despatched to me at Sens, where I had remained since parting with him in July.

"On the 13th, at five in the morning, the representative of the people Barras was nominated commander-in-chief of the Army of the Interior, and General Bonaparte second in command. The field artillery was still in the camp at Sablons, guarded by 150 men only: the remainder was at Marly, with 200 men. The depôt at Meudon was without any guard. They had at Feuillans only some fourpounders, without gunners, and not more than 80,000 cartridges. The magazines of provisions were in various places throughout Paris. In several sections drums were beating the *génerale*. That of the Théâtre Français had pushed forward advanced posts to the Pont Neuf, which they had barricaded.

"General Barras ordered the artillery to be moved instantly from the camp of Sablons to the Tuileries; caused gunners to be sought out from the battalions of the 89th, and among the gendarmerie, and stationed them at the palace. He sent to Meudon 200 men of the legion of police, whom he drew from Versailles, fifty horsemen, and two companies of veterans. He ordered the transport of the stores at Marly to Meudon; sent for cartridges, and established a manufactory of them at Meudon. He assured the subsistence of the Army of the Convention for several days, independently of the magazines which were in the sections.

"General Verdier, who commanded at the national palace, manœuvred with great coolness. He had orders not to fire till the last extremity. In the meantime, reports arrived from all quarters that the sections were assembling in arms, and forming their columns. He disposed the troops for the defence of the Convention, and prepared his artillery to repulse the rebels. He placed the cannon at Feuillans, so as to batter the Rue St. Honoré. Two eight-pounders were planted at each opening, and, in case of mischance, two pieces were so stationed in reserve as to fire upon the flank of any column that might have forced a passage. He left in the square of the Carrousel three eight-pounder howitzers, to play upon the houses whence the rebels might fire upon the Convention.

"At four o'clock in the afternoon, the columns of the rebels issued from all the streets, in order to form. This critical moment would have been seized, by even the most inexperienced troops, to overwhelm them. But the blood about to flow was that of Frenchmen. It was proper to suffer these wretched beings, steeped already in the crime of revolt, to sully themselves still more by that of fraternicide, and with having to answer for the horrors of the first bloodshed. At a quarter to five the rebels had formed. They commenced the attack on all sides. Everywhere they were thrown into confusion. French blood flowed. The crime, as the shame, fell that day all upon the sectionaries.

Among the dead were recognized everywhere emigrants, landholders, and nobles. Among those who were made prisoners, it was found that the great portion were the Chouans of Charette. Nevertheless, the sections did not hold themselves beaten. They betook themselves to the church of St. Roche, the Théâtre of the Republic, and the Palace of Equality; and, on all hands, were heard in their fury exciting the inhabitants to arms. To spare the blood which would have flowed on the morrow, it required to allow them no time to recover themselves, but actively to pursue them, without, however, engaging ourselves in difficult passes.

"The general gave orders to General Montchoisy, who was at the Place de la Revolution with a reserve, to form column, and, taking two twelve-pounders, to march by the Boulevard, turn the Place Vendôme, effect a junction with the picket at headquarters, and return thence in column. General Brune, with two howitzers, advanced by the Rues St. Nicaise and St. Honoré. General Cartaux sent 200 men, with one four-pounder, of his division, by the Rue St. Thomas du Louvre. General Bonaparte, who had had two horses killed under him, hurried to Feuillans. These columns moved forward. St. Roche and the Théâtre of the Republic were forced, and abandoned. The rebels then retired to the head of the Rue de la Loi, and barricaded themselves on all sides. Patrols were sent out, and during the night several cannon-shot were fired to oppose them. This completely succeeded.

"At daybreak, the general was informed that the students from the quarter of St. Geneviève, with two cannon, were marching to the succor of the rebels, and despatched a detachment of dragoons, who captured the artillery, and brought both pieces to the Tuileries. Notwithstanding all this, the expiring sections still made head: they barricaded the streets in the section of Grenelle, and planted cannon in the principal streets. At nine o'clock, attacks were preparing by Generals Berruyer, Vachet, Brune, and Duvigier, from different quarters; but the courage of the sectionaries failed with the dread of seeing their retreat cut off. They evacuated the post, and forgot, at the sight of our soldiers, the honor of French chivalry, which they had to support. The section of Brutus still caused some uneasiness. The wife of a representative had been arrested there. Orders were given to General Duvigier to advance along the Boulevard; and to General Berruyer to draw up in the Place de Victoire. General Bonaparte occupied the Bridge of the Exchange. The section was surrounded; a charge was made upon the Place de Grêve, filled with a multitude from the Ile St. Louis, the Théâtre Français, and the Equality Palace. Everywhere the patriots had recovered courage; everywhere the poniards of the emigrants, raised against us, had disappeared; everywhere the people had discovered their folly and their error. On the morrow, the two sections of Le Pelletier and the Théâtre-Français were disarmed."

After the 18th Vendemiaire, I returned from Sens to Paris. During the period of my short stay in the capital, I saw Bonaparte less frequently than at former seasons. I have no reason to ascribe this restricted intercourse to any other cause except the extensive duties of his new appointment. Madame de Bourrienne's notes, however, are continued thus: "In the interval (of our residence in the country), many letters were exchanged between my husband and Bonaparte: those of the latter were most pleasing and affectionate. He showed however very little solicitude about old friends. On returning to town, we found all was altered. The college friend had become a great personage; he was in command at Paris, as a recompense for the day of Vendemiaire. The small house in the Marais was exchanged for a magnificent residence in the most fashionable quarter; the modest cabriolet had given place to a superb equipage; and he himself was no longer the same. The friends of youth, indeed, were still received at his sumptuous entertainments, where ladies sometimes appeared—among others, the beautiful Madame Tallien, and the graceful De

Beauharnais, to whom he had already begun to pay attention.   But he seemed to care very little about his friends;
and no longer *thee* and *thou*-ed them, as in times past.
I shall mention one only, M. de Rey, son of a knight of
St. Louis, whose father had perished at the siege of Lyons,
and who himself had escaped almost by a miracle.   Being
an agreeable and amiable young man, and a devoted royalist, we became intimate.   He, too, went to visit his old class-
fellow of the Military College; but, being unable to bring
himself to frame his speech in the all-important plural,
Bonaparte turned his back upon him, and took no notice of
a second visit.   He never did anything for this youthful
associate beyond giving him a miserable appointment of
inspector of provisions, which M. de Rey could not accept.
Three years after, the young man died of consumption,
regretted by many friends."

I now most frequently met Napoleon at breakfast or
dinner.   One day he pointed out to my observation a lady
seated nearly opposite to him, asking what I thought of her:
my answer seemed to be highly agreeable to him.   His conversation afterward turned chiefly upon this topic, touching
her family and amiable qualities.   He gave me to understand that his probable marriage to the young widow would
contribute much to his happiness.   I easily perceived, from
the tenor of the discourse, that this connection would effectually second his ambition.   His constantly increasing intimacy with her whom he loved brought him also into
contact with those most influential at that period, thus
facilitating the means of realizing his pretensions.   He
remained in Paris only twelve days after the nuptials,
which took place on the 9th March, 1796.   A few months
later, he was on his way as Commander-in-chief of the
Army of Italy!

I shall say nothing of the military details of that brilliant
campaign, in the course of which he bore the standard of
France from the shores of the Gulf of Genoa, beyond the
Rhœtian Alps.   I limit myself to citing a few documents,

and to the relation of some facts which may prove serviceable to the historian.

Scarcely had he arrived at the army headquarters, when
Colli, the Austrian general, wrote to him, requiring the
liberation of one Moulin, an emigrant, who had been arrested, though acting in the capacity of an Austrian envoy,
and threatening otherwise reprisal on the person of a French
officer. The Commander-in-Chief of the French Army replied: "Sir, an emigrant is a parricide, whom no character
can protect. There was a want of respect toward the French
people, in sending Moulin as envoy. You know the laws of
war; and I cannot understand the reprisal with which you
threaten my Chief-of-Brigade Barthélemy. If, contrary to
all the laws of war, you permit an act of such barbarity,
every one of your prisoners in future shall answer for the
consequences. None shall be spared. Otherwise I hold the
officers of your nation in the esteem due to brave soldiers."

The executive directory, to whom these letters were
transmitted, approved the arrest, but forbade any punishment beyond safe custody, from respect to the character of
an envoy. As to a project of joining Kellermann as his
second in command, Bonaparte wrote to Carnot, 24th May,
1796: "Whether I carry on the war here or elsewhere is to
me a matter of indifference. To serve my country—to merit
in the eyes of posterity a page in our history—this is my
whole ambition. To unite Kellermann and me in Italy is
to ruin all. General Kellermann has more experience, and
will better conduct the war than I; but together, we shall
mar the affair. I cannot willingly serve with one who con-
ceives himself the first commander in Europe."

There have been published a great number of letters from
Bonaparte to his wife. Of these, I have neither the inclination nor means of contesting the authenticity. I simply give
one here, which, in my judgment, differs not a little from
the others. We shall find in it fewer of those exaggerated
expressions of affection, and less of that style, so strangely
affected, and full of pretension, remarkable throughout the

whole of that correspondence—the authenticity of which, I repeat, I do not mean to deny. He announces to Josephine the victory of Arcola:

"*Verona, 29th, midday.*—At length, mine adorable Josephine, I breathe again. Death is no longer before mine eyes, and glory and honor are once more in my heart. The enemy has been beaten at Arcola. To-morrow we repair the blunder of Vaubois, in abandoning Rivoli. In eight days, Mantua will be ours; and soon, in thine arms, I shall be able to give thee a thousand proofs of the ardent love of thy husband. On the earliest opportunity I will hasten to Milan. At present, I am somewhat fatigued. I have received a letter from Eugene and Hortense. They are delightful creatures. As my whole family is a little dispersed, the moment all have rejoined me I will send them to thee. We have made 5,000 prisoners, and have slain at least 6,000 of the enemy. Adieu, mine adorable Josephine! Think often of me. If thou dost cease to love thine Achilles, or if thy heart should ever grow cold toward him, thou wilt be very mistaken and very unjust; but I feel assured thou wilt always love me, as I shall ever remain thy most devoted friend. Death alone shall dissolve a union which sympathy, affection and sentiment have formed. Send me news of thy health. A thousand and a thousand tenderest adieus!"

I was soon to be a witness of these triumphs as, setting out to join the Army of Italy, I never quitted its youthful commander for an instant, till 1802. But I hold it of some moment to prove (in opposition to certain very ungenerous assertions already given to the public) that in this I threw myself neither as an intruder, nor as an obscure intriguer, into the path of fortune. I obeyed the dictates of friendship, rather than the impulse of ambition; and the following correspondence will show with what confidence I was then honored. The same letters, however, written in the spirit of friendship, and not for history, tell also of our military achievements; and whatever recalls that heroic period will probably be read not without interest.

"*Headquarters, Milan, 8th June, 1796.*—My dear Bourrienne: I am desired by the Commander-in-Chief to express to you all the pleasure he had in hearing from you and that he ardently desires you should join us. Set out, then, my dear B., and come quickly. Be assured of that affection with which you inspire all who know you. We shall have only one cause of regret—your not having shared our success. The campaign just concluded will be celebrated in the annals of history. Is it not glorious, in less than two months, and with less than 30,000 men, in want of everything, to have completely beaten, and in eight separate actions, an army of from sixty-five to seventy thousand; dictated a humiliating peace to the King of Sardinia; and chased the Austrians from Italy? The last victory, of which you are doubtless apprised—that of the passage of the Mincio—has ended our toils. There yet remain the siege of Mantua, and the reduction of the citadel of Milan; but these obstacles cannot detain us long. Adieu. I repeat, in the name of General Bonaparte, his invitation, and the assurance of his desire to see you. Receive from, etc. MARMONT, Colonel of Artillery, and Aide-de-camp to the Commander-in-Chief.''

I was obliged to remain at Sens, waiting my erasure from the list of emigrants, which, however, I did not obtain till 1797, after repeated instances on the part of Bonaparte. My hours, also, were devoted to study, and I preferred repose to the bustle of a camp. This double motive prevented my acceptance, at the time, of this friendly invitation. Some months after, I received a second letter from Chief-of-Brigade Marmont, dated—

"*Headquarters, Gorizia, 22d March, 1797.*—The Commander-in-Chief, my dear Bourrienne, charges me to express his desire, that you should speedily come to him. I unite with the General, in urging you, my dear B., to join the army without loss of time. You will increase an attached family, which longs to receive you into its bosom. I send inclosed the General's order, which will serve as your passport. Take post and come. We are on the point of penetrating into Germany. The language already begins to change, and in less than four days the Italian will no more be heard. Prince Charles has been beaten: we are in pursuit. Should the campaign continue successful but a little longer, we shall be in Vienna, to sign a peace so necessary to Europe. Adieu! Esteem as something the wishes of one who is yours sincerely devoted.''

Inclosed was the following order:

"Bonaparte, Commander-in-Chief of the Army of Italy. Citizen Bourrienne will repair to my headquarters, on receipt of the present order.   BONAPARTE.''

On the 19th April, 1797, I reached the headquarters of the Army of Italy, at Leoben, the morning after the preliminaries of peace had been signed. Here ceases my intercourse with Bonaparte as equal with equal, companion with companion, and now commence those relations which respect him as great, powerful, surrounded with homage and with glory. I no longer accosted him as formerly; I appreciated too justly his personal importance; his position had interposed too vast a distance in the social scale for me to remain insensible to the necessity of comporting my bearing accordingly. I made with pleasure, and without regret, a sacrifice of familiarity, intrinsically of small moment, of *thee-thou*-ing, and of other little intimacies. When I first entered the apartment, where he was surrounded by the officers of a most brilliant staff, he called out, "So, thou art come at last?'' But when we were alone, he gave me to understand that my reserve pleased him. I was immediately placed in charge of his correspondence.

The same evening I entertained him with a recital of the insurrection in the Venetian states, and the perils to which the French were exposed. "Set thyself at ease,'' was his reply; "these knaves shall pay well for this. Their republic has been!'' That republic yet stood rich and powerful; and the words recalled an expression of Naude, a writer of the age of Louis XIII. "Seest thou Constantinople, counting on its being the seat of a double empire; and Venice, that boasts the maturity of a thousand years? Their day will come!''

From the first, I easily perceived that Bonaparte was not extremely satisfied with the preliminaries of Leoben. It had been his wish to march upon Vienna. This he did not conceal from me. Previously to the proposal of peace with the Archduke Charles, he had written to the Directory, stating the design to follow up his success; but that, for this, the co-operation of the armies on the Sambre and Meuse, and on the Rhine was necessary. The Directory pronounced a diversion from that quarter impossible, and said that these armies were not in condition to pass the rivers in their front. This declaration, so unexpected, and so contrary to all his demands, forced him to set bounds to his triumphs, and to renounce the favorite idea of planting the standards of the republic on the ramparts of Vienna.

The very first paper I signed was the occasion of a little outbreak. A law of 23d August, 1794, prohibited the bearing of any name save those in the register of baptism. I wished to conform to this regulation, so stupidly opposed to inveterate habits. My elder brother was still alive; I signed "Fauvelet, junior." This made the General angry. "There is not even common-sense," said he, "in this change of designations; for twenty years I have known thee as Bourrienne: sign as thou art named, and send the long-robes with their laws to the right-about."

On the 20th April, returning to Italy, we were detained on an island by a sudden swelling of the Tagliamento. A courier appeared on the right bank, and made good the passage to our station. Bonaparte read in the despatches of the Directory that the armies on the German frontier, having arranged their dispositions for crossing the Rhine, had actually commenced hostilities on the very day of signing the preliminaries at Leoben. This news reached his headquarters seven days after that assembly had warned him not to reckon upon the co-operation of the armies of Germany. It is impossible to describe the General's emotion on the perusal of these despatches. He had signed the preliminaries only in consequence of the representations of his government that for the present a diversion by the armies on the Rhine was impracticable: now he learned that their

co-operation with the army he commanded was on the point
of being effected. So great was his agitation of mind that,
for the moment, he determined on repassing to the left bank
of the Tagliamento, and of breaking with the Austrians on
any pretext. He even persisted, till Berthier and other
generals combated this resolution. "How different," exclaimed he, "would have been the preliminaries!—if, indeed, they had ever existed." But his vexation and regret
—I might almost say despair—rose to its height, when a few
days subsequently he received from Moreau a communication, dated 23d April, announcing that he had passed the
Rhine on the 20th, most successfully, having taken 4,000
prisoners, and would lose no time in marching to his support. Who can say, indeed, what might have been the
consequences, but for this vacillating and suspicious policy
of the Directory, fomented by the basest intrigues, and jealousy of the young conqueror's fame? for, considering the
circumstances of the case, there cannot be a doubt that
the Directory, fearing his ambition, sacrificed the renown
of our arms, and the honor of our country. Had the movement on the Rhine, urgently demanded by Bonaparte, taken
place a few days earlier, he would have been enabled, without risk of defeat, to have dictated the conditions of peace,
or to have advanced upon Vienna. Strongly impressed with
a sense of this injustice, he wrote to the Directory, on the 8th
May: "Since apprised of the passage of the Rhine by Hoche
and Moreau, how deeply have I regretted that the movement
had not been effected a fortnight sooner, or at least that
Moreau had informed me of his being in a condition to
accomplish it." Information to the contrary, in fact, had
been transmitted! What becomes after this of the unjust
accusation that Bonaparte, through jealousy of Moreau,
deprived France of the future advantages of a protracted
campaign?

While traversing the Venetian States, on our return to
Milan, he discoursed often about the affairs of the republic
of Venice. He constantly asserted that in their origin he

had been entirely a stranger to the insurrections which had agitated the country. Good sense merely would have shown that, since his object was to carry the war to the banks of the Danube, he could have no possible interest in seeing his rear harassed by revolts, and his communications interrupted or cut off. "Such a combination," to continue in his own words, "would have been absurd, and could never have entered the head of one to whom his very enemies cannot deny a peculiar nicety of management." He acknowledged, however, that he did not now regret the turn things had taken, because he had already extracted advantage for the preliminaries, and hoped to profit still more in concluding a definite treaty. "On arriving at Milan," said he, "I will give orders to occupy Venice." It is, then, quite demonstrated to my judgment that, in their beginning, the Commander-in-Chief had no hand in these insurrections, which finally terminated the existence of Venice as an independent state; that, subsequently, he by no means regretted them; and, later still, turned them to good account.

The army reached Milan on the 5th May. Soon after Bonaparte established his headquarters at Montebello, a very beautiful seat, three leagues from the capital, and overlooking a magnificent view of Lombardy. Here negotiations commenced, the Marquis St. Gallo, Austrian plenipotentiary, taking up his residence within half a league of us, but the treaty was finally concluded at Passeriano. After making an excursion to the lakes of Como, Maggiore, and the Borromean isles, the General devoted his attention to the organization of Venice, Genoa, and the cities of the Milanese. He sought for mind, and found it not. "Good God," exclaimed he, "how rarely do we meet with men! There are in Italy eighteen millions of inhabitants, and I have with difficulty discovered two—Dandolo and Melzi." He had appreciated them justly. Dandolo is one of those who, during the revolutionary era, reflected the highest credit on Italy: a member of the Grand Council of the Cisalpine Republic, his subsequent administration in Dalmatia

was great, equitable and firm. The services of Melzi, Duke
of Lodi, as Chancellor and keeper of the Great Seal of the
kingdom of Italy, are known to all. But to those who have
seen a little of the world, Napoleon's reproach is only a
truism, forcibly expressed, and is more especially applicable
not to the upper, but to the highest rank of society.

While Bonaparte was thus variously engaged at a distance, efforts were making at home to deprive him of the
honor of conceiving those campaigns, the excellence of
which could not be concealed. It was an opinion generally admitted, that Carnot, from his office in the Luxembourg, drew up, or dictated for him, the plans of these campaigns; that Berthier was his right hand, whom he was
fortunate above measure in having near his person, without
whom he would have felt much embarrassed, even with the
plans of Carnot, which were often mere romances. This
twofold absurdity has survived for a moment even against
the evidence of facts. Many persons still entertain this belief, which, in foreign countries especially, finds numerous
partisans. Everywhere have I been assailed with questions
on the subject. Now, not one word of all this is true. We
must render unto Cæsar what is Cæsar's. Bonaparte was an
inventor, not an imitator, in the art of war. That no man
has here surpassed him is indisputable. At the commencement of this skilful campaign, the Directory, as a matter
of course, sent him certain instructions; but he invariably
followed his own judgment, constantly asserting in his despatches that all would be lost if movements, planned at a
distance from the scene of action, were to be implicitly or
blindly followed. Then he offered his resignation. The
Directory gave in, by acknowledging the difficulty of determining military operations at Paris: all things were arranged
by such concessions. On entering his service, I saw a despatch from the Directory, dated in May, 1796, authorizing
him to conduct the rest of the Italian campaign according
to his own views and calculations. And, most certainly,
there was not a movement, not a single operation, which

did not emanate from himself. Carnot had been obliged
to yield to his firmness.

When the Directory desired to treat of peace, toward the
close of the year 1796, General Clarke, appointed to conclude the armistice, had powers authorizing him, in case
Mantua did not fall during the arrangements, to include the
blockade as it should then stand. In this case, the Emperor
of Austria would have stipulated that the place and garrison
should be provisioned day by day. Bonaparte, convinced
that an armistice, *without Mantua*, would never be a step
toward peace, vehemently opposed this condition, to which,
indeed, he referred all assent. He carried his point—the
place capitulated—the consequences are known: the splendid campaign finished with an advantageous peace. Nevertheless, he had looked forward to the chances of war, and
was preparing, during the blockade, to gain possession by
storm. He wrote the Directory to that effect, remarking,
"A stroke of this nature depends absolutely upon luck—
upon a dog barking, or a goose cackling."

General Clarke had also again been appointed second
plenipotentiary in the negotiations now carrying on. Bonaparte more than once told me, as a fact not to be doubted,
that this officer had a secret mission, to watch, and even to
arrest him, should an occasion offer of doing so without
danger. That such suspicion was entertained, I cannot
deny; but I must add, that all my efforts failed to establish
its grounds. In daily intercourse with Clarke, he never put
a question to me; and I never heard a single expression
which could have induced the belief of his being a spy; if
one, he played his part skilfully. Even in his *intercepted*
correspondence, nothing transpired to confirm these suspicions. Bonaparte, however, could not endure him, and, by
his influence, rendered ineffective the diplomatic mission
of Clarke, who was recalled. But I must say, though esti-
mating his talents as not above par, he cherished no resentment in consequence of the conduct suspected to have been·
pursued in Italy; "having alone," observed he, "the right

to be offended, I pardon." He had even the generosity to demand, in Clarke's favor, a diplomatic mission of the second class. Such traits were not uncommon with him.

Bonaparte, excessively sensitive to whatever reached him of the reports concerning Carnot and Berthier, said to me one day, "This is so gross an absurdity! It is very easy to say to a general, 'Depart for Italy, win battles, and advance till you sign peace in Vienna.' But the execution—there's the rub!—that is not quite so easy a matter. I never set the least account upon the orders received from the Directory. There are upon the spot too many circumstances to modify such instructions. The movement of a single corps of the enemy's army will completely overturn an entire plan arranged thus by the chimney-corner. None but old women would put faith in such gossip. As to Berthier, since you have been with me, you see what he is: he is a blockhead. What! So he has done all! It is he who appropriates a great part of the glory of the Army of Italy!" In reply, I endeavored to show such ideas must in the end yield to the truth; that each would then enjoy his own; or at least, that posterity would do justice. This pleased him.

For my own part, I liked Berthier. I found him an excellent person throughout our very intimate and long intercourse. Our numerous avocations in common had occasioned his contracting a custom of thou and thee-ing me, in conversation, but never in writing: in return, I used to banter him, but very unsuccessfully, for murdering his vowels, a habit which, in speaking, gave a coarseness to his enunciation. He abounded in courage, honor and probity, with great regularity in business. Berthier, however, could neither yield with affability, nor refuse without harshness. He knew perfectly the station of all the corps, the names of their commanders, and their force: he was always ready, day and night. He dictated with precision and clearness the orders derived from the General's instructions, and was, besides, sincerely devoted to his leader. In fine, it must be allowed that he formed an excellent chief of staff.

Here let his admirers stop. He himself wished no higher praise. His talents were very limited, confined to a particular department, and united with a character of extreme weakness. Such, too, was his entire dependence upon Bonaparte, and so great his admiration of him, that he never would have presumed to oppose his plans or give advice: on the other hand, Bonaparte's friendship, the frequent occurrence of his name in bulletins and official despatches, had increased Berthier's reputation beyond its just extent. The former, speaking of the latter to the Directory, who had desired his opinion of the generals employed under him, said: "Talents, activity, courage, character, everything, is in favor of Berthier." This was in 1796, when he made an *eagle* of him; at St. Helena he has described him as a *goose*. The truth lies in between: he was neither the one nor the other. Yet, to Berthier, Bonaparte was more attached by habit than by inclination; but Bonaparte was greatly a creature of habit. He counted much upon his whereabout, and disliked new arrangements, or, in his own words, "new faces." Berthier loved him, and executed his orders well; and this made up for want of genius.

As to Carnot, when his reputation shall have ceased to depend upon temporary influences, and when his character shall be tried by the touchstone of distant history, there will remain to him nothing of his pretended portion in the triumphs of the Army of Italy, or in the glory, most unquestionably *exclusive*, of its immortal leader.

CHAPTER III

Conduct of the Directory and Augereau—The Treaty of Campo-Formio—
Return from Italy—Tributes to the Conquering Hero

BONAPARTE had long foreseen an impending struggle between the supporters of monarchy and the republicans. The contest was now on the eve of decision. The partisans of royalty were reported to abound in all quarters. Every officer returning from Paris to the army deprecated vehemently the spirit of reaction which agitated the interior.... The private correspondence of the General urged him unceasingly to declare his party, or pressed him to act for himself. At the same time, there existed in the majority of both assemblies of the legislature an evident dislike of Bonaparte. The leaders of the royalists and the orators of Clichy incessantly wounded his self-love by their discourses and writings. They overwhelmed him with abuse; they vilified his name and the reputation of his army, and censured, with asperity, the plan of his campaigns and conduct in Italy, especially with respect to Venice. His services thus obtained for recompense only hatred and ingratitude. Comparisons with other generals were instituted, and he was considered merely as a fiery and impetuous leader. He had become absolutely tired of the epithet "learned," as repeated to satiety, in speaking of Moreau's tactics.

But a circumstance which afflicted him still more was to see Frenchmen who were members of the national councils yet enemies and slanderers of the national glory. He represented to the Directory the necessity of arresting the emigrants; of destroying foreign influence; of putting down the journals named as sold to England and Austria, and which, in advocating their principles, he accused of being more sanguinary than Marat had ever been. He urged the recall of the armies, and shutting the club, society, or cabal, of Clichy, all the members of which were secret or declared enemies of revolutionary principles. The remembrance of his destitute situation in 1795, occasioned chiefly by Aubry, one of its warmest partisans, doubtless now sharpened the General's resentment against this assembly. The cause of the Revolution, embraced at this epoch by Bonaparte, was also supported by the victorious Army of Italy, which he took care to represent as indignant at the occurrences passing in France, persuaded even his soldiers to think that they were so, and to declare themselves exclusively animated with a desire of marching to the succor of liberty, and of the constitution of the year III.

His resolution to pass the Alps with 25,000 men, and advance by way of Lyons upon Paris, was well known in the capital, and all were occupied in discussing the conse-quences of this passage of a new Rubicon. Carnot, who has always appeared to me to have been sincere in his inten-tions, but whom, because in the minority of the Directory, Bonaparte deceived, wrote to the General, August 17, 1797: "Here the good people fabricate a thousand projects for you, each more absurd than the other. They cannot believe that one capable of so great things will condescend to live as a private citizen." This has reference to the General's reiterated application for leave to retire from affairs, founded on the state of his health. This he represented to be so pre-carious as to require two years of repose for its re-establish-ment, and as not permitting him any longer to mount on horseback. Bonaparte despised the Directory, accusing the members of imbecility—of wavering and pusillanimous con-duct—of numberless faults—of embezzling the resources of the state—and of persisting in a system vicious in itself and debasing to the national glory. He knew that the royalist party demanded his dismissal, and even arrest. But before declaring for either of the two factions, he first thought of his own interests. He did not consider that enough had yet been done to bear him out in a daring attempt to seize the supreme power, which, as respected the mere act of seizure, had certainly been an easy achievement in his cir-cumstances. He rested content for the present to support that party which was backed by the opinion of the moment, and by the sentiment he had himself inspired into the troops. I have mentioned his determination to march to Paris, should things appear to take a turn unfavorable to re-publicanism, which he preferred to royalty, hoping better to attain his own ends in the ascendency of the former. At this time he was even seriously arranging his plan of cam-paign. To defend this so much despised Directory appeared identical with working for his own proper windfall; that is to say, an institution seemingly of no further use, beyond keeping the place for him, until he should find it quite convenient to take it himself.

Toward the end of July, in order to be informed of every transaction, Bonaparte despatched to Paris his aide-de-camp La Valette, who possessed and merited his unreserved confidence. La Valette united to an excellent education, solidity of acquirement, an amiable disposition, a pliant temper and moderate opinions. His devotion, too, was absolute. He received instructions, and a particular cipher for his correspondence with the General-in-Chief. A few days after, Augereau set out, on 27th July. Bonaparte, on this occasion, wrote *officially* to the Directory, that "this officer had demanded leave of absence to go to Paris on his own private affairs." Bearer of the addresses of the Italian Army, and named, on the 9th August, commander of the seventeenth military division, "he came to cut the throats of the royalists." This we shall see presently. These were also his own vaunts. Such were his private affairs! Let us declare the truth: Augereau was sent expressly for the purpose of seconding the revolution preparing against the royal party, and the minority of the Directory. So decidedly, too, had Bonaparte taken his resolution, that, ten days before, wishing to instruct Augereau in the part to be played, a courier extraordinary was despatched to Vicenza, where he commanded, with an order for him to repair upon the instant to Milan; and, to insure greater secrecy, the private order bore, "You will recollect my own apartment below is unoccupied, and ready for your reception." Augereau was selected for this service, because Bonaparte knew the extravagance of his republican principles, his daring spirit, and small political capacity. He believed him quite capable of aiding a movement of which his own presence with the army did not permit a personal superintendence: while, as an agent, the former could be a rival, neither in glory nor ambition, capable of converting that movement to his own profit.

Not satisfied with two agents, Bonaparte, somewhat

later, sent Bernadotte to Paris, for a similar purpose. The pretext assumed this time was to present to the Directory four standards taken at the battle of Rivoli, which, through mistake, had been left at Peschiera. Bernadotte played no conspicuous part in the affair. He was always prudent.

By these means Bonaparte was made aware of every event, even before it was made public at Paris. A constant correspondence was kept up through La Valette, Augereau, Barras, Carnot, Bernadotte and Talleyrand, which I have preserved, and which will be found to differ in several respects from the recital of the same transaction by Napoleon at St. Helena to his noble companions in misfortune. One of La Valette's early letters shows the state of parties. "The minority of the Directory always hope the possibility of an accommodation with the Chambers. The majority will perish rather than yield more; they see the abyss dug before them. But such is the infatuation of Carnot, or the feebleness of his character, that he hesitates whether to become a supporter of monarchy, as he acted in the case of the Terrorists. He advises temporizing. Barras, on the contrary, says, 'I only wait the decree of accusation to march against the conspirators in the councils, and soon shall their heads roll in the kennels!'" The transactions of the 18th Fructidor (September 3, 1797)—which brought this crisis to an issue, gave the triumph to the republican party, and deferred for three years the demise of the pentarchy—offers one of the most remarkable events in its brief and pitiable existence. Once the resolution was formed, but the execution delayed, according to the aide-de-camp's statement, "because of disagreement respecting the proper means of carrying into effect an arrest of the obnoxious members of council; and the apprehension of ulterior results where the first success was not doubtful." A few days after, Augereau writes thus: "The determination of the Directory is the same to-day—that is to say, the project always advances, and its execution will preserve the republic, notwithstanding the apathy of the indolent and the opposition of the demagogues.

So send me the money." Four days before the final consummation, La Valette reports: "At length the movement,
so often announced, is about to take place. The Directory
will cause to be arrested to-morrow night, or the next, fifteen
or twenty deputies. It is not expected there will be any
resistance." And, on the eventful day itself, Augereau
wrote announcing its results: "18th Fructidor. At length,
my dear General [success had rendered him familiar], my
mission is fulfilled, and the promises of the Army of Italy
were this night redeemed. The Directory had resolved on
a vigorous stroke: the moment was yet uncertain, the preparations incomplete: fear of being anticipated hastened
measures. At midnight I despatched an order for all the
troops to put themselves in motion, and to march upon
the points indicated: before day all the bridges and principal
squares were occupied with cannon: at daybreak the halls of
the councils were surrounded. The council guards cordially
fraternized with our troops, and the members, whose names
are subjoined, have been arrested and committed to the
Temple prison. The prosecution of a still greater number
continues. Carnot has disappeared. Paris is tranquil, and
in astonishment that a crisis, announced so terribly, has
passed over in holiday guise. The robust patriot of the
suburbs proclaims the safety of the republic, and the black
necks (the priests) are under. It now remains for the wise
energy of the Directory, and of the patriots of both councils,
to finish the rest. The seat of the assemblies is changed,
and the first operations promise for good. This event is a
great step toward peace. It is for you to overleap the space
which still keeps us from this conclusion."

On the 24th, Bernadotte says, "The deputies arrested on
the 18th have been sent off for Rochefort, where they are
to embark for Madagascar, the place of banishment. Paris
is tranquil. The people learned of the arrest of the deputies
at first with indifference. A sentiment of curiosity by and
by drew them into the streets; enthusiasm followed; and the
cry of 'Long live the Republic!' so long unheard, resounded

throughout the whole city. Some of the neighboring departments have expressed their disapprobation. One has pro-
tested; but it will be alone. The government has at this
moment in its power the possible resuscitation of national
energy; but every one feels the necessity of surrounding it
with republicans of activity and worth. Unfortunately a
multitude of men, without talents, and without means,
already believe that the movement has been only for them.
Time will set all this to rights. The armies have recovered
stability; the military of the interior are respected, or, at
least, feared. The emigrants flee, and the disaffected priests
conceal themselves. Never was any event more auspicious
for consolidating the republic. The Legislative Body has
conceded to the Directory a great degree of power. There
remains, nevertheless, a considerable party in both councils
adverse to republican forms, who, so soon as the first
emotion of fear has passed, will endeavor to ruin all. This
the Government knows. Measures will, therefore, be taken
to guard against such a result, and to secure the patriots
against a new persecution.''—Talleyrand writes on the last
day of the same month, ''We intend publishing documents,
clearly showing that the courts of Vienna and of London
were in the best understanding with the faction just suppressed among us. It will appear in our proclamations to
what extent the negotiations of these two courts, and the
movements in the interior, have accorded. The members of
Clichy, and the cabinet of the emperor, had for a common
and manifest object the re-establishment of a king in
France, and a disgraceful peace, by which Italy should be
restored to her ancient masters.''

Bonaparte experienced an intoxication of joy on learning the happy issue of the 18th Fructidor. Its results produced the dissolution of the Legislative Assembly, and the
fall of a party which for months had disturbed his peace.
The admission of his brother Joseph into the Council of the
Five Hundred, formerly opposed by the Clichians, followed
as another consequence; but the General soon perceived that

the victors abused their power, and were compromising anew the safety of the republic, by reviving the former principles of revolutionary government. The Directory was both alarmed at his dissatisfaction and resented his censure. The members conceived the singular idea of opposing to him Augereau, of whose blind devotion they had just received proof, and this officer was, accordingly, named Commander of the Army of Germany. Augereau, whose extreme vanity is notorious, believed himself able to cope with the conqueror of Italy. His arrogance rested on the achievement of having, with numerous soldiery, arrested a few unarmed representatives, and torn the epaulets from the uniform of the commandant of their guards. The Directory and he filled the headquarters, now removed from Milan to Passeriano, with informers and intriguers. Bonaparte, informed of all, laughed at the Directory, offering his resignation, that he might be entreated to retain the command. He did not, however, cease to complain of their proceedings, sharply commenting on "the sole efficacy of wisdom and moderation in establishing the happiness of the country"; cautioning them "to take care lest, after having humbled thrones, they should allow hireling writers, and ambitious fanatics, disguised under every species of mask, to plunge them anew into the revolutionary torrent." He affected deep indignation at their doings respecting Augereau, etc. "It is evident, then, from all these facts that the government is acting toward me in much the same way as Pichegru was treated after Vendemiaire. I request you will accept my resignation, and appoint some one to succeed me. No power on earth shall persuade me to continue in the service, after this horrible instance of ingratitude on the part of government. My health, also, considerably affected, imperatively demands repose and tranquillity. The state of my mind, too, requires to recover its tone among the mass of citizens. For a long period, great power has been intrusted to my discretion: in all circumstances I have employed it for the welfare of the country—*so much the worse for those who believe not in virtue, and who may have suspected mine.* My reward exists in my own breast, and in the opinion of posterity. Now that the country is secure I may retire. In the moment of peril, I shall be found in the foremost rank in defence of liberty and the constitution." To these complaints, the Directory replied in the most soothing and even submissive strain. They also sent their agent Bottot, secretary of Barras, to headquarters, ostensibly for the purpose of reassuring the General as to their friendly intentions. This person Bonaparte regarded, and perhaps justly, as a spy; he treated him accordingly with great coldness, but never, as has been said, entertained for a moment the idea of causing him to be shot.

I shall now say a word on the treaty of Campo-Formio; not that I imagine all these treaties, pretended masterpieces of human wisdom, the offspring, so to speak, of the power of destruction, and which perish as speedily as the producing cause, will much engage posterity. In blotting Venice from the list of states, France and Austria equally partook of her spoils: a portion was given to the Cisalpine republic. Now Austria owns the whole. Venice herself, and her finest provinces, were then ceded to Austria in compensation for Belgium and Lombardy. Austria took, without scruple, these beautiful portions of the Venetian territories, though that State, ever devoted to Austrian politics, had, in fact, sacrificed herself by adhering, at a critical juncture, to those very interests. An insurrection in its rear had preserved the hereditary dominions from the prolonged occupation of the French army.

After the 18th Fructidor, General Bonaparte had more power, and Austria less of haughty confidence. The Directory, in fact, wrote "that it was no longer necessary to temporize with her, and that it was evident she had only protracted discussions of peace, waiting an expected explosion in France, and as a pretext for obtaining the requisite time to repair her losses. From the commander to the meanest soldier the Austrians at this period maintained that the three Directors, whom they termed triumvirs, should be

poniarded, and royalty proclaimed. All flattered themselves with being speedily in Paris, attended by the emigrants. Condé, the chief of the latter, was already secretly in France, and, by the aid of his connections, had
penetrated as far as Lyons." The success of the directoral
majority overturned these hopes. Accordingly, Bonaparte
received at his headquarters, about a month after their removal to Passeriano, a letter, written with the Emperor's
own hand, dated Vienna, 20th September. In this document, Francis expressed his *surprise* to learn the tardy state
of the negotiations, and his sincere desire of peace; announcing the Count Cobentzel as the bearer of his final determinations, and as possessing his entire confidence. "After this
new assurance," continued the Emperor, "of the spirit of
conciliation on my part, I doubt not you will feel that peace
is in your hands, and that on your counsels will depend the
happiness of many millions of men. Should I be deceived
in the means I considered as the most likely to put an end
to the calamities which have so long desolated Europe, I
shall at least possess the consolation of having tried all
measures depending upon myself. The consequences which
may thence result I can never be reproached with."

Not before the arrival of this document and its bearer
did negotiations seriously commence; former plenipotentiaries, Bonaparte easily perceived, were not authorized to
conclude anything definite. His first ideas on the terms
to be granted, which I have preserved, and here insert, and
which the reader may compare with the actual treaty, comprised the five following conditions: "1. The Emperor shall
have Italy to the Adda; 2. The King of Sardinia to the
Adda; 3. The republic of Genoa shall have Tortona, as far
as the Po (Tortona to be demolished), as also the imperial
fiefs (Coni to be given up to France, or dismantled); 4. The
Grandduke of Tuscany to be restored; 5. The Duke of
Parma to be restored."

The only point of great difficulty was Venice. Austria
stipulated for the line of the Adige, with that republic, in

exchange for Metz, and the boundary of the Rhine, to the confines of Holland. The Directory insisted upon these last border lines, and Mantua, for the Italian republic, without conceding the whole line of the Adige and Venice. The difficulties upon these points rendered peace so doubtful that, for a month before the final ratification, the manner of announcing the rupture was seriously discussed.

During the concluding arrangements of the negotiation, Bonaparte, tired out with so much folly—as, for instance, a proposal from the Directory to revolutionize the whole of Italy—and so many difficulties, repeated more than once his offer to resign, and expressly requested a successor. In all this there was little sincerity. So judged the Directory. In spite of this feigned indifference, therefore, his resignation was refused in terms the most flattering and urgent. This was what he wished. One cause of real discontent was the persuasion that the Directory had divined his object, and regarded his powerful aid on the 18th Fructidor as originating in personal views of ambition and power. Notwithstanding written assurances of hypocritical gratitude, and sentiments the very opposite, and although the Directory stood indispensably in need of his support, they caused him to be watched by agents, who spied his proceedings, and sought, by means of his confidential retainers, to penetrate his views. His friends wrote him from Paris; and I incessantly repeated that peace, which depended upon his decision, would prove a much more popular measure than the renewal of hostilities, exposed as war would be to new chances of success and reverse.

A premature winter hastened his resolutions. On opening my windows at daybreak, on the 18th October, I beheld the mountains covered with snow. The weather on the preceding evening had been beautiful, and, till then, the autumn had advanced as if promising to be fine and late. I entered the General's bedroom at seven o'clock, as usual, and, awakening him, related what had happened. He, at first, affecting not to believe me, jumped out of bed, ran to the window, and, having witnessed himself this so unexpected change, pronounced with the greatest calmness these words: "Before the middle of October! What a country!—Come: peace must be made." While he was dressing in haste, I read the journals to him, as I did every day. He gave little heed; but, shutting himself up with me in his cabinet, most carefully reviewed the condition of the several portions of his army. "See here," said he; "nearly 80,000 effective men: I feed and pay this number; but shall not have more than 60,000 on the day of battle. I shall win; but then I shall be reduced 20,000 in killed, wounded and prisoners. How, then, resist all the Austrian forces which will march to the relief of Vienna? A month or more will be necessary for the armies of the Rhine to support me, supposing them in condition; and in a fortnight the snow will block up the roads and passes. It is decided. I make peace. Venice shall pay the expenses of the war, and our boundary shall be the Rhine. The Directory and the lawyers may prattle as they please."

He wrote to the Directory: "The tops of the mountains are covered with snow. I cannot, according to stipulated forms, commence operations in less than twenty-five days, and then we shall find ourselves in deep snow." Fourteen years afterward, a winter, equally untimely, but in a climate far more severe, must of course have opposed to him obstacles more fatal. Why did he not exercise the same cautious foresight?

Conferences followed, and peace, as predicted, was made at the expense of Venice.

The 18th Fructidor, without doubt, powerfully contributed to the arrangements at Campo-Formio. The Directory, on the one hand, more pacifically inclined, after this stroke of policy, felt at length the necessity of putting an end to discontent by giving peace to France; while, on the other, Austria, seeing the plans of the royalists in the interior completely traversed, deemed it time to conclude with the republic a treaty, which, despite of minor objections, left her

mistress of Italy. Besides, the campaign of the French
army, so fruitful in splendid deeds of arms, had not merely
produced glory—greatness followed in the footsteps of conquest. As there had been hitherto something singular in
our public affairs, a grand moral influence, the fruit of victories and of peace, was now ready to expand over the whole
of France. Republicanism was no longer the blood-stained
and ferocious monster of former years. Treating as an equal
with princes and their ministers, but with all the superiority
derived from victory and his own genius, Bonaparte, by degrees, brought foreign courts to become familiar with republican France, and the republic to cease regarding all states
governed by kings as natural enemies.

Under these circumstances, the approaching arrival in
Paris of the General-in-Chief, occupied universal attention;
and the feebleness of the Directory yielded, in the capital of
France, to the presence of the Conqueror of Italy. On the
17th November, he quitted Milan, for the congress at Ra-
stadt, there to preside over the French delegation. Before
departing, however, he sent to the Directory one of those
messages which might well pass for fabulous, though here
simple truth only required to be related. This memorial
was the colors of the Army of Italy. One side bore inscribed, "A grateful country to the Army of Italy": the
other exhibited a simple and magnificent abridgment of
the history of the Italian campaign, its military achievements, political results, and fruits, in the treasures of art
brought to the capital of France—"150,000 prisoners, 170
standards, 550 cannons, 600 field-pieces, 5 bridge equipages,
9 sixty-fours, 12 frigates (thirty-twos), 12 corvettes, 18 galleys; Armistice with Sardinia, convention with Genoa, armistice with Naples, with the Pope, with the Duke of Parma,
convention of Montebello, treaty of Campo-Formio; Liberty given to the people of Bologna, and fifteen other states
in Italy, Corcyra, with the isles of the Egean and of Ithaca;
Sent to Paris masterpieces by Michelangelo, Guercino,
Titian, Paul Veronese, Correggio, Albano, the Carraci, Ra-

phael, and Da Vinci." This standard was destined to form
the decoration of the public hall of the Directory.

The greater part of the cities of Italy had been accustomed to behold in their conqueror a liberator; and such
magic is there in the word liberty, which now resounded
from the Alps to the Apennines, that everywhere Bonaparte
was received with enthusiasm. At Mantua he was lodged
in the palace of the ancient dukes, and, during a residence
of two days, traced the plan, and commenced the foundation, of a canal on the Mincio; celebrated a military funeral
in honor of General Hoche; and superintended the erection
of a monument to Virgil. At this period, one who had
never before seen Bonaparte, describes him thus, in a letter
to Paris: "I beheld with deep interest and extreme attention, that extraordinary man, who has performed so many
great things, and who seems to promise that his career is
not yet closed. I found him very like his portraits, small
in stature, thin, pale, having the air of one overwrought,
not in ill health, as reported. He appeared to me to listen
with more abstraction than interest, as if occupied rather
with his own thoughts than with what was said to him.
There is much of the intellectual in his physiognomy, and
an expression of habitual meditation, which reveals nothing
of what is passing within. In that thoughtful head, in that
daring mind, it is impossible not to suppose some bold
thoughts, which will influence the destinies of Europe."
We might imagine but for the date (the latter being actually
published in the newspapers of December, 1797), that this
last sentence had been written after subsequent events had
verified the conjecture.

The journey of Bonaparte across Switzerland, while to
himself a real triumph, left also useful consequences; and
his presence calmed many apprehensions. After the recent
overturnings among the Cisalpine states, the Swiss feared
some dismemberment, or, at least, some encroachment, which
the chances of war might have rendered possible. Everywhere he applied himself to restore confidence, and every-

where was received with enthusiasm, as the "pacificator"; such was the desire of seeing him speedily, that throughout the whole route, from Aix in Savoy, by Geneva and Berne, to Basel, a relay of thirty horses night and day awaited his service. At Geneva he received the envoys from Berne, whom he dismissed, satisfied by his pacific assurances. On arriving, overnight, in that city, we passed through a double line of carriages, lighted up and filled with handsome dames, who made the air ring with "Long live Bonaparte! Long live the Pacificator!"

The most magnificent preparations were now going on at the Luxembourg for Bonaparte's reception. The great court of the palace, elegantly ornamented, was crowded with spectators. On an immense amphitheatre, erected at the lower end, sat the public authorities, while the windows were filled with ladies. Opposite the principal entrance rose the patriotic altar, surmounted by the statues of Liberty, Equality and Peace. When Bonaparte entered, every one stood up, and uncovered. Notwithstanding this splendor, the ceremony was one of freezing heartlessness. All wore an air of restraint, with more of curiosity than of gratitude in their expression, each seemingly an inquisitor of his neighbor. An unpleasant accident doubtless contributed to increase this general sense of oppression. One of the under secretaries of the Directory, contrary to strict orders, had mounted upon some scaffolding on the roof of the right wing, then under repair; but scarcely had he set foot on the first plank, when it capsized, and the unfortunate functionary was precipitated from a great height into the arena below. A universal stupor fell upon all; women were taken ill, and the windows were nearly deserted. Some mischievous wits—such are everywhere to be found—amused themselves and others by foreseeing, in this fall of their subordinate, that of Messieurs the Directors themselves.

The business proceeded; harangues were not spared. Talleyrand introduced the General to the Directory, making a long discourse, listened to with some impatience, so great was the desire to hear Bonaparte. The Conqueror of Italy arose, and with a modest air, but firm voice, pronounced the following brief address to the Directors, speaking as if they had done all, and mentioning himself only once:

"The French people, in order to be free, had kings to beat down. To obtain a constitution founded on reason, eighteen centuries of prejudice were to be overcome. The constitution of the year III., and you, have triumphed over all these obstacles. Religion, feudalism, and royalty, have successively, for twenty centuries, governed Europe; but, from the peace which you have just concluded dates the era of representative governments. You have accomplished the organization of the great nation, whose territory is now bounded, only because Nature herself has fixed its limits. You have done more. The two most beautiful regions of Europe, once so famous in science, in art, and by the great men whose birthplace they were, behold, with the loftiest hopes, the genius of freedom arise from the tombs of their ancestors. These are the two pedestals on which the destinies will place two mighty nations. I have the honor to lay before you the treaty signed at Campo-Formio, and ratified by his majesty the Emperor. When the happiness of the French people shall be secured on the best practical laws, all Europe will become free."

Barras, then president, replied with a prolixity of which everybody seemed tired. Having at length concluded, he threw himself into the arms of the General, who had little liking for such affectations, giving him what was then termed the fraternal "accolade," or embrace. The rest of the members following the example of their president, surrounded and embraced Bonaparte, each striving to do his best in this scene of sentimental comedy.

The two councils would not be behind the Directory: a few days after they also gave an entertainment to the General, in the gallery of the Louvre, newly enriched with the masterpieces of painting brought from Italy. All these shows were actual punishments to Bonaparte, who, from the time of his arrival in Paris, displayed great modesty in all things. For example, the authorities of the department

of the Seine had sent a deputation, requesting to know
when he would receive them: he, himself, accompanied by
General Berthier, took his own reply to the magistracy. It
was remarked, also, that the judge of the division in which
the General resided having waited upon him at his house,
the evening of his arrival, December 6th, he returned the
visit next day. These attentions, puerile in appearance,
were not without effect upon the minds of the Parisians.
Though he lived very retired, he often attended the opera.
But, as it formed part of his plan to show himself as little
as possible, he usually took his station at the bottom of the
box behind his wife, placing me beside her. Several times
he was called for, with loud acclamations, but in vain: he
never presented himself. Once he sent me to procure the
performance of certain pieces, with a particular cast of
the characters, so as to include several distinguished actors,
if that were *possible*. "Nothing," said the gallant manager,
"is *impossible* where the wishes of the Conqueror of Italy
are concerned. Your General has banished that word from
the French dictionary." Bonaparte laughed immoderately
at the extreme politeness of the operatic artist.

In the midst of this popularity, a woman sent notice to
inform him that an attempt was to be made upon his life,
and that poison would be the means employed. Bonaparte
caused the bearer to be arrested, who, accompanied by the
judge, was conducted to the woman's house who had given
the information. They found her dead upon the floor,
bathed in blood, with her throat cut and several stabs in
different parts of her body. The men whose conversation
she had overheard and disclosed, having learned the fact,
had taken this fearful revenge.

The street in which his small residence, No. 6, stood, was
named Chantereine; but, during the night of the 10th–11th
December, received the appellation of "Victory," in consequence of a public decree. This and other incense offered
to his fame, the acclamations which everywhere followed his
appearance, altered not his view of the position which he

knew himself to occupy in public opinion. He used to say to me, "In Paris they soon forget everything. If I remain long idle here, I am lost. In this great Babylon one reputation supplants another. People will not have seen me above thrice at the theatre, when I shall be no longer an object of their regard: therefore I shall appear but seldom." When he did go, it was to a private box. "Nevertheless," observed I, "it must be agreeable to be thus besieged by the admiration of one's fellow-citizens."—"Bah! the same crowd would run after me with the same eagerness were I going to the gallows."

On the 28th December he was chosen a member of the Institute, for the class of arts and sciences. He showed himself very sensible to this tribute of a learned body, and addressed, upon the occasion, the following note to Camus, president of the class:

"The suffrage of the distinguished men who compose the Institute honors me. I feel sensibly, that before I can become their equal I shall long be their pupil. If there were any mode more expressive than another of conveying to them my sentiments of respect, that I would employ. The only true conquests, those which awaken no regret, are such as we obtain over ignorance: The most honorable, as the most useful pursuits of nations, are those which contribute to the extension of human thought. Henceforth, let the real greatness of our republic consist in not permitting the existence of one new idea which has not been added to the national intelligence.   BONAPARTE."

About this period, also, the General renewed, but still unsuccessfully, his former attempt to obtain a dispensation of age and seat in the Directory. Perceiving the field to be not yet clear, he said to me, on the 29th January, 1798, "Bourrienne, I shall remain here no longer: there is no good to be done: they will listen to nothing. I see, if I loiter here, I am done for quickly. Here, everything grows flat: my fame is already on the wane. This little Europe of ours cannot supply the demand. We must to the East: all great reputations come from that quarter. How-

ever, I will first take a turn round the coast to assure myself
what can be done. I will take you with me—you, Lannes
and Sulkowsky. If the success of a descent upon England
appear doubtful, as I fear, the Army of England shall become the Army of the East, and I am off for Egypt."

This, and many such like conversations, give a just idea
of his character. He always considered war and conquest
as the noblest and most inexhaustible sources of glory.
This glory, indeed, he loved with passion, but now there
was policy in his fervor. While, by distant exploits, fame
was kept toiling after him, he hoped that events would
occur in France to render his return necessary and oppor-
tune. His place would be ready, and he would thus appear
to claim it as a man neither forgotten nor unknown.

CHAPTER IV

Preparations for the Egyptian Campaign—Napoleon's Literary Tastes—
Malta Taken—His Occupations at Sea—Easy Capture of Alexandria—March into the Desert begun

IT WAS resolved that Bonaparte should attempt in the
East an expedition unusual in modern Europe. On
the 12th April, 1798, he was named Commander-in-Chief
of the Army of the East, which the same day also beheld
created. At the same time, Marmont espoused Mademoiselle Perregaux, and La Valette a young lady of the family
of Beauharnais, niece to Josephine. After the explanations
already given, what are we to think of the *honorable exile*,
the *ostracism*, to which the Directory are said to have
wished, by this expedition, to condemn Bonaparte? Bonaparte was scarcely the man to allow himself to be banished!
Doubtless, the project of the colonization of Egypt was not
new—it had been proposed to Louis XV. by the Duke de
Choiseuil; but the design had slumbered along with so
many others, in the forgetfulness of dusty parchments. Its

revival is entirely due to Bonaparte. At Passeriano, seeing the term of his labors in Europe approach, he first turned his serious attention eastward. There, during long evening walks in the magnificent park, this subject formed a no less interesting than inexhaustible theme of discourse with his favorite generals, aides-de-camp, and myself. "Europe," he would exclaim, "is but a mole-hill: there never have existed mighty empires, there never have occurred great revolutions, save in the East, where, 600,000,000 of people live, where the cradle of all religions is, the birthplace of all philosophies!" Monge was almost always present at these conversations. That learned man, ardent in mind and heart, falling in with these opinions, excited yet higher enthusiasm in the bold spirit and lively fancy of our General. We all joined in chorus. It is to similar scenes Desaix alludes, when, writing to Bonaparte, he said, "I have viewed, with deep interest, the fleet at Corfu. If ever it sail upon those great enterprises of which you have spoken, in pity do not forget me." He was not forgotten. I repeat, then, the Directory went for nothing, in reviving the design of this memorable enterprise, whose issue answered neither to the grandeur of its conception, nor the boldness of its plan. With any other government, success had been certain. In respect of personal will, the Directors remained as perfect strangers to his departure as they were to his return. They were but the passive official instruments of Bonaparte's inclinations. These they converted into decrees and orders when the forms of government required. They no more devised the conquest of Egypt than they traced the mode of its execution. It was he who organized the Army of the East; procured money; appointed the leaders; assembled the ships of war, frigates and transports. To him pertains, also, the happy and noble idea of adding to the expedition men distinguished in art and science; the fruits of their labors, while they have revealed the present, and much of the ancient, state of a region, the name of which is never pronounced without awakening mighty recollections, now remain the sole result of one of the most extraordinary enterprises of modern times. These eminent individuals were chosen by Bonaparte, who carried into that country, again plunged into ignorance and barbarity, the treasures of civilization and of industry—gifts alone capable of softening here below the mournful destiny of man.

His orders traversed with the rapidity of lightning the coast line from Toulon to the mouth of the Tiber. He assigned, with admirable precision, the place of meeting—to some before Malta, to others before Alexandria. All these orders he dictated to me in his own closet. It was he, not the Directory, who hastened the expedition. Doubtless, he was seconded with perfect goodwill. They dreaded his reputation, character and fame, and, therefore, were not sorry to see him remove to a distance, and refused him nothing; but we must carefully separate this selfish feeling from any desire to increase his fame, as also, from any love to France. Indeed, had not personal considerations blinded them to all other views, far from facilitating, the Directors ought to have opposed this expedition. Ultimately for themselves, immediately for France, a victory on the Adige would have been of far more value than one on the Nile. The desire of getting rid of one whose talents and competition they feared, shut their eyes to evident danger, in depriving the country of a noble army, of many illustrious generals, and to the probable loss of the fleet, while relations with foreign powers were at best but ill assured. As to Bonaparte, he was fully convinced that there remained for him no choice between this hazardous adventure and destruction. At the same time, Egypt appeared a proper field in which to maintain his reputation, and to exalt yet higher the splendor of his name.

A short time before our departure, I asked how long he intended to remain in the East? "A few months, or six years," was the reply; "all depends upon events. I shall colonize the country, and take out artists, workmen of all descriptions, women, actors. We are only twenty-nine; we must be thirty-five. These six years will suffice me, if things succeed, to reach India. Tell all those who talk of your departure that you are going to Brest. Say the same to your own family." I did so.

The following list of books, for a camp library, I copy from a paper in his own hand, given me to make the purchase. The volumes were in 18mo., and will show what he preferred in science and literature. I have, however, corrected the orthography, and cannot help remarking how, knowing the writers so well, he could have written, for instance, *Ducecling*, *Ocean*. Certainly, to divine that this latter meant *Ossian* required an intimate acquaintance with his favorite passion for the bard of Caledonia.

I. *Science and the Arts.*—Plurality of Worlds, Fontenelle, 1 vol.; Letters to a German Princess, 2; Course of the Normal School, 6; Treatise on Artillery, 1; On Fortifications, 8; On Fireworks, 1.

II. *Geography and Travels.*—Barclay's Geography, 12 vols.; Cook's Voyages, 3; La Harpe's Collection of French Voyages and Travels, 24 vols.

III. *History.*—Plutarch, 12 vols.; Turenne, 2; Condé, 4; Villars, 4; Luxembourg, 2; Duguesclin, 2; Saxe, 3; Memoirs of the French Marshals, 20; President Hainault, 4; Chronology, 2; Marlborough, 4; Prince Eugene, 6; Philosophical History of India, 12; Germany, 2; Charles XII., 1; Essay on the Manners of Nations, 6; Peter the Great, 1; Polybius, 6; Justin, 2; Arrian, 3; Tacitus, 2; Livy, vols. —; Thucydides, 2; Vertot, 4; Denina, 8; Frederic II., 8.

IV. *Poetry.*—Ossian, 1; Tasso, 6; Ariosto, 6; Homer, 6; Virgil, 4; Henriade, 1; Télémaque, 2; the Gardens (Delille), 1; Masterpieces of the French Drama, 20; Select Fugitive Poetry, 10; La Fontaine, vols. —.

V. *Fiction.*—Voltaire, 4; Héloïse, 4; Werther, 1; Marmontel, 4; English Novels, 40; Le Sage, 10; Prévost, 10.

VI. *Political.*—Old Testament and New, the Koran, the Vedas, Mythology, Montesquieu, Spirit of Laws.

The squadron set sail on the 19th May. The admiral's

ship, "L'Orient," being overloaded, drew too much water, and ran aground. She was disengaged without difficulty, accident, or perceptible delay. Yet both *before* and *after* the battle of Aboukir, presentiments were thence derived of her final misfortune. I add, with regret, that I have often heard such tales repeated by sensible men.

We arrived before Malta on the 10th June, for the non-arrival of some convoys had retarded us two days. The understanding opened with Europe, during and after the negotiations at Campo-Formio, had not so completely succeeded as to give us at once possession of that celebrated fortress. Bonaparte showed himself much irritated against those who had been sent to prepare matters. Yet Dolomieu had afterward reason to repent his reputation in the transaction; while Poussielgue had done all he could in his trial of seduction: still success was not complete. There existed misunderstandings, and a few cannon shots were exchanged. The Commander-in-Chief ordered General d'Hilliers, who had served in Italy with much credit, to land and attack the western quarter of the island. This was effected with great prudence and ability. But, as to those in the secret all this was known to be but for form's sake, these hostile demonstrations were not followed up. They were necessary to save the honor of the knights of the cross; and that was all they meant. Those who know the place, know also that it could not have been taken in two days by a fleet in our circumstances. Pursued by an enemy, we had not a moment to lose, and at any instant might have been surprised by that enemy, caught in disorder, and been totally destroyed. The impregnable fortress of Malta is so entirely secured against an assault, that General Caffarelli, after examining the fortifications with the greatest care, said, in my presence, to the Commander-in-Chief, "Upon my word, General, we were extremely fortunate in having friends within, had it been only to open the gates to us." This conquest has been magnified into an astonishing victory—a prodigy of wisdom and valor! What a pity! It was barefaced treason.

We may judge, then, of the value of Napoleon's assertions at St. Helena: "The capture of Malta was not owing to a private understanding, but to the foresight of the Commander-in-Chief. It was in Mantua I took Malta." It does not very plainly appear what is the meaning of "Malta taken by foresight in Mantua." But it is no less true that I wrote, under his dictation, a lot of instructions for this same "private understanding." Napoleon has also said to another noble companion of his exile: "Malta certainly possessed immense physical, but no moral, means of resistance. The knights did nothing disgraceful. They could not hold out against impossibility." No; but they gave themselves up. The successful capture of Malta was assured before the fleet quitted Toulon.

One of the first acts of Bonaparte was to set at liberty the Turkish prisoners, and clear the horrible galleys. This was a deed of reason and humanity. He devoted his time to providing, with equal activity and talent, for the administration and defence of the island. His only relaxation, an occasional walk in the extensive gardens of the grand master, where we regaled on the delicious fruit of the magnificent orange trees, proved alike pleasing to us all. On the 19th June, we took our departure from Malta, which our leader never imagined he had taken for the English. They requited him shabbily for that service. Several knights accompanied us, having obtained employment both in the civil and military departments.

During the night of the 22d, the hostile squadron was almost upon us, passing within six leagues of the French fleet. Nelson, having learned at Messina the capture of Malta, on the very day we left the island, made directly for Alexandria, which he conceived to be our destination. Thus, taking the shortest route, setting all sail, and unencumbered with convoys, he reached the Bay of Alexandria on the 28th, three days before our fleet. The French squadron shaped its course, first for Candia, which was seen on the 25th, and then to the southward, favored by the Etesian winds, which blow regularly from the north at this season. By this means, all arrived safe on the 30th June before Alexandria.

The remarkable saying of Bonaparte to the pupils of a school which he had one day visited, "Young people, every hour of time lost is a chance of misfortune for future life," may be considered as, in some measure, forming the rule of his own conduct. Perhaps no man ever better understood the value of time: his very leisure was business. Of this our passage appears to be a striking instance. If the activity of his mind found not wherewithal to exercise itself in reality, he supplied the defect by giving free scope to imagination, or in listening to the conversation of the learned men attached to the expedition; for he, probably, was the only man in the fleet who never experienced weariness for a single moment.

On board the "L'Orient," he delighted in discoursing with Monge and Berthollet, when the discussion most frequently ran upon chemistry, mathematics, and religion; as also with General Caffarelli, whose conversation, rich in facts, was, at the same time, lively, intellectual and cheerful. Of the two philosophers, Monge evidently appeared the favorite, because, endowed with an ardent fancy, without exactly possessing religious principles, he yet cherished that propensity toward religious ideas which harmonized with the feelings of Bonaparte. On this subject Berthollet sometimes laughed at his compatriot. Besides a cold imagination, his mind, constantly turned to analysis and abstraction, showed a leaning toward materialism, for which the General ever expressed a sovereign dislike. At other times, Bonaparte conversed with the admiral, when the subject always respected naval manoeuvres, of which he showed great desire to obtain knowledge; and nothing more astonished Brueys than the sagacity of his questions. I was present when, one day, having asked how the ships would be brought into action in case of attack, he declared, after hearing the reply, that, should the circumstance occur, he would give orders for every one to throw his luggage overboard.

Bonaparte, during the whole voyage, passed the greater part of his time below in his cabin, reclining upon a couch, which, by a ball-and-socket joint at each foot, rendered the ship's pitching less perceptible, and, consequently, relieved the sickness from which he was scarcely ever free. I remained almost always with him, reading aloud some of the favorite works composing his camp library. Of our familiar conversations Josephine almost always formed the subject. Passionately as he loved the glory of France and his own, she still engrossed many a thought in a soul thus full of high emprise: his attachment, indeed, approached to idolatry. Sometimes, too, he amused himself for whole hours with the captains of such vessels as we hailed, when, having satisfied his curiosity, he permitted them to depart, exacting a promise to say nothing of their meeting with the French squadron.

While we were at sea, he rarely got up before ten, when he breakfasted. At dinner, he had always company, in addition to the admiral, his own staff and the colonels on board, who regularly dined at the table of the Commander-in-Chief. As there were 2,000 souls on board, and among these many distinguished men, choice could be daily made. One of his greatest pleasures during the passage was, after these dinner parties, to appoint three or four persons to support, and as many to impugn, some proposition. These discussions had an object; the General thus created opportunities of studying the talents of those whom it was his interest to know thoroughly, in order, afterward, to employ them according to their capabilities. A circumstance here will not surprise those who have been admitted to intimate converse with Bonaparte: in these encounters of wit he constantly gave the preference to him who had maintained an extravagant conception with ability over the advocate of common opinion and reason. It was not solely superiority of address which determined his judgment, for he really preferred a clever defence of an absurdity to an equally able argument in favor of the rational view. He himself always proposed the subject to be discussed, generally selecting questions of religion, on the different forms of government, on the art of war. One day, "Are the planets inhabited?" another, "What is the age of the world?" a third, "Will our earth be destroyed by water or by fire?" again, "The truth or falsehood of presentiments, and the interpretation of dreams," formed the inquiry. This last, I well remember, was suggested by the remembrance of Joseph, as closely connected with the land whither we were bound. No country, indeed, presented itself to our view without calling up in the thoughts of our leader its appropriate associations of history, legislation, polity or mythology.

When the serenity of the weather invited, he went upon the quarter-deck. I recollect that, one day, walking thus with him, while steering our course through the Sicilian Sea, on a beautiful evening, at sunset, I thought I described the summits of the Alps. This seemed to the General a mistaken fancy, and he laughed at me accordingly. The admiral being referred to, confirmed my observation, after examining the horizon through his telescope. "The Alps!" At this word I think I still behold Bonaparte. I see him long standing immovable; then, all at once breaking from his trance, "No!" exclaimed he to us, "never can I view without emotion the land of Italy! Here is the East; thither I am now bound; a perilous enterprise calls me. These mountains overlook the plains where I have so often led to victory the soldiers of France. With them we shall conquer still!" It formed, in truth, at this period, one of his most agreeable employments to recall the splendor of former campaigns, seeking to read in the past a happy presage of coming triumphs. These anticipations of success he always associated with the politics of France, pleasing himself by imagining the effects which they would produce upon the public mind.

The band on board the "L'Orient" sometimes played,

but only on the gangway.   Bonaparte did not yet sufficiently admire music to hear it in his apartment.   A taste
for this art may be said to have kept pace with his power,
as love for the chase manifested itself only after his elevation to the empire: as if he had wished to prove that he possessed not only the genius of sovereignty for commanding
men, but also the instinct of those aristocratic pleasures, the
enjoyment of which is reckoned, in the eyes of their people,
among the essential attributes of kings.

In a long voyage, it is impossible to prevent accidents
from men falling overboard.   This occurrence happened
several times with us, from the crowded state of our vessel.   On these occasions, it was strange to witness the instinctive force of humanity in the bosom of one so lavish
of the blood of his fellow-creatures on the field of battle,
and who was about to shed torrents of it in that very Egypt
whither we were going.   Whenever a man fell into the
water, the Commander-in-Chief had no rest till he was
saved.   He instantly ordered the ship to lay to, showed
the most lively uneasiness till the unfortunate was recovered, and ordered me to recompense liberally those most
active in the rescue.   Sailors who had thus distinguished
themselves, when guilty of some breach of discipline, were
always exempted from punishment.   I remember, during
one dark night, a noise was heard, as of a man overboard.
Bonaparte instantly gave the word to put the ship about
till the supposed victim should be rescued from inevitable
death.   The crew hastened from all quarters, exertions were
redoubled, and at length we fished up—what?   The victim
was—a quarter of beef, which had slipped from a noose over
the side.   How did Bonaparte act?   He ordered me to reward the sailors who had exposed themselves on this occasion more liberally than usual: "It might have been a man,
and these brave fellows have shown neither less zeal nor less
courage."

After thirty years, all these things are present to my
thoughts as if they had occurred but yesterday.   Such

was the general manner in which Bonaparte passed his time during the voyage. As it drew toward an end, he busied himself with preparations for a new scene. It was then he dictated to me the famous proclamation addressed to his soldiers before landing:

"Soldiers! — You are about to undertake a conquest, the effects of which upon the civilization and commerce of the world will be incalculable. You will strike a blow, the surest and most vital which England can receive, until you deliver her deathstroke. We shall have to make some fatiguing marches, to engage in a few combats; but success will crown our exertions. The fates are favorable to us. The Mamelukes—retainers of England, tyrants of the unfortunate country—soon after our landing shall have ceased to exist.

"The people with whom we are about to be connected are Mohammedans. The first article of their faith is this: 'There is no other God but God, and Mohammed is his prophet.' Do not gainsay them; live with them as you have done with the Jews, with the Italians; pay the same deference to their muftis and their imaums as you have paid to the rabbis and the bishops; show to the ceremonies prescribed by the Koran, and to the mosques, the same tolerance as you have shown to the convents and the synagogues, to the religion of Moses and of Jesus Christ. The Roman legions protected all religions. You will find here usages different from those of Europe: it is proper that you habituate yourselves to them.

"The inhabitants treat their women differently from us; but, in every country, he who violates women is a monster. Pillage enriches only a few; it dishonors us, destroys our resources, and makes enemies of those whom our interest requires to be friends. The first city we approach was built by Alexander; every step will awaken sublime recollections worthy of exciting the emulation of Frenchmen."

To this proclamation was appended an order of the day, consisting of twelve articles, prohibiting pillage, as also every species of violence, and containing directions for collecting imposts and contributions. The punishment denounced upon delinquents were: repairing the damages inflicted, two years in irons, and death. Here I may be

permitted a reflection. Passages in the proclamation **have**
been severely animadverted upon as contrary to the doctrines of Christianity. But how absurd to have entered
Egypt with the cross in one hand and the sword in the
other! Policy and common-sense required us to respect
the religion of the inhabitants. Both this and other proclamations produced an excellent effect.

In the course of the passage, particularly between Malta
and Alexandria, I conversed often with the brave and unfortunate Brueys, and had the happiness of enjoying his
confidence and friendship. He complained bitterly of the
organization of the fleet; of the encumbered state of
the ships of war and frigates, and, above all, of the
"L'Orient"; of the great number of transports; of the im-
perfect arming of the men-of-war, and the feebleness of their
crews. He assured me it required no little resolution to
take charge of an armament so ill-equipped; and several
times declared that, in the event of an encounter with the
enemy, he would guarantee nothing. "In case of an attack," added he, "even by an inferior squadron, the confusion among such a multitude, the immense quantity of
baggage, would inevitably bring on a catastrophe by imped-
ing the manœuvres. God grant," said the admiral, with a
sigh, "that we pass without meeting the English! for, had
they only ten ships, I cannot promise success; and, even
with such a victory as we should obtain, what would
become of the expedition?"

We did escape, and made the coast of Africa on the
morning of the 1st July, the columns of Severus announcing
Alexandria. The frigate "Juno" having been despatched
for M. Magallon, the French consul, it was near four o'clock
when he arrived, a very hollow sea running. From him the
Commander-in-Chief learned that Nelson had been before
Alexandria on the 28th June, and, after a conference with
the English agent at the place, had directed his course to
the northeast. Thus, had we not been detained two days,
waiting for a convoy from Civita Vecchia, we should have

arrived before the town at the same time with our enemies.
How insignificant are often those causes upon which the
good or bad fortune of the mightiest enterprises depends!
Reckoning from the time of our leaving Malta, Nelson,
expecting to find us at Alexandria, and seeing we had not
arrived, imagined we had sailed for Alexandretta, in Syria,
there to disembark for Asia. This error saved the expedition a second time.

On hearing these details, Bonaparte resolved on an immediate disembarkation. This the admiral opposed, representing to him the state of the sea, then in violent commotion;
the distance from the coast, nearly nine miles; the dangerous reefs; the approaching night; and our total ignorance of
the most convenient landing places. But these representations, to induce a delay of about twelve hours, till the next
morning, were urged in vain: Bonaparte listened to them
with impatience and ill humor, though assured that Nelson
could not return for several days. "Admiral," said he,
impatiently, "we have no time to lose; fortune gives me but
three days; if I profit not by her indulgence, we are lost."
He reckoned greatly upon his fortune: that chimerical idea
constantly influenced his resolutions. I certify these things
to have occurred in my presence: not a single detail could
escape me. But it is false, quite false, that, upon the appearance of a sail not answering to signals, and which, for
my part, I never saw, Bonaparte exclaimed, "Fortune! wilt
thou abandon me? I ask of thee only five days!"

The General having the command of the whole armament, both by sea and land, the admiral was constrained to
yield. He took me, however, apart, to communicate his apprehensions, which, indeed, chiefly concerned his colleague,
whom he considered, in running so great hazard, as incurring too serious a responsibility. Upon my refusal to interfere, knowing the General's firmness, and also as agreeing
with him in opinion, Brueys sorrowfully gave the signal for
disembarking. This movement was effected amid many
difficulties and dangers. In getting to the boats, the troops

had to glide down the ship's side by a rope, remaining suspended till the returning wave brought the shallop up to their level. We had to lament some loss; but everything had led to anticipation of greater misfortunes than we actually experienced. About one o'clock in the morning of July 2 we first set foot on the soil of Egypt at Marabou, three leagues east of Alexandria. Two hours after, the Commander-in-Chief was in full march upon that capital, with the divisions of Kléber, Bon and Morand. The Bedouin Arabs, hovering upon our right and rear, cut off stragglers, and those who separated from the corps. On arriving within gunshot of Alexandria, we began the attack; the walls were scaled, and, in a short time, French valor had triumphed over all opposition.

The first blood which I saw flow in this war was that of General Kléber; he had been struck by a ball upon the head, not in the escalade, but in commanding the attack. Kléber always exposed himself to the first blows: he might have been named the brave where all were brave. He came to the column of Pompey, where several individuals of the staff had reassembled, and from whence the Commander-in-Chief overlooked the attack. This was the first time I had spoken to Kléber, and our intimacy dated from this day. I had the satisfaction to render him some assistance. I confess it with pain, the sentiments then awakened in his favor soon lost much of their warmth. Selfishness, I discovered, quickly displaced in his breast those benevolent dispositions toward misfortune which are the happy attribute of youth.

It has been attempted to elevate the capture of Alexandria, which fell in a few hours, into a great feat of arms. The General himself wrote, that the city was taken after a little firing; the walls, poorly defended, were very soon scaled. Alexandria was not given up to pillage.

Bonaparte devoted ten days passed in Alexandria to organizing the city and district, with that activity and talent which I never could sufficiently admire, and in preparing for the march of the army across the province of Bohahireh.

For this purpose, Desaix, with 4,500 infantry, and sixty horse, repaired to Beda, upon the route to Damanhour. This officer first encountered the privations and sufferings of the campaign. His magnanimous character, his devotion to Bonaparte, seemed ready to yield before the distress of the moment. "For God's sake," thus he wrote, so early as the 15th July, "do not leave us in this position. The detachment is discouraged, and murmurs. Give us orders to advance or to fall back, with all speed: the villages are mere huts, absolutely without supplies." In these arid plains, scorched by the heat of a tropical sun, we often contended for water, so common elsewhere: wells and springs, those secret treasures of the Desert, are hidden from the eager search of the traveller; and often, after choking marches, we found nothing to allay the imperious cravings of thirst save a brackish and disgusting fluid.

CHAPTER V

Battle of Chebreisse—Battle of the Pyramids—Fall of Cairo—Organization of Egypt—Defeat of the Fleet at Aboukir

WHAT disparity between the city of Alexandria, as represented in history, and the melancholy town of modern times! Where formerly dwelt 900,000 inhabitants were now to be numbered scarcely 6,000. That city, once so magnificent, we found without fortifications, and, strictly speaking, without even a vestige of what it had been. There appeared merely some columns torn from the ancient ruins, and applied in miserable taste to modern buildings. The quay of the *old port* is itself but a mass of broken columns of marble and granite. Two monuments only were entire and erect—the pillar of Pompéy and the obelisk of Cleopatra; but hardly any remains could be discovered of the Roman: none of that city which contained the tomb of Alexander.

Before taking possession of Egypt, Bonaparte addressed various proclamations to the Pacha, to the commandant, and, on entering Alexandria, to the natives of the country, exciting them against the beys, from whose yoke he pretended to have come to relieve them. Again, a few days after, he wrote to the Directory, describing his operations, from the time of leaving Malta to the capture of Alexandria.

The 7th July we set out for Damanhour, across the vast plains of Bohahireh: these are not, as reported, a desert. While the army toiled onward beneath a burning sun, the torments of the soldiers were augmented by the illusion of water, which the *mirage* so well known in tropical climes unceasingly renewed, at the very moment, too, when all felt the greatest sufferings from thirst. The Arabs harassed us on the march without intermission. They emptied or infected the few cisterns and springs found in these vast solitudes. Once exhausted, the wells are replenished very slowly, and the soldier who, from the commencement of a weary march, had experienced a devouring thirst, found little relief from a brackish, muddy and polluted liquid. The army traversed these wastes with the speed of lightning; but the troops already expressed their sufferings in frequent murmurs of discouragement.

On the first night of our march a mischance occurred, which might have been fatal to the staff and to the Commander-in-Chief. We were advancing through the darkness, with only a weak escort, almost all asleep on our horses. Suddenly, two volleys of a well-sustained fire were directed upon us: we awoke, rallied, reconnoitred, and learned with great satisfaction that only one guide had been slightly wounded in the hand. It was the division of Desaix, which, forming the advance, had fired, mistaking us for enemies. Our small advanced guard had not heard the challenge of the outposts.

Arrived at Damanhour, the staff established headquarters in the sheik's house, which, newly whitewashed, made a brilliant appearance externally, but within exhibited a

TALLEYRAND

primitiveness hardly to be conceived. Everything showed
the greatest poverty—scarcely a pitcher whole; and for
seats, some coarse mats, filthy and in tatters. We found
nothing, absolutely nothing, for the convenience of life.
Bonaparte knew the proprietor to be rich, and, by kindness,
having inspired the sheik with some confidence, asked,
through the interpreter, why, having wherewithal, he thus
deprived himself of every requisite, assuring him that an
unreserved answer should be attended with no ill consequences. "Look at my feet," said the old man: "some
years ago, I repaired my dwelling, and purchased a little
furniture. This found its way to Cairo; a demand for
money followed, because I was thus proved to be rich.
I refused payment; they maltreated and forced me to pay.
Since then I have reduced myself to the barest necessaries,
and now no longer repair anything." In fact, he walked
with difficulty from this infliction. Spies are everywhere
ready to denounce the mere suspicion of being rich; and, in
this unfortunate country it is only by an appearance of
the most abject poverty that the rapacity of power and the
cupidity of barbarism can be escaped.

In this our headquarters an insignificant troop of mounted
Arabs came to insult us by their presence. Bonaparte, who
was at the window, indignant at this audacity, turned to
young Croiser, an aide-de-camp in attendance, saying, "Here,
Croiser, take some of the guides, and disperse those raga-
muffins." In an instant, Croiser appeared in the plain,
with fifteen guides. The little band engaged. We beheld
the combat from the window. But there appeared in the
orders, and in the attack, a hesitation unexpected by the
General. He called out from the window, as if they could
have heard, "Advance! will you? Charge!" After a short
but pretty obstinate combat, in which our horsemen retired
as the Arabs advanced, the latter finally withdrew, unmolested, and without loss. The General's anger could not
be restrained; it was vented without measure upon poor
Croiser, on his return, and so harshly, that he retired in

tears. Bonaparte desired me to follow and calm him: all was in vain. "I will not survive this," said the youth; "I will expose myself to certain death on the first occasion that presents itself; I will not live dishonored." The word coward had been pronounced. Croiser found the death he sought at St. Jean d'Acre.

On the 10th we marched to Rahmahanieh, where Alexander's canal commences, and where those of the civil service were embarked on board the flotilla, that their horses might serve to mount a few men more. The flotilla was commanded by Perrée, in the "Cerf," formerly commodore of the naval forces of the Adriatic, with orders to keep on the flank of the army, thus giving and receiving protection. On the 13th, at night, both military and naval forces began to ascend by the left bank of the river; but the force of the wind, which at this season blows directly up the valley of the Nile, carried us ahead of the army. In this situation, we found ourselves exposed in front to seven Turkish gunboats, mounting twenty-four and thirty-six pounders, and in flank, to the fire of Mamelukes, Arabs and Fellahs, who lined both banks. Our gunboats were armed with only small cannon in the bows, so that, casting anchor, we maintained a very disadvantageous contest for three hours and a half, in which one of the Turkish gunboats blew up, while the Turks took several of our craft by boarding, and massacred the crews before our eyes, holding up to us the heads of our companions by the hair. At length, the appearance of a detachment of the army saved us from destruction, as our ammunition began to fail. Such is the true account, though historians have destroyed the Turkish squadron. They did us much injury; and sailed up the river, having suffered but little damage, after an engagement wherein twenty men were wounded and several slain on our side, and in which both parties had fired upward of 1,500 cannon-shot.

Meanwhile, the army had encountered a body of about 4,000 Mamelukes at Chebreisse. This village, as the Com-

mander-in-Chief afterward told me, it was his intention to
have turned, and, inclosing the Mamelukes between the
French and the Nile, to have utterly cut them off. Apprehending, from the cannonade, that our situation was
perilous, he had, however, changed his plan, attacked them
in front, and, after defeating and driving them back upon
Cairo, made the movement upon his left, which saved us.

We continued our voyage, and were without communications from the army until the 23d July. On the 22d, we
beheld the Pyramids; and the same day the sound of a distant cannonade, which continued to increase as the north
wind lulled, announced that a serious affair was going forward. We now beheld the banks of the Nile covered with
naked dead: the bodies, becoming more numerous at every
turn, were thrown by the waves upon the shore, or borne
sullenly along toward the sea. This horrible spectacle; the
solitude of every village, so lately in ceaseless hostility
against us; the inexplicable tranquillity of our course, no
longer troubled by musketry, now from the one bank, now
from the other, or from both at once, made us presume, with
some assurance, that a battle, fatal to the Mamelukes, had
taken place. But we had need of certain intelligence. The
misery which overwhelmed us during this navigation is not
to be described. For eleven days we had been reduced to
live on melons and water, while obliged to oppose at every
moment the fire of the Arabs and Fellahs, from which the
death of some, and the wounds of many of our companions,
seemed, in our circumstances, not so heavy a ransom as we
had reason to dread. The rise of the Nile was only commencing, and the shallowness of its stream obliged us to
leave the gunboat, and get on board a dgerm, thirteen
leagues from Cairo, where I arrived on the 23d, at three
in the afternoon.

Scarcely had I saluted the Commander-in-Chief, after
a separation of twelve days, when he accosted me in these
terms: "Ah! so you are come, then! You are the cause—
you and the others—that I failed in the object of my battle

at Chebreisse; it was to save you—Monge, Berthollet, and others on board the flotilla—that I hastened my movement on the left toward the Nile, before my right had inclosed Chebreisse, from which not a Mameluke should have escaped me."—"For my part," replied I, "you have my best thanks; but, in conscience, could you abandon us, when you had taken away our horses, and put us, whether we would or no, on board that same flotilla?" He fell a-laughing; but afterward testified how sincerely he felt the loss we had sustained. The same evening I wrote to his brother Louis: "The Commander-in-Chief charges me, my dear Louis, to announce to you the victory gained yesterday over the Mamelukes. It is complete. The battle was fought at Embabeh, opposite Boulac. The enemy's loss is estimated, in killed and wounded, at 2,000, forty pieces of cannon, and many horses. Our loss has been trifling. The beys have fled into Upper Egypt. The General enters Cairo this evening. I am desired also to say that you are to join us immediately, with the General's effects and horses; ascending the Nile in dgerms, with the battalion of the 89th, from Rosetta. Do not, my good friend, forget our baggage—we have much need of it—the books, papers, and *all* the wine."

The occupation of Cairo was the immediate consequence of the victory of Embabeh. Indeed, the march of the French army toward that city had been an uninterrupted succession of combats and of triumphs. Conquerors at Rahmahanieh, at Chebreisse, at the Pyramids, the Mamelukes defeated, their chief, Mourad Bey, forced to flee into Upper Egypt, there was no longer any obstacle preventing our entrance into the capital, after a campaign of only twenty days. Bonaparte had preceded this occupation by proclamations of a most pacific tendency, addressed to the sheiks, to the inhabitants and to the Pacha of Cairo. He wrote also to Kléber, who, on account of his wound, had been left commandant at Alexandria, giving an account of the campaign and issuing orders, finishing thus: "At the moment of writing, I find a letter from Louis, in a garden belonging to

Mamelukes, which proves that one of your couriers has been intercepted." This was his own unfortunate aide-de-camp Julian, an interesting young officer and of great hopes, who, with fifteen soldiers, as was afterward discovered, had been butchered in the village of Alkam, on the Libyan bank of the Nile. The Commander-in-Chief issued an order to burn and plunder the village. This was executed; but no trace of the fatal event could be discovered, for all had fled: only, in the dust of a distant and deserted hut, the soldiers found the regimental button of a vest, bearing the number of the corps which had furnished the escort of the hapless Julian.

On the following day after the entry into Cairo, Bonaparte wrote the letter to his brother Joseph which was intercepted and published, and whose authenticity has been causelessly questioned: "You will see in the public papers the bulletins of the conquest of Egypt, which has been sufficiently disputed to add a laurel leaf more to the fame of this army. Egypt, in corn, rice, vegetables and cattle, is the richest country which exists on the earth. Barbarism is at its height. There is not money enough here even to pay the troops. I expect to be in France in two months. Engage a house either near Paris or in Burgundy; I expect to pass the winter there." The announcement in this letter is corroborated by an autograph note in my possession of the warlike stores and necessaries to be sent out to Egypt; and both prove his intention to have colonized that country.

Immediately on the fall of Cairo, the Commander-in-Chief turned his attention to the civil and military organization of the country. He should have been seen at this season, while in full vigor of manhood. Nothing escaped his rare penetration, his indomitable activity. Egypt, long the object of his study and meditations, became as well known to him in a few weeks as if he had sojourned therein ten years. The order to observe the most severe discipline was repeated, and strictly enforced. The mosques, civil and religious institutions, harems, women, customs were scrupulously respected. A short time had elapsed when already the French, admitted into the houses, might be seen living peaceably with the inhabitants, smoking a pipe with them, assisting in their labors and amusing their children. Thus, scarcely having laid aside the sword, soon to resume it, and after a residence of only four days in Cairo, Bonaparte, with rare sagacity, laboring to secure the interests of his army, without apparently injuring the interests of the country, appointed provisional governments in all the cities and provinces occupied by our troops. These were to regulate their proceedings by a code of only four articles, but which had been drawn up after seeing, consulting and examining all from whom information could be drawn:—I. A divan of seven persons to watch over the general police of each province. II. The internal military defence of each province intrusted to an aga of the Janizaries, with sixty men, to act with the French commandant. III. An intendant, with the requisite subordinates, to collect the revenues, as formerly belonging to the Mamelukes, now to the republic. IV. A French commissary to correspond between the intendant and the general finance administration.

While the Commander-in-Chief was thus actively engaged in organizing his conquests, he learned that Ibrahim, the most powerful of the beys after Mourad, of whom General Desaix had gone in pursuit, was making head in Syria. Upon this, Bonaparte resolved to march in person against this formidable opponent, and quitted Cairo accordingly, after a residence of fifteen days. The results of this campaign, the defeat of Ibrahim at El-Arych, are known to every one; besides, I enter little into details of battles, limiting myself to facts which I have myself witnessed, and to rectifying accredited errors. Something, too, more important still, requires our attention. During this absence of the Commander-in-Chief, news arrived at Cairo of the overwhelming disaster of the French squadron at Aboukir, on the 1st of August. The aide-de-camp despatched by Kléber with the intelligence proceeded, on my recommendation, instantly to Salehyeh, where Bonaparte then was, and who immediately returned to Cairo, a distance of thirty-three leagues.

On learning the terrible catastrophe at Aboukir, the Commander-in-Chief seemed completely borne down. His condition, I will even say, gave me extreme pain. And, indeed, with all the energy of his character, could he bear up at once against so many and so great calamities? To the painful feelings aroused by the ungenerous complaints, and the moral discouragement of his companions in arms and glory, was just added a misfortune incalculable, positive, irreparable—the conflagration of our fleet. His perspicacity measured at a glance all its fatal consequences. And yet, men would have it that considerations so momentous—a present so afflicting, a future so uncertain—made not upon the spirit of our leader a profound and sorrowful impression! Truly, in feigning insensibility, then foreign to his nature, his panegyrists are deceived if they imagine thus to pronounce his eulogy. Because he was a great man, must complete divorce be made between his feelings and humanity?

Before the fatal 1st of August, it had been Bonaparte's intention, the possession of Egypt once assured, to take back to Toulon the fleet, now become useless; and, after sending troops and necessaries of every description to Egypt, to unite the fleet with all those forces of France and of her allies which the government would then have assembled against England. It is certain that, before departing upon the Eastern expedition, he had submitted to the Directory a note relative to these grand designs. Extraordinary and gigantic ideas occupied him unceasingly. He always regarded a descent upon Britain as possible; but ever as certainly fatal while we were so inferior at sea. By these different manœuvres he hoped to gain the ascendency there also. By his sudden appearance and great preparations on the coast, he purposed either to effect a descent, the English fleet being absent in the Mediterranean, or hoped, by thus exciting alarms at home, at least to prevent troops being sent against the force in Egypt; or both these objects might be successfully accomplished. He delighted himself with the sublimity of dating a despatch from the ruins of Memphis, and three months after from the rich and populous city of London! The loss of the marine destroyed all this combination, converting into an empty dream those romantic and adventurous conceptions.

Is it consistent with human nature to suppose him, with cold insensibility, beholding these mighty designs vanish into nothing? When left alone with me, he gave full vent to his emotion. I endeavored to console him, by representing how much more fatal the rencontre would have proved, had it taken place in the open sea, and before the troops had disembarked, through the simple and very probable occurrence of Nelson having remained only twenty-four hours longer before Alexandria. "All," said I, "would then have been lost beyond remedy. Since we are blockaded here, we must and will find resources in ourselves. There is money— there are provisions; let us await the future and the exertions of the Directory—" "As for your Directory," interrupted he, quickly, "they are a parcel of ——; they fear and hate me; they will leave me to perish here. And to crown the whole, see you not these faces? It is every one's cry, 'I will not remain!' "

What he said was perfectly true at the time. From the first moment the army set foot in Egypt, as can yet be proved by many witnesses, dislike, uneasiness, discontent, and longing for home, took possession of almost every individual. The illusion of the expedition had vanished at its very commencement. There remained only the reality, and that was sad enough. What bitter complaints have I not heard escape from Murat, from Lannes, Berthier, Bessières, and so many others! These continual outcries, without measure and without moderation, and which frequently even wore the aspect of sedition, caused profound affliction to Bonaparte, forcing from him severe reproaches and intemperate sallies. That this is the truth, without the least exaggeration, intercepted letters manifestly proved. For example, one from many of these intercepted letters thus proceeds: "We are in a country where all are dying of despair. If the army had known the situation of things before leaving France, not one of us would have embarked. Each would have preferred death a thousand times to the misery we now endure. We have the enemy all around; in front, in rear, and on either flank. It is exactly like La Vendée. Without exaggerating, there have died of thirst alone, in the space of five or six days, from five to six hundred men. Universal discontent prevails in the army; despotism had never attained its height till now. Our soldiers have killed themselves in the very presence of the Commander-in-Chief, exclaiming, 'This is thy doing!' We have been terribly deceived in this enterprise, so fair and so vaunted. We have beheld soldiers who, witnessing the sufferings of their companions, have shot themselves through the head; others have been seen to leap into the Nile, with arms and knapsack, and thus perish amid the waters. On seeing the generals pass, the soldiers call out, 'There go the butchers of the French!' uttering a hundred imprecations of the same sort. Of 40,000 Frenchmen, all languish to return; there are not five who think otherwise."

And, in truth, what else could be expected? Disgust had in every breast succeeded to enthusiasm. Instead of being assisted by the inhabitants, whom we were ruining, under pretence of freeing them from the yoke of the beys, we found all against us: Mamelukes, settled Arabs, wandering Arabs, Fellahs. The life of no individual was safe who removed but 200 toises, whether from our stations or from the corps to which he belonged. He fell into the hands of the enemy, who inflicted death, frightful torments, or a treatment, to Frenchmen, worse than either. Complaints were numerous, from the highest functionary to the lowest sentinel. Public opinion has been much divided on the military and moral condition of the Egyptian Army. But

the truth is, a cruel selfishness soon became the ruling sentiment. Privations and sufferings, caused by the want of food
and water, under a burning sky, whose fierceness nothing
tempered; desolate aridity on the plains; squalor in the
villages; maladies unknown in Europe; hopes deceived;
a sullen silence in reply to the constant question, What will
become of us?—such was our real position. How severely,
then, must the disaster of Aboukir have aggravated all
former ills, by taking away even the hope of ever revisiting
our native country!

Upon this subject I held a long and most confidential
conversation with the Commander-in-Chief. I hastened to
say, that the dark forebodings which had at first assailed
him soon cleared away. He quickly recovered the serenity
which is superior to events; the moral courage, strength of
character, elevation of thought, which had for an instant
bent beneath the overwhelming burden of the disaster. He
only repeated, in a tone difficult to conceive, "Unhappy
Brueys! what hast thou done!"

In regard to the catastrophe of which we now speak,
blame has been attached to the memory of Admiral Brueys.
But who are the accusers? Bonaparte and his admirers?
Upon what indictment is the accusation grounded? The
letter of the General to the Directory of the 20th August,
1798. But that letter, written fifty days after his entry into
Egypt, misrepresents facts, alters dates, affirms what is at
least doubtful, strikes the innocent, because he hoped thus
to screen himself from the misconduct which posterity might
impute to him. The simple truth would sufficiently have
pleaded his justification, without implicating another. The
loss of the fleet was evidently the result of those circumstances in which it was placed, and, above all, of the fearful
destitution which afflicted us during the first month of our
invasion, which did not allow of the naval force being
victualled, except from day to day—morsel by morsel.
Now, it is said, in the first place, that Brueys refused to
set out for Corfu, in opposition to the reiterated and most

positive orders of the Commander-in-Chief. But how could he set sail without provisions—provisions with which it was impossible he could be supplied? It is added, that the orders to depart were repeated. When, and by whom? This is carefully concealed. The truth is, that from the 8d July, to his unfortunate end, Brueys had not received a single line from Bonaparte, so impossible was it to maintain correspondence, while the latter received *all* the admiral's despatches only on the 26th, at Cairo, too late to give assistance. Brueys, also, is reproached for having obstinately awaited events in an open roadstead. But how is it possible to believe that the admiral would have remained on the coast of Egypt against the express orders of the General, who was also the commanding officer, whom he must have obeyed from superiority, if not from a sense of duty? On this part of the accusation, too, great stress is laid upon the surveys and reports of Captain Barré; but the reply of the admiral must also be taken into consideration, where he maintains, and by excellent reasons, his opinion of the entrance to the harbor of Alexandria being impracticable to ships of such size as composed the squadron.

It certainly would be unjust, under these circumstances, to ascribe the loss of the fleet to Bonaparte: but why attribute this misfortune to the misconduct of Brueys? The disaster was in reality the fault of no one, but the consequence of a chain of events beyond human control. In accordance with these facts, I presented to Bonaparte the following scroll of a letter to the Directory: "Admiral Brueys could not enter the harbor of Alexandria, which is too shallow for line-of-battle ships. Imperative circumstances obliged him to remain in the roads at Aboukir, waiting a favorable opportunity of setting sail for Corfu. His position proved untenable. The left of his line was forced, notwithstanding two mortar batteries had been planted on a point covering that wing, and each of his ships singly exposed to the fire of several opponents. The fleet has been destroyed. You will find subjoined the exact state of our loss in men and stores. This great calamity, of which a combination of unfortunate circumstances has been the sole cause, will doubtless prove to you the necessity of exerting all your care, in order to send us speedy reinforcements and other requisites for the army."

This outline of a despatch contained neither justification nor censure; but, glancing it over, he returned my sketch with a smile, saying, "It is too vague, too smooth; it wants effect. You must enter largely into details; you must speak of those who have distinguished themselves. And then you say not a word of fortune; and, according to you, Brueys is without reproach. You do not know mankind!—Leave it to me. Write."—He then dictated the famous despatch actually sent, in which the loss of the fleet forms merely an episode, concluding with the celebrated sentence, "And it was only when Fortune saw all her favors useless, that she abandoned our fleet to its fate."

I ought to declare that Bonaparte himself laughed at the disguising of unfortunate events, always endeavoring to withdraw the attention from the cause of misfortunes. He never hesitated to pervert facts, when the truth would have diminished his glory. He termed it foolishness to do otherwise. And I here state, once for all, that the whole truth never entered into his despatches, when veracity was in the least unfavorable and when he could dissemble. He knew how to disguise, or alter, or conceal it altogether, as suited his purposes.

CHAPTER VI

Syrian Expedition—Capture of Jaffa—Massacre of the Garrison— Siege of Acre

ON THE 11th February, 1799, we commenced our march for Syria, with about twelve thousand men. It has been erroneously published that our numbers amounted to only six thousand: nearly that number perished in the campaign. Nor is the statement that Kléber embarked his division at Damietta less incorrect: he only assumed the command of the division already there. We had no naval force; besides, our troops were too few for exposure in a sea covered with enemies. At the moment while such was our condition and disposable resources, and leaving hardly as many men behind in Egypt, the Directory had published at home, *according to news just received*, that we had sixty thousand infantry and ten thousand horse; that the army had been doubled by its conflicts, and, since arriving in the East, had lost only three hundred men!

Before our departure, Berthier, through persevering entreaty, had at length obtained permission to return to France. Ten days before he was to have departed for Alexandria, and thence to sail in the "Courageous" frigate, which had for some time been preparing. His instructions were already made out: Bonaparte had yielded with regret, but he could not allow to perish before his eyes, of homesickness and romantic love, one who had so faithfully served him in every campaign, and who had so earnestly entreated this proof of regard. The time was approaching when the two friends were to part, never, it might be, to meet again. The General-in-Chief thought of the separation with real pain: of this the chief-of-staff was well aware. At the moment when all imagined that Berthier was about to set out for Alexandria, he entered Bonaparte's apartment: "You are going, then, to make war in Asia?"—"You know that all is prepared. I march in a few days."—"Well, then, I cannot leave you. I voluntarily renounce my return to France: it would be too painful for me to forsake you in the moment of fresh dangers: here are my instructions and my passport!" Bonaparte felt much gratified by this resolution, and all former coldness disappeared in a most cordial reconciliation. The fact is, this amorous worship had reached a foolish height, completely unhinging the little common-sense bestowed upon Berthier by nature. Writers have placed him among the great men who have been lovers; but the homage which he rendered to a crayon portrait, remotely like the object of his adoration, often excited our mirth. One day, about three o'clock, I happened to be the bearer of an order from the Commander-in-Chief to the chief-of-staff: I found him upon his knees on a little divan, before the portrait of Madame Visconti. Berthier's back being turned to me, I had to give him a push, so intent were his devotions, to apprise him of my presence. He blustered a little, but was not at all put out.

One whose absence I regretted much was Louis Bona-parte, to whose return his brother consented, yielding to his peaceful tastes, impaired health, and languishing desire for home. Having the good fortune to escape the English cruisers, he arrived in safety, and, in passing through Sens, dined with Madame de Bourrienne, for whom he had taken charge of a beautiful shawl, the first cashmere, I believe, ever seen in France. Louis was very much as-tonished to find my wife in possession of the correspondence of the Egyptian army, which had been intercepted by the English and published in London. He thus recovered sev-eral letters which had been addressed to himself; and read others in the same volume which, as he informed me, would destroy the peace of more than one domestic circle on the return of the army.

We left Marmont behind, in charge of Alexandria, a position he regarded as a disgrace, so earnest was his desire to be with the General, who had recently conferred upon him the rank of brigadier-general of artillery, as being the first man who entered Malta. He wrote to me a few days before our march into Syria (7th February): "It is now a long time, my dear Bourrienne, since I last claimed your remembrance. I should be culpable by longer silence, for I have seen your postscript in your last letter to La Valette. I reconcile myself with difficulty to live absent from my friends and, for an age, have not seen the family where I had contracted friendships so dear to me. I do not even presume that my fate will soon call me among you: make me at least happy in the belief that you all think of me.

Adieu, my good friend. The bombardment gives us some distraction in the midst of my griefs, but does not remove them. The General is become unkind toward me. Send me your letters; I can forward them—but no politics."

We had already been several days on our march across the Desert, when, one afternoon, having reached Messoudiah, or *The Fortunate*, a singular spectacle presented itself, which was something more to us than merely amusing. This place is situated upon the shore of the Mediterranean, and surrounded with hills of very fine sand, easily penetrable by the abundant rains of winter. The water thus lodged is preserved under the sand, so that, on scooping a hole, four or five inches deep, at the base of any of the hillocks, the fluid immediately gushes up, filling the little cistern. It was sufficiently amusing to see us all sprawling upon the sand, digging miniature wells with our hands, and, with comic selfishness, putting in practice all manner of stratagems to obtain the most abundant spring. But, otherwise, this was a discovery of no small importance to us: the water, in truth, was a little turbid, and we had no time to allow it to settle; still the taste was sufficiently pleasing, and we found refreshment in the very Desert, under circumstances of almost universal privation, where the least mitigation reanimated the wayworn soldier by the renewal of hope. We touched, too, upon the confines of Syria, whose verdure, and sun, and vegetation, recalled our native land. Our soldiers bathed, also, the cool waves flowing within fifty paces of these unexpected treasures, and all were refreshed.

While we were yet near this place, so justly termed *The Fortunate*, I observed Bonaparte walking alone with Junot, as frequently happened. I was at a short distance, and know not why my attention was fixed upon the General at this particular moment. His countenance, at all times very pale, had assumed a still more pallid hue—a change for which I could assign no cause. There seemed as if something convulsed his whole frame: his looks wandered, and several times he struck his forehead. After a quarter of an hour's conversation, he quitted Junot, and turned toward me. I advanced to meet him: scarcely had we closed—"You are not my friend!" said he, in a voice broken and stern: "Women! Josephine!—Had you, Bourrienne, been attached to me, you would have told me all that I have just learned from Junot: he is a true friend. Josephine!—and I six hundred leagues distant! You ought to have told me!—Josephine to have deceived me thus!—She!—Woe to them!—I will exterminate the whole race of coxcombs and danglers!—As to her—divorce—yes, divorce—a public divorce!—I must write—I know all!—It is your fault! you ought to have told me!" These broken exclamations, the disordered mien, the altered tone, all but too plainly informed me of the nature of the conversation with Junot. My situation was extremely delicate, but by good fortune I preserved my self-possession. I saw that Junot had taken most unwarrantable liberties with his General, and had cruelly exaggerated the indiscretions of Madame Bonaparte, if such indiscretions really existed. I did not conceal this opinion; ungenerous as the conduct certainly was, both toward an absent woman, who could not defend herself, and toward our leader, to whose public anxieties—already sufficiently great—domestic afflictions were thus added; and false, as I believed the aspersions to be. These observations of mine, to which, notwithstanding, he listened with some calmness, made no impression. I spoke to him of his fame: "My fame!" cried he, "alas! what would I not give that those things Junot has told me were not true?—so much do I love that woman! If Josephine be guilty a divorce must separate us forever!—I will not be the laughing-stock of all the idlers of Paris! I write instantly to Joseph; he must obtain the divorce." The General was still much agitated, but gradually became less so: I seized the moment, when, from having some determination on which to dwell, his mind had recovered a degree of calm, to represent the danger of writing to his brother on information doubtful at best. "The letter," added I, "probably intercepted, will discover the disorder of mind under which it was written: as to the divorce, you can think of that hereafter—but with reflection." These last words produced an effect I had not dared to hope: at once he resumed calmness, listening as one who felt the necessity of even anticipating the words of consolation; and never again returned to the subject. Fifteen days afterward, at St. Jean d'Acre, he expressed to me great dissatisfaction with the conduct of Junot, whose indiscreet revelations he then began to regard as the inventions of malignity. I perceived in the sequel that he never forgave the offence, and may almost affirm with certainty that this operated as one cause why Junot was not a Marshal of France, as were several of his comrades, for whom Bonaparte had less affection. We may presume, too, that Josephine, afterward informed of the whole by her husband, exerted no great interest in favor of her accuser.

Our little army advanced upon El Arych, where we arrived on the 17th February. The fatigues of the Desert, the want of water, and privations of all kinds, excited the most violent discontent among the soldiers. They insulted those whom they saw on horseback; indulged in threatening language against the republic, the *savants*, and those whom they regarded as the authors of the expedition. Exhausted by thirst, too, individuals frequently pierced the water-skins with their bayonets; and, from this cause, hurtful to all, numerous quarrels and disturbances arose. These brave fellows, however, often showed a better spirit, softening with pleasantries the bitterness of their taunts. A soldier, perceiving that his conversation with a comrade was producing a bad effect upon others, suddenly changing his tone, called out to one near him—"Hullo, you there, can you tell me if this same Pacha of Acre has any water?"—"To be sure—I suppose so."—"Ah! very well—may the devil take as good care of him as he does of it!—not a drop does he allow to pass." We were yet forty leagues from Acre.

On the 26th of February, El Arych surrendered. We

shall see hereafter that a mistake has prevailed regarding the fate of the garrison.   On the 28th, we had the first prospect of the verdant and fertile fields of Syria.   At length we had rain—often too much.   The first of March saw us in Ramleh, the ancient Arimathea, where we slept in a small convent, inhabited by two monks, who were very attentive to our wants.   The church was given up for a hospital. These good fathers told us that this way had passed the family of Jesus Christ in their flight to Egypt, and showed the springs at which they quenched their thirst, where the pure and delicious water afforded us great pleasure.   The associations of education, nourished by the mighty events transacted in these regions, maintained their mysterious influence over our imagination.   We were only about six leagues from Jerusalem.   I asked the Commander-in-Chief if he entertained no wish to visit that celebrated city.   "Oh! as for that—no!   Jerusalem lies not in my line of operation: I court no dealings with mountaineers in their own rugged defiles.   And then, upon the other side of the mountain, I should be assailed by numerous cavalry.   I am not ambitious of the fate of Crassus."

We had, therefore, nothing to say to Jerusalem; only a manifesto was despatched to the authorities, declaring our pacific intentions with respect to them, to which no answer was returned.   After passing Ramleh, we met with two, or, it might be, three hundred Christians, in a most pitiable state of servitude, misery and destitution.   In conversing with them, I could not help admiring how much the hope of future reward tended to comfort them under present evils; but I learned from many among them that they lived not well together.   The same passions of hatred and jealousy are found wherever, and under whatsoever circumstances, men exist in society.

On arriving before Jaffa, where were already some troops, one of the first persons I met was Adjutant-General Gressieux, to whom, on asking how he did, I offered my hand. "What are you about?" said he, repelling my advances with a precipitate gesture. "Good God! you may have the plague: we never touch each other here!" This I related to the General-in-Chief, who merely said, "If he is afraid of the pestilence, he will die of it." In fact, we learned a short time after that he speedily fell a victim to the infection.

The siege of Jaffa, a paltry town, dignified as the ancient Joppa, commenced on the 4th, and terminated, by assault and pillage, on the 6th of March. The carnage was horrible. Bonaparte sent his aides-de-camp, Beauharnais and Croiser, to appease, as far as possible, the fury of the soldiery, to ascertain what passed, and report. They learned that a numerous detachment of the garrison had retired into a strong position, where large buildings or caravansaries surrounded a courtyard. This court they entered, displaying the scarfs which marked their rank. The Albanians and Arnauts composing nearly the whole of these refugees, cried out from the windows that they wished to surrender, on condition of their lives being spared; if not, they threatened to fire upon the officers, and to defend themselves to the last extremity. The young men conceived they ought, and had power, to accede to the demand, in opposition to the sentence of death pronounced against the garrison of every place taken by assault. I was walking with General Bonaparte before his tent, when these prisoners, in two columns, amounting to about 4,000, were marched into the camp. When he beheld the mass of men arrive, and before seeing the aides-de-camp, he turned to me with an expression of consternation—"What would they have me do with these? Have I provisions to feed them? ships to transport them, either to Egypt or France? How the devil could they play me this trick?" The two aides-de-camp, on their arrival and explanations, received severe reprimands; to their defence, that they were alone amid numerous enemies, and that he had recommended them to appease the slaughter, "Yes," replied the General, in the sternest tone, "without doubt, the slaughter of women, children, old men, the peaceable inhabitants, but not of armed soldiers. You ought to have braved death, and not brought these to me: what would you have me do with them?"

But the evil was done—4,000 men were there—their fate must be determined. The prisoners, each with his hands bound behind him by cords, were made to sit down grouped together, before the tents. Sullen rage was depicted in every lineament: they received a little biscuit and some bread, deducted from the already scanty stores of the army. In the General's tent a council was held, which, after long deliberation, broke up without coming to any resolution. The day following arrived, in the evening, the reports of the generals of division; these were filled with complaints on the insufficiency of provisions, and the discontent of the soldiers, who murmured because of their rations being devoured by enemies withdrawn from their just vengeance. All these reports were alarming, especially those of General Bon: they even induced the fear of a revolt. Again the council assembled, to which were summoned all the generals of division. The measures here discussed for hours, with a sincere desire of adopting and executing that which might save these unfortunate captives, were the following:

Shall they be sent to Egypt? and have we the means of transportation? In this case, it would be necessary to give them a numerous escort, and our little army would be too weak in a hostile country. Besides, how feed both prisoners and escort, when we could give them no provisions on setting out, over a tract already exhausted of resources by our passage? If it is proposed to send them by sea, where are the ships? With every telescope turned upon the ocean, we could discern not one friendly sail. Bonaparte, I affirm, would have regarded this a real favor *of fortune*. It was this hope—I have pleasure in saying so—this thought alone, that enabled him to brave, for three days, the murmurs of his army. But we ever hoped in vain for distant succor: it never came.

Shall these prisoners, then, be liberated? They will then either set out directly for Acre, to reinforce the

Pacha, or, throwing themselves into the mountainous tract of Naplouse, harass our rear and right flank, and the destruction of our own men will be the price of the life which we have spared. If this be deemed incredible, ask the question of our own experience—what is the life of a Christian dog in the estimation of a Turk? Ingratitude will here become with them an act of religion.

Shall we then disarm and incorporate these men among our own troops? Here was suggested, in all its force, the question of provisions; afterward occurred the danger of such companions in an enemy's country. What was to be done with them, in the event of a conflict before Acre? or how dispose of them beneath the walls of that city? The difficulties of provisioning and of guarding them increased more and more.

The third day arrived, yet no means of safety, so much desired for these unhappy men, presented itself. The murmurs of the camp augmented—the evil went on increasing—remedy appeared impossible—danger was real and pressing. On the 10th of March the order "that they should be shot," was issued and executed. There was no separation of the Egyptians, as has been said—there were no Egyptian prisoners.

Many of these miserable beings, composing the smaller column, which, amounting to about 1,500, was drawn up on the beach, at some distance from the main body, while the butchery was going on, escaped by swimming to some reefs out of gunshot. Perceiving this, our men laid down their muskets on the sand, and employing the signs of reconciliation and of amity, which they had learned in Egypt, invited the return of their victims. They did return, but, coming within reach, met death, and perished amid the waters. I limit myself to those details of this horrible necessity of which I was an eye-witness. The atrocious scene makes me yet shudder when I think of it, as when it passed before me: much rather would I forget, if possible, than describe. All that can be imagined, however fearful, in this day of blood, would fall short of the reality. I have reported the truth—the whole truth. I was present at all the debates, at all the conferences, at all the deliberations. I had, of course, no deliberative voice, but I owe it to candor to declare that, had I possessed a vote, my voice would have been for death. The result of the deliberations and the circumstances of our army would have constrained me to this opinion. War unfortunately offers instances, by no means rare, in which an immutable law of all times, and common to all nations, has decreed that private interests shall be sacrificed to one paramount public good, and humanity itself be forgotten. It is for posterity to judge whether such was the terrible position of Bonaparte. I have an intimate conviction of the fact; moreover, by the advice of the council of officers, whose opinion finally became unanimous, was the matter decided. I owe it also to truth to state, that he yielded only at the last extremity, and was, perhaps, one of those who witnessed the massacre with the greatest sorrow.

After the siege of Jaffa, the plague began to manifest its approach with more severity. From first to last, seven or eight hundred men were lost by the contagion during the Syrian expedition.

Our march upon Acre, which commenced on the 14th March, was by no means the series of triumphs and obstacles vaunted in certain works. All has been made out of the foolhardiness of General Lannes, who, contrary to the express orders of Bonaparte, obstinately pursued a troop of mountaineers into the passes of Naplouse. In returning, he fell into an ambuscade, losing sixty men killed, and more than double the number wounded, the Turks firing from behind rocks and down precipices upon our people. During the firing, Bonaparte manifested much anxiety, and most severely reproached Lannes for having uselessly exposed, and sacrificed without object, a number of brave followers. Lannes excused himself by saying the peasantry had insulted his detachment, and he wished to chastise the rabble.

"We are in no situation," replied the Commander, sternly, "to indulge in such bravadoes." Our evening bivouac was a melancholy one; the rain fell in torrents, and Zeta, where we halted for the night, on the 15th, afforded no resources for our wounded. The useless loss just sustained seemed a sad augury to many—a presentiment but too surely confirmed by the event.

On the 18th we arrived before Acre. The Djezzar, as we learned, had just taken the head from our envoy Mailly, causing the body to be thrown into the sea in a sack. This cruel Pacha must have ordered a great number of similar executions, for the waves often threw ashore bodies in this state, which we discovered while bathing. The details of the siege are sufficiently known. Though encompassed by a wall, flanked with good towers, having also a broad and pretty deep ditch, defended by regular works, this small fortress was judged incapable of protracted defence against French valor, and the science of our engineers. But the facility and promptitude of the capture of Jaffa blinded us not a little in regard to the similar appearance, though different condition, of the two places. At Jaffa we possessed a sufficient artillery; at Acre we did not: we had only to do with the defenders of Jaffa, left to their own resources; at Acre we were opposed to a garrison maintained by reinforcements of men and stores, supported by an English fleet, and aided by European science.

Sidney Smith, doubtless, was the great cause of our failure. Much has been said of his intercourse with the Commander-in-Chief. The reproaches alleged by the latter, of Sir Sidney having endeavored to seduce the officers and soldiers of the French army, even supposing them to have been well founded, were the more singular that such means are frequently resorted to by belligerents. As to the embarking of French prisoners on board a vessel infected by the plague, the odious accusation is repelled by its improbability alone, but, above all, by established facts. At the time, I observed Sir Sidney closely, and certainly remarked a species of knight-errantry in his disposition, sometimes leading to trifling fooleries, but I affirm that his conduct toward the French was that of a generous enemy. Several letters have been shown me, which bore witness in his favor, that the writers "were very grateful for the good treatment experienced by the French when they had fallen into his hands."

At Acre, all the arrangements, all the works, all the attacks, were conducted with that slightness and careless-ness which a too sanguine confidence inspires. Kléber, in his walks with me through the lines, often expressed his surprise and dissatisfaction on this head. "The trenches," said he, "are not knee deep; we ought necessarily to have had battering cannon. We began with only field-pieces. This encouraged the besieged, by disclosing the weakness of our resources." Our heavy artillery, consisting of no more than three twenty-fours and six eighteens, arrived, with the greatest difficulty, not before the last days of April, and already three assaults had been made, with evident loss; by the 4th of May our powder, too, began to fail. Balls also were wanting, and an order of the day fixed a price, accord-ing to the calibre, for each bullet shot from the place or the ships of war which could be recovered and brought in. The ships "Tiger" and "Theseus," stationed on each side of the bay, interrupted the communication between the camp and the trenches, but caused more noise than mischief: an officer, however, was killed by one of their balls the evening before the raising of the siege.

Upon the walls, the enemy had stationed marksmen, chiefly Albanians, of great expertness. They placed stones, one above the other, on the top of the parapet, and, putting their rifles through the openings, took aim, completely under cover, and with deadly precision. On the 9th April, General Caffarelli, so well known for courage and talent, was traversing the works with his hand resting on the hip, in order to balance the defective gait occasioned by his wooden leg. The general's elbow thus extended above the trench. He was warned that the balls, fired so near from the place, hit the smallest objects. Paying no attention to this warning, he had his elbow fractured a few instants after. Amputation of the arm was judged indispensable, which the general survived eighteen days. Bonaparte went regularly twice a day to visit him, and, by his orders, according with my own regard for the patient, I hardly ever left him. A little before his last moments, he said to me: "My dear Bourrienne, read me Voltaire's preface to the Spirit of Laws." I did so—and he fell asleep. On entering the tent of the Commander-in-Chief, he asked as usual, "How goes it with Caffarelli?" I told him what had happened, and that his end was near. "Bah! so he wished to hear that preface? It is singular." Bonaparte went to see him; but he still slept. I returned, and heard the general's last sigh, which he yielded the same night, in perfect peace. The general died universally regretted—a brave soldier and a man of learning.

In the assault of the 10th May, Bonaparte was early in the trenches, attended by Croiser, who had vainly sought death during the siege; for life had become even more insupportable since the unhappy affair at Jaffa. Aware that the termination of the siege, which he foresaw to be near, must greatly retard the desired death, he leaped upon a battery. This elevated situation necessarily drew upon him the fire of the enemy. "Croiser!" exclaimed Bonaparte, in a voice of thunder, "come down—I command you—you have no business there!" The youth remained, without returning any answer. An instant after, a ball passed through his right thigh. Amputation was performed. The day of our departure he was placed upon a litter; but he died of lockjaw between Gaza and El Arych, where I received his last adieu.

The siege of St. Jean d'Acre continued sixty days. There had been in that time eight assaults, and twelve sorties. During the assault of the 8th May, more than two hundred men penetrated into the city. Already the shout of victory arose; but the breach, taken in flank by the Turks, could not be entered with sufficient promptitude, and the party was left without support. The streets barricaded, the very women running about throwing dust in the air, exciting the inhabitants by cries and howlings—all contributed to render unavailing this short occupation by a handful of brave men, who, finding themselves alone, regained the breach, by a retrograde movement; but not before many had fallen. At this assault, Duroc, then in the trenches, was wounded by the recoil of the fragment of a howitzer-shot fired against the fortifications. Fortunately, the fleshy part only of the thigh was carried away, the bone remaining untouched. He had a tent in common with several other aides-de-camp, but, for better accommodation, I had him brought into mine, and scarcely ever quitted his side. On entering about midday, after a short absence, I found the patient in a profound sleep. The excessive heat had made him throw off all covering; and even a part of his wound lay exposed. A small scorpion, which had crawled up by the leg of the camp bedstead, was just on the point of reaching the sore. I had the good fortune to dash the reptile to the earth; but the somewhat hasty movement awoke my patient.

We often bathed in the sea. There were days when the English, *probably excited by grog*, let fly broadsides at our floating heads. I know not that any accident ever resulted from these efforts. Convinced of the impossibility of being hit, we soon paid no attention; and, indeed, the circumstance afforded us matter of diversion.

Toward the conclusion of the siege, the news from Egypt announced some inconsiderable risings in Lower Egypt. These were occasioned by a fanatic, El Mohdy, who gave himself out for an angel. They had, however, no further consequence beyond throwing upon our rear some enthusiasts, whose illusions were effectually exorcised by the musket—a potent divining rod. I expressed some surprise at the want of intelligence from Upper Egypt. "Desaix is there," replied Bonaparte; "and I am easy." A few days after, he heard from that general, unceasingly engaged in beating and pursuing the indefatigable Mourad. These despatches contained information of the loss of a very beautiful and large dgerm, built for the navigation of the Nile, and named "The Italy." The commander, Morandi, after an obstinate resistance, and despairing of escape from the Arabs and Fellahs, fired the powder magazine and perished with many of those on board; namely, the greater part of the band of the Sixty-first demi-brigade, and some armed and wounded soldiers. Those who escaped on shore, as private letters stated, were put to death amid the most horrible torments, to the sound of their own music, played by their unfortunate companions. Thus all, in turn, to the very last, became sufferers. This sad news, the frightful details, and the name of the dgerm, struck forcibly upon the General's mind. "My good friend," addressing me in a prophetic tone, "Italy is lost to France—it is all over—my presentiments never deceive me!" I combated this opinion, by endeavoring to convince him that there could be no connection between Italy and the destruction of a bark to which the name of that country had been given, at a distance of 800 leagues; but nothing could induce him to give it up. The prediction was soon realized.

CHAPTER VII

Failure of the Siege of Acre—Bonaparte Returns to Europe—Politics in France—Bernadotte and Moreau

THE troops quitted Acre on the 20th of May, when Bonaparte issued a proclamation, which insults truth from beginning to end, and is yet to be read in many works! We took our departure at night, in order to avoid a sortie from the besieged, and to place the army, having three leagues of flat land to traverse, beyond range of the English gunboats and vessels of war, in the bay of Mount

Carmel. The removal of the wounded and sick had commenced two days before. We effected our night march
along the shore of the Mediterranean, and passed Mount
Carmel.

Our little army reached Cairo on the 14th June, after
a most painful march of twenty-five days, accomplished
under every species of privation. The heat, during the
passage of the Desert between El Arych and Belbeys, had
exceeded 33° usually, and, on the ball of the thermometer
being placed on the side, the mercury rose to 45°. The
fallacious mirage was more seductive than ever; and, notwithstanding the lessons of sad experience, so real appeared
the illusion we often could not refrain urging forward our
jaded steeds, to find—only salt and arid sands. In two
days I found my cloak covered with salt left by the evapo-
ration of the night dew. The bitter waters of these deserts,
which our thirsty horses drank with avidity, occasioned the
loss of great numbers—the poor animals dropping under
their riders before they had gone a mile from the watering
place.

The bad success of the Syrian expedition gave birth to
complaints and reflections, such as our position called forth,
marked more by their justness than moderation. "Why,"
men said, "go to anticipate the movements of an army which
did not yet exist? Why, if this army was one day to attack
Egypt, spare it the difficulties and evils of a march across
the Desert? And why set out to besiege that army in its
own strongholds, in place of waiting for it on the plains of
Egypt? Was it not evident, also, that the sea, in the possession of our enemies, would be of vast importance in such
an expedition?" This reasoning of the general good sense
of the army would be incontrovertible if the real object of
the war had been, as officially announced, the destruction
of the butcher of Syria. But we have seen that it concealed
other and greater, but, in our circumstances, objects more
chimerical still.

Bonaparte announced his entrance into Cairo by one of

those lying bulletins that imposed only on fools. "I bring," said he, in this precious document, "many prisoners and colors. I have razed the palace of the Djezzar, the ramparts of Acre. There stands not one stone above another. All the inhabitants fled by sea; Djezzar is dangerously wounded." I avow a painful sentiment felt while writing these words from his dictation. Excited by what I had just witnessed, it was difficult to refrain hazarding some observation; but his constant reply was—"My dear fellow, you are a ninny, and comprehend nothing at all of the matter." And, with these words, he signed what was to go round the world, and to inspire historians! Our return to Egypt, too, has been attributed to insurrections in that country. Nothing can be more incorrect; these were trifling. The reverses at Acre, and the fear, or rather wise foresight, of a hostile disembarkation in July, were the true causes. We had enough of Syria. What should we have done any longer there? Lose men and time. Truly our leader had neither too many men nor too much time at his disposal.

On the evening of the 15th, I was walking with the General, when we perceived, advancing from the north, an Arab messenger at full speed. He was the bearer of a despatch from Marmont, who commanded at Alexandria, greatly to Bonaparte's satisfaction. The Turks had disembarked on the 11th, at Aboukir, under escort and protection of an English fleet. This news of a landing by fifteen or sixteen thousand enemies did not surprise Bonaparte, who had long foreseen such an occurrence. The event, however, was little expected by the generals, to whom he had prophesied the destruction, before Acre, of that very army now arrived in Egypt.

Immediately on perusing this despatch, Bonaparte, shutting himself up in his tent, continued till three o'clock next morning dictating to me his orders for the march of the troops, and for the conduct of those who, during his absence, were to remain in the interior. I beheld at this crisis the full development of that ardent spirit, which difficulties roused—that celerity which anticipated chances. He was all action, and never hesitated. At four o'clock on the morning of the 16th, he was on horseback, and the army in full march. At this time of his life, energy, decision, promptitude, imperturbable presence of mind and rapidity of execution, never forsook him on great emergencies. Must I not render justice to these qualities? On the eighth day, after leaving the Pyramids, we were in Alexandria, where all was prepared for that memorable conflict of the 25th July, which certainly did not repair the immense losses and fatal consequences of the naval engagement of Aboukir; yet the battle will ever recall to Frenchmen one of their most glorious achievements in arms.

The Turks being defeated, Bonaparte sent an envoy on board the English admiral's ship. Our intercourse was marked by that urbanity which ought to characterize the relations of civilized nations. The admiral presented to our envoy some little gifts, in return for those we had sent, and the French "Gazette" of Frankfort, of the 28th June, 1799. For ten months we had been without news from France. Bonaparte ran over this journal with an eagerness easy to be conceived. "Well," said he, "my presentiment has not deceived me: Italy is lost. The miserable creatures! All the fruit of our victories has disappeared. I must be gone."

He caused Berthier to be called—made him read the news. "Things," said he, "go ill in France. I must see what is passing there. You shall go with me," adding that only myself and Gantheaume, for whom he had sent, were in the secret. And he recommended Berthier to be discreet; to show no unusual elation; to change nothing in his ordinary habits; to make no purchases, nor sell anything—finishing with the words, "I am sure of myself—I am sure of Bourrienne." The chief-of-staff promised silence, and kept his pledge. He had had enough of Egypt, burned with a desire of returning to France, and feared lest his own indiscretion should ruin all. Gantheaume arrived. Bonaparte gave him an order to prepare two frigates, "La Muiron" and "La Carrière," and two small brigs, "La Revanche" and "La Fortune," with provisions for four or five hundred men, and for two months. He then confessed to him the secret of the armament, recommending the closest concealment of its object, and to act with such prudence that the English cruisers might remain also in complete ignorance of the preparations. Afterward, he settled with Gantheaume the route to be followed. He provided for every contingency.

We have just seen the sole cause of the departure of General Bonaparte for Europe. It is a very plain fact, which has been disguised by the most absurd suppositions and ridiculous conjectures. It has been attempted to assign to a simple occurrence some extraordinary origin. It is not true, as so often repeated, that he had determined on his departure before the battle of Alexandria. He would have been very well pleased had that disembarkation not taken place, in which case he would have waited for news from France, and made his plans accordingly. It is pretended that Bonaparte had received intelligence of events in Italy before the engagement of the 25th by means of his secret correspondence. There existed no correspondence, either private or official. Ten months had already elapsed, and we were still without news from Europe. It is contrary to truth that he was officially informed of the state of affairs in France, and of the critical situation of things both there and in Italy. Who is Bourbaki, or Bombachi, reported so confidently to have brought news from Joseph to his brother at Acre, which occasioned the siege to be raised? I never heard the name; and how was he to arrive at the camp *alone*, either by sea or land? And then, Madame Bonaparte —she, forsooth, told this secret to Fouché for 1,000 louis! What secret? Let us be satisfied with the truth. It was the accident, already explained, which procured news from Europe. It ought to be regarded as certain, and I affirm that Bonaparte never dreamed of his departure for France when he made his expedition to the Pyramids, nor when he learned of the disembarkation of the Anglo-Turkish army.

Writers have framed intelligence reaching him by way of Tunis, Algiers, Morocco—from I know not where! But nothing can be opposed to a certain fact. At this period, during more than two years, not a single despatch, in any circumstances, remained unknown to me. How, then, could all those mentioned escape my notice?

On the 23d August, 1799, we embarked in the frigates "La Muiron" and "La Carrière," to the number of from four to five hundred. Such was our squadron, such the formidable armament with which Bonaparte—so he had written to the Divan at Cairo—was to annihilate all his enemies. This boasting tone might impose upon those who knew not the real state of things; but as for us, what were we to think of it? The same as Bonaparte thought on the morrow. Fifteen months had elapsed since we quitted our native country. Everything smiled on our departure: all was dark at our return. Where now were the fourteen ships of war, the frigates, the three hundred sail, which then bounded over the surges of the Mediterranean to Eastern conquests? What had been the fruit of those pompous proclamations, those promises, those hopes, and even of our first success? What had availed the capture of Malta in forty-eight hours, or the reduction of Egypt in one month? Alas! times were indeed changed; reduced to conceal our flight, to embark by stealth, we read nothing that was not hazardous in the future; and, if we cast remembrance back upon the past, we had to deplore the loss of our fleet, replaced by two frail Venetian barks, fitted out in haste.

Night had already fallen when we got on board the frigates, anchored at a considerable distance from the Port of Alexandria. The feeble light of the stars, however, sufficed to show us a corvette approaching to observe, and, as it were, to be present at our silent and nocturnal embarkment. Next morning, when on the point of setting sail, we perceived a wherry making directly from the harbor. On board was M. Grand-Maison, an excellent man, whom we all loved, but who, nevertheless, had not been nominated

among those returning to France. He entreated, supplicated; but in vain. Bonaparte, desirous to be gone, would
listen to no new arrival; and only at the last moment,
Monge, Berthollet, and myself prevailed. We hoisted over
the ship's side our brother of the Egyptian Institute, with
the breeze swelling in our sails.

On the 9th October, 1799, at eight in the morning, we
entered the bay of Fréjus. The sailors not having remarked
the coast during the night, we knew not where we were. At
first there was some hesitation whether we ought to advance:
we were not expected, and could not reply to the signals
changed during our absence. Some shots were fired from
the batteries on the coast; but our frank entrance into the
roadstead, the numbers crowded on the decks of the two
frigates, our demonstrations of joy, soon dispelled every
doubt of our being friends. Already had we entered the
port and almost taken up a station, when the report spread
that one of the ships carried General Bonaparte. In an instant the sea was covered with craft. In vain we besought
the people to keep at a distance; we were fairly carried off
and landed on shore. When we represented to the crowd
of men and women which pressed around us the danger
they incurred, all cried out: "We prefer the plague to the
Austrians!"

What we felt on treading the soil of France, I essay not
to describe: Oh! how sweet it seemed to breathe the air of
our native land under the delicious sky of Provence! The
reception we had experienced; the acclamations, the delirium, of which our leader was the object; the interest
which every one was urgent to express toward us, heightened
our gladness. All this was so overpowering as to deaden,
for a space, the impression of the mournful tidings which
met us from every quarter. In the first moment of our joy,
as if by one spontaneous feeling, we repeated, with tears of
enthusiasm, the beautiful lines which Voltaire has placed
in the mouth of the Sicilian exile.

Hardly had he entered Fréjus when, eager for news, Bo-

naparte questioned everybody.   Here he first learned the real
extent of our reverses in Italy.   These completely effaced former ideas: "The evil is too great," said he; "there is nothing to be done."   The sacrifice was not made without pain.
Never shall I forget with what satisfaction, with what intoxication, he dwelt upon the effect which would be produced in
France by the simultaneous announcement of an Egyptian
and an Italian victory.   Decided thus to hasten with all
speed to Paris, he set out the same afternoon.   Everywhere
was he received with the same enthusiasm; his journey resembled a triumphal march, and it required but small gift
of prophecy to foresee in it something of the futurity that
lay beyond.

The state of things in France was indeed fearful.   Every
province become a prey to anarchy and the ravages of civil
war; the nation menaced with foreign invasion, and groaning
under a load of tyrannical laws; the government denounced
by the universal voice of the people, as without power, without justice, without morality, the mere puppet of the factious
and intriguing.   The highways were so infested by robbers
that our carriage was voluntarily escorted, not more from
respect than from anxiety for our safety.   All things wore
the aspect of dissolution; disorder reigned throughout, but
especially in the provinces; for men in large cities more
easily escape the fangs of despotism and oppression.   Any
prospect of a change could not fail of being hailed with
transports.   The majority of the French nation longed to
emerge from this debasement.   Two dangers threatened
at one and the same moment—anarchy and the Bourbons.
There was felt the pressing and irresistible necessity of concentrating the supreme power, and, at the same time, of
maintaining those institutions which symbolized the spirit
and the intelligence of the age—institutions which France
had purchased so gloriously, and at the price of ten years
of misfortune; of which she had known the sweets only in
hope; and which seemed on the point of being lost forever.
The good sense of the nation was searching for a man capa-

ble of restoring tranquillity to an exhausted and bleeding country. But the search had yet been vain. A fortunate soldier presented himself, covered with glory, who had unfurled the banners of the republic from the Capitol and from the Pyramids. All acknowledged his possession of superior talents: his character, the well-known boldness of his views, and his victories, had placed him in the first rank: his conduct hitherto had likewise appeared to proclaim the wish to render the country of his adoption free and happy. Thus, without a thought in reserve, expectation fixed upon a general whom past actions designated as the most capable of defending the republic from foes without, and liberty from false friends within; a general whom his flatterers, and even many of good faith, addressed as "the hero of liberal principles." At the least, there could not be comparison between him and the ignoble crowd of fanatical hypocrites, who, under the pretexts of republican and liberal notions, had reduced France to the most disgraceful and the vilest servitude. But, in reality, who could have imagined that, after obtaining the chief magistracy of the republic, for whose preservation he had seemed to labor so earnestly and so successfully, Bonaparte would employ the powers of that very magistracy to trample beneath his feet those principles which he had so often proclaimed—to which he had pledged allegiance?

We reached Paris on the 24th Vendemiaire (16th October). He had as yet been informed of nothing, having seen neither his wife nor brothers, who had posted through Burgundy, while we had taken the route by the Bourbonnais. The news of the General's disembarkation at Fréjus had been transmitted by telegraph to Paris. Madame Bonaparte, dining at M. Gohier's the same day on which, as president of the Directory, he received this despatch, formed the resolution of instantly setting out to meet her husband, knowing of what importance it was that she should be beforehand with his brothers. His jealous anger, caused formerly by the imprudent conduct of Junot, had left no apparent traces:

nevertheless, secret suspicion preyed upon the mind of
Bonaparte. When Josephine returned to Paris, we were
already there. Remembrance of the past, the hateful and
envenomed tales of his brothers, exaggerations of facts, had
exasperated him to the last degree; accordingly, Josephine
was received with studied severity and an expression of the
most cutting indifference. For three days, he held no communication with her, and, during that space, spoke to me
incessantly of those suspicions which imagination had now
converted into certainties. Often threats of divorce were
uttered, with no less wrath than on the border of Syria.
I again assumed, with success, the part of the conciliator:
my endeavors, seconded by his own reflections, the sincere
affection he had always entertained for Josephine, and his
love for her children, brought about a perfect reconciliation.

On the morrow after his arrival, Bonaparte paid a visit
to the Directory. The interview was cold. On the 24th he
said to me, "At dinner, yesterday, with Gohier, I affected
to take no notice of Siéyès, who was there, and I could observe all the rage with which this contempt inflamed him."
—"But are you sure he is against you?"—"I know nothing
about his plans as yet; but he is a man of system—that
I like not." In fact, Bonaparte was already contemplating
how he might turn him out, and take his place in the
Directory.

But, to follow the course of events, we must cast a retrospective glance upon the state of parties during our absence,
and at our return to Paris. The army was exclusively republican, while the Directory and the government seemed
as if constituted expressly for intrigue of all kinds. Siéyès
was reported at one time to have entertained thoughts of
inviting the Duke of Brunswick to the head of affairs, and
Barras seemed not to have been far removed from recalling
the Bourbons. Moulins, Roger-Ducos, and Gohier alone
maintained, or affected alone to maintain, the possibility
of preserving existing forms. Among the military, again,
Moreau enjoyed a high reputation, and might be considered

as representing the Army of the Rhine, which, having reared in its own ranks men of great valor, while not refusing the tribute of admiration to the Conqueror of Italy, leaned with something of personal interest in its estimation of him who had repaired the disasters on the German frontier. Bonaparte, on the other hand, had, for devoted partisans, all the companions of his Italian expedition, and, a little later, those whom he termed "my Egyptians." Bernadotte, too, though at the head of no party, occupied a conspicuous place in public attention, as a stern and inflexible republican, round whom, in the event of any great political explosion, most probably would rally all those of similar sentiments. Strange, that the affairs of Europe should since have been so changed, so intermingled, so fantastic, that the crown of Sweden has become compatible with the fidelity sworn to the constitution of the year III.! During the Egyptian expedition, Bernadotte, in his capacity of a zealous republican, had discharged the functions of minister of war. I have strong reasons for believing that Joseph and Lucien made all sorts of attempts to bring him over to their brother's party; and, with that view, had seconded his nomination to this office. At the same time, I guarantee only what I have seen or heard. It was also reported that, at first, he had yielded to their influence, but afterward, alienated by their demands in favor of their client, acted independently in his office, and even undertook to open the eyes of the Directory to the ambitious views of the Bonapartes. Certainly the subsequent conduct of Bernadotte, as witnessed by myself, went to corroborate these reports. Endowed with rare perspicacity, he was the first to penetrate clearly the ulterior designs of Bonaparte. He saw the Directory divided into two parties; one duped by the promises, the other accomplices of the Conqueror of Egypt. In these circumstances, if I may so express myself, he hawked about the offer of his services to all those in the government who were, like himself, opposed to the change so much apprehended. But Bonaparte was not the man to

be vanquished in management, and every instant beheld his
adherents increase.

Three weeks before our arrival from Egypt, Bernadotte
had resigned the war portfolio, which was now in possession
of Dubois-Crance. Some friends of the late minister, however, were attempting to recall him to his former post.
This it imported much to prevent. And how well Bonaparte already understood his position appears from a conversation held with me the second day after our arrival. After
a short silence and rubbing his forehead with his right hand,
he continued, breaking off from less important matters—
"I am perfectly aware that Bernadotte and Moreau will be
against me. But of Moreau I have no fear; he is soft, without energy. I am sure he prefers military to political
power: we shall gain him by the offer of a command. But,
Bernadotte? he has Moorish blood in his veins; he is bold
and enterprising; he has been with my brothers; he does
not like me. I am almost certain he will be against me.
If he become ambitious, he is capable of daring anything.
Yet you will remember with what lukewarmness he acted on
the 18th Fructidor, when I sent him to second Augereau.
Besides, this devil of a fellow is scarcely to be seduced; he
is disinterested; he has judgment: but we shall see." In
little more than three weeks after our arrival, Bernadotte
had dined with Bonaparte, both in the Rue Victoire and in
the country. The latter had laid himself out to persuade,
and finally prevailed on the former, if not to forward, at
least not actively to oppose his schemes. In all these advances, Bonaparte acted upon his own principle—"We must
always be beforehand with our enemies and show them a fair
outside; without this, they think we fear them, and that
gives them boldness." Moreau, again, had been brought in
the same time completely over. Such were the difficulties
in the way, such the imperative necessity of knowing our
ground well, when Bonaparte began to act. Let us now advance into a more extensive field, and view our first chances.

As a mark of high esteem for the General, the Council of

Five Hundred named his brother Lucien their president. The sequel proved the importance of this nomination, which, with the excellent conduct of Lucien, who throughout displayed a courage, activity, intelligence and presence of mind rarely united in the same individual, mainly contributed to the success of the 19th Brumaire.

The General had a fixed plan of conduct, whence he did not once depart, during the twenty-three days from his arrival till the above date. He refused almost all private invitations, as a safeguard against indiscreet inquiries; waived all unacceptable offers, and all replies which might compromise him. It was even with considerable repugnance that he consented to a project of the ardent Lucien, who, by every species of address, had brought the majority of his colleagues to take part in a public subscription dinner to be given in honor of Bonaparte. This, from the number of the guests—two hundred and fifty—the diversity of their opinions, and their mutual suspicions, the dullest affair at which I was ever present, attained, however, its object. Two parties, till then irritated against each other, were thus brought together and prepared to join against the common enemy. Bonaparte, wearied and impatient, dined quickly, rose as soon as he had finished, and, making the round of the table with Berthier and myself, addressed a few words of flattery to some, to others an unmeaning phrase, according to circumstances, and disappeared, leaving his entertainers still at table.

During this brief political crisis, nothing passed more noble, more elevated, or less contemptible, than all we have seen in these revolutionary commotions, and especially in that of the 18th Fructidor. Everything in such political dealings is so despicable, conducted with so much knavery, with so many lies and snares, so much treachery and impudence, that for the honor of the human species a veil should be drawn over the disgusting details.

CHAPTER VIII

Revolution of 18th Brumaire—The Chambers Dissolved—Bonaparte as Consul
—State of the Army left in Egypt

THE parts were well cast in the grand drama whose catastrophe approached. During the three days preceding the 18th Brumaire (9th November) every one was at his post. Lucien, with no less activity than intelligence, advanced the conspiracy in the Council of Five Hundred. Siéyès took care of the Directory. Réal, under the wing of Fouché, negotiated with the departments, and, according to the instructions of his leader, labored with admirable address, without compromising Fouché, for the destruction of those from whom that minister derived his power. Time pressed. So early as the 14th, Fouché said to me—"Tell your General to be speedy. If he delays he is lost."

On the 17th, Bonaparte was informed by Régnault St. Jean d'Angely that the overtures made to Cambacérès and Lebrun were not received in a very decided manner. "I will have no tergiversation," replied the General with warmth. "Let them not suppose I have need of them. They must determine to-day. If not, to-morrow will be too late. I feel myself sufficiently strong at present to stand alone." These individuals had remained almost strangers to the intrigues which preceded the 18th Brumaire. Bonaparte, in his arrangements, had cast his eyes upon Cambacérès, the minister of justice, in order to create him one of his colleagues, when he should be in a condition to appoint them; because, through his former life, this functionary had given pledges to the partisans of the Revolution, and he added Lebrun to counterbalance the former choice. Lebrun was well known as a man of honorable conduct and moderate principles.

By this selection Bonaparte hoped to satisfy all parties. Besides, neither was in a state to contend against his own inflexible resolution and ambitious views.

What low intrigues the 17th Brumaire beheld! That day I dined with Bonaparte. After dinner, he said to me—"To-morrow I have engaged to din with Gohier. You may well believe I shall do no such thing. I am not the less vexed at his obstinacy. To reassure him still more, my wife has just invited him to breakfast for to-morrow. It is impossible he should apprehend anything. I saw Barras this morning, and left him very ill at ease. He besought me to see him again to-night. I promised, but shall not go. To-morrow the affair will be finished. It is a little time gained. He expects me at eleven. All will be prepared for my reception. Take my carriage, mention my name, and you will be immediately admitted. Say to him, a severe headache has obliged me to go to bed, but that I shall see him to-morrow without fail: that he may be quite easy; for everything will be arranged. Avoid as much as possible being questioned; do not stay long; and come to my apartment on your return."

I arrived at eleven o'clock at night precisely, in the General's chariot. The greatest solitude and most profound silence reigned in the apartments leading to the cabinet of Barras. I was announced, when, seeing me instead of Bonaparte, he showed extreme astonishment. He had a most disconsolate air. It was easy to perceive that he looked upon himself as a lost man. I discharged my commission, and remained but a short time. On conducting me to the door, he said: "I see Bonaparte deceives me. He will not return. All is over. To me, nevertheless, he owes everything." I replied that he would certainly return on the morrow. A negative shake of the head showed me plainly he did not believe the assertion. We shall see what passed. Bonaparte, on hearing the account of my visit, appeared well satisfied. In reply, he said—"Joseph has just gone to Bernadotte's to tell him to come to-morrow."—

"From what I know," was my answer, "if he does come, he will be of no service to you."—"I believe so; but he can no longer do me any hurt: that is all I want. Come, good-night! Be here to-morrow morning at seven." It was then one o'clock.

Returning on the morrow a little before seven, I perceived a great number of generals and officers already assembled; and on entering Bonaparte's chamber—an extraordinary circumstance—found him risen. At this moment he appeared calm, as on the approach of battle: the great agitation was reserved for the day after. I had not been there more than a few minutes, when Joseph entered with Bernadotte, whom he had not been able to find the preceding evening, and had therefore brought thus early. I felt so surprised to see the latter in plain clothes, that I could not help approaching and saying, in a low voice—"General, everybody here is in uniform, except you and I."—"Why should I be so?" As he pronounced these words, Bonaparte, struck also with surprise, interrupted his conversation with several persons collected about him, and turning abruptly toward Bernadotte—"Hold!" said he, "you are not in uniform."—"I am thus every morning, when not on duty."—"But you shall be on service in a moment."—"I have heard nothing to that effect. My instructions should have reached me sooner." Bonaparte then withdrew with Bernadotte into an adjoining room. The conversation was not long—there was no time to be lost.

In another quarter, under the influence of a party of the principal conspirators, the translation of the two legislative bodies to St. Cloud was decreed on the morning of the 18th, and Bonaparte appointed to the command of the armed force.

While these various transactions were going forward, Barras probably still expected Bonaparte, while Josephine awaited Gohier for breakfast. In the residence of Bonaparte were assembled all the generals devoted to him. Never had I seen there so large a number. All were in full uniform. Some half dozen civilians also appeared, of those initiated in the mysteries of the day. The humble abode' of the Conqueror of Italy was much too small for such an assemblage: the court, and even the entrance, were crowded. Bonaparte had been informed of the decree of the Council, and, before mounting on horseback, waited for the copy which would be transmitted to him. At the very moment even of this numerous convocation of officers, that decree was passed in the Council of the Ancients by a majority which might be termed factitious, for the members had been summoned in the evening at different hours, and matters were so managed that sixty or eighty, whom Lucien and his friends had been unable to bring over, did not receive their intimations till too late.

When the message of the Ancients arrived, Bonaparte invited all the assembled officers to follow him. On the news which he announced, a small number drew back—at least I observed two groups separately quit the house. Bernadotte, addressing me, said, "I remain with you." My belief then was that a great deal of jealousy appeared in his demeanor. Bonaparte, before descending the stairs leading into the court from the small circular dining-room, which served also as an antechamber, returned hastily to invite Bernadotte to follow. He refused. Bonaparte said to me in passing: "Gohier is not come—so much the worse for him!" then he sprung on horseback. Scarcely was he gone, when Bernadotte also departed.

Thus left alone with Josephine, I became the confidant of the anxieties which disturbed her, and which I sought to tranquillize by saying that, everything being prepared, affairs would go on of their own accord. She entertained much kindness of feeling toward Madame Gohier: this sentiment extended also to her husband; and I have reason to believe that Madame Bonaparte sent her assurances to President Gohier, through a friend of his wife, that if he resigned voluntarily, without joining Barras, all would go well. But, at that moment, Gohier and Moulins were in their places in the hall of the Directory, waiting for their colleague Barras, to deliberate as a majority, not counting upon Siéyès and Ducos, respecting the translation of the two councils to St. Cloud. They were deceived in their hope. Barras had been so completely prostrated by my visit of the evening before, which had opened his eyes at midnight, that he refused to appear, however pressing the messages sent to him, but remained invisible to his brethren till the moment when Bruix and Talleyrand made him acquainted with the accomplishment of what he dreaded, and demanded his resignation; for, in the position of things, *requested* would be too mild an expression.

On leaving home, Bonaparte rode to the garden of the Tuileries, where, accompanied by Generals Beuronville, Moreau and Macdonald, he reviewed about 10,000 troops, assembled there from an early hour. He then read to the soldiers the decree of the Ancients, directing the transference of the two chambers to St. Cloud for to-morrow (19th), and interdicting all exercise of functions and all deliberations elsewhere, and before that time. The decree further invested Bonaparte with the command of all the military force, and empowered him to require the aid of every citizen if needful. After reading this document, to which the troops listened with the most lively interest, the General addressed them in a few words of explanation, showing the decree to be conformable to articles 102–3 of the constitution, and that measures were in operation for the better government of the country, which he and they were called upon, in the discharge of their duty, to assist and protect. While the General was thus laboring in his vocation, the Council of the Ancients issued an address "to the French," setting forth that "the Council of the Ancients employed the right delegated by the constitution of changing the residence of the legislative body, in order to reclaim the national representation from the dominion of factions, and to restore internal peace." A proclamation somewhat similar was also issued by Bonaparte, addressed to the citizens, and distributed throughout Paris. He was so certain of the manner in

which the Council would act, that he dictated to me this
same proclamation before receiving the decree upon which
it was founded.

During these transactions, I remained with Josephine.
We were at length considerably reassured by learning that
a message, through Adjutant-General Rapatel, had been
delivered at Joseph's house, who was absent, in name of
Bonaparte and Moreau, requesting his presence at the Tuileries. This alliance, so long unhoped, appeared to us both
a favorable omen. It was in effect a grand stroke played
and gained, by Bonaparte thus engaging Moreau on his side:
the game, too, appeared by no means without hazard, since
we all knew Moreau to be justly alive to the injurious slights
of Bonaparte, of whose projects, besides, he was not ignorant. A slave to military discipline, the former now no
longer regarded his fortunate rival save as his chief nominated by his Council of the Ancients. Orders were given
him, and he obeyed. Bonaparte assigned to the Commander
of the Army of the Rhine the Luxembourg quarter—the
command of the jailer-guard of the Directory. He accepted, and no circumstance could have contributed more
marvellously to the accomplishment of the views of Bonaparte and the triumph of his ambition. Whatever might
be the event, Moreau had been under his orders: the latter
would, more than any other, thus be compromised with
the Directors, should they prove refractory; and this stern
republican had held captive the chiefs of the republic.

At last we beheld the General return. Almost everything had succeeded; he had then to deal only with soldiers.
In the course of the evening he said to me—"They are now
engaged in decreeing, by the commission of inspectors of
the chamber, what shall be done to-morrow at St. Cloud:
I am better pleased that these people should decide—it flat-
ters their vanity. I shall obey orders which I have myself
concerted." Continuing our conversation, he expressed satisfaction at having won over Moreau, and then spoke thus
of Bernadotte's visit: "A general without uniform!—he

might as well have come in slippers. Do you know what
I told him on withdrawing?—All. He then knew what to
depend upon: I prefer plain dealing. I said his Directory
was detested, his constitution grown stale; that it had become necessary to make a clean house, and give another
direction to the government. I then added, 'Go and put
on your uniform; I cannot wait longer; you will find me at
the Tuileries in the midst of all our comrades. Bernadotte,
you need place reliance neither on Moreau nor on Beuronville, nor upon any of the generals of your side. When you
know men better, you will find that they promise much, and
hold to little. Trust them not.' He then said he would
take no part in what must be called a rebellion. A rebellion! Bourrienne, can you conceive that? A pack of im-
beciles; people who play the lawyer from morning to night
in their pettiest affairs! All was useless; I could not overcome Bernadotte's resolution: he is a bar of iron. I requested his pledge to undertake nothing against me. Know
you what he said?''—"Doubtless, something unpleasant."
—"Unpleasant! that's a good one!—much worse. He told
me, 'I shall remain quiet as a citizen; but, if the Directory
give me orders to act, I will march against all perturbators.'
After all, I laugh at him: my measures are taken, and he
shall have no command. Moreover, I may just tell you, I
completely outwitted him as to the sequel. I played off
the sweets of a private life—the pleasures of the country
—the delights of Malmaison—of, I know not what? I enacted the swain, and so parted. On the whole, things have
passed off pretty well to-day. Good-night; we shall see
to-morrow.''

On the 19th, I went to St. Cloud, accompanied by my
old acquaintance La Valette. As we were passing through
the Place Louis XV., he asked me what was to be transacted, and what I thought of the events now at issue. "My
friend," said I, "we shall either sleep in the palace of the
Luxembourg, or we finish here." Who could have told
which was to be the conclusion? Success has justified as a

noble enterprise what the least circumstance had converted into a criminal attempt.

The meeting of the Ancients opened at one o'clock, presided over by Lemercier. Discussion ran high upon the situation of affairs; upon the admission of the members of Directory; and the propriety of an immediate election. Altercation was becoming warm. The accounts brought every instant to General Bonaparte determined him to enter the hall and take part in the debate. His entrance was hasty, and in anger—no favorable augury of what he would say. The passage by which we entered led directly forward into the middle of the house: our backs were toward the door. Bonaparte had the president on his right; he could not see him quite in front. I found myself on the General's right; our clothes touched; Berthier was on his left. All the harangues composed for Bonaparte, after the event, differ from each other—no miracle that. There was, in fact, none pronounced to the Ancients; unless a broken conversation with the president, carried on without nobleness, propriety, or dignity, may be called a speech. We heard only these words: "Brothers in arms"—"frankness of a soldier." The questions of the president followed each other rapidly: they were clear. Nothing could be more confused, or worse enunciated, than the ambiguous and disjointed replies of Bonaparte. He spoke incoherently of "volcanoes"—"secret agitations"—"victories"—"constitution violated." He found fault even with the 18th Fructidor, of which he had himself been the prime instigator and most powerful upholder. He pretended to be ignorant of everything up to the very moment when the Council of the Ancients had called him to the succor of the country. Then came "Cæsar"—"Cromwell"—"tyrant." He repeated several times, "I have nothing more to tell you." And he had told them nothing. He said he was called to assume a higher command, on his return from Italy, by the wish of the nation, and, afterward, of his comrades. Out came the words, "liberty, equality." For these, every one saw, he had not come to St. Cloud.

Scarcely were they pronounced, when a member—I believe Linglet—interrupted him sharply, "You forget the constitution." Then he became animated, and we lost the drift of his talk, comprehending nothing beyond "18 Fructidor"— "30 Prairial"—"hypocrites"—"intriguers"—"I am not so" —"I shall declare all"—"I will abdicate the power when the danger which threatens the republic has passed." Bonaparte, thinking all these allegations admissible as proofs, plucked up a little assurance and accused the two directors, "Barras and Moulins, who had proposed," said he, "to place him at the head of a party whose object was to put down those professing liberal ideas." At these words, revolting from their falsehood, great clamor arose in the hall. Some demanded, with loud outcries, a general committee to examine these revelations. "No, no!" exclaimed others, "no general committee! a conspiracy has been denounced: it is proper that France hear all." Bonaparte was then invited to enter upon details: "You ought to conceal nothing." These interruptions, apostrophes and interrogations overwhelmed him: he believed himself- lost. Instead of explaining what he had said, he accused anew the Council of Five Hundred. The disapprobation became more violent, and his discourse still more wanting in method and coherence. Sometimes he addressed the representatives, now quite stultified; sometimes the military in the court, who were beyond hearing; then, without any transition, he spoke of the "thunder of war," saying, "I am accompanied by the God of war and fortune." The president then calmly observed to him, that he found nothing—absolutely nothing—upon which they could deliberate; that all he had said was vague: "Explain yourself, unfold the plots into which you have been invited to enter." Bonaparte repeated the same things —and in what style! No idea, in truth, can be formed of the whole scene, unless by those present. There was not the least order in all he stammered out, with the most inconceivable incoherence. His place was in front of a battery, rather than before the president's chair of an assembly.

RETURN FROM ELBA

Perceiving the bad effect produced upon the meeting by this rhapsody, and the progressive confusion of the speaker, I whispered, pulling his coat gently at the same time, "Retire, General; you no longer know what you are saying." I made a sign to Berthier to second me in persuading him to leave the hall; when suddenly, after stammering out a few words more, he turned round, saying, "Let all who love me, follow!" The guards stationed at the door offered no opposition to his passage; the attendant who preceded calmly drew aside the drapery which closed the entrance, and the General sprang upon his horse, in the midst of the troops which filled the court. Truly, I know not what might have been the consequence had the president, seeing the General retire, said, "Grenadiers! let no one pass." I have a notion, however, that, instead of sleeping on the morrow in the palace of the Luxembourg, he would have finished his part in the square of the Revolution.

We have just seen what a spectacle the hall of the Ancients presented: without, all wore a different aspect. Scarcely had the General appeared on horseback, when shouts from a thousand voices of "Long live Bonaparte!" rose in every quarter. This was but a ray of sunshine in the interval of the storm: the Council of Five Hundred was yet to be faced, and was quite otherwise prepared than the Ancients. All combined to produce a fearful uncertainty; but there was now no retreat, the party was too deeply engaged; the last stake must be played; some hours more, and the die would be cast.

These apprehensions were not groundless. In the Council of Five Hundred, agitation was at its height. The most serious disturbances were manifested in all its deliberations; the Council insisted that the installation of the two Chambers should be announced to the Directory, and a message despatched to the Ancients, requesting information upon the motives which had rendered necessary an extraordinary session. But already no Directory existed: Siéyès and Ducos had thrown themselves into the party of Bonaparte;

Gohier and Moulins, confided to the custody of Moreau, were detained prisoners in the Luxembourg; and, while the message was yet under discussion, the resignation of Barras, previously addressed to them, was forwarded by the Ancients to the Five Hundred. The reading of this document by Lucien, as president, occasioned a great uproar in the latter assembly. A second reading was demanded, and the legality of the resignation, with other matters connected, were yet undergoing a stormy examination, when Bonaparte appeared in the assembly, followed by the grenadiers, whom, however, he left at the door.

I was not with the General on this occasion, having been commissioned to send information to his wife by express that all would go well. But without guaranteeing things so positively as if I had seen them, I hesitate not to think, and to say, that we must rank among the grossest fabrications all that has been said of pretended acts of violence, and of imaginary daggers. This conviction is founded upon the accounts given me the same evening by individuals most deserving of credit, spectators of what passed. As to the reports then or afterward promulgated—in all, the recitals vary according to the opinions of the narrators. It is said that, on the sight of armed men, a universal outcry arose. From all parts of the hall resounded the exclamations, "The sanctuary of the law is violated!"—"Down with the tyrant!" —"Down with Cromwell!"—"Down with the Dictator!"— "What means the madman?" with others of the same kind. Bonaparte must needs hammer out a speech, but had no sooner opened his lips than the sounds were lost in almost universal cries of "Long live the Republic!"—"The Constitution forever!"—"Exile for the Dictator!" Then, it is said, the grenadiers rushed forward, calling out, "Let us save our General!" that upon sight of these, indignation reached its height, and that Bonaparte, out of his wits, fell into the arms of the soldiers, crying out, "They intend to assassinate me." I give faith to the cries, to the menaces, to the vociferations, but rank as fables the poniards and firearms with which the deputies are said to have been armed, and this irruption of the military, the more confidently as Bonaparte mentioned these circumstances neither to me nor to Josephine.

On Bonaparte's exit, the deliberations in the Five Hundred continued to be most tumultuous, and the wildest proposals were ventilated. The president, Lucien, endeavored to calm the assembly; but every sentence was interrupted by cries—"Bonaparte has tarnished his fame!" "He is become a disgrace to the republic!" "I devote him to execration!" After new efforts, he resigned the chair to Chasal, desirous to obtain a hearing as a simple member. He requested that the General might be again introduced and allowed to state his intentions, which, he maintained, were only to explain something of great moment in the situation of affairs; "for I believe none of you will, in any case, impute to him designs inimical to liberty." This proposition of Lucien was not accepted. Cries of "Exile!" "Bonaparte!" "Exile!" pervaded the assembly. Lucien a second time left the chair, that he might not, as president, be compelled to put to the vote the sentence of outlawry invoked against his brother. Braving the fury of the chamber, he ascended the tribune, abdicated the presidency, resigned his mandate as deputy, and threw off his insignia. At the moment when he thus quitted the assembly, I returned to my station on the scene. Bonaparte, perfectly informed of what was going on within, sent some soldiers to his brother's rescue. They brought him out from the midst of the hall, and the General attached importance to the circumstance of having with him the president of an assembly which thenceforth he affected to treat as rebellious. Lucien now reassumed the functions of president; but it was on horseback, at the head of the troops. Inspired by his brother's and his own danger, he pronounced, with inflammatory gestures, a spirited harangue, which showed what a man might venture who was nothing, and could be nothing, save through the splendor reflected from his brother.

Notwithstanding the shouts of "Bonaparte forever!" which followed this address, the hesitation reigning among the troops still continued. They shrank from turning their arms against the national representatives. Upon this, Lucien, unsheathing his sword, cried out, "I swear to pierce the bosom of my own brother, if ever he harbor a thought injurious to the liberties of Frenchmen!" This dramatic effort won entire success. Hesitation vanished at these words, and, on a sign from Bonaparte, Murat, at the head of the grenadiers, charged into the hall, and cleared it of the representatives. All were forced to yield to the logic of the bayonet, and here stopped the interference of the armed force on this famous day.

By ten o'clock at night the greatest calm reigned throughout the palace of St. Cloud, wherein so many tumultuous scenes had just been enacted. All the deputies had remained within its precincts. They might be seen wandering about in the saloon, in the galleries, in the courts. The majority had an air of consternation not yet quieted. The rest affected a satisfaction well got up; but all burned with the desire of returning to Paris. This they could not do till a new mandate revoked the order for their translation.

At eleven o'clock, Bonaparte, who had yet taken nothing the whole day, but who seemed insensible to physical wants in the season of great action, said to me, "Come, Bourrienne, write. I must this evening address a proclamation to the inhabitants of Paris. To-morrow, on its awakening, I shall occupy the whole capital." The proclamation dictated to me that evening proved, no less than others, how greatly its author excelled in the art of embellishing the truth to his own advantage.

The day had thus been passed in destroying one government; it was imperative to devote the night to the building up of a new one on the ruins. Talleyrand, Ræderer, and Siéyès were at St. Cloud. The Council of the Ancients assembled, and Lucien set about searching out such members of the other chamber as he could count upon. He was able to collect only about thirty, who, with their president, represented the *majority* of the numerous assembly of which they formed so small a portion. This shadow of a representative assembly was essential; for Bonaparte, in spite of the illegal proceedings of the previous day, desired to have the appearance of acting under lawful authority. The Council of the Ancients had already in the morning decided that an executive provisional commission should be named, composed of three members, and was preparing to appoint the commissioners—a measure the initiative of which belonged to the Five Hundred—when Lucien came to announce to his brother that his own chamber was unmanageable.

On these grounds, the Council of *Five Hundred*, represented now by the *majority* of *thirty*, passed with all speed a decree to the following effect: "There is no longer a Directory; and there are no longer members of a national assembly, by reason of the excess and felonious attempts to which they were continually proceeding." Then appeared a list of sixty-two deputies, noticed by name, as especially turbulent. By other articles of the same decree the Council created a provisional commission, similar to that the Ancients proposed to be instituted, decided that it should be composed of three members, and that these members should take the title of Consuls of the Republic. There were named as Consuls, Siéyès, Roger Ducos and Bonaparte. The remaining depositions comprised in this nocturnal decree of St. Cloud were merely formal. This night sitting was perfectly peaceable; indeed, it could not well be otherwise. All the members knew in advance the part they were required to play. By three in the morning all was finished, and the palace of St. Cloud, lately the scene of so much tumult, assumed its wonted character of one vast solitude.

In forming the consular administration, Bonaparte not having yet experience of the men with whom he was thus about to surround himself, procured from those whom he knew among the most remarkable individuals of that period,

and who were best instructed regarding France and the revolution, written information respecting the persons worthy
and capable of entering the senate, the tribunate, and the
council of state. These notes afford grounds for believing
that the writers considered themselves as falling in with his
sentiments, and regarded him as impressed with the current
opinions, by dwelling as strong recommendations upon the
patriotism, love of liberty, and former occupation of office
under the republic, of those nominated for the projected
functions. Bonaparte, however, thought only of organizing
a complaisant senate, a mute legislature, and a tribunate
which should content itself with a seeming independence,
existing in certain fine speeches and sonorous phrases. He
appointed senators without much difficulty; but it was not
so with members of the tribunate. Here he hesitated long,
foreseeing difficulties with that assembly. On attaining
power he dared not all at once disregard the exigencies of
the times; but consented for a season to humor the hollow
ambition of those who still continued their fine declamations
about liberty. He considered that circumstances were not
yet sufficiently favorable for the prevention of this third
power in the constitution, destined in appearance to plead
before the legislature the cause and interests of the people;
but, even in yielding to this necessity, the very idea of a
tribunate caused him a lively uneasiness. To say the truth,
Bonaparte could not bear public discussions on projects
of law.

These notes are principally in the handwriting of
Lucien, though several portions are inserted by Regnault
St. Jean d'Angely. In the autographs, an asterisk is affixed
to many names, placed there by Bonaparte himself, in order
to distinguish those upon whom he intended to have his eye
for future employments. These marks designate chiefly
practical men, merchants, bankers, former administrators,
and some few lawyers; but all were men of talent, and characterized as of moderate principles and steady habits. The
descriptions annexed are usually very brief. Several are

marked out, to be avoided as declared partisans of the
Orléans party, which is there designated as secret, active and
numerous, and likely one day to be troublesome in France!

But we must do justice: of all qualities or recommendations, that which possessed the greatest influence with the
First Consul was uncorrupted integrity; and herein he was
seldom mistaken. When Cambacérès, on his elevation, va-
cated the office of minister of justice, Bonaparte conferred
it on M. d'Abrial, a Peer of France, since dead. On remitting the portfolio to the new minister, the First Consul
addressed him thus: "Citizen Abrial, I know you not, but
am informed you are the most upright man in the magistracy; it is on that account I have named you minister of
justice." Above all, he required talent, and little as he
liked the men of the Revolution, he considered that, in this
respect, they could not be passed over. For mediocrity he
had conceived an extreme aversion, and rejected a character
of this description, whenever presented; but, if such a one
had long been in office, he submitted to the empire of habit,
dreading nothing so much as change, or, in his own words,
"new faces."

At the Luxembourg, Bonaparte occupied a suite on the
ground floor, his study being near a private stair leading to
Josephine's apartments. I had rooms above. After breakfast, which was served at ten, he chatted for a few minutes
with his ordinary guests, that is to say, his aides-de-camp,
the persons invited, and myself, who never quitted him.
There were also pretty generally present some political and
literary friends, and his brothers Joseph and Lucien, whom
he received with the greatest pleasure, and with whom he
conversed most familiarly. When we rose from table after
breakfast, it rarely happened that, having bid good-morning
to Josephine and Hortense, he did not add—"Come, Bourrienne: come, let us to work."

During the day I was occupied either in reading to him,
or writing to his dictation, or he went to council, which was
his custom, three or four times a week. On those days he

was always in bad humor, because he had to cross the
court and ascend to the council chamber by the grand stairs.
It happened, too, that the weather at this time was particularly bad. This source of petty annoyance continued till
the 25th December, when he got quit both of the grievance
and his two colleagues, Siéyès and Ducos. From this date,
he properly assumed the title of First Consul, uniting in
the consular executive Cambacérès and Lebrun. From the
council he always entered his study singing, and God
knows how wretchedly! He then examined what had been
previously ordered, signed letters, stretched himself at
length in his *fauteuil*, reading the letters of last night and
the publications of the day. When there was no council
he remained in the study, chatting with me, always singing;
notched the arm of his chair—a common amusement; and
often, in short, behaving like a great boy. Then, arousing
himself on a sudden, he would decide upon some public
work to be executed, or dictate to me those mighty schemes
which astonished and awed the world.

We dined at five. After dinner the First Consul retired
to the apartments of Josephine, where he usually received
the visits of the ministers, and with especial pleasure that
of the minister for foreign affairs, more particularly after the
portfolio had passed to Talleyrand. At midnight, and often
sooner, he gave the signal for retreat by saying, abruptly,
"Let us to bed." In the apartments of the Luxembourg,
of which the amiable Josephine did the honors with so
much grace, the word *Madame* came again into use.

In selecting the members of the consular government and
legislature, two classes of candidates were sources of apprehension to Bonaparte. On the one hand, he loved not the
men of the Revolution; he distrusted still more the partisans
of the Bourbons. The mere name of these princes filled
him with secret terror; and often did he speak to me of
the necessity of building a wall of iron between them and
France. We shall see hereafter what was his opinion of the
regicides; but, in those early times of his power, he judged

that the more pledges any one had given to the Revolution,
by the larger securities, also, did the same person appear
bound to oppose return to the ancient order of things. In
other respects Bonaparte was not the man to listen to any
consideration whatsoever where his policy had spoken out.
The notes already alluded to were unceasingly consulted.
But, besides, he often received with great kindness recommendations from private persons whom he knew particularly. It would have been hazardous, however, to have
recommended a knave or a fool. The men most cordially
disliked were those whom he designated as "people who
talked about everything and always." "*I want,*" he would
say frequently, "*more head and less tongue.*"

Though Bonaparte, on attaining the consulship, doubtless in his heart desired war, yet he was not ignorant how
much the people longed for repose, and that the appearance,
at least, of seeking peace was the interest of a government
erected on the ruins of one which had provoked an un-
popular and disastrous hostility. In this view he hastened
to notify the various foreign powers of his new dignity, and
caused a letter of like tenor to be addressed to our diplomatic
agents abroad.

With respect to all who remained in Egypt, Bonaparte
found himself in a very singular predicament. Placed at
the head of the government, not only had he become the
depositary of the information actually transmitted to the
Directory, but despatches forwarded to one address were
handed to another: thus, it was Bonaparte, First Consul,
who received the complaints lodged against Bonaparte, the
deserter of the Egyptian army. For all these complaints,
too, it must be confessed, there existed but too just grounds.
And we cannot help admiring the rapid concurrence of
events which had raised Bonaparte to the consular chair.
According to the natural order of things, according to his
own calculations, even, and desire, he ought first to have
reached Toulon, where the laws of quarantine would most
certainly have been enforced: well, fear of the English,

the uncertainty of the pilot, obliged him to land at Fréjus, where those salutary laws were violated by the very people most interested in maintaining them inviolate. Let us suppose an obligatory sojourn in the Lazaretto at Toulon. What would have happened then? Complaints and criminations would have fallen into the hands of the Directory, furnishing powerful weapons against Bonaparte. His accusation would then have become possible, and his suspension probable; for the complaints were of a nature to be certainly followed up by the former of these results. Of this there needs no other proof than the official despatch of General Kléber, which, after having read, the Consul placed in my custody.

This document, dated from Cairo, 26th September, commenced by informing the Directory of General Bonaparte's departure, and his own promotion to the chief command. "My first care," says Kléber, "has been to take cognizance of the actual state of the army. It is decreased one-half. With this diminished strength we have to occupy the principal points from the Cataracts to Alexandria and El Arych, and at the same time to contend no longer with disorganized Mamelukes, but against three great powers—thé Porte, the English, and the Russians. Arms, powder and shot are failing us, without the possibility of supply. The soldiers are naked, a state the more dreadful, as, in this country, it is the most active cause of disease; so that, with half the numerical force, we have a much greater number of sick than last year. Bonaparte exhausted all the disposable resources of the country in a few months after our landing: in revenue we are consequently in arrear twelve, in pay to the troops, four millions. The season, too, is unfavorable; the Nile has not risen. Egypt, in appearance tranquil, is anything but submissive. I am surrounded by enemies. Such is the situation in which Bonaparte remitted to me the enormous burden of the Army of the East. He left me power to conclude a peace, if this year we should lose 1,500 men by the plague. This more than all shows his own opinion of the state in which he left things. What are 1,500 men, more or less, to the extent of country I have to defend, while every day is a day of battle? The Commander-in-Chief has also written, Alexandria and El Aryoh are the keys of Egypt. The latter is a wretched fort, four days' journey in the Desert; 600 Mamelukes can cut off our communications when they please. Alexandria was sufficiently well defended; but Bonaparte carried off the artillery to fit out his frigates, and our own heavy guns were lost in the disastrous campaign of Syria. In fine, General Bonaparte was deceived in the consequences of his success at Aboukir: he did indeed destroy almost the totality of the Turks who landed; but what is the loss of 15,000 men to such a power? It has not retarded, one instant, the march of the Grand Vizier. In these circumstances, what can, what ought I to do? I will try to gain time by negotiations, proposing as terms that the French occupy all the fortified places, until peace is made with England, receiving the revenues on paying to the Turkish Pacha the tribute formerly paid. If, as is likely, these terms be rejected, I will try our fortune if, by any possibility, only 5,000 men can be got under arms."

The rest of the letters from Egypt were not less incriminating than this of Kléber's; but the word of a general (who offered to prove every allegation), become Commander-in-Chief, accusing a predecessor in terms so precise, must have had great weight, especially looking to the coincidences of the whole correspondence. A sentence must have been inevitable, and then, no 18th Brumaire—no consulate—no empire—no conquests in all Europe—but also, no St. Helena. All these hinged upon the circumstance of the English fleet having constrained "La Muiron" to voyage at a venture through the Corsican Sea, and to land at hazard.

The Egyptian expedition formed too grand an incident in the life of Bonaparte for him not to desire earnestly, and often, to recall the public mind to his conquests in the East. It was requisite, besides, that the nation should never cease to behold, in the Chief of the Republic, the first of its generals condemned to renounce military glory. While Moreau had been invested with the command of the Armies of the Rhine; while Massena received the Army of Italy, as the reward of his victory at Zurich; and while Brune was at the head of the Army of Holland, he, who had passed his youth in camps, solaced the hours of temporary inactivity by a momentary retrospect of his ancient triumphs. Fame was not to be mute for an instant on the theme. With this view, he caused to be published, at short intervals, in the "Moniteur," recitals of the Eastern expedition. Often did it furnish matter of congratulation that the damning correspondence, and especially Kléber's despatch, had fallen into his own hands.

Perfectly aware how the Egyptian expedition ought to be viewed, Bonaparte yet looked with a favorable eye upon those who extolled that adventure. The correspondence now in his possession rendered him the master of important secrets. The confidences which concerned himself were precious documents, as displaying the opinions entertained of his conduct. This was the source of much of the favor, and much of the disgrace, which, without this key, remains inexplicable. This accounts, better than anything else, for the elevation of so many men of mean abilities to places and honors, and, at the same time, reveals why so many others of real merit were discountenanced and forgotten.

CHAPTER IX

The Consul's Policy—Relations with Russia—Death of Washington—Murat—
Josephine and the Necklace

I AM almost tempted to designate as the "consulate preparatory" that period of the consular government during which Bonaparte resided at the Luxembourg. Then, in fact, were planted the first germs of those mighty enterprises which he meditated, and the foundation laid of those institutions by which he announced his accession to power. He had then two men within himself—the republican general, exposed to all eyes as the friend of liberty and of revolutionary principles; and the man of ambition, coveting in secret the overthrow of that liberty and of those principles: thus in darkness preparing the destruction of the edifice which necessity constrained him to erect in open day. These two characters he played with inconceivable address and deep hypocrisy, which, if it so please, may be titled profound policy. This was indubitably requisite for the accomplishment of his designs; but, as if not to lose the habit, he carried this dissimulation into affairs altogether secondary. ·

During his sojourn at the Luxembourg, the Consul sometimes paid visits of ceremony, accompanied by his aides-de-camp, or a minister. I did not form one in these official excursions, but frequently, or to speak more correctly, almost always, he informed me afterward what had been done or said. Only six days after his preferment, he visited the prisons and, as his arrival was unexpected, the conductors of these establishments had no time to get things dressed up, so they were seen in their real condition. I was in the cabinet on his return from the prisons. "What beasts," exclaimed he on entering, "were these directors! To what a state have these gentry reduced the public establishments! But, patience, I shall set all matters to rights. The prisons are ruinous—unhealthy—the prisoners are ill-fed: I questioned them; I examined also the jailers, for from the overseers one gets nothing; they always trump up their wares. When at the Temple prison, I could not help thinking of the unfortunate Louis XVI. He was an excellent person, but too good, too easy, and knew not how to deal with the world: and Sidney Smith!—I had his chamber shown me. If the blockheads had not allowed him to escape, I should have captured Acre! There are too many recollections associated with that said prison; I shall order it to be pulled down some of these days. Do you know what I did at the

Temple? I ordered the registers to be produced: there were hostages among the captives; I have set them at liberty. 'An unjust law,' it was thus I addressed them, 'has deprived you of freedom: my first duty is to restore it to you.' In this, Bourrienne, have I not done well?'' Here he did do well, and many blessed him for the happiness thus bestowed.

Another incident of the first consulate shows the inflexibility of Bonaparte's character, when he had once formed a decision. In July, 1799, General Latour Foissac, intrusted with the command of Mantua, contrary to its apparent means of defence, had surrendered that important fortress. The Directory had ordered inquiry, but the Consul broke off the proceedings, and pronounced sentence against Foissac, though he had as yet been only impeached before a council of war, and nothing proven. This arbitrary decision occasioned much discontent among the general officers; and some days after, I essayed to induce him to revise his decree, remarking, that in a country where honor holds the first rank among the principles of conduct, it was impossible for Foissac, if guilty, to have escaped condemnation. ''Bourrienne, you are probably right; but the resolution is passed—the blow is struck. I have explained myself in a corresponding manner before the public. I cannot retrace my steps so soon. To retreat—is to have been weak. I must not appear to have been wrong: I shall see by and by: time will bring indulgence and pardon. At present it would be premature.''

He loved contrasts; thus, while acting so severely toward an unfortunate commander, he was busy with a troop of comedians, which he desired, or rather wished to have the appearance of desiring, to send out to Egypt: not that he now attached the slightest importance to such puerilities, but they answered his purpose.

While we resided in the Luxembourg, early in January, 1800, a mission of real importance was confided to Duroc, whom the First Consul sent to the Court of Prussia. The causes of this preference were the accomplishments, education and graceful manners of Duroc, and the wish of his patron to bring him forward in the eye of France. The youthful envoy, too, had never quitted us in Italy, in Egypt, and on board "La Muiron," while Bonaparte's tact led him at once to conjecture that Frederick William would be well pleased to hear from an eye-witness the narrative of these campaigns, especially the siege of Acre. Nor was he disappointed; for such I learned from Duroc himself were the chief subjects of conversation with the Prussian monarch. The first interview continued two hours, and on the morrow the envoy was invited to dine with his majesty. When the news of this arrived at the Luxembourg, I could see the Chief of the Republic was extremely well pleased to find one of his aides-de-camp seated at the table of a king whom, but a few years later, he kept cooling his heels in an antechamber at Tilsit. The Prussian was the first court in Europe which recognized the Consul's authority.

It was at the Luxembourg, also, that Bonaparte first displayed (27th Nivose) his hatred of the liberty of the press. By a consular act, or rather act of the First Consul, it was decreed "that, whereas a portion of the journals printed in Paris are instruments in the hands of the enemies of the republic, the minister of police will take care that, during the continuance of the war, there shall be printed, published and distributed only thirteen political journals, as per margin, exclusive of those connected *solely* with science, art, literature and commerce." Certainly this may well be regarded as a preparatory step, and may serve as a scale to measure the greater part of Bonaparte's acts by which he established his own power under pretence of consulting the interests of the republic. The restriction, too, "during the war," showed only provisionally, and left a little hope for the future; but the provisional is of a nature very elastic, and Bonaparte knew how to stretch it to infinity.

The title of First Consul made him disdain even the title

of Member of the Institute—an honor which, in his proclamations, he had even preferred to that of Commander-in-
Chief. But in speaking of his nomination, I forgot to say
what he really thought of it. The truth is that, young,
ambitious, covered with glory, he received no ordinary
gratification from the title which was thus offered: it was
for the public. But in private how often have we laughed
heartily on weighing the value of these literary distinctions!
Bonaparte knew a little of mathematics, a good deal of history, and, it need not be added, possessed immense military
genius; but with only all this, he was good for nothing at
the Institute, unless to deliver a course on ancient and modern strategy. Already he no longer entertained the least
regard for that learned body, of which in the sequel he cherished so great distrust. It was a *corporation*—an *authorized
assembly;* there required nothing more to give umbrage to
Bonaparte, and Napoleon was no longer at the pains to dissemble how much he detested all that enjoyed the right
of assembling and deliberating. Even from the time of his
return, after the Egyptian expedition, he began to be weary
of a title by which *too many colleagues* had the privilege of
addressing him; and he detested colleagues. "Do you not
find," said he one day to me, "that there is something
trivial, something ignoble, in the phrase, 'I have the honor
to be, my dear colleague?' It tires me." In general all
expressions which sounded like equality displeased him
utterly. The figure of the Republic, seated, and holding
a lance, affixed to legal instruments, at the beginning of the
consulate, was not long in being trodden underfoot: fortunate would it have been had he thus treated only the *image*
of liberty!

Another preparative for the future order of things, which
dates also from the Luxembourg, was the institution of
honorary sabres and muskets. Who does not discover in
this humble means the foundation of the Legion of Honor?
A sergeant of grenadiers, named Aune, having been included
in the first distribution, *easily* obtained permission to write

thanking the First Consul. Bonaparte, desiring to reply ostentatiously, dictated to me the following letter: "I have received your letter, my brave comrade. You have no need to tell me of your actions; you are the bravest grenadier in the army since the death of the brave Beñerete. You have had one of the hundred sabres which I distributed to the army. All the soldiers agreed that you were the person who best deserved it. I wish much to see you again. The minister of war sends you an order to come to Paris." This flattery, addressed to a soldier, tended strongly to effect the object proposed. The letter could not fail to circulate in the army. The First Consul—the first general of France —call a sergeant "My brave companion!" Who would act thus but a sincere republican—an enthusiastic admirer of equality? There wanted nothing more to inflame the whole army with devoted admiration.

At this very time Bonaparte had begun to find himself straitened in the Luxembourg, and preparations were making for the Tuileries. But this grand step toward the re-establishment of monarchy was to be taken with all prudence. It behooved first to remove the supposition that none save a king could inhabit the palace of our ancient kings. What was to be done in this case? A very fine bust of Brutus had been brought from Italy; and was not Brutus the scourge of tyrants? Upon this, David was solemnly appointed to the charge of superintending the location of Junius Brutus in the gallery of the Tuileries. What greater proof of hatred of tyranny! And then a bust could do no harm—all was for the best. The reasoning was perfectly unexceptionable.

To sleep in the Tuileries, in the bed-chamber of the kings of France, was *all* that Bonaparte desired; the rest would follow. To establish a principle satisfied him in the meantime; at a fitting opportunity he could pursue the consequences: hence the affectation of not mentioning the name in the acts, but of dating them from "The Palace of Government." The first preparations were modest enough; for the stanch republican ought to have no taste for luxury. Therefore the architect only received orders to clean out the palace, a term of significant application, after the assemblies which had therein held sittings. For this so small a sum as five hundred thousand francs sufficed. The Consul's play was to conceal as much as possible the importance attached to the translation of the consular domicile.

About the same time was accomplished the organizing of a council of state, divided into five sections; namely, Home Department, Finances, Admiralty, War, Legislation. The allowance of the counsellors of state was fixed at 25,000 francs, and that of the presidents of each of the sections at 35,000 francs. The costumes of the consuls, and different orders of state officers, were also appointed. Velvet, proscribed since the monarchy, now once more came into use; and, as if from regard to the manufactories of Lyons, it was decreed that this anti-republican stuff should be employed in the robes of office. Thus, in the most insignificant details, the constant aim of Bonaparte was to efface the remembrance of the republic, preparing things so artfully for the return of monarchy that when the time arrived there should remain only a word to be changed. Beyond this, I can assert that he took little concern in these important frivolities. I never remember to have seen him in the consular habit, a costume he detested. The dress he preferred, and the only one in which he felt at ease, was that of the camp, the uniform of the guides, a corps whose devotion, conduct and courage merited the predilection.

Some time before a consular decree of another nature and of different importance had carried joy into the bosom of many families. Bonaparte, as we have seen, had reasons for bringing about the 18th Brumaire, preparatory to overturning the Directory. The Directory subverted, he had now motives, at least in part, for undoing the effects of the 18th Fructidor. He caused a report for those exiled on that occasion to be presented by the minister of police, and authorized the return of forty, merely placing them under

surveillance, and assigning a certain place of residence.
But the greater part of these distinguished men remained
not long under even this restraint. They were quickly
called to fill those high situations in the administration for
which their respective talents were adapted. All this was
natural; for Bonaparte wished, as yet, in appearance at
least, to base his government upon those principles of moderate republicanism which had occasioned their banishment
whom he now invited to assist his labors. Thus he proceeded to invite to the councils of the consulate those whom
the Directory had proscribed, precisely as, at a later period,
he recalled the emigrants, the proscribed of the republic,
into the high functions of the empire. The times and the
men alone differed—the thought was the same.

The first relations between Bonaparte and the Emperor
Paul I. commenced soon after the consulate. Circumstances
seemed a little less unfavorable. For some time, vague
rumors announced a coldness between Russia and Austria,
while an open misunderstanding manifestly existed between
the courts of London and St. Petersburg. From these transactions, the First Consul, divining the chivalric and somewhat romantic character of Paul, judged the season pro-
pitious for severing Russia from England. He was not
the man to allow any opportunity to escape, and seized on
this one with his usual sagacity. It had formerly been refused to include, in a cartel of exchange between France
and England, 7,000 Russians, taken prisoners in Holland.
These Bonaparte ordered to be armed and clothed anew, in
the uniforms of the corps to which they had belonged, and
sent back without ransom, exchange, or condition whatsoever. This ingenious munificence was not thrown away.
Paul showed himself abundantly sensible thereof, and, from
an ally, became the declared enemy of England. Henceforward, the Consul and the Czar were on the best terms.
Lord Wentworth, ordered to quit St. Petersburg, immediately retired to Riga, and English ships were seized in all
the ports of Russia. The arrival of the Baron Springporten,

as Russian ambassador at Paris, caused universal satisfaction. Through this envoy, who enjoyed the entire confidence of his master, a personal correspondence was carried on between the French Consul and the Russian Emperor. I have read the autograph letters of Paul. They were remarkable for the frankness with which they expressed admiration of Bonaparte. No courtier could have used terms more flattering; but the professions of the Emperor were sincere; and his friendship led him in all things to comply with the wishes of his hero. Of this he gave a proof as lively as it was singular. Having conceived so violent a hatred against the English government, he desired to engage in single combat all those kings who refused to shut their ports and declare war. There was given, to be inserted in the Petersburg "Court Gazette," his challenge to the King of Denmark. But declining to request officially from the senate of Hamburg its insertion in the "Correspondent," the journal of that state, the affair was referred to M. Schramm, a merchant, by Count de Pablen, the Russian minister of police. The Count intimated to M. Schramm that it would afford the Emperor much satisfaction to have inserted in the "Correspondent" the article from the "Gazette," with the request, if the insertion took place, to remit by an extraordinary courier twelve copies of the journal on vellum paper. The intention of Paul was to have sent a copy to all the sovereigns; but this folly *à la* Charles XII. produced no result. This enthusiasm of Paul for Bonaparte was to the latter a source of the liveliest pleasure he had ever experienced. The friendship of a sovereign appeared a move nearer being a sovereign himself. But he failed not, at the same time, to draw immediate profit from the friendship of the heir of Catherine. Through the instigation of the Czar, a Prussian army menaced Hanover, and, with his support, Bonaparte was contemplating the march of a French army by land against the British possessions in India. The tragical death of Paul formed the catastrophe of these intrigues of the north.

Before quitting the Luxembourg, to inhabit the Tuileries, Bonaparte resolved to strike the eyes of the Parisians by the splendor of a grand ceremony. For this, he fixed upon the 20th Pluviose, that is to say, ten days before finally leaving the quondam palace of the Directory. These fêtes were then very different from what they afterward became. They derived all their magnificence from military display; and, at all times, when the Consul mounted on horseback, surrounded by a brilliant staff, in centre of which he was conspicuous by the simplicity of his attire, he was sure that the populace of Paris would throng around his path, to salute him with unforced and unbought acclamations. The sole object of the present festival was to have been the presentation, in the Hospital of the Invalids, then called the Temple of Mars, of seventy-two stand of colors, taken at the battle of Aboukir, from the Turks. But the news of the death of Washington arriving before the arrangements were completed, Bonaparte seized with avidity the means of producing greater effect, by mingling the cypress of mourning for this great citizen with the latest laurels gathered by himself in Egypt. The greatest fuss possible was added to the publication of this intelligence; and the following order of the day, previously dictated to me, was addressed to the consular guard and to the army:

"Washington is dead! That illustrious man combated against tyranny. He consolidated the liberty of his country. His memory will ever be dear to the French people, as to the freemen of both worlds, and especially to the soldiers of France, who, like him and the warriors of America, fight for liberty and equality. The First Consul, therefore, orders that, for the space of ten days, black crape be suspended from all the standards and flags of the republic."

The death of Washington, the noble founder of rational freedom in the New World, was an event of perfect indifference to Bonaparte; but it happened opportunely, as a fresh occasion of masking his real designs under high-sounding phrases in favor of liberty. On the 20th Pluviose, accord-

ingly, Lannes, to whom Bonaparte had assigned the act
of presentation, attended by strong detachments of cavalry,
bent his way to the Hôtel des Invalides. Here, in the hall
of the council, the minister of war waited to receive the
pledges of Eastern victory. All the ministers, counsellors
of state and generals, had been convoked to assist at the solemnity. Lannes pronounced a discourse to which Berthier
replied, and M. de Fontanes joined his studied eloquence
to the military harangues of the two generals. M. de
Fontanes, along with Suard, La Harpe and some others
proscribed at the 18th Fructidor, were among the first authorized by the Consul to return to France. He was charged
with pronouncing the funeral oration of Washington; and,
as may be supposed of an *able* speaker, the flowers of his
oratory were not strewed exclusively on the bier of the
American hero. In the temple was the statue of Mars.
From the columns and the arched roofs depended the
trophies of Denain, Fontenoy and the Italian campaign—
trophies which would have still been there, had not the
demon of conquest possessed Bonaparte. Two aged veterans, in their hundredth year, stood beside the minister of
war; and beneath the trophy, composed of the standards
of Aboukir, reposed the bust of the liberator of America.
In short, every species of quackery suited to such an occasion was called into requisition. In the evening the assembly was numerous at the Luxembourg, and Bonaparte took
to himself much credit for the effect produced on this well-
contrived occasion. There now remained only ten days to
wait, before sleeping at the Tuileries. On the 10th the
national mourning for Washington ceased. Well might
the sables have been retained for the funeral of freedom!

The first report on the civil code before the Legislative
Body was also made during the stay in the Luxembourg.
There also were decreed the statutes constituting the Bank
of France, and that establishment was organized which, till
then, had been wanting in our country. In this palace, too,
was solemnized a domestic ceremony in Bonaparte's family,

afterward productive of no mean consequences to the parties. I have hitherto spoken but little of Murat, in the course of these Memoirs; but, having now arrived at the epoch of his marriage with the sister of the First Consul, it seems here the proper place to revert to certain facts of some interest anterior to that alliance; especially as this will afford me an opportunity of mentioning discreetly, but with truth, certain family details. Murat, by the beauty of his external form, his physical strength, the somewhat over-refined elegance of his manners, the loftiness of his carriage, and his fearless bravery in combat, bore less resemblance to a republican soldier than to one of those warlike knights so romantically described by Ariosto and Tasso. The nobility of his appearance quickly effaced all recollection of the lowness of his birth: he was courteous, polished, gallant; and, on the field of battle, twenty men commanded by Murat were worth a regiment. Yet, on one occasion, even Murat had a "moment of fear." The following are the circumstances under which *he* once ceased to be himself: When, in the first campaign of Italy, Bonaparte had forced Wurmser to retire within Mantua with 20,000 men, Miollis, with 4,000 soldiers only, was directed to oppose the sorties made by the Austrian general. In one of these attacks, Murat received an order to charge Wurmser. He *was afraid!* did not execute the order, and, in the first moment of confusion, said he was wounded. From that time, Murat fell into disgrace with the Commander-in-Chief, whose aide-de-camp he then was, though contrary to the rules. For, prior to this, having been sent to Paris as commissioner to present to the Directory the first colors taken by the French army in Italy, he was introduced to, and, as first aide-de-camp of the General, received with kindness by Madame Bonaparte, whose interest, and that of Madame Tallien, procured for him the rank of brigadier-general. It was a remarkable circumstance for the times that Murat, on his return, notwithstanding this accession of rank, still continued aide-de-camp to Bonaparte, whom the rules did not permit to have one of higher grade than chief-of-brigade, answering to the rank of colonel. It was, on Bonaparte's side, but an early anticipation of the prerogatives everywhere reserved for princes and sovereigns. Previously to this journey, Murat had become acquainted with the handsome Caroline Bonaparte, at her brother Joseph's, who then discharged the functions of republican ambassador at Rome. It appeared that, from the first, Caroline had not viewed him with indifference; and he found himself the favored rival of Prince Santa Croce, who earnestly sought her hand.

After the affair at Mantua, however, Murat fell into such disrepute with the Commander-in-Chief that the latter seemed to have conceived a sort of dislike for his former friend—placing him, first in the division of Reille, and subsequently in that of Hilliers. When we returned to Paris, after the treaty of Campo-Formio, Murat was not included in our party; but as *the ladies*, his patronesses, had no little credit with the minister of war, they obtained for him a place in the Egyptian expedition, and he was attached to the Genoese division. On board the "L'Orient," the former aide-de-camp constantly remained in complete disgrace. During the passage, Bonaparte never once spoke to him; and in Egypt, also, he was treated always with coldness, or sent from headquarters upon difficult missions. But the Commander-in-Chief having at length opposed him to Mourad Bey, Murat performed such prodigies of valor, and in so many perilous encounters, that he effaced, by so much bravery, the slight stain which a moment of hesitation had affixed to his name under the walls of Mantua. Finally, he contributed so powerfully to the fortunate success of the day of Aboukir, that the General, happy in bearing into France a last laurel gathered in the East, forgave the error of a moment, and wished also to forget what had doubtless been reported to his ear: for, though Bonaparte never exactly said so, I have many reasons for thinking the name of Murat was uttered by Junot in his indiscretions at the Springs of Messoudiah. The grenadier charge, led on by

Murat, on the 19th Vendemiaire, dissipated any lingering clouds; and at those seasons, when the necessity of Bonaparte's politics dominated all other considerations, the rival of the Roman prince received the command of the consular guards.

Madame Bonaparte, in seeking to captivate the chivalrous spirit of Murat by laboring for his advancement, had it principally in view to gain one partisan more to oppose the brothers and family of her husband: and she had need of support. Their jealous hatred permitted no opportunity of venting itself to escape. The good Josephine, whose only reproach was, perhaps, having been somewhat too much a woman in her love of admiration, was haunted by distressing presentiments. Carried away by the unreflecting openness of her character, she perceived not that the same coquetry which procured her defenders likewise supplied her implacable enemies with arms against her. In this situation of things, Josephine, well aware that she had attached Murat by the ties of gratitude and friendship, ardently wished to see him united to Bonaparte in a family alliance, and aided by her best influence his union with Caroline. She could not be ignorant, also, that already, at Milan, an intimacy had commenced between the parties, rendering their marriage altogether desirable; and it was she who first proposed it to Murat. He hesitated, and in his hesitation went to consult M. Collot—a good counsellor in all things, and one whom long intimacy had initiated into the family secrets. M. Collot recommended an immediate and formal application for the hand of the sister of the First Consul. Murat repaired to the Luxembourg, and presented his request to Bonaparte. Did he do well? To this step he owed the throne of Naples: had he abstained, he would not have been shot at Pizzo.

However that might have been, the First Consul listened more like a sovereign than as brother in arms to the suit of Murat. He received him with a cold gravity; he said he would think of it, without giving at first any positive answer. Murat's proposal, as may be supposed, formed the subject of the evening's conversation in the drawing-room of the Luxembourg. Madame Bonaparte employed all her means of pleasing and persuasion to obtain a favorable reply. Hortense, Eugene and I, lent our aid. Our exertions were for some time without apparent success. "Murat," we were told, among other things, "is the son of an alehouse keeper. In the elevated rank to which fortune and fame have raised me, his blood cannot mingle with mine. Besides, nothing presses. I will see about it hereafter." We returned to the charge, dwelling upon the mutual affection of the young people, and on the devoted attachment of Murat to the person and service of the Consul; nor did we fail to point out to the latter the brilliant courage and excellent conduct of the young soldier in Egypt. "Yes," exclaimed he then, with animation, "that I acknowledge; Murat was superb at Aboukir." We allowed not the moment of kindly dispositions to pass away, but redoubled our entreaties. At length consent was given. The same evening, when we were alone in his study, "Well, Bourrienne," said he, "you ought to be satisfied; for my own part I am so likewise; every reflection made, Murat suits my sister; and then no one can say I am proud or court grand alliances. If I had given my sister to a noble, all your Jacobins would have set up a cry of a counter-revolution. Besides, I am very well pleased, for reasons you can easily divine, that my wife has interested herself in this marriage. Since it is decided, I shall hasten the affair; we have no time to lose. If I go to Italy, Murat goes with me: I must there strike a decisive blow."

Next morning, when I entered the Chamber of the First Consul, at seven, as usual, I found him even better satisfied than in the evening with the resolution he had formed. I readily perceived that, notwithstanding his discernment, he had no suspicion of the true motive which had induced Josephine to take so deep an interest in the affair. In his satisfaction he even allowed me to discover that he considered her anxiety a proof of the falsehood of those indiscreet reports mentioned to him of her intimacy with Murat.

The marriage was celebrated in the Luxembourg, but without any pomp; the First Consul wisely judging the time not yet arrived for rendering his family arrangements matters of state. Previously to the celebration, however, a little comedy was to be played in which I could not dispense with accepting a character: and here I may as well explain the whole plot. At this time, Bonaparte had not much money, and gave to his sister in consequence a dowry of no more than thirty thousand francs. Feeling, also, the propriety of making her a marriage present, and not having wherewithal to purchase one suitable, he took a diamond necklace from his own wife and gave it to the intended. Josephine was not at all satisfied as to the propriety of this confiscation, and set all her wits to work contriving the means of replacing her necklace. She knew the famous jeweller Foncier had a magnificent set of fine pearls, reported to have belonged to Marie-Antoinette. Sending for them she judged they would answer admirably. But, for this purchase, two hundred and fifty thousand francs were necessary. And how raise this sum? Recourse was had to Berthier, then minister of war. Berthier, murdering his vowels as usual, consented to discharge in an easy way certain debts against the hospitals of Italy; and as the contractors who, in these times, obtained payment, showed themselves grateful to their patrons, the pearls were transferred from Foncier to the jewel-case of Madame Bonaparte.

The set of pearls thus obtained, there occurred another little difficulty on which the fair possessor had not at first calculated. How could she wear an ornament so very remarkable, and acquired without her husband's knowledge? This seemed so much the more difficult that the First Consul knew his wife had no money; and as he was—the term will be excused—somewhat of a *meddler*, he knew, or fancied he knew, what jewels she had. For more than a fortnight, then, the pearls remained invisible, Josephine not daring to display them. What a punishment for a woman! At length, one fine day, Madame Bonaparte said to me, "To-morrow there is a grand drawing-room; positively I must wear my pearls: but, you know *him*, he will grumble if he discovers anything. Now do, Bourrienne, I beg of you, keep by me, and should he ask about my pearls, I will say, without hesitation, that I had them long ago." Everything passed as Josephine feared and hoped. Bonaparte, on see-ing the jewels, failed not to inquire—"Ah! what have we got here? How very fine thou art to-day! Whence are all these pearls? they appear new to me; I never saw them before."—"Oh, yes; but thou hast seen them, ten times; it is the necklace which the Cisalpine republic gave me, and which I have put in my hair."—"It seems to me, notwith-standing—"—"Now, do be quiet; just ask Bourrienne; he will tell thee."—"Eh, well, Bourrienne, what say you to that? do you remember them?"—"Yes, General, I recollect perfectly having seen them before." I told the truth, for Madame Bonaparte had shown me her purchase some days before; and it was likewise true that she had received a pearl necklace from the Cisalpine republic, but one much inferior. Josephine played her part with admirable dexterity; I en-acted tolerably, as required, the deponent in this little drama, and the Consul suspected nothing.

CHAPTER X

The Police System in France—Napoleon's Installation at the Tuileries—His Personal Habits, Character, Appearance, Conversation, and Opinions

AT THE Luxembourg the First Consul also organized his secret police, which, at the same time, was in-tended to act as a check upon the public police. There existed, at first, the systems of Duroc and Moncey; later, those of Davoust and Junot. Madame Bonaparte termed this a vile system of spying; my observations on its inutility were disregarded. Bonaparte had the weakness to suspect Fouché, and looked upon this precaution as necessary. That minister is too well known in this line that I should here vaunt his abilities; he quickly discovered both the institution and its agents, high and low. It is difficult to form an idea of the follies, the absurdities, the romances of the bulletinists, both noble and plebeian. I shall be silent on such villanies, anticipating merely a personal occurrence, which must prove the worthlessness of the wretched and disgusting system. The adventure happened in the second year of the consulate, when we were established at Malmaison. Junot had a large sum for the secret police of the capital; of this he gave 8,000 francs to a wretched reporter; the rest passed to the police of his own stables and kitchen. On reading one of these daily bulletins I found, "M. de Bourrienne went last night to Paris. Entering a certain residence in the Faubourg St. Germain, Rue de Varenne, there, in a very animated conversation, he gave it to be understood that the First Consul desired to make himself king." I had never opened my mouth on this subject. It is to be observed, also, that I never did, nor indeed could, leave Malmaison for an instant, being liable every moment, night and day, to be called by the First Consul, and very often sent for unexpectedly. But, on the night particularly specified, he had continued dictating notes and instructions to me till three o'clock in the morning! Junot came every day at eleven o'clock; I sent for him while alone in the study. "You have not read your bulletin?"—"Yes, but I have."—"That is impossible."—"Wherefore?"—"Because you would have stopped an absurdity which concerns me."—"Ah! I am very sorry for it, but I am sure of my agent; I shall change nothing in his report."—"You are wrong." I then related to him what had passed on the night in question. He persisted, and went away.

Every morning I arranged on Bonaparte's table the papers and letters to be read. That morning Junot's report was placed uppermost. The First Consul entered, took it up and began reading. Having come to the obnoxious passage, he fell a-laughing. "Have you read this bulletin?" —"Yes, General."—"What a beast Junot is! it is long since I knew that; how he allows himself to be gulled! Is he here still?"—"I believe so; I have had some explanations with him in the spirit of good-fellowship; but he refused to listen to anything."—"Send him here." Junot entered. "Blockhead that you are, how could you hand me a report like this? So, you don't read your bulletins? What warrant have I that you do not compromise other persons as unjustly? I want positive facts, and not inventions. Your agent has long displeased me; dismiss him this very day." Junot attempted to justify himself. "Enough said! See it done." Fouché, to whom I related this affair, informed me that the contrivance was his, in order to amuse himself at Junot's expense. The former, indeed, often led the police of the palace into the snare he had previously set. This added to his own credit. Miserable police! In my time it poisoned the existence of the First Consul, often irritated him against his wife, his servants and his friends. He at length discovered and escaped from its fatal influence, but not before it had entangled him in its wiles and long held the ascendant over even his power. False denunciations, forged correspondences, the most artful coincidences, preceded by the most alarming reports—such are the means which the police will ever practice for its own preservation; by these it survives; not to use them is death. "You think, then," said Napoleon, at Elba, one day to an officer, "that the agents of the police anticipate and know all. The police invents much more than it discovers. Without doubt, mine was better than these gentry now employ; yet it was often only at the end of ten or fifteen days that mine learned something through chance, imprudence or treason. It is the same with the post-office—like the police, it catches only fools."

The period of quitting the Luxembourg having arrived,

Bonaparte, in addition to those already described, accompanied the change with many new precautions, all equally deceitful. The removal was fixed for the 80th Pluviose; the day previous had been selected for publishing the list of votes accepting the constitution. On the other hand, he had postponed for ten days the insertion, in the "Moniteur," of the speeches and proceedings in the Temple of Mars. He considered the day in which he was to make so bold an advance toward monarchy well adapted to entertain the inhabitants of Paris with great ideas about liberty and to mingle anew his name with Washington's.

On the day appointed for this decisive ceremony, I entered the chamber of the First Consul, as usual, at seven o'clock. He was in a profound sleep; and this was one of the mornings in which he begged me to let him indulge a little longer. I remarked that General Bonaparte was much less moved at the moment of executing designs which he had projected than at the time of their conception: so established was his habit of considering what he had determined upon in thought as already performed. On my re-entering, he said, with an air of marked satisfaction—"Well! Bourrienne, at length we shall sleep in the Tuileries! You are very fortunate; you are not obliged to exhibit yourself; you can go in your own way: but, with me, it must needs be an affair of display—a procession; that is tiresome: however, we must speak to the eyes. The Directory was too simple, so it enjoyed no consideration. With the army, simplicity is in place; in a great city, in a palace, it becomes incumbent on the head of government to draw attention by all possible means: but we must walk warily."

Bonaparte left the Luxembourg at one o'clock precisely. The procession was, doubtless, far from resembling those which, under the empire, displayed such magnificence; but all the pomp permitted by the existing state of things in France had been given. The only true splendor of that period was the magnificence of the troops; 8,000 chosen soldiers, especially the superb regiment of guides, were assem-

bled.   The military officers were on horseback, the civil
functionaries and counsellors of state in carriages; and, for
their transportation, it was necessary to have recourse to
hackney coaches, merely using the precaution of covering
the number with paper of the same color as the body of
the vehicle.   The consular carriage only was drawn by six
horses.   These recalled the memory of glory and of peace,
being the beautiful white coursers presented by the Emperor
of Austria after the treaty of Campo-Formio.   With the First
Consul, who was in military costume, wearing his magnificent sabre, a present also from Francis, were his colleagues
Cambacérès and Lebrun.   Everywhere on the route, through
a considerable portion of the capital, his presence called forth
shouts of joy, which then required not to be extorted by the
police.   The immediate approaches to the Tuileries were
lined by the consular guard—a royal usage, which contrasted singularly with the inscription over the entrance—
"ON THE 10TH AUGUST, 1792, ROYALTY WAS ABOLISHED IN
FRANCE, AND SHALL NEVER BE RE-ESTABLISHED!"   It was
re-established already.

   No sooner had the carriage stopped in the square of the
palace, than the First Consul, instantly alighting, mounted,
or, to speak more correctly, vaulted on horseback, to review
the troops, while his two colleagues ascended to the royal
apartments, where the council of state and ministers attended
them.   The review was prolonged in presence of an indescribable confluence of spectators; the windows were filled
with elegant women, dressed in the Grecian costume, then
the fashion; and from every quarter, as from a single voice,
resounded acclamations of "Long live the First Consul!"
Who would not have yielded to the intoxication of such
enthusiasm?   After passing between the lines, addressing
flattering expressions to the commanders of the corps, Bonaparte, having Murat and Lannes on his right and left, took
his station near the gate of the Tuileries.   Behind stood a
numerous staff composed of youthful warriors, bronzed by
the suns of Italy and Egypt, every one of whom had been

in more combats than he numbered years. When the Consul beheld pass before him the colors of the 86th, the 43d,
and the 30th demi-brigade, as these standards were reduced
to a bare pole with some tatters of silk, torn by bullets and
blackened with smoke, he took off his hat and bent toward
them, in token of reverence. This homage of a great captain to ensigns mutilated on the field of battle was hailed
by a thousand acclamations. All the troops having defiled,
the First Consul ascended with dauntless step the stairs
of the Tuileries.

The part of the General was over for that day; now commenced that of Chief of the State. And here is the proper
place to relate a fact of which I was both an eye and ear
witness, because, though occurring somewhat earlier, its
effects became daily more perceptible, after the removal
to the Tuileries. The reader will not have forgotten that
when Ducos and Siéyès bore the title of Consuls, the three
members of the consular commission were equals, if not
in fact, at least in right. When Cambacérès and Lebrun
replaced them, M. de Talleyrand was appointed at the same
time successor to M. Reinhard as minister for foreign affairs.
On this appointment, he was admitted to a private audience
in the study, where I remained alone with them. The words
addressed by Talleyrand to Bonaparte were too remarkable
in themselves, and in their effects upon the auditor, for me
to forget them: "Citizen-General," said the new minister,
"you have confided to me the department of foreign affairs:
I will justify your confidence; but I esteem it my duty at
once to declare that I will consult with you alone. There
is in this no vain haughtiness on my side; I speak only as
the interests of France are concerned. That our country
may be well governed, that there may be unity of action, it
is indispensable that you be First Consul, and that the First
Consul have in his own management whatsoever directly
pertains to politics—namely, the home and police departments, for the internal government; my department, for
external relations; and finally, the two great instruments

of the executive, war and the admiralty.   It will, therefore, be altogether proper for these five ministers to correspond with you alone.   The administration of justice, and of the finances, is doubtless connected with the executive policy by numberless links, but here the union is less inseparable. With your permission, General, I would advise that the Second Consul, very able lawyer as he is, should have the direction of legal affairs; while the Third, equally conversant in ways and means, should conduct financial operations.   This will occupy—will amuse them; and you, General, having at disposal the vital powers of government, will thus be enabled to attain the noble object of your aims —the regeneration of France.''

These remarkable words were too much in accord with the private sentiments of Bonaparte to be heard with indifference.   "Do you know, Bourrienne,'' said he, on the departure of the minister, "Talleyrand gives good counsel; he is a man of excellent sense.''—"Such, General, is the opinion of all who know him.''—"Talleyrand,'' added he, with a smile, "is quick; he has penetrated me.   What he advises you know well it is my intention to do.   But one stroke more!—he is right: they walk with speed who walk alone.   Lebrun is an excellent person, but he has no politics in his head; he writes books.   Cambacérès has too many traditions of the Revolution.   My government must be quite new.''   So punctually were Talleyrand's advices followed, that already, the very day of the installation of the consular government, when Bonaparte had entered the hall wherein the presentations took place, Cambacérès and Lebrun resembled rather spectators than colleagues of the First Consul.   On this occasion, as our republicans of the consular times were not altogether Spartans, the procession to the Tuileries, the review and the presentations were followed by grand dinners.   The First Consul received at his table the two other consuls, the ministers and the presidents of the great bodies of the state; Murat entertained the chiefs of the army; and the entire council of state, getting into the conveyances with effaced numbers, drove off to partake of Lucien's good cheer.

Before installing ourselves in the Tuileries, we had made frequent visits to the palace, surveying how the repairs, or rather *cleansings*, ordered by Bonaparte, advanced. At the very commencement, seeing the quantity of *bonnets rouges* (caps of liberty) painted upon the walls, he desired the architect, Lecomte, "See that all these smearings vanish; I will have no such abominations."

The slight changes which he wished in the interior of the suite destined for himself were of his own planning. A bed of state, not that of Louis XVI., was placed in an apartment opening from his study; but I may just mention that he slept there very rarely; for, cultivating the simplest tastes privately, he loved external splendor only as a studied means of imposing upon men. To speak in vulgar fashion, both at the Luxembourg and Malmaison, as also during the first period of his residence at the Tuileries, Bonaparte slept with his wife. Every night he descended to Josephine's chamber by a small staircase, opening into a wardrobe, which adjoined his cabinet, and formerly the oratory of Mary de Medicis. I never entered the Consul's bedroom except by this passage, which he used likewise on ascending to *our* study.

As to our study, or office, I have beheld so many events prepared therein; have witnessed in it sometimes great, sometimes little, things transacted; and finally, passed there so many hours of my life, that the whole still remains indelibly impressed on my memory. A very beautiful table for the First Consul stood nearly in the centre. When he placed himself at work in the splendid armchair, the same which he so unmercifully notched with his penknife, his back was to the fireplace and his right to the only window in the apartment. Against the opposite wall stood a large bookcase, filled with papers from top to bottom. A little to the right, a door led into the bedchamber of state already mentioned. Beyond. was the grand saloon of audience, upon the ceiling of which Lebrun had painted Louis XIV. When we took possession, a tricolor cockade, daubed upon the forehead of the *grand monarch*, still attested the base imbecility of the Convention. Beyond this was the hall of the guards, which conducted to the great staircase. My writing-table, very plain, was placed near the window, whence in summer I enjoyed the perspective of the tufted foliage of the chestnut trees; but to see those who walked in the garden I had to rise, while a slight movement of the head enabled me to face the Consul, when we had to address each other. On the right was a small apartment, or closet, appropriated to Duroc, by which, also, was held communication with the attendant in waiting and with the state apartments. Duroc being rarely present, I used the small room to see those persons with whom it might be necessary to converse. Such was the consular, afterward the imperial, study.

In reading the history of the great men of antiquity, do we not regret that their annalists have neglected to tell us of the man, occupying themselves only with the hero? In effect, though nothing more resembles an ordinary man than an illustrious personage, when one follows both into the details of private life, it is no less true that, generally speaking, the world likes to be acquainted with the most unimportant habits of those whom great talents and vast renown have elevated above their fellow men. Is this merely an effect of curiosity? or, rather, may it not be referred to an involuntary display of self-love? And do we not thus seek, without intending it, to console ourselves for their superiority in beholding their errors, their weaknesses, their absurdities even; in short, all those points of contact which they exhibit in common with the herd of mankind? In order, then, that those inquisitive in such details may find wherewithal to satisfy their longing in regard to Bonaparte, I intend to devote the following paragraphs to a physical and moral portraiture of the man, as I have seen him, in his tastes, his habits, his passions, his caprices. I draw at present from the original, as every moment exposed to my observation for so many years.

The ablest painters and sculptors have labored to fix upon the canvas, or to call forth from the marble, the features of that extraordinary man. The greater number of these skilful artists, whose talents honor France, have happily seized the type of his countenance; yet may we assert that there exists not a perfect resemblance. It is not granted even to genius to triumph over an impossibility. The noble contour of the head, the expanded front, the pale and elongated visage, and the meditative cast of the countenance might be represented; but the mobility of his glance was beyond imitation—that glance which obeyed volition with the rapidity of lightning. In the same minute might be read in his quick and piercing eye an expression, now sweet, now stern, now terrible, and anon caressing. It seemed as if every thought which agitated his soul molded his physiognomy correspondingly.

Bonaparte had finely formed hands, and highly estimated this advantage. He likewise took particular care of them, and often, while conversing, looked at them with complacency. He had also pretensions to fine teeth; but these claims appeared to me less justly founded. When he walked, whether alone or in company, in a room or in his gardens, he stooped a little in his gait, with hands crossed behind his back. Frequently he made an involuntary movement of the right shoulder, by slightly elevating it; at the same time, a motion in the mouth, from left to right, was observable. If one had not known this to be only a habit, these motions might have been mistaken for spasmodic affections. They, in reality, indicated deep cogitation—a sort of concentration of the spirit, while it cherished lofty reflections. Often, after these walks, he drew up, or dictated to me, the most important papers. It seemed almost impossible to tire him, not merely on horseback, and with the army, but in his ordinary exercise; for sometimes he walked during five or six hours in succession without being sensible of the exertion. He had a habit, too, in these walks, when accompanied by any one whom he treated familiarly, of passing his arm through his companion's and thus supporting himself.

Bonaparte used frequently to say to me—"You see, Bourrienne, how temperate and spare I am. Well, I cannot divest myself of the apprehension that, forty years hence, I shall be a great eater, and become very corpulent. I foresee that my constitution will undergo a change; and notwithstanding I take sufficient exercise. But what would you? It is a presentiment, and will certainly be realized." This idea troubled him much. As nothing then permitted me to participate in them, I never failed to argue against these fears as groundless. But he would not listen to me; and during the whole time of my remaining in his service, this presentiment haunted him continually. It was but too well founded.

For the bath he had an absolute passion, and mistook this partiality for a necessity of life. He remained habitually two hours in the water. During this time I read to him extracts from the journals or some new pamphlets; for he desired to hear all, know all, and see all for himself. While in the bath he kept continually turning the warm water valve, raising the temperature to such a pitch that we found ourselves enveloped in an atmosphere of vapor so dense as to prevent my seeing sufficiently to read. We were then forced to open the door.

I never knew Bonaparte to be otherwise than extremely temperate and an enemy to all excess. He was aware of the absurd stories circulated concerning him; and they sometimes put him out of humor. How often has it been repeated that he was subject to attacks of epilepsy! During the space of more than eleven years, I never saw any symptom which resembled in the very least that malady. He was very healthy, and of excellent constitution. But if, on the one hand, his enemies have thought to degrade by describing him as subject to a grievous periodical infirmity, his flatterers, apparently imagining sleep as incompatible with greatness, have not less belied truth in speaking of his supposed wakefulness. Bonaparte made others wake, but he himself slept, and slept soundly. He desired that I should call him every morning at seven. I was, therefore, always the first who entered his bedroom; but, pretty often, on my attempting to rouse him, he would say, his eyes still shut—"Do, Bourrienne, I beseech you, let me indulge a moment longer." When there happened to be nothing very pressing, I did not return again till eight. In general, he slept seven hours out of the twenty-four, besides dozing a little in the afternoon.

Among the private instructions delivered me in writing there was one very singular on this point: "During the night," said the rule, "you will enter my room as seldom as possible. Never awake me when you have good news to announce: with such intelligence nothing presses. But, if the matter concerns bad news, wake me immediately, for then there is not an instant to be lost." This was good calculation, and Bonaparte often found his advantage therein.

As soon as he had risen, his valet de chambre shaved him and dressed his hair. While these operations were going forward, I read the newspapers aloud, commencing always with the "Moniteur." He gave no attention save to the English and German newspapers. "Pass, pass," he would say to me, on reading the French journals; "I know all that is there. They say only what I permit." I have often been much astonished that his valet did not cut him during these readings; for, on hearing anything remarkable, he turned suddenly toward my side. When his toilet was completed, and that, too, with great care—for he dressed with scrupulous neatness—we descended together to the study. There he signed the answers to important petitions, of which the analysis had been made by myself the preceding evening. At levees especially, and on public days, he was very punctual in these signatures, because I took care to put him in mind that the greater part of the petitioners would be in the apartments, or would present themselves on his passing to the parade ground. In order to spare him this annoyance I informed them in advance what had been the decision of the First Consul. Afterward he read the open letters which I placed in order upon his table, classing them according to their importance, and to which he charged me with replying in his name. Sometimes, indeed, though rarely, he wrote answers himself. Thus passed the time till ten, when breakfast was announced by the steward of the household, while at the Luxembourg, in these terms —"The General's table is served." On adjourning to the breakfast room we found a repast of extreme frugality. Almost every morning, at this meal, he eat chickens done with oil and onions, then named, I believe, *Poulet à la Pro-vençale*, but since perpetuated in the cards of our restaura-teurs under the more ambitious designation of *Poulet à la Marengo*. He drank very little wine. What he did take was always Bordeaux or Burgundy, and the latter in pref-erence. After breakfast, as after dinner, he had a cup of strong coffee. This beverage I never saw him take between repasts; and I know not to what source to attribute the re-port that Bonaparte had a perfect passion for coffee. This supposition perhaps is theirs who pretend that he never slept during the night. The one hypothesis requires to be supported by the other. When he did work later than usual, it was never coffee he ordered, but chocolate, of which he always made me take a cup with him.

What has been said respecting Bonaparte's immoderate use of snuff is not less opposed to truth than his liking for coffee. Certainly, he had early begun to show a partiality this way. He used, however, but a small quantity, always in a box, of which he had a great many; for this was one of his fancies; and, if he resembled in anything the great Frederick, it was not in converting the pocket of his vest into a snuff canister; for I have already said he carried neatness in dress to a degree of fastidiousness.

Bonaparte nourished two real passions—fame and war.

Never was he more gay than in the camp; at no time so morose as when inactive. Building, too, gratified his imagination; plans of gigantic construction filled, more than any other thought, the void created by repose. He was aware that such monuments constitute a portion of the history of a people, which, by their long duration, bear witness to the civilization of their age, long after the nation has disappeared from the face of the earth, and that, often to the most remote generations, they hand down as true, conquests in reality fabulous. He deceived himself, however, in the means by which he hoped to attain this end. His inscriptions, his trophies, and, later, his eagles, figured nobly on the monuments of his reign; but why, by false initials, endeavor to bring within his own era even the old Louvre? The multitude of N's engraven everywhere, could avail nothing in opposition to the recitals of history; a scratch upon a wall could not alter the order of time. But what matters it? Bonaparte knew that the fine arts impart to great actions a long renown, and consecrate the memory of princes who encourage and protect them. Yet has Bonaparte affirmed to me, more than once—"A great reputation is but a great noise; the more we make of it, the further it is heard. Laws, institutions, monuments, nations—all perish, but the noise is prolonged, and echoes among other generations." This was a favorite idea. "My power," he would say again, "depends upon my fame, and my fame upon the victories I have gained. My power would fall if I gave it not a base of more fame and of new victories. Conquest has made me what I am; conquest alone can maintain that position." It was this sentiment, then reigning supreme in his mind, and probably ever forming his ruling principle, which awakened unceasing visions of new wars, and scattered the seeds of hostility throughout Europe. He believed that to remain stationary was to fall: hence, the desire ever to be advancing: and with him not to act grandly and strikingly was not to act at all. This constraining necessity flowed from his organization; it was inseparable from his

very being. "A government just created must needs dazzle
and astonish," he would say. "When it sends forth no
meteoric splendor, it fades." It was vain to ask repose
on the part of one who personified movement itself.

His sentiments toward France, finally, differed much
from those observable in youth. Long he bore with impatience the remembrance of the subjugation of Corsica, which
he then desired to regard as his country; but this feeling
subsided, and I can affirm that he passionately loved France.
His imagination kindled at the sole idea of seeing her great,
happy, powerful, the first among the nations of the earth,
and dictating laws to all others. He beheld his name indissolubly united with that of this beautiful France, and
listened to the union being repeated in the echoes of most
distant time. In his every action, the present moment disappeared before the ages to come; in every region into which
he was led by warlike enterprise, the opinion of France held
empire over his thought. Like Alexander at Arbela, who
esteemed it less glorious to have vanquished Darius than to
have conquered the suffrages of the Athenians, Bonaparte
at Marengo was haunted by the idea, "What will they say
in France?"

Before engaging in battle, Bonaparte made little pro-
vision for subsequent events, if successful; but occupied
himself much with what ought to be done in the case of
defeat. I here report a fact of which I have often been
a witness, leaving to his brethren in arms the decision on
the merits of this conduct. He was enabled to accomplish
much, because he hazarded all, grasped at all, and was
cautious in nothing. His excessive ambition urged him on
to power, and power obtained only added to his ambition.
None ever more firmly held the conviction that a nothing
often decides the greatest affairs. This supplies the reason
why he was more solicitous in watching than in tempting
events; he beheld them in their progress of preparation and
maturity, when, suddenly seizing, he directed them at will.

Bonaparte was not by nature inclined to esteem mankind, and he despised them more in proportion as he knew them better. This unfavorable opinion of the human race, the result of experience, was, in his case, justified by many striking examples. His severity was the fruit of a maxim he frequently repeated—"There are two levers whereby men may be moved—fear and interest." What esteem, for instance, could Bonaparte have for the pensioners on the opera-purse? This was a fund deriving a considerable revenue from the gaming-houses, one portion of which served to cover the surplus expenditure of that magnifi-' cent theatre, while the residue had a secret appropriation. Thence very tolerable gratuities were touched on bonds signed by Duroc. There might often be seen entering by the little private door personages invested with very oppo- site characters. Our fair Egyptian friend, whose captive husband was so maliciously released by the English, made pretty frequent visits to the fundholder of the opera. There, too, might be found, at one and the same time, a philoso- pher, an actor, a celebrated orator, and a maimed musician. One day the cashier transacted business in the same hour with a priest, a courtesan, and a cardinal, who no longer, as of old, discounted Turkish sequins for French francs at an exorbitant rate of exchange.

One of Bonaparte's greatest misfortunes consisted in his not believing in friendship, and in not feeling the necessity of loving—the sweetest aspiration of which the human heart is susceptible. How often has he exclaimed in my hearing, "Friendship is but a name: I love no one—no, not even my brothers; Joseph, perhaps, a little; still if I do love him, it is from habit, because he is the eldest of us.—Duroc? Yes, him I certainly love. But why? His character suits me. He is cold, severe, unfeeling; and then, Duroc never weeps! As for me, it is all one; I well know that I have no true friends. While remaining what I am, I can make as many of them as I like in appearance. Look you, Bourrienne, we must leave tender-heartedness to the women—that is their affair. But no sensibility for me! It is necessary to be firm—to have a heart of adamant: otherwise, let no one meddle with war or politics!"

In his social relations, Bonaparte showed himself, in schoolboy phrase, sullen; but his sulkiness was rarely disobliging. His fits of ill-humor passed like clouds, and evaporated in words. His unkind treatment, his sarcastic allusions, the bursts of his resentment—all these were calculated and prepared beforehand. When he had to express his disapprobation against any one, the presence of witnesses encouraged the attack: then his remarks were always harsh, sarcastic, and humiliating. Under these strokes it was hard to bear up; but he seldom gave way to these violent sallies, and never except on proofs received of the culpability of their objects. When he designed to take one to task, he always desired to have a third party as witness. I frequently observed that this inspired him with more hardihood: in fact, when alone with him, and when well informed of his character, there was a certainty of one's getting the better, by being cool, frank, and never appearing to wince under the castigation. To his friends at St. Helena he is reported to have said that he admitted a third on such occasions only that the blow struck might sound to a greater distance. Such was not his true motive; for then it would have been far more simple to have made a public exhibition at once. There were other reasons. During the whole time I remained in his service, I remarked that he cared not about private interviews: when he was expecting any one he would say—"Bourrienne, you will remain." And when a person was announced whom he did not expect—a minister, for instance, or general—on my rising to retire, he would say, in an undertone, "Remain now." I certainly was not detained that what might be said should thus be spread abroad; it formed no part either of my character, or of my duty, to carry about his words. It may, besides, be presumed, that the few persons admitted, as third parties, into these confidences, could not be ignorant of the inconvenience attending on indiscretions under a government that knew all. In every way, Bonaparte would have failed of his aim, in reckoning upon the talkativeness of a third person, if that had been the only object proposed.

For the sanguinary actors in the Revolution, and especially for the regicides, the Consul entertained the profoundest aversion. He endured, as a painful burden, the obligation of dissembling his sentiments; but, when he spoke to me of these men of blood, of those whom he himself named "assassins of Louis XVI.," it was with horror, lamenting the necessity under which he yet labored of employing and of constraining himself so far as to speak them fair. Many times did he say to Cambacérès, at the same time gently pinching his ear, to make palatable, by this habitual familiarity, the bitterness of the sarcasm, "My poor Cambacérès, I have nothing to do in that case; but your affair is clear—if ever the Bourbons return, you will be hanged!" Upon this, a forced laugh would contract the leaden countenance of Cambacérès, in a manner as difficult, as it would be disagreeable, to paint. This expression was uniformly the sole reply of the Second Consul, who once, however, in my hearing, made answer—"Come, now, do stop your ill-timed jokes!" If, to use a vulgar phrase, there ever was one who laughed only from the teeth outward, it was Cambacérès.

Bonaparte exhibited some singular habits and tastes. Whenever anything went wrong, or when some disagreeable thought occupied him, he uttered a humming sort of noise, far, indeed, from resembling an air, for he was very unmusical, as already mentioned. In this mood, seating himself by his writing-table, he poised himself on his chair, leaning backward so dangerously that a hundred times have I called to him to beware of falling heels over head. In this situation he vented his ill-humor against the right arm of his elbow-chair, slashing it with his penknife, which, indeed, was of no other use to him. I took great care to have always within his reach the very best pens, for, charged with deciphering his writing, I was more interested than any

one else that he wrote—not well, which was out of the question, but the least badly possible.

The sound of bells produced upon Bonaparte a singular
effect, for which I have never been able to account. When
we were at Malmaison, and while walking in the avenue
leading to Ruel, how often has the booming of the village
bell broken off our most serious conversation! He stopped,
lest the moving of our feet might cause the loss of a tone
in the sounds which charmed him. He was even inclined to
be angry with me for not feeling the same impressions
as were made upon himself; the influence, indeed, was so
powerful, that his voice trembled with emotion, while he
said—"That recalls to me the first years I passed at Brienne.
I was happy then." The bell ceased to vibrate—and he,
resuming the current of gigantic revery, would launch into
the future, encircle his head with a diadem, and hurl kings
from their thrones!

Nowhere, unless it were on the field of battle, have
I seen Bonaparte more pleased than in his gardens at Malmaison. During the early period of the consulate, we retired thither every Saturday evening, staying over Sunday,
and sometimes Monday. Nor can I describe his joy, on
getting to his beloved retreat, more happily, or more truly,
than by saying, that it resembled the buoyant gladness of
a youth just let loose from school. At Malmaison, the
Consul made study give place *a little* to walking, overseeing
in person the improvements which he had ordered. At
first, he sometimes visited the environs, until the report
of the police poisoned his native feeling of security, by
insinuating fears of royalist partisans lying in wait to carry
him off. For the first four or five days, on getting possession, he amused himself, after breakfast, in calculating the
annual income, omitting nothing, not even the care of
the park, and the price of the vegetables. He found the
whole amount to be 8,000 francs. "That is not so bad,"
were his words; "but, to live here, one would require an
income of 30,000 francs." I fell a-laughing heartily to see

him seriously study this out. These humble desires were
not of long duration.

In the country, one of his greatest pleasures was to see a
lady, of a tall and slender figure, dressed in white, walking
in a shady avenue. He could not endure colored dresses,
especially those of a deep shade; and for women with too
much *embonpoint* he had a sovereign dislike. Ladies in the
situation wished by those "who love their lords," inspired
him with invincible repugnance, so that very rarely were
they invited to his parties, or dinners. He possessed all
the requisite qualifications for being what is termed in the
world an agreeable man—except the will to be so. He was
too imposing to attract, and, unless by those who perfectly
knew him, a sentiment of involuntary fear was experienced
in his presence. In that saloon where the excellent Josephine presided with so much grace and affability, all
breathed freedom and gayety in the absence of her lord:
on his arrival, a change came over the scene, and every
eye rested on his countenance, to read there the disposition
of his mind, whether he was to be communicative or silent,
gay or gloomy.

Often he talked a great deal, sometimes even a little too
much; but he conversed in a manner than which nothing
could be more agreeable, or more truly engaging. His conversation seldom ran upon light or humorous subjects, never
upon frivolous matters. He so much loved discussion that,
in the heat of argument, it was easy to lead him into disclosures. Sometimes he amused himself, in a little circle,
by relating anecdotes of presentiments and spirits. This
occurred always in the evening, when the day was closing.
He prepared his auditors by some solemn observation. On
one occasion, for example, he began by saying, in a grave
tone, "When death strikes at a distance a person who is
dear to us, a presentiment almost always announces the
event, and the individual whom death removes appears to
us at the moment of our loss." After this introduction, he
related to us the following instance: "A great personage

in the court of Louis XIV. happened to be one in the
gallery at Versailles when that monarch was reading to his
courtiers the bulletin of the battle of Friedlingen, gained
by Villars, in Germany.   Suddenly, at the very moment,
the courtier beheld, at the extremity of the apartment, the
shade of his son, who was in the army with Villars, and exclaimed, 'My son is no more!'   An instant after, the king
named him among the slain."

All Bonaparte's narratives overflowed with fascination
and originality.   He was particularly talkative on a journey.   In the warmth of discourse, always delightful, always
abounding in noble views and elevated ideas, he sometimes
permitted to escape involuntary disclosures upon his future
plans, or, at least, revealed things which might serve to give
insight into those which he still wished to conceal.   I took
the liberty of remarking on this imprudence, and he received
my observations in good part, acknowledging his failing,
saying at the same time that he was not aware of going so
far.   He did not pretend to dissemble this species of heed-
lessness, of which he has made frank confession in his notes
at St. Helena.

When in good humor, his ordinary caresses consisted in
slight fillips with the first and second fingers, or in gently
pinching the tip of the ear.   In his most friendly conversations, with those admitted to unrestrained intimacy, he was
in the habit of repeating, "You are a simpleton—a ninny—
a blockhead—an ass—a fool—an idiot."   These six words
served to vary his catalogue of compliments; but he never
applied them seriously, and the tone with which they were
pronounced rendered their significance one of entire kindness.

Bonaparte put no faith either in medicine or in the pre-
scriptions of physicians.   He spoke of physic as of an art
altogether conjectural, his opinion in this respect being fixed
and immovable.   He possessed a masculine reason which
admitted only of demonstrated truths.

He had great difficulty in recollecting proper names and
dates, but possessed a prodigious memory for facts and locali-

ties. I remember that, once, in going from Paris to Toulon, he made me observe six different places adapted for great battles, and he never forgot them; for, at that time, the recollection was one of the earliest journeys of his youth, and he described to me the surface of the ground, and explained the positions he would have occupied, even before we had reached the places themselves.

Insensible to the charms of poetic harmony, Bonaparte had not even sufficient ear to appreciate the measure of the verses, nor could he recite a single line without altering the rhythm; but the sublime thoughts of poetry charmed him. He was a worshipper of Corneille, and to such a degree that one day, after the performance of "Cinna," he observed to me—"If a man like Corneille lived in my time, I would make him my prime minister. It is not his poetry that I admire, but his good sense, his great knowledge of the human heart, in short, the profundity of his politics."

Politeness in his intercourse with women did not form an habitual trait in the character of Bonaparte. Rarely had he anything agreeable to say to them; often, indeed, he addressed unlucky compliments, or made the strangest remarks. Sometimes it was, "Ah! good God! what red arms you have got!" at others, "Oh! what a villanous head-dress!" or, "Who has bundled your hair up in that fashion?" Sometimes, again, "You have got a very dirty dress! Do you never change your gown? I have seen you in that dress twenty times before." In this he had no mercy, and generally liked to see money lavished. Often present at the toilet of his wife, who had most exquisite taste, he had become hard to please as respected the costumes of other ladies. At first, elegance was what he chiefly required; a little later, he looked to expense and magnificence, but always to propriety. At the commencement of the consulate, he complained more than once of the fashion which left the neck exposed.

Bonaparte did not like cards, which was so far very for-

tunate for those invited to his parties; for when he sat down
to a card table, as he sometimes considered himself obliged
to do, nothing could be more tiresome than the game, whether
at the Luxembourg or the Tuileries. On the contrary, when
he walked about through the numerous assembly, every one
felt pleased, for he addressed a great many people. It was,
however, always with the learned men present that he held
conversation, especially with those who had accompanied
the Egyptian expedition, or with some popular author.
But, on the whole, it was not so much in a drawing-room
as at the head of his troops that one must have seen him, to
have formed a high idea of Bonaparte, and appreciated his
powers. Uniform became him much better than the most
splendid civil costumes, and, in these latter, his first essays
were not by any means happy. I have been told that the
first time he appeared in official robes he wore with them
a black stock—a singular contrast, as was remarked to him.
"So much the better," replied he; "that leaves something
at least of the soldier, and there's no harm done."

The First Consul was sufficiently punctual in paying his
personal expenses, but he disliked discharging public accounts, arising out of former transactions with ministers
for the various services of the state. These payments he
put off as long as possible, by every sort of chicanery and
difficulty, having recourse to the very worst reasons. Hence,
had accumulated so immense an arrear of expenses as occasioned the necessity of a committee of liquidation. It was
with him a fixed opinion, a settled conviction, that "Whoever writes himself contractor signs himself knave." Whatever was not paid to this class of functionaries he considered
as a just restitution; and the sums deducted from their accounts seemed to him as recovered from a robbery. The
less a minister paid upon his budget the more favorably was
he regarded; and this ruinous economy can alone explain
the protracted credit of the claims against the French marine.

On religion Bonaparte had only vague ideas. He was
wont to say, "My reason keeps me in unbelief .regarding

many things, but the impressions of childhood and the feelings of early youth throw me back into uncertainty.'' I
have already mentioned the effect produced upon his mind
by the sound of bells, and it is a fact which I have twenty
times witnessed. He liked very much to converse about
religion. I have very frequently, at Passeriano, in Egypt,
on board the ''L'Orient'' and ''La Muiron,'' heard him take
a most active share in animated conversations on this subject. He readily conceded whatever was proved, and everything that appeared to him to come from men and time; but
he would never hear of materialism. I remember that,
being on deck one beautiful night, surrounded by several
persons, who were talking in favor of this distressing theory,
Bonaparte, raising his hand toward the heavens and pointing
to the stars, said, ''Gentlemen, your arguments are vain—
who made all these?'' The perpetuity of a name in the
memory of men was to him the soul's immortality. To all
religions he extended entire toleration, and could not conceive how men should be persecuted on account of religious
creeds.

Among Bonaparte's singular habits I may cite that of
sitting sidewise upon every table within reach. He used
to seat himself in this manner upon mine, resting his left
arm upon my right shoulder and balancing his left leg,
which did not touch the floor, thus continuing to dictate,
shaking the table all the while, very much, of course, to the
improvement of my penmanship.

Bonaparte felt great repugnance to reverse a decision,
even when aware of its injustice. In little as in great things
nothing could induce him to withdraw a step: to recede was,
with him, to fall. Here his heart was at variance with his
conduct: he felt this, too; but his good inclinations were
silenced by what he regarded as a political exigency.
Never, perhaps, did Bonaparte say, ''I have done wrong'';
his favorite expression was, ''I begin to suspect all is not
right.'' Nevertheless, and in opposition to this maxim,
more becoming a disappointed theorist than the head of

a government, Bonaparte was neither rancorous nor vindictive. His character was not sanguinary. I cannot, of
course, justify all those sentences drawn from him by the
inexorable laws of war, and the cruel necessity of circumstances; but I am able to say that, in this respect, mankind
has often been most unjust toward him. Outrageous fools
only could have given him the appellations of Nero and
Caligula. There existed nothing in his actions or character
which ought to have exposed him to such insult. I believe
I have remarked with sufficient sincerity on his real faults
to be taken at my word: well, then, I can assure the reader
that, setting aside political considerations, Bonaparte was
sympathetic, kind, accessible to pity. He was very fond of
children; and rarely does a wicked man show such an attachment. In the habits of private life he had—yes, the
word is not too strong—he had much benevolence and great
indulgence for human weakness. A contrary opinion is too
deeply rooted in some minds that I should flatter myself
with being able entirely to remove the impression. I shall
have, it is to be feared, some opposers; but I address myself
to those who seek for truth. I lived in the most unreserved
confidence with Bonaparte for six-and-twenty years, and I
advance nothing lightly. At all events, allowance must be
made for differences of times, circumstances and characters.
The Collegian must be distinguished from the General, the
Consul from the Emperor, if we would pronounce an impartial judgment.

CHAPTER XI

Duties of Bourrienne—Second Italian Campaign

THE following instructions, dictated for me by the First
Consul to General Duroc, and of which I have carefully preserved the original, will show the confidence
reposed in my services, and the manner in which Bonaparte
entered into the details of his government.

Duties of Bourrienne

"I. Citizen Bourrienne will take charge of opening *all letters* addressed to the First Consul, and present them to him three times a day, or when they arrive, should there be anything pressing. The letter-basket will be kept in the study, where the letters are also to be opened. He is to report all those of secondary importance, writing upon each letter the decision given by the First Consul. The hours shall be—when the First Consul rises, eleven o'clock at night, and a quarter of an hour before dinner.

"II. He is charged with the superintendence of the *Topographical Office*, and *Office of Translation*, in which there shall be a German clerk and an English clerk. Every day he will present to the First Consul, and at the same hours, the journals of these countries, with the translations which may have been made from them: in the Italian journals he is only to mark what the First Consul should read.

"III. He will keep one register for nominations to places in the administration; one for nominations to places in the justiciary; one for nominations in foreign affairs; and another for the places of receivers and important officers in finance. In these registers he is to inscribe the names of all those individuals which the First Consul may transmit to him. These registers must be written with his own hand, so that no person can have knowledge of them.

"IV. The secret correspondence, and the different reports of police, are to be addressed directly to him, and transmitted from *his own hand into the hand* of the First Consul. He will peruse these, so that no one may have knowledge of them.

"V. There shall be a register for everything connected with the secret expenditure extraordinary, and whatever may have reference to that department. He is to write the whole with his own hand, in such manner that no one may have any knowledge thereof.

"VI. He will take care to expedite all that shall be transmitted to him, whether from the office of Citizen Duroc, or belonging to the private study of the First Consul, taking care to arrange his work and class the whole in such a manner that all may continue to be secret.

(Signed)   "The First Consul, BONAPARTE.

"PARIS, 13th Germinal.   Year VIII."

The official occupations assigned in these instructions were by no means my only labors; I had to write to the Consul's dictation during a great part of the day, or to decipher what he had written himself—always the most painful of my functions. So unremitting were my avocations, that they scarcely ever allowed me to leave the study during the day, and if by any chance I dined in town, I could arrive only as the company sat down to table, and was obliged to retire at the coffee. Once a month, at most, I went to the Théâtre Français, without Bonaparte, but could remain not later than nine o'clock; at that hour we recommenced work. My medical friend constantly told me he trembled for my health; but zeal carried me on, and if the Consul spared not others, neither did he spare himself; nor can I say how happy I found myself at this period in the unreserved confidence of that man upon whom the eyes of all Europe were turned.

In these early times of the consulate it was wonderful to behold the eagerness with which every one strove to second the activity of the First Consul in his exertions for the social regeneration of France. All seemed animated with new life, and struggled as if competitors in doing good. Already might it be said that France, especially in her moral aspect, no longer resembled the France of the Directory, and yet five months had not elapsed since the expulsion of the directors. The course of events, too, seemed to concur in the benevolent intentions of the Consul. Vaccination, which perhaps has saved as many men as war has mown down, was introduced into France, and Bonaparte, who had a keen spirit of appreciation, highly approved the discovery. New institutions were organized, and the members of the ancient constitutional assemblies of France invited to return. Management here was doubtless necessary, and the invitations were limited or modified to suit the various parties whom he could not yet set at defiance. The personal sentiments, however, of the First Consul appear from the following fact, which occurred at this time, when none of his actions was without a motive. "Bourrienne," said he to me one day, "I still can venture nothing against the regicides; but I shall show them what I think of them. To-morrow I am to be engaged with Abrial in organizing the tribunal of appeal. Target, who is President of this court, refused to defend Louis XVI. Eh, well! do you know whom I shall name instead of him?—Tronchet, who undertook the defence! They may talk as they like; I care not."

At that period Bonaparte often spoke of his desire to improve public education, to which he thought a proper direction had not been given. The central schools were not to his satisfaction; but he could not refuse praise to the Polytechnic School, the best establishment for instruction ever founded, and which in the sequel he spoiled by giving it a military organization. A single college had preserved at Paris the remembrance of ancient studies: this was the college of Louis XIV., to which had been given the appellation of the Pritanée. This establishment the First Consul visited unexpectedly one day, accompanied by Lebrun and Duroc. He remained upward of an hour, and, in the evening, mentioned to me his visit with much interest. "Do you know, Bourrienne, that I have been acting the professor to-day?"—"You, General!"—"Yes, indeed, and acquitted myself not so ill. I examined the students of the mathematical class; I still remember my Euclid pretty well, and gave them some demonstrations on the board. I went through the class-rooms, the bedchambers, the eating-hall. I tasted their soup; it is better, in truth, than ours was at Brienne. I must give serious attention to the state of public instruction and the regulation of the colleges. There wants a uniform for the scholars: I observed some who

were very well, and others poorly dressed. That serves
no good purpose; it is at college, above all places, where
equality should reign. We must plant for the future."

Of the students who had been examined, seven or eight
of the most distinguished, after consultation with the rector,
received pensions of 200 francs, and three were placed in the
foreign office as students of diplomacy—an excellent method
of rearing men of business, and a project due to Talleyrand.
This visit to the college recalls the memory of a fact in some
measure connected therewith, and which shows all the loftiness of the Polish character. Among the students of the
Pritanée was a son of General Miackzinski, who died fight-
ing under the banners of the republic. This young man was
then between sixteen and seventeen years of age. Soon
after, having left the college, he enlisted, and, being in
one of the corps reviewed by Bonaparte on the plain of
Sablons, was pointed out to the Consul, who said to him,
"I knew your father; he was a brave man; act like him and
in six months you shall be an officer." Six months passed;
young Miackzinski wrote to the First Consul reminding him
of his promise. Another month passed. He wrote again,
"You desired me to be worthy of my father; I shall be so.
You said I should be an officer in six months; since that,
seven months have elapsed. When you receive my letter,
I shall be no more: I will not serve under a government
whose chief fails in his word." The youth was but too
faithful to his own. After having thus written to the First
Consul, he retired to his room, and with a pistol shot himself through the head. A few days after this tragic event,
the nomination of Miackzinski arrived at his regiment, for
he had not been forgotten. A delay in the war office occasioned the catastrophe. The Consul seemed greatly affected, and said to me—"These Poles! they are all honor!
—My poor Sulkowsky was just such another!"

Just about the same time occurred the escape of General
Mack, who broke his parole and escaped from Paris, when
the Consul merely said, "Mack may go where he pleases;

I never met such mediocrity in any man. I have not the slightest fear of him, and if he ever be opposed to any of our good generals, there will be good sport. But a thought strikes me—there are other Austrian officers prisoners also. One of these, Count Dietrichstein, belongs to a great family in Vienna. I will set them all at liberty. On the point of commencing the campaign that will look well; they will see I fear them not—and then, who knows? that will perhaps procure us friends there." The order was expedited for liberating the Austrian prisoners. It was ever thus—his acts of generosity, his choice of agents, his very severities, were the results of premeditated aims. He was always governing. And this aptitude, this continual preparation for measures of government manifested itself in all things. While thus occupied with so many important cares, he was arranging and authorizing the celebration of sacred operas and the promenades at Longchamps discontinued since the Revolution. While the republican calendar was still observed in all public acts, the ancient times and ancient calendar were imperceptibly recalled in the seasons of pleasure. Good Friday was marked by the first ball, and the holy weeks by promenades and concerts. Apropos of these trifles, I must here relate a *coincidence* which greatly diverted the First Consul. A day had been fixed for the *début* of the son of Vestris the opera dancer, and the grandfather was to reappear on the occasion. The same day had been appointed for a solemn meeting of the Institute, at which Bonaparte was to preside. One morning I observed in some journal, and could not refrain reading to him, a notice—"The appearance of young Vestris is advanced a day, in order that there might be no competition with the First Consul, whose presence at the Institute ought to draw a great audience." He laughed most heartily at this *delicate* attention on the part of citizen Vestris.

From the commencement of the month Germinal (April, 1800), the First Consul had been exerting himself with fresh activity in reorganizing the Army of Italy. His own presence in Paris, the fine body of consular guards, the desire, so natural to young people, for splendid uniforms, had stimulated the military ardor of the youth of good estate in the capital. This was a feeling of which the First Consul was too wise not to take advantage by thus inviting to join his cause many families of consequence, and diffusing more widely the spirit of the army. Of these Parisians he formed a body of volunteers, destined for the army of reserve, then concentrating at Dijon. Their uniform was yellow, and, on that account, in certain saloons, where everything was apt to be turned into ridicule, the volunteers got the name of *canary birds.* Bonaparte, who did not always understand a joke, took this very seriously, and frequently expressed to me his dissatisfaction. In other respects he viewed with pleasure in this corps a first essay toward establishing privileged soldiers, an idea he had always entertained and subsequently often put in practice.

The constitution of the consular government forbade the First Consul to go out of France as commander of an army. He therefore desired that his long meditated design of putting himself at the head of the Army of Italy should not be divulged. I remarked that by the promotion of Berthier to the command of the Grand Army, so named for the first time, no one would be deceived; all would see clearly that he had made the choice in order to command in person. The First Consul smiled at the observation, and explained himself openly to the new minister, in my hearing—"Well, Carnot," said Bonaparte, having sent for him to the private study, "I am going to Italy. A grand stroke is contemplated. The campaign will be short. Italy has echoes to repeat my name. I want you; and will take you with me." Carnot gave the First Consul to understand that he must decline the commissariat with the present commander. "Pillage will be the word," said he, "and it will be impossible to establish good order in the service."—"Ah, bah!" replied the Consul; "it is all for form's sake. Can you suppose I would have confided my army to Berthier, if I were not to be there myself? Berthier knows not how to command, but he executes my orders better than any other; and I am accustomed to his manner. You must really come." Carnot had still an air of being very indifferent about the campaign, but was at length prevailed upon by Bonaparte's entreaties, and even caresses. For this consent Carnot suffered afterward, as constantly happened. For in such cases—and it may be remarked as a peculiar trait in his character—Bonaparte showed himself a perfect male coquette.

The 6th of May (16th Floreal) had been fixed for our departure from Paris. The arrangements of the First Consul were settled and his orders given, but even yet he wished it to be believed that he was not to command the army. The evening before, having assembled the two Consuls and the ministers, he said to Lucien, "Prepare for to-morrow morning a circular for the prefects. Fouché, do you cause it to be published in the papers. Say I am gone to Dijon to inspect the army of reserve. You may add that perhaps I shall go as far as Geneva, but give positive assurance of my return within a fortnight. Cambacérès, you will preside to-morrow at the council of state; in my absence, you are the head of government. Speak to the same purport to the council; say my absence will be short, without specifying anything; express to the members of council my entire satisfaction; they have already rendered important services; I am content; let them persevere—Ah! I forget. You will announce, at the same time, that I have named Joseph counsellor of state. If anything happen, I will return like the thunderbolt! I commend to you all the great interests of France. I hope to be soon talked of in Vienna and London."

At two o'clock in the morning we took our departure, following the route through Burgundy so often traversed in circumstances very different. Conversation was of war—of the warriors of antiquity—and I then learned the preference which the first General of modern times gave to Alexander over Cæsar.

"Whom do you prefer," asked I, "Cæsar or Alexander?"—"I place Alexander in the first rank. Still I admire Cæsar's fine campaign in Egypt. But my reason for preferring the king of Macedon is the conception, and especially the execution, of his Asiatic campaign. Those who blame that prince for having spent seven months in the siege of Tyre cannot have the least idea of war. Great discussions are held on this subject in the schools; but, for my part, I would have spent seven years before that city, if necessary. I regard the siege of Tyre, the conquest of Egypt, and the march to the oasis of Ammon, as proofs of the genius of that consummate captain. He wished to give the king of Persia, whose feeble vanguard only, so to speak, he had beaten at the Granicus and at Issus, time to assemble all his forces in order that he might overthrow, by a single stroke, the colossus which he had only shaken. Alexander, by pursuing Darius into his states, would only have thrown a greater distance between himself and his reinforcements, while he encountered but scattered troops which would have drawn him into deserts, where his army would have found a tomb. By persevering in the siege of Tyre he secured his communications with Greece, that country which he so dearly loved, for whose sake he had undertaken all, in like manner as I perform all for France, and in whose glory he placed his own. By taking possession of the wealthy province of Egypt, so powerful at this era, he forced Darius to march to its defence or deliverance, and to march half the way in order to meet him. He made a useful impression upon the always fervent imagination of the Orientals in causing himself to be acknowledged the son of Jupiter. It is well known how all this tended to his success. Dying, too, at the age of thirty—what a name has he left!" Though a stranger to the noble profession of arms, I could not but admire the strong sense and profound remarks of my companion, and found it impossible to forbear saying, "General, you are always reproaching me with being no flatterer; now in truth you fill me with admiration."

It is not to be dissembled that, though the affairs of the interior, from the 18th Brumaire to the period when Bonaparte entered upon the campaign now about to commence, had experienced innumerable improvements, external relations presented a very different aspect. Italy was lost; and from the frontiers of Provence might be discerned the smoke of the Austrian bivouacs. Bonaparte was not ignorant of the difficulties of his position, which urged him to the daring enterprise on which he had entered. Here he practiced no delusions on himself or others. Often would he repeat to me at this time, "We must play our all against all."

The army to be attacked was numerous, warlike, victorious; ours, with little exception, was composed of new levies, but officered by chiefs of unequalled ardor. The fate of Bonaparte hung upon the winning or the loss of a battle. He saw the danger, but without being daunted, confiding in himself and the devotion of his soldiers. "It is true," he would exclaim, "I have many conscripts in my army; but are not these conscripts Frenchmen? Four years ago, with a feeble army, did I not chase before me the Austrian and Sardinian hordes and sweep Italy? We will do the same. The sun which now shines upon us is the same light that shone at Arcola and at Lodi. I rely on Massena; I hope he will hold out in Genoa. But if he be forced to yield to famine, I will recover Genoa in the plains of the Scrivia. Ah! with what pleasure shall I then revisit *my* beautiful France." My beautiful France! This at such a time! At the very moment when a possible, nay, probable, chance seemed on the point of wresting from him forever the possession, he ventured for the first time to call it his own!

In this promising frame of mind, the First Consul reached Martigny on the 20th May. This is a convent of Bernardines, situated in a valley into which the rays of the sun scarcely penetrate. The army was now in full march for the great St. Bernard. In this sad solitude, Bonaparte tarried three days, impatiently waiting for the surrender of the fortress of Bard, on the other side of the mountain, which covered the road to Yvrie. The town had been carried on the 21st; but on the 28d he learned that the fort still held out, and that nothing foretold its approaching surrender. Venting his resentment in complaints against the commandant of the siege, he said to me, "I am tired of this convent: yonder fools will never capture the fort: I must go and see things with my own eyes: they force me to interfere in so paltry an affair." The order was given for instant departure.

The invasion of Italy, by the pass of the great St. Bernard, was a grand conception, altogether the Consul's own, and which has fixed the admiration of the world. A solitary hospice, built on the summit, between the valleys of Martigny and Aosté, destined for the reception and relief of travellers, attests the danger of these storm-ridden heights. But here the question was not of single travellers, who were to pass Mount St. Bernard, but of a whole army. Cavalry, baggage, ammunition wagons, artillery, were to defile along paths so narrow that the goatherd there picks his steps with caution. On one side overhanging snows might every moment carry down our squadrons in their avalanches; on the other, a single false step was death. We all passed, men and horse, one by one, along these chamois tracks. The artillery was dismounted; the guns, inclosed in hollow trunks of trees, were dragged along with ropes.

I must here mention that the First Consul had despatched money for the purchase of provisions. The good fathers had collected from both valleys, but especially from the Swiss side, store of cheese, bread and wine. Tables were spread in front of the hospice between the house and the road. Each soldier, as he defiled, emptied his glass of wine, took his portion of bread, with a slice of cheese, and gave place to another. The fathers served out and renewed the repast with admirable zeal, and their warrior-guests were thankful for the brief pause from toil.

The First Consul climbed St. Bernard with that steady coolness and air of indifference which never forsook him when he felt the necessity of setting an example or exposing his person. He interrogated his guide concerning the two valleys, entered into all details respecting the means of livelihood and manners of the inhabitants, and inquired whether accidents were so common as reported. To this last question the guide replied that a succession of facts, treasured up in the course of time, enabled the mountaineers to foretell so certainly the approach of warm weather, that they were rarely deceived. Bonaparte was dressed in his gray riding-coat, and went on foot, with a whip in his hand, ever and anon casting an angry and somewhat anxious look to see if any one approached to announce the surrender of Bard. During the ascent, I never quitted him for an instant; and despite the excessive difficulty of the route, we incurred no personal hazard and came off with merely great fatigue.

The First Consul, on arriving at the hospital, was received in a hall upon the ground floor. He visited the chapel, with its three little libraries, and even found time to read a few pages in some old volume whose title I have forgotten. Our repast was very frugal. The small garden was still covered with snow. "You must have very few vegetables here," said I to one of the fathers. "Sir," was his reply, "we draw every resource from the valleys. In the month of August only, in warm seasons, we raise small cabbages." The good monks further entertained us with relations of the deaths of travellers who, contrary to their advice, had attempted to scale two pointed rocks of ice, about eighty feet high, and not far distant.

When we had reached the extremity where commences the descent on the Italian side, a great many of us slid down, seating ourselves on the snow. The first who passed rendered a service to those that followed, by smoothing the snow and tracing the course. This rapid mode of conveyance caused us great laughter; and we were only prevented from any occasional flight, after some 8,000 feet, by the termination of the snows.

On the 23d we arrived within sight of Bard. On the left is Mount Albaredo; on the right, the Doria-Baltea, a moun-

tain stream; between lay our route, commanded by the fort.
To avoid the fire, our army crossed, or rather escaladed
Albaredo; but as the cannon could not thus be carried over
an almost inaccessible steep, it was resolved to traverse with
our whole train the town of Bard, which is not fortified, and
separated from the fort by the inconsiderable torrent already
mentioned. Advantage was taken of the approaching night;
the wheels of the carriages, and even, in many instances, the
feet of the horses were bound round with straw and boughs
of trees; the whole thus passed with noiseless rapidity
through the little town. Our men were, indeed, under the
enemy's fire; but the houses afforded sufficient protection
against its worst effects. A great part of the army had thus
passed before the surrender of the fortress which so completely commands the narrow valley that, but for the negligence and carelessness of the Austrians, it might have
rendered fruitless the passage of the great St. Bernard
When the 'Commander-in-Chief arrived within gunshot, he
gave the order to cross at full speed the intervening space,
gain a small goat-track on the left, conducting to the summit
of Mount Albaredo, and thus turn the town and fort of
Bard. We scrambled up this track on foot with much difficulty. Having reached the plateau on the summit, which
commands the fort at a small distance, Bonaparte, resting
his telescope upon the grass, and concealing himself from
the view and shot of the besieged, surveyed the fortifications
most carefully. After putting several questions to those
who had come to give information respecting the place, he
pointed out, with impatient dissatisfaction, the errors into
which the besiegers had fallen, and with that glance which
so rarely deceived him, indicated the position of a new
battery and the point against which its fire was to be directed, insuring surrender on the first few shots. Scarcely
had he issued these orders when, descending the opposite
side of the mountain, he left Bard in the rear and slept at
Yvrie. On the sixth day after, he learned that the place
was in our possession.

We arrived at Milan on the 2d of June, almost without resistance. For the country was completely exposed, with the exception of some weak detachments, incapable of retarding our progress, and, to the affairs with these, we could scarcely give the name of battles since success was not for a moment doubtful. Our leader had detected and struck through the gap in his opponent's armor—had completely surprised and astonished the Austrian, who now conceived that nothing better could be done than to retrace his steps and renounce the invasion of France. It is in such circumstances that audacity in war becomes the veritable inspiration of genius. But the bold enthusiasm which fired Bonaparte inspired not Melas. The latter, instead of returning, to place himself in communication with the hereditary states, ought to have imitated the daring of the former, and boldly advanced upon Lyons. He had nothing to fear from Masséna; Suchet was incapable of opposing him; Italy was secured, by its strong places being in his own possession, and in France there were only open towns, and no combatants. Fortunately for us, Melas proved himself to be no Bonaparte. The citadel of Milan was immediately blockaded; Murat, despatched against Piacenza, seized that post without obstacle; and Lannes beat General Ott at Montebello. He little imagined then that by this exploit he had made conquest of a future duchy.

The First Consul passed six days at Milan. On the second, a spy who had been very serviceable to us in the former admirable campaigns in Italy sent in his name; he was remembered, and ordered to be admitted. "What! not yet shot!" was the address of the First Consul.— "General," replied the spy, "when the war recommenced, I entered the service of Austria, because you were far from Europe: I attach myself to the fortunate; I have always found my account in so doing: but I am tired of my profession; I wish to leave off business, make up my little fortune and live in tranquillity. Sent into your lines by General Melas, I have it in my power to render you im-

portant service. But I must report to my employer. You
are sufficiently strong to communicate to me some real information, which I may impart to him."—"As to that," said
the First Consul, "it imports nothing though the enemy,
while ignorant of my designs, knew my force and position,
provided I am well informed of his force and position.
You shall be satisfied; but attempt not to impose upon me.
These thousand louis shall be forthcoming—but only after
you have done me good service." I then wrote, from the
mouth of the spy, the names of the Austrian corps, their
force, their position, the names of their generals, etc. The
First Consul marked with pins, upon a map, all the disclosures thus made relative to localities. The spy afterward
added that Alessandria was not provisioned, and Melas far
from expecting a siege; that there were many wounded in
the place, and medicines wanting. Berthier, in return,
received authority to give him a note, pretty nearly correct,
on our position. The thousand louis were paid after the
battle of Marengo; for the information had proved exact
and important. The spy afterward informed me that Melas,
enchanted with his manner of serving the Austrians, had
also handsomely rewarded him: "I am now," added he,
"able to bid adieu to my villanous trade." This little
event the First Consul regarded among the favors of his
good fortune.

CHAPTER XII

Battle of Marengo—Kellermann's Charge—Conditions of Armistice with Austria
—Return to France—Renewed Hostilities with Austria—Ceracchi's
Conspiracy—Fouché—Tyrannical Resentment of Napoleon

THE day now approached when all must be lost or won
The First Consul was busied in making his arrangements and directing the different corps of his army
upon the points of occupation designed. Murat, at Piacenza,
had intercepted a courier from Melas, with despatches to the
Aulic Council at Vienna. These reached headquarters on

the night of the 8th June. Melas announced the surrender
of Genoa on the 4th, and spoke with inconceivable disdain
of our supposed army of reserve, and of Bonaparte's presence in Italy as a fable, declaring him to be at Paris. It
was scarcely possible to carry delusion and ignorance further. It was three in the morning when I received this
precious document, written in German, and by four had
finished that translation which was afterward published.
On entering the chamber of the First Consul, I was forced
to shake him gently by the arm; for, with bad news, as
the reader is aware, he desired to be awakened. I read my
translation; so greatly did its contents surprise him that
he exclaimed, "Nonsense! Surely you have forgotten your
German!" Scarcely, however, had he vented this pleasantry, when he sprang up from bed, and, before eight
o'clock, the necessary orders for retrieving the possible
consequences of this unexpected event, the fall of Genoa,
and to hasten the march of the troops upon the Scrivia,
were expedited. On the same day, the 9th, he left Milan
with his personal staff, fixing headquarters at Stradella on
the 12th.

By one of those effects of chance, often so singularly
coincident, Desaix, who was destined to aid the victory and
arrest the retreat at Marengo, reached Toulon the very day
we quitted Paris. The capitulation of El Arych, on the 4th
January, 1800, had enabled him to leave Egypt. After a
tedious voyage on board a Ragusan vessel, he had been
taken by the English cruisers and carried to Admiral
Keith's station at Leghorn. The French general here demanded his release in terms of the capitulation of El Arych,
and in virtue of the English and Turkish passports which
he produced. But he was placed in quarantine and treated
as a prisoner of war, till advice arrived from England ordering his release. In the letter addressed to Bonaparte, giving an account of his adventures, the autograph of which
is in my possession, toward the conclusion, he says: "Yes,
my dear General, I wish most ardently to be engaged, but,

by preference, against the English. I have sworn an eternal
hatred against them: their insolence and bad treatment are
ever present to my memory. Whatever rank you assign me
I shall be satisfied; you know I neither wish nor aspire to
the first commands. I shall serve, with the same pleasure,
as a private volunteer, or a general; only, let me know my
destination immediately, that I may not lose an instant: a
day not well employed is a day lost.'' On recovering his
liberty, in consequence of communications from England,
he was captured a second time by pirates in crossing to the
coast of France, but not detained. Arriving at length, he
wrote to me, from Toulon, on the 6th May. This letter I
received at Martigny, and, showing it to the First Consul,
''Ah! would we had heard this at Paris!'' said he, and instantly the order was issued for General Desaix to repair
with all despatch to headquarters. He joined us at Stradella on the morning of the 11th, and was received with
the most cordial friendship, remaining closeted with the
First Consul upward of three hours. On the morrow, an
order of the day published to the army the appointment
of Desaix to the command of the division of Boudet, who
had been killed in a previous engagement. That general
was intimately connected with, and, without doubt, much
lamented by the First Consul, yet, on receiving the news
of his death, he merely said, ''How the devil shall I replace Boudet?'' On expressing to General Bonaparte my
astonishment at the long conversation he had just held with
Desaix, he replied, ''Yes, I have been long with him, but
you know that I esteem him most highly. Immediately on
my return to Paris I make him minister at war: he shall
always be second only to myself: I would make him prince
if I had the power.'' In two days, Desaix was no more.
He fell at the age of thirty-three.

On the 12th we moved forward from Stradella. On the
13th, in concentrating toward the Scrivia, we passed through
Montebello, and beheld the scene of the conflict between Lannes and the Austrians on the 9th. The churches were still

full of wounded, and the traces of death, which everywhere presented themselves, testified but too clearly how well this bloody victory had been disputed. The fight had been terrible. In conversing some days after with Collot, and me, Lannes uttered these remarkable words, which I might well remember—"Bones crashed in my division like hailstones against windows." He merited the title (Duke of Montebello) afterward borne with so much simplicity and so much honor.

On the 18th, the First Consul rested at Torre di Gallifolo. In the course of the evening, an officer of the staff, sent to reconnoitre whether the Austrians had a bridge upon the Bormida, while I was present, reported in the negative. This information tranquillized the Consul, who then retired, well satisfied, for the night. But on the morrow, when the Austrian cannon were heard early in the morning, and learning that the Austrians had debouched, and were engaged on the plain, he expressed the greatest disapprobation, accused the officer, whose name I conceal, of being a coward, and spoke even of bringing him to trial. Mounting on horseback, Bonaparte, in all haste, sped to the scene of the contest, and I saw him no more till six o'clock in the evening. According to instructions, I repaired to St. Juliano, the village indicated, as already mentioned, in the consular cabinet at Paris, as the field destined for the decisive battle, and not above two leagues from the spot where the combat actually commenced. About midday I beheld a number of wounded, with their escort, passing through, and soon after, a great many fugitives. These talked of nothing but retreat, which, it was said, Bonaparte alone opposed with firmness. They then advised me to quit St. Juliano, where I had just received a courier for the Commander-in-Chief. In retiring I fell in with the division of Desaix, which, in the morning, had been sent off toward Novi, to watch the road toward Genoa, but had been countermanded when the engagement began. With this division I returned to my former station, struck with the numerical weakness of a corps thus in march to succor an army alike weak, and now much broken and even dispersed. All regarded the battle as lost, and it was so, in effect: for the First Consul, having asked Desaix what he thought of it, that honest and brave general replied, without any boasting, "This battle is completely lost: but it is only two o'clock; we have still time to gain one to-day." The First Consul himself reported to me, the same evening, these simple and heroic words. Who would have thought that this little column, and a handful of heavy cavalry under Kellermann, would be able to change, before five o'clock, the fate of the day.

Hardly two hours had elapsed from the moment of the departure from St. Juliano of Desaix's division, when, most agreeably surprised, I beheld that army returning in triumph, which, from morning, had caused me the deepest anxiety. Never, in so brief space, had Fortune shown herself under aspects so very opposite: at two o'clock, all wore the desolation of defeat, and its unhappiest consequences; at five, victory had returned, faithful to the flag of Arcola: Italy was regained at a single stroke, and the crown of France gleamed in prospective.

While returning to headquarters with the First Consul about seven in the evening, I witnessed the sorrow for Desaix, for whose loss he expressed the most lively regret. Afterward he said, "Little Kellermann made an excellent charge, and most opportunely: we owe much to him. Observe upon what accidents affairs may depend." From these few words it is evident he could appreciate the service which he refused to acknowledge. He was unwilling that a result so decisive should be attributed to any other cause than the combinations framed by his own genius and foresight. That genius, too, had been displayed so fully, so greatly, on so many occasions, that, less informed respecting his insatiable thirst of glory, I should have felt surprised at a kind of half discontent at the cause of success in the midst of the success itself. It must be acknowledged that in this he resembled neither Jourdan, nor Hoche, nor Kléber, nor

Moreau, who on all occasions showed themselves eager to render justice to the service of those who had fought under their standards. On the contrary, when Kellermann presented himself at table where the First Consul was seated surrounded by a number of generals and officers, the latter merely said, "You made a pretty good charge, Kellermann," and, as if in opposition to this coldness, turning immediately toward Bessières, who commanded the horse grenadiers of the guard, speaking very loud he said, "Bessières, the guards covered themselves with glory." The real truth, however, was that the guard had taken no part in the charge made by Kellermann, who had not been able to assemble more than five hundred heavy cavalry. This handful of brave fellows cut in two the Austrian column, which was on the point of overwhelming the division of Desaix, and made 6,000 prisoners. The guard did not charge at Marengo till late in the afternoon.

On the morrow, at headquarters it was reported that in the first impulse of feeling, Kellermann, hurt by so dry a reception, replied to Bonaparte—"My pretty good charge has placed the crown on your head!" I did not hear this reply, and therefore am not sure it was made; but this I can affirm, that such a sentiment was written, and the fact known to Bonaparte. The director-general of the post-office, M. Delaforrest, sometimes transacted business with the First Consul. Everybody knows what sort of business would engage the attention of the postmaster-general and the head of government. During one of these *laborious* sittings, the First Consul discovered a letter from Kellermann to Laselle, and read therein—"Would you believe it, my friend? Bonaparte has not made me general of division—me! who have just placed the crown upon his head!" The letter, neatly resealed, was forwarded to the address; but the contents Bonaparte never forgot. Hence the small share of favor enjoyed ever afterward by Kellermann.

But be this as it may, whether the general did or did not give the crown of France to the First Consul on the day of

Marengo, certain it is that at night he gave him a supper; and not him alone, but all his famishing staff. This, be it noted, was no small service, destitute as we were of everything. We enjoyed ourselves most heartily, profiting by the precaution of General Kellermann, who had sent to search for provisions in one of those pious retreats, always well furnished, which one is extremely fortunate in discovering while in campaign. On this occasion it was the convent of Del Bosco which had been put under contribution; and the worthy fathers, in just recompense for the ample store of good things and capital wines made forthcoming to the commandant of the heavy cavalry, were presented with a protection against all other claimants on their hospitality.

After supper, the First Consul dictated to me the bulletin of the battle. The following is an abstract:

"After the battle of Montebello, the army moved forward, in order to pass the Scrivia: the advanced guard, on the 24th Prairial (13th June), defeated the enemy, who defended the approaches of the Bormida, and those near Alessandria. Melas was shut up between the Bormida and the Po. On the 25th (14th June), at daybreak, the enemy passed the Bormida by three bridges; surprised our advanced posts; and commenced with the greatest fury the battle of Marengo. Four times, in the course of the conflict, we were in retreat, and as often in advance. Upward of sixty pieces of cannon on both sides were taken and retaken during the day. More than twelve charges of cavalry were made, with various success. At three o'clock, 10,000 men and horse, supported by artillery, charged our right flank, in the vast plain of St. Juliano, in which were stationed the guards, as a redoubt of granite. Cavalry, artillery, infantry, were directed against this battalion; but in vain. This obstinate resistance kept in check the enemy's left, and our right carried at the point of the bayonet the village of Castel-Canolo. Our left, already disordered, was forced to retreat by an overwhelming charge of cavalry. The enemy then advanced along his whole line, pouring in a fire of grape from upward of one hundred pieces of cannon. The roads were covered with fugitives, wounded, and ruin. The battle seemed lost. The enemy advanced within musket shot of the village of

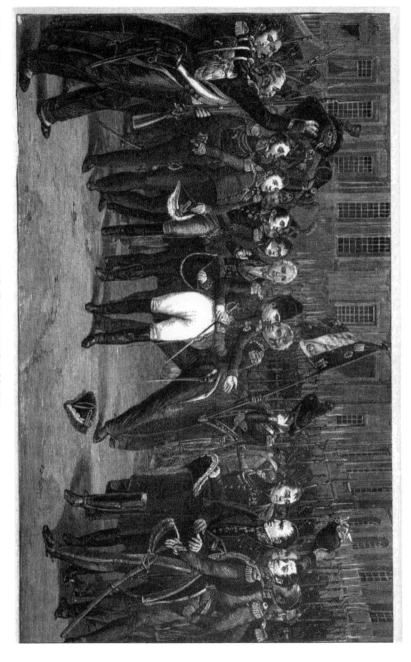

THE ADIEU AT FONTAINEBLEAU

St. Juliano, where was drawn up the division of Desaix, behind whose columns the fugitives rallied. The enemy had now committed faults which presaged the catastrophe: his wings were too much extended. The presence of the First Consul reanimated the confidence of the troops. 'My children,' said he, 'recollect, my custom is to sleep upon the field of battle!' Shouts of 'Long live the Republic!' replied. Desaix charged: in an instant the enemy were overthrown. General Kellermann, who, with a brigade of heavy cavalry, had protected the retreat on our left, charged so vigorously, and with so much skill, that 6,000 grenadiers, with General Zack, chief of staff, remained prisoners in his hands. Our whole army followed up this movement. The enemy's right was cut off; consternation spread through their ranks; their cavalry, attempting to protect the retreat, were dispersed by Bessières, with the guard. We have taken fifteen standards, forty pieces of cannon, and from six to eight thousand prisoners. Of the enemy more than 6,000 have been left on the field. We have lost 600 killed, 1,500 wounded, among whom are three generals, and 900 prisoners. But the loss of Desaix, who was struck by a ball as his division commenced the charge, shuts the heart to joy. He died almost immediately, having only time to say to young Lebrun— 'Go, tell the First Consul I die with regret, not having achieved enough to live in the remembrance of posterity.' In the course of his life, Desaix had four horses killed under him, and received three wounds. He had joined headquarters only three days before, and, on the evening preceding, had repeatedly said to his aides-de-camp—'It is a long time since we last fought in Europe: the balls no longer know us: something will certainly happen.' When, in the hottest of the fire, news arrived of his death, the First Consul allowed only the single expression to escape— 'Why am I not allowed to weep?' "

The manner of Desaix's death has been differently related; and I need hardly say that the words given to him in the fabulous bulletin just quoted were imaginary. He did not fall into the arms of his aide-de-camp, Lebrun, as stated by the First Consul; nor did he utter the fine sentiment which I wrote at his dictation.

Early on the morning after the battle, Prince Lichtenstein, representing General Melas, arrived at the headquarters of the First Consul with proposals of peace. The conditions did not suit Bonaparte, who declared his willingness to grant liberty and the honors of war to the army shut up in Alessandria, whither the Austrians had retired after the defeat at Marengo, but on the condition that Italy and its fortresses should be delivered to France. The prince requested leave to confer with his commander: he returned again in the evening and made numerous observations on the severity of the conditions. "Sir," replied the First Consul, with marked impatience, "carry my last resolves to your general, and return quickly: they are irrevocable. Know that I am perfectly acquainted with your situation: I am not a soldier of yesterday. You are blockaded in Alessandria; you have many wounded and sick; you are in want of provisions and medicines. I occupy your rear; you have lost, in killed and wounded, your best soldiers. I might demand more; my position authorizes it; but I moderate my claims out of respect for the gray hairs of your general, whom I honor." This reply was given with great nobleness and energy. The prince agreed to all. As I conducted him to his escort he complained that "these conditions were very hard, especially the surrender of Genoa." This latter seemed the more severe, as the Emperor of Austria learned by the same post the capture and restitution of the city.

How few the events, and how brief the period which may sometimes reverse the fate of nations! We quitted Milan on the 13th June; on the 14th had conquered at Marengo; on the 15th were in possession of Italy. A suspension of hostilities between the French and Austrian armies proved the immediate result of a single battle; and, in virtue of a convention, we obtained entrance into all the fortified places with the exception of Mantua. As soon as the convention was signed, Bonaparte dictated to me the following note, at Torre di Galifolo: "The day after the battle of Marengo, Citizen-Consuls, General Melas sent to inquire at the outposts if he might be permitted to send to me, as envoy, General Skal. During the day was signed the convention of which a copy is here adjoined. It has been signed in the course of the night by Generals Berthier and Melas. I hope the French people will be satisfied with their army.—BONAPARTE.''

We returned to Milan: the appearance of the First Consul was everywhere saluted with almost continual acclamations. From the first, indeed, we had been well received; but now any little clouds formerly overcasting the *sincere* joy and love of a conquered people were dissipated. During this second sojourn at Milan, Bonaparte saw, for the first time since his return from Egypt, Masséna, who having been left behind in the command of Alexandria, had thrown himself into Genoa, upon returning to Europe, in consequence of the convention of El Arych. The First Consul praised him most highly for his admirable defence of Genoa, and appointed him successor in the command of the Army of Italy.

After some days passed at Milan, engaged in settling the affairs of Italy, the First Consul set out for France, by way of Turin. Here he remained some hours, chiefly to inspect the citadel, just given up to us, in consequence of the capitulation of Alessandria. Crossing Mount Cenis, we met Madame Kellermann: the Consul stopped his carriage and offered congratulations on the brave conduct of her husband at Marengo. I shall not attempt to describe the manifestations of joy and admiration with which Bonaparte's return was hailed in France. At Lyons, the assembled multitude, with continued acclamations, demanded to see him: he appeared at a balcony, and next day consented to lay the foundation stone of new public buildings designed to efface the very remembrance of the revolutionary_scenes.

At Dijon, the rejoicing of the inhabitants really partook of delirium. I have seldom seen a sight more pleasing or more touching than a procession here of young females, of remarkable beauty and elegance, who, crowned with flowers, attended the carriage of Bonaparte, recalling the triumphs of the Grecian and Roman conquerors.

At Paris the First Consul took pleasure in declaring his presence by evident proofs of his incredible activity: thus, on the second day after his arrival from Italy, he affected to promulgate a great number of decrees. Subsequently, he distributed military honors: Kellermann he named general of division, which, in all justice, ought to have been done on the field of battle. On the sabres of honor awarded at the same time was engraven this inscription, flattering to himself: "*Battle of Marengo: First Consul commanding in person;* presented by the government of the republic to General Lannes." Four similar sabres were presented to Generals Victor, Watrin, Gardanne, and Murat. A great number of swords, inferior in value, were distributed to other officers; as also badges of honor to the privates and drummers of such regiments as had distinguished themselves at Marengo and in the Army of the Rhine; for Bonaparte was too politic not to include among those deserving national rewards the officers and soldiers who then fought under the orders of Moreau. A medal was even struck commemorative of the entrance of the same army into Munich. But it is worthy of remark that, amid all the official fables and exaggerations published on the short Italian campaign, a false modesty was thrown over the whole by retaining the name of the Army of *Reserve.* Through means of this artful precaution, the honor of the constitution and of the First Consul was saved in appearance: he had not violated its acts; if he had made war it was only by accident with a body of reserves. Yet he had saluted this said army of reserves as the grand army, and his own bulletins witnessed against him. Truly I never could comprehend how, with ideas so grand, often so noble, Bonaparte could descend to such contemptible and shallow frauds. Strangers, and even his own prisoners, were the objects of his calculating attentions. I recollect his saying one evening about this time—"Bourrienne, write to the minister of war to choose from the manufactory at Versailles a pair of the finest pistols, and send them in my name to General Zack. He dined with me the other day and very much praised our manufactory of arms; I wish him to have a specimen, and besides, this can be productive of nothing but good. People will talk of the circumstance, and perhaps it may find echoes at Vienna. Write.''

The 14th July had been appointed as a festival in honor of the republic, and upon this day Lucien, minister of the interior, had made preparations for solemnizing the victory of Marengo. Certainly, since the establishment of the republic, France had never beheld the future through a vista of brighter hopes.

On that day, in the Temple of Mars, Lucien pronounced a discourse upon the promising situation of France as compared with the horrible Reign of Terror, and the disgraceful period of the Directory. Lannes had the merited honor of presenting to the government the colors taken at Marengo, and accompanied the presentation with words becoming his own frank and generous character. After other speeches and the distribution of five medals to as many veterans, declared by their companions most deserving of this distinction, the First Consul spoke as follows: ''The colors now presented to the government, before the people of this mighty capital, bear witness to the genius of Generals-in-Chief Moreau, Masséna, and Berthier; to the military talents of the generals, their lieutenants; and to the bravery of the French soldiers. On returning to the camps declare to the armies that, for the day of the 1st Vendemiaire, when we celebrate the anniversary of the republic, the French people expect either peace or—if to this the enemy oppose invincible obstacles—more standards, the fruits of new victories.''

After this address of the First Consul, the vaulted roofs of the Temple resounded to the notes of Méhul's military hymn. But, of all the occurrences of the day, the most striking was the arrival of the consular guard, returning from Marengo. I was at a window of the Military College when this body of brave men arrived on the ground; and

never shall I forget the electric movement, so to speak, of
enthusiastic feeling called forth by their appearance. These
soldiers defiled before the First Consul, not in fine uniforms
as if on parade. Hurried from the field of battle on the
morning after the contest, they had traversed Lombardy,
Piedmont, Mount Cenis, Savoy, and France, in the space
of twenty-nine days. They presented themselves, worn
down with the fatigues of a long march, bronzed by the
sun of an Italian June, and with arms battered and accoutre-
ments torn in the murderous conflict.—Reader! would you
form an idea of this? Look at the grenadier in Gerard's
picture of the battle of Austerlitz.

The First Consul, in stating that the French people
looked for peace, could not think that the moderate conditions proposed after victory would not be accepted by
Austria. In this hope, which everything seemed to favor,
the deputies of the departments had been convoked for the
first time since the commencement of the consular government. This meeting had been fixed for the 1st Vendemiaire,
a date already designated in the Consul's speech, and at this
precise date further remarkable as ending the old and beginning a new century (28d September, 1800). To this and
similar festivities, however, it appeared as if peace were
not destined to add the expected gladness. The armistice
concluded after the battle of Marengo, at first broken and
subsequently renewed, had continued to be observed for
some time between the French and imperial armies; but
Austria, engaged by a subsidy of two millions sterling,
refused to treat definitely unless conjointly with England.
She never lost hope of recommencing a more fortunate contest. The court of Vienna refused to ratify the preliminaries signed by M. de St. Julien, at Paris; and Duroc, commissioned to present them for the Emperor's ratification,
was not permitted to pass the Austrian advanced posts.
This inconsiderate step, the result of the all-powerful influence of England, excited the reasonable indignation of the
First Consul. "I have need of peace," said he to me, "in

order to organize the interior [he did not say to mature my plans for seizing the supreme power], and the French people cherish the same desire. Austria, a second time beaten, is offered the same terms as she accepted at Campo-Formio. What would she more? My demands might have been higher; but tranquillity is necessary. I will not, however, be trifled with—I must be decided." On this, Moreau received orders to break the armistice and declare hostilities unless the bridges of the Rhine and the Danube—that is, the towns of Philipsburg, Ulm and Ingoldstadt—were delivered up to the French. The Austrian cabinet then acquiesced so far; and on the very day which he had purposely appointed in his ultimatum, 28d September, the First Consul was informed of the occupation of these three places.

Before speaking of a circumstance connected with the date at which we are now arrived—namely, the conspiracy of Ceracchi and others—I deem myself usefully employed in assigning its true value to an expression used by Napoleon at St. Helena, where he is made to say, "The two attempts on my life, which placed me in the greatest peril, were those of the sculptor Ceracchi and of the fanatic at Schœnbrunn." I was not at Schœnbrunn, but believe, as will appear hereafter, in the danger incurred by Napoleon. With regard to the attempt of Ceracchi, the following are the real facts, in their most scrupulous fidelity: The conspiracy was a shadow, but to give it a body, served a purpose. There was then upon the town one named Harrel, formerly a colonel in the army. He was in want, and consequently discontented. Harrel united himself to Cerrachi, Aréna, Topino-Lebrun, and Domerville. From different motives all these individuals were violently exasperated against the First Consul; and, concerting together how to take him off, fixed for the day of assassination the 10th October, at the opera. Thus far Bonaparte's life might have been in danger. But what follows? On the 20th September, 1800, Harrel came to inquire for me at the Tuileries. Here he unveiled the whole, engaging to betray his accomplices in

the very act, and asked money, as he said, to nourish the
plot and bring it to maturity. I could make only general
observations to Harrel, but, without assuming too serious
responsibility, dared not dismiss him, before informing the
First Consul of this singular confession; and he ordered me
to give the money to Harrel, but forbade any intimation to
Fouché, to whom he wished to prove his own superiority in
police. Harrel came almost every night at eleven to give
me an account of the proceedings. But time pressed. The
First Consul became impatient. At last Harrel came to
state that they only wanted money to purchase arms. It
was given. But next night he returned to say that the
armorers had refused to sell without an order. Fouché
was then informed of the whole, and gave the order, as I
had not the power. The day having arrived, the Consuls,
after transacting business, entered the cabinet of their chief
colleague, who asked in my hearing if they thought he
should go to the opera. They advised in the affirmative,
as there could be no danger, all precautions being taken,
while it would be of advantage to prove the nullity of all
such attempts. After dinner Bonaparte threw a greatcoat
over his little green uniform, and got into his carriage, accompanied by Duroc and myself. He arrived and entered
his box without interruption. In about half an hour, keeping Duroc alone with himself, he desired me to go into the
corridor and observe what passed. Scarcely had I left the
box when, hearing a great noise, I learned that a number
of persons had been arrested. I returned to inform the First
Consul, and we drove instantly back to the Tuileries. Harrel was replaced on the army list, and named commandant
of Vincennes, a circumstance to which I shall have to refer
hereafter under details of most melancholy interest.

As to the conspiracy itself, it is evident that the actors
therein wished to take the life of the First Consul; but it
is no less clear that their machinations, being every one of
them known through an accomplice, could readily have
been suppressed. In fact, Carbonneau, one of those con-

demned, while he made frank confession of the part he had acted in these extravagant conceptions, declared also that they had assumed consistency only through the countenance of the agents of the police, ever eager to evince their zeal by some fresh discovery to their employers.

Although three months elapsed between these watched machinations, which might easily have been prevented altogether, and the horrible plot of the 3d Nivose, it may be proper here to consider these two events in succession. The plots also had no further resemblance than in their object. The former conspirators belonged to the revolutionary faction, and, as if to establish a similitude between Bonaparte and Cæsar, had prepared those who were willing to act the part of Brutus. The second, I say it with profound grief, were of the royalist party; and, in order to murder the First Consul, these men felt no restraint from the fear of hurling to destruction a great number of their fellow-citizens. On this account it is impossible for an author who cherishes sentiments of self-respect, whoever may have been the abettors of such an act, to avoid stigmatizing this as one of the most atrocious crimes committed since there were miscreants in the world. Here more than ever do I feel how much it may sometimes cost to render homage to truth; but when truth commands, who would refuse to obey?

On the 3d Nivose, the Consul had appointed to be present at the first representation of Haydn's magnificent oratorio of the Creation. On leaving the cabinet for dinner—for I did not dine with him on that day—he said, "Bourrienne, you know I go to the opera to-night. You may go, too; but I cannot set you down, as I take Lannes, Berthier and Lauriston with me." Much pleased with this arrangement, I set out before, and was in the house when the First Consul arrived. On entering his box, as usual, he took the front seat; and, as all eyes were fixed upon him, he affected the greatest calm. Lauriston, on seeing me, came in all haste to the box and informed me what had happened—"The First Consul has narrowly escaped assassination in the Rue

St. Nicaise, by the exploding of a barrel of gunpowder,
which broke the glasses of the carriage. He escaped,"
added Lauriston, "by not more than ten seconds. When
the coachman, on turning Rue St. Honoré, pulled up to
receive orders, Bonaparte merely said, 'To the opera.'"
On hearing this, I returned immediately to the palace, well
assured the First Consul would soon require me. He was
not long in retiring; and, as the explosion had been heard
over all Paris, the grand saloon was thronged in an instant
with a crowd of functionaries, who came to observe the eye
of the master, that they might know how to think. Nor
did he keep them long in suspense. "This is the work of
the Jacobins!" cried he, with a loud voice; "it is by the
Jacobins this attempt to assassinate me has been made.
Neither nobles, nor priests, nor Chouans are implicated
here. Since we cannot chain, we must crush them. France
must be purged of such disgusting filth. No pity for such
miscreants!" It would require to have beheld the animated
countenance of Bonaparte—his gestures, always few, but expressive—to have heard the sound of his voice—before an
idea can be formed of the bitterness with which he pronounced these words. In vain some of the counsellors of
state, and especially Fouché, represented that there existed
no proof against any one; Bonaparte repeated, with increased vehemence, what he had already said regarding
the Jacobins; and if the proverb be true that the wealthy
get the reputation of greater store than they actually possess, the First Consul was excusable in attributing to the
Jacobins one crime more.

Fouché had many enemies. It was not surprising, then,
that several of those at the head of administration sought to
widen the difference of opinion between him and the First
Consul. The minister of police, like the rose in the fable,
bent, but only to elude the tempest. The ablest comedian
could not give to the life his attitude of serenity during
Bonaparte's bursts of rage—his evasions of direct reply—
his patience of accusation—his negative silence—and, above

all, his half revelations. I saw clearly he did not believe the Jacobins guilty. I stated the same opinion privately to the Consul; but nothing could undeceive him. "Fouché," was his reply, "has reasons for being silent. He knows how to manage, for he seeks to screen his own partisans, a mass of men practiced in blood and crime! Was he not one of their leaders? Do I not know how he acted at Lyons, and on the Loire? Well, Lyons and the Loire furnish me with the key to Fouche's conduct." This is the exact truth. I oppose it to a thousand fictions of which this event has been the subject. These are mere inventions. The First Consul merely said afterward to Fouché, "I do not confide in your police. I make my own police, and wake till two in the morning." This was true only in rare instances.

On the morrow it rained congratulations. The prefect of the Seine had assembled the twelve mayors of Paris, and attended the consular audience at their head. To these worthies Bonaparte addressed himself thus—"So long as a handful of brigands attacked me directly, I left the law to punish; but since, by a crime without example, they have endangered the population of the capital, chastisement shall be as prompt as it is exemplary. We must transport some hundreds of wretches who have calumniated liberty by committing crimes under that name, and thus take from them the possibility of committing new ones." The council of state several times assembled. The First Consul's opinion being known, every one strove to confirm it. Even Fouché, making his conviction yield to the delicacy of his ministerial position, addressed to the Consul a report which made large concessions to the consular will. The public journals played their part by filling columns with revolutionary remembrances against those who were now to suffer from a retrospective enactment. Upward of 100 individuals were sentenced to transportation, and the senate took its date from inexhaustible compliance, on this occasion, with the desires of the First Consul. This list was filled up from those whom it pleased their accusers to qualify as Jacobins. I

was fortunate enough to obtain the erasure of some, who
may, perchance, be among my readers. I name only M.
Tissot, and who, in turn, was not ungrateful when my day
of political influence had passed away. In writing this I
tremble to think that men were struck at hazard, strangers
to the crime with which they were branded, without proof,
nay, without inquiry. A simple act of the Consul's, 4th
January, 1801, confirmed on the morrow by decree of the
senate, sufficed to banish beyond the territory of the republic and to place under especial observation 130 individuals,
of whom nine were merely designated *Septembrisers!* Such,
too, had been the odium excited against these men as actors
or contrivers in the plot of the "infernal machine," that they
narrowly escaped being massacred by the populace at Nantes
on their way for embarkation, and were only saved by the
vigorous interference of the armed force. "If," said Bonaparte, at one of the sittings of the council, "there are no
proofs, we must take advantage of popular excitement. The
event is to me only an opportunity. We can now transport
men for all that is past." Again, he told me, on leaving
one of the sittings, where the question of the *special tribunal*
had been agitated, "that he had been a little too warm; that
he had declared it necessary to strike like the thunderbolt;
to shed blood; to shoot as many of the guilty as the explosion had made victims—from fifteen to twenty; transport
200, and purge the republic of such miscreants." In all
this the tyrant was so evident that, in its decree, the senate
did not once mention the attempt of the 8d Nivose; but it
did not the less declare the act of the Consul's to be a measure for the preservation of the constitution. This by way
of a blind. If, under the designation of Jacobins, the First
Consul included all those whom France could boast as devoted supporters of her liberties, we can hardly reproach
him with his hatred of such men. He could not pardon
them for having judged with unbending severity the oppressive acts of his magistracy, nor for having opposed the
destruction of those national rights which he himself had

sworn to maintain and to defend, but which, nevertheless, he labored incessantly to overturn. These were the true motives of his resentment. It was thus his own injustice had, in his eyes, rendered culpable those who refused to wink at that injustice. This was the cause why he showed more suspicion of those whom he termed Jacobins than of the Royalists. But I extenuate, while I point out, the errors of Bonaparte. Any other in his situation would have done the same, and perhaps more. Already truth reached him with difficulty. He was surrounded by men who uttered not what they themselves thought, but what they divined were his thoughts. Only in so far did he admire the wisdom of his counsellors, and Fouché, to maintain himself in favor, was forced to give up to him 130 proscribed persons chosen from among his own most intimate associates.

But this minister, induced thus to act, though not convinced, was never deceived in the true authors of the attempt of the 3d Nivose. With his usual sagacity, therefore, he put in motion the whole machinery of the police. For some time his efforts were fruitless. At last, on Saturday, 31st January, 1801, that is six weeks subsequently, about two hours after our own arrival at Malmaison, we beheld Fouché alight, and found that he brought irrefragable proofs of the soundness of his first opinion. There was no longer room for doubt: Bonaparte saw clear as noonday that the attempt of the 3d Nivose had been a plot hatched among the partisans of royalty. But as the act of proscription had gone forth against those whom he termed Jacobins in the mass, there was no receding. Thus the final result of this affair was that the innocent and the guilty suffered together; but with this difference, that the latter were at least tried previously. When the former were so precipitately condemned, Fouché had been unable to substantiate their innocence; their arbitrary condemnation is, therefore, not to be imputed to him. Enough of criminal associations attach to his memory; let it be cleared of this crime. I even venture to assure the reader that he opposed courageously the first

burst of the Consul's anger, and arrested his arm when up-
lifted to strike. He never came to the Tuileries without
asserting to me the innocence of those first condemned.   He
did not, indeed, dare to hold this language with the First
Consul; but I frequently repeated the presumptions of the
minister of police. As proofs, however, were wanting, I
was answered with a triumphant air—"Ah, bah! Fouché!
He is always harping on that string; he halts on that foot.
As to the rest, what signifies it to me?—for the present I
have got rid of them. If the guilty be found among the
royalists, they shall be seized next."   When the real crimi-
nals were at length discovered through the exertions of
Fouché, St. Regent and Carbon, the only immediate actors
who had escaped the eyes of the police, because true to
each other, insensible alike to fear and bribery, were executed, paying with their heads the price of an infamous
crime. In this manner the First Consul got rid of them
too. Thus all his wishes were accomplished. He had his
part, and justice had hers.

CHAPTER XIII

Napoleon's Pamphlet—His Encouragement of the Monarchical Idea—Death
of Paul I.—The King of Etruria—Napoleon's Estimate of Religion

I HAVE had occasion to remark on the innumerable
means employed by Bonaparte to arrive at sole power,
and to prepare the public mind for so great a change.
He held it as a maxim—of which, indeed, the events of this
life prove the truth—that, such preparation accomplished
by the people becoming accustomed to a report, all energy
is taken from opposition at the moment when any plan
comes to be actually executed. The following is a curious
history of a pamphlet launched into the world as tentative
on the subject of hereditary power. In December, 1800,
while Fouché was in pursuit of the real contrivers of the
plot just described, appeared a pamphlet entitled "Parallel

between Cæsar, Cromwell and Bonaparte." He was absent
when I received and read this production, which openly
preached hereditary monarchy. I had no information respecting the publication, but speedily found it had been
issued with lavish prodigality from the office of the home
department. Scarcely had I laid it on his table when he
entered, and, seeming to run it over, asked, "Have you read
this?"—"Yes, General."—"Well! what think you of it?"
—"That pamphlet, General, is of a nature to do much harm
in public opinion; it appears to me ill-timed, for it reveals
your designs prematurely." The First Consul seized and
threw the tract on the ground, as he had the habit of doing
with all the absurdities of the day, after running rapidly
through them. I was not the only one who judged thus;
for next day arrived copies from the prefects nearest Paris,
with complaints of the mischievous effects it was producing.
I remember one of these representations stated that such
a document was sufficient to unsheathe against him the daggers of fresh assassins. He glanced over this correspondence—"Bourrienne, send for Fouché; let him come hither
with all speed and render me an account." In half an hour
Fouché was a third in our study. "What about this pamphlet?" said the Consul, beginning and continuing the
dialogue with the greatest warmth; "what is said of it in
Paris?"—"General," replied the minister, with a coolness
that was imperturbable and slightly sardonic, "all pronounce it to be extremely dangerous."—"Eh, well! why
then have you allowed it to appear?—it is an insult."—
"General, some delicacy was to be observed in regard to
the author."—"Delicacy! What mean you? You ought
to have clapped him into the Temple."—"But, General,
your brother Lucien has taken this said pamphlet under his
especial protection; the printing and publishing were by
his order; in short, it came from the ministry of the interior."—"It is all one to me! Then it was your duty,
as minister of police, to have arrested Lucien and incarcerated him in the Temple. Blockhead that he is! he contrives

always to compromise me." At these words the Consul left
the cabinet, pulling the door after him with violence.
"Put the author into the Temple!" exclaimed Fouché,
who, from the half smile on his lips during Bonaparte's
wrath, I clearly perceived had something in reserve; "that
would be difficult indeed! Do you know," continued he,
turning to me, "that, alarmed at the effect which the
'Parallel' was calculated to produce, on getting notice of it
I hastened immediately to Lucien to make him aware of his
imprudence. Upon this, in place of answering, he set about
rummaging in a drawer, whence he drew forth a manuscript
and showed it to me. And what think you I saw there?—
Corrections and annotations in the handwriting of the First
Consul!"

Lucien, informed of the First Consul's displeasure, came
also to the Tuileries, reproaching his brother with having
pushed him on, and afterward abandoning him. "It is your
own fault," said the First Consul; "you have permitted
yourself to be entrapped. Well! so much the worse for
you! Fouché has been too dexterous—too able for you: you
are but an ass in comparison." Lucien gave in his resignation, which was accepted, and set out for Spain. This diplomatic exile turned out a good thing, though but a disguised
banishment. The Spanish mission became a mine of riches
to Lucien and Godoy.

At this time M. Otto was in London, negotiating both
for an exchange of prisoners and on the Austrian affairs.
But matters proceeded very slowly. The English cabinet
would not listen to an armistice by sea, in like manner as
France had concluded one by land with Austria. For this
it was alleged, that in the case of a rupture France would
derive from the cessation of maritime hostilities greater advantages than Austria from the truce concluded with her.

With regard to the latter power, if, after the victory of
Marengo, the First Consul had shown himself punctilious,
the manner in which Genoa was delivered up would have
furnished grounds of complaint. There was here, in fact,

some hesitation. When Masséna presented himself before the place, in order to receive possession of it, Prince Hohenzollern, whom Melas had left as governor, with a considerable force, refused to give it up, not conceiving why he ought so speedily to leave, as one defeated, a city into which his commander had so recently made his triumphal entry. But the nobleness of the aged general, tried in so many difficult contingencies, did not desert him on this occasion: he ordered the place instantly to be ceded, or the refusal to be maintained at the prince's own peril. Obedience was the word, and the First Consul winked at the transaction. Far however from taking it in good part, his enemies seemed only to derive new audacity from this forbearance. Thenceforward orders were given to assume the offensive in Germany and Italy. The chances of war were for some time doubtful. Upon a reverse, Austria made promises; after a victory she eluded her promises. At length Fortune declared for France; her armies passed both the Danube and the Mincio, and the celebrated battle of Hohenlinden carried the French advanced posts within thirty miles of Vienna.

During these tergiversations of Austria and the deep policy of England, the lively anxiety of the First Consul may easily be conceived. He knew full well the intrigues set on foot for the restoration of the Bourbons. In these circumstances, still so fluctuating and doubtful in their issue, Moreau, on the 3d December, 1800, gained the memorable victory which threw a preponderating influence into the vacillating scale. On the 6th, the First Consul received the news. His joy may be imagined. It was on Saturday: he had just entered from the theatre when I laid the despatch before him. So extravagant was his glee that he jumped up and fell back upon me, being only thus prevented from tumbling on the floor. I ought to say that he did not expect so great results from the movements of the Army of the Rhine.

On the evening previous to the battle, Moreau, being at

supper with his aides-de-camp and several general officers, received a despatch which he read beside his guests. Although no boaster, he could not help saying on this occasion, "I am informed of the movements of Baron de Kray [the Austrian commander]; they are all I could desire. To-morrow we shall take from him 10,000 men." The Marshal was better than his word: he took 40,000, with many standards.

The day after the fortunate intelligence from the Rhine, M. Maret, the secretary-general, came, as usual, about four o'clock, to get some decrees of the Council signed. While in the act of signing, and without raising his head, the First Consul asked, "Maret, are you rich?"—"No, General," replied the secretary, who was standing at his right hand, holding some papers.—"So much the worse. You ought to be independent."—"General, I wish never to be dependent except upon you." The First Consul then fixed his eye upon Maret, saying, "Hem! not so bad, that!" And when he had withdrawn, turning to me, "Maret is a sharp fellow; he does not want sense; he answered adroitly."

The victory of Hohenlinden gave a new turn to the negotiations for peace, and led to the opening of the Congress of Luneville, which took place on the 1st of January following. Instructed by the past, the First Consul would hear no more of a suspension of hostilities till Austria should agree to treat separately, to which she was obliged to consent, and abandon her dependence upon England. This power demanded to be admitted as a third party at Luneville, which was acceded to, on condition that war should cease between France and England, as between France and Austria. All this adjourned the preliminaries till 1801, and the peace between the two former powers till 1802.

On the 9th of February, 1801, six weeks after the opening of the Congress at Luneville, peace was signed between France and Austria. This alliance, termed, as usual, in the treaty, *perpetual*, lasted *four years*. This was a long while too! The plenipotentiaries were Joseph Bonaparte and Count Lcuis de Cobentzel. Joseph met the latter on the way to Paris, he having passed Luneville for the purpose of sounding the dispositions of the French government. On this, both returned to the capital, and, having held an interview with the First Consul, set out on the morrow for the seat of Congress.

Bonaparte now began to interfere with the very amusements of the people, when these tended to excite popular ideas of liberty or government. New pieces were interdicted at the theatre, and their authors prosecuted. It was thus with the author of "Edward in Scotland." The piece had escaped the licenser, and been given during Bonaparte's absence at St. Quentin, whither he had gone to inspect the canal, and, if possible, to rescue that undertaking from its everlasting uselessness. The play was a great success; royalist and emigrant crowded to the representation; numerous applications were made to the Bourbons. But the spirit of liberty breathed by the Scottish patriots seemed too animating to the First Consul, who, on his return, attended the second exhibition. "It is too palpable," said he; "I wish it not to be played. What a blockhead to license such a piece! Why permit political dramas to be acted at all, without first consulting me?" The author, M. Duval, was obliged to leave France. One poor playwright narrowly escaped banishment because accused of aping the manners of the First Consul and his colleagues, in a piece called the "Antechamber"; wherein two lackeys addressed each other thus: "I am in service."—"And I also."—"We are colleagues." The dress of these valets, too, was considered as a burlesque on the consular costume. "This," said the First Consul to me, "forms a pendant to Edward; things cannot be suffered thus. If the imitation be as is said, the dresses shall be stripped off in the Place de Grève, and torn by the hands of the hangman." M. Dupaty, the author, narrowly escaped being treated to the same toilet. It came out, on investigation, that the piece had been writ-

ten years *before* the consulate! These successive triumphs.
engaged flatterers to get interdicted many of our ancient and
long-admired masterpieces, from the applications that *might*
be made. The piece most agreeable to the First Consul was
"Cinna": this on account of the long and admirable invec-
tive against popular power. The same year, 1801, beheld
the fatal creation of Special Tribunals, justified neither by
the urgency nor gravity of the circumstances to which their
erection was referred. These courts were both the foundation and cornerstone of succeeding despotism; they judged
without appeal, in secret, and on evidence upon which they
sat, at once as judge, jury, and executioner.

About the commencement of the same year, Fulton presented his memorial on steamboats. I endeavored to bring
the First Consul to give it a serious examination. "Bah!"
said he, "all these projectors, and these inventors of schemes,
are either intriguers or visionaries. Say no more about it."
I pointed out to him that the person he designated as an
intriguer did nothing more than renew an invention already
known, since Franklin, in 1788, had written to one of his
friends, "There is nothing new at present in physical science,
except a boat propelled by a steam-engine, which of itself
ascends against the stream. It is thought the construction
of the machine may be simplified and perfected so as to become generally useful." He would listen to nothing on the
subject. Fulton afterward went to America, where, availing himself of the knowledge he had acquired in France
and England, he constructed at New York, five years later,
the first steamboat which was tried successfully. We might
have enjoyed the priority of this powerful agent in navigation and commerce. Distrust of projectors may easily be
carried too far: nothing obliges one to accept their propositions, but neither can a refusal be justified without
examination.

In the month of March, of the same year, Paul I., by
a domestic revolution, fell beneath the daggers of assassins.
On this news the First Consul, yielding only to a painful

sentiment awakened by a stroke so unexpected and which influenced so powerfully his political connections, ordered me instantly to send to the "Moniteur" the following note:

"Paul I. died on the night between the 23d and 24th March. The English squadron passed the Sound on the 30th. History will instruct us in the relation existing between these two events."

Thus were associated in his mind the crime of the 26th, and the mark, justly discerned, I believe, of its authors. The amicable correspondence between Paul and Bonaparte had begun to assume great regularity. "I was certain," said the latter to me, "in concert with the Czar, of giving a mortal blow to the English power in India. A revolution of the palace upsets all my plans." This resolution and the admiration entertained by the autocrat for the ruler and republic of France must unquestionably be reckoned among the causes of his death. Of this crime those were at the time chiefly accused who had been threatened with so much ardor and perseverance, and who had the greatest interest in the change of an emperor. I have read a letter of a northern potentate which leaves me without doubt on this head. The letter of this august personage even exhibited the wages of the crime and the part of each actor. But it must also be confessed that the character and conduct of Paul, his tyrannical acts, his violent caprices, the frequent excess of his despotism, had kindled strong hatred against him; for patience has its limit. These motives probably did not *create* the conspiracy, but they greatly *facilitated* the execution of the plot which deprived the Czar of his life and throne.

On the death of Paul the Consul's system in respect to Russia underwent a change. Already, in Egypt, had he expressed to Sulkowsky his great desire of seeing Poland re-established. Now he often dictated to me, for the "Moniteur," notes in which the object of various reasonings was to prove that Europe could never enjoy repose till these national spoliations had been avenged and repaired:

but frequently these notes were torn instead of being sent
to press. The idea of a war against the empire unceasingly
agitated him, and undoubtedly the conception of the fatal
campaign, which dates eleven years later, was now first
formed. The subsequent motives, indeed, were very different; for the restoration of Poland was a mere pretence.
Nevertheless, Duroc was sent to St. Petersburg to offer
congratulations to the Emperor Alexander on his ascending
the throne.

Soon after a new royal acquaintance supplied for a little
the loss thus sustained, and, before investing his own brow
with two crowns, Bonaparte judged it politically useful to
place one on the head of a prince—and that prince a Bourbon. He rejoiced in an opportunity to accustom the Parisians to the sight of a king. The Infant Louis de Bourbon,
eldest son of the Duke of Parma, had gone to Madrid, in
1798, for the purpose of contracting a marriage with Maria
Amelia, sister to Maria Louisa. The prince fell in love
with the latter; Godoy favored this inclination, and, using
all his influence, succeeded in bringing about the match.
To a son, born six years subsequently, was given the name
of Charles Louis, after the King of Spain. France occupied
Parma, which, according to the treaty signed by Lucien
Bonaparte, was to revert to that power on the death of the
reigning Duke. On the other hand, France was to cede to
Prince Louis of Parma the grandduchy of Tuscany. Spain
paid a considerable sum, according to agreement. On going
to take possession, Don Louis and his spouse passed through
France, under the name of Count and Countess of Leghorn.
At Paris they were received as King and Queen of Etruria.
The circumstances were yet budding which brought, from
the same hand that now gave a king to Tuscany, the temporary overthrow of the house of Spain. The literature of the
day is filled with descriptions of fêtes given to the youthful
pair. The one given by Talleyrand was especially remarkable for elegant splendor. The King and Queen of Etruria
came also several times to dine at Malmaison. Upon one

of these occasions, the king fainted. This indisposition he himself attributed to a weakness of stomach, but his people let out that it proceeded from some more serious malady. On their first visit, Bonaparte left the cabinet for a moment to see whether the saloon was properly arranged for their reception. He returned almost immediately, quite flurried— "Bourrienne, can you imagine such stupidity—they had exposed in full view a picture representing me pointing out Italy from the summit of the Alps, and commanding its conquest—a fine compliment to an Italian king!" During these visits to Malmaison, the prince amused himself in the most childish and ridiculous sports. In these the Consul never joined, and indeed saw very little of his royal visitor, being always engaged with business. "What a pity," said I, "that the people of Tuscany must be governed by such a ruler."—"Politics will have it so," replied he; "besides, there is no harm in showing our men, who have seen no kings, what they are made of." The arrival of the youthful sovereigns in the capital, however, threw a kind of splendor over the first years of the reign of Bonaparte, who was everywhere hailed in the words of Voltaire—

"I create monarchs, but would not be one"—

a verse which was applauded to the echo. This applause he thought signified oblivion of his unfortunate pamphlet. Moreover, the reception given by the public to a king of his creation was by no means a consideration of indifference: it began the habit of admitting what he decreed. As to the new-made king himself, he was, in the language of the First Consul, *a poor man*. "I am tired of them," said he to me one day, after spending several hours alone with the two. "He is a perfect automaton. I asked a variety of questions; he could not reply to one. He seemed to consult his wife, who, poor thing, did her best instructing him what to say. This poor prince sets out for a kingdom without knowing what he is to do. He will not pass the Rubicon."

These occurrences recall the mission of Lucien into

Spain, of which we see they were in some measure the fruit. Among other instructions, Lucien had received orders to employ every possible means to determine Spain to declare war against Portugal, with intention of constraining the latter power to separate from England, of which the First Consul had always looked upon that portion of the Peninsula as a colony. Charles IV. was thus prevailed upon, through Godoy aiding these views, to commence a war which was but of short continuance, terminating almost without bloodshed by the capture of Olivenza. On the 6th June, 1801, Portugal signed the treaty of Badajos, engaging to cede Olivenza, Almeida, and other places of less importance, to Spain, and to shut her ports against Britain. In reference to this peace, which Bonaparte at first refused to guarantee, until some new conditions of small moment had been added, it behooves me to relate an important fact. In order to obtain the recovery of Olivenza and its territory, Portugal made a secret offer to Bonaparte, through communications with me, of the sum of eight million francs as the price of his concurrence. This offer he repelled with indignation, declaring that never would he consent to sell honor for money. Those who have accused him of similar transactions must have indeed known little of his inflexible principles.

At this time a considerable party urged Bonaparte to throw off the yoke of Popery and to establish a Gallican Church whose head should be in France. They imagined his ambition would be captivated by this new power, bearing some resemblance to that of the first emperors of the Romans. But his sentiments did not coincide with the project. "I am convinced," observed he to me, "that a part of France would become Protestant, especially if I seemed to countenance such a disposition; but I am also as certain that the great majority would remain Catholic; nay, that this majority would struggle with the greatest zeal and fervor against the schism of one portion of their fellow-citizens. I dread religious contests, which resemble dis-

sensions in families. In re-establishing the religion which
has always reigned in the land, and which yet keeps its hold
on the heart, and in leaving the minorities freely to exercise
their worship, I am in harmony with the whole nation, and
give satisfaction to everybody."

The First Consul judging, like a man of superior mind,
that the re-establishment of religion would be of great assistance to his government, had, in fact, been occupied from
the beginning of the year 1801 in arranging a Concordat with
Pope Pius VII. Cardinal Gonsalvi arrived in Paris in June,
and the Concordat signed in July, 1801, passed into a law of
the state in April, 1802. A solemn "Te Deum" was chanted
in the metropolitan cathedral of Nôtre Dame, on Sunday the
11th April. The crowd was immense, the greater part being
obliged to stand. The ceremony was imposing; but who
will venture to say that the general demeanor harmonized
with the devotional act? Had the season not yet arrived
for this innovation? Was it too rude a transition from the
twelve preceding years? Be the cause what it might, certain it is that a vast proportion of those present exhibited
in their countenance and gestures more of impatience and
hostility than satisfaction or reverence. On all sides were
heard murmurs indicative of discontent; whisperings, which
I might rather call conversations, sometimes interrupted divine service; the expressions employed were even far from
being measured; finally, I know not through what fatality
hunger had seized upon so many of the auditory, but sure
it is, every moment might be seen those who turned round
their head to crunch a piece of chocolate. I affirm even to
have seen people taking lunch without putting themselves
to any trouble or even seeming to give attention to what
was going forward.

The consular court, generally speaking, was very irrelig-
ious; nor could it be otherwise, being composed chiefly of
those who had most powerfully contributed to the overthrow of religious worship in France, and of men who, having passed their life in camps, had more frequently entered

the churches of Italy to carry off pictures than to hear mass. Those who, without being alive to any religious impressions, had received that education which leads us to respect the faith of others, though we ourselves have no belief therein, attached no blame to the First Consul, and comported them- selves with decency. But on the way from the Tuileries to Nôtre Dame, Lannes and Augereau wished to get out of the carriage on finding they were to be carried to mass; and would have done so, had not an order from Bonaparte pre- vented them. They went then to church; but on the mor- row, when the Consul asked Augereau how he liked the ceremony, he replied—"Oh, all was very fine; there only wanted the million of men who devoted themselves to death in order to destroy what we are now establishing." Bona- parte was much irritated at this observation.

While negotiations were carrying on with the Holy See, he one day remarked—"In all countries religion is useful to the government: we must employ it to work upon men. I was a Mohammedan in Egypt; I am a Catholic in France. It is fitting as far as policy is concerned that the religion of a state should be entirely in the hands of the ruler. A great many urge me to found a Gallican Church and to make myself head of it; but these people know not France. If they knew her, they would understand that she is—speak- ing of the majority—far from desiring this rupture with Rome. The Pope must push me very hard before I resolve upon it; but I do not believe he will force me so far."— "You have reason to think so. You recollect, General, what Cardinal Gonsalvi said—*The Pope will do everything which the First Consul may desire.*"—"He will do well: let him not suppose he has to do with an idiot. Guess what they place in front—the good of my soul! But as for me —this immortality—why, it is the remembrance left in the memory of men. That idea incites to great deeds. Bet- ter never to have lived than to leave no traces of one's existence."

CHAPTER XIV

Egyptian Affairs—The Peace of Amiens—Saint Domingo—Louis Bonaparte's
Marriage—Recall of Emigrants—Napoleon's Illness and Irritability
—Extravagance of His Brothers—La Fayette

FOR the last time I revert to the affairs of Egypt—to that episode in the life of Bonaparte which occupied so brief a portion, yet holds therein so conspicuous a place. Of all his conquests, he attached most importance to this, because it had spread the fame of his name in the East. All was tried, all was done, for the preservation of this colony, but in vain.

One evening in April, 1801, arrived at Malmaison the English "Gazette," announcing the successful disembarkation in Egypt of the army commanded by Abercromby, the battle which the British had fought, and the death of that general. The importance of the intelligence raised doubts of its veracity; at least, the principal personage affected disbelief, and in unison arose the chorus of officers, and aides-de-camp present in the saloon when I laid my translation before them. All agreed with his view, particularly Lannes, Bessières and Duroc. They probably imagined that, by acting thus, they paid agreeable court to the First Consul, who said in a bantering tone—"Pshaw! Bourrienne, you don t understand English, and then you are such a strange mortal, always disposed to believe bad rather than good news." These words, and the approving simper of the bystanders, put me out of humor: I answered accordingly—"How, General, can you allow yourself to believe that the English government would publish officially, unless true, so great an event, yet so little beyond probability, that you yourself have entertained apprehensions of its occurrence? Have you ever found news of this importance false when

published in the British 'Gazette'? However these gentlemen may talk, I believe it but too true, and, unfortunately, their laughter will not gainsay the information."
Other and bitter retorts of the optimists and flatterers were
probably cut short by the First Consul saying, in his usual
way, "Come, Bourrienne! come, let us to work." In our
short passage from the saloon to the library, he added—
"Now, what a strange fellow are you! why trouble yourself
about so trivial an affair? Eh! my God! I surely believe
the news, but they consider themselves doing me a pleasure
by calling its truth in question. Let them alone; you know
them."—"Is it even so? I entreat your pardon, but I do
think my attachment is better proved by telling you my real
mind. You desire me never to delay an instant informing
you of bad news: to dissemble would be much worse."

That Bonaparte entertained a high opinion of the value
of Egypt there can be no doubt. In a letter to Kléber, he
wrote—"You can appreciate as well as I how important the
possession of Egypt is to France. The Turkish power,
which threatens ruin on every side, now begins to fall in
pieces, and the evacuation of Egypt would be a misfortune
the more grievous that we should behold that fine province
pass into other European hands—in our own days too."
But the choice of Gantheaume was unfortunate. He had,
indeed, participated in the dangers of the homeward passage, and naturally enjoyed the consequent confidence yielded -
to one under similar circumstances. This predilection for
mediocrity, awakened by an honorable feeling, failed in its
recompense. Gantheaume made a poor return. The First
Consul seeing him still at Brest, notwithstanding he had received his orders, could not refrain exclaiming, from time
to time—"What the devil is Gantheaume about now?" In
one of the daily reports was sent the following quatrain,
which set Bonaparte a-laughing most heartily:

> No ballast in head, no freight in the hold,
>   Such is the trim Admiral Gantheaume;
>   From Brest he sets out, to go to Bertheaume—
> From Bertheaume to Brest returns he full bold.

This conduct of the admiral, his tergiversations, his arrival at Toulon, his tardy departure thence on the 19th February, 1801, only ten days before Admiral Keith had appeared before Alexandria with Sir Ralph Abercromby, completely blasted all the prospects of the aid and reinforcements which the First Consul zealously labored to send to the colony. At the same time, it is no less true that his own retreat in 1799 had paved the way for the loss of that country. The death of Kléber, and the choice of Menou as his successor, decided its fate.

One of the surest means of paying useful court to Bonaparte was to unreservedly applaud his views with respect to the consolidation of the Eastern colony, or to contribute thereto. It was by the former means that Menou gained his confidence. From the first year of the occupation he began to reveal to the General his dreams about Africa and spoke to him in a long letter of the negroes of Senegal; of opening a communication with Mozambique; of recommencing the culture of sugar, which he maintained to have first come from Egypt to Europe and America; of cochineal being easily cultivated, and thus of ruining the commerce of England. The remembrance of this adulation procured for Menou the governorship of Piedmont, on his return from Egypt, which he had betrayed to the English, by absurd measures of defence, and by sending against Abercromby isolated detachments, instead of falling upon him with all his disposable force, and thus certainly annihilating the invading army. When he named Menou governor in Italy, the First Consul, at my request, had likewise the goodness to appoint my elder brother, commissary-general of police in Piedmont. I am obliged to confess that this mark of favor was subsequently withdrawn; for my brother abused the confidence thus reposed in his integrity.

In like manner, by flattering this Oriental mania, Davoust, on returning from Egypt in 1800, in consequence of the convention of El Arych, also insinuated himself into his good graces, and, if he did not merit, at least obtained, favor.

At this period, Davoust possessed absolutely no claim to the sudden fortune which he made. He obtained, without previous rank or services, the command of the grenadiers of the consular guard. From that day dates the enmity which Davoust bore me. Astonished at the length of the interview with which Bonaparte honored him, I asked, immediately after it terminated, "How could you endure to remain so long with a man whom I have always heard you term a confounded blockhead?"—"But really then I did not know him well: he is better than his reputation bears: you will find so likewise."—"I ask nothing better," was my answer. The First Consul, imprudent as he ever was, made no scruple to report to Davoust my opinion of his merits. His hatred died only with himself. I shall have to speak repeatedly, and under remarkable circumstances, hitherto little known, of this man, who, without reputation, without merit, attained all at once to the highest favor.

The First Consul did not forget his cherished conquest; it was the constant object of his thoughts. Toward the end of 1800, at length sailed from Brest six ships of war and four frigates, selected from those in the best condition for sea, and forming but a small portion of the number that ought to have been ready. Every circumstance attending the sailing of the expedition seemed to announce the bad success of the enterprise. A fearful tempest fell upon it on leaving harbor. The squadron, thus dispersed, rallied at Cape Finisterre, passed the Straits, and had reached, without encountering any new danger, the neighborhood of Cape Bon. Here, by a strange manœuvre, and for which no cause was ever assigned, we learned that the fleet had tacked and entered Toulon, instead of making directly for Alexandria. The most frivolous pretexts were alleged in justification of this inconceivable conduct. Thus, whether he would or no, the Consul was forced to attempt other expedients for the relief of Egypt. A second enterprise was accordingly set on foot, which alone shows his clear-sightedness and eager desire to save the colony. On board four ships of the line, and as many frigates, under the orders of Admiral Brueys, at Rochefort, which, with others at L'Orient, were to join Gantheaume at Toulon, he embarked troops and necessaries of all kinds, so that each carried a portion of every sort. This precaution had in view that a little of everything might reach Egypt, should only one, two or three vessels arrive at their destination. Where there is nothing, a little is of great moment. Had this junction been effected there would have assembled at Toulon eighteen ships of war, with 7,500 troops in every department of the service, with a great variety of stores which Bonaparte had noted as useful or necessary to the colony. But all things were adverse to the sailing of this armament—season, wind, and the action of the commanders. The adjournment of its departure rendered it useless: Egypt was in the meantime evacuated.

This brings us to the most brilliant period of the consulate and of France—the epoch of the Peace of Amiens. I except neither the era of the conquests of Louis XIV., nor the most brilliant years of the empire. The consular glory was then unsullied, and held in prospect the most flattering hopes; while those accustomed to examine the real situation of affairs could readily discern great disasters under the laurels of the empire.

The proposals made by the First Consul to induce a pacification proved that he really wished peace. He perceived that to unite his name and first acts of administration with a transaction so desirable was to gain the love and gratitude of the French. His offers were—to give up Egypt to the Grand Seignior; to restore all the ports in the Gulf of Venice and the Mediterranean to the respective powers; to cede Malta to the Order, and even to raze the fortifications, should England judge such proceeding needful for her interests. In India, Ceylon remained in our possession, and we made a demand for the Cape of Good Hope and all that England had taken in the West Indies. Britain—who had resolved on retaining Malta, her second Gibraltar of the Mediterranean, and the Cape of Good Hope, her caravansera

of the Indies—relaxed in favor of the former isle by proposing an arrangement rendering it independent both of
Great Britain and France.   But we had no pledge that this
was not a feint, since, whatever might be the determinations,
it seemed not likely that a maritime power would resign
a station which commands the Mediterranean.   In fact, we
shall see that war broke out anew on this very point.   I
speak not of the discussions about the American islands.
These, in my opinion, ought to have but small attraction
for us: they cost more than they bring us.   Our colonial
system is absurd, obliging us to pay for colonial produce
almost double what our neighbors give.   This, both in date
and circumstance, leads to the St. Domingo expedition,
which left the shores of France on the 14th December, 1801.
The fatal issue is well known: shall we never be cured of
such absurd enterprises ?

After the First Consul had dictated to me, during the
course of nearly a whole night, the instructions for this
expedition, he sent for General Leclerc, and, in my presence, addressed him, to the following effect: "Here are your
instructions.   Now is your time: go, get rich, and trouble
me no more with your everlasting importunities for money."
The regard entertained by Bonaparte for his sister Pauline
entered not a little into the motives for this wholesale
method of enriching her husband.

Leclerc's instructions provided for everything; but it
was painful to remark that the appointment of one of the
youngest and most inefficient generals left no hope of a successful result.   The belief, too, is forced upon us, that no
other motive determined the First Consul's choice save the
desire of getting rid of, by enriching, a brother-in-law who
possessed, at least, the talent of being utterly displeasing to
him.   The inconceivable influence held over him by the
members of his own family constantly asserted itself.   The
St. Domingo expedition is one of the grand faults committed
by Bonaparte: every one consulted dissuaded him from it.
Hence, he has deemed justification necessary through his

organs at St. Helena: but has he succeeded, by asserting to his historians there "that he was obliged to yield to the advice of his council of state?" Was he the man to submit to a council the discussion, far less the dictation, of a warlike enterprise?

Bonaparte dictated to me, for Toussaint, a letter containing the most honorable expressions and flattering promises. He sent back, also, his two sons, who had completed their education at Paris, with an offer of the vice-governorship, provided Toussaint would lend his aid to bring back the colony to the mother country. This chief, either dreading deception or entertaining more ambitious views, resolved on war, after, for a moment, having shown some inclination toward an arrangement. He was easily reduced by an army yet vigorous, well conditioned, and warlike. He capitulated and retired to a plantation, whence he was not to remove without permission from Leclerc. A pretended conspiracy furnished the pretext for sending him a captive to France. Placed, at first provisionally, in the Temple prison, on arriving in Paris, he was afterward incarcerated in the Château de Jou, under rigorous confinement. This, so different from his former habits, the change of climate, and his recollections of the past, were sufficient to shorten his days without recourse to poison—a report unworthy of credence. Toussaint, I ought to say, did write to the First Consul; but I never saw the expressions attributed to him— "Toussaint, first man of the blacks, to the first man of the whites." Bonaparte acknowledged him to be possessed of energy, courage, and great talent. I am certain he would have rejoiced in a different conclusion of relations with St. Domingo than this kidnapping and sudden deportation. Probably, too, another than Leclerc would have brought Toussaint to reconcile the interests of the colony, and the rights of humanity, with the claims of the mother country, moderated as these had become through time and events. The yellow fever, which carried off Leclerc, spread its ravages among the army: desertion became general. Ro-

chambeau succeeded Leclerc, and, by his severity, completed
the loss of the colony. He abandoned the island to Dessa-
lines, and gave himself up to an English squadron in 1803.
Thus terminated this unfortunate expedition, which cost us
a fine army, and of which the original expense was furnished
by the plunder of the navy chest for the support of invalids.
This sacrilegious spoliation boded no good. Unable to
wrest liberty from the colony by force, we have sold it. Will
the colony pay? I answer beforehand—No.

Bonaparte often suffered from extreme pain, and I have
now no doubt from the nature of his sufferings that these
already originated in the commencement of the complaint
of which he died at St. Helena. The pains, of which he
almost constantly complained, affected him with more than
usual severity during the night, while dictating to me the
instructions for General Leclerc. I led him to his apartment
at a very late hour. We had just taken a cup of chocolate,
as usual at all times when our labors extended to one
o'clock in the morning. He always ascended to his chamber
without a light, being well acquainted with the passage
through his very neat library. He was leaning on my arm.
Scarcely had we left the small staircase leading into the
corridor, when an individual, making at full speed for
the stair, ran violently against the First Consul, who was
supported from falling by clinging to me. On reaching
his chamber, we found Josephine, who had heard the noise,
awake and greatly alarmed. Inquiries, immediately set on
foot, proved the aggressor to be simply one who, having
like a fool exceeded the proper time for such manœuvre,
was retreating from an amorous appointment. The meeting,
as may well be supposed, did not take place—at least at
Malmaison. It was thought unnecessary to take any precautions beyond having the corridor better lighted, and
the unlucky issue of this assignation only spoiled others
of the same kind.

It was on the 7th January, 1802, the evening previous to
the departure for the convocation at Lyons, that the mar-

riage of Mademoiselle Hortense with Louis Bonaparte took place. At this period, as the practice had not yet been resumed of joining to the civil act the nuptial benediction, the religious rite was performed in the private domicile, Rue Victoire, where a priest attended for this purpose. At the same time, Bonaparte caused the marriage of Caroline, performed by the magistrate two years before, to be also religiously solemnized. He did not follow this example; from what motives does not appear. Did he already entertain ideas of a divorce, which the sanction of religion would have rendered more difficult? or was his conduct the result of an indifference not experienced in the case of the others? It could not proceed from fear of being accused of weakness, since he thus revived the ancient usage where both his sister and daughter-in-law were concerned? The few words I heard from him on the subject evinced perfect indifference.

Napoleon has said, at St. Helena, speaking of Louis and Hortense, "Their union arose from attachment: each was respectively the other's choice. As to the rest, this marriage was the result of Josephine's intrigues, who found her advantage therein." I shall clear up these facts, here somewhat misrepresented. Louis and Hortense were by no means attached: this is certain. The First Consul knew it, as he was also well aware of Hortense's decided preference for Duroc, who did not return her affection with equal warmth. The First Consul consented to their union, but Josephine looked forward to the marriage with much pain; she exerted all her efforts to prevent its conclusion; and often spoke to me of it, though, unfortunately, somewhat late. "My two brothers-in-law," she would say, "are my most determined enemies; you see all their intrigues, and know how much uneasiness they have caused me; this projected marriage will leave me without any support. Besides Duroc, independent of Bonaparte's friendship, is nothing; he has neither fortune, rank, nor even reputation; he cannot be a safeguard to me against the declared enmity of the brothers: I must

have some more certain reliance for the future. My husband loves Louis very much; if I can succeed in uniting
my daughter to him, he will prove a strong counterpoise to
the calumnies and persecutions of my other brothers-in-law."
I replied, that she had too long concealed her intentions
from me; that I had promised my services to the young
people the more willingly knowing the favorable sentiments
of the First Consul, who had often said to me, "My wife
labors in vain; they suit each other; they shall be married.
I love Duroc; he is well born. I have properly given
Caroline to Murat, and Pauline to Leclerc; I can as well
give Hortense to Duroc, who is a brave fellow. He is as
good as the others—he is general of division—there can be
no objection to their union. Besides, I have other plans
for Louis." I added, in my conversation with Madame
Bonaparte, that her daughter burst into tears when a marriage with Louis was even mentioned.

The First Consul, indeed, had caused to be expedited,
by an extraordinary courier, the brevet of a general of
division to Duroc, in order to meet him as he returned
through Holland from St. Petersburg, whither he had been
sent, as already stated, to compliment the Emperor Alexander on his accession. This piece of politeness had its
probable origin in the prospect of the marriage taking place.
During this absence, the correspondence of the youthful
lovers had passed through my hands, at their own request.
Almost every evening I made one of a party at billiards
with Mademoiselle Hortense, who played extremely well.
When I whispered to her "*I have a letter,*" the game quickly
ceased; she ran to her chamber, where I followed, and delivered the note. Her eyes filled with tears, and she did
not descend again to the saloon till long after I had returned
thither. All was without result for her: Josephine required
in the family a support *against* the family. Seeing her so
firmly bent on this resolution, I engaged no longer to oppose
her views, of which I could not disapprove, but pointed out
to her that it was no longer possible for me to preserve

silence and neutrality in these domestic debates. She appeared satisfied. During our stay at Malmaison intriguing continued. I mention no details; it was always the same scenes—the same irresolutions. On our return to the Tuileries, things were in similar condition; but probabilities favored Duroc. I even offered him my congratulations, which he received with wonderful coolness. In a few days, Madame Bonaparte, absolutely resolved on the marriage of her daughter with Louis, contrived to change the whole face of affairs, and to bring over the First Consul to her opinion. On the 4th of January, after dinner, he entered our study where I was at work. "Where is Duroc?"— "Gone out—I believe to the opera."—"Tell him, as soon as he returns, that I have promised him Hortense: he shall marry her. But I wish that this take place at latest in two days. I will give him 500,000 francs. I name him commandant of the eighth military division. He must set out for Toulon, with his wife, the day after his marriage, and we shall live separate. I will have no son-in-law in the same house with me. As I wish the affair settled, send me word, this same evening, if this suits him."—"I don't think it will."—"Very well; she shall marry Louis."—"Will she have him?"—"She must have him."

Till toward the middle of 1801, those emigrants proposed for removal from the list had always been named by the minister of police. The First Consul having obtained proof that such erasures were often due to urgent solicitation, to favor, to intrigue, and even purchased by money, decided on concentrating this department of business in his own study. Other affairs, however, suffered from this tedious labor, which, in spite of all my exertions, produced not above ten or twelve erasures weekly. I brought this repeatedly under his notice. At first he paid no attention to my remarks. Soon after the "Te Deum" had been celebrated for the Concordat and the Peace, I profited by a moment of good humor and benevolence, in which he seemed to be at Malmaison, to hazard anew the proposal of a general return of emigrants. "You have," said I laughing, "reconciled the French to God: reconcile them to each other. There never have been true lists of emigrants, there have been only lists of absentees: as a proof of this, we have been going on·constantly erasing, and may continue the same occupation to the end of time." He embraced the idea. "Good!" said he, "we will consider it; but I must except one thousand individuals of the principal families, especially those who have held offices in the establishments of the kings or princes, or at the old court." The number of exceptions was afterward reduced to one half.

Having completed the schedule of his decree, the First Consul convoked, for the following day, a grand council, composed of the ministers, the two consuls, and five others of the chief public functionaries. I remained in the cabinet attached to the library, and which communicated with the circular saloon, in which the council assembled. The discussion was long and warm. I heard the whole, for they spoke very loud; sometimes, in fact, shouted. The First Consul combated, forcibly, the numerous objections urged against his proposal. He was answered with equal warmth. In the sequel, the Revolution rejected all restitutions. She consented, indeed, to recall her victims, but determined to retain their spoils.

On returning to our study, the First Consul was completely engrossed with the bad effect produced upon the council by the proposal of a decree such as the one just deliberated upon. I took the liberty of saying to him, "You have too much good sense, General, not to perceive that your scheme has failed. The refusal to restore to the emigrants what may still remain in possession of the state, destroys, with this concession, all that is noble, or grand, or generous, in their recall. I cannot conceive how you yielded to an opposition so unreasonable and so grasping." —"How is this?" said he, still in anger. "You must have overheard all. The Revolution had the majority in the council; what would you have had me do? Am I strong

enough to overcome all these obstacles?''—''General, calm
yourself, I wish not to pain you; but you are quite able to
return to the attack, and to oppose these people.''—''That
will be difficult,'' replied he, softening a little. ''I repeat,
they have still the upper hand in these affairs; time is necessary for all that. Besides, nothing is definitely fixed: we
shall see.'' Fifteen days after this conversation was decreed
the *Senatus Consultum* of the 6th Floreal, year X. (April
26, 1802). That act, as is well known, granted the recall
but refused the restitution of property. We have just seen
what were the intentions of the Chief of the State; but once
more he was constrained to yield to the Revolution: Bonaparte would otherwise have adhered to his original design.

From the commencement of the same year, 1802, Napoleon began to feel violent pain in his right side. I have
often seen him at Malmaison, in the evening, while at work,
and when midnight approached, recline on the right arm of
the sofa, unbutton his coat and vest, and give vent to a sob
of anguish. If I spoke to him, he generally replied, ''How
I suffer!'' A few minutes after I would conduct him to his
bedroom. I have several times been obliged to support him
on the small stair which led from the inner cabinet to the
corridor leading from his apartments. It was at this period
that he used to say, ''I have an apprehension that, on attaining forty years, I shall become a great eater; I feel the presentiment of an excessive corpulence.'' This fear caused
him much disquiet, in which, as I told him, it was impossible to participate. I was mistaken. Some six months
before he had inquired who was my physician; I replied,
''M. Corvisart.''—''How did you get acquainted with him?''
—''Your brother, Louis, recommended him to me: to
him he is indebted for the cure of the complaint with
which, as you know, he was afflicted. He places great
confidence in him.'' A few days after he took Corvisart
for his medical attendant, and, three years after, appointed
him first physician to the Emperor. The Consul speedily
became accustomed to this gentleman, and, in my time,

always saw him with pleasure come to chat a little: his open
and good-humored manner pleased him much. Corvisart
frankly acknowledged that medicine could do little for him,
and that the little which it could effect would arise more
from regimen than from drugs.

The pain experienced by the First Consul increased his
irritability. Perhaps to this cause may be attributed many
acts of this period of his life: his ideas were then no longer
the same in the evening as they had been in the forenoon,
and very often he tore up in the morning, even without the
smallest remark, notes which he had dictated to me during
the night, and considered excellent. Sometimes even I took
upon me not to send to the "Moniteur," as he desired, remarks which, dictated at night under irascibility and suffering, might have produced a bad effect throughout Europe.
When he did not see the article on the morrow, I alleged,
as excuse, the lateness of the hour, or the delay of the
courier: "But there is nothing lost," I used to say, "to-
morrow will do as well." He did not reply directly, but
remarked, probably a quarter of an hour afterward, "Don't
send my note to the 'Moniteur' before showing it to me,"
and was sometimes astonished at what he had dictated, saying in a good-humored way, "Pshaw! you must surely have
misunderstood me"—or, "This is not *too* good, is it?"—
"By my faith, I can't say *too*."—"Oh! no, it is good for
nothing; what say you?" Then, with a slight shake of the
head, he would tear up the paper. He sent me once, at two
o'clock in the morning (we were then at the Tuileries),
a note in his own hand, running thus:

"For Bourrienne.—Write to Maret to erase from the note
which Fleurieu read at the Tribunate the phrase relative
to Costaz. Soften, as much as possible, what has reference
to the report of the proceedings."

Such changes were often made in consequence of sug-
gestions of mine, which, at the time, he had rejected with
impatience.

In 1802, Jerome had arrived at the rank of *Enseigne de Vaisseau*, and, finding himself at Brest, indulged in expenses far above his fortune and the appointments of his place— expenses which he could liquidate only by charging them to the state. He often drew upon me, by letters of exchange, which the First Consul accepted with many angry remarks. One of these letters, in which Jerome described his pleasures, and the entertainments given him, and then announced that he had drawn upon me for 17,000 francs, excited the choler of the First Consul, who wrote to him:

"I have your letter, M. Enseigne de Vaisseau. I am displeased to find you on board your corvette, studying a profession which ought to be the theatre of your glory. Die young, and I shall be pacified. But I shall not be, if you live sixty years without fame—without being useful to the country—without having left traces of your existence. Better would it be never to have existed.—Paris, 6 Messidor, year X. [27th June, 1802].—For Jerome, Enseigne de Vaisseau."

The above letter contradicts positively what has been published in the biographies—that Jerome Bonaparte served, in 1801, as lieutenant in the expedition against St. Domingo. He sailed on board "L'Epervier," after reception of his brother's letter, only as lieutenant. On the 23d November he wrote to me as follows:

"This is to inform you, my dear Bourrienne, that I have drawn upon you, by bill of exchange, for *twenty thousand francs.* I have written to the Consul by the last ship, and without doubt he has spoken to you about it. At St. Pierre I met with an old friend of yours, General Castella, in command there, and with whom I remained till the 18th Brumaire, having passed only seven days at *Fort de France.* Adieu, my dear B. I embrace you.　　J. BONAPARTE."

"P.S.—All the Europeans, my dear Bourrienne, die in this country. Here I have already twenty-three men less in my corvette, which is a very bad vessel; judge, after this, whether I can be at ease on board 'L'Epervier.' To-night I prepare for a trip to the English islands: that voyage will keep me from twenty to thirty days at sea. Adieu, my dear B. I embrace you."

Jerome never answered either the hopes or the wishes of his brother, who seldom gave him another name than *a dirty little rascal.* We have just seen his conduct as a naval ensign. From the earliest years of his life he had been a cause of sorrow to his brother and the whole family. Westphalia will never forget that he was her king; nor without reason did *his people* call him a *miniature of Heliogabalus.*

Speaking generally, the First Consul was harassed by the continual craving of his brothers for money. To finish with Joseph, he made M. Collot commissary of provisions for the navy, under condition of remitting yearly to Joseph, from the income of his situation, 1,500,000 francs. Lucien had feathered his nest in Spain. I believe this commissariat, which continued only for a short time, turned out very well for Joseph, but proved a bad speculation for M. Collot, who was very irregularly and very ill paid, while the stipulation of the Consul left him no means of repaying himself. He demanded an audience, which, through the interference of Junot, was granted. As usual, where a third man was required as witness, the *vous resterez,* "you will remain," was addressed to me on this occasion. M. Collot came to Malmaison: it was in the evening. He spoke to the First Consul with dignified firmness, exposed his wrongs and complained of the condition in which he was left, and of the enormous encumbrance with which he had been burdened. He explained that already several millions were owing on a service of from 20,000,000 to 24,000,000 francs, and gave it clearly to be understood that the articles furnished were necessarily overcharged on Joseph's account. The First Consul replied, with intemperate violence—"Eh! —for what do you take me? Think you I am a Capuchin? I had to give 100,000 crowns to Decrès, 100,000 to Duroc, 100,000 to Bourrienne, you ought to take measures to pay yourself and not come troubling me with such stuff. I have ministers: it is for them to render me an account. I will see Decrès; enough at present. Leave me and dun me no more with your bills: I have nothing to do with such affairs."

In April, 1802, the First Consul bent all his efforts toward getting himself declared Consul for life. We shall revert to the actual proceedings hereafter. This, perhaps, was the epoch in his career during which were most completely developed those principles of falsehood and dissimulation, commonly called maxims of Machiavel. Never have stratagem, untruth, craft, seeming moderation been practiced with more talent or success. Lucien was the most violent propagator of the doctrines of hereditary power and the stability of a dynasty—phrases which, since the month of March, had engrossed all conversation. M. de Talleyrand, whose ideas *could not be* anything save monarchical, held the cabinets of Europe in train. Bonaparte branded as ideologists and terrorists the real friends of constitutional liberty. Rœderer, Régnault d'Angely and Fontanes followed with zeal and constancy the same apostleship as Lucien. Madame Bonaparte courageously opposed the influence of those counsels which she regarded as fatal to her husband. The latter very seldom spoke confidentially with her about politics or public affairs. "Let her mind her spinning and knitting," was his usual observation.

While the First Consul thus aspired to the throne of France, his brothers, and especially Lucien, affected a superciliousness and pretensions perfectly ridiculous. The following is an instance, almost incredible, but which I witnessed· On Sunday, the 9th May, Lucien paid a visit to Madame Bonaparte, who asked, "Why did you not come to dinner last Monday?"—"Because there was no place appointed for me. the brothers of Bonaparte ought to have the chief seats after him."—"What do I hear!" replied Josephine; "but if you *are* Bonaparte's brother, recollect what you *were*. In my presence, all places are equal. Eugene would never have made so ill-mannered a proposal."

During the negotiations at Campo-Formio we have seen that Bonaparte was occupied in another, and, by his own account, even more difficult mission—obtaining the liberation of the prisoners at Olmütz. Since that period M. de La

Fayette had remained in a neutral country, refusing to participate in those measures adopted in France after the 18th Fructidor. He had, indeed, been received by the First Consul after the battle of Marengo. On that occasion Bonaparte discoursed above two hours with him in private, and, when he was gone, I remember the latter said to me—"There is nothing to be done with him; I am vexed at it; he will listen to nothing. He is a man whose principles are estimable, but they are mixed up with some obstinacy and much exaggeration." A short time thereafter, on the occasion of the fête given to the Americans, La Fayette accepted Joseph's invitation to be present. Though an offer of a place in the senate was subsequently declined, he continued, notwithstanding, to visit the First Consul and to maintain an intercourse of reciprocal esteem. The epoch of the consulate for life put an end to these amicable relations. On this question La Fayette refused his vote; and, in justification, addressed to Bonaparte the following letter:

"GENERAL—When a man, deeply sensible of the gratitude he owes you, and too feelingly alive to fame not to love yours, places restrictions on his suffrage, these are so much the less liable to suspicion, that none will more rejoice to see you First Magistrate for life of a free republic. The 18th Brumaire saved France, and I at this moment enjoy the blessings of home through the liberal policy to which you have pledged your honor. Since then we have beheld the consular power, that healing dictatorship which, under the auspices of your genius, has accomplished so great things, less great, however, than will be the restoration of liberty. It is impossible that you, General, the foremost in that order of men, whom to compare and to place we must pass in review of all ages, can desire that such a revolution—so many victories and so much blood—numberless sorrows and exertions—should leave for the world, and for you, no other result save arbitrary rule. The French people were too well acquainted with their rights to have forgotten them beyond recall; but they are to-day, perhaps, in a better condition than during their excitement to retrieve them usefully; and you, by the influence of your character and the public confidence—by the superiority of your talents, of your station,

of your fortune—are able, in re-establishing liberty, to provide against all dangers, and to dispel all anxieties. I can,
then, have only patriotic and personal motives for desiring
that you may establish, to your own glory, a permanent magistracy. But it comports with my principles, with my engagements, with the actions of my whole life, to pause before giving my voice to such a measure, until it be founded
on a basis worthy of the nation, and of you. General, I
hope you will herein discover, as you must have already
perceived, that with the integrity of my political principles
are united sincere attachment to your person, and a profound
sense of my obligations to you.—Health and respect.

"LA FAYETTE."

To this letter was subjoined the following note:

"Shall Napoleon Bonaparte be Consul for life? I cannot
vote for such a magistracy, until political liberty be sufficiently guaranteed; then I give my voice to Napoleon
Bonaparte."

The First Consul, as may be imagined, was not at all
pleased with the scruples of M. de La Fayette. He read
his letter with impatience, and afterward remarked to me
—"I have often told you M. de La Fayette is a political
monomatist—an obstinate person. He does not comprehend
me: I am very sorry for it; for he is an honorable man. I
wished to make him a senator; he has refused; truly so
much the worse for him. I can very well afford to do without his vote." In discoursing on the consular government
of the United States, on their triennial consulate, as well
as the new liberty of consular France, Bonaparte and La
Fayette, as may well be supposed, differed in opinion: even
the manner in which the latter had re-entered France grievously displeased the former. "I left my country when liberty fled, and I return with her," said La Fayette; "for she
has returned, since Napoleon is her high-priest." And,
sooth to say, Napoleon found it very bad in the apostle of
American liberty to return to his *diocese* without a passport!

But not only on these topics did La Fayette oppose the
ideas of the First Consul; he found fault with the Concordat

also. He would have wished that Bonaparte, permitting
equal liberty to all religions, had kept them all, as in the
United States, entirely without the support of government
—the followers of each sect maintaining their own church,
and paying their own clergy. I recollect, on this occasion,
how Bonaparte said to me—"La Fayette is perhaps right in
theory; but what is it beyond mere theory—a folly when
applied to masses of men! And then he is constantly harping upon America, as if the French were Americans! The
French he does not understand. Among them the Catholic
religion is paramount; and, besides, I need the Pope, who
will do anything I desire. Do you know," continued the
Consul, smiling, "La Fayette made use of a strange expression: he said, 'You seem to have a desire *of getting the little
fiddle broken over your head.'* We shall see—we shall see."
And, in effect, we have seen.

CHAPTER XV

Bernadotte—Bonaparte's Private Theatre—Dismissal of Fouché—Quarrel with
Lannes—Difference with Bourrienne—The Consulate for Life

I SHALL now revert to some facts which had either
escaped my recollection, or which I reserved in order
to class them with analogous events. My first retro-
spections concern a man called, by the inexplicable combination of events, to a throne, and who still governs for the
happiness of his people. Bernadotte, we have seen, necessarily fell into disgrace, by refusing to second the designs
of Bonaparte for the overthrow of the Directory. Neither
were there wanting tale-bearers and their tales to maintain
or to heighten the animosity which this opposition had inspired. This enmity the First Consul could not venture
at first to display openly; but he watched every occasion of
removing Bernadotte to a distance, placing him in difficult
positions, and giving him missions without any precise in-

structions, in hopes that by the commission of faults he would draw upon himself all the responsibility. In the first period of the consulate, the deplorable war of La Vendée raged in all its intensity. The organization of the Chouans was complete, and the anxiety caused to Bonaparte by this civil war exceeded that from the side of the Rhine or of Italy, because by its success his internal government and ulterior views would be more affected. The mission, then, of putting an end to the struggle was a difficult one; but, for that very reason, Bonaparte resolved on consigning it to Bernadotte. The conciliatory measures of that general, however, his chivalrous manners, and a happy mixture of prudence and address, enabled him to succeed where others had failed: He finally established good order, and submission to the laws.

Some time after the pacification of La Vendée, an insurrectional movement manifested itself at Tours, where the fifty-second regiment refused to march till the men had received their arrears of pay. Bernadotte, Commander-in-Chief of the Army of the West, without showing any surprise at such insubordination, merely gave orders that the regiment should draw up in the square at Tours; then at the head even of the corps, he caused the ringleaders to be arrested, without one daring to offer resistance. This bold measure Bonaparte first blamed in a note added to the report; but was subsequently obliged to give it tardy and indirect praise.

Time augmented more and more Bonaparte's resentment against Bernadotte, and the go-betweens and flatterers were not idle in their insinuations concerning the latter. One day, on which a grand public reception was to take place, I saw the First Consul in such a state of impatient ill humor as induced me to ask the cause. "I can no longer endure it," replied he with violence: "I am resolved on an explanation this day with Bernadotte. He will probably be here. I will break the ice, come what may. He may do his worst, but we shall see. It is time that this were ended." **Never**

had I seen him so angry, and dreaded the meeting accordingly. When he retired, before descending to the grand
saloon of audience, I took advantage of a moment to descend
before him, which was easily accomplished, since the saloon
was not twenty paces from the study. By good luck, the
very first person I saw was Bernadotte alone in the embrasure of a window looking into the Carroúsel. Rapidly to
cross the hall and to approach him was the work of an instant. "General, believe me, you had better retire; I have
strong reasons for advising you thus." Bernadotte, seeing
my extreme anxiety and knowing the sincere sentiments of
esteem and friendship which attached me to him, consented
to retire. This I regarded as a triumph; for, certainly,
from the frankness of Bernadotte's character and his quick
sense of honor, he would not have borne the cutting remarks
which Bonaparte appeared in the humor to address to him.
My stratagem had all the success I could have hoped.
Nothing was suspected. One thing only attracted notice—
the victim had escaped. After the audience, the First
Consul on entering exclaimed, "Can you conceive it, Bourrienne? Bernadotte did not come."—"So much the better
for him, General," I merely said. Nothing ensued; for,
on reascending, after a momentary absence in Josephine's
apartments, he found me in the cabinet as if I had never
left it, five minutes sufficing for my little negotiation.
Bernadotte always showed himself sincerely grateful for
this proof of friendship; and, in truth, from a feeling I cannot well explain to myself, the more I beheld Bonaparte's
unjust hatred increase, the greater became my interest in the
noble character which was its object.

The scene just mentioned occurred in the spring of 1802.
At this date the First Consul had established himself at St.
Cloud—a residence to which he was very partial, as there
enjoying more freedom than at the Tuileries, where it is
impossible for the sovereign even to breathe the air at a
window without immediately becoming the object of public
curiosity and attracting the gaze of multitudes. At St.

Cloud he could leave his cabinet when he chose, and prolong his walk without fear of importunate solicitations. One of his first cares was to order the repairing of a cross-road conducting to Malmaison—a distance which he usually traversed in a quarter of an hour. This proximity to his favorite country house rendered St. Cloud still more agreeable. Here, too, so to speak, he made the first rehearsals of the grand drama of empire; here he commenced with introducing, in external forms, the customs and etiquette which pertain to the usages of royalty. He quickly observed what influence may be exercised over the mass of mankind by the pomp of ceremonies, the splendor of audiences and richness of costume. "How deserving," he would say, "are men of the contempt they inspire! All my virtuous republicans, forsooth!—I have only to gild their livery, and they are my humble servitors."

From the first months of the year 1802, the republic had been but a name—a historical reminiscence. There remained, indeed, a lying inscription over the gates of the palace, but both the trees of liberty erected in the court Bonaparte had caused to be cast down, even before his instalment in the Tuileries—proceeding thus against vain symbols before attacking realities. After the *Senatus Consultum*, however, of the 2d and 4th of August, it was apparent to the least clear-sighted that there no longer wanted anything to complete the sovereign power of the First Consul, save a designation. On the passing of the decrees, indeed, Bonaparte readily came to regard the different bodies of the legislature merely as so many instruments necessary to the exercise of power. Still he found the pear not yet ripe for the full development of his ulterior projects of sovereignty, with its forms and privileges. "All that will come," said he one day: "but look you, Bourrienne, it is requisite, in the first place, that I myself assume a title, whence will naturally flow all other honors, which I shall confer on these people about us. The greatest difficulty is surmounted; there is no longer anybody to be deceived;

all the world sees as clear as day that there is but one step from the consulship for life to the throne. Some management is yet necessary; there are still refractory spirits in the Tribunate—but they shall pay for it."

At Malmaison we had also our company and our dramatic entertainments, and everything was conducted with the greatest decorum: and since we are on the subject, I may as well introduce the reader behind the scenes. The First Consul had given orders to construct for our use a very pretty theatre. Our ordinary troop consisted of Eugene Beauharnais, his sister Hortense, Madame Murat, Lauriston, Didelot, prefect of the palace, and myself. Forgetting the cares of government, which we left as much as possible behind at the Tuileries, we were often very happy in our colony at Malmaison. At that time, too, we were young; and what does not youth embellish?

The pieces which the First Consul liked best to see us perform were "The Barber of Seville" and "Defiance and Malice." Our list contained also "Proposals of Marriage," "The Wager," "Lovers' Quarrels," where I was the *Valet*, and "Rural Wit," in which I played the *Baron*, having for *Baroness* the young and beautiful Caroline Murat. Hortense played exceedingly well, Caroline tolerably, Eugene very well, Lauriston was a little heavy, Didelot so so, and, be it said without vanity, I was not the worst of the company.

We possessed, in theatrical phrase, an establishment, in point of scenery and decorations, admirably arranged. Bonaparte had presented to each a collection of pieces, beautifully bound, and, as the natural patron of our troop, had caused to be procured rich and elegant dresses. He took great pleasure in our performances. He liked to see plays acted by those with whom he was intimate. Sometimes he even complimented us on our exhibition. Although the thing amused me quite as much as the others, I was more than once obliged to observe to him that my occupations left me no time to study my parts. On this he would assume one of his most coaxing moods and say, "Come,

now, that's a good fellow: you have such a memory! you
know it amuses me: you see very well these assemblies
render Malmaison quite gay: Josephine is very partial to
them. Rise earlier in the morning. Really, I sleep a great
deal—now is it not so?—Come, come, Bourrienne, do oblige
me in this; you all make me laugh so heartily! Don't
deprive me of this pleasure: you know very well I have
not too much amusement. Ah! upon my word, it is not
me alone that you will deprive of enjoyment."—"I am
charmed to have the power of contributing to your amusement," I would feel constrained to reply, and I set to work
to learn my parts.

On the days we played, the company at Malmaison was
always very numerous. After the play, the apartments
were crowded. The most animated and varied conversations took place, and gayety and ease formed the soul and
charm of the whole. Refreshments of all kinds were in
profusion, and Josephine did the honors with so much kindness that no one felt himself overlooked. After these delightful parties, which usually broke up about midnight,
the company returned to Paris, where the cares of business
awaited us.

It is a maxim especially applicable to absolute governments, that a prince ought as seldom as possible to change
his ministers and never save for weighty reasons. In the
business of administration, experience goes a great way.
The First Consul acted upon these principles, which were
also those of the Emperor; often he yielded to unjust causes,
but never dismissed a minister without cause. Sometimes
even he carried these views too far and retained for a space
those whom he ought to have superseded.

In his agents, and in men generally, Bonaparte beheld
only means and obstacles. On the 18th Brumaire, Fouché
had been a means; it was now feared he might become an
obstacle: it was necessary, therefore, to think of getting rid
of him. Bonaparte's most sincere friends had from the
commencement opposed this man's admission into the gov-

ernment; but their own disgrace had been the only result of their disinterested counsels, so influential a personage had Fouché become. How could it be otherwise? Fouché had retained power under the Republic by the death of the king for which he voted—under the Reign of Terror, by his bloody atrocities at Lyons and Nevers—under the Consulate, by his real services, although these were a little exaggerated —with Bonaparte by the charm, so to speak, by which he had fascinated him—and with Josephine through the enmity of the First Consul's brothers. In all Paris—throughout all France—there prevailed a belief in Fouché's extraordinary ability; and the opinion was so far well grounded that no one has ever shown himself so skilful in persuading the world to regard him as a man of talent. His secret in this particular is the secret of the greater part of those who are termed statesmen.

Be it as it may, the First Consul regarded with no favorable eye the peculiar influence which Fouché had contrived to acquire. To the repugnance always lurking at bottom against the minister were now joined other causes of discontent, and his dismissal was resolved. Yet even thus, Bonaparte, still under the spell, dared not proceed, except with circumspection: when he spoke of him it was with violent bitterness; Fouché present, the tone became softened. Adopting the abolition of the office as preparatory to the removal of the functionary, who had been minister of police since the 18th Brumaire, the First Consul proposed to Fouché this abolition, which he represented still distant, merely as a proof to the people of the security and tranquillity of the government. Unable to allege any reasonable objection, Fouché stipulated for two years longer as necessary to establish completely the political security of the government, hoping in that time to add *enough* to his already enormous wealth—for he was no less greedy of gold than his master of glory, equally ambitious of increasing the limits of the estate of Pont Carré, as the latter of extending the boundaries of France.

The determination thus formed to suppress the administration of police, Bonaparte would not wait the delay which he had feigned as conceding to be necessary. On Saturday, the 12th September, we set out for Mortfontaine, and there, on the Monday, pressed by the united instances of Lucien and Joseph, he signed the decree of abolition. On our return to Paris on the morrow, Fouché came to Malmaison as usual, to transact business; the First Consul could not decide to inform him of his dismissal, and afterward deputed Cambacérès to announce it. Endeavoring still further to soften the blow, he wrote to the Senate, of which he had appointed the ex-minister a member:

"In difficult circumstances, Citizen Fouché, by his talents, activity and attachment to the government, has shown himself equal to all contingencies. Placed in the bosom of the Senate, should circumstances again require a minister of police, the government will not find one more worthy of confidence."

This letter the subject of the eulogium even regarded as a promise, and thenceforward all his subterranean batteries had but one aim—that of forcing Bonaparte to realize it. We shall see in the sequel with what success these efforts were attended. The aversion, too, of Bonaparte, had strangely blinded him in the means selected for replacing this dangerous engine. For the administrations of justice and police being united, two departments, most discordant, were placed in the hands of Régnier. The minister of the former, Abrial, so honorably preferred, as already mentioned, was in equal honor dismissed to the Senate, with these words: "The police being joined to the administration of justice, I cannot longer retain you in office; you are too honest a man for the police." A compliment this, by the way, not overflattering to Régnier, the new minister.

I have already spoken of the distresses of Josephine, who was much affected at the dismissal of Fouché, whom she looked upon as an adherent, and may here introduce some occurrences of which, about this period, Malmaison was the scene. Madame Louis Bonaparte was advanced in her first pregnancy, and Josephine, who tenderly loved her children, looked forward with that solicitude so natural to a mother's heart. She had long been aware of the calumnious reports respecting Hortense and the First Consul, which base accusation caused her many tears. Poor Josephine! how very dearly did she purchase that splendor in which she moved! Meanwhile Bonaparte, dazzled by the attachment then everywhere manifested toward him, aggravated this grief through a foolish infatuation. He endeavored to persuade her that these reports owed their publicity only to the wish formed by the French to see him a father. In this manner these intended consolations, addressed by self-love to maternal sorrow, rendered more acute the terrors of the wife by awakening anew the dread of a divorce.

Josephine's inquiries on this subject, at first timid, became more decided when the consulship for life had placed Bonaparte on the steps of the throne. I remember one day, about the period of the unseasonable publication of the famous "Parallel," that, having entered the study without being announced—a step she sometimes ventured upon when the good humor of the breakfast hour induced the hope of a continuance of sunshine—Josephine approached the First Consul very gently, seated herself on his knee, passed her fingers lightly through his hair and over his face, and, judging the moment favorable, exclaimed in a burst of tenderness: "Bonaparte, I beseech thee, do not make thyself king! It is that Lucien who urges thee to it: do not listen to him." Bonaparte answered, without unkindness, and even smiling—"Thou art foolish, my poor Josephine! It is thine old dowagers of the Faubourg St. Germain —thy Rochefoucaulds who tell thee all these tales. You interrupt me; leave me alone." I now remember, like an almost forgotten dream, that being sometimes constrained to witness certain small conjugal explanations such as the above was by no means the most agreeable function of the confidential secretary of the First Consul. What he

ˉthen said in a tone of kindly feeling, I had, in truth, heard him state in sober earnestness, and had been five or six times present during such altercations. Misunderstanding, too, on this question, undoubtedly reigned between the families of Beauharnais and Bonaparte. Fouché was, at this season, for Josephine, and Lucien one of her bitterest foes. One day, Rœderer broke out with such violence against Fouché, in presence of Madame Bonaparte, that she replied to him, with extreme bitterness—"The real enemies of Bonaparte are those who give him ideas of hereditary empire—of a dynasty—of divorce and marriage." The good Josephine could not contain herself, knowing Rœderer to be of that party, and a propagator of such opinions, under the training of Lucien.

In his dazzling progress the Consul neglected none of those means which were adapted at once for the gaze of the multitude, and to win the approbation of men of sense. Thus, he displayed sufficient attachment to the arts, and rightly judged that industry demanded the protection of the head of the state; but it must be acknowledged, at the same time, that he himself rendered sterile the very seeds he had sown, by denying them the free air of liberty, the only invigorating atmosphere. Yet had he reason to be proud of the exhibition made during this autumn of the pro-·ductions of national industry, which was held at the Louvre, under the direction of M. Chaptal. In particular, he enjoyed the admiration thus excited among foreigners, who, since the peace, had flocked in crowds to Paris. In fact, during the year 1802, the capital offered to the eye a new spectacle for a new generation, and, never, since the assembly of the States-General, had Paris presented a more gratifying aspect. The funds, too, that great thermometer of opinion, as he termed them, were equally satisfactory. If, after the 18th Brumaire, they had doubled in value—from seven to sixteen—they were now tripled even from that rise, having attained, on the institution of the consulate for life, to fifty-two.

With regard to our foreign relations, peace everywhere prevailed. The court of Rome, which since the Concordat had been, so to speak, at the service of the First Consul, exhibited under all circumstances proofs of adherence to the interests of France and compliance with the desires of her ruler. It had been the first to recognize the erection of Tuscany into the new kingdom of Etruria, as also the Helvetian, Cisalpine and Batavian republics. Prussia speedily followed this example, and the other powers of Europe in succession. All these new states, whether kingdoms or republics, were under the immediate influence of France. Piedmont, divided into six departments, was united to that country, and the news of a "Te Deum," chanted at Turin as a thanksgiving for this union, left Bonaparte in no doubt on the readiness with which Italy would bend beneath his yoke. The island of Elba, which his own banishment was subsequently to render so famous, also was under the shadow of the French republic. Thus all seemed to concur in the assurance of absolute power to the First Consul—the only kind of government of which he was able to form any idea. Although I had not been privy to his most secret thoughts, I should never, on this subject, have been mistaken as to his ulterior designs. One characteristic distinction of his government, even under the denomination of consular, gave no doubtful evidence of his intention. Had he designed to found a free constitution, it is quite evident he would have assigned to his ministers a personal responsibility, while, on the contrary, they were responsible to himself alone; he beheld in them only instruments, to be thrown aside at pleasure. This one circumstance sufficed to unveil his future intentions; and, better to conceal these, all government acts were signed only by M. Maret, the secretary of state. Thus the consulate for life was but a disguised empire, the usufruct of which did not long satisfy the First Consul's ambition. His brothers urged him on, and a new dynasty was resolved upon. But circumstances demanded caution and delay.

It was not only an absolute, but, much worse still, a military government also, which Bonaparte labored to establish in France. He conceived a decree, signed by his hand, to be endowed with some magic power, capable of at once transforming generals into able diplomatists; so they were appointed to embassies, as if to forewarn the different sovereigns that he would one day take their several crowns by storm. Among these military envoys appears Lannes, whose nomination to the court of Lisbon arose out of circumstances an account of which will not be read without interest, as displaying the character of Bonaparte and exhibiting the methods he disdained not to employ when desirous of removing even his most faithful friends as soon as their presence became inconvenient.

Bonaparte never *thee* and *thoued* Lannes, but Lannes continued the practice, and it is impossible to describe how unendurable to the former this persisting in kindly familiarity by one of his most valiant companions in arms became. The increasing power of the First Consul, every day demanding fresh sacrifices on the part of friends, made no change in the blunt frankness of Lannes, the last, in fact, who still dared to treat Bonaparte as an equal, or tell him the undisguised truth. There wanted nothing more to decide his banishment. But under what pretext remove the conqueror of Montebello? That must be contrived, and in this truly diabolical machination we shall see Bonaparte put in play that superabundance of craft with which he was so amply provided.

Lannes, careless of the morrow, prodigal of his gold as of his blood, gave away a great deal to poor officers and to his soldiers, whom he loved as children: his whole fortune thus consisted in the debts which he owed. When he wanted money, which often happened, he came quite simply to the Tuileries, and asked for so much of the First Consul, who, I must own, never refused him. Knowing his situation, Bonaparte said to him one day—"My good fellow, you must get settled in a manner befitting your rank. Let us see—rent the Hôtel de Noailles: order it to be furnished with becoming magnificence." Lannes, whose very openness prevented him from suspecting a thought in reserve, followed the advice of the First Consul. The house was engaged and splendidly fitted up. After having thus conformed to Bonaparte's instructions, the General came to ask him for 400,000 francs, being the amount of expenses incurred in some sort by his orders. "But," said the First Consul, "I have not the money."—"How, thou hast not the money! what the devil am I to do?"—"Is there none in the chest of the guard? Take what you want—we will arrange that." Ever without distrust, Lannes went to the treasurer of the guard, who at first made some difficulty, but yielded when he understood the consent of the First Consul to have been given. Not twenty-four hours afterward, the treasurer was called upon for his cash account, and Lannes' acknowledgment for the 400,000 francs refused, as not representing that sum. It was in vain that the treasurer alleged the authority of the First Consul: he had on a sudden lost all recollection of the matter—never gave such an order— where was it? It was quite clear Lannes must restore the money—and, as I said before, poor Lannes! he was rich only in debts. On this he went to Lefèbvre, who loved him as a pupil, and related all that had passed. "Awkward this," said Lefèbvre to him: "why didst thou not apply to me? Why hadst thou anything to do with that —— at the Tuileries? 'Sblood! there's the money: carry him his francs, and bid him be ——."

Lannes arrived in a fury at the apartments of the Consul. "How," cried he, "couldst thou condescend to such an unworthy act!—play me such a trick!—lay so disgraceful a trap for me, after all I have done for thee—after all the blood I have lavished to serve thine ambition! Is this all the recompense which thou reservest for me?—thou forgettest, then, the 18th Vendemiaire, when I did more than thou! Dost remember Millesimo? I was a colonel before thee. To serve thee, I again became a soldier—better I had remained a grenadier. For whom did I fight at Bassano? Thou sawest me at Lodi, at Governolo, where I was wounded— and yet playest me such a scurvy trick? But for me, Paris would have revolted on the 18th Brumaire: without me, thou wouldst not have gained the battle of Marengo. By myself alone—yes, alone—I passed the Po at Montebello, with my whole division, though you wished to give the honor to Berthier, who was not present. I—I have paid in my person to see myself disgraced! That cannot—shall not be. I must—" Bonaparte heard all this, motionless, and pale with rage: Lannes was on the point of challenging him, when Junot, attracted by the noise, rushed in hastily. His unexpected presence somewhat reassured the First Con-sul, and at.the same time calmed the general's fury. "Well, then," said Bonaparte, "go to Lisbon; you will make money there, and when you return will need no one to pay your debts." Thus was attained the object proposed. Lannes set off for Lisbon, tormented him no longer with familiarities, and, on returning, never used the obnoxious *thee* and *thou*.

It is not, I confess, unintentionally that I here record this scene: it conducts me naturally to the explanation of the true causes which led to my own separation from the First Consul. Always faithful to the law self-imposed, I shall dissemble nothing. Nine months previously I had offered my resignation; for the work had become too severe, and the confinement too unremitting for my health. The physician had, doubtless, spoken to the same effect with the First Consul; for the latter said to me one day, in a tone little soothing, "Why, Bourrienne, Corvisart tells me you have not a year to live." The compliment was not overkind on the part of an early friend; especially as the doctor's pre-diction seemed not unlikely to be fulfilled. I had formed the resolution of retiring, which was urged also by my family; but various considerations kept me in a state of uncertainty: of these, affection for the First Consul—a friend from seven years of age, and this friendship only interrupted once by Joseph's machinations—was not the least. An unforeseen occurrence ended my indecision.   On the 27th of February, at ten in the evening, Bonaparte dictated to me a diplomatic despatch of great importance and very urgent for M. de Talleyrand, who was, at the same time, directed to repair to the Tuileries at an hour mentioned.   According to established usage, I remitted this letter to the officer on duty, to be forwarded to the minister.   This was on a Saturday.   On the morrow, Sunday, M. de Talleyrand arrived, as if for audience, about midday.   The First Consul having immediately addressed him on the subject of the despatch was extremely surprised to find it had been received only that morning. He rang instantly for the attendant to call me.   As he was in very bad humor, he pulled the bell-rope with so much precipitation that he struck his knuckles violently against the corner of the chimney-piece.   I entered in all haste. "Why," cried he, addressing me abruptly, "why was my letter not delivered last night?"—"I know not; I gave it instantly to the functionary appointed to transmit all letters."—"Go, inquire about the delay, and return quickly." Having rapidly informed myself how matters stood, I returned to the cabinet: "Well?" said the First Consul, whose ill temper had rather increased than otherwise.— "Well, General, no one is in fault; M. de Talleyrand was to be found neither at the office, nor at home, nor in any of the circles he usually frequents."   Not knowing on whom to vent himself, restrained by the impassibility of Talleyrand, but choking with rage, Bonaparte started up, hurried from the cabinet, and went to interrogate the officer in waiting, which he did in an abrupt manner, putting the latter quite out, who stammered and replied incoherently, thus exciting more and more the irritation of the inquirer.   Seeing the Consul thus beside himself, I had followed, and, on his returning toward the cabinet, endeavored to pacify him, entreating him not to make so much noise about an affair which, after all, was not of such moment.   I know not if his violence arose from seeing the blood streaming from his fingers, at which he looked every instant, taking, as the

reader knows, great pride in his hands; but a most outrageous fury, such as I had never before witnessed, seized upon
him, and, as I was about to enter the cabinet at the same
time, he flung the door from him with such violence that
most infallibly, had I been two or three inches nearer, I
should have had my face broken. This almost convulsive
action he accompanied by a speech quite unbearable, calling
out to me in presence of M. de Talleyrand, "Leave me alone!
—you are a —— beast." At these unheard-of words, I confess the rage which filled the First Consul on a sudden fired
me also, and that, transported by a resolution, quick as lightning, I opened not less rudely than he had shut the door, and
cried, being really no longer in my senses, "You are a hundred times a greater beast than I!" This said, I shut the
door, and ascended to my own apartments on the floor above.

Such a separation was as far from my wishes as from my
expectation; but what was done could not be undone. I
seized the occasion, however, without leaving time for reflection, and, still trembling with excitement, wrote, in these
terms, the offer of my resignation—"General: The state of
my health permits me no longer to continue my service
near your person. I beg you to accept my resignation.—
BOURRIENNE."

Some minutes after, I saw from my windows saddle-
horses brought upon the terrace. This was contrary to
custom, Bonaparte seldom riding out on horseback on Sunday. Duroc accompanied him. I descended soon afterward to the study, and laid my letter on his table. Returning at four o'clock, and seeing it, he said to Duroc, before
breaking the seal—"Ah ha! a letter from Bourrienne," adding almost immediately—for to read the billet required brief
space—"He is in a pet—Accepted!" I had quitted the Tuileries at the moment of his return. Duroc sent me the following note, while at dinner: "The First Consul, my dear
Bourrienne, commands me to say that he accepts thy resignation and requests thee to inform me about his papers.
I embrace thee.—P.S. I shall call presently."

About eight o'clock he came for me. The First Consul was in the study when we entered. I immediately began to explain to Duroc the necessary arrangements. Piqued to find I did not speak to him, and at the coolness with which I talked to Duroc, Bonaparte addressed me in the harshest tones, "Have done, you ——! there is quite enough of that: leave me!" I leaped from the steps upon which I had mounted for the purpose of showing Duroc the situation of some papers, and retired instantly. I, too, had quite enough of that!

In looking out for a convenient domicile, two days more were passed at the Tuileries. On the Monday, I descended to the apartments of the First Consul, to offer my adieus. We conversed long and amicably together: he expressed regret that I was leaving him, and said he would do everything for me in his power. I mentioned several places; and finally hinted at the Tribunate. "That does not suit you," said he: "they are declaimers and speechifiers, whom I will send about their business. All the disturbances in other quarters proceed from the harangues of the Tribunate: I'll have no more of them." He went on in such a tone as left no doubt of the uneasiness caused him by this assembly, in whose ranks were to be found men of great talents and noble characters. In fact, during the same year, 1802, it was reduced to fifty members, and, somewhat later, entirely suppressed.

On the morrow (Tuesday) the First Consul asked me to breakfast with him. After breakfast, while he was conversing with some one, Madame Bonaparte and Hortense pressed me to make some advances, pointing out, with all the gentleness and kindly feeling they had ever shown, that I ought to do so, seeing I had also been wrong, and had forgotten myself. I replied that the evil seemed past remedy, and that, besides, I really required repose. At that moment, the First Consul called me and, in a long conversation, renewed his promises of kindness.

At five o'clock I was about to quit the Tuileries altogether, when I was informed the First Consul wished to see me. Duroc, who was in the antechamber leading into the cabinet, said, as I passed through—"My good fellow, he wants you to remain. I beseech thee not to refuse: do me this favor. I have declared to him that I cannot manage these affairs: I am not accustomed to them; and, between us, they are too annoying." I entered the cabinet without replying. The First Consul approached with a smile, and, taking me by the ear, as in his gracious moments, said: "What! still in the sulks?" and, in this way, conducted me to my usual place. "Come, seat yourself there." To judge of my situation, the reader must have known him. He had, when he chose, a most winning manner. I had not the power to resist: I could not even reply; and resumed my wonted tasks. A few minutes after, dinner was announced. "You will dine with me to-day?" said he. "I cannot; I am expected where I was going when you sent to call me: I cannot break my engagement."—"In that case, I have nothing more to say; but give me your word that you will be here at eight."—"I give it you." Thus, I found myself reinstated as confidential secretary of the First Consul, and believed our reconciliation sincere.

I now throw a retrospective glance over the most important acts of the consular government previous to the consulate for life.

The Tribunate had emitted the proposition that some *splendid mark* of public gratitude should be conferred upon the First Consul. This expression was indefinite, and it remained to show what this *splendid proof* should be. Bonaparte knew well what he himself desired; but determined, notwithstanding his impatience often prompted him, sword in hand, to seize the prize, not to commit himself. He resolved to have the appearance of yielding only to the necessities of France, and thus to enslave it, through excess of seeming love for the country. Such a combination could not have sprung up or been matured in a vulgar brain; but Bonaparte's was not fashioned like any other head. It required a most powerful volition to curb for a length of time the boldness so natural to him, and which resulted more from his temperament than from his character. I acknowledge, for my part, who so well knew him, that I always admired in him more the courage which he displayed in refraining till fitting season, than all the most audacious acts he ever performed.

According to form, the proposition of the Tribunate was transmitted to the Senate. Thenceforward the senators upon whom the Consul reckoned the most frequently appeared at the Tuileries. La Place, whom Bonaparte had deemed so incapable as a minister, and Lacepède, disputed for the palm of assiduity; but in that respect both these learned men were outdone by the two consular colleagues. On this occasion, Cambacérès, in particular, showed himself grateful for the license granted to transport, per mail, to Paris, the gastronomic products of France. But on sounding the minds of those who frequented the committees of rehearsal, preparatory to the full senatorial discussion, as it was discovered that the majority would not be for the consulate for life, it was agreed to limit the *splendid mark* to a prorogation of the consulate for ten years, in favor of the First Consul. Lacepède, the mover, took his measures accordingly and limited his motion to the appointment for ten years, commencing from the termination of the ten years already granted by the constitution. I have forgotten who proposed the question of the consulate for life, but this I recollect, that Cambacérès was eager in his assurances of its success. Bonaparte, on hearing these assertions, whether dictated by flattery or conviction, I cannot say, tossed his head with a gesture of impatience and doubt, and afterward remarked to me, "They will probably play off some grimaces, but to it they must come at last."

In the Senate, an attempt to have the question of the consulate for life first considered, failed; consequently, that of the decennality being passed, it became needless to discuss the former. There was something very curious in the

Senatus Consultum delivered on this occasion. The Senate, speaking in name of the French people, said that the act had been agreed upon "as an expression of the people's gratitude *to the Consuls* of the republic," though the consular reign was proposed to be prolonged in the person of the *First Consul* only. In fact, such an extension of power voted in favor of Cambacérès and Lebrun could only have been toward them an act of bitter mockery.

The First Consul, strongly dissatisfied as he felt with the decision of the Legislative Assembly, nevertheless veiled his discontent under ambiguous words. When Tronchet, at that time president, had read to him, in solemn audience, at the head of a deputation, the Decree of Prorogation, he replied, in a brief address, the last sentence of which was the only important one—"You consider that I owe to the people a new sacrifice of ease: I will make it, should the votes of the people command from me what your suffrage authorizes." He would not accept of the offer of the *Senate*, under a feigned respect for the wishes of the *People*, though, in reality, he refused because he wished more. Thus the question assumed a new form, and could not receive its decision save from the people; and since the people had the right of refusing what the Senate offered, they possessed, by that same admission, the power of granting what the Senate had not offered. Such were the calculations of Bonaparte, and they proved correct.

Things being thus disposed, the time had arrived for consulting the Council of State, in order to determine how the votes of the people should be solicited; what questions were to be submitted to them, and, finally, when their suffrages should be collected. Though a member, I never assisted at the deliberations of the Council. My avocations in the cabinet and delicate position with regard to the First Consul prevented me taking my seat. This was no subject of regret, and my position necessarily rendered me acquainted with all that passed. Some opposition was manifested, but without acrimony, and, on the whole, the discussion was calm and even cold. A strong majority carried the measure of appeal in favor of the First Consul, and he, ever faithful to his plan, ever ready, for his own purposes, to caress the sovereignty of the people which he held in horror, promulgated the following decree:

"The Consuls of the Republic, considering that the resolution of the First Consul is a splendid homage rendered to the majesty of the people, and that the people, consulted on their dearest interests, ought to recognize no other limits than those interests, decree as follows:

"Article I. The French people shall be consulted on this question: *Shall Napoleon Bonaparte be Consul for life?*

"Article II. In each commune registers shall be opened, in which the citizens are to be invited to inscribe their votes on this question.

"Article III. These registers shall be opened at the secretariats of all the administrations, at the offices of all the tribunals, and at the dwellings of all mayors and notaries.

"Article IV. The space allowed for voting in each department shall be three weeks, dating from the day on which this decree arrives at the prefecture, and seven days, reckoning from the time of its publication in each commune."

In this decree the policy of the First Consul showed itself under a new aspect, and his craft shines forth in all its splendor. At one and the same moment he refused the less, while he strove to grasp the more; in reality, he himself proposed the greater, that he might exalt his moderation in not accepting the less. Thus the Senate found itself outplayed; the resolution was transmitted to the Tribunate, and from the moment that, through dexterous management, Bonaparte had brought it round to the people, the question might be regarded as already decided in his favor, both from the means of influence which a government has always at command, and because, hitherto, the *outward* acts of the First Consul had been such as to secure popularity.

While merely the necessary forms were thus waited for—in other respects there could be no doubt—the First Consul went to pass some days at Malmaison. This was pretty generally his custom after an event out of the ordinary routine of government. There he reflected upon what he had done, and, by the success attending his most daring actions, was encouraged in the belief of his fortune and in the species of worship he rendered to audacity. While passion urged him on, he saw but his object; that attained, he examined the obstacles which he might have encountered. The first day of our retreat, it being then about the middle of May, and consequently the evenings fine, on our rising from table Bonaparte said to me—"Come, Bourrienne, let us take a turn." He was very serious, and we had walked out in the park for two or three minutes without his uttering a single word. Ignorant of the cause of this silence, and wishing to break it in an agreeable manner, I spoke to him of recent transactions. He seemed scarcely to hear me, so completely did he appear absorbed in his own reflections. Then, stopping on a sudden, "Bourrienne," said he, "do you think the pretender to the crown of France would renounce his rights were I to make offer of a large indemnity or even of a province in Italy?" Surprised at this abrupt question on a subject of all the least expected, I answered at once that the thought was not to be entertained, and though the Bourbons could not, with any likelihood, hope to return while he was chief of France, yet, it was to be supposed, they did regard their return as probable. "How so?"—"General, for a very simple reason: Do you not find that your agents daily flatter your desires, or conceal the truth from you, in order to show forth their own importance in your service? Are you not often indignant when the truth at length reaches you?"—"Yes; well?"—"Very well, General, must it not be the same with the agents of Louis XVIII. in France?"—"You are right; your idea is good. But keep yourself easy; I fear them not. Notwithstanding something, perhaps, may be done: I will think of it. We shall see." The conversation dropped on this subject; but it will be seen erelong that this thought did not germinate in Bonaparte's brain without bringing forth its fruit.

In the interval between the acts of the legislature relative

to the consulate and the collecting of the votes, Lucien renewed his intrigues, or, to speak more correctly, gave them
a new bent on the question of succession, so that hereditary
power also might be included. Circulars on this subject,
but without name, which had been dispersed over the country, were transmitted, by different prefects, to the minister
of the interior, with complaints of the mischief they were
producing in their prefectures. These came from Lucien.
Whether Bonaparte knew of them this time, as in the case
of the famous pamphlet, is not certain; but I believe him
to have been not quite a stranger to their contents, for they
were from the pen of Rœderer, at the instigation of Lucien,
and Rœderer was then in high favor at the Tuileries. I only
recollect the First Consul getting into a great passion about
a pamphlet by Camille Jordan, who, though he voted favorably on the question of the consulate for life, demanded also
the liberty of the press, and wrote in support of this demand.
The suspended vote of La Fayette was but a peccadillo in
comparison. Bonaparte ran over the fatal brochure, breath-
ing invectives against its author. "How!" said he, "am
I never to have done with these firebrands?—babblers, who
see politics upon paper as they look at the world on a chart!
Forsooth! I have only to allow them to order things, and all
will go well! On my word! Camille Jordan, whom I received so kindly at Lyons—he also demands the liberty
of the press! No! assuredly they shall not have it! I might
as well get into the stage at once, and set off to live on a
farm some hundred leagues from Paris!" As a conclusion
to this violent sally the first act of the First Consul in favor
of the liberty of the press was to seize the pamphlet in which
Camille Jordan had set himself to show forth its advantages.
Everything tending to popular interference, whether in
writing or speaking, was the raw-head-and-bloody-bones to
Bonaparte—hence his profound hatred of lawyers, orators
and writers.

There was still in France, and even in the legislature,
a considerable number of men who silently opposed Bona-

parte in the headlong career of his ambition—who had saluted with enthusiasm the dawn of the Revolution, but who had subsequently turned with abhorrence from its mockeries and its crimes. These yet cherished the possibility of a constitutional government in France. From such opponents, however, Bonaparte deemed no danger to be feared; he even turned their honorable aspirations into a lure by promises of liberty and by an appearance of popular forms. He could now say—"Do you require the voice of the nation?—behold it is in my favor. Three million five hundred and seventy-seven thousand two hundred and fifty-nine citizens have given in their suffrages; well! of that number how many are for me? Behold again: three million three hundred and sixty-eight thousand one hundred and twenty-five. Compare; you have not wherewith to oppose me—one vote to forty-five in my favor. I obey the voice of the people." He might also have added—"Besides, what are those suffrages given against me? Those of ideologists, lawyers, haranguers, Jacobins and peculators of the public revenue under the Directory? What! object to such arguments?" Nor must the reader imagine that I have invented the words here put into Bonaparte's mouth; in fact, he used them oftener than once.

The result of the voting being declared, the Senate found itself compelled to repair the only fault yet committed in the eyes of the First Consul, by presenting to him, in full audience, a decree thus conceived:

"Article I. The French people appoints, and the Senate proclaims, Napoleon Bonaparte Consul for life.

"Article II. A statue of Peace, holding in one hand the laurel of victory, and in the other this decree of the Senate, shall witness to posterity a nation's gratitude.

"Article III. The Senate shall convey to the First Consul the expression of the confidence, love, and admiration of the French people."

Bonaparte replied to the deputation of the Senate in presence of the members of diplomacy, whose day of audience had been fixed on purpose for enabling the ambassadors speedily to inform their respective courts that Europe reckoned a king more. In his reply the only thing worthy of remark is the appearance, once more, of the high-sounding words, *Liberty* and *Equality:* "Through my efforts, through your concurrence, Citizen Senators, through the concurrence of all the authorities, aided by the confidence and the wishes of this great people, Liberty and Equality, and the prosperity of France, shall be established beyond the vicissitudes of chance and the uncertainties of the future. The best of nations will be the happiest, as the most worthy of being so, and the felicity of the French people will contribute to that of all Europe. Then, satisfied with having been called, by the fiat of Him from whom all emanates, to bring back to earth Justice, Order, and Equality, I shall hear the stroke of my last hour without regret, and without anxiety as to the opinion of the generations to come. Senators, receive my thanks on this solemn occasion. The Senate desired what the people has now willed, and henceforth is more closely associated in all that remains to be done for the good of the country."

On the day of this solemnity, besides the diplomatic body, there was a prodigious assemblage of generals, officers and superior functionaries of government. In the grand apartments of the Tuileries all wore the aspect of rejoicing and bustle. Not so in the apartments of Josephine, who could not but see, in each step which her husband made toward the throne, a step which removed him from her. Sad, oppressed with secret grief, she had yet to sustain the honors of the evening's receptions. She acquitted herself with her wonted grace. But, on that evening, the tone of conversation was unusually serious: little was spoken of besides the ceremony of the morning and the happiness of France, now assured during the life of the Consul. His words were recalled—were dwelt upon—each, in some way or other, expressed his admiration of the great man, who would owe all to the award of the people. Bonaparte enjoyed his triumph with well-enacted modesty, while the farseeing Cambacérès, in the midst of a numerous circle, affected to put restrictions on his approbation, as if the First Consul had manifested principles too popular!

CHAPTER XVI

Accusations against Bourrienne—Political Questions regarding England—The Poem on Hortense

I NOW return to my own private circumstances as consequent on my first fall from favor, from which the preceding details have carried me over six months. On the morning after resuming my functions, I entered as usual the chamber of the First Consul, to call him at seven. He showed no coolness, but treated me in all respects as if absolutely nothing had occurred between us. On joining me in our study he spoke of affairs with his wonted tone of confidence, and I saw from the great number of letters left in the basket during the few days of my suspended functions that Bonaparte had still as little taste as in times past for that work. Thus, then, I found myself re-established in my old intimacy, but soon discovered that henceforward, from the scene witnessed by Talleyrand, my continuance in the study of the Tuileries would be only provisional—longer or shorter, according to circumstances.

Some time afterward the First Consul addressed me with an expression of interest and kindliness by which, however, I was not deceived. "My poor Bourrienne, you really cannot do all. Business increases, and will continue to do so. You know what Corvisart says. You have a family; I wish to spare your health, and not kill you outright: you shall have assistance. Joseph, to whom I have spoken on the subject, tells me he is willing to resign to me his own secretary, with whom he is much pleased. He will be under your orders, make your copies, and you will give him in charge whatever you can dispense with doing yourself with-

out injury to my service. At least, you will be considerably
relieved in your work."—"I ask nothing better," said I,
"than to have some one to assist me; he will become accustomed to your service and be able to replace me one day."

Joseph, in effect, did give up to his brother M. Mennevalle, a young man of excellent education, laborious, quiet
and discreet, with whom I was perfectly satisfied, and never
had occasion to regret the time passed in his society. I soon
remarked that the First Consul set himself to form Mennevalle, and to habituate him to his business and his ways.
As he never pardoned me for having dared to quit him, now
that he had attained so high a degree of power, my punishment had been resolved upon. I had seized the opportunity
that offered, in order to separate myself from him: he took
advantage of an unfortunate occurrence to separate himself
from me.

I proceed to explain the misfortune in which I got involved, more deserving of consolation and assistance than
of punishment. The circumstances have been very incor-
rectly related. I shall not attempt to refute all the errors
that have been printed on the subject, but quote only from
the "Memoirs of the Duke of Rovigo" (Savary).

"The life of Napoleon was one of continual labor. He
employed as confidential secretary M. de Bourrienne, the
companion of his boyhood, and who participated in all
his toils. Bourrienne had a prodigious memory, spoke and
wrote several languages, his pen was as rapid as speech.
These were not the only advantages he possessed; he was
acquainted with administration and with law, which, with
his devotedness and activity, rendered him an invaluable
man to the First Consul. I have witnessed many instances
of the confidence reposed in him by his chief, but cannot
speak with the same assurance of the causes of his dismissal.
Bourrienne had many enemies; some he owed to his character—more to his place. He could not be attacked on the
score of ability or discretion. They set a watch upon his
habits, and discovered that he dabbled in stocks: imputation thus became easy. He was accused of peculation: this
was to attack him on the unguarded side. The First Con-

sul abhorred nothing so much as illegal means of acquiring gold. But a single vice was not sufficient to ruin a man whom he was accustomed to love and esteem. Whether the accusations were well founded or not, nothing was neglected to bring them under the eye of the First Consul. For this purpose they employed a means which, originally intended for the discovery of truth, was often perverted to the purpose of conveying falsehood to the ear of the state. During the reign of Louis XV., or under the Regency, a system of observation had been established at the post-office, exercised not over all letters, but over such only as there were motives for suspecting. These were opened, and, when not convenient to suppress them, the inspector took a copy and despatched them by the regular course. By the aid of this institution, an individual who lodged information against another could give weight to his accusation. It sufficed to put into the post-office letters conceived in terms to confirm the opinion wished to be supported. The most honest man in the world might thus find himself compromised by a letter which he had never read, or, at least, which he had not understood. I myself have had experience of this. I opened a correspondence on some fact that had never taken place. The letter was opened, and a copy transmitted to me, because such were then my orders. But when this copy reached me I had already in my possession the originals, which had arrived through the ordinary channel. Summoned to answer to the inquiries which these essays provoked, I thence took occasion to expose the danger of blindly adopting information derived from such a source, and thus the system fell into discredit. But as yet it enjoyed full confidence, at the period of Bourrienne's downfall. His enemies took care not to neglect this means: they contrived, also, to blacken him with M. de Barbé-Marbois, who gave to the accusation all the weight of his probity. The opinion of this rigid functionary and other additional circumstances determined the First Consul to separate from his secretary."

By peculation is meant the crime of those who convert to their own use moneys levied for the public service. But, never having been intrusted with the administration of the resources of the state; never having either touched or collected the public funds; having ever remained an entire

stranger to such responsibilities—the reproach of peculation cannot rest upon me. The inconceivable version of
M. de Rovigo, so little in harmony with the introductory
eulogy, must, therefore, be the fruit of misapprehension,
for I have proofs that he esteemed me more than any one.
The whole is a calumny which cannot be his own work, but
to which he has lent himself as the echo. However it may
be, this singular accusation has procured from the austere
magistrate, of whose venerable name the Duke had too
lightly made use, an occasion of giving to the world a
fresh proof of a love of justice. I was still ignorant of
the Memoirs of the Duke of Rovigo, except from seeing
their announcement in the newspapers, when my family
transmitted the following letter, addressed to me by M. de
Barbé-Marbois:

"SIR—In certain Memoirs, recently published, I have
been led to remark the following article. (Here is transcribed the passage above quoted.) This assertion is not
true. And I consider it a debt of justice, as respects you,
sir, and as respects myself, to declare that I was ignorant
at the time, and still am ignorant of the causes of the separation alluded to. I request you to accept," etc.

There needs, I believe, nothing more than this noble and
spontaneous act to justify me and rebut the indiscreet accusation of peculating, uttered in ignorance of the true causes
of my rupture with the First Consul; which are as follows:

One of the principal houses in Paris had engaged to furnish stores for the war office. With the knowledge of Berthier, the minister with whom the house had concluded
the engagement, I purchased an interest. Unfortunately,
the house in question, unknown to me, had become also
deeply implicated in speculations on 'Change. The unskilfulness of agents, together with the permanent causes
of ruin in a game where the cards are too dear, produced
their usual consequences, and the house found itself in a
deficit of several millions. This raised such a rumor that
the First Consul, who had always a false idea of the public

funds, believed the slight depression to be the consequence of this failure. The stocks were represented to him as over-turned, and insinuations were made that I was accused of abusing the confidence of my situation to excite a by-play of fall and rise. Thus, though in truth a loser to a very considerable amount, I became an object of resentment to the First Consul, who informed me "He had no further occasion for my services." Had I been desirous of pacify-ing him, I might have pointed out to him that I could not be blamed for *purchasing* with my own money such an inter-est, when he had considered himself legally entitled to stipu-late for a *gratuity* of 1,500,000 francs for his brother Joseph with the commissioner of naval stores. But for some time, M. Mennevalle had begun to replace me in the cabinet. There wanted, then, only an occasion to decide the First Consul on paying off old scores, by dispensing, for good and all, with my services. I have given the true pretext for our separation; and I defy any one to substantiate a tittle of Rovigo's accusation, or of any exaction or extortion.

Our rupture happened on the 20th October, and it was not till the 8th November that I received the following letter from the First Consul:

"Citizen Bourrienne, Minister of State—I am satisfied with the services you have rendered since near my person; but henceforth they are no longer necessary. My intention is that you cease from this date to discharge the functions or to bear the title of my confidential secretary. As to the rest I am disposed to embrace the earliest occasion that may present itself, of placing you in a manner suitable to your activity and your talents, and most conducive to the benefit of the public service.   BONAPARTE."

In the course of the nine months between my resignation and final dismissal, two great events, as already explained, took place—the Consulate for Life and the Peace of Amiens. Of the latter, and of my newly-acquired liberty, I was inclined to take advantage by making a tour in England, whither some affairs called me.

The First Consul had never believed in a long duration of the peace with England. He had concluded without desiring the measure, because it was so ardently wished throughout all France that, after ten years of war, he judged it indispensable in founding his new government. Peace seemed necessary in order to enable him to conquer the throne of France, in like manner as war became the instrument to strengthen and enlarge the basis of his power at the expense of the other thrones of Europe. Such was the secret of the Peace of Amiens, and of the speedy rupture that followed: though the explosion, on the side of Great Britain, took place sooner than the First Consul could have wished. He had too much acuteness to be deluded for a moment as to the intentions of England; he was fully assured that she would not have concluded a peace but because, deserted by her allies, she could not do otherwise, and that she would never allow France time for reorganizing a navy. On these grand questions of peace and war, the Consul entertained ideas of the most elevated order; but in the discussions of this period he always declared in favor of war. When others spoke of the advantages of peace, he acknowledged their importance. But he maintained, on the other hand, that all these advantages could be only conditional, so long as England might throw, at will, into the balance of the world, the preponderance of her navy, and insinuate the influence of her gold into the cabinets of Europe. "The peace ought to be broken, since England will evidently do so. Why not anticipate her hostility? why permit her to take her advantages? We must astonish Europe: we must change the political aspect of the Continent! We must strike a great blow, and let it be terrible—unexpected!" Thus reasoned the First Consul, and it is known how his actions accorded with his thoughts.

The conduct of England but too well justified these apprehensions. Already, in fact, was she preparing the strong arm of her subsidies, an arm even then powerful in diplomatic concerns. In profound secrecy these manœuvrings

were carried on, and the English government sought, under
the veil of unjust complaints, to cover the sources of real
injury inflicted by underhand dealings. In fact, the King
of England had addressed to Parliament a message which
spoke of armaments preparing in the ports of France,
and precautions necessary to be taken against aggressions.
Irritated at seeing his prospects of peace cut short, the First
Consul, in a wrathful ebullition, thus addressed the English
ambassador, Lord Whitworth, in the saloon in presence of
the other ambassadors: "What means this? Are you weary
of peace? Must Europe be once more deluged in blood?
Preparations for war! Does your nation think to overawe
us? Eh, well! we shall see. France may be vanquished,
destroyed perhaps—intimidated never!" The British envoy,
astonished at this sally, made no answer. He contented
himself with writing to his own court the details of this
interview, in which the First Consul had certainly too far
forgotten himself, if, indeed, his had not been wilful forgetfulness.

From the first day in which England showed dissatisfaction, it might have been taken for granted that she desired
war. Malta she had promised to give up, but retained;
Egypt she should have evacuated, but remained in possession of; the Cape of Good Hope she ought to have yielded,
but continued to hold; she had signed at Amiens a peace,
without any intention of observing its conditions. The
assembly at Lyons had awakened her suspicions, and the
British ministry had seen too clearly not to discern a future
King of Italy in the modest President of the Cisalpine Republic. England, whose policy is always so consistent with
itself, so far-sighted and so solid, beheld St. Domingo in the
hands of the French: St. Domingo must be free, and
the French navy compelled to suffer for the efforts it had
made to recover itself a little. England opposed ambition
to ambition, stratagem to stratagem. She asserted, without
proof, that France had not executed the clauses of the treaty,
and had certainly taken her resolution when she signed the

peace at Amiens, which wise men had foreseen was only
a truce.   These dispositions of England produced their
inevitable result.   Henceforward communications became
reserved at first, then hostile; explanations were recipro-
cally demanded with equal haughtiness, passports were re-
quested--and war quickly followed.   England, upon this
occasion, showed an eager violence, the more shocking that
she of all the powers of Europe was the only one which had
suffered no reverse and could come into the field with unbroken force.   Who knows not, moreover, that it is during
war English commerce flourishes most profitably, and that
by involving the Continent in perpetual wars she prospers
and enriches herself?

The First Consul having calculated upon a longer continuance of the Peace of Amiens, found himself in rather
a doubtful position on its abrupt termination.   The great
number of discharges that had been granted, the deplorable
state of the cavalry, and the temporary nullity of the artillery, caused by the, too inconsiderate adoption of a plan of
Berthier's for recasting the field-pieces, demanded all Bonaparte's energy and promptitude.   The conscription was called
forth to fill up the ranks of the army; the artillery scheme
abandoned; contributions levied in all the great towns; the
cavalry remounted with horses from Hanover, which, on its
occupation, furnished a great number.   Into all, Bonaparte
seemed to possess the art of infusing his own incredible
activity of spirit, and the essential sinews of war were
created as if by enchantment.   It is impossible to describe
the labors undertaken and executed.   The whole extent of
Channel coast presented the aspect of one vast arsenal; for
on this occasion, Bonaparte formed his troops on the model
of the Roman legions, causing the tools of the artisan to
replace, in the hands of his soldiers, the weapons of the
warrior.   They excavated the harbor at Boulogne and repaired and finished the works at Ambleteuse, commenced
under Louis XVI., and interrupted during the Revolution.
And what is worthy of remark, the soldiers were at the

same time no less diligently employed in their military exercises, their time, so to speak, being as completely occupied as that of their chief. During the year 1803, and while the camp at Boulogne continued to be kept up, one may say the First Consul was everywhere. The papers announced his arrival at St. Cloud; two or three days later, they stated that he had inspected the works, superintended reviews, ordered new enterprises; and almost immediately after a public audience, preceded by a parade in the Carrousel, showed he had again returned to the capital.

For these frequent visits, sometimes to one coast, sometimes to another, Bonaparte generally set out in the night, stopping next morning at the post-house of Chantilly, where he made a temperate breakfast in all haste. Rapp, whom I continued to see when at Paris, was constantly speaking to me of these affairs, for he almost always accompanied the First Consul; and well had it been if none save such as Rapp had been admitted near his person. In the evening he supped at Abbeville, and arrived the second morning very early on the coast. "Imagine," said my informant, "this kind of life; one would absolutely require to be made of iron to support it; for scarcely have we alighted from the carriage, when away we go on horseback, with the First Consul, for ten or twelve hours together. He sees all— examines all—often talks with the men: how they love him! When shall we pay a visit to London with all our brave fellows?"

In the midst of these continual active operations, every part of government, and the proceedings of the Council, received the usual attention. I had not yet left him at the time of agitating the question in what manner treaties of peace were to be concluded. Some members of the Council, among whom Truguet took the lead, proposed that, in accordance with an article of the constitution, treaties should be brought forward by the heads of the government, discussed in the Legislative Assembly, and afterward passed and promulgated as laws. Bonaparte maintained an opinion decidedly the reverse, and his remarks perfectly coincided with my sentiments when he observed, "It is for the pleasure of showing that they can get up an opposition when they thus invoke the constitution; for, if the constitution direct in this manner it knows not what it says. There are matters which cannot be the subject of discussion in an assembly. How! when I treat with Austria, for example, even should my ambassador accede to the propositions, must there be nothing done if these conditions be rejected by the legislative body? It is an absurdity without parallel. Upon my word, things would thus come to a fine pass! Lucchesini and Markow would give every day dinners like those of Cambacérès; they would make their money go; would buy those who are for sale; would get our propositions outvoted; and that, doubtless, would be an excellent method of conducting business!" Such was Bonaparte's language while yet he affected to observe the constitution—and he was right.

His conversation when he talked with me about what had passed in the Council was habitually a singular compound of citations from antiquity, historical allusions and original ideas. He was ever speaking of the Romans; and I recollect, during Mr. Fox's visit, that he thus set himself to shine before the foreign statesman, whom he admired prodigiously. In his manner of viewing the world he beheld but two states on the globe, the East and the West. "What signifies it," were his words, "that two nations are separated by rivers or mountains—that they employ a different idiom? With slight shades, France, Spain, England, Italy have the same manners, the same habits, the same religion, the same dress; there a man can marry only one wife; in these countries there are no slaves—such are the grand distinctions separating the civilized man from the savage. With the exception of Turkey, Europe is but one province of the world; when we go to war among ourselves it is but civil strife. There is, indeed, another way of dividing the globe—into land and water." Then he would run over the whole circle of European interests; speak of Russia, whose alliance he courted; of England, mistress of the seas; and he rarely failed to terminate this flow of elevated thought without reverting to what was then a favorite project—an expedition to the great Indian continent.

When, from these generalities, Bonaparte descended to the special interests of France, his language was still more that of a sovereign, and I must say, he spoke as a prince more jealous than any other has ever been of the dignity of France, whose sole representative he considered himself to be. Having learned that a captain in the English navy had visited the dockyard of Brest as a merchant, whose passport the officer had borrowed, he became quite furious that no one had arrested the impostor; and, as nothing was lost upon him, he made this a pretence for augmenting the police establishment, saying, in full council—"Had there been at Brest a commissary of police he would have caused this English captain to have been arrested, and sent him immediately to Paris. As he had undertaken the part of a spy, I should have caused him to be shot as one. No Englishman—no lord—not even the ambassador of England, ought to be permitted to enter our ports." "I shall in future see all this righted," said he, on speaking to me of his outburst in council; "there are enough wretches who sell me every day to the English."

Upon another occasion he said, in presence of a great number of generals, senators and high functionaries, who had assembled previous to an audience of the ambassadors— "The English believe I am afraid of war: I fear it not. Were we to yield to England now, she would presently interdict our navigation of certain seas, demand our ships— and what not! But patience; I am in no humor to endure such humiliations. Since England wishes war she shall have it: I shall not let her wait, and we shall see."

Yet was he very ambitious of standing well in public opinion in England. Of this I had a singular proof, and of the importance which Bonaparte attached to the judgment formed in that country of the actions imputed to him.

What I am going to relate will serve also to throw new light upon his inclination to employ tortuous and petty ways to attain his end. He gave a ball at Malmaison, when Hortense had reached the seventh month of her time, and, though well-known to have an aversion to women in her condition, above all to their dancing, begged Hortense to stand up, if but for a single country dance. She declined, but he insisted, using every species of cajolery—"Now, let me beg it as a favor; I have such a desire to see you dance: come, do it to please me"; and at last Hortense did dance. What was his object? We shall see. On the morrow there appeared in one of the papers a poetical piece, composed in a very gallant strain, on the country dance in which Hortense had joined, notwithstanding her condition. Hortense was extremely vexed, and, when the journal arrived at Malmaison, complained of the affair, and, above all, would not believe, in spite of the facility of our small wits, that these verses could have been composed and printed on a fact which happened the night preceding. Bonaparte answered vaguely, and in a laughing way: as to myself, he could tell me nothing about an affair of which I was equally well informed with himself. When Hortense knew I was alone in the study she came and pressed me with questions. I judged it best to tell her what had occurred. The verses had been composed by order of Bonaparte, before the ball, by a poet whose name I have now forgotten: the ball had been given expressly for the verses, and the First Consul had set himself to entreat her to dance in order to verify the poetry. All this petty contrivance had been arranged in order to give the lie to an English newspaper announcing her accouchement. This premature notice had, in fact, excited Bonaparte's indignation; for he well knew its object to be to accredit those infamous reports which we have already refuted. Yet such were the little machinations which often found place in that mind wherein were matured so many gigantic designs.

On reading again the manuscript of this portion of my

Memoirs, I observe that, carried away, as often happens, by the analogies of ideas, I have spoken of events posterior to the breaking up of the treaty of Amiens without sufficiently dwelling upon the peace itself, one of the greatest events in the present history. Here I may be permitted to make one short reflection: The transactions, of which I may subsequently treat, though occurring after my separation from the First Consul, were but the consummation of earlier designs, communicated to me by himself. If, then, I beheld the development of certain effects, I had been present at the birth of their causes; and I believe I hazard nothing in asserting that my long and uninterrupted study of Bonaparte's character enables me, better than any one else, to estimate those acts of power to which I have always possessed a key. How often have I told my friends Duroc and Rapp the true sense of what they supposed themselves explaining to me for the first time! Here, indeed, I except those transactions which the First Consul had himself confided to my discretion—such as his real views with regard to a descent on the English coast, in which almost every one believed. On that, and similar confidences, I have reason to think he was aware and approved of my secrecy.

At the conclusion of the Peace of Amiens, one of those circumstances which went most directly to prove that it would be of short duration was Mr. Pitt's retirement from office. I made this observation to Bonaparte, but without insistence, as I quickly perceived, from the abrupt manner of his asking, "What is it you say?" although understanding me perfectly, that my observation had displeased him. It required, however, no extraordinary acuteness to perceive the true motive here. That illustrious minister considered a short truce, to which people gave the name of a treaty, as indispensable to England. However this may be, I have always considered the measure as a fault in the British cabinet, whatever need England might have had of peace. And the error was not long in being discovered. Lord Whitworth, the English ambassador, quitted Paris on the

night of the 12–13th May, 1808, while the English government, without their being demanded, gave his passports to
the French envoy at London. In this state of things, France
proposed to the British government to receive, with common
accord, the mediation of Russia, but as England had declared war only in order to repair the fault committed
in concluding peace, all overtures of pacific tendency were
rejected. Thus, the Consul, in the eyes of the public, was
enabled to assume the garb of great moderation and sincere
love of peace. Henceforth commenced between England
and France one of those furious contests which had marked
the reigns of King John and Charles VII., and which furnished our wiseacres an occasion for comparisons with the
ancient rivalship of Rome and Carthage, whence they
concluded, in their plenitude of political wisdom, that, as
Carthage had fallen, England must be undone. Such were
the empty sounds with which flatterers every instant saluted
the ears of the First Consul. And here I may just remark
that never before had adulation attained to so remarkable a
height. Never had the nation so revelled in the luxury of
addresses. They poured in from the four winds of heaven.
Not a prefect, not a sub-prefect, mayor nor corporation,
however constituted, failed to send in his or its speech.
One would have thought that Bonaparte had proclaimed
a competition in baseness and that all France had entered
for the prize. In the grave circumstances of the times he,
however, was not wanting to himself, but put forth all his
activity of intellect; and greatly had he changed in the
course of six months, if he felt not his soul stirred into
ecstasy at the bare idea of one vast war whose extent would
gratify his illimitable ambition.

Bonaparte was at St. Cloud when Lord Whitworth quitted
Paris. A fortnight passed in fruitless attempts to renew the
negotiations. Nothing, therefore, now remained but to prepare for war. On this occasion the First Consul addressed
to the Senate, the Legislative Assembly and the Tribunate
a message full of dignity and free from those gasconades in

which he so frequently indulged. The Senate's reply was accompanied with the present of a first-rate ship of war, paid for from its own resources.

The manifesto of the British cabinet had struck like a thunderbolt upon the French government, which, though aware of the intrigues going forward in London, was by no means prepared for such an outbreaking. The primary subject of complaint regarded commercial arrangements. The union of Piedmont to the French republic, also of the states of Parma and Placentia, to which Bonaparte had constituted himself heir, on the death of the Duke, and the continued occupation of Holland by our troops, were added as separate grievances. The mission of General Sebastiani, sent into Turkey and Egypt for the purpose of exciting the native powers against England, and of preparing for a prospective attack upon the Anglo-Indian possessions, formed the subject of strong remonstrance in the manifesto. When that officer went out on his mission I was still in the secrets of the First Consul; and, it must be acknowledged, the English ministers here showed themselves but too well informed. Sebastiani's memorial, as published, abounded in expressions and disclosures calculated to give offence. The sum of all is, that, amid this mutual recrimination, neither government had kept good faith.

England was desirous of retaining all her advantages: and it has more than once happened that a state has boasted its fidelity to treaties because not exactly the first to infringe them. This was Bonaparte's situation. England, too, alleged only her ostensible reasons. In a communication to the legislative body, touching the state of France, the First Consul had said, "England, single-handed, is unable to contend with France." This proposition sufficed to rouse to arms the whole susceptibilities of British pride; and the cabinet chose to construe it into a menace. It was not so; for, when Bonaparte threatened, his words were more firm and more energetic. The expression simply tended to reassure the confidence of the French people; and if we carefully examine by what increasing efforts, at what sacrifices, England has persisted in creating enemies to France on the Continent, we shall probably be authorized in the conclusion that, in secret, the British entertained the same opinion as Bonaparte. Alone against France, England, doubtless, would have done much mischief, especially by falling upon the remnant of the French navy, scattered throughout the entire globe; but against continental France she could undertake nothing, and supposing allies on neither side, these two powers might be long at war with but little of actual hostility.

The first consequence of the declaration of war by England was the invasion of Hanover by the French troops, under the command of General Mortier. The telegraphic despatch conveying the intelligence to Paris was no less true than brief, containing the whole history of the expedition—"The French are masters of the Electorate of Hanover, and the enemy remain prisoners of war." When informed of this circumstance, the First Consul conceived the hope of exchanging the Hanoverian troops for the French prisoners already taken by sea, and made a proposition to that effect; but the English cabinet decided that, though the King of England was also Elector of Hanover, there existed no union between the states of which he was the head; and, in consequence of this subtile distinction, rejected the proposal. Nothing could then equal the animosity of the two governments against each other; and Bonaparte, at the moment of declaring war, showed his indignation in a manner which cannot be approved. I speak of his arresting every English subject found in France—a barbarous order; for it is dreadful to inflict upon individuals, who have entered a country relying upon the laws of civilized nations, that resentment which ought to be exercised only as respects the government whose subjects they are.

CHAPTER XVII

Bonaparte's Opinion of Polite Literature—The Preparations for the Invasion of
England—Conspiracy of Cadoudal, Pichegru, and Moreau—Murder
of the Duke d'Enghien—European Resentment Thereat

ABOUT the same period various of the old usages were
re-established. Among others the Institute of France
was remodelled and separated into four classes, intended to recall the remembrance of the ancient Academies
—a denomination, however, which the reformer rejected,
notwithstanding the desire and the intrigues of several persons, and, among others, of Lucien. Neither in this division
did the classes of the Institute retain the same rank they
formerly held as Academies. He placed in the principal
station the class of science, degrading to the second the
ancient academy of literature. Bonaparte, in fact, held
polite literature in light esteem. He was very fond of
St. Pierre's tale of "Paul and Virginia," because he had
perused it in early youth; but I remember well his having
one day tried for about a quarter of an hour to read the
"Studies of Nature," by the same author, when, tossing
the book contemptuously from him, he said—"How can
people read such trash? It is insipid, vapory stuff; there
is nothing in it; these are the reveries of a visionary. What
is this nature? Nature! the phrase is vague—void of all
meaning. Men and passions, to be sure; these are what
ought to be depicted: these tell something—have meaning.
Such gentry are good for nothing under any government!
I shall give them pensions, nevertheless, because I ought
to do so as head of the state; they occupy and amuse idlers:
but I will make Lagrange a senator; that man has a head."

But though speaking of them in this manner, it must not
be supposed that Bonaparte treated men of letters ill: on
the contrary they were objects of his solicitous courtesy,

and the number of poets was considerable who, from time
to time, visited Fouché, and afterward Savary, for their
guerdon of fifty or a hundred louis; and from among these
laureates—by pay if not by laurels—afterward arose the
strains which celebrated the burning of Moscow as one of
the proudest results of the Russian campaign!

While I thus expose, however, the general dislike in
which all men of letters were included by the First Consul, it must also be remembered that this arose less from
prejudice than from the necessities of his position. Time
is required to appreciate, even to peruse works of literature,
and time was so precious to him that he would have wished,
so to speak, to shorten the straight line. For this reason he
preferred those authors who treated of the practical and exact sciences; the more especially as these are circumscribed
by a boundary within which strictures on administration or
thoughts on government do not easily penetrate. He regarded suspiciously political economists, juris-consults—in
short, all writers who meddled in any manner with legislation, institutions, or moral improvements. In the remodel-
ling of the Institute, while admitting a literary class of forty
members, he altogether abolished that of the moral and political sciences. Of the two classes thus remaining, Bonaparte continued in the first, that of science, while Lucien
entered the second, or that of literature. The utility attaching to realities was with him so paramount that in the
sciences, even, he preferred those which applied to the earth:
thus he never treated Lalande with so much distinction as
Monge and Lagrange. Astronomical discoveries could not
conduce so directly to his personal greatness; and besides,
he never forgave Lalande the design of placing him in a
dictionary of atheists at the very time he was establishing
relations with the Holy See.

All the intriguers of Europe were now at work. They
daily arrived from England, but unable to penetrate into the
interior of France they took up their abode in all the frontier
cities. There they established correspondences, and thence

issued pamphlets which reached Paris by post in the shape of letters. On his side, the First Consul, beholding in every-thing the influence of England, yielded entirely to his desire of vengeance. He was not, of course, ignorant that the most fatal war for his rival would be a hostility directed against her commerce. As a prelude to the gigantic folly known under the name of "The Continental System," he accord-ingly issued the most peremptory orders for the interdiction of English merchandise. A long decree was promulgated by which it was rendered incumbent upon all military posts, upon the national guards, the police and all functionaries whatsoever, to arrest all individuals who should introduce articles of English manufacture or origin, or who should sell or warehouse them in the interior of France; or who should even attempt to introduce these contraband goods. The *suspected* were immediately on their capture to be conducted to the nearest prison, and those who had used force in land-ing prohibited commodities were to be sued before the spe-cial tribunals. And every one knows what judgments were at this time rendered by a special tribunal. In short, Bona-parte had in this decree accumulated all that the laws could authorize in the way of severity. To this system I shall return hereafter, for peculiar circumstances enabled me to study both its progress and effects.

The First Consul wanted not for causes of irritation against his active enemies: the news which reached Paris from the coasts of the Channel were by no means encour-aging. The English fleets not only blockaded the French ports, but had commenced the offensive by bombarding Granville.

This brings me to the question of an actual descent upon England. I have already stated that Bonaparte never enter-tained the idea of a real invasion. The interview and con-versation I am now to relate bears still more directly on the same subject.

There had been nearly seven months of war since the rupture of the Peace of Amiens when, on the 15th Decem-

ber, 1803, the First Consul sent for me to the Tuileries. I
held still in mind his incredible proceedings, and, as I had
not seen him for some time, I felt by no means at ease at
this summons. However it might be, I knew not, but to
be candid, on receiving this invitation I took the precaution
to fortify myself with a nightcap, apprehending the notion
had seized him of sending me to sleep at Vincennes. My
fears, however, turned out to be unnecessary. Rapp was
master of ceremonies on that particular day, and I sought
not to conceal from him the ideas I harbored on the possible
result of the visit. "You may set yourself at ease," said
Rapp, "the First Consul wishes only a little chat with you";
and then he announced me.

Bonaparte, on entering the grand saloon, where I was in
waiting, accosted me in his most gracious manner. After
the usual little *drolleries*, he asked, "Pray, what say the old
women of my preparations for a descent?"—"General, there
is much diversity of opinion; each person speaks after his
own way. Suchet, for example, whom I often see, has no
doubt that it will take place, and hopes then to give you
new proofs of his gratitude and attachment."—"But Suchet
tells me you do not believe in the invasion?"—"That is
true; I put no faith in it."—"And why?"—"Because five
years ago, at Antwerp, you told me you would not stake
France upon the cast of such a die—that it was too hazardous. In this respect nothing has been changed."—"You
are right; those who credit the intention of a descent are
blockheads: they see not the thing in the true light. Doubtless I might land with 100,000 men: the English would encounter me in a general battle: I should win it; but I must
reckon upon 30,000 men killed, wounded and prisoners. If
I march upon London, a second battle awaits me under its
walls. Supposing me victorious here, also, what should I
do in London with an army diminished by three-fourths,
without hope of reinforcements? This would be madness.
Without a superiority gained by our navy, it is vain ever
to think of such a project. The grand mustering of troops

yonder in the north has a different object. My government must either be the first of all, or it falls.''

Bonaparte then evidently wished to practice deceit upon all as respected his true designs here. It was his object to fix the eyes of all Europe upon his pretended invasion of England in order to withdraw attention from his real designs: nor was this one of the least inglorious of those devices which he played in the grand game of politics. The trick, however, was an expensive one. The cities voted ships of war which were never finished; and even Paris fell to constructing boats, destined for the transport of the invading army, but which were never to see British shores. The immense quantity of shallops and flat-bottomed boats only begun, or preparing, or finished, were good for nothing and excited, I well remember, a general smile. Still people were deceived; even Duroc and Rapp gave credence to the reality of the scheme; yet the state of our marine, in point only of men, might have sufficed to dispel the delusion. Soldiers, so to speak, may be *improvised*, but sailors must be formed by long experience; and our few experienced seamen were then parcelled out in distant settlements —a double misfortune; for they thus fell into the hands of the enemy while removed from the defence of their native shores.

On the 8th March, 1804, while very grave matters were going forward, I had another unsolicited audience of the First Consul, at eight o'clock in the morning. After conversing about indifferent matters, asking how I was employed and what were my expectations, he said I might depend upon him. He afterward uttered some vague expressions relative to the conspiracy of Pichegru and Moreau, which had just been discovered. Then, suddenly changing, ''Apropos,'' said he, ''reports are still spread of my connection with Hortense: scandalous stories were set afloat about her first child. I then hoped that the public gave heed to such things only from a desire of seeing me have a child. Since you and I have been separated have you heard them

repeated ?''—''Yes, General, frequently; but 1 confess at
the same time I had believed that such a calumny could not
have so long survived.''—''It is truly atrocious; you know
that it is; you have seen all—heard all; the slightest transaction could not have escaped your observation; you enjoyed
her unlimited confidence at the time of her correspondence
with Duroc.   I expect from you, if ever you write anything
about me, that you will redeem my memory from this infamous slander; I would not that it follow me to posterity.
I count much upon you.   You have never given credit to
this odious imputation ?''—''No, never, General.''   He then
entered upon a number of details on the past and present
life of Hortense, and on the turn her marriage had taken.
''Things have not prospered,'' said he, ''as I wished: their
union is not happy.   This hurts me, for I love them both,
and also because it is calculated to strengthen these infamous
reports.''   He ended the conversation by saying, ''Bourrienne, I sometimes think of recalling you, but, as there
exists no cause, people would still say I have need of you,
and I would have the world know that I stand in need
of no one.''   He spoke again for a moment of Hortense.
I replied that, upon my own conviction, I would do as he
desired, and that he might depend upon the truth being
known through me.   I have already redeemed my pledge.
Let his memory be freed from the imputation of evil he did
not commit!   Let impartial history reject this slander!   His
principles on this point were severely pure, and, to close the
subject forever, I declare that such a connection accorded
neither with his ideas, his manners, nor his tastes.

Before my first visit to the Tuileries, as already mentioned, and prior even to the rupture of the treaty of
Amiens, intriguing speculators, whose excessive zeal was
not less fatal to the cause of the Bourbons than the blind
devotion of unprincipled followers proved to the First
Consul, had engaged in certain dark manœuvres which could
produce no favorable result.   These machinations at this
time had in view the reconciliation of Moreau and Pichegru.

The latter, proscribed on the 18th Fructidor as one of the obnoxious deputies, unable to obtain the First Consul's permission to return to France, had taken up his residence in England, waiting a favorable opportunity of executing his projects. Moreau lived in Paris, but appeared neither at the audiences nor in the circles of the First Consul; and the hostility of these two generals against Bonaparte—declared on the part of Pichegru, still veiled by Moreau—was a secret to no one. But, everything smiling on the First Consul, he viewed this enmity with more disdain than fear, reassured also by the banishment of the one and the character of the other. The name of Moreau posssesed far greater influence with the army than that of Pichegru, and those who were plotting the overthrow of the consular government perfectly understood that nothing could be successfully attempted without the aid of the former. The crisis was, in truth, unfavorable; but some in the secret, knowing also something of the plans of the British cabinet, and that the peace was only a truce, resolved to take advantage of the brief interval to effect, in advance, a reconciliation which might bring round a community of interests. Moreau and Pichegru were, in fact, on bad terms ever since Moreau had sent to the Directory the papers seized among the baggage of General Klinglin, and which so clearly demonstrated the treason of Pichegru in leaguing with the Bourbons while he was at the head of the Army of Germany. From that period the name of Pichegru had lost its influence over the soldiery, while the fame of Moreau remained dear to all who had seen victory under his command.

These attempts had only the effect of compromising Moreau, without determining him to anything. His natural indolence, and perhaps good sense, had dictated as his rule of conduct the maxim to let men and things take their course; for often in politics, as in war, to temporize is no bad activity. Besides, Moreau was then a stanch republican, and most certainly would not have labored to bring back the Bourbons—the aim of Pichegru.

Such is the introduction to transactions of far deeper interest which happened at the close of the consulate, namely, the conspiracy of Georges Cadoudal, Moreau, Pichegru and others, and the everlasting stain on Napoleon's name, the murder of the Duke d'Enghien.

On the conspiracy of Georges different opinions have been expressed. I contradict no one; I shall merely relate what I learned and saw, which may throw some light upon that horrible and mysterious affair. I am far, however, from believing that the whole was a conspiracy to prepare the way to the imperial throne. But I am inclined to think that, planned by those implicated therein, it was aided by Fouché, in order to accelerate his return to the ministry. I combat no one's opinion, but it will be permitted me to support my own by the exposition of facts.

Fouché knew Bonaparte well; nor had he forgotten that, in his message to the Senate on the 15th September, 1802, the First Consul had said that, if circumstances required a minister of police, the government could find none better qualified than the ex-functionary. Fouché, in my opinion, matured such *circumstances* with unpardonable ability. Let not this be deemed a harsh conclusion; not one generous sentiment could harbor in the mind capable of writing the soul-harrowing correspondence of Fouché during his mission to Lyons. The daily and necessary intercourse which for years I had held with Fouché, previous to the suppression of his department, placed me on a footing which gave me the privilege afterward of visiting him when he became lost in the Senate and I in the crowd. Fouché, in all his conversations, assured me, with a confidence I could not well account for, that the First Consul in the end would again have recourse to him. "Régnier," he would say, "is too dainty, and too great an ass to play the policeman well; he will allow the First Consul to fall into some snare." I confess that at the time I attached little value to such assertions, attributing them to vanity and to a desire of recovering his place, knowing, also, his real dislike of the First

Consul. Circumstances corroborated these remarks, and now strengthen my opinion as respects his participation in the subsequent manœuvres.

While attempts were making, as already described, to bring about a reconciliation between Moreau and Pichegru, Fouché set about Moreau men of his own party and way of thinking, encouraged, probably, without knowing it, by the subtle Fouché, to exercise an influence over him and to irritate his mind. The Abbé David, a common friend of both generals, was first employed as an instrument of reconciliation, but, being arrested and consigned to the Temple, he was replaced by a man named Lajollais, whom everything confirms to have been employed by Fouché. This agent repaired to London, where he intrigued without engaging in the conspiracy, preparing the departure of Pichegru and his friends from thence, returning to Paris to announce their arrival, and to prepare all things for their reception and—destruction. The sole foundation of this intrigue was the discontent of Moreau.

One day in the end of January, 1804, I recollect having visited Fouché about two o'clock; the horses were put to his carriage, he himself was alone in his cabinet and about to seal a letter for the First Consul, then at St. Cloud. He read me this note just written; it was short and concluded with these words, which struck me forcibly: *The air is full of daggers.* What preceded was a little obscure, but tending to the same vague and astounding conclusion. In a postscript the writer said, "*I am setting out for Pont Carré.*"—"How!" said I, "the air full of daggers, and you quit Paris without going to St. Cloud to give your explanations to the First Consul!"—"I thought you had known him better; I send my letter by an express messenger; I shall not be one hour at Pont Carré before receiving an order to repair in all haste to St. Cloud. Look in upon me to-morrow; we will have some talk together." Fouché despatched his letter and drove off. I called next day and learned from himself that everything had fallen out as he expected.

Scarcely had he arrived in the country when a courier arrived, bearing an order for his immediate attendance at St. Cloud. Here the First Consul affected to treat his intelligence as invented to increase his own importance. "What will you say," answered Fouché, "if I inform you that Georges and Pichegru have been in Paris for some time on this very plot?"—"Ah!" returned Bonaparte, with a look of pity, as if delighted to catch Fouché napping, "how truly you are informed! Régnier has just received a letter from London that Pichegru, only three days ago, dined at Kingston in the house of one of the English ministry." Fouché persisted; Régnier was sent for, and Bonaparte soon discovered that the latter had been mystified by agents better paid by his rival. The new functionary was dismissed, but the ancient minister of police objected to the immediate revival of his office, fearing thus to awaken suspicion, stipulating merely that the conduct of the affair should be intrusted to Réal, with orders to obey all instructions received from himself.

There appears then no reasonable ground for doubting that the conspiracy, if not originated, was fomented by Fouché and the police in his pay. The want of concord among the pretended leaders; the facilities afforded them in disembarking, coming to and residing in Paris; their almost simultaneous arrest and consequent depositions—all prove such connivance, and that their temporary tranquillity arose from their being, so to speak, in a chamber of glass, as respected the police. Moreau never for an instant favored the return of the Bourbons; this I could not but know from my connection with his most intimate friend, M. Carbonnet: it was, therefore, quite impossible for him to make common cause with Georges and Pichegru. Polignac, again, De Rivière and some others had no intention of acting at all; they had come to Paris to view the actual state of things and certainly to inform the Bourbon princes how they were to value the foolish hopes given them by inferior agents, always eager to exalt their own services at the expense of

BATTLE OF WATERLOO

truth. These gentry, unquestionably, had set on foot a conspiracy; but it was against the treasury of London, whence they had hoped to draw salaries. There can likewise be no question that the secret agents of Fouché, who also misled the regular police—agents formed of false friends to persons disposed by previous sentiments to favor a conspiracy of this nature—also encouraged them to attempt its accomplishment. I fully believe that a large proportion of the accused actually entertained the design of overturning the government and restoring the Bourbons; but I maintain that they would have made the attempt neither at the time, nor in the manner they did, if the means had not been facilitated—if they had not' been encouraged by perfidious insinuations and deceitful hopes.

The greater part of the conspirators were already in the Temple, or the prison of Laforce, when one of them, Bouvet de Lozier, made an attempt to hang himself in the former place of confinement. The wretched man had but too nearly succeeded, having made use of his cravat for the purpose, and was on the point of expiring when, by chance, the jailer entered his dungeon. Recalled to life, De Lozier exhibited a striking but not uncommon example of great courage with little moral fortitude. He did not fear death, yet knew himself incapable of confronting the interrogatories of justice, and had resolved to kill himself lest he should be led to make confessions. He did make them, and on the morrow (that is, on the 15th February), Moreau was arrested while returning from his estate of Grosbois to Paris. From the declarations of De Lozier, also, the *regular* police—the police not in the pay of Fouché—first learned the particulars of three successive disembarkations effected in silence, and that a fourth was expected.—But let us come to the official details.

"Georges and his band of assassins had continued in the pay of our enemies: his agents traversed Vendée and the neighboring departments. Georges and Pichegru contrived their machinations: and in the year XI. Moreau and Piche-

gru were criminally reconciled—two men whom honor ought
to have placed at eternal variance. The police seized one
of their agents returning for the second time from England,
upon whose person documents were found attesting this combination. Lajollais, the friend and confidant of Pichegru,
made two journeys between London and Paris, carrying on
the correspondence: in the meantime all things were prepared in Paris by the scoundrels of Georges."—Here I interrupt the report of Régnier, who thus describes Lajollais as
the friend of Pichegru, to state that before the writing of the
report it had become clear as day that Lajollais was an agent
employed to connect with the conspiracy the two chiefs
marked for such implication.—"A retired spot was assigned
between Dieppe and Tréport for the landing of the conspirators, who were brought there in English ships of war. Here
they found men corrupted and paid to guide them from
station to station, as previously agreed upon: at Paris,
places of safety were provided in houses rented in advance,
and in the charge of connivers. The first landing consisted
of Georges and eight of his men. The former remained on
the coast to aid the second arrival, composed of Coster St.
Victor and ten other ruffians. Early in December, Pichegru,
Lajollais, Galliard, the brother of Raoul, Jean Marie, one of
the first associates of Georges, and other rascals of the same
sort, effected a third landing. A fourth was prevented.
Georges and Pichegru were lodged in the same house in
Paris with thirty men, commanded by the former. They
travelled by night: their accomplices, the order of their
journey—all are known. Three interviews took place with
Moreau, the last two in the general's own house; another
was appointed, but not held."

Such is the substance of this famous report; the concluding details are from the confessions of an accomplice, and
the whole composition bears as if the grand judge, Régnier,
had labored to earn for his administration a brevet of incapacity.

Having learned the arrest of Moreau, on the evening of
the 15th February, I went at an early hour next morning
to the house of his uncle, M. Carbonnet, with whom I
longed to converse on the affair. What was my surprise!
He had just been arrested also. "I advise you, sir," added

the porter—"for I have the honor to know you—to retire
without persisting; those who call here are watched."—"Is
your master still within?"—"Yes, sir, they are examining
his papers."—"I must see him."

I remained but a moment with M. Carbonnet, who appeared far more downcast on account of the general's arrest
than his own. His papers being sealed, he was consigned
to a secret prison at St. Pelagie, and did not recover his
liberty without paying for it, and that only after Moreau
had left France. I witnessed the rigorous search of this
house, and know nothing of the grounds upon which dealers
in informations and calumny could pretend that it had been
fitted up for the Duke d'Angoulême. The adroit Fouché
regarded as a masterstroke the compromising of Moreau; he
well knew that Bonaparte would pardon all his contrivances,
should they be discovered, solely because they had resulted
in removing a man whom those about him endeavored to
represent as a dangerous rival.

The events which succeeded each other with such rapidity in the commencement of the year 1804 are so interwoven
—run so into each—that they would require to be taken one
by one, dwelt upon, and returned to again and again. All,
however, in these machinations had one main object: the
foundation of a French empire in favor of Napoleon. A vital
consideration to the accomplishment of this scheme existed
in the state of parties both at home and abroad. While
Bonaparte was at peace with the rest of Europe, the cause of
the Bourbons had no longer a support in foreign cabinets,
and the emigrants, now without a rallying point, and no
longer an organized body, had no alternative but to submit
or give up the contest. But, war breaking out afresh, the
whole assumed a new aspect; the cause of foreign belligerents became the cause of the Bourbons, since it was one
opposed to the interests of Bonaparte; and as numerous ties
connected the emigrants still abroad with those who had
returned but half satisfied, or rather disappointed, into the
bosom of their country, risings in the interior, combined

with the powers already in arms against Bonaparte, were to be apprehended.

In France itself, again, all that had passed during the two preceding years favored Bonaparte's views on the crown and encouraged him to the erection of a new dynasty. But, to the men of the Revolution, to the republicans, and to his own party, sprung from the ranks of both, a pledge seemed to be necessary that, in re-establishing the throne, he set it up, not for the Bourbons, whose return these partisans had just reason to fear would be fatal to those whose hands were yet red with the blood of a Bourbon, and a king. It behooved him to bind to himself those of whom he stood in need, or rather of whom he thought he stood in need, by rendering himself as guilty as they were. The Duke d'Enghien was selected as the victim whose blood might calm the conscious terrors awakened in the men of the Revolution by the sole name of the Bourbons, Bonaparte believing that they judged themselves as he himself judged them. Besides, the death of the Duke d'Enghien, by filling with grief the breasts of all the royalists who had successively rallied round the government of the First Consul, would produce a new separation, and places, honors, dignities, must become the exclusive property of the men of the Revolution. Such were the mutual advantages of the mutual services and concessions of the parties concerned. How do the facts agree?

In February, 1804, the principals and accomplices in the conspiracy of Georges were arrested. Then comes the fatal 21st March, the murder of the Duke d'Enghien. Next follows the 30th April, the proposition made by the Tribunate to found in France a government with a single head. To this succeeds the 18th May, when the decree was published declaring Napoleon Bonaparte Emperor. The 10th June closed the tragedy by the condemnation of Georges and several of his accomplices, in which bloody drama the death of a Bourbon, and the crown of France placed upon the head of a fortunate soldier, were acts purposely introduced.

Machiavel has said that when the author of a crime is unknown, we must search out whom it profits. Here the advice of the Italian finds an obvious application, since the crime profited Bonaparte alone, and since he even deemed it indispensable to the possession of the crown of France. How, in the first place, can it be said that the Duke perished as the accomplice of Georges? This is one of those suppositions that do not merit examination; or, if it be made a subject of positive assertion, it is one of the grossest falsehoods which it is possible to conceive in history.—Let us compare facts. That unfortunate prince resided at Ettenheim, on account of a young lady to whom he was attached, and had no understanding with the plotters in the interior. Moreau was arrested on the 15th February, Georges and Pichegru were seized during the same month, and the Duke D'Enghien not till the 15th March. But, if the prince had really engaged in the conspiracy, or even had known of it, let me ask, would he have remained, almost within sight of the frontier, nearly a whole month after the seizure of his pretended associates, an occurrence of which he could have been informed in three days? So completely was he a stranger to the conspiracy that he said to those who mentioned it to him at Ettenheim, that his father or grandfather should have informed him, for his own personal security. Would they have delayed so long to send this assurance? Alas! sad experience proved that he could be reached in a few hours.

The sentence of death against Georges and his companions was not pronounced till the 10th of June, 1804, and the Duke was shot on the 21st March, at which time the pleadings had not even commenced. How explain this haste? If, as Napoleon has asserted, the young Bourbon was an accomplice of these conspirators, why was he not arrested at the same time? Why was he not confronted with them, either as an accomplice or as compromised by their declarations, or, in fine, as a useful witness against them, whose deposition might throw some light on that dark affair?

How comes it that the name of the illustrious accused was never once pronounced in the whole course of that terrible suit? The prince was no more when, at last, the accused were brought before the special tribunal: there would have been no risk in making the dead speak, and yet not one had the conscience to involve him by a single word, either as participating in or concealing the conspiracy.

But the responsibility must rest upon Bonaparte alone, for who would have dared to suggest it to him? He knew not what he was doing. A prey to ambition, whose "fiery fever" urged him on ever to madness, he understood not to what fearful extent he sunk in the world's opinion, because he was ignorant of the real nature of that opinion for which he was ready to sacrifice all. How terrible—and the more terrible because too late—must have been the intimation conveyed by the unusual silence of his counsellors! For three days after the fatal execution not a voice was raised in the Council of State!—Sublime or ridiculous might have been the thoughts which passed his own lips, but not a sound was uttered in opposition or reply—in praise or censure. They had not, however, been silent while the deed was yet to be done. In a Council held on the 18th March, where the arrest and death of the Duke D'Enghien was canvassed, it was violently opposed. Cambacérès, the second man in the state, distinguished himself in this opposition: yet he had voted, with little hesitation, for the death of Louis XVI. Bonaparte, in cruel mockery, merely replied to his arguments, "You, Cambacérès, are *become unusually* chary of the blood of the Bourbons!" To this Council Fouché was called, though only a senator, with no official employment and consequently with no legal right to be present. Fouché, like his evil genius, was urging him on to empire, and, from the moment of disclosing the conspiracy which he himself had nurtured, had said there was not an instant to lose—that he must decide. And Bonaparte *did* decide.

While these events were going forward in France the unconscious victim remained at Ettenheim, where he lived on "soft hopes," and not in conspiracy. The Duke d'Enghien thought as nobly as his grandfather, and, like him, would have scorned the proposal of assassination had it been brought to his knowledge. It was known, nor was the First Consul ignorant of the fact, that an individual had offered to the Prince de Condé, under certain conditions, to assassinate the First Consul. The indignant prince nobly refused to retrieve the rights of the Bourbons at the price of crime. In the sequel the conspirator was recognized to be an agent of the police in Paris, sent on a special mission to involve the Princes in a plot which would have ruined them forever in the public mind, opposed to murder on either side. But to return to the attempt of tracing the bloody scene which closed in the castle of Vincennes.

General Ordener, commandant of the horse grenadiers of the guard, received instructions from the minister of war to repair to the Rhine, where the chiefs of the gendarmes of New Brissac were placed under his command. General Ordener despatched a squadron of these to Ettenheim, where, on the 15th March, they seized the Prince. He was immediately conveyed to the citadel of Strasburg, and there detained till the arrival of orders from Paris. These were speedy, and as promptly executed; for the carriage which brought the unfortunate Prince arrived at the Barrier on the 20th, at one o'clock in the morning. There the cavalcade halted for the space of five hours, and afterward took the road to Vincennes, by the outer ramparts of Paris, reaching its destination at nightfall. Everything in this horrible transaction passed during the reign of darkness; the sun was not to enlighten even its tragic close. The escort received orders to enter Vincennes at night; at night the fatal gates closed upon the captive; during the night assembled the Council which tried, or rather which condemned without having tried, the accused; while the clock was yet striking six the command to fire was given, and at six o'clock, before the sun had yet risen, the Prince had ceased to live. Here I may be permitted a single reflection. Even should it be admitted that the Council of the 10th March exercised an influence on the arrest of the Duke, there was no Council held between his arrival at the Barrier, in the morning of the 20th, and the moment of execution; it could then have been no one save Bonaparte only who gave the final orders —too punctually followed.

Here, as aiding the narrative, I may insert an extract from the examination and other official documents.

"*Consular Decree.*—The Government of the Republic decrees as follows:

"Article I. The former Duke d'Enghien, accused of having borne arms against the Republic, of having been and still being in the pay of England, of taking part in the plots formed by the above power against the safety, both external and internal, of the Republic, shall be arraigned before a military commission, composed of seven members, to be named by the Governor-General of Paris, and to assemble at Vincennes.

"Article II. The Grand Judge, the Minister at War, and the Governor-General of Paris, are charged with the execution of the present decree.

"The First Consul,   (signed)   BONAPARTE.
"By the First Consul,   (signed)   HUGUES MARET,
                                                War Minister.

"Commander-in-Chief,
   Governor of Paris,   (signed)   MURAT."

Conformably to the dispositions in the above decree, Murat named the commission, which assembled on the night of the 20–21st March, the Prince's deposition in the meantime being received by an officer appointed for that purpose, as follows:

"*Year XII. of the French Republic.*—This day, 29 Ventose, at midnight, I, Captain Major of the *gendarmerie d'élite*, by order of the commanding officer of the corps, presented myself before the Commander-in-Chief Murat, governor of Paris, who immediately gave me orders to repair to the Castle of Vincennes and report myself to General Hullier, commanding the grenadiers of the consular guard, from him to receive further instructions.

"For the execution of the dispositions in the Consular Decree, and in virtue of an order from the President of the Military Commission, immediately assembled in the Castle of Vincennes, the captain reporter of the case entered the bedchamber of the Duke d'Enghien, accompanied by a colonel of the *legion d'élite*, a lieutenant, and two foot gendarmes of the same corps. The captain reporter, assisted by a captain of the 8th regiment, as registrar chosen by reporter, received the following replies in answer to questions put in order."

To these questions, the greater part of which referred to the Prince's proceedings after leaving France in 1789, the most explicit and candid answers were received. This part of the deposition implicated the Prince not more deeply than many thousands of *returned* emigrants, who had borne arms along with him. The reader will judge whether he was compromised, in the slightest degree, by the subsequent portion, directly relative to the alleged cause of his arrest:

"Asked if he corresponded with the French Princes at present in London, and if he had seen them lately? Replies, That naturally he corresponded with his grandfather, since the period of separating from him at Vienna, whither he had accompanied him, after the disbanding of the Corps de Bourbon; in like manner he corresponded with his father, whom he had not seen, as far as he could remember, since 1794 or 1795.

"Being asked if he knew General Pichegru, if he had had correspondence with him? Replies, I have never, to the best of my belief, seen him: I never had any correspondence with him. I congratulate myself on not having known him, after the vile means of which, it is said, he wished to make use—if the report be true.

"Asked if he knew ex-General Dumourier, and if he had been connected with him? Replies, Not at all; I never saw him.

"Being asked if, since the peace, he had carried on any correspondence in the interior of the Republic? Replies, I have written to some friends who are yet attached to me, and who have served with me, respecting their affairs and mine. [These were not such correspondences as those which he supposed the question implied.]

."In attestation of the foregoing, the present has been signed by the Duke d'Enghien and the other persons present."

In the Duke's own hand, in a separate note, before the signatures, was added:

"Before signing this examination, I urgently request a private interview with the First Consul. My name, my rank, my principles, and the horror of my situation, induce me to hope that he will not deny this request.
"L. A. H. DE BOURBON."

On this deposition the military commission passed judgment, or *two* judgments, one *before*, the other *after*, the execution. The former, and, of course, that upon which the Duke was executed, ran as follows:

"This day, the 30th Ventose, year XII. of the Republic —The military commission, constituted in execution of the decree of the government of the 29th current, assembled in the Castle of Vincennes in order to try the former Duke d'Enghien on the charges contained in the said decree. The president directed the accused to be brought in unbound, and without irons, and ordered the captain reporting the case to read the documents both for and against, one by one. After the reading of the decree aforesaid, the president put the following questions:

"Your names, surnames, age, and place of birth? Replied, Louis Antoine Henri de Bourbon, Duke d'Enghien, born at Chantilly the 2d August, 1772.

"Asked if he had taken arms against France? Replied, That he had served throughout the whole war, and that he adhered to the declaration which he had signed, and added, moreover, that he was ready to make war, and desired to be employed in the new war of England against France.

"Being asked if he was still in the pay of England? He replied that he was, and received one hundred and fifty guineas monthly from that power.

"The commission, after having caused to be read, by the organ of their president, the declarations of the accused in his hearing, and having asked him if he had anything to add in the way of defence? He replied that he had nothing more to say, and persisted therein.

"The president directed the accused to retire, the Council deliberating with closed doors. The president collected the votes, commencing with the junior in rank, the president giving his opinion last. The Council unanimously declared the accused guilty, and applied to him article —— of the law of ——, thus expressed ——, and, in consequence, condemned him to suffer death.—Ordered, that the present judgment be carried into immediate execution, at the instance of the captain reporter, after being read to the condemned, in presence of the different detachments of the garrison corps. Written, closed, and tried in one sitting at Vincennes, the day, month, and year aforesaid, as witness our hands."

Here follow the signatures, with the exception of the registrar's, which was not affixed to the judgment upon which the Prince was executed, an omission sufficient to render it void. But what is that compared with the blanks showing that the commission was unable even to quote either the article of the law or the law itself in virtue of which they passed the sentence of death. On the morrow there appeared a second judgment, vamped up in greater form, when it was no longer time. Even then it became necessary to go back to the revolutionary laws of 1791— a code, the destruction of which by Bonaparte had been hailed with enthusiasm, and to which he absolutely owed, in no small measure, his elevation in France. These laws he invoked anew for the destruction of the Duke d'Enghien, and even then, with senseless effrontery, the captive was designated as a *spy!* "Every individual," so runs the clause, "whatever be his rank, quality, or profession, convicted of spying for the enemy, shall be punished with death." The only other clauses quoted refer to plots and conspiracies, and had no reference to the Prince in a particular capacity, and, as respecting emigrants who had borne arms, they had been repealed.

On the 22d, the day after the execution, I was informed that some one wished to speak with me: it was Harrel, commandant of Vincennes. The following is word for word what he said. Harrel perhaps thought he owed me some gratitude, to be repaid by these particulars; but he was not my debtor; it was much against my will that he had kept up Ceracchi's conspiracy, and received the reward of a feigned accomplice.

"The evening before last," said he, "when the Prince arrived, I was asked if I had the means of lodging a prisoner? I replied, No; that there remained only my own apartment and the council chamber. I was then told to have a chamber immediately prepared in which a prisoner who would arrive in the course of the night might sleep. I was also desired *to cause a grave to be made in the court.* I replied that would not be easy, the court being paved. What other place, it was asked, would answer? The ditch was fixed upon, and there, in fact, the grave was dug.

"The Prince arrived about seven o'clock in the evening. He was perished with cold and hunger; he did not appear sad. He requested of me something to eat, and desired to be shown to bed after his repast. His chamber not being yet warmed, I received him in my own and sent to the village for some food. The Prince placed himself at table and invited me to be seated with him. Afterward he put a number of questions about Vincennes, what was passing, and a great many other things. He told me he had been brought up in the neighborhood of the castle, and conversed with much affability and condescension. Among other inquiries he asked, 'Why do they want me? What is their purpose with me?' But these questions produced no change in his tranquillity, and he showed no uneasiness. My wife, who is sick, was in bed in an alcove of the same apartment, separated from us only by a grating: she heard, without being seen, all this conversation, and experienced the most lively emotion; for she recognized the Prince, whose foster-sister she had been, and the family had settled a pension upon her before the Revolution.

"The Prince was in haste to retire to rest. He had need of some: but before he could have been well asleep the judges ordered him to be brought into the council chamber. I was not present at the examination. On its conclusion the Duke again ascended to his chamber, and when they went to seek him in order to read the sentence to him, he was in a profound sleep. A few moments after they were leading him to execution. He had so little apprehension of this, that, while descending the stair which conducts into the moat, he asked where they were taking him: no one made reply. I walked before the Prince with a lantern: feeling the cold which came from below he grasped my arm, and said—' *Will they throw me into a dungeon ?*' '

Such was Harrel's simple narrative: the rest is too well known. I think I yet behold him shudder when thinking of this action of the unhappy Prince. Savary was not in the ditch at the moment of the execution, but most certainly on the glacis above, whence he could easily overlook the whole. Much has been said of a lantern, reported to have been fixed to a buttonhole on the Duke's breast. That circumstance is pure invention. Captain Dautancourt, having weak sight, caused the lantern carried by Harrel to be brought close, in order to read the sentence to the unhappy Prince—and what a sentence!—by which he was condemned, not only unjustly, but without even the forms of justice. It was probably this use of the lantern which gave rise to the outcry spread abroad; besides, it was six o'clock in the morning when the fatal event took place, and on the 21st March it is light at that hour.

General Savary dared not take upon himself to delay the execution, although the Prince urgently demanded an interview with the First Consul. Had Bonaparte seen the Duke, I believe it may be considered as a matter beyond doubt that he would have saved his life. How, indeed, could he have acted otherwise ? Thus all that can be laid to Savary's charge is not having suspended an execution which, in all probability, had it been delayed, would not have taken place. Of this there appears almost a proof in the uncertainty which must have reigned in the mind of the First Consul. Had he not wavered, all his measures would have been determined in advance; and, had they been so, to a certainty the Duke's carriage would not have been kept waiting for five hours at the Barrier. It is a known fact, also, that at first the intention was to convey the Duke to the prison of the Temple. But from all this, the final inference is to me clear as day that an order had been received from Bonaparte to destroy the Duke d'Enghien—an order so full and explicit as rendered it impossible to speak with Bonaparte again till all was concluded. Savary, then, did nothing but obey; and it had been better for him, in his late Memoirs, to have acknowledged this with regret, than to attempt, with heroic but mistaken devotion, to palliate, even at his own expense, this crime which will eternally stigmatize the name of the master whom he so faithfully served. I promised to tell the truth on this melancholy subject, and have fulfilled my promise, regardless of the pain which the avowal has caused me. Of the correctness of my general inferences can there be a more convincing proof than the circumstances of Harrel's narrative, which permit me not to entertain the doubts I could have wished still to have cherished? A grave prepared beforehand—a grave dug in the ditch of a fortress, while the unconscious captive, its destined inmate, yet lived but by the permission of him who gave that order.

The immediate consequences of the death of the Duke d'Enghien were not confined to the consternation with which this stroke agitated the capital. The news filled the provinces with equal fear and hatred, and foreign courts with indignation not less deep because silent. One entire class of society, and that the most influential, which we may here term the *Faubourg St. Germain* of the provinces, namely, the country gentlemen, was, by this act, to a man alienated. The disposition of the landed interest had till then been not unfavorable to the First Consul. On it had pressed, in its heaviest rigor, the law of hostages, and, with the exception of some families grown inveterate in the belief that they were to the world what they appeared to be in a circle of some two leagues—illustrious personages—all wise people in the provinces, even while preserving a sincere attachment to the ancient order of things, had seen with satisfaction the Consular substituted for the Directoral government, and certainly bore no hostility to the person of the chief magistrate.

The consequences were still more fatal at foreign courts, universally changing the sentiments of the sovereigns toward the First Consul. Every crowned head and every princely family in Europe regarded the murder of the Duke d'Enghien and the violation of the neutrality of the states of Baden as insults to their rank. The slow policy of the cabinet of Vienna, however, and the vicinage of the French troops in Hanover, which overawed Berlin, prevented either of these courts from testifying resentment by any public remonstrance. But, at St. Petersburg, Alexander openly proclaimed his indignation, and henceforth England found it more easy successfully to negotiate with Austria and Prussia as well as Russia, though the two former continued silent. The English press for long after designated Bonaparte only as the murderer of the Duke d'Enghien; and I know for certain that Mr. Pitt observed to some one, "Bonaparte has just wrought himself more mischief than we have been able to inflict since the first declaration of war."

Of all the monarchs of Europe, however, the injury affected most nearly the Kings of Naples and Spain, since theirs was the blood that had been shed; but they could only suffer and be silent. Not so Louis XVIII., more of a king, though without subjects, than those of his family actually seated upon thrones. Immediately on the execution of the Duke he wrote to the King of Spain as follows:

"SIRE, SIR, AND DEAR COUSIN—It is with regret that I return to you the insignia of the Golden Fleece which his Majesty, your father, of glorious memory, intrusted to me. There can now be nothing in common to me with the grand criminal whom audacity and fortune have placed upon my throne, since he has had the barbarity to shed the blood of a Bourbon in that of the Duke d'Enghien. Religion might engage me to forgive a murderer, but the tyrant of my people must ever be mine enemy. In the present age it is more glorious to deserve than to wield a sceptre. Providence, for inscrutable purposes, may condemn me to end my days in exile, but never shall my contemporaries or posterity be able to say, that, in the season of adversity, I showed myself unworthy, even to my last sigh, of occupying the throne of my ancestors.   LOUIS."

CHAPTER XVIII

Arrest and Trial of Cadoudal and other Conspirators—Death of Pichegru—Moreau before the Court—The Sentences

THE death of the Duke d'Enghien presents a horrible episode thrown into the grand action, then in progress, and soon afterward consummated, of Bonaparte's elevation to the imperial throne. The trials of the real or supposed conspirators belonged, in part, to the same events. These I attended throughout, and thus obtained conviction of the fact that Moreau was not in reality a conspirator, though I believe the First Consul might naturally enough have supposed him such. And I am also convinced that the machinations of the police had induced the actual conspirators to regard the victor of Hohenlinden as their accomplice and their chief.

The declarations of Bouvet de Lozier led to the arrest of Moreau; Pichegru was taken through the most infamous treachery of which man can be guilty, being betrayed by one named Leblanc, to whose friendship he had implicitly confided his liberty and life. The official police, at length informed of the general's presence in Paris, had in vain endeavored to discover his retreat, when this wretch, who had, in fact, provided the very asylum he was now to violate, came voluntarily to state that the price of a friend's blood was one hundred thousand crowns. Comminges, the commissary of police, was thus furnished with an exact description of Pichegru's place of concealment, Rue de Chabanais, and with false keys to his very bedchamber. This functionary, with a party of strong and resolute men, repaired to the spot during the night of the 22–23d February. These precautions were rendered fully necessary by the prodigious personal strength of Pichegru, and by knowledge of the fact that, with means of defence at hand, he would never allow himself to be taken without desperate resistance. This party gained admittance by means of the false keys which Leblanc had had the baseness to get made for himself. Their victim was asleep. A night-lamp burned on a table by the bed. The light was instantly overturned and extinguished, and the whole threw themselves upon the general, who struggled, nevertheless, with great force, uttering loud cries for help. He was at length overpowered and pinioned, and thus they conducted the conqueror of Holland to the dungeon which he never left alive.

Pichegru, I confess, was far from inspiring the same interest as Moreau. The army never forgave his negotiations with the Prince de Condé, before the 18th Fructidor.

Fifteen days after the arrest of Pichegru, Georges was seized, on the 9th March, in company with another of the accused named Leridant, about seven in the evening, while crossing, in a cabriolet, the square of the Odéon. To this spot he had, doubtless, been conducted by the agent of the police, in order that a public capture might strike with greater effect upon the minds of the multitude. If such was the calculation, it cost the life of one man, and had nearly proved fatal to another; for Georges, who always went armed, shot dead the police officer who seized the reins, and, in like manner, wounded the first who advanced to lay hold of himself. Besides his pistols there was found upon his person a dagger of English manufacture, and, though all this might have been expected, the journals next day failed not to raise a great outcry, as if Georges had for months been lurking in the capital for the purpose of assassinating the First Consul.

Georges' last place of concealment had been in the house of a fruit-woman named Lemoine, whose daughter had gone on before with a packet belonging to him, and the young woman was in the act of getting into the vehicle at the moment of his arrest. At the instant of firing he called out to this person to save herself; but the police were quickly upon her traces, and she was discovered in a neighboring house, where she had given the packet to another female; this, among other things, contained a bag of 84,000 francs. It was also discovered that the parcel had been opened, "merely through curiosity," by the husband of the woman to whom it had been intrusted, though, as turned out, he had been somewhat more than curious, in contriving to abstract therefrom, in an extremely brief space, rather better than a thousand crowns. All these persons were arrested, and Georges the same night was conducted to the Temple prison. After his arrest there still remained several individuals, of less note, implicated in the conspiracy, and who had found means to elude pursuit, but were all secured within five days after the death of the Duke d'Enghien. They were taken by the famous Commissary Comminges, in the house of one named Dubusson, who had furnished a retreat to several of the proscribed. It may show the nature of such researches to explain how the last captures were effected here, namely, by the police firing at suspicious-looking furniture, doors, or hiding-places throughout the premises. By this means, Villeneuve, who was shut up in a cupboard, being wounded in the arm, the whole were discovered. It is worthy of remark, also, that the day after Georges' arrest the Council assembled in which Bonaparte decided the fate of the Duke; that is to say, when all those of note or consequence among the alleged conspirators were in the hands of the government, and when there no longer existed a pretext for alleging the presence of any mysterious personage in Paris: for Pichegru, with daring peculiar to himself, had made his nightly appearance in several saloons of the Faubourg St. Germain, exciting the fears, yet eluding the researches, of the police. This mysterious personage it was attempted to pass off as the Duke d'Enghien, and thence reasons were found for defending his murder! More than a hundred captives now crowded the Temple, who, Moreau excepted, were all treated with extreme rigor. They dared not hold com-

munication with, for fear of mutually compromising, each
other; but all exhibited a courage and resolution which
awakened fears as to the outcome of the trial. Neither
promises nor threats of punishment could draw from them
any disclosures in the course of examination. Pichegru in
particular displayed such firmness that Réal, on leaving the
dungeon, where he had just been examining him, exclaimed
aloud, before several witnesses, "What a man that Pichegru is!"

Forty days had elapsed from the arrest of that general
when, on the morning of the 6th April, he was found dead
in the cell which he occupied in the Temple. During this
space Pichegru had undergone ten examinations; he had
not made a single confession; not one individual had been
compromised by his replies; all his declarations showed his
readiness to speak out, but that he would do so only in public and during the solemn proceedings of the legal tribunals.
"When I am before the judges," said he, "my language
shall ever be conformable to truth and the interest of my
country!" What, then, would have been the tenor of that
language? Doubtless it was feared the spirit of it would
prove anything but convenient. It was resolved, therefore,
it should not be heard, for Pichegru would have kept his
word: he was no less able as a general than firm and resolved as a man, in which respect he showed himself
infinitely superior to Moreau.

The day on which Réal expressed himself as above was
the last of Pichegru's examinations, and of his life. On
this occasion, as I afterward learned from unquestionable
authority, Pichegru, always careful not to implicate any of
his fellow sufferers, took no care to conceal his detestation
of him who had resolved on his death, but expressed his
determination to expose to the eyes of the nation the odious
contrivances of the plot by which the police had insnared
him. He declared, likewise, that he and his companions in
captivity no longer thought of anything save how to leave
Paris as speedily as possible, and escape the pitfalls dug

around them, having one and all renounced any design against Bonaparte—a design into which they had been led by the police, when they were arrested. To this frank and stern avowal I attribute the premature death of Pichegru. M. Réal, who examined that unfortunate man, knows better than any other the substance of his confessions. I am ignorant whether the examiner, who is still alive, either now or later will lift the veil which covers these mysterious events; but I know he dare not contradict a single fact which I now advance. To me it is demonstrated, to the fullest conviction, that Pichegru was strangled in prison; a theory of suicide is consequently inadmissible. I have read all that has been published on this subject; the truth has not been declared till now.

The body was discovered lying on the bed, about half-past seven in the morning, by the domestic, on entering to light the fire. About the neck of the corpse was a black silk cravat, through which had been passed a piece of wood as a turning stick. This had been twisted round till suffocation ensued, and one end still remained resting against the left cheek, being thus prevented from recoiling. Upon the same cheek had been inflicted a considerable abrasion from the forcible and irregular movement of the stick. Some struggling had been heard in the chamber, but not such as to excite inquiry, and the marshal of the prison declared that the key of the general's chamber had been ·brought to him at ten, and continued throughout the night in his possession, till the moment of lighting the fire! Such are the principal details of the investigation. It was reported, very awkwardly, at the time, that Réal had said, "Now, though nothing can be more clearly demonstrated than this suicide, all is vain; people will always say that, not being able to convict him, we strangled the prisoner." Réal never said this—it bore too near a resemblance to the truth.

I have here no intention to justify those who engaged in a conspiracy; crime is ever to be condemned, whatever inducements may have been used to excite to its commission; though such excitement, in the hands of those who afterward punished the delinquents, necessarily diminishes our indignation. That such encouragement was given by the secret police appears from what has already been stated, and from a fact reported to me by M. Carbonnet, who witnessed the entrance of Pichegru, accompanied by Rolland and Lajollais, into Moreau's library, the general being there to receive them, and, after the interview, related its object to my informant as follows: Pichegru said he had been informed by mutual friends that Moreau and the senate reckoned upon bringing about a change. Moreau assured Pichegru he had been deceived, that he knew nothing which warranted Pichegru's journey; he treated it as madness, and declared that every attempt to overturn the government was impracticable and absurd.

While the process was in preparation, Georges and the other principal conspirators were held in the most rigorous and secret confinement. The catastrophe of Pichegru was communicated to them separately; and as none credited the report of suicide, it is not easy to conceive the consternation and terror thus excited among the captives. I grieve to say Louis Bonaparte, certainly the best of his family, indulged the cruel curiosity of visiting Georges in this situation. What an unworthy spectacle! Louis appeared surrounded by a brilliant staff; the royalist chief was stretched upon a couch, his hands crossed in front of him, and heavily bound with irons. Lauriston informed me of these particulars, and, notwithstanding his devotion to the interests of the First Consul, could not forbear from voicing his disapprobation of what he had witnessed. Nor did this surprise me. Lauriston was not, like too many of Bonaparte's aides-de-camp, a stranger to the feelings of humanity.

The indictment being drawn up, the prisoners were permitted to have communication with each other, and in that reckless indifference of life inspired by youth, misfortune, and courage united, they actually amused themselves with

childish sports! An order for their transfer to the Conciergerie put an end to these games thus strangely played; and
for this abode of new and more certain sorrow they prepared
as if setting out on some ordinary visit. Before departing,
Georges harangued his companions in captivity, encouraging
them to constancy and mutual forgiveness—"Show to the
world by your demeanor and your discourse that you possess
the courage and resolution which inspired me with such confidence in you, which would have rendered us triumphant
over the enemies of our king and of our faith had we not
been so unworthily betrayed!"

Everything being now prepared, Hémart, the regicide,
was named president of the special tribunal before which the
prisoners were to be cited. This choice filled Paris with
general horror; it seemed to seal the doom of the accused.
Napoleon had now been about ten days Emperor when the
trials, which had hastened his elevation, commenced on
the 28th May. It is impossible to describe either the con-
course in the Palace of Justice during all the twelve days
of the proceedings, or the anxiety, consternation and doubt
which prevailed. The judge; the selection of the jury; the
recent death of the Duke d'Enghien; the more immediate
and mysterious fate of Pichegru—all threw a fearful and
gloomy apprehension into the minds of men. In my own
individual case I cannot yet recall without emotion my feelings on seeing the prisoners one by one enter and take their
places between two officers of justice, all wearing a grave
but firm expression of countenance, save Bouvet de Lozier,
who dared not raise his eyes to his companions, whom weakness, not inclination, had seduced him to criminate. Of the
whole forty-nine accused, among whom were several women,
I knew only Moreau and Georges. All eyes were turned
upon the victor of Hohenlinden, and every look was one of
respect and admiration. In the course of the whole proceedings, which I followed with equal interest and attention, not
the shadow of a fact occurred to inculpate his conduct for
one instant. Scarcely one of the hundred and thirty-nine

witnesses for the prosecution knew him, while he declared, during the fourth sitting, that not one of the accused had either been known, or, to the best of his knowledge, even seen by him. His appearance was constantly untroubled as his conscience; he repelled the attacks of his accusers with a calm dignity and modest assurance, although from time to time there burst from him an expression of just indignation. I remember, on the president accusing him of a design to assume the dictatorship, the electric effect produced when Moreau exclaimed—"I dictator! make myself dictator with the partisans of the Bourbons? Where, then, were to be found my own supporters? I will tell you—they would have been the soldiers of France, nine-tenths of whom I have commanded, and fifty thousand of whom I have saved! These warriors, however, would have aided me in a cause against which the partisans you now give me have combated since 1792!" But for the cannon bullet which struck down Moreau amid the ranks of the enemies of France—but for the foreign badge which disgraced the hat of Hohenlinden, his fame had been unsullied! I still seem to see the worthy friend of Moreau, General Lecourbe, unexpectedly entering the court, holding an infant in his arms, and saying, in a strong voice, which yet trembled with emotion—"Soldiers, behold the son of your general!" All the military in the immense hall, as if by spontaneous sympathy, presented arms to the child, and a murmur of approbation rose from the auditory. Unquestionably if, at this moment of enthusiasm, Moreau had but spoken the word, the court would speedily have been cleared, and the prisoners set at liberty. He remained silent, and, of all present, seemed the only unconcerned spectator. The same respectful admiration actuated the soldiery who guarded Moreau in prison, and rendered it no easy matter for the government to provide effectually for his security without increasing an admiring guard, so as to render it a formidable point of support in the event of an insurrection. The general's docile and unambitious character, however, proved the best guarantee for his safe custody. Such was the respect he inspired, even when accused, that in the court, whenever he rose to speak, the gendarmes appointed to guard him rose also of their own accord and stood uncovered till their prisoner had sat down.

Georges was in no degree to be compared with Moreau; the former inspired less of interest than of curiosity; and, apart from their former position in society, their behavior in the present emergency exhibited a striking contrast. Moreau - appeared calm and dignified and secure in conscious rectitude: Georges, resigned to the fate that awaited him, viewed his situation with an almost barbarian firmness. As if to avenge himself on death before suffering its pains, he assumed a tone of bitter sarcasm against all concerned. Thuriot, another regicide, and one also of the judges, he always addressed, pronouncing his name Tue-roi (Kill-king), and when obliged to reply to the judge's interrogations, exclaimed, on finishing, "Give me a glass of water, that I may wash my mouth!" But under this assumed tone and manner of a rude soldier, Georges concealed the soul of a hero: throughout the whole proceedings he discovered unshaken firmness. Of all that concerned himself personally, he concealed nothing. On everything which might compromise others neither insinuation, reproaches, nor arguments could open his lips. The following dialogue will give some idea of the manner in which Georges' examination and replies were conducted. When the witnesses to his arrest had answered the interrogatories of the president, the latter, addressing Georges, asked—"Have you anything to reply?"—"No."—"Do you admit the facts?"—"Yes." Then, as Georges affected to pay no attention, but to be looking at some papers which lay before him, Hémart was obliged to remind him that he ought not to read during his examination, and the dialogue recommenced thus: "You admit having been arrested in the place mentioned by the witness?"—"I know not the name of the place."—"You admit having been arrested?"—"Yes."—"Did you fire two pistol shots?"—"Yes."—"Did you kill a man?"—"It might be so: I

know nothing of it."—"You had a poniard?"—"Yes."—
"And two pistols?"—"Yes."—"Whom had you with
you?"—"I do not know the person."—"Where did you
lodge in Paris?"—"Nowhere."—"At the moment of your
arrest did you not lodge with a fruiterer, Rue Montagne
St. Geneviève?"—"At the moment of my arrest I was in
a cabriolet: I lodged nowhere."—"Where did you sleep the
night before?"—"Nowhere."—"What were you doing in
Paris?"—"I was walking about."—"What persons did you
see there?"—"I shall name no one—I know them not."
Offers, too, had been made to him in prison; and I heard
M. Réal, who had been the organ of communication, say to
Desmarets and others, "I have just seen Georges; he has
rejected all my offers of pardon and employment under the
imperial government; he put an end to my commission
by saying, 'My companions followed me into France—I will
follow them to death.'" And yet the man to whom solicitations on behalf of the Emperor were thus made in a dungeon by a councillor of state was stigmatized as a *brigand*
in placards stuck about the walls of Paris!

Coster Saint-Victor had something chivalrous in his bearing and language which prepossessed all in his favor: he
presented no bad likeness to one of the Fiesco conspirators
or cavaliers of the Fronde—votaries at once of pleasure and
of politics. An anecdote was about this time placed to his
account which I may here give, though considering it merely
imaginary. Saint-Victor, having no fixed place of abode in
Paris, had found for one night a lodging with a certain fair
actress well established in the good graces of the First Consul. By chance, Bonaparte happened to pay her a secret
visit on the same evening, and found himself in presence
of Saint-Victor, who thus might easily have disposed of his
man; but in this interview of rival gallantry there passed
only exchanges of mutual courtesy. The story is ridiculous;
Bonaparte never went abroad at night, and certainly would
not have commenced a course of nocturnal adventures when
he believed "the air to be full of daggers." The invention

was calculated to render him more odious should Saint-
Victor not be pardoned.

Wright was heard during the sixth sitting, as thirty-
fourth witness for the prosecution. He declared that he
would reply to no question; that, as prisoner of war,
he claimed all the rights of one; that he owed any account
of his proceedings to his own government alone. The
advocate-general requested the president to order his examination of the 21st May, and one still later, to be read
to Captain Wright. After the reading, Wright replied that
they had not inserted in the report the threats of delivering
him up to a military commission and shooting him unless he
betrayed the secrets of his country.

In the course of the proceedings the most tender interest
attached to MM. de Polignac, Charles d'Hozier, and De
Rivière—all young, all heirs of illustrious names, which,
notwithstanding the proscription of the nobility, still held
influence over the spirits of men even when opposed to their
principles, especially when accompanied with the steadfast-
ness and heroism manifested by these young victims. All
seemed reckless of their own fate and solicitous only for
the honor of the cause they had espoused. Even under the
sword of the law, these faithful servants of the Bourbons
seized every opportunity of displaying their attachment.
A medallion, with the likeness of the Comte d'Artois, was
produced as evidence against De Rivière; he requested a
nearer view; it was handed to him, when he pressed it to his
lips and returned it, saying he merely wished thus to testify
his homage to a prince whom he loved. But the immense
audience were still more moved, when the two brothers
Polignac each in turn implored the judges to let the vengeance of the law fall upon himself, but to spare his brother.
There was not a dry eye in the court; yet in my memory
does there contrast horribly with this tender scene the figure
of Hémart putting an end to this touching rivalry by saying,
in a tone more vindictive than befitted magisterial gravity,
"The proceedings are closed."

For four hours we waited the return of the judges—the crowd was every moment increasing. A general stupor fell upon all when, at length, Hémart resumed the president's chair, holding the sentence of the court in his hand. Death was pronounced against Georges Cadoudal, Bouvet de Lozier, Rusillon, Rochelle, Armand de Polignac, Charles d'Hozier, De Rivière, Louis Ducorps, Picot, Lajollais, Roger, Saint-Victor, Deville, Gaillard, Joyaut, Burban, Lemercier, Jean Cadoudal, Lelan, and Merille. Only two years' imprisonment was awarded to Jules de Polignac, Leridant, Rolland, Hisay, and General Moreau.

At this sentence consternation spread throughout Paris; it was a day of general mourning and, though Sunday, the usual places of public resort were deserted. To the horror of such wanton condemnation to death of so many, the greater part of whom belonged to the most distinguished class of society, was added the ridicule of Moreau's condemnation—a thing to which no one could be more sensible than Bonaparte himself. He is reported to have said to the judges on this occasion—"Gentlemen, I am but your pupil; it is your duty to be well informed before presenting your report. But when I have once your signature, on your heads be it if an innocent man suffer."

The language is like his, and, in substance, the same as we shall find he himself expressed to me some days after. In the commencement of this catastrophe, I have not hesitated to lay the whole odium of the Duke's murder on Bonaparte; but, in the affair of Georges and Moreau, he was less guilty than the judges and accusers, and far less so than the grand instigator of so many hateful machinations. The language above quoted, however, though it might have been well placed in the mouth of a sovereign whose ministers were responsible, could only be an ironical excuse from the lips of an absolute ruler.

The condemned appealed, less from inclination than through the pressing entreaties of their friends. Moreau also put in an appeal; but, yielding to his fate, he withdrew

it before the sitting of the court, consoled by the thought
that he owed his misfortune to a too splendid reputation.
I obtained at the time the most unquestionable assurance
that Murat immediately applied to the Emperor for a general
pardon, on the grounds both of humanity and policy, urging
that such an act of clemency, at the commencement of the
imperial reign, would evoke goodwill throughout France
and Europe far more than equivalent to any security gained
by the execution of the conspirators.   The application was
unfavorably received; but Josephine, who, on becoming
Empress, lost none of her matchless benevolence or attachment to old friends, succeeded in obtaining mitigation of
some of the sentences.

Bouvet de Lozier, by his revelations, Rusillon de Rivière,
Rochelle, Armand de Polignac, and D'Hozier, as also, in all
probability, Armand Gaillard, through this intercession, and
Lajollais as a matter of course, were pardoned.   As to the
other victims of the dark contrivances of base police spies,
they underwent their fate on the 25th June with the same
courage and resignation they had throughout displayed.
Georges, aware of a report having arisen that he had been
received into favor, requested one privilege at least, which
was to die first, that his companions when dying might carry
with them the assurance that he had not survived them.

I have said that the judges composing the special tribunal were tampered with; and this I assert on personal proof.
Bonaparte knew that I was very intimately acquainted with
M. Desmaisons, one of the members of the court and brother-
in-law of Corvisart; he knew, besides, that this judge inclined to the opinion that Moreau was innocent, and ought
to be acquitted.   One morning very early, during the progress of the trial, Corvisart paid me a visit with a very embarrassed air—"How now," said I, "what bad news do you
bring?"—"None," replied the man of medicine; "but I
come by order of the Emperor; he desires you will speak
with my brother-in-law; his words were, 'Desmaisons is the
senior judge—a considerate man; his opinion will have great

weight. I know he is favorable to Moreau; he is wrong. Go find Bourrienne, and come to an understanding with him, to bring his friend to more rational ideas; for, I repeat it, he is wrong; he deceives himself." I need not repeat the indignation and astonishment with which I listened to this proposal, nor that, during the whole course of the proceedings, I took care not once to visit or speak to M. Desmaisons, who, however, would have been as far from suffering himself to be influenced as I could have been from making the attempt. There were also other honorable men among the judges, for all were not Hémarts and Thuriots. History will preserve, as a noble contrast to the turpitude of the period, the reply of Clavier to the president, who urged him to give his voice against Moreau—"Well, sir, and if we condemn him, who will absolve us?"

CHAPTER XIX

Bonaparte made Emperor—The Formalities—Titles Bestowed—Josephine's Dislike of the Change

I HAVE all along stated that the events narrated in preceding chapters either conduced or became subservient to the elevation of Bonaparte to the imperial throne. Revert we now to the progress and proceedings of this most important consummation, which have in some degree been anticipated, that the foregoing details might be kept together.

For a long time the agents of the government had been trained throughout France to demand for the First Consul, in the name of the people, that which the people were far from desiring, but which Bonaparte wished to assume under show of according to the general inclination—the sovereign power, without restrictions, limits, or subterfuge of denomination. A conspiracy against his life was not an opportunity to be omitted, but, on the contrary, was eagerly laid hold of by all the authorities, civil, military and ecclesiastic: a new and most abundant shower of addresses, congratulations, and rendering of thanks inundated the Tuileries. Knowing what would prove most pleasing to their master, the greater part of these addressers did not limit themselves to mere felicitations; they insinuated, more or less adroitly, that France called upon her glorious chief to place himself so high as to be beyond reach of any new attempt—to *consolidate his work;* which, being interpreted, implied that he should assume imperial and hereditary power.

Bonaparte, in this scene of the grand drama, played his part with his wonted superiority, suffering nothing to appear outwardly at first, leaving to others the care of preparatory measures. The Senate took unto itself the due honors of precedence in congratulating the Consul on his escape from "the daggers of England"; for so, in official parlance, had the imaginary conspiracy been designated: the Senate besought the First Consul *not to defer finishing his work.* This address was presented only ten days after the death of the Duke d'Enghien. Whether Bonaparte suffered compunction from his useless crime and perceived the bad effect produced on the public mind by that catastrophe, or whether he found the terms employed by the Senate somewhat too vague, does not appear; but he allowed the address to remain nearly a whole month without reply. When he did answer, it was only to invite a clearer exposition of sentiment. These negotiations were secret; for Bonaparte liked publicity only in results. But to the Tribunate belonged the initiative of all measures; and in the Tribunate the project now ripening was proposed.

The member Curée had the honor of first proposing officially the conversion of the Consular Republic into an Empire, and the elevation of Bonaparte to the title of Emperor, with hereditary right. Curée brought out his proposition in the meeting of the 30th April, at which I was present. He commenced by exposing the misfortunes which had overwhelmed France, from the Constitutional Assembly down to the 18th Brumaire—a revolution which he justly characterized as a deliverance. He then passed in review the brilliant career of the present head of the Republic; enumerated his claims to the gratitude of France; showed that her flourishing condition depended on him—"Let us haste, then, to demand the hereditary transmission of the supreme magistracy; for, in voting for a hereditary chief, as Pliny said to Trajan, we bar the return of a master. But, at the same time, let us give a great name to a great power; let us choose a title which, while it carries the idea of the highest civil functions, may recall glorious remembrances *and breathe no taint upon the sovereignty of the people.* I can see, for the guardian of a *national* power, none more fitting than the title of Emperor. If it signifies 'victorious Consul,' who better merits to receive it? which people, what armies, were ever more worthy that such should be the title of their leader? I move, therefore, that we transmit to the Senate our wishes, which are those of the whole nation, to the following effect:

"I. That Napoleon Bonaparte, now First Consul, be proclaimed Emperor, and, in this quality, continue to take upon him the government of the French Republic.

"II. That the imperial dignity be declared hereditary in his family.

"III. That those of our institutions which are as yet but traced out be definitely settled."

Such was the apologetic harangue of Curée; and I beheld a crowd of the members of the Tribunate eagerly pressing forward to have their names inscribed on the roll, each following with a speech more and more laudatory than that of the author, or rather proposer of a motion so evidently emanating from him upon whom ultimate effects would touch. But could there be any doubts on the complaisant part thus enacted by Curée, they would vanish before the fact that, ten days previously, Bonaparte had taken care to have the whole proceedings rehearsed in a private sitting of the Council of State. About the middle of April, that assembly having met, as if for the ordinary despatch of business, Cambacérès entered instead of the First Consul, who was expected, and, as Second Consul, assumed the chair—the councillors remarking that his air was more solemn than usual, though he habitually affected a grave exterior. Régnault de St. Jean d'Angely, a member of the Council, with whom, though not precisely connected, I had pretty intimate relations, informed me of all. "The First Consul," said he, speaking with the enthusiasm which he really then entertained, though he subsequently acknowledged having been deceived, "has convinced me that he desires supreme power only in order to render France great, free, and happy, and place her in security against faction. He asked me to take the lead in this matter before the Council; and I did not hesitate. After Cambacérès had given us to understand the object of the meeting, and had retired, I frankly proposed the question, for which the members were thus all prepared, expressed in these terms: 'Is it expedient to place the government of France upon the base of hereditary power?'" The proposer of this the fundamental question followed up the subject with a long address, showing, "from history, and from the present state of Europe, that a hereditary government alone promised security to the state and happiness to the people." Régnault did not, however, conceal from me that his motion experienced considerable opposition, especially from Berlier. "With hereditary succession," said this latter, "there no longer remains to France anything of that Republic for whose sake she has exhausted her treasury and sacrificed millions of her people. Besides, I do not believe the French nation disposed to renounce what they still possess of a good so dearly purchased." Others spoke to the same purpose, but with less force; and finally the partisans of hereditary power found themselves in the majority of twenty to seven, and resolved to present an address to the First Consul. The minority of seven, on the other hand, had prepared a counter address. To prevent this collision of opinion, Bonaparte, informed of all, gave the Council to understand that he desired each member individually to send in his separate opinion. By a strange chance it became Berlier's duty to present these separate overtures. Bonaparte received them graciously, and assured the Council that he sought hereditary power only for the greater good of France. "Never shall the citizens be *my subjects*, yet never shall the French people be less *my people!*"

Such had been the preliminaries in the Council of State regarding the proposition officially brought forward in the Tribunate by Curée; but after reflection it was agreed that, since all opposition would be useless, and perhaps might prove dangerous to its authors, the minority should accede to the majority. And so it was arranged.

It had now become no longer necessary to keep the secret; *the pear was ripe:* the address of the Senate was accordingly published forty days after date. In this its first address the Senate had taken for its text the events passing in France and the intrigues abroad, especially those of Drake, an agent sent by England to Munich. This text, obscure in itself, naturally led the addressers to hint obscurely at what they termed the wants of France. To give more solemnity to their proceedings the Senate repaired in a body to the Tuileries, and Cambacérès, as president, pronounced the address.

"On viewing," said this document, "those attempts from which Providence has saved the hero necessary to its designs, we are struck with one prime reflection, namely, that by the destruction of the First Consul is meditated also the destruction of France. The English and the emigrants know that your destiny involves that of the French people. Give us, then, institutions so combined that their system may survive you. You found a new era, but you ought to render it immortal; splendor is nothing without duration. Great man! complete your work by making it eternal as your own glory! You rescued us from the chaos of the past; you fill our hearts with gratitude for the blessings of the present; guarantee to us the future!"

For nearly a month, as already stated, this address remained unanswered. Then Bonaparte replied to the Senate, at greater length than usual, and in substance as follows:

"Your address has formed the object of my most constant meditations. You have declared the hereditary succession of the supreme magistracy to be necessary in order to secure the French people against the plots of their enemies and the agitation excited by ambitious rivals." [Here it is very worthy of remark that the expression "hereditary succession" had not once been pronounced in the address.] "Several of our institutions have at the same time appeared to you calculated to assure, without reversion, the triumph of equality and of public liberty, and to offer to the nation and to government the twofold security required. We have always been guided by this great truth, that sovereignty resides in the French people in such a way that all— all things without exception—should be made to work together for the interest, happiness, and glory of the nation. In proportion as I direct attention to these grand objects, I am the more convinced of the truth of the sentiments I have expressed to you, and I feel more and more that in this conjuncture, new as it is important, the counsels of your wisdom and your experience are needful to confirm my ideas. I invite you, then, to lay before me your full and unreserved opinion."

This message to the Senate expressed the will of Napoleon. And that body, created for the preservation of those institutions consecrated by the constitution of the year VIII., had no other resource than to submit to intentions so unequivocally manifested. Accordingly, a response was framed to the above message of which it could be deemed nothing more than an amplified explanation. The grand principles were here positively announced, "that hereditary government was essential to the happiness, glory, and prosperity of France; and that such government could be confided only to Napoleon Bonaparte and to his family." Still the Senate affected, as Bonaparte had done in his message, to season their reply with the high-sounding phrases of liberty and equality. That body had even what might be termed the audacity to say that the arrival of Bonaparte at hereditary power would secure the liberty of the press —a freedom which he held in such abhorrence, and without which all other liberties are but vain illusions.

In all these proceedings I believe the Senate to have been more accomplice than dupe: for it was no longer possible to shut one's eyes to Bonaparte's ambition and his design of establishing, for his own advantage, a power more absolute than had been even the despotism of Louis XIV.

By the reply of the Senate the most important move had been effected: there remained little more than ceremonies to regulate and forms to contrive. These different arrangements occasioned a delay of fifteen days. At length, on the 18th May, NAPOLEON, for the first time, was saluted SIRE by his ex-colleague Cambacérès, at the head of the Senate, who had come in state to present the decree relative to the foundation of the empire. The interview took place at St. Cloud. This organic *senatus consultum*, which changed entirely the ancient constitution, being read, the Emperor replied:

"Whatever can conduce to the good of the country is essentially interwoven with my happiness.

"I accept the title which you consider to be useful to the glory of the nation.

"I submit to the sanction of the people the law of the succession. I hope that France will never repent those honors with which she may surround my family.

"At all events, my spirit shall not abide with my posterity beyond that day on which they cease to deserve the love and confidence of the great nation."

The Senate and its president afterward waited upon the Empress with congratulations; and thus was realized the prediction I had made to Josephine three years before at Malmaison.

The first act of Bonaparte, now Emperor, on the very day of his elevation to the imperial throne, was to nominate Joseph to the dignity of Grand Elector, and Louis to that of Constable of the Empire; each with the title of Imperial Highness. On the same day Cambacérès and Lebrun were appointed to the dignities of Arch-chancellor and Arch-treasurer of the Empire; and the first letter signed by Bonaparte as Emperor, and under the name Napoleon, was the following:

"Citizen-Consul Cambacérès, your title is to be changed: your functions and my confidence remain the same. In the high dignity with which you are about to be invested, you will manifest, as in your office of Consul, the wisdom of your counsels and the distinguished talents which have obtained for you so important a share in whatever of good I have been able to accomplish.

"I have then only to desire from you a continuance of the same sentiments toward the state and toward me. Given at St. Cloud, this 28th Floreal, year XII.   NAPOLEON."

This note, countersigned "By the Emperor—H. B. Marat," shows the art of Bonaparte in managing transactions. It is to the *Second Consul* this letter is addressed by the *Emperor*, and the republican dates are preserved! Of the republic there remained only these and the mendacious legend on the reverse of the coin!

On the morrow the Emperor came to Paris to hold a grand levee at the Tuileries: he was not the man to waive the enjoyment of that pageant which his pride drew from his new title. The assembly was the most brilliant and numerous that had yet been known. Bessières presented an address, in the name of the guards, and the Emperor replied—"I constantly behold with increasing pleasure my companions in arms, escaped from so many dangers and covered with honorable wounds. I ever experience a feeling of satisfaction when I think, while viewing them ranged under their standards, that there is not one battle, not one combat for the last fifteen years, and in the four quarters of the globe, which has not among their ranks witnesses and actors." At the same time were presented, by Louis Bonaparte, in the exercise of his functions as Constable, all the generals and colonels then in Paris. In a few days everything assumed a new aspect. Public admiration was loud; but, in secret, the Parisians laughed at the somewhat stiff forms of the new courtiers. This gave sovereign displeasure to Bonaparte, whose ears the circumstance reached through the most charitable intentions possible, in order that he might be cured of prepossessions in favor of the men of the old court.

Napoleon, studious of giving every solemnity to his elevation, ordered that the Senate itself should publish and proclaim in Paris the decree which established the imperial dynasty. This decree, which might have been termed the constitutional charter of the empire, consisted of 142 articles, ranged under the following heads: 1. The government of the republic is confided to an emperor, who takes the title of Emperor of the French. 2. Succession hereditary. 3. The imperial family. 4. The Regency. 5. The grand dignitaries of the empire; namely, grand elector, arch-chancellor of the empire, arch-chancellor of state, arch-treasurer, constable and high admiral. 6. The great officers of the empire. 7. Oaths. 8. The Senate. 9. Council of State. 10. Legislative Body. 11. Tribunate. 12. Electoral Colleges. 13. Supreme Imperial Court. 14. The Judiciary order. 15. Proclamations. 16. The imperial dynasty hereditary in the descendants of Napoleon. This head to be presented for the people's acceptance. By one of those unlucky coincidences which I have sometimes known to occasion much remark, the promulgation of this decree was fixed for Sunday, 30th Floreal: this was to be a festival to all Paris, while the unfortunate beings accused of attempting the life of the man whom it profited languished in the dungeons of the Temple.

From the day following the imperial accession of Bonaparte the ancient formulas were re-established. The Emperor decided that the princes and princesses of the empire should bear the title of Imperial Highness; that his sisters should assume the same designation; that the grand dignitaries should be styled Serene Highness; that the princes and grand dignitaries should further be addressed *Monseigneur;* the secretary of state should have the rank of minister; that ministers should retain the title of Excellency, and be addressed Monseigneur in all petitions; that the president of the Senate should be styled Excellency.

At the same time Napoleon nominated the marshals of the empire, and appointed that they should be called Monsieur le Maréchal, in speaking, and Monseigneur, in writing,

to them. The following are the names of those children of
the republic, transformed, at the fiat of a brother in arms,
into supports of his empire: Berthier, Murat, Moncey,
Jourdan, Masséna, Augereau, Bernadotte, Soult, Brune,
Lannes, Mortier, Ney, Davoust, Bessières, Kellermann,
Lefèbvre, Perignon, and Serrurier.

It will have been remarked that, in the list of dignities
lavished by Bonaparte upon his family and favorites, the
name of Lucien does not occur. The two brothers were no
longer on good terms; not, as has been said, because Lucien
wished, so late in the season, to play the part of republican,
but because he refused to submit to the imperious commands
of Napoleon in a circumstance where Lucien's docility might
have served the interests of his policy. In the committees
preceding the grand change, it was not Lucien, but Joseph,
who, to discover the state of opinion, got up a republican
opposition with skill sufficient to catch one or two dupes.
As to Lucien, having in reality rendered great services to
his brother, and appreciating himself these services beyond
their value, he deemed no recompense less than an independent crown a sufficient reward. Certain it is that, during his
sojourn in Madrid, he had carried his pretensions so high
as to attempt playing the agreeable to one of the Infantas of
Spain. On this various reports were circulated on which
I do not place much reliance, never having been able to
verify them. What I know amounts to this, that, Lucien's
wife being dead, Bonaparte thought of marrying him to a
princess of Germany, in order thus to commence with the
first grand alliance. Lucien refused to meet the views of
Napoleon, and privately espoused the wife of a broker,
named, I believe, Jouberton, who, for convenience, had
been sent to the colonies, where he died a short time afterward. When Bonaparte was informed of this marriage by
the priest, who had been sent for privately to the Hôtel de
Brienne, he became furious, and from that moment resolved
not to confer upon Lucien the title of a French prince, on
account of what he termed his *mésalliance*. He remained,

then, only a Senator; while brother Jerome, by following a quite opposite course, became a king. As to Lucien's republicanism, it survived not the 18th Brumaire; he had ever shown himself, as we have seen, the most strenuous advocate of hereditary right and the succession.

On Sunday, the 15th July, the Emperor had occasion to exhibit, for the first time, to the eyes of the Parisians, all the splendor of imperial pomp. As the commencement the members of the Legion of Honor, present in Paris, took the oath, conformably to the new formula. For the first time there now appeared, so to speak, two distinct cortèges: the Emperor's and that of the Empress. When Bonaparte took possession of the Tuileries he alone had been surrounded with the scanty appurtenances of grandeur permitted by infant luxury; and Madame Bonaparte, nothing more than the First Consul's wife, modestly conveyed herself thither, without parade and without attendance, and took her station, as already noticed, at one of the windows in the apartments of the Second Consul. But times had greatly altered. Here was now the imperial procession of the Empress in carriages which traversed the gardens of the Tuileries, until then exclusively reserved for the public; next appeared the military cavalcade of the Emperor, who desired to show himself on horseback, surrounded by his chosen generals, become marshals of the empire. M. de Ségur had, by this, been appointed grand master of the ceremonies, and consequently took charge of the manœuvres of etiquette. Conjointly with the governor he received the Emperor at the entrance of the Hotel of the Invalids. They, in like manner, conducted the Empress to a seat prepared for her, fronting the imperial throne, which Napoleon occupied alone, on the right of the altar. I was present, spite of my repugnance to witness these brilliant juggleries; but, as Duroc had called upon me two days before with tickets of admission to a particular station, I dared not dispense with going lest the searching eye of Bonaparte should detect my absence, if Duroc had acted by his order.

I enjoyed my position, for at least an hour, in observing the haughty demeanor, sometimes indeed not a little ludicrously overacted, of these new grandees of the empire; I could mark all the evolutions of the clergy, who, with Cardinal Belloy at their head, went to receive the Emperor on his entrance into the church, no longer, as formerly, the temple of Mars. What strange reflections shot across my mind while beholding mine ancient comrade of Brienne seated on an elevated throne, surrounded by the colonel-generals of his guard, the grand dignitaries of his crown, his ministers and marshals! Involuntarily my cogitations reverted to the 19th Brumaire; and this majestic pomp vanished away when I thought of Bonaparte's stammering to such a degree that I was obliged to pull him by the coat to warn him to withdraw. It was neither a spirit of enmity nor of jealousy which awakened these reflections; in no circumstance of our career would I ever have exchanged situations; but whoever has reflected—whoever has been present at the unexpected elevation of one formerly but barely on a footing of equality, will probably conceive the strangely mingled nature of those emotions with which, for the first time, I was assailed on this occasion.

From this train of thought I was aroused by a movement throughout the vast interior, on the termination of the religious ceremony; the church then resumed, in some sort, the appearance of a profane temple. The audience were more attached to the Emperor than to the God of the Christians; and their piety, therefore, equalled not their enthusiasm. Mass had been listened to with indifference; but when M. de Lacepède, grand chancellor of the order, after pronouncing a laudatory harangue, finished by summoning the grand officers of the Legion of Honor, Bonaparte assumed his hat, as did the ancient kings of France when they held a court of Justice—a profound silence, a kind of religious awe pervaded the assembly. He stammered not then, as at the Council of Five Hundred, while announcing with a firm voice, "Commanders, officers. legionaries, citizens, soldiers!

You swear upon your honor to devote yourselves to the service of the empire; to the preservation of its territory in . full integrity; to the defence of the Emperor, of the laws of the republic, and of the rights which these have consecrated; to combat, by all means which justice, reason and laws authorize, every enterprise which shall tend to re-establish the feudal system; in fine, you swear to aid, with all your power, in the maintenance of liberty and equality, the prime basis of our institutions! Do you swear this?"

All the members of the Legion cried aloud, "This I swear!" adding the exclamation, "Long live the Emperor!" with an enthusiasm impossible to describe, and in which the whole audience united. Yet what, after all, was this new oath ? With few changes, that of the Legion of Honor under the Consulate, with this exception, that the "Emperor" now took precedence of the "laws of the republic," and that such change was not merely a form. It was, besides, not a little amusing or even audacious to dictate an oath for the maintenance of equality at the very moment when so many titles and distinctions had just been re-established.

Three days after this ceremony, as had been announced by the Emperor at its close, he set out for the camp at Boulogne, in order to distribute the decoration of the order among the members in the grand army there assembled. Availing myself of her invitation, I went to visit Josephine at St. Cloud, some days after Napoleon's departure. My visit was not expected: I found the Empress engaged with four or five ladies of the court, who were soon to take the titles of ladies of honor and ladies in waiting. The fair assembly, on my entrance, which immediately succeeded my announcement, seemed every one occupied with some of those brilliant gewgaws which the jeweller Leroi and the famous milliner Despeaux furnished at such enormous prices. For of whatever painful reflections Josephine might be the victim, she was too much a woman not to contrive, even amid her sorrows, always to have some moments to spare for the affairs of the toilet. On this occasion the party was in deep consultation upon the question of the dresses to be worn by the Empress in her tour through Belgium with Napoleon, whom she had appointed to meet at the Castle of Lacken near Brussels.   Notwithstanding the importance of discussions on the cut of sleeves, the shape of hats, and the color of gowns, Josephine received me as usual, that is to say, in the most gracious manner; but, not being able to converse with me, said, quite simply, though in such a way that I might understand the hint as an invitation, that she intended passing to-morrow forenoon at Malmaison.   I soon after took leave; and about midday on the morrow presented myself in that delicious retreat, which I could never behold without emotion.

Madame Bonaparte was walking in the garden with her favorite companion, Madame de Rémusat, the daughter of Vergennes, the minister of Louis XVI., in whose service, though his talents may, neither his honor, probity, nor devotion can be disputed.   These ladies I met at the turning of the alley leading to Ruel.   I paid my respects to Josephine, inquiring at the same time for his Majesty, and never shall I cease to remember with what touching expression she said, "Ah! Bourrienne, for Heaven's sake allow me, at least here, to forget that I am Empress! be always our friend." As Josephine had nothing to conceal from her companion, with the exception of certain domestic afflictions, of which most probably I was the sole confidant, we talked as if without witnesses.   As may be supposed, too, we spoke of him who was the sole object of Josephine's thoughts.

After speaking of the journey into Belgium which she contemplated, Josephine continued—"How much is it to be regretted, Bourrienne, that the past cannot be recalled!   He set out in the best disposition; he has granted several pardons to the conspirators, and I beheld him for the moment gratified by the good which he had it in his power to perform; and but for these wretched politics I am certain he would have extended favor to a still greater number.   Recent events have been to me the cause of much sorrow; but I

constrained myself to conceal my griefs because I have remarked that they displease him and render him only the
more gloomy. Now, in the midst of his army, he will forget everything else. How great has been my affliction that
I could not succeed in all the applications made through my
means! The excellent Madame de Montesson came all the
way from Romanville to St. Cloud to intercede for De Rivière
and the Polignacs. We contrived that Madame de Polignac
should obtain an audience. How very beautiful she is! Bonaparte was much affected on seeing her and said, 'Madame,
since it was only my own life which your husband would
have attempted, I can pardon him.' You, who know *him*,
Bourrienne—you are aware that *he* is not a bad man; it is
his counsellors and his sycophants that induce him to commit villanous actions. Rapp conducted himself in the best
possible manner: he went to the Emperor, and would not
be refused till he had obtained the pardon of another of the
condemned, whose name has escaped me. [Rusillon, I believe, the Empress here meant.] How these brothers Polignac interested me! There are at least some families who
owe *him* gratitude! Let us endeavor as far as we can to
forget the past; the future has sufficient to alarm me! Be
assured, my dear Bourrienne, I shall not fail during our tour
in Belgium to quicken the good intentions which I know
him to entertain toward you; so soon as I learn anything
certain, I will let you know. Adieu!''

CHAPTER XX

Madame de Staël—Pius VII. at Fontainebleau—Bourrienne made Minister to
Hamburg—Bonaparte Crowned King of Italy

ENGLAND was never more the dupe of Bonaparte than
during the encampment at Boulogne. Believing in
the attempt of a descent, she exhausted herself
in providing the means of a defence round her whole
coast, lest she might be taken at any point unprovided.

Such are the advantages possessed by the party acting on
the offensive. But, though keeping herself on the defensive, she attempted several acts of hostility through the
superiority of her navy and command of the sea. Fortune,
however, seemed inclined to protect the arms of Napoleon;
at least these attacks did us little injury; and, in spite of
the rockets and infernal machines of Admiral Keith, which
were reported to have wholly destroyed our flotilla, the
English, in their enterprises, lost as many men as we did.

But Napoleon, then in the vigor of his genius and activity, had always his eyes fixed far from those things which
surrounded him, and upon which his attention seemed to be
bent. Thus, during the preceding journey, the object of
which was to organize the territories on the Rhine, he sent
out two squadrons, one from Toulon, under Villeneuve, the
other from Rochefort, commanded by Messiessy. With the
operations of these armaments I have little to do; but
the orders thus given obtained me an opportunity of seeing
Lauriston, who, despatched by the Emperor, whom he accompanied in his progress, to assume the command of the
troops in the squadron of Villeneuve, passed some days
with me in Paris. I loved Lauriston very much, and we
naturally held long conversations on the way in which the
Emperor passed his time. "You cannot have an idea," said
Lauriston to me, "of his vast activity, nor of the species of
enchantment which his presence produces upon the troops.
But, more than ever, is he enraged against the contractors,
and has been very severe upon some." This gave me no
surprise; I knew, of old, Bonaparte's sentiments on this
point: he used to term these agents the "scourge and lep-
rosy of armies"; asseverating that he never would raise one
of them to honors, and that their aristocracy was to him the
most insufferable of all. They were now no longer important personages: he not infrequently proceeded with them
in much the same sort of way as with the Beys of Egypt.
When a contractor had become too rich, or when the origin
of his fortune rendered him suspected, he was ordered to

give in a report. Upon this Bonaparte decided, in an arbitrary manner, whether prosecution was to be employed; in which case he wrote under the report, "Remit to the minister of justice, who will take care to have the laws put in force." I ought, at the same time, to state that one circumstance tended greatly to confirm Napoleon in this bad opinion of contractors, namely, that, in most cases, on being informed of the above, or similar marginal reference touching them, the hint sufficed to bring them to an arrangement with the treasury—to speak plainly, to disgorge two or three millions, under the title of a restitution. But, unfortunately, Bonaparte, extreme in all things, made no exceptions; and some men of probity, as Collot and Carbonnet, were thus nearly ruined.

Lauriston was the best informed of all Napoleon's aides-de-camp, and with him the latter generally conversed on literary subjects. He had then left the Emperor and Empress at Aix-la-Chapelle; but at Lacken, when on duty one day, as he informed me, Bonaparte sent for him after the Empress had retired to her apartment and talked of the decennial prizes; of a tragedy by Carion de Nisas, called "Peter the Great"; and of a new novel by Madame de Staël. "On this authoress," continued Lauriston, "and on her 'Delphine,' the Emperor made several remarkable observations, among others, 'I dislike masculine women as much as I despise effeminate men. All to their own parts in the world. What means this vagrancy of imagination?— what remains of it? Nothing. It is all the metaphysics of sentiment—a disorder of the fancy. I cannot endure that woman, just because I detest women who throw themselves at my head—who make a dead set at one; and, God knows, her flatteries were broad enough in all conscience.'" I gave the more credit to these words, as reported by Lauriston, that they squared with my recollections of the manner in which Bonaparte had often spoken to myself of Madame de Staël, and that I had, besides, frequently witnessed her advances to the First Consul and even to the Commander-in-Chief of the army of Italy. Bonaparte had heard of Madame de Staël only as being the daughter of M. Necker—a man for whom he entertained very small esteem. The lady, too, knew nothing of him as yet, save from the reports of fame concerning the youthful conqueror of Italy, when she addressed him in letters full of enthusiasm. Of these Bonaparte would read aloud to me some snatches, then burst out a-laughing and say, "Can you conceive, Bourrienne, such extravagance?—the woman is certainly mad." I recollect in one of these letters Madame de Staël, among other things, said they had been created for each other; that, through an error in human institutions, the mild and peaceful Josephine had been united with his fate; that nature seemed to have destined a soul of fire like hers for the adoration of a hero like him. All these extravagances disgusted Bonaparte to an indescribable degree. On finishing the perusal of these fine epistles he either threw them into the fire or rumpled them up and tore them with marked displeasure, observing to me—"Truly, indeed! a female wit, a manufacturer of sentiment, compare herself to Josephine! Bourrienne, I will not condescend a reply to such letters!"

At the same time I witnessed what the perseverance of a woman of spirit can accomplish. In spite of Bonaparte's prepossessions against Madame de Staël, and which were never removed, she contrived to get admission to his receptions, and, if anything could have disgusted him with flattery, it would have been the admiration, or, to speak more correctly, the species of worship, which she lavished upon him. She compared him to a god descended upon the earth—a simile which, somewhat later, seemed to me exclusively reserved for the use of the priests. Unfortunately, however, it appeared that no god could please Madame de Staël save Plutus; for, in military phrase, under cover of her eulogiums, she threw forward a claim of 2,000,000 francs, due, as she pretended, to the good and loyal services of her father. Bonaparte, on this occasion, replied that, whatever value he might attach to the suffrages of Madame de Staël, he did not think himself authorized to purchase them at so dear a rate with the money of the state. It is well known how the enthusiasm of this celebrated woman changed into hatred, and by what annoyances, unworthy of himself, Napoleon harassed her, even in retirement at Coppet. With these things I have nothing to do; since the circumstances reached me, as they did the public, by report; but of the early intercourse of Bonaparte and De Staël I have now related what I know to be facts and coming within the sphere of my personal knowledge.

The mission of Caffarelli, who had been despatched to feel the pulse of pontifical compliance, and endeavor to induce the Holy Father to come to Paris and crown the Emperor, was successful. Caffarelli, whom I knew intimately, bore a striking resemblance to his brother, the general, who died in Egypt. He possessed the same delicate tact, the same pleasant humor and pliancy of character. But, in truth, there existed, from the first, little doubt as to the Pope's mind. Since the Concordat, the best relations had reigned between the courts of Rome and Paris; nor could Pius VII. have forgotten how much the success of the French arms in Italy had contributed to his own elevation. His election, in fact, had been so opposite to the wishes of the Aulic Council that, the conclave having been held in Venice, Austria refused to the successor of St. Peter a passage through her Italian states, and Pius was obliged to embark for Ancona. I shall hereafter speak of Bonaparte's conduct to the Head of the Church. His religious ideas have been already described, as consisting rather in a species of instinctive sentiment than as being the result of a belief grounded on reason and reflection. Still he attached much importance to the power of the church; not that he feared it, far less could it have entered his head that a sovereign, wearing a crown and a sword, should kneel to a priest of Rome, or lower the sceptre to keys, nicknamed keys of St. Peter. His was a mind far too virile and too great for all this. But the alliance of the church with his authority he deemed a happy influence by which to work upon the opinion of the people; and as one tie more for insuring their attachment to a government thus blessed by the solemn sanctions of religion. On concluding the Concordat he had said, "I leave the generals of the Republic to cry out as much as they like against the mass; but I know what I am about; I labor for the future." He was right, and now reaped the fruits of his own foresight.

As to the church, in placing upon the head of Napoleon the right of seniority which had been prudently conceded to the kings of France, she only renewed the action of Stephen III., when, nearly eleven centuries before, he came to consecrate, in France, Pepin the Short and his sons. Probably, too, the Romish clergy—good, easy men—were beholding in their visions a return of those golden days of the people's ignorance and the church's power, when kings were her vassals and she enjoyed the monopoly of both worlds. At least, I recollect to have heard the Cardinal de Bayonne assert a very general sentiment among his cloth that the consecration of Napoleon was an event extremely favorable to the power of the Papal See, since it proved that none other save the Pope could give a legitimate right to the crown of France! I was by no means of the same opinion with his Eminence; but certain it is, that the consecration of Napoleon removed much of the religious scrupulosity entertained by those honest people who conceived themselves still bound to the Most Christian King. Even in England, though no longer connected with the Romish Church, the arrival of the Pope in Paris produced perhaps a greater sensation than elsewhere; and I subsequently learned that the Cabinet of St. James and Mr. Pitt were greatly stirred, so justly did they appreciate the influence of this event in adding weight to the crown of the new sovereign.

When the Emperor understood that the mission to Rome had been successful, of which he was informed while on his progress through the states of the Rhine, he lost no time in returning to St. Cloud, in order to prepare for his corona-

tion. He desired, without delay, to have the sceptre of
Charlemagne confirmed in his grasp, his right to which had
already been acknowledged by all the powers of Europe,
with the exception of England. The Emperor of Germany
had, at first, shown some hesitation in recognizing the Emperor of the French, waiting to know what part he of Russia
would take; but, pressed by the necessity of declaring himself, he sent in his acknowledgment of the Empire, assuming
to himself the new title of Emperor of Austria. This determination of Francis, in all probability, was the result of information which could not fail to reach him that Napoleon
had been visited, during his progress on the Rhine, by the
majority of the Princes of the Holy Empire.

Orders had been given in the meantime that everywhere
throughout the French territories the Pope should be received with the highest distinction, and the Emperor himself, accompanied by the Empress, set forward to meet the
Holy Father at Fontainebleau. From this chateau, now
become, like all others, an imperial palace, and lately most
splendidly refurnished, the Emperor advanced on the road
to Nemours, when he learned by the couriers the near arrival
of Pius VII. His object in this was to avoid the ceremonial
which had been previously settled. Under pretence of the
chase he contrived, as if by chance, to be upon the road
when the Pope's carriage passed. He dismounted from his
horse, and Pius alighted from his travelling carriage. Rapp,
who was present, described to me with amusing originality,
and in his German accent, this grand interview. I think
I still hear the comic recital of this independent Alsatian.
"Imagine," said he, "how this singular comedy was played.
In order that they might be on a footing of equality the Emperor and the Pope, after properly hugging each other, got
into the same vehicle, each by his own door, so as to enter
at one and the same time: all this had been arranged. At
the entertainment which followed the Emperor had taken
his measures so as quite naturally to find himself seated on
the Pope's right; and all fell out as he desired. As to the

rest," added Rapp, "it must be owned that I have nowhere seen a better looking or more respectable old gentleman than his Holiness."

After this conference at Fontainebleau between the Pope and Napoleon, who, as we have seen, commenced their personal correspondence by the first of Christian Kings taking the precedence of the Head of the Church by a subterfuge, Pius departed first for Paris. All the honors usually given to the Emperor were conferred upon him, and he was lodged in the Pavilion of Flora. By a delicate attention the Pope found his bedchamber arranged and furnished exactly as in his own palace on Monte Cavallo. His Holiness became the object of public respect and of general solicitude. His presence in Paris furnished a singular contrast to the state of that capital, where, only four years before, every altar was still lying prostrate. I wished to see the old man, and had my desire gratified when he visited the imperial printing office, situated where the Bank of France now stands. The director of the establishment caused to be printed, in presence of his Holiness, a volume which was dedicated to him, namely, "The Pater Noster," in one hundred and fifty different languages. Upon the occasion of this visit the Pope made the remarkable observation which so well merits preservation. A young man kept his hat on in presence of the Holy Father; some persons, indignant at such gross and ill-placed disrespect, went to pull it off, when the Pope, observing the disturbance, and having learned the cause, approached the young man, and, addressing him in a manner truly patriarchal, said, "Young man, uncover, that I may give you my blessing; the benediction of age never yet did harm to any one." I remember well that the greater part of those present were deeply affected by this paternal allocution. Pius VII. possessed a figure which commanded respect; as may be proved even to those who have not seen him, for he yet lives in the admirable portrait from the pencil of David.

The Pope arrived in Paris on the 28th November, and

no time was lost in preparing for the solemnity which had brought him thither. Two days after, that is to say, on the 1st of December, the Senate presented to the Emperor the result of the votes of the people on the question of hereditary succession; and next day the consecration took place. It was pretended that the title of Emperor changed nothing of the republic, and that the succession of this dignity in one family was the only innovation introduced under the empire. On this question, therefore, Napoleon affected to desire the sanction of the people. Throughout the whole of France, then divided into 108 departments, 60,000 registers had been opened. There had voted 3,574,898 individual citizens, of whom only 2,569 had given their voices against hereditary succession. I know that Napoleon caused the list of these opponents to be transmitted to him and frequently consulted it. They were not royalists, but, for the most part, old and stern republicans; and, to my knowledge, many royalists abstained from voting, not wishing uselessly to compromise themselves, yet unwilling to give their support to the author of the Duke d'Enghien's death. As for myself, I gave my vote for the succession in Napoleon's family, my situation, as may be conceived, not permitting me to act otherwise.

I turn now to matters of personal concern, although relating immediately to Napoleon. I mean my nomination to the office of Minister Plenipotentiary to the Dukes of Brunswick and Mecklenburg-Schwerin and the cities of the Hanseatic League, or, generally, to the circle of Lower Saxony.

This nomination took place on the 22d of March, 1805, that day twelve months precisely from my visit to Josephine at Malmaison after the death of the Duke d'Enghien: a singular coincidence of dates. The Empress, always excellent, ever mindful of her friends, had promised, as the reader is aware, to inform me of the Emperor's intentions in my behalf; and accordingly announced my nomination by an express, and that I might expect an order to make my appearance at court. The very day on which I received this kind message from Josephine arrived an official intimation to wait upon the Emperor next morning at Malmaison. I shall not attempt to conceal how much rather I preferred meeting him there than at the Tuileries or even St. Cloud. It may easily be imagined that our former intimacies at Malmaison placed me much more at ease during an interview which, from my knowledge of Bonaparte's character, gave me always a little uneasiness. Was I to be received by my old companion of Brienne or by his imperial majesty? It was the ancient college friend who received me.

Immediately on my arrival at Malmaison, I was ushered into the alcoved apartment leading to the library. The devil of a man!—let me be excused the expression—played the coquette in a manner that surprised even me, who knew him so well in his arts of seduction. He came up to me, a smile upon his lips, took my hand, a thing he had never done since the consulate, pressed it affectionately; it was impossible to see in him at this moment the Emperor of France and the future King of Italy. Still I was too much upon my guard against the susceptibilities of his pride to permit my intimacy to exceed the bounds of affectionate respect. "My dear Bourrienne," thus he addressed me, "surely you do not think that the elevated rank to which I have attained can change me as respects you? No! The trappings of the imperial theatre do not constitute my value; but these are necessary for the people. I claim esteem in myself. I have been very well satisfied with your services, and have appointed you to a post where I shall have need of them: I know I can rely upon you." He then inquired about my family and my occupations with the most friendly interest: in short, I never beheld him in a mood more free, more open, or exhibiting more of that captivating simplicity which he displayed with greater frequency in proportion as his greatness had become unquestionable. "You know," added Napoleon, "that in a week I set out for Italy to make myself king; but that is only a stepping-stone: I have

greater designs regarding Italy. It must become a kingdom comprising all the transalpine country from Venice to
the maritime Alps. The union of Italy with France can
be but transient. It is, however, necessary, in order to accustom the population of Italy to live under common laws.
The Genoese, the Piedmontese, the Venetians, the Milanese,
the Tuscans, the Romans, and the Neapolitans detest each
other. Not one of these would acknowledge the superiority
of the other; and yet Rome, by her associations, is the
natural capital of Italy. But to accomplish that the power
of the Pope must needs be restricted to affairs purely
spiritual. I do not think just now of accomplishing all
this; but we shall see hereafter: I have as yet only crude
ideas, but these will ripen with time; and then everything
depends on circumstances. What was it that told me when
we were strolling, like two idle fellows as we were, through
the streets of Paris, that I should one day be master of
France? My wish; but then a vague wish—circumstances
have done the rest. It is then wise to provide for what may
come; and it is what I am doing. Regarding Italy, as it
would be impossible to unite her at once into one power,
yielding submission to uniform laws, I commence by making
her French. All these little good-for-nothing states will
thus become habituated to live under the empire of the
same laws; and when habits are formed, enmities extinct,
then there will again be an Italy; and I shall restore her to
independence. But for this twenty years are requisite; and
who can count upon the future? At this moment, Bourrienne, I take a pleasure in telling you these things; they
were shut up in my thoughts; with you I think aloud."

I do not believe I have changed two words of what
Bonaparte said to me on Italy, so interesting was the subject, and such my habitude of retaining his words. After
speaking of these vast projects, without any other transition
save that produced by the crossing of his own rapid ideas,
Bonaparte continued: "Apropos, Bourrienne, one thing
I must tell you! Do you know Madame Brienne has re-

quested me to pass through Brienne, and I have promised
her: I do not conceal it from you.   I anticipate great pleasure in revisiting the scenes which for six years were the witnesses of our youthful sports.''   Seeing the kindly humor of
the Emperor, I thought I might venture to say how happy
I should feel in being permitted to accompany him and
participate in those emotions of the past; to recall on the spot
our walks, our studies and our recreations.   Napoleon was
silent for a moment, seeming to reflect; then, with an accent
of extreme kindness, replied, ''Listen, Bourrienne.   In your
situation and in mine that is impossible.   It is more than
two years since our separation.   What would be said of a
reconciliation so sudden?   I will frankly confess that I
regret the loss; and the circumstances in which I have
frequently been placed more than once inspired me with
the idea of recalling you.   At Boulogne I had resolved
upon it; my resolution was taken.   Rapp may have spoken
to you on this subject; for he loves you, and told me with
all the frankness of his nature that your return would delight
him.   But reflection came; and if I did not carry out my
intention it is because, as I have repeated to you more than
once, I will not that the world can say I have need of any
one.   No!   Go to Hamburg.   I have designs upon Germany
in which you can be very useful to me.   There will I strike
England to the heart.   I shall shut the whole Continent
against her.   I have ideas besides that go further; but these
are not matured.   There is not sufficient similarity among
the nations of Europe; European society requires to be re-
generated; there wants a superior power which may so far
bear sway over the other powers as to constrain them to live
in good intelligence with each other; France is well placed
for that.   As to details, you will receive instructions from
Talleyrand; but what I commend to you, above all things,
keep strict observance upon the emigrants.   Woe to them
should they become too dangerous!   I know there are still
among them those who will not be quiet—certain of the old
leaven of the Marquis de Versailles.   They are fools who

come like moths to burn themselves at the candle. You
have been an emigrant, Bourrienne; you have a weak side
toward them; and you know I have recalled more than two
hundred on your recommendation. But it is no longer the
same thing. Those still in exile are incorrigible; they no
longer stand in need of revisiting their country. Keep good
watch over these: that is the sole recommendation I have
to give in particular. You are to be Minister of France at
Hamburg; but your mission is a special one. I authorize
you, in addition to the official correspondence with the
Minister for Foreign Affairs, to address myself directly
when you have anything special to say to me. You will
correspond likewise with Fouché."

I perceived that Bonaparte had still something to say.
As we continued walking up and down the alcoved saloon,
he stopped on a sudden, and, regarding me with an expression almost of tenderness, said, "Now, Bourrienne, before
I go into Italy, you must thus far oblige me. You sometimes visit *my wife;* and that is well; it is quite proper; you
have been too long one of the family not to continue so.
Go and see her; endeavor once more to induce her to listen
to reason about these foolish expenses. Every day I hear
of new extravagances, and this really puts me to the torture.
When I speak to her on the subject, I get angry—I speak
harshly. She weeps; I excuse all—pay all. She makes the
best of promises; but the very next day comes the same
thing; and we have always to begin anew. And then—had
she but given me a child! It is the torment of my life not
to have a child. I perfectly comprehend my position; it
never will be secure till I have offspring. Should I die,
not one of my brothers is capable of succeeding me. All
is commenced; nothing is completed: God knows what will
be the issue. Go and see Josephine; omit nothing of what
I have told you." He then resumed the gayety which had
marked the former parts of our conversation, for clouds
driven by the tempest do not traverse the vault of heaven
with such rapidity as ideas and sensations succeeded each

other in the spirit of Napoleon. He finally dismissed me, with the habitual nod; and, seeing him in good humor, I turned, in leaving the room, and said—"Well, sire, you are going to hear the old bell at Brienne; I wager you find the sound sweeter than the bells of Ruel."—"That's true; you are right: do not laugh at me—come, good-by."

Such are my recollections of an interview which lasted above an hour and a half. We walked the whole time, for Bonaparte was indefatigable in these audiences, and would have walked a whole day, I believe, while conversing, without being sensible of the exertion. I left him better satisfied than ever with my friendly reception, and, according to his desire, went upstairs to the apartments of Madame Bonaparte, which, in truth, had previously been my intention.

I found Josephine with Madame Rochefoucauld, an amiable woman and lady of honor to the Empress. On stating that I had just left the Emperor, thinking, doubtless, I had something to communicate, she made a sign to her attendant and we remained alone. I had no difficulty in bringing the conversation to the subject on which Napoleon had spoken; for Josephine herself, without knowing, put me upon the track by first speaking of a violent scene which had occurred only two days before. "When I wrote yesterday," said she, "to inform you of your appointment and that Bonaparte would require you, I hoped you would come to see me on leaving him, but did not think he would send so soon. Were you still with him, Bourrienne, you would persuade him to hear reason. I know not who takes pleasure in carrying him reports; but really I believe there are people employed everywhere searching out my debts in order to inform him." These complaints, so gently hinted by Josephine, rendered my mission less difficult than it otherwise might have been; which, notwithstanding, seemed but a sorry introduction to my new office of diplomatist. I related all the Emperor had said, reverted to the first affair of the twelve hundred thousand francs arranged for half the sum, and ventured to allude to the promises then made.

"What would you have me do?" said she; "is it my fault?" These words Josephine repeated with an earnest sincerity which rendered them touching at once and comic. "People bring me fine things, show them to me, extol their beauty: I buy, they ask no money, and then demand payment when I have none: this reaches his ears and he gets into a passion. When I do have money, Bourrienne, you know how I employ it; I give the greater part to the unfortunates who apply to me, and the poor emigrants. Come, now, I shall try to be more economical; tell him so if you see him again. But is it not a part of my duty to give as much as possible—to do all the good I can?"—"Certainly, madame," replied I, "but permit me to say nothing requires more discernment than properly to apply your bounties. Had you passed your life upon a throne, you might have known whether your favors were truly bestowed upon misfortune; but, as it is, you cannot be ignorant that they are oftener the spoil of the intriguing than the portion of necessitous merit. I cannot dissemble that the Emperor was very much in earnest when touching upon this subject, and desired me to speak with you."—"Did he utter no other reproach against me?"—"None, madame; you know the influence you have over him in everything not pertaining to politics; let me, as a sincere and devoted friend, beseech you to give him no more uneasiness on the subject of expense."—"Bourrienne, I promise you this. For the present, adieu, my friend!"

In relating to Josephine what the Emperor had stated to me, I had taken especial care not to touch upon a chord far more sensible, alas! than even the very distressing expostulations she had to undergo on the subject of her expenditure. The poor woman! I should have reduced her to despair had one word escaped me touching the regrets expressed by Bonaparte at having no child. On this subject she had ever cherished an invincible presentiment of what would one day befall her. As to the rest, Josephine really spoke truth when she said that it was not her fault: order and economy,

while I knew the two, were as incompatible with her disposition as moderation and patience with the temperament of
Napoleon. The sight of the least waste put him beside
himself; and this species of emotion his wife rarely spared
him. With what dissatisfaction, on the other hand, did he
view the greed of his own family for wealth! the more
he heaped upon his relations the more insatiable was their
craving. With the exception of Louis, whose desires were
always honorable and his wishes moderate, all the rest im-
portuned him with incessant demands. "Truly," he once
observed, "to hear these people one would say I had devoured the inheritance of our father!"

Voltaire has said—I forget in what place—"that it is
very well kissing the feet of popes provided that hands be
tied." Bonaparte had little esteem for Voltaire, and probably was not aware of this irreverent remark of the phi-
losopher of last century; but he seemed to construe the
pleasantry seriously, or at least to act gravely upon the principle. The Pope, or rather the cardinals who advised him,
thinking that so great an act of complaisance as a journey
to Paris ought to pay somewhat more than its own expenses,
otherwise it was, in their opinion, thrown away, demanded
as a recompense the restoration of Avignon and Bologna,
with some other territories in Italy. This really was great
awkwardness in a court whose policy is usually so fine and
so well adapted to the occasion. To ask the reward after the
service had been rendered!—the fable of the stork and
the fox! Had the Papal See, *before* the Pope's journey,
asked, not Avignon, which most certainly it would not have
got, but the Italian territories, Bonaparte might have given
these—in order to take them back again. Be this as it may,
those tardy claims, authoritatively rejected, occasioned extreme coldness between the Pope and the Church's eldest
son: and the former, after conferring the title of Emperor
of the French, refused the same consecration to the King
of Italy.

As he had stated to me in the preceding interview,

Napoleon set out for Milan just seven days after, on the 1st of April, in order to assume the iron crown. The Pope remained behind for some time, and his prolonged presence was not without effect on the spirit of men, when afterward the times of his own persecution arrived. It had been better for Bonaparte had Pius VII. never come to Paris; for it subsequently became impossible to behold as other than a victim one whose truly evangelical meekness had there been observed.

Napoleon was in no haste to seize the crown of Italy, because it could not escape him. He remained three weeks at Turin, where he inhabited the elegant palace of Stupinis, the St. Cloud of the kings of Sardinia. Here he received the report from the camp of Boulogne, and arranged the embarkation with such minuteness that those who executed his orders were the first dupes. Here, too, he was residing when the Pope passed through Turin, and thither he went to take leave of the Holy Father, affecting the greatest deference in all the relations of personal intercourse. Thence the Emperor set out for Alessandria, where he had already begun those immense works which absorbed so much treasure. After the battle of Marengo, he said one day to Berthier and me, "With Alessandria, I shall always be master of Italy. It must become the first fortified place in the world, with a garrison of forty thousand men and provisions for six months. The French troops, in case of revolts, or should the Austrians send formidable armies into Italy, will always find a refuge there; and wherever I am, that time will be sufficient for me to fall upon Italy, overwhelm the Austrians, and raise the siege of Alessandria."

So near the plain of Marengo, the Emperor did not fail to visit that celebrated field of battle, and, to give greater solemnity to the occasion, passed in review thereon all the French force then in Italy. Rapp afterward told me there had been brought from Paris, expressly for this purpose, the uniform and hat which he wore on the day of that memorable conflict. It was remarked, also, that the worms, who spare neither the costume of living kings nor the bodies of deceased heroes, had been busy with these trophies of Marengo, which, nevertheless, Bonaparte wore at the review.

Thence, by Casal, he repaired to Milan, where th most brilliant reception which had yet greeted any entrance into the capital of Northern Italy awaited him. In the month of May, 1805, Napoleon was crowned at Milan with the iron crown of the ancient kings of-Lombardy, which, on this occasion, was drawn from the dust wherein it had reposed for ages. The ceremony of this new consecration took place in the cathedral of Milan, next to St. Peter's the vastest interior of Italy. Upon. this occasion, taking the iron crown from the hands of the Archbishop of Milan, Napoleon placed it upon his own head, calling aloud, "*Dieu me l'a donnée ; gare à qui la touche*," which remarkable expression afterward became the legend of the Order of the Iron Crown founded by the Emperor in commemoration of this event.

At Milan, too, the last Doge of Genoa, M. Durazzo, came to add one gem more to the crown of Italy. His mission had for its ostensible object to supplicate the Emperor in name of the republic to permit the state of Genoa to exchange her independence for the signal honor of becoming a department of the French empire. This offer, as may well be conceived, was nothing but the result of previous intrigue, the whole being concerted beforehand. The prayer was accepted with a protecting air; and while the country of Andria Doria ceased from the list of nations, her last duke, his representative, was flung back among the crowd of senators. This city, once so opulent and proud of her surname "superb," became the headquarters of the 27th military division. The Emperor went in person to take possession, and slept in the Doria Palace in the bed whereon Charles V. had reposed centuries before.

Descending from these lofty reminiscences I cannot here omit the opportunity of setting to rights one of those inconceivable mistakes into which Bonaparte at St. Helena cannot have fallen otherwise than voluntarily. I find in the "Memo-

rial" that "the famous singer, Madame Grassini, first drew
his attention at this coronation." Afterward Napoleon is
represented as saying that this celebrated woman addressed
him at this period, and has amused himself with putting into
her mouth the following speech: "When I was in the full
splendor of my beauty and genius, I desired to gain but one
look, nor was that wish gratified; and behold, you now regard me when I am no longer deserving of attention—when
I am no more worthy of you." I confess my utter inability
to explain, or even conceive, what could have tempted Napoleon to invent such a fable. This I know, that in 1800,
not 1805—before the battle of Marengo, not at the coronation
—I have very frequently been one of three with Napoleon
and Madame Grassini at supper in the General's chamber,
whereat I was not especially well entertained. Another circumstance is also among my recollections, that when I awoke
him on the night that information reached me of the capture
of Genoa by the Austrians, Madame Grassini awoke likewise. But I write not for the lovers of scandalous chroni-
cles—only the whole is so ridiculous.

I continue my recital of the Italian journey, though
before the Emperor's return to Paris I had already taken
up my residence in Hamburg. Before leaving Milan the
Emperor caused to be erected on the Great St. Bernard a
monument in commemoration of the victory of Marengo.
M. Denon, who accompanied Napoleon, and who was always
charged with the execution of such plans, subsequently informed me that, after fruitless search for the body of Desaix,
in order to entomb it beneath this monument, the discovery
was made by General Savary. It is thus certain that the
ashes of the brave Desaix rest upon the summit of the Alps.

The Emperor arrived in Paris toward the end of June
and departed instantly for the camp of Boulogne. Then
arose anew the belief of an immediate descent upon Britain,
the more so that Napoleon caused several trials at embarkation to be made under his own eye. But these led to nothing. A circumstance which then occurred furnished a fresh

proof of the inferiority of our navy.   A French squadron of
fifteen sail fell in with an English one under Admiral Calder
of only nine ships, and in the engagement which ensued,
which ought to have been favorable to us, we had the misfortune to lose two of our fleet.   This new journey to the
coast had then no connection with the project of invasion of
which Napoleon had long foreseen, if not the impossibility,
at least the inutility.   The only object was to show himself
a second time as Emperor, with the new dignity of King of
Italy, to the finest and best disciplined army which Europe
had for a long time beheld.   He wished also, by empty
menaces against England, to inflame the enthusiasm of his
soldiers and to conceal the intention that these armed masses
had been organized in order to overrun Germany and repel
the Russian forces already in march toward the frontiers of
Austria.   The dissatisfaction and intrigues of these two
powers, and certain other movements in the North, as we
shall find, had not escaped the eagle glance of Napoleon
amid the pomp and splendors of his coronation.   We shall
soon behold him fall like a thunderbolt on Germany, and
render himself master of the Austrian monarchy by the
day of Austerlitz, as in like manner the field of Marengo
had hailed him victor of Italy.

CHAPTER XXI

Treaty between Russia and England—Bernadotte in the Field—Capitulation of Ulm

ON MY first arrival in Germany, the Emperor of Austria had not yet acknowledged Napoleon as King
of Italy, though his ambassador had remained at
Paris.   From that moment, however, Austria prepared for
war.   England, glad to be rid of even the apprehension of
an invasion, urged on the cabinet of Vienna.   But I have
reason to believe that Napoleon *was not absorbed* in his pretended expedition when the hostile intentions of Austria

manifested themselves; he desired such manifestation, and this lifting of bucklers in another quarter caused to be forgotten, without regret, his useless and expensive preparations against England. This power was, in the meantime, making immense efforts to resist the invasion which threatened her, and expended considerable sums in transporting troops from Hanover. Never, in fact, had such precipitation been witnessed. Vessels could not be procured in sufficient abundance, and immoderate prices for transports were given. These troops were those of General Walmoden, captured in Sublingen, by Marshal Mortier, who first commanded the army of occupation in Hanover. The British government had refused to ratify the capitulation because it stipulated that the troops should remain prisoners of war. Bonaparte had two motives for not insisting upon this harsh condition; he wished to retain possession of Hanover in lieu of Malta, and as the means of more easily attacking Prussia, whose intentions had begun to excite his suspicion. He thus secured his left flank, in the event of marching to the north. Mortier, therefore, received orders to modify the capitulation, and the transport of the troops thus liberated, with the supposed urgency of their presence at home, occasioned the haste now described, by which many of the Hanoverian houses realized fortunes.

Marshal Bernadotte succeeded Mortier in Hanover. We resumed our former friendly relations both officially and privately. Before my arrival two Irishmen had been recommended to the marshal by Berthier as spies. One of these, MacMahon, I quickly found to be more a spy of England than on our side. Of this I apprised Bernadotte; he had made the same discovery, and wrote me, "I never had any confidence either in the capacity or the devotion of the said MacMahon. I never intrusted him with any commission of importance, and if he received employment, it was from his having been recommended by the minister of war and that his unfortunate situation inspired pity. I gave him at first 400 francs per month, but, detecting his incapacity, I reduced this allowance to 250—a pittance barely sufficient to keep him alive." After the occupation of Hanover, Mr. Taylor, English minister at Cassel, had been obliged to quit that court, but had returned notwithstanding the opposition of France. Bernadotte's letter to me on this subject is interesting:

"MY DEAR BOURRIENNE—I have just received advices which remove all doubt on the transactions at Cassel in Mr. Taylor's affair. That minister has been received, notwithstanding the representations of ours (M. Bignon), which, indeed, till now had been merely verbal. I know the Elector wrote to London, requesting that Mr. Taylor might not return; in reply, the English government sent him back: our minister did everything to induce the Elector to dismiss him; but the grand consideration of the Elector's pecuniary interests carried the day; he could not afford to quarrel with a court on which he depends for twelve million francs. The British ministry, to be sure, have been again addressed on the subject, and the Elector himself, by a private letter, has requested the King of England to recall Mr. Taylor; but it is very likely the court of London will elude the demand. Under these circumstances our troops have approached Cassel. Until then, the whole country of Göttingen had been exempt from military occupation; new dispositions required by the scarcity of forage determined me to send a squadron of horse chasseurs to Münden, a little town twelve miles from Cassel. This movement placed the Elector ill at ease; he has expressed a desire to see things reinstated in their former position, and begged M. Bignon to write me in these terms, charging him to repeat the assurance that he should be delighted to cultivate my acquaintance at the waters of Neuendorff, where he is to be for some time. But herein I shall act, as already stated to you. I believed, my dear Bourrienne, you would not be sorry to learn all these particulars: you may rely on their accuracy. I salute you.
"BERNADOTTE."

Our information, however, was not always so legitimately obtained, as the following incident which happened about the time of my arrival at Hamburg will show: A courier from Vienna, on his route to England, was waylaid in a forest through which he had to pass, and his despatches seized by order of the Emperor. His hands were then tied, and he himself in this condition bound to a tree. The unfortunate man remained in this frightful situation till an old woman, passing accidentally, discovered and released him from almost certain death. During the six years I remained in Germany no such order reached me: it was well; for I would not have directed its execution.

In the beginning of the month of August, a treaty was talked of between Russia and England. I had previously learned, upon unquestionable authority, that the Emperor Alexander had made overtures to General Moreau, to induce him to accept the command of the Austrian infantry. The Emperor made offer of twelve millions of rubles to defray travelling expenses. Moreau, as is well known, had not the misfortune to accept these conditions till long after, when he died in the ranks of the enemy.

This treaty persons of high rank and versed in these affairs, who saw the original, communicated to me by the following extracts: 1. The object of the treaty to be the re-establishment of the equilibrium of Europe. 2. The Emperor of Russia shall place thirty-six thousand men at the disposal of England. 3. Neither of the two powers to lay down arms till the King of Sardinia be restored to his dominions, or have received an equivalent in the northeast of Italy. 4. Malta to be evacuated by the English, and occupied by the Russians. 5. The two contracting powers guarantee the independence of the Ionian Republic, and England engages to aid Russia in her war with Persia. Had this project of a treaty been realized—and of its existence I have no doubt—it is impossible to calculate what might have been the consequences to Europe.

At this epoch no one in the north questioned the near approach of a continental war. I affirm that, had not Napoleon assumed the initiative, and renounced in good time his extravagances at Boulogne, France would have been overwhelmed. I was not slow in advising him of the danger which threatened the country. Of this, more hereafter.

The movements of the Hanoverian army, which occupied a vast extent of position, required its force to be concentrated, in order to approach the line of those military operations which events announced to be at hand. Bernadotte was thus *obliged* to abandon Cuxhaven, which belonged to Hamburg, and took occasion of this necessity to elicit certain aids from that city, under pretext of the evacuation being a mark of respect for the municipality! The following is his letter to me on this subject:

"You have good reason, my dear Bourrienne, to complain of me; I had, from the first, intended to advertise you of the movements taking place in the army, but supposed that in twenty-four hours you must be informed of everything. I have completed preparatory dispositions for concentrating the troops upon Verden and beyond that upon Ganove; I have also assembled some regiments at Göttingen. Up to this moment all is conjecture; but, so soon as I have anything positive, be assured, my dear B., you shall know. I feel how important it is that you should be *au courant* as to how matters go here. As the movement I have just made carries me a little from Cuxhaven, I may abandon that post entirely. Could you not turn that circumstance to advantage for the army? I think you would perform something agreeable to his majesty by procuring supplies for his army in Hanover. Accept, my dear B., renewed assurances of my regard.   BERNADOTTE.

"*September 3, 1805.*"

The Marshal soon after set out, in full march, for the south of Germany. Napoleon, remembering the successful mission of Duroc to Berlin, under the Consulate, despatched him a second time, in order to appease the King of Prussia, who took very seriously the violation of his neutrality by the passage of Bernadotte's army through Anspach. Duroc's mission, however, was this time not so agreeable. The easy progress of the troops through Hesse had encouraged this new infringement; but there existed a mighty difference between a petty state and the kingdom of Prussia. In his first letter Duroc wrote me:

"I know not how long may be my sojourn at Berlin. By my last news, the Emperor is still at Paris, and numerous armies are assembling on the Rhine; the hopes of peace become more and more overcast: Austria is at the bottom of all. I have heard from Marshal Bernadotte. His passage through Hesse has been effected in the best manner possible; the Marshal lauds the Elector to the skies."

To this was subjoined a note in the handwriting of M. Laforest, our minister at the court of Prussia, desiring copies of the Russian Military Regulations, and the Austrian Almanac—"A circumstance," to borrow my correspondent's words, "which, if it showed how far we are behind in these matters, proved at least our good faith." Duroc's second letter was in a different strain; the kindness of the King of Prussia had vanished with the news of the march through Anspach. Much misconstruction has been put on this no doubt illegal violation of the rights of a neutral power: but a letter from a servant of the Emperor, dictated in the confidence of friendship, may place things in their proper light:

"The corps of Marshal Bernadotte has traversed the marquisate of Anspach, and an order, issued in the best possible faith, but misconstrued, through certain underhand dealings, has been here at Berlin represented as an insult offered to the King and an outrage to his neutrality. But is it to be supposed that the Emperor, in the present circumstances especially, would think of insulting or of offering violence to an ally? Besides, reports have been exaggerated, or invented by those who are greater friends to our enemies than to us. I am very ready, however, to admit that Marshal Bernadotte's seventy thousand soldiers are not seventy thousand virgins. Whatever may be the extent of damage—and I am very sure it has been far from fatal—it is not the less injurious to us. Laforest and myself have been very hardly looked upon, though in no degree culpable. All the idle stories set afloat here must have reached you. Perhaps Prussia will not forget that France was the only power which took an interest in her aggrandizement and has still the same views to maintain."

The junction of the Marshal's corps with the grand army, prior to the battle of Austerlitz, was of too much importance to Napoleon not to be expedited by all means and by the shortest road. Gustavus of Sweden, always engaged in some scheme, proposed to form an army composed of his own troops, the Prussians and English; and unquestionably a vigorous attack in the north had prevented Bernadotte's departure from the Weser and the Elbe to reinforce the grand army in its march upon Vienna. But this coalition confined its operations to besieging the insignificant fortress of Hameln. Prussia would not yet break with us, and the King of Sweden, thus abandoned, only drew upon himself the heavier resentment of Bonaparte, while his reverses alienated the affections of his own subjects.

Such was the state of affairs after I had been three months in Hamburg, when at length intelligence reached me that the Emperor had set out for the army. This event was preceded by the abolition of all that now remained of the Republic, namely, its calendar. This had been one of its most foolish inventions; for the designation of the months could not be generally applicable, even when confined to France. A decree of the 9th September decreed that, from the commencement of January, 1806, the months and days should resume their ancient divisions and names.

It was Napoleon's constant policy to represent his enemies as aggressors—himself as forced to declare war. In this he had two objects in view—to maintain an appearance of sincere love of peace, and to remove the responsibility of a contest which he seemed not to have sought. His career offers few examples of this policy so striking as the operations previous to the first conquest of Vienna. Nothing could be more evident than that the transformation of the Cisalpine Republic into the Kingdom of Italy, and the union of Genoa to the empire, were acts contrary to the existing treaties; yet the Emperor did not the less complain of these treaties being violated by Austria. The truth is, Austria had armed in the most secret manner and assembled her troops on the frontiers of Bavaria. An Austrian corps had even penetrated into some of the provinces of the Electorate.

From that moment Napoleon could assume for a pretext the necessity of marching to the succor of the allies of France.

In this spirit he published a singular manifesto, intended for the Diet then assembled at Ratisbon. In this document he exposed his grievances, and threw the odium of all that might follow upon the previous bad faith of Austria; here the facts were, of themselves, true, but presented only one side of the question.

"In such grave circumstances," so concluded the document, "and after vainly endeavoring to bring the court of Vienna to sentiments truly pacific, notwithstanding the reiterated asseverations of that court of having no hostile intentions against France, the Emperor of the French regards himself bound to declare that he will consider as a proclamation of war, formally directed against himself, every aggression to the detriment of the Germanic body, and especially against Bavaria; the Emperor being fully determined never to separate the interests of his empire from those of the princes of Germany, his allies."   .

This note reached me on the 15th September. Twelve days after, on the 1st Vendemiaire, which was to figure, for the last time, among the festivals of the Imperial Republic, Napoleon presided in the Senate and departed on the morrow for the army.

Were I to attempt merely to give an idea of the brilliant campaign of 1805, I should be obliged, in extracting from despatches and letters, to make my narrative in some measure like an almanac, marking each day by one victory at least, or one of those rapid movements which the presence of Napoleon impressed upon his army, and which so powerfully contributed to the prodigious results of a campaign of sixty days. In truth, was not the celerity of the first operations of the Emperor a thing till then unimagined? On the 24th of September he left Paris, and hostilities had commenced by the 2d of October. On the 6th and 7th the French passed the Danube, and turned the army of the enemy. On the 8th, Murat, in the battle of Wertengen, on that river, made two thousand prisoners, with many Austrian officers of distinction. On the morrow the defeated Austrians sustained another discomfiture at Günzburg, by our valiant squadrons, who, following up their advantage, entered Augsburg on the 10th, and Munich on the 12th of the same month. On receiving these despatches, I could almost fancy myself perusing legends of romance. Two days after the entry of the French into the Bavarian capital, that is to say, on the 14th, an Austrian corps of six thousand laid down their arms to Marshal Soult at Memmingen, while, on the same day, Ney won, by force of arms, his dukedom of Elchingen. Last, the 17th of October beheld the famous capitulation of Ulm; and, in another quarter, the same date witnessed the commencement of hostilities in Italy between Masséna and the Archduke Prince Charles. I am persuaded that Napoleon felt great disappointment that the Prince was not opposed to him, for often have I heard him complain of the unskilfulness of the enemy's generals, whose faults, though he ably profited by them, seemed to take from him the full honors of victory. Never, perhaps, did any man more anxiously desire to encounter enemies worthy of his arms.

With respect to the capture of Ulm, the report which I am now to render is that which was laid before the Emperor. He had paused, for a brief space, at Augsburg, with the venerable prelate and former elector of Treves, who was gratefully attached to his person, in order to consider the movements by which he was to operate upon the Austrian army. The pause was the crouching of the tiger before he springs: he rushed forward with such incredible rapidity that the Archduke Ferdinand deemed himself but too fortunate in being barely able to recross the Danube. All the other Austrian forces, however, were shut up in Ulm, and the garrison of a place deemed to be impregnable had thus been augmented to thirty thousand men.

General Ségur, afterward in the service of Murat, had been intrusted with conveying the first overtures to Mack. His report on this subject will be read with interest.

"Yesterday, 24th Vendemiaire (16th October), the Emperor sent for me to attend in the cabinet. I received orders to repair to Ulm, to request Mack to surrender in five days, or, if he should stand out for six, to grant them. These were my only instructions. The night was dark; a fearful hurricane raged; the rain fell in torrents; it was necessary to pass by cross-roads, and avoid gulfs in which man, horse, and mission might have met an untimely end. I had almost reached the gates without lighting upon our advanced posts. There were none, in fact: sentinels, videttes, mainguards— all had got under cover; even the parks of artillery were deserted; no fires—no stars. I continued to wander about for three hours in search of some means to make known my approach. I traversed several villages; questioned those in them; all to no purpose. At last I found a trumpeter of artillery, half drowned in the mire, and stiff with cold, under a carriage. We were doubtless expected; for, at the first summons, an officer, M. de Latour, appeared, who spoke French very well. He bandaged my eyes and led me under the fortifications. I remarked to my conductor how useless were all these precautions in such darkness; but customary observations could not be dispensed with. The distance appeared long. I entered into conversation with my guide, endeavoring to discover what troops were shut up in the city. From his replies I conjectured we held inclosed all the remains of the Austrian army. At length we reached the inn where the commander-in-chief held headquarters. He speedily made his appearance—tall, aged, pale, and with an expression which announced a lively imagination. On his countenance was obviously impressed an anxiety which he labored to conceal. After the exchange of some compliments, I gave my name, stating I had come from the Emperor to summon the Austrian general to surrender, and to arrange with him the terms of capitulation. These expressions appeared to him insupportable, and at first he would not listen to their being necessary. I insisted, observing that having been received it must be obvious to the Emperor that the General was aware of his own situation. He replied quickly that his situation would soon be changed; that the Russian army was approaching to his succor; that we should be between two fires and might find it our turn to talk of capitulating. I replied that in his position it was not wonderful he should be ignorant of what had taken place in Germany; that in consequence I had the honor to inform him of Marshal Bernadotte's occupying Ingoldstadt, and his advanced posts being on the Inn, where the Russians had not yet shown themselves. 'May I be ——,' exclaimed General Mack in great wrath, 'if I am not certainly informed that the Russians are at Dachau! Do you suppose you can deceive me thus! or treat you with a child? No, no! M. de Ségur, if in eight days I am not relieved, I consent to surrender the place, my soldiers to remain prisoners of war and their officers to be prisoners on parole. Then there will be time for relieving me, and I shall have done my duty. But help will reach me: of that I am certain.'—'I have the honor to repeat, general, that we are not only masters of Dachau, but of Munich. Besides, supposing you right—which is not the case—if the Russians be at Dachau, five days will be sufficient for them to come and attack us, and these his Majesty grants you.'—'No, sir,' replied the general, 'I demand eight days; they are indispensable to my responsibility.'—'Thus,' resumed I, 'all the difficulty consists in three days. But I cannot understand the importance your Excellency attaches to these when his Majesty is before your gates with an army of one hundred thousand men, while the corps of Marshal Bernadotte and General Marmont are able to retard for three days the march of the Russians, even supposing them to be whence they are yet far off.'—'They are at Dachau, I repeat,' interrupted General Mack.—'Well, be it so, M. le Baron,' said I, 'or, if you will, at Augsburg; we are so much the more pressed to a speedy termination of your affair. Do not force us, then, to carry Ulm by assault; for then, instead of five days, the Emperor will be here in the morning.'— 'Ah, sir!' replied the commander-in-chief, 'do not imagine that fifteen thousand men will allow themselves to be forced so easily; it will cost you dear!'—'Some hundreds of brave fellows, doubtless,' replied I, 'and you the destruction of your army and of Ulm, with which Germany will reproach you; in short, all the evils of an assault, which his Majesty would spare by the proposition offered through me.'—'Say,' cried the Marshal, 'that it will cost *you* ten thousand men! The strength of Ulm is no secret.'—'It consists in the heights which surround it—and these are in our possession.'—'Then, sir, is it possible that you do not know the strength of Ulm?' —'Doubtless we do, Marshal, and so much the more completely that we can look down upon your works.'—'Very well, sir,' said the unfortunate general, 'then you see men ready to defend themselves to the last extremity if your

Emperor does not grant them eight days. I can hold out long enough here. There are in Ulm three thousand horses upon which we will feed rather than surrender, with as much pleasure as you would do if in our place.'—'Three thousand horses!' answered I; 'ah, Marshal, the straits to which you are already reduced must be considerable since you so early think of such wretched resources.'

"The Marshal hastened to assure me that they had ten days' provisions; but I gave no credit to the assertion. The day began to break; I arose, saying my instructions directed me to return before day, and, in case of refusal to surrender in five days, to transmit the order, in passing, to Marshal Ney to begin the attack. Here General Mack complained of the severity of the Marshal in refusing to receive his flags of truce, and I embraced the opportunity to represent the character of Ney as fierce, impetuous, impossible to be restrained, that he commanded the most numerous and nearest force of the army, and waited with impatience the order for the assault. The old general was not to be intimidated, insisted upon eight days, and pressed me to carry his request to the Emperor. I might have proposed six, but saw no advantage in the measure, and wished not to compromise myself. He held out for the only thing now left him to defend—time.

"On the 25th, at nine in the morning, I again saw the Emperor at the Abbey of Elchingen and gave an account of this negotiation, with which he appeared satisfied. On being recalled, I received from Marshal Berthier new propositions in writing, which General Mack was to be required to sign immediately. By these the Emperor granted eight days to the Austrian general, but to date from the 28d, the first day of the blockade, which, in fact, reduced the time to six days; but, in case of obstinate refusal, I was authorized to date from the 25th. About midday I entered Ulm, always with the same precautions; but this time General Mack was at the gate. I presented the Emperor's ultimatum, he retired to consider it with some officers, among whom I thought I perceived Prince Lichtenstein and Generals Kleinau and Giulay. In a quarter of an hour he returned to dispute with me about the date. From a misunderstanding he had conceived that the eight days were clear, exclusive of the 25th, and, with a strange emotion of satisfaction—'M. de Ségur,' cried he, 'my dear M. de Ségur, I reckoned on the generosity of your Emperor, and have not been deceived.

Tell Marshal Berthier I respect him; say to the Emperor
that I have only some slight observations to make, and will
sign all he requires.   But tell his Majesty that Marshal Ney
has been very harsh; that generals do not treat each other
in the fashion he has treated me.   Be sure you repeat to his
Majesty that I confided in his generosity.'   Then, with
an effusion of increasing delight, he added—'M. de Ségur,
I value your esteem; I attach much importance to the
opinion you may entertain of me; I will show you a writing
which I had signed, for I was determined.'   While speaking thus he unfolded a sheet of paper, inscribed with these
words—'*Eight days, or death!*' signed '*Mack.*' ''

Prince Maurice of Lichtenstein had also been sent to the
imperial headquarters with a flag of truce, and, conformably
to usage, was conducted on horseback with his eyes bandaged.   Rapp afterward described to me this interview:

"Conceive the astonishment," said he, "or rather confusion, of the poor Prince on the bandage being removed;
he knew nothing at all of the real state of affairs, having
no idea that the Emperor had yet arrived.   On finding himself in presence of Napoleon, he could not forbear an involuntary expression of surprise, which did not escape the
Emperor, and frankly avowed that Mack was not aware of
his being before the walls of Ulm.   The Prince asked to
capitulate on condition that the garrison should be permitted
to return to Austria.   That request drew a smile from the
Emperor.   'That is not to be thought of,' replied he; 'I can
have no motive for granting your demand.   What should I
gain?   Eight days?   In eight days you are mine without
conditions.   Do you suppose I am not informed of all?
You expect the Russians?   If they be in Bohemia, it is
the nearest.   If I allow you to depart, who shall assure me
that you do not join their army, and afterward fight against
me?   Your generals have too often deceived me; I will not
again be their dupe.   At Marengo I had the weakness to
allow the troops of Mélas to march out from Alessandria.
What ensued?   Two months after, Moreau had to fight the
garrison of Alessandria.   Besides, the present is no ordinary
war.   After the conduct of your government, I can trust
to no engagement.   You have attacked me.   If I consent to
what you demand, Mack would pledge himself—that I know;
but has he the power to keep his word?   As respects him-

self, yes; but no, as concerns his army. Were the Archduke Ferdinand still with you, I might confide in his word,
because he would be responsible for the conditions, and because he would not dishonor himself; but I am aware he
has quitted Ulm; he has passed the Danube—I know how
to reach him, though.'—You cannot conceive," continued
Rapp, "the embarrassment of Prince Lichtenstein. Recovering a degree of composure, however, he said, 'that unless
upon these concessions, the army would not capitulate.'—
'In that case,' replied Napoleon, 'you may return to Mack,
for I will never grant such conditions. Do you make game
of me? Hold, there is the capitulation of Memmingen;
show that to your general; let him surrender on the same
terms: I will consent to none other. Your officers only
shall return to Austria, but the soldiers must remain prisoners. Tell him to make haste. I have no time to lose. The
longer he delays, the worse he will render his own situation
and yours. I shall have the corps to which Memmingen
surrendered here to-morrow—and we shall see. Let Mack
know that there remains no other part to be taken save
conforming to my will.' "

The imperious tone which Napoleon employed with his
enemies almost always succeeded and produced upon Mack
its usual consequences. Ulm became, as he had predicted,
the "Caudine forks" of the Austrian army. The defenders
marched out with what are termed the honors of war, and
were sent prisoners into France. I may here remark, that
of all the troops which Napoleon had to combat in his military career, the Austrians most readily surrendered themselves prisoners of war.

How great the change which fifteen days of success,
crowned by the capture of Ulm, had effected in the position of affairs! The hopes of our enemies had risen to a
pitch of folly. The security of the cabinet of Vienna was
really inexplicable. Some had even disposed of France as
a conquered country; and among other presents, at her expense, had awarded Lyons to the King of Sardinia, in compensation for the temporary occupation of Piedmont!

It was a singular trait in the character of Napoleon that,
however irritated he might feel against opposition, and its

authors, his resentment disappeared with success. He consoled the misfortune of the vanquished generals when admitted into his presence: nor did this arise from a feigned generosity or emotion of dissembled pride. Often have I heard him say, "How miserable must be the general, on the morrow, after a lost battle!" He had himself experienced the feeling at Acre, and I believe, at that moment, would have strangled the Djezzar; but had the latter surrendered, he would have treated him with the same distinctions as were lavished upon Mack and the other captive commanders at Ulm. These amounted to seventeen, among whom were Prince Lichtenstein, Kleinau and Giulay, both enjoying reputation acquired in the preceding wars, and General Fresnel, whose situation was delicate, as being an emigrant and a Frenchman. It was really painful, as Rapp informed me, to look upon these generals, while they defiled, with Mack at their head, bowing respectfully, as they passed the Emperor, who addressed them as follows:

"Gentlemen, I regret that so many brave men should be victims of the folly of a cabinet which entertains absurd projects, and scruples not to compromise the dignity of the Austrian nation by trafficking in the services of its generals. Your names are known to me, and are honorably remembered wherever you have fought. Examine the conduct of those who have compromised you. What more iniquitous than to attack me without declaration of war, and unawares? Is it not criminal to bring upon the nations a foreign invasion?—to betray Europe, by thus introducing into her disputes hordes of Asiatics? In sound politics, the Aulic Council, in place of attacking me, ought to have sought my alliance, to drive back the Russians to the north. The union now formed by your cabinet will stand eternally in history as a monstrous thing; it is a compact of the dogs and shepherds with wolves against the sheep. Such a conception would never have entered the head of a statesman. It is fortunate for you that I have not been worsted in the unjust contest to which I have been provoked, otherwise the cabinet of Vienna would have but too late perceived its error—an error for which it will in all likelihood pay dearly some day."

On these successes Napoleon addressed to his army a proclamation, which has always appeared to me a master-piece of military eloquence. For, while he commended their past exploits, he stimulated the ardor of his troops to fresh exertions. He congratulated his soldiers on having, in a campaign of fifteen days, chased the Austrians from Bavaria, annihilated a force of one hundred thousand men by the capture of sixty thousand prisoners, two hundred pieces of cannon, ninety standards, and all the generals, fifteen thousand soldiers only having escaped. At the same time he roused their emulation by announcing:

"But we must not stop here; you are impatient to begin a second campaign. That Russian army which English gold has transported *from the extremities of the universe* must experience from you the same fate. In the approaching struggle the honor of the French infantry is especially concerned: then will be decided, for the second time, the question already determined on the plains of Holland and amid the mountains of Switzerland, whether the French infantry is the first or the second in Europe. There are no generals against whom I can acquire fame. All my care will be to obtain victory by the least possible effusion of blood. My soldiers are my children."

The reader must have witnessed, as I have done, the prodigious excitement into which his soldiers were wrought by the words of Napoleon, to conceive the effect of such an address.

CHAPTER XXII

Capture of Vienna—Battle of Austerlitz—Prussia Isolated—Hanover
Exchanged—Battle of Trafalgar

THE second campaign speedily opened, and was hailed with undiminished enthusiasm. There is no exaggeration in saying that the exploits of our troops surpassed the rapidity of thought. Every courier brought me reports more favorable than I had even dared to hope. Two days after the capitulation of Ulm, Murat, on his side,

had shut up General Warnuk, and forced him to capitulate
at Trochtelfrugen. With him were ten thousand men; so
that, exclusive of killed and wounded, the Austrian army
found itself diminished by fifty thousand in the course of
twenty days. On the 27th October, the French troops, by
crossing the Inn, first penetrated into the Austrian dominions, and immediately occupied Saltzburg and Braunau.
Masséna also obtained important advantages in Italy, having, on the same day that these two fortresses surrendered,
that is, on the 30th, gained the sanguinary battle of Caldiero,
and taken five thousand prisoners from the Austrians. On
the 2d of November, Lintz was captured; and the bold
march of Ney upon Innspruck had rendered us masters of
the Tyrol. Still I was not prepared for a letter received
by an extraordinary courier from Duroc, who, after leaving
Berlin, had rejoined the Emperor in Lintz. This laconic
epistle ran as follows: "We are in Vienna! The Emperor
is well, and better satisfied than ever; he is much pleased
with your services at Hamburg, and appears equally pleased
with my mission to Berlin, although you are aware that I
succeeded in nothing; but he had no doubts of my zeal.
He expected me with impatience. I did not conceal from
him the tergiversations which I had witnessed. As much
as possible hold yourself informed of proceedings at Berlin,
and send us word." This letter, dated on the 13th, and
these words, "We are in Vienna!" appeared to me like a
dream. The capital of Austria, that city which from time
immemorial had not beheld the face of an armed foe, become the prey of the *imperial eagle* of France, which, after
three centuries, at the close of a campaign of forty days,
had thus avenged the humiliation of Francis I., imposed
by the *griffin eagle* of Charles V.

Austria, however, did not fall without an effort, both in
the field and in the cabinet. An attempt was made through
Giulay, already mentioned, with the too palpable design of
retarding us in the career of victory, by proposing an armistice, preliminary to a peace, of which the Austrian govern-

ment professed to be sincerely desirous. The snare was too gross. Napoleon said he too desired peace, but kept pushing on—bidding Giulay report to his master for answer that he was ready to treat, though as yet he saw no reason for suspending operations. Bonaparte could not, in effect, without the greatest imprudence, listen to Giulay, since he brought no powers from Russia, who therefore might easily have disavowed the armistice and interposed in time to defend Vienna, the occupation of which had become so important to the French army.

The Russians were, in fact, marching in front of our troops, and the division commanded by Mortier received a check in the first encounter which occasioned the Emperor very great displeasure. For the first time during the campaign he had thus experienced anything like a reverse; it was in truth very slight, but the capture of the first three eagles of which the enemy had obtained possession vexed him exceedingly, and detained him for some days longer than he intended at St. Poulten, where he then was.

The capture of Vienna was due to the fortunate temerity of two men, Murat and Lannes, who yielded to each other in nothing where bravery and daring were concerned. At the time, much was talked of the bold stratagem by which these two marshals prevented the destruction of the bridge of Tabor: without this, our troops could not have gained possession of Vienna, save after incredible difficulties, since that capital is defended by the Danube and its branches. This act of courage and presence of mind, which exercised such essential influence over the rest of the campaign, was subsequently related to me by Lannes himself, who spoke of it as an excellent joke, and seemed much more delighted with having outwitted the Austrians, than considering himself as having performed a splendid action. The most hazardous enterprises were so simple and so natural for him that he was very often the only one who saw nothing unusual in them. What men have been the victims of Napoleon's ambition!

"Conceive," said Lannes to me, I think during the Prussian campaign; "I was one day strolling with Murat along the right bank of the Danube, upon which lay our respective divisions of the army, when, reaching the extremity of the bridge of Tabor, we saw the Austrians at work on the opposite side, evidently employed in preparations for blowing up the bridge on the approach of our troops. These rascals had the assurance to work under our very noses; but we gave them a lesson. Our plan being settled and properly arranged, we returned to give orders. I confided the command of my column of grenadiers to an officer on whose courage and intelligence I could rely. Our dispositions made, Murat and I, with two or three other generals, returned to the bridge. Here we advanced along quite at our ease, and with so much composure that they took us for simple officers. We entered into conversation with the commander of a post established on the middle of the bridge, conversed innocently on an armistice speedily to be concluded, and in this way contrived to divert the attention of the Austrian officers to the left bank. On this, according to previous orders, my column rushed upon the bridge. The Austrian artillerymen on the left bank, seeing their officers in the midst of us, dared not fire; my grenadiers, with Murat and myself at their head, charged forward; and thus we arrived at the opposite bank. All the materials prepared for blowing up the bridge were thrown into the river, and my men took possession of the batteries destined to protect the passage. The poor devils of Austrian officers remained perfectly stultified on my telling them that they were our prisoners: it was even necessary to bully them a little."

Such was the recital of Lannes, who laughed most heartily on recalling the figure cut by the Austrian officers in their consternation on discovering the blunder they had committed. Lannes, however, had not foreseen the importance of the enterprise which he had accomplished, though it soon became evident. Not only was a passage into Vienna thus secured to the army, but an insurmountable barrier interposed between the junction of the Austrian corps under the Archduke Charles with the Russian army. The Archduke, pressed by Masséna, had retreated in all haste to the heart of the hereditary states, not doubting that a general battle would there be decided. I may just advert, in passing, to the disagreeable situation of Prince Charles: forced to take part in a war of which he had highly disapproved, but intrusted only with a secondary command in Italy, his reputation was exposed to a compromise, while he had never been brought fairly into the contest. Thenceforth he renounced all command in the Austrian armies.

As soon as the corps of Murat and Lannes had taken ' possession of Vienna, the Emperor ordered all the other divisions of the army to direct their march upon the capital, which became, in some sort, the capital of the French army; and he himself, as if at St. Cloud, established his headquarters at Schœnbrunn, whence he issued his directions both for forcing the Archduke Charles to retire upon Hungary and for leading his own army against the Russians. Leaving in Vienna and the environs only four divisions, under Mortier and Marmont, he took the route for Snaim (Moravia), where the mass of the Russian army was believed to be concentrated. The Russians, however, had marched upon Brünn, toward which Napoleon then eagerly hastened: the two armies, in mutual search of each other, could not thus allow the question to remain long undecided.

During these forced and next to miraculous marches Murat and Lannes constantly commanded the advanced guard. The lofty foresight of the Emperor seemed to grow during the operations preceding the battle of Austerlitz: it is certain—and too many officers, witnesses of the fact, have spoken to that effect in my hearing for me to doubt its truth —that he himself pointed out the ground in advance upon which he would engage the Russian army, and commanded his generals carefully to examine its sinuosities, for they would there have to play a great game. Still, to keep up the

persuasion that he desired peace, he had caused the minister
for foreign affairs to follow the army close at hand, and sent
also Savary as envoy to the Emperor of Russia, offering
peace before coming to blows with him. The conditions,
however, were of a nature which he knew could not be accepted without dishonor and such as the gain of a battle
could not more than authorize. It is evident to every reflecting mind that he acted thus for the purpose of assuming
the air of a pacificator, while he could securely indulge his
passion for war.

At length arrived the great day when, according to the
expression of Napoleon, "the sun of Austerlitz arose."
All our forces were concentrated on the same point, about
forty leagues beyond Vienna. There remained only the
wrecks of the Austrian army, the division of Prince Charles
not having been able to triumph over the skilful manœuvres
which held it distant from the line of operations; but the
Russians, of themselves, were superior to us in number,
while their army was composed, in greater part, of fresh
troops. Illusion had reached a high pitch in the enemy's
camp. The north of Europe has its Gascons no less than the
south of France: the Russian youth, as I afterward learned,
expressed their confidence in loud boasting. The evening
before the battle, the Emperor Alexander having sent the
Prince Dolgorouki, one of his aides-de-camp, to Napoleon,
with a flag of truce, this young man could not govern his
petulance, even in presence of the Emperor. As the conference took place in private, no one knew the nature of
the "impertinence"; but Rapp, being in attendance, heard
Bonaparte exclaim, in dismissing the messenger, "When
you are on the heights of Montmartre I shall reply to such
impertinence only with my cannon." A singular phrase
while in thought we transport ourselves to the time when
it became a prediction. As to the battle, I am able to speak
of it almost as if I had been present, having had the lively
satisfaction of seeing my friend General Rapp soon after in
Hamburg. His graphic relation was as follows:

"When we arrived at Austerlitz, the Russians, ignorant of the Emperor's skilful strategy to draw them to the ground upon which he had resolved to engage, and beholding our advanced guards yield before their columns, conceived the victory won. According to their notions, the advanced guard would suffice to secure an easy triumph. But the battle began—they found what it was to fight, and, on every point, were repulsed. At one o'clock the victory was still uncertain; for they fought admirably. They resolved on a last effort, and directed close masses against our centre. The imperial guard deployed: artillery, cavalry, infantry, were marched against a bridge which the Russians attacked, and this movement, concealed from Napoleon by the inequality of the ground, was not observed by us. At this moment I was standing near him waiting orders. At once arose on our left the rolling of a heavy fire of musketry; the Russians were repulsing one of our brigades. Hearing this sound, the Emperor ordered me to take the Mamelukes, two squadrons of chasseurs, one of grenadiers of the guard, and to observe the state of things. I set off at full gallop, and, before advancing a cannon-shot, perceived the disaster. The Russian cavalry had penetrated our squares, and were sabring our men. In the distance could be perceived masses of Russian cavalry and infantry in reserve. At this juncture the enemy advanced; four pieces of artillery arrived at a gallop, and were planted in position against us. On my left I had the brave Morland, on my right General d'Allemagne. 'Courage, my brave fellows!' cried I to my party; 'behold your brothers, your friends, butchered; let us avenge them, avenge our standards! Forward!' These few words inspired my soldiers; we dashed at full speed upon the guns and carried them. The enemy's horse, which awaited our attack, were overthrown by the vigor of the same charge, and fled in confusion, as we pursued, over the wrecks of our own squares. In the meantime the Russians rallied, but, a squadron of horse grenadiers coming to our assistance, I could then halt and await the reserves of the Russian guard. Again we charged, and this charge was terrible. The brave Morland fell by my side. It was veritable butchery where we fought man to man, and so mingled together that the infantry on neither side dared to fire, lest they should kill their own men. The intrepidity of our troops finally bore us in triumph over all opposition: the enemy fled in disorder under the eyes of both Emperors of Austria and Russia. These sovereigns had taken their station on a rising ground, in order to be spectators of the contest. They ought to have been satisfied, for I can assure you they witnessed no child's play. For my own part, my good friend, I never passed so delightful a day. The Emperor received me most graciously when I arrived to tell him that the victory was ours; I still grasped my broken sabre, and as this scratch upon my head bled very copiously, I was all covered with gore. He made me general of division. The Russians returned not again to the charge—they had had enough; we captured everything—their cannon, their baggage, their all, in short, and Prince Ressina was among the prisoners.''

Such was Rapp's recital, and in many long and interesting conversations with this excellent man I learned other details, which will appear in their proper place. What now remains of Austerlitz? The remembrance—the glory—and magnificent picture of Gérard, the idea of which was suggested to the Emperor by the sight of Rapp covered with blood.

The day after the battle the Emperor, being still in the Château of Austerlitz, Prince Lichtenstein, the former envoy at Ulm, arrived in the evening with a message from Francis, proposing an interview. This was accepted, and the ceremonial arranged to take place on the morrow, the 4th; for the battle had been fought on the 2d December, exactly the first anniversary of Napoleon's coronation. The French Emperor on horseback found himself first at the place appointed for the meeting, at a windmill, about three leagues from Austerlitz. Immediately after, the Emperor of Austria arrived in an open carriage. When Napoleon observed him approaching, he alighted, advanced on foot, surrounded by his aides-de-camp, and embraced Francis on accosting him. During the interview, Napoleon was attended by Berthier only, and Francis by Prince Lichtenstein; so that the aides-de-camp—from one of whom, Lauriston, I received these details—could not overhear the conference, the subject of which it is easy to divine. I can portray to myself Bonaparte endeavoring to seduce his vanquished enemy by those insinuating words of which he possessed the secret in so great a degree, seeking in some sort to palliate his own glory by the exterior of affected modesty: we may, in like manner, paint the humiliation of the future father-in-law, forced to obey the imperious dictate of necessity. What a situation for the successor of Charles V.! The Emperors remained together nearly two hours, and separated as they had met, with an embrace. On returning slowly toward his army, the Emperor must have experienced the internal complacency of gratified pride: he seemed wholly absorbed in meditation, which he suddenly broke off to send an aide-de-camp to the Emperor of Austria. Savary was selected for this purpose. The object of the mission was to inform Francis that the messenger had orders to proceed to the headquarters of Alexander, to receive his adherence to the terms as agreed upon by the two Emperors in their conference. Alexander agreed to everything, saying, that since the King of the Romans (the only title yet vouchsafed to the Emperor of Austria) was satisfied, so was he; that for his sake only had he interfered, and consequently now found himself disengaged—having no wish to form for himself. Thus terminated the hostilities of this campaign, which elevated the glory of Napoleon to the highest pitch. The diplomacy of France and Austria assembled in Pressburg, and there the negotiations were begun and carried on till the 25th, when all was concluded on that day three months from the time Napoleon left Paris. Russia, though she had taken part in the war, took none in the negotiations: hostilities ceased between her and France, but without any treaty of peace being established.

The Emperor had solemnly announced to his Senate, on leaving Paris, that he wished no aggrandizement for France; and he kept his word. Judging, apparently, that the promises of the Emperor of the French did not bind the King of Italy, he so ordered matters that, by the treaty of Pressburg, were conceded—not to France but to Italy—the ancient

territories of Venice in Dalmatia and Albania. In virtue
of the same treaty, the Elector of Bavaria, with the title of
king, received the principality of Eichstett, a part of the
territory of Passau, the Tyrol, and the important city of
Augsburg. The Elector of Würtemberg was likewise raised
to the regal dignity, and all the Austrian possessions in
Swabia, Bresgaw and Ortenau were divided between the
two new kings and the Elector of Baden created Grandduke.
To have the appearance of granting some concessions, Saltzburg and Berchtesgaden were yielded to Austria, while to
the Archbishop of Saltzburg was assigned the principality
of Würtzburg, erected into a grandduchy, Napoleon thus
rewarding the good ecclesiastic with a province for the hospitable reception he had given him on his way to conquest.
The same treaty recognized the independence of the Batavian
and Helvetian republics, while it annulled the Teutonic
Order. Thus was explained to me the expression, "I have
views on Germany," as employed by the Emperor in our
last interview.

After the battle of Austerlitz, Napoleon established himself for a few days at Brunn, in order to superintend
the cantoning of his troops. Here he ascertained the losses,
sent his aides-de-camp to visit the hospitals and to present,
in his name, each wounded soldier with a napoleon. To all
wounded officers, also, he caused gratifications to be distributed, from five hundred to three thousand francs, according to their rank.

The Emperor then set out for Schœnbrunn, where he arrived without stopping at Vienna, through which he passed
during the night. On the morning after his arrival he
received for the first time the Prussian minister, M. de
Haugwitz, who had been for some time in Vienna, negotiating with Talleyrand, and who found himself as critically
situated as can well be conceived for a diplomatist. The
Prussian envoy was very saucily received, as may be supposed, and treated with haughtiness and severity. "Is that
loyal conduct," demanded the Emperor, "which your master

holds toward us? It would have been far more honorable to have declared war at once, although he has no cause for so doing. Then he would have served his new allies, for I should have had to look two ways before giving battle. You would be the friends of all parties: that is not possible; you must choose between them and me. If you wish to side with these gentlemen, go—I oppose it not; but, if you hold with me, I desire sincerity or I separate myself from you: I prefer open enemies to false friends. What sense is there in that? you call yourselves my allies, and you permit, in Hanover, a body of thirty thousand Russians to communicate with the grand army across your states: nothing can justify such conduct; it is an overt act of hostility. If your powers are not sufficiently ample to treat of all these questions, inform yourself: I shall march against my enemies wherever they are to be found.'' The Emperor was so excited, said my informant, Lauriston, and spoke so loud that we heard him very distinctly, although in a different apartment.

The situation of the Prussian envoy was a delicate one; the more-so, too, that the grievances of which Napoleon complained were not without foundation. The truth is, that Haugwitz had come from Berlin solely as an observer and having only conditional instructions. Had the Emperor been beaten by the coalition, the cabinet of Berlin had instructed its representative frankly to declare for the victors; but the result of the battle being so eminently in favor of the French, the object of the mission dared not even be assigned. Seeing that Prussia was likely to be alone against triumphant France—that peace unquestionably would soon be agreed upon—urged on, moreover, by the menacing words of Napoleon, who never threatened in vain, M. de Haugwitz, finding no other means of averting the storm ready to burst upon his country, took upon himself, unauthorized by his sovereign, to sign a treaty, in virtue of which the margravates of Bareuth and Anspach were exchanged for Hanover I am far from any intention of justifying such a procedure, but, doubtless, the same reproaches are not to be laid upon the ambassador, as if he had acted under ordinary circumstances. In that case his incredible want of judgment could not have been too severely reprobated in exchanging two provinces for Hanover, which belonged to England, and for which his master would have to account to that government. But hope was still at Berlin, though despair only presented itself to Haugwitz at Vienna, and he thought by thus sacrificing a part to save the whole.

While these things were transacting in the Austrian capital, I learned by my bulletins that the Count de Harden-berg, *by order of his master*, had concluded a new treaty with England—a circumstance which rendered the position of Prussia, with regard to her simultaneous allies, exceedingly hazardous and complicated. How get out of this embarrass-ment? Yet get free of it they must, while Frederick William and his cabinet saw no means of safety. To Napoleon they could no longer allege even a dubious plea of neutrality. Thus, war could not be avoided: the only question was, shall it be with France or England? The former was in the strength of recent victory, and the latter had granted a sub-sidy of fifteen millions. Haugwitz, having signed his treaty at Vienna, set out immediately for Berlin. On the road he met Colonel Pfuhl, despatched to inform him of the treaty concluded by the cabinet at home. The two returned to Berlin together. At this moment all the diplomatists were in motion, although Bonaparte had greatly simplified their calling; for, as far as concerned him, only two principles now composed the diplomatic code—"My will, or war."

His Prussian Majesty, as may well be imagined, ex-pressed the most lively dissatisfaction with the proceedings at Vienna. Never, perhaps, had sovereign been placed in more cruel perplexity. Under the difficulties of the case, recourse was had to one of those political shifts which may retard but can never avert the danger. It was conceived that the clause of the treaty which respected Hanover might be refused, at least until the sanction of England should be obtained—a sanction which, very obviously, would not be procured. To escape the immediate resentment of Napoleon, the two margravates were sacrificed, and Hanover was received as in pledge till the conclusion of a general peace. After all, the Emperor in thus dealing away Hanover absolutely bestowed nothing: it belonged not to him—not even by military occupation; for the occupying division had been recalled at the commencement of the campaign.

Still there were hopes for Prussia. The Russians, indeed, had retired from the field of battle at Austerlitz, but without renouncing all hostile action: the Emperor Alexander had not acknowledged Napoleon either as Emperor of the French or King of Italy. I remember to have heard even, that, having occasion to write before the battle, the superscription of his letter ran—"'To the Chief of the French government." In fact, at this very moment, while the French cabinet at Vienna knew nothing of the new treaty with England, and entertained no doubts of the validity of the one just signed by Haugwitz, the Russian general, Buxhoewden, at the head of a corps of thirty thousand men, after passing the Vistula at Warsaw, was in full march for Bohemia. This was one of the fruits of Alexander's journey to Berlin: that prince had induced the King of Prussia to make common cause with the coalition; but the fortune of Napoleon had anticipated the declaration. Duroc had witnessed the interviews of the two sovereigns; but their political negotiations had been so adroitly managed under this, in appearance, amicable intercourse, that neither he nor our minister, Delaforest, spite of their rare sagacity, could discover, certainly, to which party the Prussian cabinet would adhere. Probably the King himself had not exactly made up his own mind; and, besides, there existed a difference of opinion among his counsellors, of whom M. de Hardenberg and the Queen inclined more directly to hostility against France than did Frederick William.

Amid these various diplomatic arrangements, the results of his late brilliant successes, the Emperor received intelli-

gence of the disaster of Trafalgar, which had been nearly
contemporaneous with the surrender of Ulm to his own
arms. Admiral Villeneuve, who, with Gravina, commanded
the combined fleets of France and Spain, sailed from Cadiz
with the intention of attacking the English fleet under the
orders of the famous Admiral Nelson. The southern shores
of the Peninsula witnessed this naval combat, in which thirty-
one French engaged thirty-three British ships, and, notwithstanding this equality of force, eighteen of our fleet were
captured or destroyed. This great battle gave to the world
a new proof of our inferiority at sea, both in material and
seamanship. Admiral Calder had given us a lesson which
Nelson completed—but at the expense of his life. A blood-
ier naval engagement had not taken place since the renowned
Armada. Its issue was equivalent to the destruction of our
whole fleet, since the thirteen ships that escaped to Cadiz
were almost wrecks. For a space, courage gave hope to the
French, as I learned by my information from Vienna; but
finally they were obliged to yield to the superior tactics of
the enemy. Our naval power was thus definitely paralyzed,
and an end put to every thought of an attempt upon England. The day was fatal to three admirals; Nelson lost his
life in the fight, Gravina died of his wounds, and Villeneuve, a prisoner, was carried to England, where he committed suicide.

CHAPTER XXIII

Bourrienne's Spies—Dr. Gall—Occupation of Hanse Towns—Bernadotte,
Governor of Hamburg—The Continental System

I NOW enter my minister plenipotentiary's study; wherein
events not a little curious occasionally took place. The
year 1806 began my troubles with the effects of the literary propensities of Louis XVIII., in shape of a "Declaration," transmitted by post on the 2d of January. This
production had been diffused in vast numbers, being in

a form easily transmissible, even into France, as a letter. On the 16th I received a despatch from Fouché, with three envelopes of the work of the *Pretender*, urging me to procure as many such as possible and transmit them to him. From this duty I got free by pleading its impossibility, knowing well that the object was to compromise individuals, who had received a letter without being aware of its contents. In this dispersion, Dumouriez, whose carriage was loaded with copies, had been very active; indeed, his occupation had now dwindled to vending pamphlets, more or less indifferent. At this date Germany, and especially the Hanse Towns, were inundated with such writings. Before the proclamation one of the most odious of these pamphlets had appeared under the title, "Bonaparte, which art in Heaven, hallowed be thy name.—Rome, printed by the Pope." The expressions were horrible, and I never could discover the author, though I prevented the circulation of this fearful tract.

In February I was enabled to answer fully an information received from the ministry of police in Paris, relative to one named Dranob, who, with Lesemple, had formed a plot against the life of the Emperor. The name was an anagram of Bonard, the true appellation of the former, who, in female disguise, had escaped from the Conciergerie in 1798; and represented himself to me as having been an officer in the light artillery. Few examples occur of knaves with so much courage and address.

Arriving in Hamburg, about the commencement of 1805, to fulfil these engagements, which, as he had told me, were entered into with the English government, Bonard, instead of killing the Emperor, thought it would be better to inform against his accomplice Lesemple. Discovering, probably, that my agents were in search of him, he called upon me of his own accord and placed in my hands certain papers which he had long concealed about his person. These documents, written in a very small character and rolled up carefully, were inclosed in a tin case, very nicely made, very slender, and about six inches long. This case was concealed about his person so as not by any possibility to be discovered, and in a way which I dare not attempt to describe. It contained, likewise, a small file of a brownish metal, which cut iron as a knife cuts paper—an instrument several times discovered by the police of Paris on the persons of other malefactors. All these papers were written by Lesemple and contained extracts from the correspondence of the two relative to their nefarious enterprise. That nothing might be wanting in the chain of evidence, I found a quarrel had taken place between the two villains at the moment of embarking at Harwich, and a combat fought in the burying-ground of that town, with the knives which they had been using at the tavern. While relating this horrible transaction, Bonard suddenly uncovered his right side and showed me a frightful gash, still bleeding. Let the reader imagine my situation; alone, with the most athletic man I have ever beheld, baring his breast, covered with gore, and confiding to me his fearful design of murder—not from repentance, but from the belief that its discovery would be more profitable than the accomplishment, producing at the same time the proofs of his own villany, concealed in a manner so incredible! While his schemes were thus denounced, Lesemple was on his way from Holland. Assured by Bonard that his prompt arrival might be expected in Hamburg, I took measures to have him arrested, and had begun to entertain apprehensions, when at length he did appear, having been detained by the Russians as a spy, and, on the 19th, I had him suddenly seized, with his papers, of which he could thus conceal none. I examined him, and his confession confirmed the horrible details before given by his associate. In his pocket-book were three passports fabricated by himself, and a bill of exchange, the product likewise of his own manufacture. Upon his person were found several packets carefully made up, and each ticketed *fifty louis*, but which, on being opened, were discovered to be filled with copper only, as also a purse with counters of the same metal.

These he used for deceiving at the gaming tables. He was at once pickpocket, spy, forger and assassin. I had promised Benard to send him to Paris free, in order to reply in person to the examination of the minister of police; but as such characters cannot be a single day in a place without being sullied with some crime, he was accused of being accessory to several robberies in Hamburg, and accordingly consigned by the prefect to the care of the police. Fearing such recommendation, however, he contrived to escape, but was taken some days after and sent under a good escort to Paris.

Yet, among such degraded men have I found rare instances of courage and presence of mind. I had an agent among the Swedo-Russians, named Chefneux, who was detected almost in the act of spying with a bulletin just ready to be sent off to me, though fortunately addressed to a merchant at Hamburg. He had also a letter of recommendation, which I had procured from a gentleman intimately known to the Russian minister, which saved him summary punishment from the Cossacks. With all these precautions it was still suspected that he had some connection with me. After many fruitless examinations, a last effort remained. Chefneux, condemned to be shot, was led out to the plain of Lüneburg with a bandage over his eyes; he heard the word, "Make ready," given to the squad and the ticking of the locks of the muskets. At this moment a person approached and whispered in his ear, in a tone of interest and kindness, "I am your friend; only say you know M. de Bourrienne and you are saved."—"No!" cried Chefneux, with astonishing firmness; "I should then lie." The bandage fell from his eyes and he was restored to liberty, with the assurance of not getting off so easily a second time. It would be difficult to mention an instance of more extraordinary presence of mind.

Sometimes, too, I had it in my power to do good even by instruments of evil. In March of this year a M. de la Ferronays, at Brunswick, was denounced by the Parisian police as a very dangerous man. I sent the same Chefneux, giving him five hundred francs per month, to live as a gentleman, and he quickly insinuated himself into the good graces of the suspected and his friends. I was obliged to send his information to Paris; but, from the manner I had otherwise heard De la Ferronays mentioned, he had awakened a lively interest in my mind, and I resolved to save him. Orders had been given for his arrest as he passed through Hamburg for England, notice of this journey having been forwarded by his friend, my agent. Travelling under another name, with the further protection of secretary to Lord Kinnaird, a title granted by his lordship, and a momentary stay only in passing to Altona saved him here. But he was soon after guilty of an imprudence which had nearly proved fatal to himself and compromised me. One evening, while at the opera, the prefect of police came up to me, saying M. de la Ferronays was in the house, and requiring an order for his arrest. He directed my attention to a young man wearing powder, whom I at once recognized from Chefneux's description. I still desired to befriend the young emigrant—but how save him now? "You must arrest him," said I to the prefect; "but first I shall take precautions to have it done quietly, without alarming the house," and, slipping out, I begged one on whom I could rely to pass the unsuspecting victim so as not to be observed, and whisper to him to flee. Returning instantly to my box, "Now, do your duty," said I to the prefect; but before he had shut the door upon me I saw the intimation given, and Ferronays was on the road to Altona.

But while execrating spying and spies, I am constrained to acknowledge the necessity under which the Emperor lay of being on his guard against the multitude of intrigues hatched in the vicinity of Hamburg, especially surrounded as that place was by the Russians, Swedes and English, still in arms, and when the treaty with Prussia stood on such dubious terms. On the 5th of January the Swedish monarch had approached with his troops to the very gates of

Hamburg. He had menaced the hapless senate with the utmost weight of his displeasure for having, on my demand, ordered the colors to be removed which had been hung out over the Austrian recruiting office. Deputies from the city were, after some delay, received into the royal presence, and the storm blew past. The king, with his six thousand men, seemed resolved on playing the part of the restorer of Germany, and of exhibiting himself as the Don Quixote of the treaty of Westphalia. At this time his headquarters were Boetzenburg, on the north bank of the Elbe. As a resource against dulness in this stationary warfare, the king sent for Dr. Gall, then at Hamburg, where he lectured on his system, at first rejected by false science and prejudice, subsequently adopted, in consequence of his arguments, which, to my mind, are unanswerable. I had much intercourse with Dr. Gall, who has done me the honor of inscribing with my name one of his works on cerebral organization. On taking leave for the camp of his Majesty of Sweden I observed, "My dear doctor, you will certainly find on his cranium the organ of vanity." In truth, had the learned doctor been permitted to feel all the crowned heads in Europe at that time, he would have got hold of some curious craniological studies.

The King of Sweden was not the only enemy to be feared. Prussia made many flattering overtures to be admitted to the protectorship and occupation of the city. This to Hamburg will be the last misfortune. The political and fiscal system of Prussia is one, of all others, most to be dreaded by a commercial city. Besides, England would never have consented to a measure which must have excluded her from the Elbe, and from one of the richest markets and most convenient points whence to extend her policy. At this time the recruiting in Hanover, no longer occupied by French troops, was carried on by England to a great extent. She scattered gold with both hands, and employed in this service an establishment of one hundred and fifty carriages with six horses each. The recruiting was intended for the Hanoverian legion, and I had little doubt the Anglo-Russians would attempt a diversion in Holland. Of these transactions I informed Napoleon, by an extraordinary courier, a means of intelligence in the use of which I had orders to stand on no hesitation; and Heaven knows how many I received and expedited. Russia, in all her dispositions, manifested extreme hatred of France, and from the movements of her corps in the north of Germany, of which I sent a fresh despatch, with all the intelligence to be collected, had no doubt in my mind of an approaching rupture in those parts. Of all these circumstances—the movements of the Russians at Wilna, Brode in Austrian Moldavia, and Prussian Poland, the names of their generals, the strength of their corps, where they labored most assiduously on their fortifications—I sent information to government in a despatch addressed to M. de Talleyrand. Russia, the reader will recollect, had merely retired from Austerlitz, for, at this time, there existed neither convention nor peace —not even an armistice. Of this she seemed inclined to take advantage; but Napoleon watched, and to outplay him was not easy.

Notwithstanding the impending war, which I judged inevitable, some attempts were made to bring about a general peace. I was not deceived, for, even in the least things, I remarked a feeling of determined hostility to pervade all foreign nations against France. I often received, for instance, from the minister of marine, packets for the Isle of France, to the preservation of which settlement the Emperor attached much importance. I had great difficulty in prevailing upon the captains of privateers, who made occasional visits to that colony, to take charge of my commissions. The hopes of peace were founded on the demise of Mr. Pitt, and especially on the entrance of Mr. Fox to the ministry. It was well known that the deceased premier was personally hostile to France, while between his successor and the Emperor there had existed reciprocal esteem; and really Mr. Fox did show himself frankly dis-

NAPOLEON ON BOARD H.M.S. BELLEROPHON

posed for peace. The possibility of this consummation he had always advocated when in opposition to Mr. Pitt. Bonaparte, likewise, moved by the high regard he entertained for Mr. Fox, might have been induced to some concessions he had formerly repelled. But two obstacles, I may say insurmountable, presented themselves: the conviction, on the part of England, that such peace would only be a truce, of longer or shorter duration, from Napoleon aspiring to universal dominion; and, secondly, that he meditated an attack upon England. Had he essayed this invasion, it would not have been more to strike his rival to the heart, and to destroy her commerce, so superior to that of France, than to blast the liberty of the press, which he had rooted up in every other place. The spectacle of a free people, separated by a strait of only six leagues, presented in his mind too seducing an example to France, and would eventually arouse the emulation of all those generous spirits who bend beneath no yoke.

During the first days of the administration of Mr. Fox, a Frenchman called upon him offering to assassinate the Emperor. The English minister wrote immediately to M. de Talleyrand on the subject, and stated that the British laws did not authorize the detention of any foreigner for a length of time who had not committed some offence, but that, nevertheless, he should not release this miserable wretch till such period as would allow the head of the French government to be informed of the proposal, and to take precautions against its effects. Mr. Fox, in his letter, further said that he had done the fellow the honor of *taking him for a spy;* an expression strongly significant of the English minister's indignation. This information, so nobly given, was the key which opened a door to new negotiations. The Emperor directed Talleyrand, in reply, to express to Fox how deeply he was touched by his honorable procedure, and that he congratulated himself on contemplating what might be expected from a cabinet guided by those principles which such conduct evinced. Napoleon did not confine himself to this

diplomatic courtesy: he thought the occasion favorable for
creating a belief of his sincere love of peace.   He sent from
Paris Lord Yarmouth, one of the most distinguished of those
Englishmen who had been so scandalously detained prisoners
at Verdun, at the rupture of the Treaty of Amiens.   To this
nobleman he consigned proposals to the English government
to enter upon negotiations, voluntarily offering to recognize,
in favor of England, the possession of the Cape of Good
Hope and of Malta.   Some have thence attempted to elicit
an occasion of praising the moderation of Bonaparte, while
others have affected to discover too great concessions in
these advances, as if the Cape of Good Hope or Malta could
have entered into competition with the title of Emperor, the
establishment of the kingdom of Italy, the acquisition of
Genoa and all the states of Venice, the dethroning of the
King of Naples and the gift of that realm to Joseph—in fine,
the new form given to Germany—all posterior to the peace
of Amiens, of which changes Bonaparte said not one word,
and from which he certainly would not have departed.

I distrusted all accounts of peace, therefore, and too well
knew Bonaparte to place any reliance on the sincerity of the
Emperor, especially after the success of the campaign of
Vienna; in fact, every day I saw his ambition extending.
He already coveted possession of the Hanseatic Towns, the
last asylums of the wrecks of liberty in Germany.   This
design he veiled under pretence of offering or rather selling
his protection.   In this negotiation, I know not why, I became agent; although, from my own knowledge of the state
of men's minds, with little hope of success, I did my duty:
that is to say, in many conferences with the municipalities
I endeavored to persuade the towns of Hamburg, Bremen
and Lubeck to accept the Emperor's protection, at a small
sacrifice of six millions, which they were required to pay
for this honor.   They, too, were faithful to their duties by
acting in the way I would have done in their place; they
declined the Emperor's generous proposal.

The Elbe renders Hamburg the natural emporium of Germany. That beautiful river, traversing the whole length of the city, receives into its bosom the riches of the east and south. Here the agriculturist and the manufacturer receive in exchange every product of the earth which taste and refinement have rendered, from being luxuries, essential necessaries to the descendants of the ancient Germans, as well as to every inhabitant of civilized Europe. At the same time, the most unsullied probity of commercial relations had gained for the merchants of the Hanse Towns universal confidence. When the sacrifices, voluntary and forced, which these small states were condemned to make before they were engulfed in the empire are considered, we can hardly believe it possible for them to have possessed such resources. In such states we discover the true secret of liberty.

We have seen what brought the Emperor in haste to Paris in the end of January, 1806, where, on arriving, he learned that his troops occupied Malta. Having made kings in Germany, he now deemed the time arrived for surrounding his own throne with new princes. At this time he named Murat Grandduke of Berg and Cleves; Bernadotte Prince of Ponte-Corvo; M. de Talleyrand Prince of Benevento; and his two ancient colleagues, Cambacérès and Lebrun, Dukes of Parma and Placenza. He granted also to his sister Pauline, some time before married, in second nuptials, to the Prince Borghese, the investiture of the Duchy of Guastalla. Strange turn of events! who could then have foreseen that the duchy of Cambacérès, the colleague of the First Consul, was to become the place of retreat to a princess of Austria, the relict of Napoleon, before his death?

We now approach the moment when war was to ravage Germany anew; for, in proportion as the hopes of peace diminished, Prussia redoubled her menaces. The remembrance of the Great Frederick agitated her; peace had become odious. Her measures, until then sufficiently moderate, all at once assumed a threatening tone from the time

when the English ministry had stated to Parliament that
France had declared her willingness to restore Hanover.
The French cabinet, on the other hand, assured Prussia that
this restitution was the nearest step to peace, and held out
large indemnities. But the Prussian monarch, well informed of all, and convinced that the house of Hanover
attached great importance to the possession of an ancient
domain, which gave a certain preponderance in Germany,
regarded himself as deceived, and resolved on war. At this
period the whole of Prussia was animated by the same warlike sentiments. The public mind, and her youth especially,
were exasperated. The king aspired to the character of
liberator of Germany. Prussia, therefore, rejected every
offer of compensation for Hanover; she knew that Napoleon
would sacrifice her twenty times over to insure peace with
England. In these circumstances, Lord Lauderdale having
been recalled from Paris by his government—notwithstanding the personal esteem of Pitt's successor for the Emperor
—we continued at war with Britain, and were on the eve of
having Prussia also on our hands.

The cabinet of Berlin sent an ultimatum replete with expressions, in which little measure was observed, and amounting almost to a defiance. Napoleon's character is known,
and, as may well be believed, this ultimatum roused his
choler. Berthier, who had remained at Munich, pressed him
to anticipate the Prussian preparations. After an abode of
eight months, passed in the chances of peace and uncertain
negotiation, the Emperor departed on the 25th of September
for the Rhine. We have works so excellent on the campaign which ensued, called the Campaign of Saxony, that I
may dispense with entering upon its details. I shall merely
mention some private events, omitting all public transactions. Who does not remember with what giant strides the
first captain of modern times traversed Prussia, and planted
his eagles in the capital of the Great Frederick?

M. Jacobi, Prussian envoy to London, remained at Hamburg with visible impatience. The crisis between France

and his country approached, and he felt the need of union with England, and support from her subsidies. England was then like an open bank to all our enemies. On the 1st of October, a courier from the headquarters at Nauemburg arrived, with an order for M. Jacobi to embark for England immediately. On the morrow he went on board a cutter sent for the purpose. He assured me, before parting, that the subsidies for Prussia were to be sixteen millions sterling. He had no great hope of the approaching contest with France. I spoke to him of Hanover; he informed me that one of the conditions of a compact between England and Prussia was the *restitution* and guarantee of that province to Britain.

On the 10th October hostilities commenced between France and Prussia. I demanded of the Senate that the recruiting in the city for the Prussian service should cease. The news of a great victory gained by the Emperor over the Prussian army reached Hamburg on the 14th; but, though the disaster of our enemies was evident, from the crowds of fugitives of all ranks and ages from the north of Germany, the accounts were so contradictory I knew not whether to rejoice or grieve, when, on the 28th, arrived official intelligence of the victory of Jena. On the day following, in his 72d year, loaded with infirmities, and grievously wounded in the battle of Auerstadt, the Duke of Brunswick entered Altona. His arrival in that city presented a new and striking proof of the instability of fortune. A sovereign prince, enjoying, right or wrong, a great military reputation, but very lately powerful and tranquil in his own capital, was now beheld, beaten and mortally wounded, borne into a foreign town in a miserable litter, carried by ten men, without officers, without domestics, escorted by a crowd of boys and rabble, who pressed about him from curiosity, deposited in a bad inn, and so worn out with fatigue and pain in his eyes, that the morrow after his arrival the report of his death was generally credited. During the few days the Duke continued to live, he was attended by his wife, who joined

him on the 1st of November; he refused all visits, and died
on the 10th. The death of this prince created little sensation in Germany, where the war occupied all minds. The
small number of emigrants whom he supported, displayed,
indeed, sincere sorrow. After the battle of Jena the prince's
faculties appear to have been much impaired. He possessed
remarkable qualities. He had served Prussia since 1792.
The violent proclamations which he published against
France had caused him to be regarded as one of the bitterest of our enemies.

At this time Bernadotte returned to Hamburg. I asked
him how we were to construe his conduct with regard to
Davoust, in refusing to assist him in his attack on the Prussian army at Nauemburg? "I am informed, by letter, that
you took no part in the battle of Auerstädt. This I did not
believe; but you have read the account which I myself received somewhat later, in which it is stated that Bonaparte
said at Nauemburg, before a great many officers, 'Were I to
deliver him to a council of war he would be shot. I shall not
speak to him on the subject, but neither will I conceal what
I think of him. He has too much honor not to perceive that
he has committed a disgraceful action.'"—"I believe him
very capable," replied Bernadotte, "of using such language.
He hates me because he knows I love him not; but let him
talk to me, and I will answer him. I am a Gascon, but he
is still a greater one. I might have been piqued on almost
receiving orders from Davoust; but I did my duty."

It is said that the Emperor, on arriving on the field of
battle of Rosbach, going from Menneburg to Halle, pointed
out the spot where the column erected by Frederick the
Great could be found, and the direction to be taken in order
to reach it. This I can readily believe, so perfect was his
knowledge of ground, and of the relative positions of armies
on a day of battle. He caused the column to be removed, a
contrast, it must be confessed, with the sentiments which
I had always heard him express. He hoped, at least, that
the monuments of his own victories would be respected.

Toward the commencement of November, the Swedes entered Lubeck; but on the 8th the town was taken by assault, and these Swedes, the remnant of the corps which had been at Jena, were made prisoners. In like manner a detachment of Prussians appeared before Hamburg, and already the citizens had stood to their defence, when Major Ameil attacked, routed, and took many of the Prussians at Zollenspieker. The danger, however, was far from removed. The major announced his intention to enter with his prisoners. Ameil could not be depended upon; he was a leader of a band of partisans, in the whole force of the phrase, and made war rather upon his own account than as contributing to the success of the operations of the army. His troop did not exceed forty men; but these were sufficient to pillage and carry dismay into the neighboring villages. Besides, his boldness was unquestionable, and when he threw himself upon Hamburg with this handful of marauders, he made the good people believe in a vanguard of twenty thousand men. He had plundered along his whole route, made nearly three hundred prisoners, and carried off a great number of horses. It was nightfall when he presented himself at the gate, leaving his followers and booty at the nearest village. Entering alone, he made for the residence of the French legation. I was very quickly sent for where I had gone on a visit, about seven o'clock in the evening, and, on entering, saw the major —the perfect *beau ideal* of a brigand. It caused me, therefore, no surprise to learn that his tone, air and gigantic mustaches had struck terror into the inmates of my saloon. He then began to entertain me with the recital of his late exploits, talked of making a dash to-morrow with his troop upon Hamburg, and rioted in the idea of pillage and of ransacking the bank. I endeavored long, in vain, to dissuade him, for the thought of such plunder had intoxicated his imagination; but, assuming on this a higher tone, I said, "Know you, sir, that such is not the fashion in which the Emperor desires to be served. During the space of seven years which I passed with him in his campaigns I con-

stantly observed the expressions of his indignation against
those who aggravate to the peaceful inhabitants the terrors
of war. The will of the Emperor is that no damage be done
to Hamburg or its territory.'' This brief address produced
instantaneously an effect greater than all my entreaties; for
the sole name of the Emperor made the stoutest tremble.
The major then had recourse to a plan of selling his booty;
this affair concerned the Senate, who had the good nature to
consider, and the weakness to grant, his petition for a sale
of the product of his robberies on the morrow in one of the
villages. They even bought his horses and gave him guards
for his prisoners. The service I had rendered in ridding
them of this freebooter was appreciated by the authorities,
who next day presented to me a vote of thanks, expressed
in a letter full of courtesy.

But the military occupation of the Hanse Towns could
not be long averted. In his march upon Berlin, after the
grand army had passed the Rhine, Napoleon detached a
corps, under Marshal Mortier, for the purpose of securing
the Electorate of Hesse and occupying Hamburg. On the
19th of November the city was taken possession of in
the Emperor's name. The greatest order and tranquillity
reigned on this occasion, though I make no secret of having feared the reverse. On the approach of the army the
utmost consternation prevailed; and, on the pressing entreaties of the magistrates, I did not hesitate to assume
other powers than those of diplomatist, and, going out to
meet Marshal Mortier, endeavored to prevail upon him to respect the neutrality of the port. All my remonstrances were
vain: he had a formal command from the Emperor.

No preparations having been made for his reception,
Marshal Mortier, with the staff, established headquarters
in my house, and the few troops he had brought formed
an encampment in the court. Thus the residence of the
minister of peace assumed the appearance of a warlike
leaguer, until such time as other arrangements could be
effected. The demands which the marshal was obliged to

make, in consequence of this occupation, were hard. But my representations suspended for a season the order given by Napoleon to seize the bank. I cannot do otherwise than render a tribute to the uprightness of the marshal's conduct, who forwarded my representations to Napoleon at Berlin, announcing that he had delayed acting till the arrival of fresh orders. The Emperor read and approved my views —a circumstance fortunate for France—perhaps not unprofitable to Europe—and most beneficial to Hamburg. Those who recommended to the Emperor the pillage of this noble establishment must have been profoundly ignorant of its utility; they thought only of one thing, the ninety millions of marks stored up in the vaults of the bank.

The successive commandants at Hamburg were Mortier, not more rigorous than could be avoided; General Michaud, who, at least, inflicted no evil he could prevent; and Marshal Brune, who has been misrepresented: his moderation gave displeasure, and he was recalled. These were succeeded by Bernadotte, when, by the battle of Jena, Napoleon, now master of Prussia and the north of Germany, no longer was reasonable with the states composing this portion of Europe, but gave way to the most incredible exactions without opposition—for weakness could offer none. Subsidies, stores of every description, quarterings unceasingly renewed, contributions for table allowances—such were a few of these demands. During a long period the general-commandant had 1,200 francs per day. The Dutch, under General Gratien, as also the inhabitants of Lübeck and of Bremen, respectively enjoyed their share of similar *advantages*. The Prince of Ponte-Corvo softened and moderated, as far as possible, these vexatious burdens. His noble character preserved Hamburg from the extortions to which he might have subjected that unfortunate city. Never did he refuse to aid me in any measures which might tend to combat the system of ruin and persecution. Under his government the Hanseatic states reposed for a space, and, happily, his governorship continued longer than that of his

predecessors. Everywhere he exerted himself to modify
the excessive rigor of the custom-house regulations; his
name was cherished by the inhabitants; it is, I am sure,
never repeated without benedictions; and the opinion thus
won proved far from injurious, when, four years after,
public favor hailed him Crown Prince of Sweden.

The famous Continental System now demands my attention; and more to me than to any other, perhaps, were its
knaveries and its fatal consequences exposed from my situation in the principal commercial city of the Continent. This
system arose during the war of 1806, and was promulgated
by a decree, dated at Berlin on the 21st of November. The
edict was the result of bad counsels. Seeing the just indignation of the Emperor against the duplicity of England,
against her repugnance to come to serious negotiations with
him, and, in short, against the hostilities which she unceasingly stirred up on the Continent, these short-sighted ad-
visers urged him to launch forth that decree which I can
regard in no other light than as an act of madness and of
European tyranny. It was not decrees but fleets that he
wanted: without fleets, without naval resources, it was
ridiculous to declare the British isles in a state of blockade, while English squadrons did actually and effectually
blockade every port in France. This, however, was what
Napoleon declared by the Berlin decrees; and such was
what is termed the Continental System, a system of peculation, of injustice, and of plunder!

It is difficult at this day to conceive how Europe could
for a single hour have endured that fiscal tyranny which
exacted the most exorbitant prices for articles become indispensable necessaries of life, both to rich and poor, through
the habits of three centuries. It is so far from being the
truth that this system had, for its only and exclusive aim,
to prevent England from disposing of her merchandise, that
licenses were sold at a high rate to those who had influence
sufficient to procure them; and gold alone gave that influence. The quantity and the quality of articles exported

from France were exaggerated with incredible impudence. It became imperative, indeed, to purchase such articles, in submission to the will of Napoleon; but they were bought only to be thrown into the sea. And yet none was found who had the conscience to tell the Emperor that England sold to the Continent, but that she bought almost nothing from thence!

The traffic in licenses was carried to a scandalous extent, and that only to enrich certain flatterers and to gratify the wrongheadedness of the contrivers. This system proves, what is engraven in the annals of the heart and understanding of man, that the cupidity of flattery is insatiable and the errors of obstinate folly incorrigible. Let me cite one example out of thousands. At Hamburg, while under the government of Davoust, a poor father of a family narrowly escaped death for having introduced, into the department of the Elbe, a small loaf of sugar for the necessities of his family, while, at the very moment, perhaps, Napoleon was placing his signature to a license for the introduction of a million of loaves. Smuggling, on a small scale, was punished with death, because government had undertaken the trade in the gross. The same cause filled the coffers of the French treasury with gold and the prisons of the continent with victims.

The legislation of the custom-house—that deadly legislation, which was in open war against rhubarb, which armed the coasts of the continent against the importation of senna —could not prevent the Continental System from falling to pieces. Ridicule had attended the installation of the odious coastguard courts. At Hamburg the president of their court, a Frenchman, delivered a harangue, setting forth that from the time of the Ptolemies there existed extraordinary custom-house tribunals, and that Egypt had owed its prosperity to these institutions! Thus the agents of government introduced its terror with their own folly. Compared with these courts, the common revenue officers, held in sufficient detestation, were regretted.

The counsellors of Bonaparte in this system advised him
to an act of folly and stupidity, requiring that each ship for
which a license had been obtained should carry out home
manufactures equal in value to the colonial products authorized by license to be imported. What was the consequence?
The refuse of silk warehouses—whatever time and fashion
had rendered completely unsalable—was purchased at almost
nothing, and as these articles were prohibited in England,
they were thrown overboard without any loss to the speculation by this slight sacrifice. The profit of the license infinitely surpassed the value of a nominal cargo, the tossing
of which into the sea only furnished matter for laughter. It
was published, I believe, by order of Napoleon, that the
forest of Fontainebleau, planted with *red beet*, would supply
all Europe with sugar! I cannot understand how he came
to allow such an absurdity to appear in the "Moniteur." I
do not, however, pretend to say that such culture should not
be encouraged.

This odious and brutal system, worthy of the times of
ignorance and barbarity which, when it had been admissible
in theory, had proved impracticable in application, has not
been sufficiently stigmatized. Men have had the folly to maintain that the continental blockade must, in the end, have
overwhelmed England under the weight of her own products! What absurdity! Those who invented and those who
set the system to work incurred alike the derision and hatred
of their contemporaries; posterity will not for a moment
entertain their dreams. The mutual wants of society, without exception, struggled with advantage against measures
so fatal. The prohibition of commerce, the severity so
unceasingly and unsparingly cruel in the execution of this
hateful conception, were, in truth, but an impost on the continent. Let the reader take only one proof of many which
I might produce from my own experience. The line of
custom-houses along the frontier, from Hamburg, between
Germany and Holland, was very strong. Enormous quantities of English merchandise and colonial products had ac-

cumulated in Holstein, where they had arrived almost all by way of Kiel and Hudsum, and all passed the line at an advance of from thirty-three to forty per cent. Convinced of this by a thousand facts, and wearied out with the vexations of the custom-house system, I took upon myself to explain my views to the Emperor directly, as, the reader will recollect, I had authority from himself to do. I despatched accordingly an extraordinary courier to Fontainebleau, where he was then residing. In this document I declared to him that all passed in spite of his custom-houses, the profit on the sale in Germany, Poland, Italy, and even France, being too great not to induce men to run all hazards. I proposed, that when he was about to unite the Hanseatic Towns to the empire, he should allow a free passage to colonial products, at a duty of thirty-three per cent, equivalent nearly to the premium of insurance. The Emperor adopted without hesitation my proposal, and in 1811, in Hamburg alone, the revenue from this speculation amounted to above sixty millions. Yet the toad-eaters of the court kept crying out with enthusiasm, "We are ruining England by shutting against her the outlets of colonial produce." The same system was afterward in part adopted in Prussia, with regard to articles seized, and that also produced considerable sums. Still the Continental System was not the less extolled and pursued.

That accursed system embroiled us with Sweden and with Russia, who would not submit to a strict blockade, while Napoleon himself lavished his licenses, and grumbled when they took the same advantage. Bernadotte, on his way to Sweden, passed through Hamburg in October, 1810. He remained with me three days, which we passed together in the greatest intimacy. He would see no one. Among other things, he consulted me how he should act with regard to the Continental System. I never hesitated to declare, that, in his place, at the head of a poor nation, which cannot live without exchanging its commodities with England, I would open my ports, and give freely and generally to

the Swedes that license which Bonaparte sold in detail.
The irrational decree of Berlin acted most powerfully
against the Emperor, by exciting the population of entire
countries against him.   Twenty kings hurled from their
thrones would have drawn upon him far less of deadly
enmity than this disregard of the people's wants.   This
profound ignorance of the maxims of political economy occasioned general misery and privation: these, in their turn,
stirred up an inevitable and wide-spreading insurrection.

The system, too, could succeed only in the impossible
case that all the powers of Europe entered fully into its combinations.   A single free port was sufficient to annihilate
the whole.   To its complete success, the conquest and constant occupation of all countries were requisite.   As a means
of ruining England, it was foolishness and impossible in exe.
cution: as an impost it was practicable, but too execrable
and oppressive to be tolerated.   Some one has termed it
"the materialism of supremacy."   This expression desig-
nates the system completely.   To lodge the destructive
array of retainers, it became necessary to convert several
prisons into custom-houses.   The jails that remained were
so encumbered with offenders against the revenue laws that
one-half of the prisoners were forced to stand while the other
half lay down to rest!

A captain reporter had coincided in a judgment favorable
to a poor peasant, taken with a loaf of sugar which had been
purchased beyond the barrier of the custom-house.   This
officer was at dinner with Davoust: in the middle of the
repast, the marshal addressed him—"So, sir captain, you
suffer from a tender conscience."—"Nay, but, my lord—"
—"Begone to headquarters; there is an order for you."
This order sent the captain eighty leagues from Hamburg.
But it would require the reader to have been a spectator,
as I was, of the vexations and miseries caused by the
deplorable Continental System, to conceive what mischief
its authors inflicted upon Europe, or what hate and vengeance it amassed against Napoleon's day of retribution.

CHAPTER XXIV

The Advance against Russia—The French Army in Poland—Affairs at Hamburg—Battle of Eylau—Gardanne's Mission to the Shah

NOT only was Bonaparte the greatest captain of modern times, but he may be said to have changed the art of war itself. He converted it into a fearful game, no longer subject to the vicissitudes of the seasons. The greatest masters of the science had regulated their operations by the ordinary divisions of the calendar; and formerly, throughout Europe, the practice had been to brave the cannon and musket only from the first fine days of spring to the last fine weather of autumn; then on both sides to put off their armor amid the frost, snow, and rain of the intervening months, and to house their wearied soldiers in what they called winter quarters. Pichegru, in Holland, had set the first example of disregarding temperature; Bonaparte, also, at Austerlitz, had set at naught the ice of winter. The plan had succeeded: he resolved on trying it again. His military genius and incredible activity seemed to double his power, and, proud of his soldiers, he determined on conducting a winter campaign under a sky more inclement than had yet canopied his fields. He only required men such as he had chained to his destiny, who would brave the storms of the north as they had dared the meridian sun of Egypt. Skilful above all generals in choosing his battleground, he would not tamely await the Russian army till it should come to measure strength with him on the plains of conquered Prussia; he resolved to march forth to the encounter and rush upon his enemies ere they could cross the Vistula. But, before quitting Berlin to explore as conqueror the regions of Poland and the confines of Russia, he told his soldiers:

"You have justified my hopes and fully replied to the confidence of the French people. You have endured privations and fatigue with fortitude equal to your intrepidity and steadiness in the conflict. You are worthy to be the defenders of my crown, and of the glory of the great nation. While animated by this spirit nothing shall be able to resist you. Behold the result of your toils—one of the first powers in Europe, which, in its delirium had lately dared to propose to us a shameful capitulation, is annihilated! The forests and defiles of Franconia—the Saale—the Elbe, which our sires would not have traversed in seven years, we have crossed in seven days, and have fought in the while four engagements and one great battle. We have been preceded in Potsdam and Berlin by the fame of our victories; we have taken sixty thousand prisoners, captured sixty-five colors—among which are those of the guards of the King of Prussia—six hundred pieces of artillery, three fortresses, and above twenty generals; yet more than one-half of you regret not having fired a single shot. All the provinces of the Prussian monarchy as far as the Oder are in our power. Soldiers! the Russians vaunt they are on the road to meet us; we will march to encounter them—we will spare them half the journey. They shall find another Austerlitz in the midst of Prussia. A nation which has so speedily forgotten our generosity toward her, after that battle wherein her Emperor—her court—the wreck of her army, owed safety wholly to the capitulation we had accorded, is a nation that cannot successfully contend with us.

"In the meantime, while we are marching against the Russians, new armies, organized in the interior of the empire, approach to occupy our place and guard our conquests. My people have arisen as one man, indignant at the shameful compact which the Prussian cabinet, in its delirium, had proposed to us. Our highways and our frontier cities are filled with conscripts, who ardently long to follow our steps. We will no longer be the sport of a treacherous peace; we will not again lay aside our arms till we have forced the English, those eternal enemies of our nation, to renounce their design of troubling the Continent, and surrender their tyranny of the seas. Soldiers! I cannot better express the sentiments I entertain for you than by saying that I wear nearest my heart the attachment which you daily manifest toward me.''

The word delirium, applied in this proclamation to the ultimatum of Frederick William, was really not too strong.

When Napoleon, on the point of commencing the campaign, sent to treat about peace, Prussia returned for answer that the Emperor was *ordered* to renounce all his conquests. The Prussian monarch, blinded by the enthusiasm of his troops, and led away by the ardor of Blucher and the Duke of Brunswick, *threatened us with his resentment*, if the French forces should cross the Rhine. I know that Napoleon, with this singular manifesto in his hand, could not finish the perusal, but, tearing it in rage, and throwing the fragments to the earth, exclaimed, "Does he deem himself already in Champagne? How! would he come to Paris—and in seven-league boots? Truly, I am sorry for Prussia, I pity William. He knows not what absurdities they have made him write. It is much too ridiculous. They send us a challenge; a fair queen wishes to be spectator of the combat —Bravo! Let us be courteous!—March!—the place of meeting is in Saxony—Forward! In the devil's name let us not keep them waiting!"

If activity had been requisite in the commencement of the campaign, everything now urged him to meet the Russians; for, if he waited till they had passed the Vistula, there probably would be no winter campaign, and circumstances would have constrained him to take up miserable quarters between that river and the Oder, or even to have repassed the latter to receive his enemies in Prussia. His military genius and indomitable activity served him well here; and the preceding proclamation, dated from Berlin, before his departure from Charlottenburg, proves that he acted not fortuitously, as often happened, but that his calculations had been previously fixed. But, splendid as such combinations of military talent may appear on the immediate scene of glory, how different is the effect upon the sufferers at a distance! Thus, for instance, at the commencement of the Russian campaign, the Emperor demanded from the city of Hamburg fifty thousand greatcoats; these I caused to be furnished immediately, knowing the importance of such defence to our soldiers in a climate of untried

rigor. On his side, Marshal Mortier was ordered to seize
all the timber fit for shipbuilding, amounting in value to
£60,000. Again, at Lubeck, my directions were to take
possession of four hundred thousand lasts of grain, and
forward them to Magdeburg. The grain and the timber,
indeed, nominally belonged to Russia. In short, the Hanse
Towns were drained like so many milk cows, at the moment
when the Continental System was beginning to dry up the
sources of their prosperity. Such were the evils of conquest, wrought for the greater glory of the empire, or rather
of the Emperor—evils aggravated by agents who cloaked
their imbecility or cupidity by overacted zeal. Of these, the
secondary chiefs of the army gave me the greatest trouble,
and against their exactions I never failed strenuously, and
often successfully, to oppose my civil authority. These
were the evils, however, which, some few years later, caused
the people, at this time disarmed, as one man to put a
term to their present sufferings and to avenge their past
misfortunes.

Meanwhile, our troops, always pushing on, marched with
such rapidity that Murat, leader of the vanguard, and whose
passion for war surpassed the ardor of all his comrades,
arrived in Warsaw before the end of November. The headquarters of the Emperor were then established at Posen, and
from all parts arrived deputations praying the re-establishment of the kingdom of Poland and the restoration of her
independence. After having received the deputation from
Warsaw, as I subsequently learned from himself, he said to
Rapp, "I love the Poles—their ardor pleases me. I would
willingly constitute them a free people, but to do so is very
difficult. Too many have got a finger in the pie—Austria,
Russia, Prussia, have each had a slice. The train once
fired, who knows where the conflagration might stop. My
first duty is to France, and I must not sacrifice her to
Poland: that would carry us too far. And then, we must
defer to the arbiter of all things—time; time will show erelong what we should do." Had Sulkowski lived, Napoleon

would have remembered his own words in Egypt, and most probably would have restored a power whose dismemberment, toward the close of last century, began to break down the species of political equilibrium which the Peace of Westphalia had established in Europe.

At the headquarters in Posen, Duroc rejoined the Emperor, after the last mission to Prussia. I learned with pain that, on the journey, he had been thrown from his horse and broken his collar bone. Every letter which I received was but a series of complaints of the miserable roads, wherein the army fought, as it were, with the mud; nor, without extreme difficulty, could the artillery and tumbrels be brought forward. I have since been told that the carriage of Talleyrand, whom Napoleon had summoned to headquarters in hopes of concluding a treaty of peace, became so imbedded that the minister stuck fast for nearly twelve hours. The soldiers were in bad humor at being in water and mud almost to the knees, and asked who it was that stopped the way? They were told, "The minister for foreign affairs." —"Ah, bah!" replied gruffly the Sancho of the company, "what the devil have they to do with diplomacy in this dog-hole of a country!"

The Emperor made his entrance into Warsaw on the 1st of January, 1807. The majority of reports previously received spoke in unison of the discontent of the troops, then suffering from severe weather, bad roads, and privations of all kinds. Bonaparte upon this inquired of the generals, who informed him of the discouragement which had succeeded to enthusiasm in the spirit of his army— "Have you spoken to the troops of the enemy. Does their courage quail on beholding their foes?"—"No, sire."—"I thought so; my soldiers are ever the same." Afterward, he said to Rapp, "*I will now stir them!*" and dictated the following proclamation:

"Soldiers! On this day twelvemonth, at this very hour, you were upon the battlefield of Austerlitz. The terror-struck battalions of Russia were flying in disorder, or, surrounded, yielded up their arms to their conquerors.   On the morrow they proffered terms of peace; but their words were fallacious.   Hardly escaped, through a generosity perhaps blamable, from the disasters of the third, they contrived a fourth coalition.   But the ally, upon whose co-operation they founded their principal hope is already no more: his fortresses, capitals, magazines, arsenals, two hundred and eighty standards, seven hundred field-pieces, five fortified cities, are in our possession.   Neither the Oder, the Wartha, the deserts of Poland, nor the tempestuous season—nothing has been able to arrest you for a moment; you have braved all, surmounted all; every foe has fled on your approach. In vain have the Russians endeavored to defend the capital of ancient and renowned Poland; the eagle of France soars over the Vistula.   The brave and unfortunate Pole, on seeing you, deems he beholds the legions of Sobieski returning from their memorable expedition.   Soldiers! we will not lay aside our arms until a general peace has established and secured the power of our allies, and restored to our commerce its freedom and its colonies.   Upon the Elbe and the Oder we have regained Pondicherry, our establishments in India, the Cape of Good Hope, and the Spanish colonies.   What shall give the Russians a right to hold the balance of our destiny?   What should give to them the right of interposing in these our just designs?   They and we are still the soldiers of Austerlitz.''

When Bonaparte dictated his proclamations (how many have I written under the circumstances described!) he exhibited for the moment the air of one inspired.   His imagination kindled like the fancy of the improvisatori of Italy; he was, so to speak, upon the tripod, and it became necessary to write with incredible rapidity in order to keep pace with him, for his dictation was then a torrent.   He was at this time serious, and caused to be read over to him what he had dictated.   On such revisals I have seen him, more than once, with a laugh applaud the effect to be produced by such or such a phrase.   Generally speaking, his proclamations turned upon three points—boasting to the soldiers of what they had performed; showing in perspective what remained to be accomplished; and blackening his enemies. The last proclamation just mentioned was dispersed in profusion all over Germany, and it is impossible, without having witnessed it, to conceive the wonderful impression thus produced upon the whole army. The divisions stationed in the rear burned to traverse, by forced marches, the space which still separated them from headquarters; while those near the Emperor forgot their fatigues, their sorrows, their privations, and desired to be led on to the combat. At the same time they comprehended very little of what Napoleon had said to them: I do not believe, for instance, they understood how they had reconquered Pondicherry or the Cape of Good Hope, on the Elbe or the Oder; but they repeated to each other, as usual, "The Emperor has said so." They recalled the battles in which they had been present—marched on gayly, though without shoes—passed the long hours without victuals and without complaint. Such was the prodigious enthusiasm, or rather fanaticism, with which Napoleon could inspire his soldiers when he felt the necessity of "*stirring*" them.

My own occupations meanwhile in Hamburg were, as usual, of a mixed description—some agreeable enough, others the reverse. Among my most pleasing avocations was the intercourse of good offices which my situation enabled me to maintain with several of the German princes, whom the fate of war had deprived of their states and forced to seek refuge in the precarious independence still enjoyed by this part of the Continent. Of the Duke of Mecklenburg-Schwerin and his family, especially the Princess Charlotte and her royal spouse, the prince royal of Denmark, I have already spoken. The former, through his minister at Hamburg, requested my permission to visit occasionally that city from his retreat in Altona. He came so frequently—for there existed a secret source of attraction—that I was constrained to make some friendly remonstrances, lest both should be compromised. But as we were on the best footing with Denmark I continued to see generally his son-in-law and beautiful daughter. The latter, indeed, after being separated from her husband, came to visit Madame de Bour rienne. Almost every day I had the pleasure of receiving the Duke of Weimar, a man of cultivated understanding and excellent heart. I had the happiness of living with the Duke in such intimacy that my house might be called his home, and finally had the satisfaction of contributing, in my degree, to the restoration of his states. It is of a truth no impulse of vanity which thus induces me to recall my relations with these illustrious personages: I have beheld too closely how human greatness is elevated and cast down to be now seduced by its illusions. There is, however, pleasure in proving by what means of moderation, even while the instrument of executing the stern behests of an iron rule, I retained the confidence of many princes of the Outer Rhine. For this purpose I may just cite, out of many in my possession, the following letter from Prince Charles, Grand Elector of Baden, dated December, 1806:

"I have the honor of addressing you in this letter, and to inform you that I have recommended to my sister to repair to Hamburg in order to be nearer her husband, the Prince of Brunswick-Oels. I beg, M. le Minister, that you will be pleased to interest yourself in her behalf during her residence in Hamburg—a favor for which I shall ever feel most grateful, and which will tranquillize my apprehensions for my sister in her present unprotected situation. I embrace this opportunity to assure you of the distinguished consideration with which I have the honor to be," etc.

Such were some of my agreeable relaxations—by contrast. Truly the difference was great between those who were pleased to look in upon my drawing-room and the people whom duty constrained me to admit into my closet. Custom, it is said, reconciles us to all things: not so; the saying, at least with me, has its exceptions. Notwithstanding my habitual necessity of employing spies, I never yet could see one of these miscreants without a feeling of disgust amounting even to horror, especially when the individual had been born in a rank from which his own inherent love of baseness or of lucre had degraded him. It is impossible to conjecture by what combinations such men are · capable of masking their design of betraying those whose confidence they have gained. An apposite example just recurs to my mind. One day a self-degraded man of this stamp came to offer me his services. He was named Butler, and had been commissioned from England as a spy upon the French government. Speedily disclosing his business, he palliated his conduct by complaining of pretended enemies, of injuries sustained, and finally expressed an ardent desire to attach himself to the cause of the Emperor, for whose service he professed his readiness to make every sacrifice. The true reason of changing here, as in every other like case, was the hope of being better paid. I believe, however, no agent of this description ever carried to a greater extent his precautions to conceal double play from his original employers. To me he kept constantly repeating a desire of avenging himself upon his enemies in London; requested to be sent to Paris, in order to be examined by the minister of police himself; and for greater security had himself shut up in the Temple on arriving, and got the following paragraph inserted into the English journals: "John Butler, commonly called Count Butler, has just been arrested and sent to Paris under a strong guard, by the French Minister at Hamburg." After the lapse of some weeks, Butler, upon receiving his instructions from *our* minister, set out for London; but, as a part of his own system of precautions, and because, according to his own advice, he could not be sufficiently vilified to be useful, he requested to have the following article published in the French journals: "The individual named Butler, arrested at Hamburg and conducted to Paris as an English agent, is ordered to quit France and the territories occupied by the French or their allied army, and prohibited from appearing in any of the dominions of France or of her allies before a general peace." In England Butler thus assumed all the honors of French persecution. In him was beheld a victim who merited the entire confidence of the enemies of France. Fouché, mean-

while, obtained through his means much useful information;
and yet Butler was not hanged! Who, in fact, would not
have been deceived by such bold-faced villany? Verily,
these are crimes of which one would almost require to be
capable before it were possible to suspect their existence!

Notwithstanding the supposed necessity for entertaining
secret agents, Bonaparte discouraged, even under this pretext, too numerous communications between France and England. Fouché, however, went on as usual, ordering the dark
evolutions of his subterranean forces. This latter had given
offence to the Emperor, in reference to the affair of the deputation of the Senate. "Fouché," said Napoleon, "ought, as a
Senator, to have dissuaded his colleagues from such a step;
and, if persuasion had been unavailing, he ought to have
employed the means at his disposal as minister of police to
hinder the deputation from passing the frontier." In truth,
Fouché's means were most ample; for, during the absence
of the Emperor, the police might almost have been termed
the regency of France. Always ready to favor whatever
might lend additional importance to his branch, and flatter
the dark suspicions of the Emperor, Fouché wrote to me
of government having certain intelligence that many French
subjects found their way to Manchester as commercial agents
for the purchase of English manufactures. This was quite
true: but how apply a remedy? These agents of French
and even Parisian houses embarked in the ports of Holland,
whence a run to England could be accomplished in not many
hours. But this was a cause of double alarm: not only were
the commercial or rather non-commercial laws thus violated,
but it was argued if French agents can so easily reach England, will not English agents with equal facility enter the
continent? This mysterious syllogism furnished fresh work
to our luckless ministers, chargés des affaires, and consuls.
Not only were we required to keep an eye upon all those
who evidently did, but upon all those also who might, come
from England. Admirable this in the conception; but the
execution?—In vain were vexatious informations, inquisi-

torial perquisitions, spies, menaces employed. English manufactures continued to inundate the continent. The reason of this is obvious; the necessities of mankind will always have more weight than the will of any sovereign, however powerful.

Return we now to Napoleon and his victorious army, who, as I have already stated, entered Warsaw on the first day of the year 1807. During his sojourn at Posen, the imperial headquarters, the Emperor, ever careful to realize the fruit of his victories, founded under the title of a treaty concluded with the elector the new kingdom of Saxony; and consequently, by the annexation of this kingdom to the confederation of the Rhine, extended his power in Germany. In terms of this treaty, Saxony, justly celebrated for her cavalry, furnished to the grand army a contingent of twenty thousand men. This aid was valuable, not only on account of the men, but especially for the horses which Saxony could furnish, and furnish abundantly, to the French troops. It was a spectacle quite novel for princes of Germany, accustomed as they were to the practices of feudal etiquette, to see an upstart sovereign treat them as subjects, and by his boldness oblige them to look upon themselves as such. Those famous Saxons who had made Charlemagne tremble threw themselves into the arms of the Emperor; and certainly it was to him no indifferent matter to see the chief of the house of Saxony attach himself to his fortune; for the new king, by his age, his tastes, and his character, was the most venerated prince of all Germany. From the moment of arriving at Warsaw the Emperor continued to receive new solicitations in favor of re-establishing the throne of Poland, and restoring to its chivalric independence the ancient empire of the Jagellons. On this subject he remained in great perplexity, but finally adhered to his first determination, which, indeed, was his usual practice— to submit to events in order to seem more fully to command them. At Warsaw he passed the greater part of his time in pleasure, in festivities, reviews, and audiences, all which did not prevent him from watching that no part of the public service, exterior or interior, should be deficient. He himself remained in the capital of Poland; but his vast intelligence was present throughout. I learned from General Duroc, when we had occasion to talk of the campaign of Tilsit, that never had Napoleon shown himself more fully or completely. He delighted to offer himself to the view and enthusiasm of his soldiers, to receive princes who came timidly to beg the restitution of their estates; afterward to show himself in brilliant audiences; and, anon, to plan gigantic designs upon the East. The war between the Turks and the Russians allured him on by hopes, or rather chimeras, favorable to his ambition. Meanwhile his universal capacity, descending to grave details, provided for all: thus, from the enormous quantity of despatches I re-. ceived, as well by extraordinary couriers as in the common way, I must regard as a masterpiece of administration the manner in which the Emperor, at Warsaw, established the mode of provisioning his army, which wanted for nothing.

Another very remarkable circumstance in the imperial wars is that, with the exception of the interior police, of which Fouché was the evil spirit, the whole government of France existed at headquarters. At Warsaw, Napoleon not only turned his cares to the wants of his army, but there governed France as if he had been in her capital. Daily expresses, and from time to time the useless auditors from this council of state, brought with more or less exactness despatches from the shadow of government left at Paris, and the most curious revelations frequently invented by the police. The portfolios of the ministers arrived weekly, with the exception of those of the minister for foreign affairs, who, after remaining some time at Mayence with the Empress, had been called to Warsaw, and of the minister of war, Clarke, who, for the misfortune of that city, governed at Berlin. This order of things continued for the ten months of the Emperor's absence from Paris. Louis XIV. remarked, "I am the state." Napoleon did not say the same thing in words, but in fact the government of France was always at his headquarters, an inconvenient arrangement.

The month of January the Emperor employed in military dispositions for the approaching attack on the Russians, but at the same time did not neglect the affairs of the cabinet: all marched in the front with himself. Whatever information reached me from Warsaw concerning his incredible foresight, intelligence, and activity, could not surprise me: I had beheld the same—and, however hazardous his position then was, in circumstances still more difficult. At Warsaw, indeed, the Emperor had not merely to think of battles: affairs were much more complicated than in the campaign of Vienna. It became necessary, on the one hand, to watch Prussia, which we occupied; and, on the other, to anticipate the Russians, whose movements and preparations announced a determination to assume the initiative in hostilities. In the preceding campaign, Austria, before the fall of her capital, had found herself alone engaged: it was no longer the same case. Austria had had only soldiers, and Prussia, as Blücher observed, began to have citizens. No difficulty had existed in returning from Vienna; but, in the event of failure, much was to be apprehended in a retreat from Warsaw, notwithstanding the creation of the kingdom of Saxony, and the provisional government of Prussia, and of the other German states we had conquered. None of all these considerations escaped the eagle eye of Napoleon; and so complete was the understanding throughout the whole of his administration, that it frequently happened to myself to receive the same information from headquarters which I had previously transmitted in such a way that the couriers had passed each other. Thus, for example, I sent intelligence to the Emperor of the arming of Austria, and received a despatch, to the same effect, from the seat of government, only a few days later. Austria, in fact, since the Prussian campaign, had been playing the same part as Prussia acted during the Austrian warfare—indecision, on the one hand, and indecision repeated on the other. As Prussia, prior

to Austerlitz, had waited for the success or defeat of the
French armies, before resolving on remaining neutral or
declaring against France, so Austria, supposing, doubtless,
that Russia would be more fortunate when united to Prussia
than when her own ally, assembled in Bohemia a corps of
forty thousand men. This body she termed an army of observation; but every one knows what such observation
implies. The truth is, these forty thousand armed Austrians were intended to act with Russia, in case of success;
and who could blame Austria for cherishing hopes of legitimate vengeance, by which she might wash away the disgrace
of the treaty of Pressburg?

In this state of things the Emperor had not a moment to
lose: it was necessary to anticipate Russia, and maintain
Austria undecided, in like manner as he had hastened the
success of Austerlitz and kept Prussia in doubt.

Napoleon, therefore, set out from Warsaw toward the
end of January, having issued the necessary orders for attacking the Russian army early in February. But, despite
his eagerness to engage, the Emperor was anticipated. The
Russian army attacked him on the 8th of February, at seven
o'clock in the morning, in the midst of dreadful weather.
Notwithstanding the snow, which fell in great quantity, the
Russians continued always to advance. They advanced to
Eylau, in Prussia, where the Emperor then was, and the imperial guard first arrested the further progress of the Russian
column. Nearly the whole of the French army was engaged
in this battle, one of the most sanguinary which, until then,
had been fought in Europe. The corps under the command
of Bernadotte was not present, because he had been stationed
on the left, at Mohrungen, whence he menaced Dantzic.
The issue of the contest would have been very different
had the four divisions of infantry and two of cavalry, composing Bernadotte's section of the army, arrived in time;
but, unfortunately, the officer despatched with the order for
him to move in all speed upon Preussich-Eylau was intercepted by a cloud of Cossacks, so that Bernadotte neces-

sarily remained stationary. Bonaparte, who always desired
to throw the blame upon some one, when things did not fall
out as he wished, attributed the doubtful success of the day
to the non-arrival of Bernadotte's division. This was true;
but, at the same time, to make it a subject of reproach to
the marshal, showed the greatest injustice. He was accused
of having refused to march upon Preussich-Eylau, although,
as asserted, General Haupolt had apprised him of the
necessity of his presence. But how dispute this fact, since,
on the same day on which the order is said to have been
delivered, General Haupolt was slain? Who could give
the assurance that this general directly and personally
had communicated with Bernadotte? Whoever has closely
studied Bonaparte, his craft, and the construction frequently
given by him to words placed in the mouth of the dead,
will find no enigma here. Let the reader recall Brueys and
Aboukir.

But, be this as it may, the day of Eylau was terrible;
the French, in vain looking for the advancing columns of
Bernadotte, after considerable loss enjoyed the mournful
honor of encamping on the field of battle. Bernadotte came
up, but too late, having fallen in with and engaged the
enemy, in full and unmolested retreat toward Königsberg,
the only capital yet remaining to Prussia. The king himself
was at Memel, thirty leagues distant.

When, subsequently, at Hamburg, I mentioned to Bernadotte the accusations concerning his conduct at Eylau, he
said, "You see him—always calumnious assertions on the
part of that man; but it is all the same to me—I care not
a fig for him." He afterward explained the whole in a
manner favorable to himself, and indulged in some reflections against certain generals which, in my opinion, were
improper. As the individuals are living, I say nothing
more, for fear of inducing a quarrel with their former comrade, now the king of Sweden.

After the conquest of the field of battle, covered with
the dead of both armies, the French remained in position,

as did also their adversary; and several days passed in unimportant events. The Emperor's offers of peace, made, indeed, with small anxiety, were rejected with proud disdain. It seemed as if a victory, disputed with Napoleon, was to be regarded as a triumph; and one would have said that the battle of Eylau had turned the heads of the Russians, for they caused a "Te Deum" to be sung on the occasion. But while the Emperor made preparations to advance, his distant policy had operated a successful diversion by rousing against Russia her ancient enemies, the Turks. Napoleon had advanced to Finkenstein, where he awaited the proper time for placing himself at the head of his troops, when he learned that a revolution in Constantinople had caused the sultan Selim his life and raised Mahmoud to the Moslem throne. The able negotiations of General Sebastiani had rescued the Porte from the influence of England, and brought the former so ardently into hostility with Russia that the standard of the Prophet was unfurled.

At the time of receiving this intelligence the Emperor had ordered forth the contingent of Spanish troops, conformably to a treaty of alliance with that monarchy. These were destined for the line of the Elbe, and we shall see the result hereafter. Somewhat later occurred General Gardanne's embassy to Persia, an opening for which had already been prepared by the successful mission of my friend Jaubert.

Gardanne's affair was none of those pompous embassies despatched by our former kings to the East; it pertained to those ideas which had germinated in the head of Bonaparte in the very dawn of his power: a light from the East had, in fact, first cast the shadow of his coming greatness before him and had never ceased to rivet his attention. I knew, from an unquestionable source, that the legation had been conceived by the Emperor on a much grander scale; in fact, that he had resolved to send to the Shah of Persia four thousand infantry, commanded by chosen and experienced officers, ten thousand muskets and fifty pieces of cannon.

I am certain the orders were issued for these arrangements. The object proposed by the Emperor, and which he avowed on maturing this design, was to enable the Shah, in person, with eighty thousand men, to make a formidable diversion upon the provinces of eastern Russia. But there existed another long cherished, real and abiding motive which reigned paramount in the recesses of his thoughts—the desire of striking at England in the heart of her Asiatic possessions. Such was the chief cause of Gardanne's mission, but circumstances permitted not the Emperor to give it all the importance he would have wished: he was constrained to rest satisfied with merely sending some engineer and artillery officers, who, on their arrival, were greatly astonished at the numbers of English whom they found in Persia.

CHAPTER XXV

Bonaparte's Exactions from Hamburg—Treaty of Tilsit—Bombardment of Copenhagen—Junot's Incapacity—The Code Napoleon

TO REVERT for a moment to more private and personal occurrences: Josephine had accompanied the Emperor as far as Mayence, and remained there for some time after his departure, when she returned to Paris at the period, I believe, when M. de Talleyrand, who had also remained at Mayence, received orders to join him at Warsaw. Well assured of the pleasure I should experience from being able to gratify her in anything, the Empress had the goodness to recommend various persons to my notice, and I need not say that such recommendations always called forth my utmost zeal. The following note, among many similar ones, falls in with the present date and shows that, since my removal from Paris, she at least had not changed:

"MONSIEUR BOURRIENNE—M. Fuzy, a native of Geneva, goes to Hamburg to follow out a lawsuit relative to a property, his claims to which are contested. He requests me to recommend him to your good offices, and I address you in his favor, so much the more willingly that I can profit by the opportunity to send you the renewed assurance of my friendship. JOSEPHINE.

"PARIS, *11th February, 1807.*"

During the early months of this year my occupations in Hamburg, as respected the domestic affairs of my diplomatic circle, gave me more trouble than ever. The genius which can wield the whole energies of warfare may have charms upon the field of battle; a rapid movement, impressed by a single will upon vast masses of living men, may dazzle the multitude as a flash of lightning blinds, by its excess of brightness, the eye that gazes; but when, at a distance from the theatre of glory, we behold its sad results weighing the people down to earth, we curse the genius of conquest as the genius of destruction. What a cruel spectacle was opposed to my view! I was doomed continually to hear the complaints of universal distress, and, far from giving relief, to execute orders which augmented the evil by increasing sacrifices already immense. In the midst of so much unavoidable suffering, too, there were those agents of the Emperor who, to show off their own importance, or to forward their own interest, rendered calamities still more grievous. I had to contend not with the excusable prejudices of the sufferers, but against their oppression by the French authorities, and, above all, the military functionaries. The greatest misfortune of the empire, in my opinion, was the abuse of that power arrogated by the wearers of great epaulets. My situation then enabled me to judge of all that is odious in military government—the worst, in my judgment, that can exist. Bernadotte, indeed, was a solitary example of disinterestedness: but then he loved to be talked about. The more the Emperor labored to depreciate, the more he strove to draw public attention to his actions. He sent me an account of the brilliant affair of Braunsburg, where his division had been particularly distinguished. The following are the terms on which he desired his relation to be published, and one of many examples will serve: "My dear Minister—I send you a note upon the affair of Braunsburg; probably you will find it essential to communicate it: in that case I shall be obliged by your getting the account inserted in the Hamburg journals." I did as he wished, for really the Emperor's injustice rendered it necessary that Bernadotte, for his own honor, should establish the truth of facts.

The surveillance of the emigrants was at this time, as always, my most disagreeable function. Fouché continued to pretend that they were formidable, in order to enhance the importance of his own ministrations. Count Gimel, who had so long resided in Altona as agent for the emigrants, being dead, after various changes M. Hué was definitively settled in that capacity by Louis XVIII., whose faithful servant he had been, as formerly of Louis XVI., whose captivity he had shared and who has consigned his name to honorable memory in his testament. That name must have recalled strange remembrances to Fouché, and he charged me, accordingly, to redouble my watchfulness. This distrust, whether real or well feigned, was carried to such extremes that I frequently received advices to watch those who were far from suspecting themselves objects of such care. Often, too, upon informations purchased at a dear rate in Paris, the minister of police would set the accredited envoys of France in foreign countries to arm themselves with rigor, and lose their time in searching out personages denounced who had never been within the circle of their influence. I, for one, never allowed an opportunity to pass of tempering the severity of Fouché's instructions.

Another of my duties, incessant during the last campaign, was to provide necessaries for the army. So many articles of clothing were demanded by the Emperor that the whole commerce of Hamburg, with Lubeck and Bremen to boot, could not have supplied the orders. I entered into an engagement, therefore, with a house in Hamburg, authorizing the partners, notwithstanding the Berlin decree, to import the requisite articles from England. I thus obtained cloth and leather by a sure way and at half the price. Our soldiers might have perished of cold a hundred times over had we ridiculously stood upon punctilio with the Continental System and the confused mass of inexplicable decrees relative to English merchandise.   Neither Hamburg, for instance, nor its territory, possessed any manufacture of coarse cloth; according to M. Eudel, director of the custom-house, every article of woollen stuff was prohibited; and yet I had to supply fifty thousand greatcoats to one order. Another arrived for sixteen thousand coats and thirty-seven thousand vests, to be made up and sent off with all despatch. The Emperor demanded of me two hundred thousand pairs of shoes, in addition to forty thousand just transmitted; yet M. Eudel said *tanned and curried hides* cannot enter Hamburg. The director took my proceedings in high dudgeon: I was quite easy. My woollens and my leather arrived; greatcoats, coats, vests, and shoes were all quickly made; and our soldiers thus found themselves fortified against the rigors of a winter campaign. My representations at length induced government to hear reason with me; I carried on my trade with England, to the great comfort of our troops, who found themselves well clothed and well shod. But could anything in the world be more absurd than commercial laws enforced to our own detriment?

After the battle of Eylau, I received a despatch from Talleyrand, accompanied by a French account of that murderous conflict, more fatal to the conquerors than to the opposite party—for I dare not say, vanquished, applied to the Russians. Had anything been wanting to confirm the unsuccessful result of that day, it would have been supplied by the anxiety evinced on the part of Napoleon that his version should, by all possible means, be first dispersed throughout Germany. The Russian account, coming previously, might have produced troublesome results. But perhaps the reader may complain that I maintain an almost total silence on the manœuvres which followed this engagement, and brought on the memorable battle of Friedland, the success of which was incontestably in our favor. But there needs not to be repeated what is known to all Europe in the immense results of that victory. The interview at Tilsit is one of the culminating points in modern history, and the waters of the Niemen reflected the star of Napoleon in its meridian splendor. Until then it had been rising—for some years longer it retained the ascendant. But the sequel! What passed externally at Tilsit, the friendship of the two emperors, and the sad situation of Prussia's monarch, all the world knows.

I give, however, some interesting private particulars. And, first, of what passed in the apartment of the Emperor at Tilsit when he received the visit of the King of Prussia. That unfortunate prince, whom his Queen Wilhelmina had accompanied, was banished to a windmill beyond the city, his only habitation, while the two Emperors occupied each his own quarters, separated by the Niemen. The fact I am now to relate was reported to me by the colonel who on that day commanded the imperial guard, and was on duty in the interior of the saloon; I give it therefore with confidence, though not entirely pledging myself. After Alexander had entered, the two Emperors remained conversing together in a balcony, while an immense multitude below hailed their reconciliation with enthusiastic acclamations. Napoleon began the conference, as in the preceding year with the Emperor of Austria, by addressing to Alexander some polite expressions on the mutability of warlike success. While they were thus conversing, the King of Prussia was announced. His emotion, which was visible, may easily be conceived, since, hostilities being suspended and his dominions overrun, he had no longer any hope save in the generosity of the conqueror. Napoleon himself, it is said, appeared touched with his situation, and invited him, together with his queen, to dinner. While seating themselves at table, Napoleon with much politeness announced to his fair guest that "he restored to her Silesia." This province the queen had very much wished should be retained in the new arrangements which were necessarily to take place.

The Prince de Wittgenstein, of whom I have not yet spoken, holds an important place in these my recollections; we lived, I may say, familiarly together during his residence in Hamburg, as will afterward appear. Here, without occupying any ostensible situation, he enjoyed the confidence of his sovereign, the King of Prussia, to whom his political talents and sage counsels proved of great utility on various occasions. After the Treaty of Tilsit, in the summer of 1807, the Prince made a voyage into England. On returning, he came to see me: our conversation naturally turned upon the grand political interests which were agitating around us, and, as he had reason to repose perfect confidence in me, I learned many things on the aspect of English politics, then useful, now curious; and which constitute the grand occupation of those who put faith in diplomacy. Prince de Wittgenstein told me that a courier, expedited from Tauroggen, did, on the 30th July, remit to M. Alopœus, the Russian plenipotentiary in London, very important despatches. One of these, which the Prince assured me he had read, stated that time did not permit *to send a copy of the treaties which had just been signed at Tilsit.* The same day, M. Alopœus sent a courier to Russia with the commercial treaty just concluded; and it may give some insight into the policy of England, though the treaty itself be now of no importance, to state that, in every respect, it was identically the same as the one offered in March by the Russian envoy on his arrival. Then the English ministry would not even hear it mentioned; but, as one French victory followed another, so concession followed concession, till finally the treaty was concluded such as first proposed. Yet I know not why England should give herself the trouble to affect squeamishness about conditions, which, when interest serves, are found to bind her to nothing.

On the morrow, continued the Prince in substance, after M. Alopœus had received the laconic despatch from Tilsit,

he offered, officially, to the court of London, the mediation
of Russia to bring about a new treaty of peace between
France and England, preparatory to a general peace. On
the 1st of August, a privy council assembled at Windsor,
at which George III. was present. Two days after, Mr.
Canning replied, but verbally, to M. Alopœus—and every
one knows the difference in diplomacy between things said
and things written—"that the British cabinet accepted the
mediation of Russia, but on condition of being furnished
with copies of the public and of the secret treaty, the King
being desirous of assurance that nothing contrary to the
interests of his crown and of his people had been stipulated." Mr. Canning added, that "Austria, before the
opening of the campaign, having offered her mediation
between the belligerents, it would be just that she acted
in concert with Russia in the mediation actually proposed;
a proceeding the more proper that the court of Vienna had
formerly offered such mediation voluntarily." On the 8th,
M. Alopœus despatched a courier, with the verbal reply
of Mr. Canning. The latter had, at the same time, declared
to M. Jacobi, Prussian minister at London, "That the King
deplored the misfortunes which had befallen his master, and
condoled with him thereon, but that, the ports of Prussia
being shut against British ships, the interests of his people,
and the honor of his flag, forced him to adopt hostile measures against Prussia." The Prince added, to all these
interesting pieces of information, that the Prince of Wales
and Mr. Canning strongly inclined to peace, and that the
majority of the English nation earnestly coincided in
the same desire.

By the treaty of Tilsit, concluded on the 7th and ratified
two days after, the map of Europe was not less altered than
by that of Pressburg the preceding year. Russia, indeed,
suffered no shameful impositions, since her territory remained inviolate. But Prussia! Yet are there historians
who extol the moderation of Napoleon in having respected
some shreds of the monarchy of the Great Frederick.—

Vaunt his glory, his genius, the rapidity of his decisions, the omniscience of his judgment—and all the world comprehends you: but to commend his moderation at Tilsit! Of a truth, gentlemen, you thus run the risk of getting discredited and laughed at. This is no moot point: to accuse Napoleon of moderation, "fixes upon him a most wrongful sentence," more especially in reference to the transactions of 1807. But there is one accusation pertaining to this date from which his name and policy must be redeemed. He has been blamed for not restoring the kingdom of Poland. Such an expectation at this period can arise—I shall be excused the expression—only from French impatience. I, too, ardently wished the re-establishment of the Polish monarchy, and do still regret, both for the interests of France and of Europe, that Poland was not restored; but because a desire, even when founded on reason, has not been gratified, are we therefore to conclude that it ought to have been fulfilled despite of all obstacles? Now, at the close of the campaign of Tilsit obstacles to the re-establishment of Polish independence were insurmountable. Had the whole of that unhappy country been seized by Prussia, nothing more easy for Napoleon than to have given freedom to its inhabitants by declaring himself their protector. But several of the Polish provinces had fallen to Austria's share, and a still greater number had been pounced upon by Russia in the successive divisions of the monarchy. Any attempt at restitution roused these two powers to make common cause; our right flank would have been inclosed by the Austrian army of *observation*, Russia remained almost unbroken in our front; Napoleon must either have revoked his declarations of independence, or have maintained them by the sword. In either case the Treaty of Tilsit, so advantageous and so necessary to him, would not have taken place. These reflections, it is most important to remark, apply exclusively to the period of which we now speak, and have no reference to the final establishment of Poland. At a later date, as we shall see—*when the pear was ripe*—the intrigues of inferior chiefs, the ambition of a secondary class, interposed to prevent Napoleon from accomplishing the views which he had ever cherished of elevating the heroic Poniatowski from the ranks of his guard to the throne of his own heroic nation.

One throne, however, was at this time added to the monarchies of Europe—that of Westphalia, in favor of the "little blackguard" who, from petty officer of a corvette, was now transformed into a king, that his brother might have under orders one royal prefect more. The kingdom of Westphalia was composed of the states of Hesse-Cassel, which formed the nucleus, a portion of the provinces torn, through the Emperor's *moderation*, from Prussia, of Paderborn, Fulda, Brunswick, and part of Hanover. At the same time, though no favorer of half measures, Napoleon planted upon the banks of the Vistula the grandduchy of Warsaw, and bestowed it on the King of Saxony, so that he might, as occasion served, either enlarge or abolish it. Meanwhile, the Polish provinces of Austria and Russia were left untouched, partisans were conciliated in the north, and still a hope for the future given to the Poles. Alexander, yet more the dupe than his father had been of the political coquetry of Bonaparte, consented to these arrangements; he recognized in the lump all the kings manufactured by Napoleon; he accepted several provinces which had belonged to his despoiled ally, by way of consolation, doubtless, for having failed in the attempt of getting more restored to him. And then the two emperors separated, the best friends in the world.

Napoleon returned to Paris toward the end of July, after an absence of ten months. Recent events had given to public opinion in his favor a moral force greater than had yet obtained since his coronation. Still the game was doubtful on more than one point. The war raged in all its intensity with England; the Swedish King had resumed his Quixotism—this, indeed, was a trifle, but it served to disturb the political susceptibilities; and war still continued between

Russia and the Ottoman Porte. The influence of the Emperor had here kindled a flame which all the exertions of Sebastiani, seconded by those of Guilleminot, and aided by his own intervention, could not extinguish. England even (a strange proceeding on her part) attempted to allay the ferment; but Mustapha Baractar continued inflexible in his enmity to Russia. Nor, indeed, was it easy to answer the Turk's logic; Russia, though beaten, demanded from him the two pachalics north of the Danube. What could she have done more, asked he, had she been victorious?

On the 3d of August an English squadron of twelve sail of the line, and as many frigates, passed the Sound, under Admiral Gambier. At the same time the British troops in the isle of Rügen were re-embarked. We in the north could not divine what was to be undertaken with forces so considerable. Alas! our uncertainty soon ceased. M. Didelot, French minister at Copenhagen, arrived at Hamburg on the 9th, at nine in the evening: he had the good fortune to escape through the Great Belt, in sight of the English, without being pursued. I instantly despatched his report by an extraordinary courier to Paris. Twenty thousand British troops, under the command of Lord Cathcart, had likewise been sent into the Baltic, and the coasts of Zealand were blockaded by ninety sail. Mr. Jackson, British envoy to the court of Copenhagen, backed by these troops the demands which he had been directed to propose to the Danish government. England pretended to apprehend an invasion of Denmark by French troops. Her demands, therefore, were nothing less than the surrender of the whole Danish fleet and stores. These, it is true, were to be held only in trust, but there existed a condition, an *until*, which presented but small security for the future; the deposit was to be retained until there should be no further need of such precaution. The threat and its execution followed close upon this insolent demand. After a noble but vain resistance and a terrific bombardment, Copenhagen surrendered and the Danish fleet was destroyed. It would be difficult to find in history an abuse more cowardly and revolting of force against weakness.

Some of the principal consequences of the Treaty of Tilsit I have already enumerated, but it is more than probable that had the bombardment of Copenhagen preceded those arrangements the Emperor would have treated Prussia with still greater severity. He could have erased her from the number of states, but withheld to gratify Alexander. The destruction of Prussia, however, was no new idea, and I had noted on this subject a remark of Bonaparte to the poet Lemercier, during our early residence at Malmaison. The man of letters had been reading to the First Consul a poem in which occurred some allusion to the Great Frederick. "You are a zealous admirer of his," said Bonaparte; "what, then, do you find in him so astonishing? He is not equal to Turenne."—"General," replied Lemercier, "it is not merely the warrior that I esteem in Frederick; you would not forbid our admiration of a man who, even on the throne, cultivated philosophy." The First Consul replied in a tone half conciliating, half sarcastic, "Certainly, my good Lemercier, such is not my intention; but that shall not the less prevent my blotting his kingdom from the map."

Peace being concluded with Russia, it became necessary to choose our ambassador, not only to maintain the new situations of amity, but to prompt Russia in her promised mediation between the courts of Paris and St. James's. This mission the Emperor confided to Caulaincourt, against whom there existed ill-founded prejudices because of some circumstances connected with the death of the Duke d'Enghien. This sentiment, at once vexatious and unjust, had preceded Caulaincourt's arrival, and, as was feared, would occasion his reception at St. Petersburg to be less honorable than was due to the minister of France and his own personal merits. I know, however, for certain that, after a short explanation with Alexander, that monarch not only retained no doubts unfavorable to the ambassador, but treated him, individually, with much esteem and friendship. Caulain-

court's was a difficult mission; England, having resolved
never to permit the conquest of the Continent, which Napoleon so evidently meditated, showed invincible repugnance
to admit the mediation of Russia. She counted on the
indignation of kings and on the spirit of the people, and
was not discouraged at the gigantic strides toward universal
dominion with which Napoleon had successfully advanced
for the last two years. He, on his part, armed in his imagination new combinations and dreamed of arousing new
enemies against his rival.

It will not be forgotten that in 1801 France had constrained Portugal to make common cause with her against
England. In 1807 the Emperor repeated what the First
Consul had done. Through inexplicable fatality, Junot received the command of the troops destined to march against
Portugal. I say against, because such is the truth, though
we presented ourselves as protectors to deliver Portugal
from the influence of England. The Emperor's choice
astonished all. Was it really to Junot, a worthless compound of vanity and mediocrity, that he confided an army in
a distant country where prudence and great military talents
were alike indispensable in the commander? For my own
part, knowing Junot's incapacity, the appointment filled me
with amazement. I afterward learned, however, by a letter
which Bernadotte had received from Paris, that the Emperor
had sent Junot to Lisbon as a pretext for depriving him
of the governorship of Paris. In that capacity he had disgusted Napoleon by his bad conduct, folly, and incredible
extravagance. Junot had neither firmness, dignity, nor any
one elevated feeling. The invasion of the unfortunate
country, thus placed at the mercy of such a man, through
imperial caprice, offered no difficulty: it was an armed
promenade, not a war; but how many events were germed
in that invasion! Unwilling to betray England, to whom
he was bound by treaties, and unable to oppose the whole
power of Napoleon, the Prince Regent of Portugal embarked
for Brazil, declaring defence impossible, and recommending

to his subjects at the same time to receive in a friendly manner the French troops, and announcing that he confided to Providence the issue of an invasion for which no motive could be alleged. It was replied, in the Emperor's name, that, Portugal being the ally of England, war was carried on against England by seizing the dominions of the house of Braganza.

But while our eagles were advancing upon Lisbon, England captured the island of Heligoland. To this feat of arms much more importance has been attributed than it really merited. The garrison, when brought into Gluckstadt, consisted of only thirty invalids. The sole consideration which gave some importance to the conquest is its situation at the mouth of the Elbe and Eyder; the island supplies the pilots required by vessels entering either river.

On returning to Paris the first act of Napoleon had been the abolition of the Tribunate. Thus was cast out from the fundamental institutions of his government the only shadow of a deliberative assembly and the last remnant of a popular administration: thus had he seized power by force and turned, as occasion served, the prestige of military success to the destruction of what remained constitutional in his authority. There was ingratitude, too, in this act, for to the Tribunate he owed the consulate for life—to the Tribunate, again, Napoleon was indebted for the empire. But he willed that there should no longer be any deliberative body, save a Senate—not to deliberate, but to vote soldiers; and a Legislative Assembly—not to legislate, but to vote money.

In the following November another great change took place in the executive by the introduction of the code of French law, under the designation of the Code Napoleon, throughout all the states of the empire. Without doubt this monument of legislation, upon which the most learned men had labored with indefatigable diligence since the commencement of the consulate, will throw credit on Napoleon in history. But was it practicable in application to an empire of such vast extent as that of France had now become? I think not. At least, under my own eye, I had proofs both of its inefficiency and inconvenience. The same coat will not fit all statures. I made my representations on this subject, but received no answer. The jury trial took pretty well; but the inhabitants of that part of Germany, accustomed to the infliction of penalties less rigorous than the punishments decreed in the Code against certain offences, felt a repugnance to be accessory to this aggravation. Hence resulted the very frequent and very serious abuse of absolving delinquents whose guilt had been demonstrated to a jury, who chose rather to acquit than condemn in terms of a sentence which was judged too severe. I recollect the instance of a man convicted of having stolen a cloak, but who pleaded in extenuation that he was intoxicated at the moment of committing the theft. When the jury came to vote, the foreman pronounced the accused not guilty, assigning as a reason that the syndic Doorman, when dining with him one day, having drunk a little more freely than usual, carried away his (the foreman's) cloak. This bacchanalian defence succeeded; for how punish the criminal for a delinquency committed also in his cups by their own chief magistrate? But, to be serious, the best institutions, and those involving the gravest affairs, become, it may be, ridiculous, when rudely forced upon a country unprepared to receive them. I know, also, at a period anterior to the present date, that extreme rigor was used to introduce the French code into unhappy Italy. Throughout the greater part of the Italian kingdom the paternal laws of Beccaria were in force. These authorized no capital punishment, and wherever they prevailed murders were less frequent than in any country whatsoever. The first time a sentence of death was executed at Placenza the city became at once deserted, and it seemed as if the fire of Heaven had fallen upon a devoted place. Matters in Italy assumed, in fact, the aspect of revolt; but, though the peaceful Hamburgers were not inclined to proceed to such extremity, it certainly showed great folly to think of attaching even the most patient by thwarting all

their habits and ideas.   The Romans always reserved a
niche in the Capitol "for the gods of the vanquished nations"; they desired only to annex provinces and kingdoms
to the empire: Napoleon, on the contrary, desired to extend
the empire—to realize the Utopia of ten different nations
united into one people.   How, for example, could justice,
that safeguard of human rights, be rendered to the Hanseatic
cities after they became departments of France?   In these
new departments were placed many judges who knew not a
word of German and were completely ignorant of law.   The
presidents of the tribunals of Lubeck, Stade, Bremerle, and
Münden, were obliged to have the pleadings translated to
them in the very council chamber.   To all this add the impertinence and levity of many of those young masters who
were sent from Paris to serve their apprenticeship in juris-
prudence and administration in the conquered provinces, of
whose language and usages they were ignorant, and we may
conceive the love of the inhabitants for Napoleon the Great.

CHAPTER XXVI

The Emperor's Dealings with Spain—Louis XVIII. in England—Louis
Bonaparte as King of Holland—Abdication of Louis

THE transactions with Spain, which soon after became
so prodigiously complicated, date from the close of
1807.   Though distant from the theatre of events,
I possessed sure means of information; but as this is one
of the portions of our history most generally if not best
known, I shall expunge from my notes all that might appear repetition to those of some little reading on this subject.   One fact sufficiently surprising, and which strikes
us at first, I verify, namely, that Bonaparte, while yet his
greatness existed only in idea, and while bending an eye
by turns upon every kingdom of Europe, never once entertained views upon Spain.   When descanting to me of the

future and the coming destinies of his star, Italy always or Germany, the East or the destruction of the power of England engaged his meditations—Spain never. Consequently, when first informed of the disorders in that country, he allowed considerable space to elapse before taking any active part in those events which were to exert so great an influence on his fortune.

Let us consider the state of things: Godoy reigned in Spain through the imbecility of the feeble Charles IV. That favorite had become the object of execration to all not attached to his fortune; and even his creatures, while consulting their own advantage, entertained for their patron the most profound contempt. The people's hatred is almost ever the just reward of favorites, because such a character implies something abject, menial and base. If this be the inference applicable to favorites in general, how much more so in the case of Godoy, who, to the knowledge of all Spain, owed his interest with the king, a royal marriage, and, as Prince of Peace, precedence over all the nobles of Castile, to the guilty favor of the queen. Godoy was a fatal man: his influence over the royal family was boundless; from a private guardsman he had become chief of the state: nor can there be a doubt that he was one of the principal causes of those misfortunes which under so many varied forms have overwhelmed Spain.

The hatred of the Spaniards against the Prince of Peace was universal. Ferdinand, Prince of Asturias, heir to the Spanish monarchy, partook in the national resentment and declared himself openly the enemy of Godoy. The latter united himself to France, through whose powerful assistance he hoped for protection against his numerous enemies. This alliance rendered him still more detested in Spain and caused France to be looked upon with an unfavorable eye. The Prince of Asturias found sympathy and support in the grievances of the Spaniards, who to a man desired the fall of Godoy. On his part Charles IV. regarded as directed against himself every attempt in opposition to the Prince of Peace. From the month of November, 1807, the king accused his son of a design to dethrone him.

At this period our ambassador in Spain was M. de Beauharnais, a relative of Josephine's first husband and a person of great circumspection, but, perhaps, not quite competent for such a situation at such a conjuncture. Nevertheless, though not gifted with the highest talents, he possessed a certain tact, which enabled him clearly to see the state of things; and he it was who first informed the government at home of the misunderstanding between the king and the prince. He could, in fact, no longer preserve silence consistently with duty, since he had repeatedly interfered, as I have been informed, but without effect, though employing the weight of his situation as minister from France. Could he allow the Emperor to remain ignorant that, in the excess of resentment against his son, Charles IV. had strongly expressed his intention of revoking the law which gave to the Prince of Asturias the succession to one of the thrones of Charles the Fifth? Nor did the king limit his proceedings to verbal manifestations; he had recourse to action, or rather the Prince of Peace acted in his name, and the warmest adherents of Prince Ferdinand were arrested. The Prince of Asturias, aware of the king's sentiments, wrote to Napoleon requesting his support. Open war was thus declared between the father and son, each appealing against the other and claiming assistance from the man whose nearest wish was to get rid of both and thus place one brother more as junior in the European college of kings; but, as I have already stated, this was a new ambition; nor, which will hereafter appear, was the throne of Spain offered to Joseph till after its refusal by Louis.

The Emperor, however, had promised his support to Charles against his son; and, averse from intermeddling in these troublesome family affairs, he certainly did not reply to the prince's first letters. But, seeing that intrigues at Madrid assumed a serious aspect, he began, as a precautionary measure, to send troops into Spain. The

Spaniards were offended at this. The nation, in fact, had
nothing to do with France; nor was it implicated either in
the infamies of Godoy or the bickerings of the royal family.
In the provinces through which the French troops passed
the inhabitants demanded why this invasion had been undertaken: according to the party which they espoused, some
attributed it to the Prince of Peace, others to Ferdinand;
but all were indignant at the result, and disturbances broke
out at Madrid with a violence which is inseparable from the
Spanish character.

In these circumstances, fearful in themselves, and still
more threatening for the future, Godoy proposed to Charles
IV. to conduct him to Seville, where he would be in better
condition to employ severe measures against the factious.
A proposition from Godoy to his master was less advisory
than peremptory. Charles, therefore, resolved to depart;
but thenceforth the people regarded Godoy as a traitor.
The populace rose, surrounded the palace, and the Prince
of Peace was on the point of being massacred in a garret,
whither he had fled for refuge. One among his pursuers
had the presence of mind to invoke in his favor the name
of the Prince of Asturias. This saved Godoy from certain
death.

But Charles IV. could not preserve his throne. Easily
intimidated, advantage was taken of a moment of terror to
demand from him an abdication which he possessed neither
the courage nor the power to refuse. He yielded his rights
to his son, and thenceforth disappeared the insolent influence of the Prince of Peace, who remained a prisoner; and
the Spanish people, like every unenlightened population,
easily excited, expressed their joy in barbarous enthusiasm.
In the course of these transactions the unhappy monarch,
removed by his very weakness from the violence and danger—more apparent, however, than real—which he had incurred, changed his mind on perceiving himself in security,
and seemed no longer satisfied with the mere privilege of
living in exchange for his crown. He resumed the desires

of royalty and wrote to Paris protesting against his own abdication and placing in the Emperor's hands the decision of his future fate.

During the progress of these internal dissensions the French army pursued its march toward the Pyrenees. These mountains were quickly passed, and Murat made good his entrance into Madrid about the beginning of April, 1808.   His presence in that capital, far from producing a beneficial effect, still more increased the disorder. The truth is, Murat regarded the Peninsula as a prey which he had been despatched to seize for himself, and for none other; nor is it surprising that the inhabitants of Madrid discovered this, for, such was his imprudence, that he made no secret of his desire to become King of Spain.   Of this I received unquestionable assurance at the time by my private correspondence from the Peninsula.   The Emperor, informed of these doings, gave him to understand, in very significant terms, that the throne of Spain and the Indies was not intended for him, but that he should not be forgotten.   Murat, then Grandduke of Berg, of Cleves and of Juliers, was not satisfied!   Verily, nowadays, when calmly reflecting upon the epidemic ambition which, like contagion, spread from Bonaparte to his lieutenants, I become as one bewildered in my recollections.

Still even the remonstrances of Napoleon were not sufficiently efficacious to restrain the inconsiderate conduct of Murat; and if in the game of effrontery he missed gaining the crown of Spain for himself, at least he contributed powerfully toward losing it for Charles IV.   That monarch, whom inveterate habit had attached to the Prince of Peace, petitioned the Emperor to restore his favorite to liberty; and a descendant of Louis XIV., a successor of Charles of Anjou, solicited as a favor to be allowed to live in any place of refuge with his family, provided the paramour of his wife accompanied him.   Both the king and queen, addressing Murat in like manner, besought him to liberate Godoy.   The grandduke, whose vainglory was agreeably tickled by royal solicitations, took the Prince of Peace under his especial protection, but at the same time declared that, notwithstanding the abdication of Charles, he could not acknowledge any other as king of Spain till he should receive contrary orders from the Emperor. This declaration, and his friendship to Godoy, placed Murat in formal opposition to the whole Spanish nation, who naturally hated the Prince of Peace, and consequently, from the influence of that sentiment, embraced the party of the heir to the crown in whose favor Charles had abdicated.

It has been stated that Napoleon found himself in a perplexing situation with regard to this disputed right between the king and his son. This is not correct. Charles, though subsequently denying his own deed as one of constraint and violence, had nevertheless abdicated voluntarily. Napoleon could hold him to his act. By that act Ferdinand was really king; but the father asserted that the renunciation had been contrary to his inclination, and retracted. The Emperor's recognition was required; he could have given or withheld it; and so, in either case the perplexity vanished, for the revolution of Aranjuez had the general consent. But then, adieu Spain for Joseph! There consequently remained only the mode which he adopted—to get possession of both princes and say to them, Gentlemen, neither of you must be king, but I shall send to Madrid a third person to occupy your throne.

Such was the situation of affairs when Napoleon arrived at Bayonne. Ferdinand allowed himself, after some hesitation, to be persuaded by deceived friends to repair thither, in order to arrange with the Emperor the differences existing between himself and his father. On reaching Vittoria reflection again returned; he distrusted the intentions of the Emperor and suspected some snare. Don Urquijo, besides, assured the youthful monarch that the pretended arbiter wished only to secure his person and place the crown of Spain upon the head of one of his own family. Ferdinand then perceived, but too late, the error he had committed.

Already was he almost in the midst of the French troops; no longer were his inclinations free; he hesitated, and would remain at Vittoria, tortured by the thought that, once at Bayonne, he should not be suffered to return. All his friends, and crowds who had hastened to Vittoria to see their prince, conjured him to remain. It was necessary to return to Bayonne for new instructions and new advices from the Emperor. He who was charged with this commission came back with a letter to Ferdinand from Napoleon, full of the most perfidious assurances and crafty promises, and containing the declaration that he would assign the throne to one or other, according to his conviction of the truth of what Ferdinand alleged or of the violence of which Charles complained. It is incomprehensible how any reasonable being could allow himself to be entrapped by such a device. To the letter of Napoleon the envoy added a *viva voce* asseveration that the crown of Spain would devolve on Ferdinand, and that all necessary preparations were then making at Bayonne with this intention. Victims of such matchless perfidy, it is well known what happened both to the son and to the father, who arrived soon after at Bayonne with his inseparable Prince of Peace. He had just retracted his abdication; and at Bayonne were seen Charles, denuded of his throne by a voluntary act which he now disclaimed; his son, king in right of succession; and Napoleon, arbitrator between the two, settling the difference by taking the crown from both and giving it to Joseph. It was the fable of the lawyers and the oyster; but the unfortunate princes had not even the consolation of a shell. The revolt of the 2d May at Madrid hastened the fate of Ferdinand, to whose charge it was laid—the suspicion, at least, fell upon his friends and adherents.

Charles IV. refused, it is said, to return to Spain, and requested an asylum in France. He signed a renunciation of his rights to the Spanish crown, which instrument bore also the signatures of the Infantas.

At the close of these transactions I saw the prince royal

of Sweden, who, with the representatives of all the powers
at Hamburg, strongly reprobated the conduct of Napoleon.
I cannot attest that Talleyrand dissuaded from this attempt
to overthrow a branch of the house of Bourbon; his enlightened mind and elevated views might have suggested such
advice; but all agreed that, had he retained the administration of foreign affairs, this revolution would have terminated
in a way more generous and noble than by the tragi-comedy
played off at Madrid and Bayonne.

I shall have occasion to revert to this subject: meanwhile
it behooves to return to other affairs, the dates of which
have been anticipated. After the Treaty of Tilsit the hopes
of the Bourbons must have seemed lost indeed. If they
still cherished expectations, doubtless these were chiefly
founded on the imprudence and mad ambition of him who
had usurped their throne. On this subject it was a remark
of Lemercier to Bonaparte himself, a few days before the
foundation of the empire—"General, if you make up the bed
of the Bourbons, you will not lie in it ten years."

The treaty with France and Russia being concluded,
Louis XVIII., whom we then designated in his own kingdom under the name of the Count de Lille, conceived the
Continent to be shut against him. But if he feared that
Alexander, in imitating the first act of his father in making an alliance with Bonaparte, might likewise imitate his
second, and dismiss the French princes from his dominions,
I have proof that Louis greatly deceived himself. This is
a fact upon which I consider it a duty to insist. It was
quite unexpectedly, and of his perfect free will, that Louis
XVIII. left Mittau. It is as true that Alexander knew not
even the King's intention to withdraw from the asylum
which he enjoyed under his protection at Mittau, and
learned the circumstance only through his own officer, the
brave Baron de Driensen, governor of that city. There
exists also on this circumstance another grave misapprehension, if indeed it be not a wilful mistake, into which some
writers have fallen who assert that Louis left Mittau for

the purpose of exciting troubles in France. The time had never been less favorable for such an attempt. At Hamburg a letter was communicated to me, written by the Abbé de Boulogne to the Duke d'Aumont, dated 22d October, consequently a short time only before the royal departure, stating that the object of the King's journey to England was the hope of forming a new coalition against the French government. A vain hope also. But one characteristic of the emigrants was the entertaining of constantly renewed chimerical expectations. Another letter was subsequently communicated to me, of the 3d November, giving an account of the King's arrival at Yarmouth on the 31st of October. I found that Louis had been constrained to await, in this port, the removal of the difficulties which were presented to his disembarkation, and also to the continuance and future direction of his voyage. It was said, among other things, in this letter, that the King of England had judged it proper to refuse permission to the Count de Lille to enter London or its environs. Finally, the palace of Holyrood, at Edinburgh, was appointed for his residence. Mr. Ross, secretary for Mr. Canning, carried to Yarmouth the determination of the English monarch. These precautions were singular, considering the relative positions of the two governments of France and England, and seemed to corroborate the preceding remarks of Prince de Wittgenstein as to the pacific dispositions of Mr. Canning. But the affairs of Spain quickly intervened to render friendly relations between Bonaparte and any honest government impossible. It was not, however, till 1814 that Lemercier's happily expressed prophecy had its accomplishment, after Napoleon had occupied the bed of the Bourbons for precisely nine years and nine months.

Fouché, grand investigator of the secrets of Europe, had been set freshly to work by the affairs of Spain; and I had my share of annoyance in the shape of inquiry upon inquiry about M. de Rechteren, formerly Spanish minister to the Hanse Towns. My information was not of a nature to please. I had nothing ill to say of Count Rechteren, who left that situation four months after my installation in 1804. This was diving pretty deeply into the past in order to explain the present.

About this time I received one of Josephine's frequent notes in favor of merit or misfortune, thus expressed—"M. Melon, now in Hamburg, requests me, my dear Bourrienne, to intercede in his favor for your protection and interest. I have the more pleasure in writing to you on his behalf as it gives me an opportunity of renewing the assurance of my regard." This note was dated from Fontainebleau, whither, in imitation of the old court, Napoleon made frequent excursions. To keep up the etiquette he sometimes hunted, but with as little relish for the sports of the field as Montaigne had for chess. The green woods afforded him no pleasure, for his mind was ever on the rack in schemes of distant ambition.

Instructed as I was, perhaps better than any other, in the hopes and designs of Bonaparte on the north of Germany, it gave me great pain to see him adopt so many measures tending directly to alienate the spirits of men from their author. Thus an order for the inhabitants to pay the French troops quartered in their territory was not only a grievous burden, but had something humiliating—and humiliation is never forgiven. Of these orders some bore the stamp of most profound ignorance: thus I was directed to impress three thousand seamen in the Hanse Towns. Three thousand sailors on a population of two hundred thousand! I procured five hundred, and these were too many, for numbers were unfit for service—but they were men.

. In the spring of 1808 I experienced a great loss in the removal of the Prince de Ponte-Corvo, with whom it was always so easy and so agreeable to transact affairs. He received an order to take the command of the French troops sent to Denmark, after the cowardly bombardment of Copenhagen. It was during his government of Hamburg and residence in Jutland that he quietly and unconsciously prepared the votes which ultimately conducted him to the throne of Sweden. Bernadotte, I remember, placed reliance on certain presages—in short, he believed in astrology; nor can I forget that upon one occasion he said to me quite seriously, "Would you believe it, my good friend, it was predicted to me at Paris that I should one day be a king, but that I must cross the sea?" We laughed together at this weakness of mind from which even Napoleon was not altogether exempt. No supernatural influence, however, elevated Bernadotte to the rank of a European sovereign— it was his character for benevolence and justice. He had no other talisman than the wisdom of his administration and his promptitude in opposing all measures of oppression. He left Hamburg on the 10th, and I heard from him on the 18th March, giving an account of his friendly reception in Denmark. On the 6th April I had a second letter requesting me to give orders to all postmasters to retain every letter addressed to the Spanish troops in his army, of which the corps of Romana formed a part. These letters the postmaster-general had directions to detain until an order arrived for their delivery. Bernadotte deemed this measure indispensable in order to prevent intrigues among the Spaniards under his command.

I had proposed to postpone the affairs of Holland to a later portion of my "Memoirs," but the present seems a fitting opportunity for the introduction of the subject.

While Bonaparte remained Chief of the French Republic, it appeared not inconsistent to have on the south the Cisalpine and on the north the Batavian, like two satellites, gravitating upon the grand republic. But, this latter transformed into an empire, it behooved that its secondaries likewise should undergo a change. The republican government of Holland had in fact been long but a shadow; still, even under the dominion of France, it preserved at least those forms of internal liberty which reconcile men to dependence. In these circumstances it was easy for Napoleon, who maintained his secret influence in the country, to get up a depu-

tation, entreating him to name a king for Holland. The
deputation, consisting of Verhuell, vice-admiral; Brantzen,
resident ambassador at Paris; Van Styrum, member of the
Supreme Council; Gogel, minister of finance; and William
Six, councillor of state, arrived in Paris in May, 1806, and
explained their object in a speech the first sentence of which
contained the substance of the whole: "Sire—We are deputed to express to your majesty the wish of the representatives of our people; we beseech you to yield to us, as
supreme chief of our republic, and king of Holland, Prince
Louis, your majesty's brother, to whom we wholly and respectfully confide the guardianship of our laws, the defence
of our political rights, and all the interests of our beloved
country, under the sacred auspices of Providence and *the
glorious protection of your majesty.*" To this humble request
the Emperor replied in kind; then turning to Louis, his
words marked well the import that he attached to the word
protection—"You, prince, are thus called to reign over a
people whose sires owed their independence to the assistance
of France. Since then Holland became united to England;
she was conquered; a second time she was indebted to
France for her existence. Let her owe to you kings who
may protect her liberties, her laws, her religion. *But never
do you cease to be a Frenchman. The dignity of Constable of
the Empire shall remain to you and your descendants ; it will
recall those duties you have to perform toward me.*" Louis
afterward replied rather to his brother than to the deputation of his new subjects. His speech, however, was probably the only one which contained some sincerity, since it
touched gently upon the regrets "which he experienced
in removing from the presence of the Emperor." Louis, in
truth, had objected to his own elevation to the full extent
of safe opposition. To his ostensible argument—the weakness of his health and the unsuitableness of the climate—
Bonaparte replied in these harsh and unbrotherly terms:
"Better die a king than live a prince!" There thus remained no remedy but obedience. Louis set out for Hol-

land accompanied by Hortense, who, however, did not long continue with her royal husband. The new king desired to render himself beloved by his people; and as this could only be effected by encouraging commerce among a trading people, he failed in strictly enforcing Napoleon's system. Hence the ground of quarrel between the brothers.

I know not if Napoleon held in mind the motives which Louis had alleged on first refusing the crown of Holland, namely, the wintry climate of that country, or whether the Emperor counted upon more explicit devotion in one of his other brothers; but certain it is that Joseph was not called to the throne of Spain till after it had been offered to and declined by the King of Holland. The following is the letter which Napoleon wrote to Louis on the occasion, a copy of which got into my possession: it is without date or place, but, from the contents, must be referred to April, 1808:

"MY BROTHER—The King of Spain, Charles IV., has just abdicated. The Spanish nation have loudly appealed to me. Certain that I shall never have solid peace with England, unless by impressing one grand movement on the Continent, I have resolved to place a French prince upon the throne of Spain. The climate of Holland does not agree with you; besides, Holland will never emerge from her ruins. In the whirlwind of the world, whether there be peace or not, she possesses no means by which to maintain herself. In this situation of things I think of you for the crown of Spain. Answer me categorically what is your opinion of this plan? If I name you king of Spain, do you accept? Can I count upon you? Answer me, in the first instance, only these two questions, thus: 'I have received your letter of such date; I reply, *yes*'; and then I shall conclude that you will do as I desire: or, on the contrary, '*no*'; which will imply that you do not agree to my proposition. Admit no one into your confidence, and speak, I request of you, to none whomsoever on the subject of this letter; for the thing ought to be done before we avow having even thought of it.   NAPOLEON."

Before his final seizure of Holland, Napoleon had formed the design of dismembering Brabant and Zealand in exchange

for other provinces, possession of which was more dubious.
Louis, however, successfully resisted this first aggression;
for Napoleon, then deeply engaged with Spain, cared not to
risk a commotion in the north. He even affected indifference, as appears from this letter to Louis on the subject:

"MY BROTHER—I received your letter relative to the
one written by the Sieur de la Rochefoucauld, your ambassador. He was not authorized to do anything, except
indirectly. Since the exchange displeases you, it is no more
to be thought of. It was useless to make me a display of
principles, since I never said that you ought not to consult
the nation. Many well informed men among your own
subjects had expressed their opinion that it would be indifferent to Holland to give up Brabant, crowded as it is
with fortresses which are very expensive, and having more
affinity with France than Holland, in exchange for provinces
in the north rich and convenient for you. Once more, since
that arrangement does not suit, there is an end of the matter.
It was needless even to speak to me on the subject, since the
Sieur de la Rochefoucauld had no instructions to do more
than feel the way."

The correspondence of the two brothers remained at this
stage for some time; but Louis was none the less exposed
to vexations on the part of Napoleon. The latter having
called to Paris, in 1809, the kings who might justly be
styled feudatories of the empire, Louis was also cited; but,
caring little to leave his states, he convoked and consulted
his council, who deemed this sacrifice necessary to Holland,
and their king acquiesced; for, upon the throne, the life of
Louis was a daily sacrifice. At Paris he lived very retired,
a mark for the police; for, as he had come unwillingly, it
was believed he would not prolong his stay to such a period
as Napoleon wished. In this opinion his persecutors were
not deceived; but every attempt at compromise failed. The
spying, circumventions and indignity to which he was thus
exposed, roused a spirit and strength of character for which
he had not received credit. Amid the silence of his royal
fellows in slavery, the voice of Louis was heard to say to

the Emperor, in presence of all, "I have been deceived by promises never intended to be fulfilled; Holland is weary of being the puppet of France." The imperial ears, little accustomed to such sounds, were fearfully shocked, and, thenceforth, there remained no choice between yielding implicity to the demands of Napoleon, or seeing Holland united to France. Louis chose the latter, though not till he had essayed his feeble opposition to the utmost, in favor of the subjects confided to his care; but he refused to be an accomplice in sacrificing them to a blind hatred of England. Louis, however, received permission to return to his kingdom, but only to behold the misery of a commercial and industrious country without commerce or employment. Once more he wrote to his brother, on the 23d March, 1810, to the following effect:

"If you would consolidate France in her present situation, and obtain a maritime peace, it is not by means such as the blockade that you will attain these ends; it is not by the destruction of a kingdom created by yourself; it is not by enfeebling your allies, and by respecting neither their most sacred rights nor the commercial principles of equality and justice between nations; but, on the contrary, by causing France to be beloved, by strengthening and protecting allies so faithful as your own brothers. The destruction of Holland, far from being a means of distressing England, will prove a source of prosperity to her, by all the industry and all the wealth which will seek refuge in that country. There are only three means of really attacking England—detaching Ireland from her, capturing her Indian possessions, or by a descent. The last two, though the most effectual, are impossible without a navy; but I am astonished that the first has been so easily abandoned. These present a more certain means of securing peace, and on advantageous conditions, than a system which does injury to yourself and your allies, in an attempt to inflict greater hurt on your enemy.

"LOUIS."

But written were become as disagreeable as spoken remonstrances. This letter had, in fact, given sovereign displeasure; and the Emperor replied, two months afterward, from Ostend—where he had stopped during one of his frequent advances—in the following terms:

"MY BROTHER—In our present situation it were best always to speak out frankly. I know your most secret views, and whatever you may tell me to the contrary goes for nothing. Holland is in a troublesome situation, that is true. I conceive you desire to extricate yourself. It is not I who can do anything, but you—you alone. When you conduct yourself in such a manner as to persuade the Dutch that you act by my instigation—that all your sentiments are conformable to mine, then will you be beloved—then you will be esteemed, and acquire the consistency necessary to reconstitute Holland. When to be the friend of France and mine shall be a title grateful to your heart, Holland will find herself in a natural situation. Since your return from Paris you have done nothing toward this. What will be the result of your conduct? Your subjects, finding themselves vacillating between France and England, will throw themselves into the arms of France, and demand with loud cries a *union* as the only refuge against so much uncertainty. If your knowledge of my character, which is, to go straight to my object without being stopped by any consideration, has not enlightened you—what would you have me to do? I can dispense with Holland; but Holland cannot dispense with my protection. If, committed to one of my own brothers, dependent upon me alone for her security, she finds not in that brother my image, you destroy all her confidence in your administration—you break your sceptre with your own hands. Love France—love my fame! These are the only means by which you can be of service to the kingdom of Holland. Holland become a portion of my kingdom—had you been what you ought to have been—would become so much the more dear to me, that I had given to her a prince who was almost my son. In placing you upon the throne of Holland, I had thought to have seated thereon a citizen of France. You have pursued a course diametrically opposite. I have seen myself forced to interdict you from France, and to seize part of your territories. When you show yourself a bad Frenchman to the Dutch, you become less than a Prince of Orange, to whom they owe the national rank and a long succession of prosperity and glory. It is proved to Holland that your recession from France has lost to her what she would not have lost under Schimmelpenninck, nor under a

Prince of Orange. Be at once a Frenchman and brother of the Emperor, and be assured that you are then in the way of the interests of Holland. The die is cast—you are incorrigible; already you desire to chase from your presence the few Frenchmen who remain with you. Neither counsel, nor advice, nor affection—but only menace and force—can move you—What mean those prayers and those mysterious fasts which you order? Louis! you seem to have no desire to reign long; all your actions—even more plainly than your confidential letters—manifest the sentiments of your mind. Return from your false course; be truly a Frenchman in heart, or your people will expel you; and you will leave Holland an object of derision—of the derision of Dutchmen. It is by reason and policy, not by a bitter and vitiated temper, that states are governed.   NAPOLEON.''

Scarcely had this letter been received by Louis, when Napoleon was informed of a menial brawl, to which the Sieur de la Rochefoucauld, doubtless aware that he would serve his master agreeably by affording a pretence for a rupture, wished to give an importance quite diplomatic. According to his statement, the honor of his coachman had been compromised by an insult from a citizen of Amsterdam. This provocation grating harshly upon the dignified susceptibilities of the wearers of livery, they demanded *satisfaction!* Upon this a scuffle ensued, which *might* have become serious, since it began to assume the character of a dispute between the Dutch and French, when the guard of the palace put an end to the fray. On the report of his ambassador, which reached the Emperor three days after the last missive had been despatched to his brother, Napoleon fulminated from Lille, where he then was, the following letter —and all about Count de la Rochefoucauld's coachman!

"MY BROTHER—At the moment when you make me the fairest protestations I learn that my ambassador's people have been maltreated in Amsterdam. My intention is that those who have rendered themselves so culpable toward me be delivered up in order that the vengeance which shall overtake them may serve as an example. The Sieur Serrurier has tendered me an account of the manner in which you conducted yourself at the diplomatic audience. I declare to you, therefore, I will no longer allow an ambassador from Holland to be in Paris. Admiral Verhuell has orders to depart in twenty-four hours. I want no more phrases and protestations; time it is I should know whether you intend being the misfortune of Holland, and by your folly to cause the ruin of that country. It is my pleasure, also, that you no more send an ambassador to Austria. I wish, likewise, that you send back all Frenchmen who are in your service. I have recalled my ambassador; I shall no longer have any, save a *chargé d'affaires* in Holland. The Sieur Serrurier, who remains there in that capacity, will make known to you my intentions. I do not again wish to expose an ambassador to your insults. Write no more of your usual sentiments; for three years, now, you have conned them over, and every instant proves their hollowness.

"This is the last letter I shall ever write to you.

"NAPOLEON."

Reduced, thus, to the last extremity, placed between the cruel necessity of ruining Holland by his own act, or of leaving her to the care of the Emperor, Louis did not hesitate; he resolved to lay down a sceptre whose rule it was not permitted him to render beneficent. This determination taken, he addressed a message to the Legislative Assembly, setting forth the too legitimate grounds of his abdication. What, in fact, could be a more lawful motive than the invasion of a country united to France by a compact termed a family alliance? But there was nothing then to withhold Napoleon in the career of his despotism. Under the command of the Duke of Reggio, more king in Holland than the king himself, the French troops had invaded that country and threatened to occupy Amsterdam, the capital. Louis descended from his throne. "Long have I foreseen," said the king in his message to the legislature, "the extremity to which I am reduced; but I could not avoid the evil without a betrayal of my most sacred obligations and sacrificing those rights which ought indissolubly to unite my fate to that of Holland." Louis subsequently promulgated his act of abdication. This he also founded upon the unfortunate situation of the kingdom, which he attributed to the hostile intentions of his brother, whom no efforts of his, no sacrifices consistent with the welfare of the country, had been able to mitigate; in fine, that he had been led to regard himself as the cause of the misunderstandings continually renewed between France and Holland. But so that he should deem it a consolation to think his individual renouncement of honors had been productive of good to his subjects, he renounced his rights only in favor of his sons, the Prince Royal, Louis Napoleon, and his brother, Prince Louis Charles Napoleon. Her majesty the queen became regent by the constitution, and meanwhile the regency was confided to the privy council.

This seems to me really worthy of remark. Louis, in renouncing the crown of Holland, believed he had the power of doing so in favor of his children. Four years after Napoleon flattered himself he could abdicate the throne of France in favor of his son, the infant king of Rome. And if, in the history of Napoleon, we examine coincidences, how often do we find him, in the mightiness of his reverses, struck by precisely the same blows as he had levelled against others in the greatness of his power!

After having taken leave of his subjects in a proclamation, Louis retired to Tœplitz, in Bohemia. It was here he learned that his brother, far from respecting the conditions of his abdication, had united Holland to the empire.

CHAPTER XXVII

The Campaign of 1809—Schill—Jerome's Impecuniosity—Abduction of the Pope—Napoleon Excommunicated—Seizure of Rome —Marriage with Maria Louisa

DURING the campaign of 1809, and at its commencement especially, the advance of Napoleon was even more rapid than in the struggle of 1805. But I do not attempt a full detail of the proceedings: I limit myself as formerly to recollections, interesting in themselves, little

known, and which fell under my own knowledge, but which
at the same time throw light upon the whole campaign.
When the Emperor had been informed of the attack directed by the Austrians against Bavaria, his orders were
instantly despatched to all officers commanding divisions
to hasten their march toward the theatre of action. The
Prince of Ponte-Corvo was called among the rest and received the Saxons under his orders—a situation with which
he was by no means satisfied. Bonaparte never forgave the
18th Brumaire. "We are," writes Bernadotte to me on the
6th, "in presence of the Austrians: they are very strong in
Bohemia and in my front; and I have scarcely got together
fifteen thousand Saxons."

The promptitude of Napoleon was never more necessary
than during the campaign of 1809; his decision in marching
upon Vienna was a masterstroke, and anticipated the plots,
well laid as they were, in case of a check to overturn his
government in the north. England, intoxicated by success
in Portugal and Spain, had employed the whole machinery
of her intrigues and had arranged an expedition in our
direction, which the prowess of the grand army alone prevented. This expedition was to consist of ten thousand
men. Field artillery, clothing, muskets and stores of every
kind were already collected in Heligoland, and Mr. Canning
had been written to by the Austrian cabinet, urging the
descent. It was the Archduke's design to concentrate in
the heart of Germany a great mass of troops, composed of
the corps of Generals Amende and Radozwowitz, and the
English troops, who were to be joined by the expected
insurgents on their march through the northern states. The
English cabinet would have wished that the Archduke had
advanced a little way further; but he preferred hazarding
the diversion to compromising the safety of the monarchy
by departing from its habitual inactivity and risking the
passage of the Danube in the face of an adversary never to
be surprised, and who calculated all possible contingencies.
To insure the success of the expedition, however, Field-

marshal Kienmacker was sent with a large reinforcement and a numerous staff to take the command in Saxony and Franconia, with directions to prosecute the invasion vigorously. In adopting this plan of campaign the Archduke hoped that the Emperor of France would either detach a strong division to the support of his allies, or would leave them to their own defence. In the former case, the Archduke would have retained great superiority over the grand army, thus diminished; and, in the latter, all was prepared in Hesse, Hanover, and other northern states for a revolt of the inhabitants on the approach of the English and Austrian armies.

But all these arrangements were rendered naught by the Emperor's new system of war, which consisted in pouncing upon the capital, thus paralyzing the enemy in the very centre of his strength and forcing him speedily to sue for peace. He was master of Vienna before England had even organized the intended expedition. In the commencement of July, indeed, the English did approach Cuxhaven with twelve small vessels of war. Here they disembarked four or five hundred seamen, with some fifty marines, and planted a standard upon one of the outworks. The day after this landing the English in Denmark evacuated Copenhagen after destroying a battery erected by the naval forces. On quitting Cuxhaven they arrested Desarts, agent for the consulate at Hamburg, who, on being reclaimed as a citizen, was provisionally set at liberty by Lord Stuart.

But to return to the Emperor's progress. Setting out from Paris on the 11th, we have seen him on the 17th at Donawerth in active operations at the head of the Bavarians; on the 23d he was master of Ratisbon. In the engagement which preceded his entrance into that city Napoleon was wounded in the heel; the hurt, slight indeed, could not induce him to quit for an instant the field of battle. Between Donawerth and Ratisbon, also by a brilliant achievement, as skilful as it was daring, Davoust gained and merited his title of Prince of Eckmühl. Before quitting Ratisbon the Emperor issued to his soldiers another of his brief addresses:

"You have justified my anticipations and have replaced numbers by bravery. In the course of a few days we have triumphed in the three battles of Thann, D'Abensberg and Eckmühl, also in the engagements of Peissing, Ladshut and Ratisbon. The enemy, blinded by a perjured cabinet, seems to have no longer preserved any remembrance of us. You have shown yourselves to be more terrible than ever. Lately our enemies have invaded the territories of our allies; but a little while, and they flattered themselves with carrying the war into the bosom of our country; to-day, defeated and terror-struck, they are in disordered flight. Already my advanced guard has passed the Inn: in less than a month we shall be in Vienna."

Fortune seemed then to sport her favors in terms of this boasting, for a month had not elapsed when another proclamation from the Emperor announced to his soldiers their entrance into the Austrian capital. But, while he was thus marching from triumph to triumph, we at Hamburg and the places adjacent had a neighbor whose presence inspired anything but security. This was the famous Prussian partisan, Major Schill, who, after exercising his freebooting in Westphalia, had thrown himself into Mecklenburg, whence, as I learned, he designed to surprise our city. He had said in Westphalia that in Hamburg should be paid the contributions levied from Jerome's kingdom. At the head of six hundred hussars, well mounted and full of audacity, with some fifteen hundred foot badly armed, he carried the small fortress of Domitz, in Mecklenburg, on the 15th May. From this station he sent out parties who raised contributions on both sides of the Elbe, stopped and plundered the public stage coaches, inquiring eagerly after news from England. This partisan inspired great terror in his progress; requisitions when not granted were taken by force. He advanced to Bergdorf, within twelve miles of Hamburg, capturing Wismar, summoning Stralsund, and forcing the Duke of Mecklenburg, though he had protected and granted lands to the officer, Count Moleke, who pursued him, to seek safety in flight. The alarm at Hamburg became general. Some even talked of bribing Schill to depart, but firmer counsels prevailed. I consulted with the magistracy, took measures for a defence, and sent under a strong escort into Holstein the custom-house chest with a million in gold. At the same time I despatched to Schill's leaguer a clever spy, who so frightened the marauder, bold as he was, by descriptions of our means and resolutions of defence that, breaking up his camp and leaving us on his left, he marched upon Lübeck, which, being without defence, could offer none. A single hussar of his band had outstripped the main body and, presenting himself alone at the gate, demanded admittance and billets for two or three thousand men who were coming. The guard of the custom-house were about to fire upon this daring prowler, when he scampered off at full gallop. Such was the spirit of the foray. But Schill's further progress was soon barred. Lieutenant-General Gratien set out from Berlin in pursuit, by order of the Prince of Neufchatel, with three thousand five hundred Swedes and Hollanders. These, some days after, having hemmed in his corps at Stralsund, Schill defended himself to the last, and after an engagement of two hours, the chief being killed, the whole band was destroyed or dispersed.

A war of brigandage such as that carried on by Schill cannot be honorably acknowledged by any power which respects itself; yet the English government, always on the watch to excite and support wars of sedition and marauding, sent to Schill the brevet of colonel and the complete uniform of his new rank, with the assurance that his whole band should thenceforth be in the pay of England. This famous partisan had soon an imitator of a more elevated rank in the Duke of Brunswick-Oels, who, in August of the same year, pursued an equally adventurous and more successful career. At the head of about two thousand men, more or less, he spread dismay along the left bank of the Elbe and entered Bremen on the 5th. An officer of the Duke presented himself at the house of the French consul, who had fled, and demanded two hundred louis, otherwise he would give orders to pillage. The person who had been left in charge persuaded the officer to accept eighty louis, for which the honest robber gave an acknowledgment in the Duke's name. The Brunswickers, being pursued by the troops at Westphalia under General Reubell, quitted Bremen on the evening of the 6th, endeavoring to reach Holland in all haste. On the 7th the pursuers entered that town and set out again in pursuit. Meanwhile three to four thousand English disembarked at Cuxhaven, but, as before, without effecting anything. The Duke of Brunswick, always pursued, had traversed Germany from the confines of Bohemia to Elsfleth, a small seaport on the left bank of the Weser, where he arrived on the 7th, one day's march in advance of his pursuers. Here he seized all the means of transport and, embarking his troops, reached Heligoland in safety. General Reubell was very improperly disgraced, as if by his negligence the Duke had escaped. This unjust punishment produced a bad effect upon the public mind.

Such is the history, or rather adventures, of two men, of whom the former was really remarkable for his dauntless bravery: they both inflicted much mischief and might have opened all eyes to what the free bands of Germany would be able to achieve, when the day of her emancipation arrived.

Rapp, who had resumed his functions near the Emperor's person as aide-de-camp during the second campaign of Vienna, related to me one of those traits or judgments of Napoleon which, from him, when compared with events which have since occurred, seemed like sympathetic forecasts of his own destiny. One day, while a few marches from Vienna, the Emperor, who kept a guide by him to give the names of all the villages and explain the smallest ruin which he passed on his march, perceived crowning an eminence the decayed remains of an ancient fortalice. "These," said the guide, "are the ruins of the castle of Diernstein." Napoleon suddenly stopped, assumed a meditative air, and continued for some time motionless, gazing on the ruins. Then turning to Marshal Lannes, who accompanied him on horseback, "Look," said the Emperor; "behold the prison of Richard Cœur de Lion. He, like us, went to Syria and Palestine. The Lion-Heart, my brave Lannes, was not braver than thou, though more fortunate than I, at Acre. A duke of Austria sold him to an emperor of Germany, who shut him up yonder. These were the times of barbarism. How different from our civilization! It has been seen how I treated the Emperor of Austria, when I could have made him my prisoner. Well, well; I shall treat him again exactly in the same way. Yet it is not I who wish this—it is the age; crowned heads must now be respected. A conqueror in a stronghold!"

A few days afterward the Emperor was at the gates of Vienna; but, this once, access to the capital was not so easy as in 1805. The fortunate hardihood of Lannes then opened the gates; but the marshal's days were numbered; he fell soon after the conversation above, in the battle of Wagram. The Archduke Ferdinand, shut up in the city, determined on defending his post, though the French were already in possession of the principal suburbs. In vain were different flags of truce sent in; the bearers were not only refused admittance, but even maltreated, and one of them almost massacred by the populace. A bombardment then commenced, and the city was soon wrapped in flames. The Emperor being informed that one of the archduchesses had remained in Vienna detained by illness, gave orders to cease firing. Strange destiny of Napoleon! this archduchess was Maria Louisa! Vienna at last capitulated, and the Emperor then, as of old, established at Schœnbrunn, did not fail to remind his soldiers in a new proclamation what he had predicted in his last address:

"Soldiers!—A month after the enemy had passed the Inn, on the same day, at the same hour, we entered Vienna. Landwehres, levies *en masse*, ramparts created by the powerless resentment of the princes of the house of Lorraine, have been unable to support your mere looks. The princes of that house leave their capital, not as soldiers of honor, who yield to the circumstances of war, but like perjured men pursued by their own remorse. Flying from Vienna, their adieus to its inhabitants were murder and conflagration. Like Medea they have strangled their children with their own hands. Soldiers! the population of Vienna, using the words of the deputation from its suburbs, disheartened and abandoned, will become the objects of your attention. I take under my especial protection all the peaceable inhabitants; as to turbulent and wicked men I shall make them examples of summary justice. Soldiers! be kind to the poor peasants —to that honest people who have so many claims to your esteem; let us cherish no pride of success; let us behold therein a proof of that divine justice which punishes the ungrateful and the perjured!"

Who would have thought after this proclamation, in which the Emperor of Austria was treated with so little respect, that the campaign would terminate in Napoleon becoming his son-in-law? Besides, I have always thought that this mania of Bonaparte in insulting his enemies was bad policy; but my observations on this point were invariably ill received.

If again it be asked, why I thus convert to my own purposes Napoleon's proclamations, while preserving a religious silence in respect to his bulletins? the answer is obvious: the former, with the exception of predictions not always verified, were founded in fact; they stated particulars known to those who had been personally actors; but the latter were intended for the people of France and foreign countries, and too well justified the proverb, "Mendacious as a bulletin."

At this time the King of Westphalia was on a tour through his states, and had advanced to no great distance from Hamburg. Of all Bonaparte's brothers he had been least known to me; and, of all the family, evidently possessed the smallest claims to personal esteem. I have in my possession only two of his letters, one of which, dated 23d November, 1802, is already before the reader. The other, of the 6th September, 1809, runs as follows:

"MONSIEUR BOURRIENNE—I shall be at Hanover on the 10th: if it were possible for you to come there and· pass twenty-four hours, it would be agreeable to me. I should then be able to remove all the difficulties which may arise in negotiating the loan which I wish to raise in the Hanse Towns. I have pleasure in believing that you will do all in your power to forward the affair. At the present moment this loan, as respects my kingdom, is an operation of extreme importance. I offer *securities more than sufficient;* but it will be of no service to me unless granted for at least two years.

"JEROME BONAPARTE."

Now, I ask, is it not most amusing, on comparing these two letters, seven years distant in date, to find that Jerome, lieutenant of a cutter, and Jerome Napoleon, King of West-phalia, had but one and the same object in writing—to ask for money? The naval officer's concern was easily got over at the expense of only a few epithets, launched by the First Consul against *the dirty little rascal,* as he then termed Jerome; but the affair of his Majesty of Westphalia required more delicate management. Jerome wished to borrow from Hamburg the sum of three millions of francs; but, notwith-standing his Westphalian Majesty's "more than sufficient securities," no lenders would untie their purse-strings. However, without employing my influence as minister of France, which I dared not do without consulting the Em-peror, I prevailed upon the senate to grant one hundred thousand francs toward paying the arrears due to his troops, and a further sum of two hundred thousand for clothing and other necessaries, for his soldiers were in want of every-thing. This will appear from the fact that he first equipped twenty-five of his own bodyguard, the members of which had before been literally naked. The poverty which at this time reigned throughout Germany, both among the allies and enemies of France, may be gathered from an expression of the King of Bavaria. I use his very words to one of the imperial household: "If things continue thus we may shut shop and put the key under the door."

Jerome, though sadly disappointed, seemed to consider

himself under some obligation, and sent me, some days after, his portrait, in a box set with diamonds, with a letter thanking me for what I had done for his unfortunate soldiers. This, I can safely say, gave me no pleasure, as I wished to have no favors from the Bonaparte family; but it never entered my brain to refuse a present from a crowned head. Napoleon was not of the same opinion. Courier after courier brought reproaches for having accepted without consulting him, and orders for me to return "this mark of special regard," for so had I designated the miniature in a general despatch to the foreign minister. I sent back the box with the diamonds and retained the portrait. Napoleon, however, had been led to apprehend that there was something irregular in the loan, which probably irritated him, and I had great trouble in proving, though he was at last convinced, that Jerome had behaved with all due propriety. As to the loan actually effected, the senators rejoiced in coming off so well; for they dreaded a visit from the Westphalian division, and that would have cost much more.

We return to Napoleon at Vienna, who, after the decisive battle of Wagram, became involved in apparently endless negotiations with Austria. His patience failing, he formed a plan to revolutionize and dismember Hungary, but, though the design was at this period maturely considered and even settled, the urgency of other affairs caused its being abandoned. I was not, however, surprised in the least on receiving the intelligence of the proposed revolution, for it only recalled one instance more of a return by the Emperor to the projects of Bonaparte which I myself had assisted in raising. Thus, I had noted that one evening, before the Treaty of Campo-Formio, he said to Berthier and me—"There might be something done with Hungary; if the Austrian government does not speedily come to a conclusion an insurrection in that country would do no harm; and nothing can be more easy. The Hungarians have not the same apathy as the inhabitants of the other Austrian provinces."

While negotiations were going on, the Emperor visited all the corps of his army, and the field of battle of Wagram, which had lately witnessed one of those feats of arms success in which is the more glorious that it has been bravely contested. In the camp before Vienna, also, he instituted the order of the "Three Fleeces," an institution which was never practically realized. But he did not always amuse himself so harmlessly in conceiving designs; he now executed one which alienated many minds in France. Five days after the bombardment of Vienna, that is to say on the 17th of May, Napoleon promulgated a decree by which the Papal States were united to the empire and Rome declared an imperial city. Whether this was good or bad policy we shall see hereafter; meanwhile it was a cowardly usurpation, and, considering the individual relations which had subsisted between the parties, an act of base ingratitude.

At Vienna, too, Napoleon received intelligence of the disaster at Talavera de la Reyna. My letters from headquarters described his being greatly affected, and making no secret of the pain inflicted by the loss thus sustained by his arms. I believe him to have been strongly attached to the conquest, just in proportion to its difficulties: this conquest he now beheld, if not wrested from his grasp, at least become doubtful in the dark chances of futurity. At Talavera began also to be known in Europe the name of a man who, perhaps, might not have been without some fame had not a great reputation been prematurely claimed for him. This was the brilliant *début* of Arthur Wellesley, whose final successes, however they might have been gained, were attended with such vast results.

While we experienced this check in the Peninsula, the English attempted an expedition into Holland, where they had already made themselves masters of Walcheren. This conquest, indeed, they were obliged speedily to abandon; but as the peace between Austria and France was still under discussion, in consequence of the armistice of Znaim, the reverses of the latter prolonged the settlement of conditions, the former expecting that new defeats might render these less objectionable. These delays occasioned Napoleon great irritation. He burned to be revenged on the sole enemies that remained, Spain and Britain. The Spanish affairs especially engaged his attention, for the battle of Talavera had struck at his military renown. This was not, however, the sole motive which induced him to relax somewhat in his pretensions toward Austria.

I return to some intervening events. We have seen by the decree of the 17th May that the papal states were united to the empire. This was an impolitic measure, with respect both to Protestants and Catholics; the former beheld the oppression of a feeble old man, the latter saw in that oppression an insult to the head of their religion. Napoleon again calculated that the triple tiara of Rome would easily bend before the new double crown of France, and rushed without consideration into an act of violence which he did not foresee would arm both prejudice and humanity against him. On the other hand, the Pope miscalculated his means of resistance and renewed the papal extravagances of the dark ages. I was sure of my agents, yet could scarcely credit the veracity of the following document, which, as I never saw it elsewhere, may here gratify and astonish the reader who finds that a papal excommunication was actually pronounced and promulgated against an Emperor of France in the nineteenth century.

"By the authority of Almighty God, of the holy apostles, Peter and Paul, and by Our own, we declare that you, Napoleon, Emperor of the French, and all your abettors, in consequence of the outrage which you have committed, have incurred excommunication, under which (according to the form of our apostolic bulls, as in similar instances, published in the usual places of this city) we declare all those to have fallen who, since the last horrible invasion of our city, which took place on the 22d February last, have committed as well in Rome as in the ecclesiastical states, the outrages against which we have remonstrated, not only by the numerous protestations made by our secretary of state, which have been successively renewed, but also by our two consistorial instruments of the 14th March and 11th July, 1808. We equally declare excommunicated all those who have been mandataries, abettors, and counsellors, and whosoever has co-operated in the execution of those acts or shall have himself committed them."

In the supposition that the above must surely have been one of the apocryphal writings of the church, I transmitted a copy to Fouché, who, in his reply, left me in no doubt as to its authenticity. I know also that, when the Emperor was informed at Vienna of the moral opposition, the only weapon to which he could resort, employed by the Pope, he showed some uneasiness as to the probable consequences of the affair. But as he never drew back, especially when he found himself engaged on the worse side, he explained his intentions so as to let his devoted partisans seem to act without compromising himself by positive orders. These facts I give for certain; the rest is known to all the world, namely, that during the night between the 5th and 6th July, the Pope was carried off from Rome by General Radet. The unfortunate pontiff was passed from city to city, for then it was the question as to who should *not* receive the illustrious captive. From Florence, Eliza forwarded him to Turin; from Turin, the Prince Borghese sent him into the interior of France; and finally, Napoleon sent him back to reside in Savona under keeping of his brother-in-law. In these pleasure jaunts his Holiness's guard of honor was a squad of gendarmerie. But in all the varied phases of this troublesome transaction, and blamable as it certainly was, the Pope could not easily persuade men that Heaven took pleasure in avenging promptly the cause of the chief of holy mother church, since the very morning which followed his abduction from the chair of St. Peter lighted up the day of Wagram.

It was at Fontainebleau, during the residence, as mentioned above, which preceded Napoleon's hurried entrance into Paris, that Josephine, who had gone to meet him at the former place, first heard of the divorce, the design of which

Napoleon had again agitated even at Schœnbrunn. It was also at Fontainebleau that Montalivet was named minister of the interior. At this period the letters from Paris entertained us with perpetual accounts of the brilliant condition presented by the capital during the winter of 1809–10, and above all, of the magnificence of the imperial court, where the Kings of Saxony, Bavaria, and Wirtemberg attended the levee of the Emperor, eager to thank the hero who had elevated them to the rank of sovereigns.

I was the first at Hamburg who received intelligence of the projected marriage of Napoleon with the Archduchess Maria Louisa. This news reached me by two different expresses within two days. The first courier announced merely the intention; the second, confirming the despatches of the preceding evening, represented this grand alliance as a thing settled. Who would have said of Bonaparte, on the day he pawned his watch at my brother's, that the hand of an Archduchess of Austria awaited him? All was fantastic, prodigious, inexplicable, in his destiny. At the same time it is impossible to describe the effect produced by that event in the north of Germany. From all parts merchants received orders to purchase Austrian stock, in which an extraordinary rise took place immediately. The joy was universal and deeply felt; the confidence of long peace seemed confirmed, the hope of a termination to the bloody rivalship of France and Austria appeared certain; and, if I may judge by the intelligence received from the interior of France and other countries, the sentiment was the same throughout. While all minds were thus absorbed in the reflections awakened by this alliance, the Emperor caused notification to be made to the different courts of Europe that the grandduchy of Frankfort had been ceded to Prince Eugene, the prince primate having constituted him his heir.

We have already seen, that in the commencement of 1810 broke out the difference between Napoleon and his brother Louis, and that Holland was then united to the empire. This province first received the visit of its new empress. The journey took place immediately after the pompous ceremonies of the marriage at Paris, on the 2d of April. Napoleon returned to Compeigne, where he had first met his bride on the 28th of March, and remained there with her eight days. Afterward he set out for St. Quentin, once more visited the canal, and was joined by the Empress Maria Louisa. After visiting various parts of Holland and Belgium, the greatest rejoicings everywhere hailing their approach, they returned by way of Ostend, Lille and Normandy, to St. Cloud, on the 1st of June, 1810.

Notwithstanding the universal and sincere joy occasioned by the events just narrated, war with England and Spain still continued, and increased the misery arising from the Continental System, which every day augmented. The Hanse Towns had refused to pay the French soldiers, who had neither money nor necessaries. There must be a term to all sacrifices; and from these towns, once so flourishing through commerce, that source of wealth being dried up, nothing more could be extracted. Present want and former exactions rendered them unable to satisfy this unjust requisition. Holland again was utterly ruined by the same antisocial system which, in the end, proved the ruin, or principal cause of ruin, to its author. In this state of things the spirits of men were kept in perpetual agitation and uncertainty by the almost daily promulgation of decrees of the senate, announcing the union of states to the empire. During the present year, or since the Treaty of Schœnbrunn, the limits of imperial France had thus been extended by the swallowing up of small communities on all sides, and seemed progressively and indefinitely advancing. In the midst of this complication of distress all minds were filled with a desperate hatred by a decree which I cannot call other than infernal, issued by Napoleon and worthy of the darkest ages of barbarism, commanding the destruction of all the colonial produce and manufactures of England, throughout the empire, and wherever his power could enforce this mad sacrifice. In the interior of France this was severe enough; but no conception can be formed of the desolation thus wrought in commercial districts. What so cruel as to burn in vast quantities, before men's eyes, the very articles—the first necessaries of life—for which they were starving? This insane measure was urged by an impatient animosity against England, rendered still fiercer by the capture of the Isle of France, of which she had just gained possession. To prevent such miserable devastation in the north, I proposed to the Emperor to admit such colonial produce as might be bonded in Holstein, at an *ad valorem* duty of thirty, and upon some articles forty per cent. I knew the holders would willingly agree to pay a legal duty not more than the expense of smuggling, while all consequent risk was removed, and, by this measure, which fortunately was conceded, a saving to the treasury accrued of forty million francs.

CHAPTER XXVIII

Bernadotte Crown Prince of Sweden—The Hanse Towns Annexed to the Empire—Josephine's Presentiment of the Divorce—Savary replaces Fouché —The Peninsular Campaign—Birth of an Heir—The Pope Detained by Napoleon

BERNADOTTE had just been elected Prince Royal of Sweden; and this brings me to a circumstance in my life which I recall with the greatest satisfaction—the prince's residence with me at Hamburg on his way to the capital of his future kingdom. But it will be necessary to recur to antecedent events in order to explain how the opposer of the 18th Brumaire came to be seated on the throne of Sweden. On the 13th March, 1809, Gustavus Adolphus was arrested. I omit the circumstances, though these would occupy a large space in the history of a period less fruitful in great events. The duke of Sudermania, uncle to the king, assumed the reins of a provisional government, and Gustavus a few days after gave in an act of abdication, which in the state of Sweden, in both foreign and domestic relations, he could not withhold. In the Month of May following the duke was elected king by the Swedish diet convoked at Stockholm. This monarch had an only son, Prince Christian Augustus, who thus became Prince Royal of Sweden, from the fact of his father's election to the throne. He died suddenly in the end of May, 1810, and Count Fersen, who in the court of Marie Antoinette had formerly been known as the "Handsome Fersen," was massacred by the populace, too ready to believe that the count had hastened the prince's death. On the 21st of August following Bernadotte was elected in his room Prince Royal of Sweden.

Count Wrede made the first overtures at Paris to Bernadotte; who, after this interview, repaired to St. Cloud. Napoleon listened coldly to his recital, and replied "that he could be of no service to him; that events must take their course; and that he might accept or refuse, as suited him; that he, for his part, would place no obstacle in his way, neither would he give any advice." But of the Emperor's being violently opposed to this choice there can be no question; and, though disavowing such a proceeding, he certainly used his endeavors in favor of the Prince Royal of Denmark. Bernadotte in the interval visited the springs of Plombières, and soon after announced to me that his election had taken place. This news I received on the 22d August, the announcement being in the following terms:

"MY DEAR MINISTER—This letter will be presented to you by M. de Signeul, Swedish consul-general at Paris, who precedes me by some days. I recommend him particularly to you. Have the goodness to receive him with your usual kindness. You will be much pleased with him. I hope in a very little to have the pleasure of seeing you. Meanwhile I renew the assurance of my sincere and affectionate sentiments. JOHN, P. R. of Sweden.

"P.S.—I request you to present my compliments to Madame, friendship to my little cousin, and to your amiable family."

All on a sudden exchange fell greatly against Russia, which was attributed to this election, Alexander having supported the Prince of Denmark. The consternation at St. Petersburg, however, which certainly did exist, proceeded less from the choice itself than from the apprehension that it had been influenced by France.

Bernadotte reached Hamburg on the 11th October and remained with me almost entirely during the three days of his stay. Our conversation was interesting in the extreme. I ventured first to speak of the unfavorable reports concerning the Prince's conduct at Wagram. He took my frankness in good part and answered in the same strain:

"The Emperor refused to see me, and assigned as his reason that he was astonished and indignant; that, after complaints, of which I could not but know the justice, I continued to boast of having gained the battle, and had published felicitations to the Saxons whom I commanded. These he had caused to be pronounced ridiculous by all those who are jealous of the superiority of others." Bernadotte then showed me his bulletin, and the private order issued to the marshals respecting it by the Emperor.

During the three days which the prince passed with me we had much conversation on the Continental System. He knew the obstinate resolution of Napoleon on that head. When he asked me what I thought of the treaty of the 1st January, 1810, by which Sweden had bound herself to the observance of this system, I was aware he asked my opinion only to be confirmed in his own. I gave mine without hesitation, which the reader already knows was against the system. "Sell your iron," said I, "your timber, hides and pitch; take in return salt, wines, spirits and colonial produce, of which you stand in need; you will thus gain the affection instead of incurring the hatred of your Swedish subjects."

Since we have proceeded thus far in the history of Bernadotte's rise we may continue the narrative through the subsequent phases of his intercourse with Napoleon.

The latter had beheld with no gracious eye the events now related: he easily divined, from the character of the former, that in him he would not possess a political puppet, nor one who would bend to the theory of conduct prescribed to French princes, and outlined, with such plain, unsophisticated despotism, in the letters to Louis. The secret discontent was not long in breaking out into open rupture. The Emperor had permitted the Crown Prince to take with him, for at least one year, those French officers attached to his staff in the quality of aides-de-camp. This permission was retracted almost immediately after; indeed, as Bernadotte stated in his letter, "while he was just thinking of writing to thank his imperial majesty for the favor." This letter changed into decided resentment the bad humor of Napoleon; he repented having granted permission for departure, and stated before the courtiers "that he had a great mind to send the Crown Prince to finish at Vincennes his studies in the Swedish language." Bernadotte received information of this threat, yet he could not believe that such a design would be attempted to be executed. The attempt, however, was made, but it proved fruitless. It was discovered that a plot had been contrived by a set of foreign desperadoes to carry off the prince from the neighborhood of Haga, and the conspirators had to embark without their prey.

At the same time the Emperor took possession of Swedish Pomerania and the island of Rugen by a division of the army under command of Davoust. Upon this the Prince wrote a temperate but firm letter, requesting an explanation.

I was in Paris at the time when the Emperor received this communication, and know that on perusing it he became frantic, and cried out, "Submit to your degradation, or die with arms in your hands!" No answer being received to his remonstrances, the King of Sweden was under the necessity of breaking entirely with France, and, unable to support a neutrality on the fermentation which ensued after the disastrous campaign of Moscow, joined, as we shall see, the alliance of England and Russia.

As the Crown Prince had remained with me in October, I had the honor of entertaining also the princess, who merely passed through on the 4th December, on her way to join her husband. She remained, however, but a very short time— only two months, I think, in Stockholm: the ancient Scandinavia was not to her taste. I may here, too, just mention, as a proof of Bernadotte's good inclination toward France, in the first place, that war was declared against England one month after his arrival as Crown Prince. In truth it was not till constrained by the Emperor's unjustifiable aggression that the Prince Royal declared to that power and to Russia that war existed between France and Sweden. Upon that occasion Count Löwenghelm, aide-de-camp to the King of Sweden, was the bearer of a letter from the Prince Royal to Alexander which stated "that the occupation of Swedish Pomerania by French troops, and the successive occupation of the shores of the Baltic, by at once violating treaties, and showing that no faith could be put in any for the future, had induced the King of Sweden to send the bearer, who possessed his entire confidence, and would explain his views to the Emperor." The letter concluded with these remarkable words—"In the midst of universal despondency àll eyes are turned upon your imperial majesty —they are already fixed upon you, sire, with the confidence of hope. But permit me to observe to your majesty that in all events there is nothing equal to the magic effect of the first instant; while its influence endures all depends upon him who has the power of acting. Men's spirits, struck with astonishment, become incapable of reflection, and all yield to the impulse of the charm which they fear and by which they are impressed." This letter also replies to reports that had been spread abroad of Russia having sought the alliance of Sweden, while it was the latter who claimed the support of the former power, forced to that step by the unanswerable law of necessity. When, for the first time, the fortune of Napoleon had failed, he made overtures to Bernadotte after the campaign of Moscow.

To these advances, in the shape of diplomatic notes, the Prince Royal replied in respectful but measured terms: "Expressing the sentiments of attachment with which he had quitted France; that in Sweden he had found this amiable disposition toward the empire common to his subjects; and that friendship had been turned into suspicion and then hostility by the French ambassador at Stockholm, who had assumed the part of a Roman proconsul, forgetting that he had not to dictate to slaves. During twenty years the human race has suffered too much: your glory is at its height; and if your majesty desires the King of Sweden to intimate to the Emperor Alexander the possibility of an arrangement, I answer for that monarch's magnanimity and willingness to concede whatever is equitable, both for your empire and for the north. Should such be your majesty's sentiments, the benedictions of the Continent will rise to heaven in your favor. Sire, one of the happiest moments of my life, since I left France, was that in which I was assured your majesty had not entirely forgotten me. You have only done justice to my sentiments of attachment; they are consecrated by the brilliant achievements of our brotherhood in arms; and, though a Swede by honor, by duty and by religion, never can I forget our beautiful France: yet never will I sacrifice the least of the interests of that country which has adopted me, and bestowed on me confidence unlimited." Such are some of the principal relations which I know to have taken place between Napoleon and the Prince Royal of Sweden, in the interval between the elevation of the latter and the fall of the empire.

But my own sojourn in the north had now drawn to a close; the hour of the Hanse Towns, like that of Venice, had struck. On the 8th December I received a honeyed missive from the minister for foreign affairs that "the Emperor wished to consult me respecting affairs in Germany, where the information I had acquired promised to be useful to the public service—a consideration which would prove my sweetest recompense," and concluding with a high

eulogium on the manner in which I had fulfilled my duties.
On the morrow I was off for Paris.   On arriving at Mayence
I met a courier, who announced that the Hanse Towns were
united to the empire.   So much for the value put upon
my information with regard to them.   I confess Bonaparte
fairly outplayed me here; like Moreau, I broke my nose
against the Tuileries and had no audience.   Only the very
first "Moniteur" I read informed me that my diplomatic
functions had ceased by the union to the empire of six new
departments, with Hamburg as their capital.   However,
I had my revenge.   This new usurpation so far northward
excited still more strongly the growing displeasure of Russia, which soon broke into open hostility, notwithstanding
the whitewashed friendship of the two Emperors.   In short,
the Continental System, destroying every kind of trade
in the ports of the Baltic, reciprocal accusations of bad
faith between her and France united Russia closer to England, and brought on that famous war the fatal issue of
which was so exquisitely characterized by Talleyrand as
"the beginning of the end."

The Emperor, instead of admitting me to an audience,
had given certain directions, as follows, to his minister for
foreign affairs, the commission being faithfully discharged
by M. de Champagny, in one of our first conferences.   "The
Emperor," said that excellent person, "has given me in
charge the order which I now deliver.—'When you see
Bourrienne say I wish him to replenish your coffers with
six millions, to pay for building the new palace of foreign
affairs.'"   Astonished at this brutal demand, I could at first
make no answer: the minister naturally desired to know
what he should say.   I was still silent—he insisted.   "Well,
then, tell him he may go to the devil!"   The minister very
naturally declined having any concern with such a message.
I would give no other reply; and, as I afterward learned
from Duroc, the Duke de Cadore was absolutely constrained
to deliver the laconic one above.   "Well, Champagny,"
said Napoleon, "have you seen Bourrienne?"—"Yes, sire."

—"Did you tell him about the six millions I wish him to re-
fund to you?"—"Yes, sire."—"What was his answer?"—
"Sire, I beg to be excused repeating it."—"What said he?
I desire to know."—"Since your majesty insists, M. de
Bourrienne said, 'That your majesty might go to the
devil!' "—"Ah! ah! he said so, did he?" Upon this,
the Emperor retired into the embrasure of a window, and
there continued for seven or eight minutes quite alone,
biting his thumbs, and doubtless giving free scope to his
projects of vengeance; but, after reflecting, he came forward and spoke to the minister about something else.
Bonaparte, however, continued to cherish the idea of making
me pay; and every time he passed the building remarked to
those present, "Bourrienne must certainly pay for that."

At Paris, of all the wonderful transactions which had
taken place, what chiefly engaged my attention was the
marriage of the Emperor; and whoever places himself in
my situation will conceive the tenor of my reflections when
I thought of my ancient college comrade, beginning life
with views hardly equal to my own, urged on by his fate,
and now son-in-law to the Emperor of Germany. Berthier
had been sent to Vienna to espouse by proxy the new Empress of the French; before him, M. de Laborde, a discreet
man and chamberlain, had been charged with the first overtures for this alliance, while Napoleon was yet uncertain
whether he should throw the imperial handkerchief to
a princess of Saxony, Russia, or Austria. When it was
settled in favor of the court of Vienna, which has given
so many queens to France, and generally with misfortune
for their dowry, the presenting of the Empress Maria
Louisa to French commissioners took place at Braunau.
The ceremonial observed on this occasion is a curious
document when we think of the Exile of St. Helena, and
General Neipperg become *factotum* of the Grandduchess
of Parma and Placenza. As to the divorce, the Pope required that all the religious formalities should be observed:
they were so, as also all the canons of the church, which

occasioned a delay of several months. The procedure was terminated, and the sentence rendered by M. de Boislève, grand official of the Archbishop of Paris. It may serve to show how Bonaparte, at this period, respected the laws in his private life, that the considerable sums required for public proceedings were paid—the treasury had its dues, but the private claims of the legal profession were not discharged; only the grand order of Réunion was sent to Boislève, who, ashamed of his honor, concealed it as long as he dared. This order, in fact, never enjoyed any respect in France.

On returning from the last Austrian campaign, Napoleon stopped at Fontainebleau, and Josephine there joined him. For the first time the communication which had previously united his own with his wife's apartments was shut up, by his order. While I lived as one of the household their domestic arrangements had been still more direct—Bonaparte's bedchamber, as the reader knows, having been only an apartment of ceremony. Josephine did not deceive herself as to the fatal forecast to be deduced from this conjugal separation. Duroc, having been sent for one day, found her alone and in tears—"I am undone," said she, in a tone the recollection of which still moved Duroc; "I am undone! all is now over with me! How shall I hide my shame? You, Duroc, you have always been my friend—you and Rapp: neither of you has advised him to separate from me; my enemies have done this—Savary, Junot, and others: alas! they are still more his enemies than mine. And my poor Eugene! what will become of him when he knows I am repudiated by an ingrate? Yes, Duroc; ungrateful he is. My God! my God! what shall we do?" Josephine sobbed convulsively while speaking thus to Duroc; and I myself witnessed the tears which she still wept over the separation.

Before the singular demand of M. de Champagny, I had requested Duroc to ask the Emperor why he would not see me. The grand marshal of the household faithfully delivered my commission; but all the answer returned was in these ironical words—"Ah, truly, have I nothing else to do than give an audience to Bourrienne? that would set all Paris a-buzzing. At Hamburg he always took the part of the emigrants. He would speak to me of former times; he is for Josephine! My wife is near being brought to bed, Duroc. I shall have a son, I am certain of it!—Bourrienne is now antiquated; since his departure I have made grand strides. I don't wish to see him; besides, it would be useless. He is a grumbler; he is so by character; and besides, you know, my good Duroc, I love him not!"

My position at Paris had thus become one of extreme delicacy; this refusal of the Emperor to see me cast something questionable over my relations with society, and at first I hesitated before visiting Josephine. Rapp, too, much to my sorrow, was absent; he had played some slight part in the ceremonial of the nuptials; but, having ventured some remarks on the Faubourg St. Germain, of which this marriage was conceived to have made the conquest, he had been ordered off to his governorship of Dantzic. Duroc, however, having assured me that Napoleon would not take such a visit amiss, I wrote the Empress, requesting leave to pay my respects. Josephine's reply arrived the same day, and on the next I repaired to Malmaison. Alas! under what circumstances and with what recollections did I now revisit this retreat. How many sweet and bitter remembrances crowded upon my mind while passing through the veranda in front to the small circular drawing-room, where I found Josephine walking with her daughter Hortense. On entering, Josephine held out her hand to me, pronouncing only these words, "Well, my friend!" But the tone was one of such profound emotion that, to this moment, the sounds vibrate upon my heart: tears prevented her saying more. Seating herself on an ottoman, placed on the left of the fire, she motioned me to take my seat beside her; while Hortense remained still standing, leaning against the mantelpiece, and vainly endeavoring to hide her tears.

Josephine had taken one of my hands, which she held

pressed between both her own, and for a long time wept in
silence, unable to utter a single word; at length, recovering
a little command over her feelings, she said, "My good
Bourrienne, I have suffered the full extent of my misfortune. He has cast me off—abandoned me: the empty title
of Empress conferred by *him* has only rendered my disgrace
the more public. Ah! how truly did we estimate him! I
never deluded myself as to my fate; for whom would he
not sacrifice to his ambition?" At this moment one of the
ladies attendant on Queen Hortense entered, announcing a
visitor to her royal mistress, who remained a few moments
longer, to recover from the effects of the distress under
which she was too visibly laboring, and then left us alone
—a situation alike desired by both; for Josephine sought
relief in disclosing her sorrows, and I longed to hear from
her own lips the story of her misfortunes and tribulations.
Women throw a touching charm into the recital even of
their griefs.

Josephine confirmed what I had learned from Duroc
respecting the shutting up of the communication between
the two sleeping apartments in the palace of Fontainebleau;
then, coming to the period when Bonaparte disclosed to her
the necessity of a separation, she thus continued: "You, my
good Bourrienne, were for years a witness of what passed
between us—you saw all, knew all, heard all; you are aware
that I never had a secret from you, but confided to you my
sad forebodings. He accomplished his resolution, too, with
a cruelty of which you can form no idea. I have now played
to its end my part of wife in this world. I have endured all
—and am resigned." At these words one of those melancholy smiles wandered across Josephine's countenance which
tell only of woman's suffering, and are so inexpressibly affecting.—"In what self-constraint did I pass that season in
which, though no longer his wife, I was obliged to appear
so to all eyes! what looks, my friend, are those which courtiers allow to fall upon a divorced wife! In what stupor,
in what uncertainty, more cruel than death, did I live, from

that period to the fatal day in which he avowed to me the thoughts I had so long read in his countenance: it was the 80th of November. What an expression he wore on that day; and how many sinister things appeared in his looks! We dined together as usual; I struggled with my tears, which, despite of every effort, overflowed from my eyes. I uttered not a single word during that sorrowful meal, and he broke silence but once to ask one of the attendants about the weather. My sunshine I saw had passed away; the storm was coming—and it burst quickly. Immediately after coffee, Bonaparte dismissed every one, and I remained alone with him. What an expression, Bourrienne! what a look he had! I watched in the alterations of his features the struggle which was in his soul; but at length I saw that my hour had come. His whole frame trembled; and I felt a shuddering horror come over mine. He approached; took my hand; placed it on his heart; gazed upon me for a moment without speaking; then at last let fall these dreadful' words—'Josephine! my excellent Josephine! thou knowest if I have loved thee! To thee—to thee alone do I owe the only moments of happiness which I have enjoyed in this world. Josephine! my destiny overmasters my will. My dearest affections must be silent before the interests of France.'—'Say no more,' I had still strength sufficient to reply; 'I was prepared for this; I understand you; but the blow is not the less mortal.' More I could not utter," pursued Josephine; "I cannot tell what passed within me; I believe my screams were loud: I thought reason had fled; I remained unconscious of everything; and, on returning to my senses, found I had been carried to my chamber. Your friend, Corvisart, will tell you better than I can what afterward occurred; for on recovering I perceived that he and my poor daughter were with me. Bonaparte returned to visit me in the evening. No, Bourrienne, you cannot imagine the horror with which the sight of him at that moment inspired me; even the interest which he affected to take in my sufferings seemed to me additional cruelty. Oh! my

God! how justly had I reason to dread ever becoming
an Empress!"

I sincerely pitied Josephine, yet knew not what consolation to give. Of all I said to alleviate her sorrows that to
which she seemed most alive was the public reprobation
pronounced against Bonaparte's proceedings in the divorce.
Here I told her nothing but the truth. Josephine was universally beloved; it had become a popular belief that the
good fortune of Napoleon depended upon her presence; and
it must be confessed that events subsequent to his illustrious alliance were of a nature to encourage this superstition. I recollect, also, while at Hamburg, that correspondence reached me from various quarters, showing that a
vague feeling—an anticipation undefined, yet generally
prevalent, beheld a source of misfortune for France in
the alliance of her chief with the House of Austria: this
union gave rise to comparisons with the fate of Marie Antoinette; and, as there wants only an unexpected occurrence
to give consistency and weight to a current prejudice, the fire
which happened at a ball given by Prince Schwartzenberg,
the Austrian envoy at Paris, was pronounced to be a coun-
terpart of the accidents which occurred on the marriage of
the Dauphin of France with the aunt of Maria Louisa.

I had left my family at Hamburg, where they continued
during the winter of 1810–11. Davoust had succeeded to
the military command of the new departments. Misery
attained its height, for Dupas was regretted. One of the
prince-marshal's first acts on arriving was to assemble the
officers and instruct them to play the spy in private houses.
Some were indignant, and advised Madame de Bourrienne
to remain on her guard. But Davoust never forgave my
free opinion of his abilities expressed to Bonaparte. Soon
after my arrival in Paris, in the commencement of 1811, I
received intelligence from an excellent friend in Hamburg
that I would soon get a letter intended to compromise me,
Talleyrand, and Rapp. This information I laid before the
Duke de Rovigo. Three weeks had passed and no letter

came. Savary was inclined to believe the alarm a false one; but in a few days the letter did arrive. To what a degree of infamy may not men descend! The letter was written by one whom I had known in Hamburg, whom I had obliged, and to whom I had given bread by employing him as a spy. After a long account of an infamous transaction in which he affirmed he had been engaged, managing it for me, Talleyrand and Rapp in England, he desired 60,000 francs to be remitted by return of courier as payment for this affair. Happily this precious document contained its own confutation. The transaction was laid in 1802, when I was not only not plenipotentiary, but still secretary to the First Consul. I copied and carried this document to Rovigo. The duke went immediately to the Emperor. Scarcely had he entered when the latter, advancing, said, "Well, I learn fine doings of your Bourrienne, whom you are always defending!" Whence, the reader will ask, arose this apostrophe? from the simplest of all causes—a copy of the letter had been forwarded by the same post to the Emperor. Rovigo explained, and produced the documents. "What baseness, what horror!" exclaimed Napoleon: "Let the rascally writer be arrested and sent hither." The order was promptly executed. What was the result? No sooner had the prisoner arrived than he was examined. His confession declared that the missive in question had been written by order and at the dictation of Marshal Davoust, and that he himself had received a small sum of money as secretary's salary in the business. It came out further that the said letter, on being put into the post-office, had been designated by the marshal to the director of the "black cabinet" as one to be opened, copied, resealed and forwarded to its original address, and the copy transmitted to the Emperor! The miserable scribe was banished to Marseilles, or to the Island of Hières, I forget which; but the grand criminal, who contrived and directed the whole, continued, as if nothing had happened, marshal of France, prince of the empire and governor-general of the circle of the Hanse Towns.

Such was the distributive justice awarded to the subjects of the empire.

Savary, Duke of Rovigo, had replaced, as minister of police, Fouché, Duke of Otranto. It had by this time been discovered that my opinion of the latter was well founded; and when the former, as new minister, came to investigate the arcana of polices, counter-polices, systems of observation and hierarchies of spying, he discovered that all these were but so many scarecrows set up to frighten the Emperor. Verily Fouché had acted much in the same way as gardeners do who place effigies in their cherry-trees to scare the sparrows and get all the fruit for themselves. Thanks to such artifices, the eagle had looked upon these with the same terror as the sparrow. But at length, the Emperor having detected a correspondence which Fouché carried on with England through the agency of Ouvrard, he dismissed the minister with fewer palliations certainly than during the consulate, but still with a good deal of management. As to Ouvrard, he was arrested, and this was the last arrest effected by Savary in his subordinate capacity; for immediately after the Emperor, sending for him to St. Cloud, placed in his hands the portfolio of general police. If, in these circumstances, Savary had known Fouché as I did, he would not have committed the egregious blunder of allowing him to remain for fifteen days afterward in quiet possession of the hotel of the police. This space Fouché employed in burning all his really useful papers, instead of arranging them as he had pretended; so that, after his *classification* of documents, Savary found himself utterly without guides, save such as his predecessor chose to leave him, and to which it would have been extremely silly to have yielded implicit confidence. Fouché concealed all the names of those heroes of his system whom he honored with the name of *observers*, and revealed only his *spies*. The former played their part in the gilded drawing-rooms in the houses of ambassadors, and contrived to have a periodical infirmity toward strong waters at all times when the great personages of diplomacy found the said waters necessary to set the stomach to rights. Thus Savary got acquainted with only the populace of Fouché's subterranean subjects; and it must be acknowledged that the spies of Rovigo were far inferior as genteel company to the myrmidons of him of Otranto. But the absence of such gentlemen was far more desirable than their best politeness; and, though I will not venture to say that they were entirely banished from the saloon, they were, at least, far more rare under Savary, who simplified the whole system and afforded something like a very respectable liberty. It is but justice to explain that though he endeavored to simplify the machinery of his administration and insensibly to diminish everything most vexatious therein, he was not always the master; and I here avow that, not without much impatience, I have seen in his "Memoirs" a voluntary assumption of responsibility in several instances when a single word would have consigned the obnoxious facts to their true author.

I continued in Paris to the month of May before returning to Germany for my family: during this period the war in Spain and Portugal occupied all minds. The year 1811 had commenced under auspices sufficiently favorable to the French arms. On New Year's Day, Suchet had carried Tortosa; and, almost at the same time, we obtained important advantages in Portugal, where Oporto and Olivenza were taken by Girard. We gained also some other advantages, as the capture of Pardaleras and the battle of Gebora, fought by the Duke of Dalmatia. But in the beginning of March fortune changed. The Duke of Belluno, notwithstanding the valor of his troops, could not fix her inconstancy in the contest of Chiclana; and from that hour the French could effect nothing against the Anglo-Portuguese army. Masséna himself was no longer the beloved child of victory, as under the walls of Vienna and in the mountain defiles of Zurich. The combined forces increased, and ours diminished daily. Nothing was spared by England to insure success in the struggle. She lavished gold; her army paid well in return for everything; and our troops, in order not to throw the inhabitants into the enemy's party, paid also for their provisions, though far from possessing the same resources. But all would not do; numerous partial insurrections broke out in different provinces, which rendered communications with France extremely difficult, and armed bands cut off our straggling and dispersed soldiers wherever they were to be found. England encouraged and supported this spirit; for otherwise the idea is not to be entertained for a moment that Portugal could, for one day, have held out against France. But combat, a deadly season, privations and misery had thinned the French ranks, and repose had become doubly necessary where exertion had ceased to be followed by results. Masséna was recalled; for the state of his health had rendered him physically incapable of the activity necessary for restoring the army to a respectable attitude. In this state of things Napoleon sent Bertrand into Illyria instead of Marmont, who then assumed Masséna's command in Portugal. The army he found in a woful state of destitution and disorder; yet, by good and prudent measures, Marmont re-established affairs, and in a short time placed himself at the head of thirty thousand well appointed infantry with forty pieces of artillery; though he could assemble but few horsemen and these badly mounted. Matters were not greatly different in Spain; at first, success was ours throughout, but so dearly purchased that the issue of the struggle might then almost have been predicted. When a people fight for their independence, every day, every hour, every death diminishes the assailants, but swells and inspirits the ranks of the patriots. A regiment destroyed is replaced with difficulty and delay, while a village burned, among an energetic population, arms the inhabitants of a whole province. In vain did Soult and Suchet cover themselves with glory; that glory, dyed in Spanish gore, was rendered fruitless. Resistance had become to all Spaniards a holy duty; and the assembling of the Cortes in the Isle of Léon gave consistency to their efforts. On this subject I remember a remark of Alfieri, written fifteen years before the present war. That author, throwing a retrospect over the different nations of the Continent, says—"I behold in the Spaniards the only nation which yet possesses sufficient energy to combat foreign rule." Certainly, if I had been then with Napoleon, I would have ventured an honest artifice, which had often proved successful, by laying the book upon his desk, open at the passage. Sometimes, indeed, he paid no attention to the volume, but most usually the passage I had selected caught his eye and provoked a discussion on the analogous thoughts then dominant in his spirit.

Throughout the summer there occurred nothing very decisive in the Peninsula. Sometimes success, most dearly bought; sometimes defeat; always blood—never results. Some brilliant affairs still bore witness to the bravery of our troops and the talents of our generals. Such were the battle of Albufera and the taking of Tarragona by Suchet, while Wellington was forced to raise the siege of Badajos. These advantages were productive only of glory, though flattering to Napoleon's hopes of finally triumphing in the Peninsula. But doubts began to prevail even at Paris; for it was pretty well known that the official intelligence was not all gospel. Duroc even confessed his illusions had fled! He said, "Good news from the Peninsula were little less to be dreaded than bad." At the same time he assured me that more than once the Emperor had expressed regret at seeing himself engaged in the war; but, because the English had taken part in it, no consideration could induce him to withdraw from the contest.

One of my old friends whom I met at Paris was Murat. He had come to offer his congratulations on the expected increase of the imperial family, and the news of his presence in the capital had not reached me, when, one morning about nine o'clock, while passing along one of the alleys in the Champs-Elysées, he accosted me before I recognized him. He was alone and dressed in a long blue overcoat. We were exactly opposite the palace of his sister-in-law, the Princess Borghese. "Hollo, Bourrienne! my good fellow, how are you?" said Joachim, for we had been on the best understanding; and he, to do him justice, never played the king, save with his attendants and those who had known him only as a sovereign. After exchange of greeting he asked, "But do tell me what are you about now?" I recounted how I had been tricked by Bonaparte in reference to Hamburg. Imagination still portrays the noble and animated countenance of the King of Naples, when, on my accosting him with sire and majesty, he replied, with indignant frankness, "Pshaw! my dear Bourrienne, prithee, no more of that; are we not always old comrades?" Then continuing, almost in the same tone, "So the Emperor has been unjust toward you! and to whom is he not unjust? His displeasure is more to be valued than his favor, so dearly does he make one pay for the latter! He says he made us kings! but did we not make him Emperor? Look you, my friend, to you, whom I have long known, I can repeat my confession of faith: my sword, my blood, my life, are the Emperor's; let him but say the word, I am in the field to combat his or the enemies of France: there I am no longer a king; I become, as of old, a marshal of the empire; but let him not urge me beyond this. At Naples I will be King of Naples, and pretend not to sacrifice to his false calculations the life, the wellbeing, the interests of my subjects. And let him not think to treat me as he treated Louis! for I am ready, if needs must, to defend against himself the rights of the people whom he called me to govern. Am I then only a vanguard king?" This last phrase seemed peculiarly appropriate in the mouth of him whose fiery valor had ever placed him in the van of our armies, to whom, in fact, had always been confided the command of the advance, and very happily expressed the situation of the soldier and the monarch.

During even this our first conversation he did not conceal from me that the greatest of his grievances arose from the Emperor's having promoted him and afterward deserted

him. "When I arrived at Naples," resumed he, "I was
told they intended to assassinate me. How did I act? I
made my entrance into Naples alone, in broad day, in an
open carriage, and would have preferred being assassinated
the first hour to living in constant apprehension of such
a fate. I immediately undertook an expedition against
Ischia. It was successful; I attempted another against
Sicily, and should also have succeeded, I am certain, had
the Emperor, according to promise, sent round the Toulon
fleet to second my operations: but he issued contrary orders:
he wished to play Mazarin to my adventurous Duke of
Guise. At present, I clearly see his aim. Since he has got
a son, on whom he has conferred the title of King of Rome,
he contemplates making the crown of Naples a temporary
deposit on my head. He looks upon Naples only as a
country to be annexed to the kingdom of Rome, in which
I perceive it to be his intention to engulf the whole of Italy;
but let him not drive me to extremities, for I will mar the
scheme or perish sword in hand." Murat was right in his
anticipations, but I had the prudence not to tell him so. It
was the Continental System, however, not these apprehensions, which wrought the final schism—which separated the
cause of Murat from the Emperor's, and constrained the King
of Naples to seek allies among princes at war with France.

About a week previous to this interview the long-
cherished wish of Napoleon's ambition had been fulfilled.
He had a son of his own, an heir of his name, of his power,
and of his crown. Here I must state, because true, that the
reports then spread abroad respecting the birth of the King
of Rome were utterly false and without foundation. My
friend Corvisart, who never for an instant quitted Maria
Louisa during her long and painful labor, left me in no
doubt on this subject, and it is just as true that the young
prince who was held over the baptismal font by the Emperor
of Austria was the son of Napoleon and Maria Louisa, as it
was false that Napoleon was the father of Hortense's eldest
son. It is also a fact, for my sensibilities, torn as they then

were, cannot render me unjust, that the birth of this infant
heir to the imperial throne was hailed with universal enthusiasm.   Never had child beheld the light under circumstances promising greater glory.   In fact, from the birth
of his son to the first of his reverses beyond the Moskwa,
the Emperor was in the zenith of his power.   The empire,
exclusive of the ill-assured throne of Spain, contained fifty-
seven millions of inhabitants.

In the meantime, the venerable old man whose capital
(the ancient abode of the Cæsars) had been deeded to an
infant successor, remained still at Savona, where he lived
in the greatest simplicity.   No agreement had been brought
about.   It has even been certified to me on the best authority that the million offered by Napoleon to the Pope for
his expenses was refused.   To conceal this refusal the money
was regularly sent, and Cæsar Berthier, who had charge of
the household, took care that the sum uniformly disappeared
in the management of an establishment for the Pope which
had been forced on his Holiness.   Truly the thunders of the
Vatican were not much dreaded at this time; nevertheless,
precautions were multiplied to lay asleep remembrance of
the excommunication.   But this was in vain, and the Pope
began to have a party.   The dissensions between the throne
and the Church produced a vague uneasiness, to which,
though not dangerous, it was desirable to put an end.
Napoleon deputed the archbishops of Nantes, Bourges,
Treves, and Tours to make some compromise, and they
also failed.   A second deputation was not more successful;
for the Pope would listen to nothing short of restoration
to Rome, with all his spiritual and temporal rights.   Such
restitution lay entirely beyond Napoleon's ideas of concession.   That Cardinal Fesch even had joined the Pope's party
is a fact which I can guarantee, but not so the following
anecdote, which I only report.   One day the Emperor was
discussing with the Cardinal the subject of the Pope's re-
cusancy; the latter made some remarks which put the former
in a passion, and calling both his uncle and the Holy Father

two old fools, he added, "The Pope is an obstinate old fellow and will listen to nothing! No, most assuredly, I shall
not permit his return to Rome!"—"He refuses to remain at
Savona."—"Eh, well! where does he suppose I mean to send
him then?"—"To heaven, most likely," added the Cardinal,
with great coolness.

These discussions continued throughout the whole summer of 1811. At length Napoleon bethought himself of calling a council, which, after the six or seven hundred already
held since the first ages of the church, he imagined might
devise some plan of restoring her to peace. This council
assembled at Paris. The attendance of Italian bishops was
numerous. The great object of dispute lay in the discussion
of the temporalities apart from the spiritual concerns of the
church. To this the Pope would never agree. It was hoped
a council would get on without his Holiness. However well
disposed toward this separation a number of prelates, chiefly
from Italy, might be, the influence of the church was still
too strong in the council, and certain members, both bishops
and archbishops, being convicted of sending secret instructions to Savona, those of Ghent, Troyes, Tournay and
Toulouse were superseded in their sees and confined in the
castle of Vincennes. The Emperor finally resolved to dissolve the council, and, fearing some act against his supreme
authority, caused each member separately to sign a declaration that the propositions relative to resumption by the
Emperor of the temporalities were conformable to the usages
of the church. In these individual declarations the members were unanimous, though when assembled in council
their opinions had been divided on the very points which
they afterward signed, doubtless for the sake of peace.

Subsequently, Napoleon, before setting out for Germany,
in the commencement of 1812, transferred the Pope to Fontainebleau, under the friendly care of Denon, our amiable
fellow-traveller in Egypt. Two motives induced this change
of residence—fear of disturbances in Italy while his Holiness
remained so near, and apprehension that the English in the

Bay of Genoa might make a dash and rescue the venerable captive. There was delicacy, however, in placing near his person one of Denon's accomplishments, character and disposition. "The Pope," I use Denon's own words, "conceived great friendship for me, always addressed me 'my son,' and delighted in conversing on our Egyptian expedition. One day he asked me for my book: as you know all is not quite orthodox therein, and I hesitated; but he insisted. After having finished the perusal the holy father said it had interested him very much, and I endeavored to gloss over the objectionable points relative to the Mosaic account of the creation. 'It is all one, my son,' he repeated on several occasions; 'it is quite the same; all that is extremely curious; in truth, I did not know it before.' Then," pursued Denon, "I thought I might venture to tell his Holiness the cause of my hesitation, and that he had formerly excommunicated both the work and its author. 'Excommunicated thee, my son!' returned the Pope, with the most touching kindness; 'have I excommunicated thee? Truly I am very sorry! I am sure I never intended to do so.'" Denon assured me that he was greatly touched by the virtues and resignation of the Holy Father; who, still, would sooner have become a martyr than yield the temporal sovereignty of Rome.

As the first step in the grand expedition in which he was speedily to be involved, Napoleon, accompanied by Maria Louisa, who expressed a desire to see her father, set out for Dresden on the 9th of May, 1812.

CHAPTER XXIX

Expedition to Moscow—Napoleon's Return—Battle of Leipsic—Napoleon's
Fallacious Financing—Strength of the European Coalition

FROM the month of March, 1811, suspicions of an approaching war with Russia began to be entertained, and in October, on returning from an excursion to Holland, upon which he had set out soon after the birth of the King of Rome, Napoleon perceived that such a rupture had become inevitable. In vain he sent Lauriston as ambassador, to replace Caulaincourt, who would no longer remain at St. Petersburg. Nothing could be done with a cabinet whose measures were already decided upon. These measures, too, had been greatly assisted by the information conveyed from time to time by Czernischeff, aide-de-camp to the Emperor Alexander, who, on various pretexts for carrying compliments from and answers to his master, contrived to be almost continually on the road between Paris and St. Petersburg; so that in the space of four years it was calculated he thus travelled thirty thousand miles, and, during all that time, had been engaged in the deepest mysteries of spying. His object, indeed, was not unknown. The Emperor treated him with all apparent confidence; and the police, under Savary, underplotted him to a considerable extent, by doubly corrupted informers; but in the month of April, 1812, it became too evident that he had obtained real and valuable information, from one Michel, a functionary in the war office. This unfortunate wretch was condemned to death. The motives which moved the Russians to war were numerous, but all springing from one grand source—the ambitious aggressions of Bonaparte, in adding to his empire state after state, to the very borders of Russia. The Hanse Towns, and the right bank of the Elbe, formed into imperial departments, we have seen, awakened into active resolution this slumbering jealousy. The seizure of Oldenburg, belonging to Alexander's brother-in-law, the invasion of Pomerania, and the operations in Poland, followed the conviction, or tended to enforce it, that if Russia wished to prevent the mighty wave, thus rolling on northward over Europe, from overwhelming her own estates, she must meet and repel it with an armed bulwark.

Napoleon, on his part, prepared for the gigantic enterprise on a scale so immense that the conquest of the world might well have seemed in prospect. From the month of March, 1811, the Emperor held at his disposal almost the entire military force of Europe. It was astonishing to behold the union of nations, languages, manners, religions, and diverse interests, ready to fight for a single individual against a power which had done them no injury. This vast expedition, the greatest conceived by the genius of man since the age of Alexander's conquest of India, fixed all attention, absorbed all minds, and transcended the calculations of reason. Toward the Niemen, as if that river had become the sole centre of all action, men, horses, carriages, provisions, baggage of every description, were directed from all points of the European continent. The army of Napoleon was not composed solely of French, nor of those troops drawn from countries subjected to her immediate influence, as Spain, Italy, Switzerland, and the Confederation. Neither Prussia nor Austria possessed the courage, or rather could claim the power, of remaining neutral; the former supplied a contingent of fifteen thousand men, under General Yorck, and Austria an army of thirty thousand troops, commanded by Prince Schwartzenberg, who nevertheless retained his station of ambassador to the French imperial court, or rather headquarters. As if victory had been already secure, Napoleon, on this occasion, for the first time, included among his own preparations for the campaign some of those splendid articles which had served to decorate his coronation, and which were now intended to swell the pomp of a triumphal entry into the most ancient capital of Muscovy. What afterward became of these is well known: the imperial carriage, used at the coronation, became the object of a speculation in London. But in his military and diplomatic arrangements there was no trifling. Before departing, Napoleon, having removed all the disposable force of the empire, issued a senatorial decree for calling out the national guards, divided into three *bans*. The national guard!—a civil militia, the bare convocation of which was a solecism in his absolute government.

So early as February, 1812, a treaty of alliance, offensive and defensive, had been concluded with Prussia, in virtue of which each of the contracting powers guaranteed recipro-

cally the integrity of their estates, and by implication those
of Turkey, then at war with Russia; a similar treaty was
concluded with Austria, toward the end of the same month;
and the confederation was renewed between France and
Switzerland.

But, while public attention, the hopes and wishes of all
our generals, and the fears of all wise men, were directed
toward Russia, the war in Spain was suffered to languish or
become daily more unfortunate. Officers most distinguished
in the art of war regarded it as a disgrace to be sent to or
retained in the Peninsula. No great foresight, therefore,
was required to predict the period when our soldiers would
be forced to repass the Pyrenees. The enemy had everywhere assumed the offensive: he had sixty thousand men,
while we had scarcely one-half of that number; further, our
troops were scattered, separated into small divisions, and
obeying different impulses; for, though Joseph had returned
to Madrid, not one of our generals considered himself as
under his orders. The enemy was abundantly supplied with
provisions, while we, objects of national hate, were in want
of everything, our soldiers having no other resource but pillage, which necessarily exasperated their difficulties for the
future. Already had Ciudad Rodrigo and Badajos fallen
into the hands of the English. I can assert, also, that however truth might sometimes be concealed from the Emperor,
the disastrous situation of Spanish affairs was fully laid before him, in the spring of 1812, previous to his departure
for Dresden. The period of his abode in that capital has
frequently been assumed as the era of Napoleon's greatest
glory: not so; but it was certainly the most imposing exhibition of the imperial splendor. In the Saxon palace, indeed, was a *hall of kings*, as at the Tuileries a hall *of princes
and marshals*. But to any one who would scrutinize the sentiments which had thus transformed monarchs into the courtiers of a soldier of the French Republic, it appeared evident
that what this assemblage possessed in brilliancy it wanted
in solidity.

From Dresden the Empress returned to Paris, while the Emperor speeded forward to Smolensk. But, before commencing his grand operations on the Niemen and the Volga, he took Dantzic on his way.

From Dantzic the Emperor led his army forward to Smolensk, crossing the Niemen on the 24th of June. But into the details of a campaign known to all the world I, as usual, enter not, especially as the reader can here be referred to the excellent work of Count de Ségur. The first affair of importance, Smolensk, had not all the success expected. Napoleon accused Junot of not having cut off the retreat of the enemy by intercepting their retreat beyond the river, after the Russian legions had been beaten under the walls of the city. This error, however, allowing it to be one, could have but little influence on the result of the campaign. Still victory was ours; but, at the same time, we lost the battle of Salamanca, and Wellington entered Madrid.

The character of Bonaparte presents the most inexplicable contrasts; though the most obstinate of mortals, no man ever more easily allowed himself to be led away by the charm of illusions; in many respects to desire and to believe were with him one and the same act. And never had he been more under the empire of illusion than during the early part of the campaign of Moscow. The easy progress of his troops, the burning of towns and villages on their approach, ought to have prepared him for a Parthian warfare, where retreat, drawing him into the heart of the country, was only preparatory to rendering the advance more fearful. All wise men, too, before those disasters which marked the most terrible of retreats recorded in history, were unanimous as to the propriety of spending the winter of 1812-13 in Poland—there to establish, though only provisionally, a grand nursery for the mighty enterprise of the following spring. But the illusions of an impatient ambition urged him on, and his ear was deaf to every other sound save "Forward!" Another illusion, justified perhaps by the past, was the belief that Alexander, the moment that he should behold the van of the French columns on the Russian territory, would propose conditions of peace. At length the burning of Moscow revealed to Napoleon that it was a war to the death; and he who had been hitherto accustomed to receive propositions from vanquished enemies, now for the first time found his own rejected. The Emperor Alexander would not even hear of negotiations. The prolonged stay at Moscow cannot be explained on any other supposition than a delusive hope that the Russian cabinet would alter its resolution and treat for peace. As to the regulations, dictated from the ancient capital of Muscovy, touching the Comic Theatre of Paris, these were just a petty contrivance of his policy, in order to put a deception upon the Parisians and make them believe all was going well, since he had leisure for such matters; and this persuasion, circulated by the leaders of public opinion, tended marvellously to support the fictions of his bulletins. These, though false in so many respects, were looked for with the utmost anxiety. How many were the wives and mothers in France who could not, without a palpitating heart, break the cover of the "Moniteur"! How many were the families who, in that series of calamities, lost their support and their hope! Never were more tears shed; in vain did the cannon of the Invalids thunder forth the announcement of a victory;—how many thousands, in the silence of retirement, were preparing the external symbols of mourning! It will yet be remembered that, for a long space of six months, the black dresses of Paris presented a very striking sight throughout every part of the city. Fate had declared against Napoleon; and, after he had taken a too tardy and vainly prolonged leave of a capital in ashes, the rigor of the climate showed itself of one accord with the Russians for the destruction of the most formidable army that had ever yielded obedience to a single chief. To find in history a catastrophe comparable to the disaster of the Beresina we must go back to the destruction of the legions of Varus.

Napoleon, setting out precipitately for Paris, intrusted the broken remains of his army to the most experienced of his generals—to Murat, who had so bravely commanded the cavalry, but who forsook his post to return to Naples; to Ney, the hero, rather than prince, of Moskwa, whose name will be immortal in the records of glory and his death an everlasting disgrace to the vengeance of party. Eugene, more than any other leader, was enabled to preserve some degree of discipline among the Italians in the midst of the universal rout; and it was remarked that these children of the south endured the frozen horrors of this campaign better than the soldiers of less genial climes: as if nature, in their constitution, had tempered one extreme by the opposite.

The return of Napoleon in nothing resembled former triumphal entries into his capital; and it was remarked that the very first great reverse he had experienced attended on his first enterprise after the marriage with Maria Louisa; then, more than ever, did the belief become popular that Josephine's presence had brought him good fortune. Superstitious as he was in some respects, I will not swear that he himself, at the bottom of his heart, did not participate in this persuasion.

From this date Napoleon began to pay regard no longer even to the forms of legal proceedings in the acts of his government. He gave himself at once to arbitrary measures, thinking the serious position in which he stood would justify everything. Nor can it be denied, while we unreservedly condemn this conduct, that his necessities were great and that he impressed an almost incredible activity upon every means of repairing losses and bringing back victory to his standard. All advanced together; a new artillery was created; men were called forth in masses; the greatest sacrifices were required, or, to speak properly, enforced by the still magic power of Napoleon: the eye of the Emperor was everywhere. He was obeyed; but what complaints throughout the whole extent of the empire! Young men who had already satisfied the exigencies of former conscriptions were now torn from their homes. Those who had paid for substitutes to the enormous amount of fifteen thousand francs were called upon to serve near his own person in the guard of honor, an institution now established for the first time. This creation struck a species of terror into the upper ranks of society, against whose members it was particularly directed. In no part of the empire, however, was it more hardly endured than in Holland; but nothing could bend Napoleon. Everywhere he now acted upon the principle that the last man and the last crown were his.

Notwithstanding this activity, the disasters of the Russian campaign were daily pressing heavy on his cause. Prussia, constrained to play one part, now resolved to act in her own interest; and General Yorck, who commanded the Prussian contingent which had been attached to the corps of Macdonald, went over to the Russians. I dare not trust myself to characterize the conduct of the king on this occasion, who, though in his heart approving this defection, yet had the general tried and condemned for having acted contrary to his orders, and, in a little time, was seen commanding in person his armies ranged against ours. The moral effect produced by this desertion was far more to be dreaded than its real amount; for in the immense levies that were daily raising a few thousands more or less in the enemies' ranks could be of no consequence. But the signal thus given it was to be feared would be speedily followed by other allies in Germany, and Napoleon foresaw in the event all of misfortune which it foreboded for the future. Assembling a privy council, composed of ministers, officers of state and a few of the great functionaries of the household, he demanded whether in such a conjuncture he ought to make overtures of peace or prepare anew for war? Cambacérès and Talleyrand, who, with the president of the senate, had been called to the council, argued in favor of peace—no gracious proposition to the ears of Napoleon, especially after defeat; so they were not heard. But the Duke de Feltré, Clarke, knowing how to touch the sensitive chord in the soul of Bonaparte, had the audacity to say that he

would consider the Emperor as dishonored if he consented
to abandon the smallest village which had been united to
the empire by a senatorial decree.   What a fine thing it is
to talk!   This opinion prevailed and the war proceeded.
Nor can I say that the Emperor was blamable in hesitating
to treat at this stage; but I blame him much for having
neglected to do so seriously and in good faith at Dresden
after the victories at Lutzen and Bautzen had proved that
in the retreat from Moscow the climate rather than the
Russians had vanquished us.

Napoleon at length quitted Paris, on the 15th April,
having under his standard a new army of one hundred and
eighty thousand effective men, excluding guards of honor.
With such physical resources and the aid of his own genius,
men rightly foresaw he could yet play a high game, and
might, perhaps, prove the winner.   This reflection was by
no means reassuring to those who had already made movements in opposition, and filled with an especial apprehension
the Hanseatic countries.   Along the line of the Elbe and
in Saxony was the grand theatre of events.   In the former,
insurrectionary and hostile movements had taken place on
a large scale.   Carra St. Cyr had precipitately retreated from
Hamburg, which had been occupied by the Cossacks under
Colonel Tettenborn, and also by the Swedish and Russian
regular forces.   In conjunction with the other towns of the
Hanseatic league, this city, besides the friendly reception
of the enemy, had raised ten thousand men for the service of
the allies.   These troops, by the disorders which they subsequently committed, justly merited their designation of
Cossacks of the Elbe.   St. Cyr being under arrest for this
injudicious and even cowardly retreat, Vandamme took
the command of the forces of this quarter, while Napoleon
marched to the grand theatre of Saxony.   The former,
during the night of the 2d of May, attacked and carried the
islands of the Elbe.   On the 9th the corps of Vandamme
and Davoust formed a junction, composing a body of forty
thousand men, on their way to the grand army.   Though

Napoleon, urged by strong necessity, desired the speedy arrival of this reinforcement, he gave orders to the Prince of Eckmuhl not to leave Hamburg in the rear, cost what it might. After a siege of twenty days the Prussian, Swedish and Russian garrisons evacuated the place, and, after seventy days of independence, Hamburg was again united to the empire. Vandamme made the inhabitants pay for this brief enjoyment of their privileges. Of this general the Emperor said at Dresden, "Were I to lose Vandamme, I know not what I would give to have him restored; but, if I had two, I should be obliged to shoot one of them." One, indeed, was quite enough in all conscience: his principle in the conquered countries was, "We must first begin by shooting a few rascals, which prevents the trouble of future explanation."

In the meantime had been fought, on the 2d of May, the battle of Lutzen, at the close of which, both parties claiming the victory, "Te Deum" was chanted in either camp. The subsequent motions of the two armies and the advance of Napoleon inclined opinion to his side. His was in reality the advantage on a field illustrious two hundred years before as the scene of the triumph and death of Gustavus Adolphus. Eight days afterward the Emperor was in Dresden; not as in the spring of last year, like the sovereign of western Europe, surrounded by his grand vassals; yet still counting on fortune. He remained ten days in the beautiful capital of the sole king, of all those whom he had created, that continued faithful to the declining star of his benefactor, and whose honorable adherence to his word subsequently cost him half his kingdom. Departing from Dresden, the Emperor set out in pursuit of the Russian army, which he encountered on the 18th at Bautzen. This battle, followed on the morrow and the next day by those of Wurtchen and Ochkirchen, continued during three consecutive days, which speaks sufficiently for the keenness of the contest. Victory declared at length in our favor. But Napoleon, and I may say France, sustained a great loss; for the same cannon ball killed General Kirschner, as he conversed with Duroc, and mortally wounded the latter in the abdomen.

The time was now come for Austria to declare herself, and all her amicable demonstrations were limited to an offer of mediating between the belligerent powers. This brought on the armistice of Plesswitz, and subsequently the congress of Prague. In these conferences the allies demanded the restitution of all they had lost since the campaign of Ulm, in 1805. This left us Belgium, Piedmont, Nice, and Savona. But nothing would induce the Emperor, ill advised as he then was, to recede to such an extent. Yet can we not easily conceive how he could have expected more. Between the 20th June and the 8th July, when the armistice was to cease, arrived news of the battle of Vittoria and the conquest of the whole of Spain by the English. This greatly improved the aspect of affairs in the allied camp, without altering the resolutions of the Emperor. But had he been advised with courage and by men of good sense, the profound grief which that victory caused would have induced him to yield to the necessity of peace.

Toward the end of July, Napoleon made an excursion to Mayence, where the Empress met him for a few days; thence he returned to Dresden, and allowed the armistice to expire on the 17th August. The congress at Prague having thus separated without attaining any result, hostilities recommenced on the 17th, and on the same day—a fatal blow for France—Austria declared against us; the Emperor alleging to his son-in-law that the greater the number of his enemies, the greater was the chance of bringing him sooner to reasonable terms. This addition of two hundred and fifty thousand men to the allied ranks, arrayed against Napoleon upward of a million of combatants.

On the 24th, seven days after the rupture of the conferences, was fought the battle of Dresden: victory remained with Napoleon; but the defeat and capture of Vandamme in Bohemia rendered fruitless the success in Saxony. This conflict will ever be memorable by the death of Moreau.

All the corps of the army which were in action at this time suffered a reverse; yet though constantly talking of fortune, we could not perceive that she was now abandoning our standards. The example once given, even Bavaria deserted, and those troops whom the Emperor had adopted, as it were, on the field of battle—whom he had trained to victory, joined the hostile ranks. The month of October opened with the conflict of Wachau, in which success and disaster were nearly balanced. Soon after the battle of Leipsic, fought on the 14th, 15th, 16th and 17th of October, decided the fate of France, and became the signal of our grand disasters. The Saxon army, the last which had remained faithful to us, went over to the enemy while the battle yet raged—a piece of treason ill rewarded, though so useful to the allies.

This great battle commenced on the 14th October, the anniversary of the famous victories of Ulm and Jena, continued four days, and decided the fate of Europe. During these days of desertion half a million of men engaged together on a surface of three square leagues. From this bloody field Napoleon retreated to Mayence, which he entered, but not without more conflicts, on the 2d of November, and thence to Paris. During this campaign of Dresden the regency of the Empress had given general satisfaction, because she had refused to place her name to sentences of death; but she had signed with great alacrity every pardon which the nature of the crime would permit. These circumstances I learned from the Duke of Rovigo (Savary), who, I must in justice say, of all Napoleon's ministers, then most truly appreciated and most honestly declared the true state of things. I recollect, also, that he solicited permission to join the Emperor at Mayence, during the conferences at Prague, with the intention of urging him to peace, at whatever sacrifice. He entertained the persuasion that he should have succeeded. I partook not in his illusions; but he was not permitted to leave Paris; and besides, as already stated, Napoleon and Maria Louisa passed there only a few days.

When the signal of our final disasters had been heard, the stocks and rate of exchange fell progressively. After the battle of Leipsic, especially, the fall became considerable. I have already said that Napoleon entertained the falsest notions on public credit, and, consequently, was ever terribly alarmed by any depression in the funds. And the admirable plans which he conceived to remedy this! One was to purchase stock in order to keep up the rate. This was a hobby which the most prudent counsels could not persuade him to abandon. But the consequences?—When public affairs suffered a check, down came the funds, and as sellers were always sure to find *one* good buyer, stock to be sold glutted the market. But this play was not enough. He had recourse to trickeries which might be termed even childish—for instance, announcing in the "Moniteur" the course of exchange at 80 when it actually stood at 60. When the crisis had passed, and things had resumed their ordinary direction, an erratum would appear, stating that an 8 had appeared in a former paper instead of a 6. In this illusive play the Emperor expended upward of 60,000,000 francs, which would have been much better employed in purchasing bills in London upon Paris. Bonaparte never could comprehend that the rise or fall of the public funds depends on a proper or improper financial administration; on the good or bad faith of the debtor; on a state of peace or war; and finally, on a judicious or imprudent system of sinking fund. To the Emperor, however, a sinking fund was merely a resource whence he could draw, upon an emergency.

At this time, namely, the autumn of the year 1813, the more the imperial government verged toward decline, a circumstance difficult to explain, the more extensively it multiplied vexatious measures. From the first disasters of the campaign of Moscow it had seemed good, in order to prevent the truth from circulating, to intercept all communications; to cut off all means of giving vent either to grief or friendship; and the order was accordingly issued to seize at the post-office all letters coming from, or destined for, foreign parts. This mode of investigation, however, as Napoleon at St. Helena has well remarked, being stale at Paris, *black cabinets* were established in the conquered countries. They were placed at Ostend, Brussels, Hamburg, Berlin, Milan, and Florence. All that was required was an order from a superior authority for a letter to be seized, and a copy transmitted to the Emperor. This intolerable abuse influenced not a little the fate of the empire. Similar cruel abuses had aided in bringing about the Revolution and the expulsion of the Bourbons, and they assisted in their restoration. At this period, however, Europe, armed against us, had most certainly not yet begun to think of recalling these princes to the throne of France.

The month of November, 1813, was fatal to the fortune of Napoleon; on all hands our armies were driven back and forced to the Rhine. In every direction the allied columns advanced toward that river. The fall of the empire evidently approached; not that the foreign sovereigns had yet resolved upon its destruction, but because it was impossible for Napoleon to contend against all Europe; and I well knew, however desperate the situation of his affairs, he would not consent to a peace falsely regarded as dishonorable. Even before the battle of Leipsic, the loss of which was to Napoleon incalculable, and the consequences ruinous, he had felt the necessity of demanding from France, as if she had been inexhaustible, a fresh levy of two hundred and eighty thousand men. The commission devolved upon the Empress, who, for this purpose, proceeded for the first time to the senate in great state. She succeeded; but the splendor of the empire was on the wane. Hardly were these men enrolled when war devoured them. The defection of the Bavarians had much increased the difficulty of the retreat; for, getting before the wrecks of the army, they had preoccupied Hanau, situated about four leagues from Frankfort, with the design of cutting off our retreat. French valor once more roused its energies; the Bavarians were at-

tacked, defeated with great slaughter, and our army reached
Mayence. But in what a condition, good Heavens! Could
the name of an army be given to some masses of men without resources, discouraged, borne down by fatigue and privations, and, in short, reduced through misery to a kind of
brutishness? At Mentz no preparations had been made for
their reception; these wrecks of soldiers and of themselves
were attacked by contagious maladies; and the horror of
their situation became complete. The disasters even of 1812
and of Moscow had been remedied by the activity of her
chief and the sacrifices of France; but those very sacrifices
had rendered irreparable the misfortunes of Leipsic.

Without including the small remnant which had escaped
from that fatal field and its consequent miseries, and without
counting also the two hundred and eighty thousand whom
Maria Louisa had obtained from the senate, in the month
of October, the Emperor had still one hundred and twenty
thousand veteran troops. These, however, had been left in
the rear, shut up in fortresses—such as Dantzic, Hamburg,
Torgau and Spandau, or scattered along the Elbe. Still,
such was the horror of their situation and of ours, that we
could not resolve to abandon, while it was impossible to
relieve, them. Meanwhile, the allies were advancing on an
immense base of operation, and in one month after the first,
a new levy of three hundred thousand men was demanded
from France. Then only her wounds seemed probed to the
bottom. After the events of Leipsic, which thus lost to
France a second formidable army, all the powers of the
coalition pledged themselves to each other, at Frankfort,
on the 9th of November, never to separate before a general
peace had been established, and to reject all armistices or
negotiations which had not such peace for its object. As
the basis of this peace the allied powers declared that France
should be permitted to retain her natural boundaries of the
Rhine, the Alps and the Pyrenees.

At this deplorable period every day brought new misfortunes—inevitable consequences of the fatal campaign of Mos-

cow. Dresden, still occupied by a French garrison, fell into the power of the allies; and the sentiments of other powers were so far changed toward Frenchmen, before whom they had so often trembled, that it was not scrupled to violate the faith sworn to the garrison of the Saxon capital. Scarcely had the French troops marched beyond the walls when they were disarmed, in the face of an engagement upon which they had surrendered, to allow them to enter France with arms and baggage. Ah! had Napoleon once more resumed the ascendency he would have been excusable in signally avenging this perfidy—this insult offered to misfortune! Holland, at the same time, welcomed with joy the hour of enfranchisement, and the arrival of a Russian corps countenanced a general but almost bloodless insurrection. Such was the love which the countries bore us, and such the happiness we had conferred upon them! But defection was not confined within the limits of the empire: Murat had come to an understanding with the English because otherwise he entertained a well-grounded fear that the throne of Naples would not long be his. Still it presented not one of the least strange of the eventful occurrences of the period to behold Neapolitans, with Murat at their head, swelling the armed million arrayed against Napoleon and France.

In the conflict of difficulties which thus assailed the Emperor he threw his eyes upon M. de Talleyrand, who, unfortunately for France, had been long absent from the affairs of government. But Napoleon having required that he should lay aside the dignity of vice-grand-elector, on becoming foreign minister, Talleyrand preferred one of the first posts in the state to a situation of which caprice might soon deprive him, while it exposed him to many ambitious machinations. Perhaps, too, Talleyrand's perspicacity led him to view the situation of affairs as desperate, and his acceptance as of doubtful good in circumstances so difficult. I have been assured that, viewing things in their source, he proposed, in a conversation with the Emperor, the very extraordinary advice to call into play the ambition of the

English family of the Wellesleys, and to awaken in Wellington's mind, the splendor of whose fame had now begun to shine forth, ambitious views and projects which would have disturbed the coalition. To this scheme Napoleon lent no attention; the issue appeared to him too uncertain, and especially too distant, for the pressing exigencies of the season. Caulaincourt was then called to the administration of foreign affairs, and Maret became home secretary, where he was much better placed. Regnier quitted the portfolio of justice and was succeeded by M. de Mole; and, at the same time, M. de Cossac resigned to Count General Daru the ministry of war.

During these slight changes of his servants the Emperor himself was unceasingly engaged in preparing the means of repelling the attack now directed against him. He created all—superintended all—performed all. Though age might have been thought to have taken from him some of his activity, yet in this crisis I beheld him as in his most vigorous youth. That he might be enabled to direct the full force of his arms against the allies who menaced him on the side of Switzerland, he took a resolution with regard to Spain which might have exercised a decisive influence upon affairs. This was the resignation of the crown, the renunciation of Joseph's rights over that country, and the immediate restoration of Ferdinand to his states. Joseph made this sacrifice at the instance of his brother, but reluctantly, and in a manner which showed how hard it is to quit a throne. The treaty was signed, but executed with inconceivable tardiness, while the torrent advanced upon France so rapidly as to interrupt the execution. Ferdinand indeed recovered his crown, but by causes very different.

The march of the allies occasioned to the Emperor intense anxiety. It was important to destroy the bridge of Basel. The Rhine, easily crossed, would throw the enemy in masses upon France. I had at this time a correspondence with a foreign diplomatist whom I shall be excused naming: this correspondence assured me the bridge would be allowed to remain, and that such agreement had been made with the allies at Berne. This astonished me, since, on our side, I had contrary information. I despatched an emissary on my own private account, being deeply interested in knowing the truth. He returned to tell me that the bridge would be suffered to stand.

On the 19th December the legislative body was convoked. M. Lainé presided under Régnier. The house formed itself into a committee to consider and report upon the communications addressed to it by the Emperor. The majority of the members sensibly felt the deplorable situation of France; they expressed these sentiments in their report. This was not what had been wanted by the Emperor, who desired that they should coincide in his views of resistance: the report was therefore seized, and the house adjourned. This proceeding I have ever regarded as a great error. Had the Emperor and his legislature frankly communicated with each other, the defects of a diplomacy always so artificial and vacillating might have been supplied. Who can doubt that a noble and candid conduct on the part of the legislative body of France, declaring that she accepted the propositions of Frankfort, would have been listened to by the allies? Would they not have preferred an honorable peace to the dangers of invading a great country, defended by an ardent and valorous people? But the remark, "You will be dishonored if the meanest village, united to the empire by a *senatus consultum*, be dismembered," continually sounded in Bonaparte's ear, whose secret wishes it flattered, and rendered him averse from every pacific measure.

Those who attentively observed events will still remember the general stupor which fell upon Paris on learning what had occurred in the legislative assembly. That body, according to custom, waited on the Emperor in order to take leave. He received the *revolters* not over graciously, and dismissed them without hearing any explanation. Afterward he observed concerning them, "The members of the

legislative body come to Paris only to obtain some special
favors.   They importune ministers from morning to night,
and grumble if not instantly satisfied.   Invite them to dinner—they seem bursting with envy at the splendor which
surrounds them.''   These words I had from Cambacérès,
who was present.

CHAPTER XXX

Siege of Hamburg—Defection of Murat—Napoleon Contemplates Joining with
the Jacobins—The Congress of Châtillon

THE reader is already aware that numerous garrisons
had been left in different parts of Germany.   Dresden
had fallen into the power of the enemy by a capitulation which was not respected; for the troops, who had
surrendered on condition of being sent into France with
arms and baggage, had no sooner marched beyond the walls
than they were stripped.   Magdeburg, under Lemarrois,
still held out, and was expected to do so for some time.
Davoust resolved to make Hamburg a similar point of resistance.   Of the extensive foreign correspondence which
I maintained at this time, my information from Hamburg
interested me especially.   During the campaign of 1818 the
allies, having driven the French out of Saxony, and constrained them to march for the Rhine, formed the siege of
Hamburg, wherein Davoust had shut himself with thirty
thousand men, in the resolution of rendering the defence
no less memorable than that of Saragossa, and of delivering
up the post only when the town had become a heap of
ashes.   Such were his own expressions, and, it must be
acknowledged, he displayed much ability in carrying his
resolution into effect, though at a fearful expense of life and
property to the miserable inhabitants.   He began by laying
up vast quantities of provisions.   Generals Dejean and
Haxo, of the artillery, were sent by Napoleon to mark out
the lines of fortification; in the formation of these Davoust

employed fifteen thousand men. At the same time General Bertrand commenced the erection of a bridge uniting Hamburg and Haarburg by joining the islands of the Elbe to the Continent—a distance of six miles. This bridge, constructed of wood taken by force from all the timber yards, was finished in eighty-three days. It presented a magnificent appearance, bestriding a waterway of five thousand and fifty-eight yards, exclusive of communications across the two islands. Many millions would not replace the houses thrown down to complete the fortifications and to uncover the approaches of the enemy. But these defences were upon so extensive a scale that sixty thousand men would have been required for their full occupation. All this was effected at incalculable loss to the inhabitants. From the immense stores heaped up in the place the garrison was plentifully supplied, while provisions in the town were to be obtained with much difficulty, in very small quantities, and at exorbitant prices. All horses, without exception, were seized for the artillery; the best were selected, the others slaughtered in the streets, and the flesh distributed to the soldiers. The inhabitants, pressed by famine, bought the hides at a dear rate. The garrison, composed of French, Italians, and Dutch, upon the evacuation of the place, in May, 1814, was found to be reduced to a moiety, having lost upward of 15,000 men. The process of demolition, in levelling the outer defences, was so complete that even the tombs and vaults were thrown down. Neither the living nor the dead were spared; for, in executing their work of destruction, the soldiers might be seen wrenching off the silver plates from the coffins, and even breaking them up, in order to get at the rich stuffs in which it is there customary to wrap the deceased. In this rage for plunder were braved even the exhalations of putridity, which doubtless aggravated, perhaps had occasioned, the pestilence that broke out at a subsequent period of the siege. To these acts of barbarity succeeded a most strict blockade, formed by the troops of Russia and Sweden, and all external communica-

tion was cut off. The King of Denmark, even, the faithful
ally of Napoleon, found himself constrained to abandon the
garrison to its fate. To this he was forced by the Prince
Royal of Sweden, who, as we have seen, joined, at an early
period, the league of the north. In one of the first sorties
General Vandamme and a considerable number of men were
uselessly sacrificed. In the month of December provisions
began to fail the inhabitants, and all useless mouths were
turned out, under every aggravation of cruelty. On the
18th one of those proclamations of expulsion was issued,
for departure, in forty-eight hours, under pain of destruction of the houses—the commandant of the gendarmerie
having it in charge to inflict on the recusants fifty strokes
of the bastinado before expelling them. But if there are
ways of dealing with Heaven, so are there with the gendarmerie. The bastinado was remitted for a sum of money,
and, in the case of females, French gallantry substituted
scourging! But such is the tie that binds us to our natal
soil that still the wretched inhabitants clung to their hearths,
and a new order of the 25th became necessary, which declared
that, out of compassion, twenty-four hours longer were
granted, after which all found within the city who could
not contribute to the defence should be considered as in
league with the enemy, and consequently liable to be
delivered to the Provost's Court and shot! This was not
enough: lingerers were still found; and, in one of the last
nights of December, all who fell under the proscription,
without distinction of age or sex, sickness or health, were
torn from their beds, and, during an intense frost, taken
outside the walls. By a refinement of cruelty the escort
was composed of citizens. In the course of the night many
aged persons perished. To misfortune the most deadly
insults were added. I have seen—I have read—I do not
invent, an order of the police declaring all female servants
subject to domiciliary visits, unless they had certificates of
health from their masters! All those evils were increased
to an incredible degree of desperation by the avarice and

barbarity of Davoust's favorite agents. One of these, a native of Auxerre, retained a valet whose business it was to carry off by force, or inveigle by fraud, for his master a daily victim from the honorable young females of the place. These are facts so well known that though, for the sake of his family, I do not mention the name of this commissary, when these pages, even at this distant date, are read in Hamburg, every one will repeat that name. Meanwhile filth and putrescence accumulated everywhere: the streets were encumbered with the carcasses of slaughtered horses: the Alster and its lake, poisoned by every species of uncleanness which there was no longer means of transporting beyond the city, sent forth deadly exhalations: as the season advanced, epidemic and febrile complaints were converted into pestilence: from sixty to eighty died daily in the hospitals, of which no care was taken: and, on the bastions, on the ramparts, and in the highways, the dead were flung into trenches rather than buried; so that the living could not make a step without treading on the remains of their relatives or friends. All pecuniary resources being at length exhausted the poor remains of the bank were seized, amounting to about eight millions of marks; and thus, while Hamburg, so lately rich and hospitable, was completely ruined, the shock was extended to distant places. Napoleon had accused Hamburg of Anglomania, and, in ruining it, thought he was ruining England. Through all these persecutions that city had been an unresisting sacrifice. Like Jerusalem—whence, it is said, during the siege by Titus, *the sound of lamentation was heard in the night*—Hamburg could only wail in silence.

Such was the state of the French interest in Germany, where we were expelled from all save a few isolated points, in which crime and useless resistance maintained a sinking cause. In Italy, Eugene commanded, that country having been confided to his care after the campaign of 1812. To the preservation of Italy, Bonaparte attached great importance, both from the recollection of his early fame and its

present value. The actual possession of its rich provinces
would be of great weight in a treaty of peace which might
call for their resignation, while they afforded a strong and
convenient point whence to threaten Austria. The Viceroy
did everything in his power to second the intentions of the
Emperor. But Eugene's army, in reality, differed greatly
from its appearance on the muster-roll. That, indeed, bore
the number of regiments, but, in many instances, the regiments themselves had remained beneath the snows of Russia
or been buried in the plains of Poland. By dint of exertion,
however, and the care taken of his soldiers, he assembled
a corps of fifty thousand men, of whom five thousand were
cavalry. After the failure of negotiations in the shadow of
a congress at Prague, the Viceroy entertaining no doubt
of an approaching attack upon Italy, marched with his
whole disposable force, and took up a position as near as
possible to the Austrian frontier, his headquarters being
at Udine. Until April, 1814, he was enabled to preserve
an imposing attitude and to protect the entrance to the
Italian kingdom with that skill which might have been
expected from one trained in the school of Napoleon, and
ranking among his best generals. Two defections, however,
afflicted the excellent heart and disconcerted the prudent
arrangements of Eugene; namely, those of Murat, his
brother-soldier, and of the King of Bavaria, his father-in-
law. Thus exposed in rear to the Neapolitan army, and in
flank to the Bavarians approaching through the Tyrol, he
commenced a series of retrograde movements in the autumn
of 1813, falling back, first upon the Tagliamento, and subsequently upon the Adige. There he took up a position with
troops considerably diminished by sickness and battles.

Toward the end of November, Eugene understood that
one corps of the Neapolitan troops had seized Rome, another
Ancona, and that the army was on its march for Upper
Italy. The King of Naples wished to turn to his own advantage the situation of Europe, and became the dupe of
offers promised as the reward of his treason. He was here

doubly a traitor; for not only had he entered into a treaty with the enemies of France, but, as nothing certain was yet known respecting his desertion, and flying reports were discredited as impossible, he continued to profess friendship for the Emperor and to receive provisions and stores from Eugene. Such, too, was the confidence at Paris, that the war minister never once thought of refusing those demands; yet, at that very moment, the King of Naples was engaged to join the Austrian troops and to make common cause against the French arms in Italy. Here Murat's conduct became perfidious and inexcusable. To disown his native for his adopted country, when the interests of the latter demanded it, was a measure standing on its own merits and liable to be judged differently, as men's opinions or their feelings differ; but to join perfidiousness to desertion can admit of only one sentiment—that it was at once unmanly and criminal. When first informed of this treachery Napoleon refused to give credence to the fact. "No," exclaimed he to those around him—"No! that cannot be! Murat, to whom I gave my sister! Murat, to whom I have given a crown! Eugene must be deceived. It is not possible that Murat should declare against me!" It was, however, not only possible, but true. At that very moment Miollis, with a handful of men, was blockaded in the castle of St. Angelo, as were also the garrisons of Ancona and Loretto in their respective citadels. The treaty between Austria and Naples was definitely signed on the 11th of January, 1814. Soon after Eugene, mistrusting Murat's conduct, retired behind the Mincio and cantoned his army. Here, on the 8th of February, the Austrian army came up with his position: he engaged and defeated the Austrians, and thus for some time prevented their invasion and junction with the Neapolitan forces. Not till eight days after this conflict did Murat officially declare war against the Emperor by sending in his declaration by his chief of staff to General Vignolles, who held the same situation in the army of Prince Eugene. Immediately all the French officers in the Neapolitan service left the king and went over to Eugene. Murat exerted every effort to retain them, but in vain. "No Frenchman," said they, "who really loves his country, can now remain in your service."—"Do you suppose, then," cried he, "that my heart is less French than yours? Believe, on the contrary, that I am much to be pitied: from the grand army I hear only of disastrous events. I have been forced to make a treaty with the Austrians and an arrangement with the English under Lord Bentinck, in order to save my kingdom from a threatened invasion by the English and Sicilians. Such a disembarkation would infallibly have excited a revolt in the interior: remain then with me."

Immediately on receipt of Joachim's declaration Eugene issued a proclamation to his troops: "Soldiers," said the prince, "my motto is, Honor and Fidelity; let the same be your device: with this in our hearts and God for our aid we shall yet triumph over all our enemies." In the same proclamation he expressed his hopes of a solid and lasting peace; these were not realized: another portion of it, in which he promulgated the imperial decree for the recall of all French officers in the Neapolitan service, had become useless from the voluntary retirement of all whom the regulation concerned; and unfortunately he possessed not the means of fulfilling his promises of victory. The Austro-Neapolitan army obtained advantages which could not be disputed; Leghorn and Ancona were taken, and the French obliged to evacuate Tuscany.

I return to affairs in France at the end of 1813. These presented a spectacle no less afflicting than in Italy. The imperial diadem, like the iron crown, tottered on the head of Napoleon. The treachery of Murat had proved doubly fatal in itself and in its effects upon the mighty combinations in which he had been destined to act an important part. In the gigantic scheme of defence and offence which he now meditated, Bonaparte's intention had been that Eugene and Murat, uniting their forces, should march upon Vienna, through the Tyrol and Carinthia, and thus get to

the rear of the allies and shake Austria to the centre.
Meanwhile he himself, with the soldiers and on the soil
of France, would have multiplied obstacles in the enemy's
front, and might have decided the campaign before their
timid million, measuring every step, had polluted Paris with
their presence. On hearing of this immense project I could
not but recognize the daring spirit which I had known to
meet greater disasters by great resources. The impress of
genius was there, but rendered powerless in the means of
execution. In the campaign of Paris, Napoleon was all himself; again he unfolded that fervid mind which, as in youthful conquests, annihilated time and space and seemed omni-
present in its energies. But the chances of success were no
longer the same: victory, even, if dearly purchased, must
become fatal to him. In France new hopes had sprung up
in the room of those that had been deceived and which had
heralded him to consular power. Now must he have felt in
all its simple honesty the counsel of Josephine—"Bonaparte,
do not, I beseech thee, make thyself king."

Napoleon was still Emperor; but the man who had imposed upon all Europe treaties of peace not less disastrous
than war itself could not now obtain an armistice. His
ambassador, Caulaincourt, commissioned to treat for one,
passed twenty days in idleness at Luneville, without being
received into the allied camp or permitted to pass the advanced guards of the army of invasion. In vain Caulaincourt entreated—supplicated Napoleon to sacrifice, or rather
provisionally to lay aside, a portion of the glory acquired
in so many combats. No concession could be obtained: he
wrote, however, to his minister—"I shall sign whatever you
will. To obtain peace I ask no condition. I shall not dictate my own humiliation." This was equivalent to a prohibition to sign or concede anything. In the course of the first
fifteen days of 1814 one-third of France was invaded and a
new congress proposed at Chatillon upon the Seine. Of the
proceedings I shall speak hereafter; meanwhile, let us consider the last moments of Napoleon's stay at Paris before

setting out for that adventurous campaign of France wherein
he displayed military talent superior even to the reverses
which he experienced, and where these were often balanced
by the fortunate daring of his vast combinations.

Affairs were approaching daily to a crisis. Strongly
pressed by the allies, he was counselled to seek extraordinary resources in the interior of the empire. He was reminded of the fourteen armies which, as if by enchantment,
sprung forth from the soil of France to defend her at the
commencement of the Revolution. In short, he was advised
to throw himself into the arms of a party who still possessed
the power of raising the mass—to join the Jacobins. What
a trial for him who had so often manifested the justifiable
loathing which these inspired! Nevertheless, for a moment
he cherished the idea of adopting this advice. He made the
round, on horseback, of the suburbs of St. Antoine and St.
Marceau; flattered the populace; replied to their acclamations with attentive eagerness, and believed he beheld in these
dispositions something which might be turned to advantage.
On returning to the palace some prudent people took upon
them to make remarks, recommending him to have recourse
rather to the upper classes—to the nobility and select of the
nation. Perceiving thus that several blamed this ridiculous
popularity, he replied—"Gentlemen, you may talk as you
please, but, in my present situation, I find no nobility save
in the rabble of the Faubourgs, nor any rabble save in the
nobility I have made." A happy device this to please
everybody, since, according to Napoleon, all were rabble
together.

At this time the Jacobins were disposed to serve and
to strain every nerve to save him. But they required that
he should leave them alone to act freely, to arouse every
revolutionary passion, to abandon the press to their management and to have sung in the streets and in the theatres
their favorite airs—with other propositions no less extravagant and not less revolting. I do not in this repeat hear-
says, but what I witnessed and heard at two meetings at

which I was present, though certainly by chance, and when
these proposals were brought forward with the more assurance
that success appeared certain. Though years had passed
since the times of my familiar intercourse with Napoleon,
I knew his opinions regarding the Jacobins too well to be
under any apprehension as to the result here. In fact, disgusted by their demands and the price which they put upon
their services, he broke off the correspondence. "It is too
much," he said; "I shall find in battle some chance of
safety, but none with these hare-brained fools," adding
afterward—"There can exist no connection between the
demagogues of 1793 and monarchy; between furious clubs
and a regular ministry; between a Committee of Public
Safety and an Emperor; between revolutionary tribunals
and the reign of law. No! if I must fall, I will not be-
queath France to the Revolution from which I saved her."

Golden words these! And Napoleon followed up a resolution worthy of himself by calling forth a truly national
and more noble instrument to parry the threatening danger. This was the National Guard of Paris, which he
placed under the command of Moncey, a man estimable
in every respect, who had loyally fought under the standard of France, and now, at an advanced age, preserved
the freshness, both mental and bodily, of youth. The Emperor could not have made a worthier choice; but the staff
of the National Guard became a focus for every species of
intrigue, save that which tended to the defence of Paris;
and when the moment came, without seeming to wish the
overthrow of Napoleon, all its members had that overthrow
uppermost in their minds. However that may be, as captain
of the guard, I was convoked with my brother officers to
meet the Emperor in the Tuileries on the 23d of January,
when we received Napoleon's farewell, previous to his setting out on the morrow, for the first time, to fight for the
hearth with the foe in the land. What a day for me! how
many recollections assailed my memory! We were introduced into the grand saloon which I had so often traversed

as a familiar of the house. Better to view the ceremony I had mounted along with others upon a bench placed against the wall. Napoleon entered with the Empress; he advanced with a noble air, leading by the hand his son, not yet three years old. For a long time I had not been near him with whom I had lived so intimately and for so many years. He had become very corpulent, and upon his extremely pale countenance sat an air of sadness and displeasure. The ordinary movements of the muscles of his neck were stronger and more frequent than I had formerly remarked.—No, I cannot describe what I felt stirring within me, on beholding this friend of my youth, so long master of Europe, on the point of sinking beneath the efforts of his enemies. The ceremony had something grave and solemn, and at the same time mournful. Rarely does silence so profound reign in so numerous an assembly. There prevailed throughout some indescribable and vague uneasiness—an eager listening for the voice of Napoleon. Nor was that voice long unheard. In strong and sonorous tones, as when he harangued his soldiers in Italy or Egypt, but without the expression of self-confidence and satisfaction with others which then beamed from his countenance, Napoleon thus addressed us:

"Gentlemen, officers of the National Guard, I have pleasure in beholding you assembled around me. I depart this night to place myself at the head of the army. On quitting the capital I leave behind, with confidence, my wife and my son, upon whom so many hopes repose. I owe this acknowledgment of security to all those acts by which you have never failed to manifest your attachment in the principal eras of my life. I shall depart with a mind freed from a weight of inquietude when I know these pledges to be under your faithful guardianship; to you I confide all I hold most dear in the world, next to France, and recommend them to your care.

"It may sometimes happen, from the nature of the manœuvres which I am now to execute, that the enemy may find an opportunity to approach your walls. If such an event should occur, bear in mind that it can be the affair only of a few days, and that I shall speedily arrive to your assistance. I recommend to you to be united among your-selves, and to resist every insinuation tending to introduce disunion. Endeavors will not be wanting to shake your fidelity to your duty; but I depend on your repelling all these perfidious instigations."

I listened to Bonaparte's words with the deepest atten-tion; and, though he pronounced them with a strong voice, it was not unmoved—he felt or feigned emotion. But that emotion, whether real or assumed, was shared by a vast number of those present; and I confess, for my own part, that I was greatly overcome, especially when he uttered the words, "I confide to you my wife and my son." I fixed my eyes upon the child; the interest he inspired was altogether distinct from that excited by the grandeur which sur-rounded, or the misfortunes which threatened, him. I be-held in the boy, whose countenance, moreover, displayed much innocent loveliness, not the King of Rome, but the son of my earliest friend. During the whole day I could not escape from a feeling of sadness, on comparing what I had that morning witnessed with our first occupation in the Tuileries. How many ages in the fourteen years that sepa-rated those events!

It will be deemed a circumstance worthy of remark, by those who take an interest in comparing dates, to find that Napoleon, the successor of Louis XVI. and nephew of that monarch by marriage with Maria Louisa, should have taken his farewell of the National Guard precisely on the anni-versary of the too famous 21st January, after twenty-five years of terror and disgrace—of hope, of glory and reverse. On the morrow he set out to join the army; but, alas! his journey was not so long as it used to be, before reaching headquarters. Eastern France was already occupied by five hundred thousand men, and Napoleon had wherewith to oppose this host only, at most, one hundred thousand; but his genius, far from failing him, seemed to renovate its youthful vigor in this terrible conjuncture.

Meantime, the congress at Chatillon-sur-Seine had opened,

where assembled the Duke of Vicenza as representative of France; Lords Aberdeen, Cathcart, and Stewart, British envoys; Count Razoumowsky, for Russia; Count Stadion, for Austria; and Count de Humboldt, from Prussia. As I received the most complete intelligence on whatever was transacted in this assembly, I believe the present portion of my "Memoirs" will deeply interest every one who seeks for the truth on the negotiations of this period. In the terms of his instructions the Duke de Vicenza demanded an armistice on the opening of the congress, according to the usual practice while negotiating treaties of peace. This Napoleon both desired and greatly wanted, to repair former losses and to prevent the fresh disasters of immediate warfare. But, instructed by past experience, the allies resolved to continue military operations, and answered the proposal of an armistice by requiring the immediate signature of the proposals of peace. These, however, were no longer the proposals of Frankfort. The allies now established, as a basis of the treaty, the limits of the ancient monarchy. They regarded their success as sufficient to authorize this; and who, in their situation, would not have acted in the same manner?

The Congress opened on the 5th of February; on the 6th there was no sitting; but on the 7th the plenipotentiaries of the allied powers declared themselves categorically. They drew up a protocol that, in consequence of the success which had attended their arms, France should be confined within her ancient limits, such as these were under the monarchy, before the Revolution; that France should renounce all influence beyond her immediate frontiers; and that, consequently, all titles implying protection in Italy, Germany or Switzerland were instantly to cease. This proposition, so different from the one sent to Frankfort to our envoy, M. de St. Aignan, appeared so extraordinary to M. de Caulaincourt that it obliged him to request a suspension of proceedings, the conditions being of a nature which did not authorize him to proceed immediately. The plenipotentiaries acceded to his wish, and adjourned the meeting till eight o'clock the same evening. In this night sitting the Duke of Vicenza declared his willingness to make the greatest sacrifices for peace, however remote the propositions of the allies, as explained that morning, had been from the terms offered at Frankfort, but requiring a definite statement of those sacrifices and of the compensations to be given in return. This was, indeed, fulfilling his recent instructions to prolong the discussions and to gain time; but the duke has been unjustly accused of opposing the peace, and throwing unimportant and even trifling obstacles in the way. Such were the private instructions of the Emperor.

On the following day, some success obtained by the allies, and their capture of Troyes and Chalons, determined Napoleon to empower his plenipotentiary to state, "That he was ready to consent to the ancient limits of France, provided the allied powers immediately consented to an armistice." This would have exactly suited Napoleon; time would have been gained. The East and the North would have risen; reinforcements could have arrived from the South of France; and he would have been able to bring up his troops from Spain and the German fortresses: besides, fortunate chances might present themselves, and, to a certainty, intrigues might be set on foot. On the 9th of February this unexpected proposal was laid before the Congress by Caulaincourt, and M. de Razoumowsky, convinced that England would accede, her object in the surrender of Antwerp and the evacuation of Belgium being thus attained, demanded, in the name of the Emperor Alexander, a suspension of the discussions. But the allies rejected this subterfuge of Napoleon; and they did right. He had given his ambassador to understand that the *first* word of the allies was not to be taken as an *ultimatum;* that he must reply by assuming the propositions of Frankfort and demanding an armistice: but that their answer even to this was not to be an ultimatum. "There are many other concessions," he added in his letter; "but, if the allies are satisfied, you may close; if not, the terms will afford room for discussion." In the same letter occurred the following remarkable expression, which describes the whole intention of the Emperor—"You may go, *verbally*, as far as you judge convenient, and, when you shall have obtained a positive ultimatum, refer to your government for final instructions concerning it." Is this clear?

In the sitting of the 10th March the Duke of Vicenza inserted in the protocol that the last courier despatched to him had been stopped and detained for a long time by several general officers in the Russian army, who had forced from him his papers, which had not been delivered to the duke till thirty-six hours afterward at Chaumont. Caulaincourt justly complained of this infraction of the rights of nations, and of established usages, as the only cause of delay in concluding the negotiations. He then laid before Congress the instructions of his master, in which the Emperor acceded to the conditions of the allies at Frankfort, from which they had receded without comprehensible motives. He, however, was careful not to communicate his secret orders—*to insist—to demand all, in order to obtain nothing.* He then inserted a long note in the protocol setting forth all the commonplaces about the balance of power, the partition of Poland, the inferiority to which France would be reduced, compared with Austria or Russia, by accepting the new basis proposed by the allies, namely, her border lines before the Revolution, and maintained, with truth, that without France the balance of power could not be preserved. He continued to state, in support of these views, that Belgium and the right bank of the Rhine, having been constitutionally united to France, and recognized by existing treaties, the Emperor neither could, nor would, consent to their dismemberment. To these propositions of Napoleon the allies replied that they contained nothing distinct or definite as respected the preliminaries presented by them on the 17th February, and which were to have been answered on the 28th, after the term of ten days fixed upon by Caulaincourt himself: they, therefore, proposed breaking up the Congress. To prevent this, the duke replied *verbally*—"1. That Napoleon was ready to renounce all influence beyond the limits of France. 2. To acknowledge the independence of Spain, Italy, Switzerland, Germany and Holland; and to make such concessions to England as should be judged necessary, and for a reasonable equivalent."

Upon this declaration the sitting immediately broke up without reply. Nor was this to be wondered at. What did Bonaparte comprehend under the *limits* of France? Those unquestionably which he had been offered, but refused, at Frankfort, and which the allies now retrenched to the limits of the monarchy. And what was the "reasonable equivalent expected from England?" Is it surprising that this obscurity and vagueness inspired no confidence? In fact, three days after this sitting of the 10th March, the allies declared that they could not enter upon the discussion of the verbal protocol of the French minister, and demanded from him within twenty-four hours an explicit declaration for or against the treaty proposed by them, that the limits of France should be those of the monarchy before the Revolution, or to propose a counter project. Always guided by his secret instructions, the Duke of Vicenza inserted in the protocol an ambiguous reply at the same meeting of the 13th March. The allies answered by repeating their demand. The former then requested a suspension of the meeting till eight the same evening, which, after some discussion, was granted. The meeting having resumed, M. de Caulaincourt, much to the surprise of all, said he would give in a counter project, but could not finish it before the evening of the 14th, or morning of the 15th March. The allies were pressed, but, from personal consideration to the French envoy, said they would adjourn to the morning of the 15th. On that occasion, to the astonishment of all, in this counter project, so long delayed, the duke modified nothing of his verbal protocol. The Emperor was to retain the Rhine, renounce Holland, Italy, his supremacy over Switzerland, and to recognize the independence of Spain; but the crown of the kingdom of Italy was to be guaranteed to Prince Eugene Napoleon. The Princess Eliza was also to retain the sovereignty of Lucca and Piombino, and the Prince of Neufchatel his principality; the Grandduke of Berg (son of Louis) was also to retain possession of his duchy; the King of Saxony was to be reinstated in his kingdom; and the Ionian Isles were to belong to the kingdom of Italy. The greater part of these conditions were received with derision by the allies. It became evident that Napoleon had never intended to treat seriously of peace at Châtillon.

In fact, on the 19th, the plenipotentiaries of the allies, perceiving that all these diplomatic stratagems had evidently no other object than to gain time, and likewise struck with the inconsistency of Napoleon's refusing for a formal peace what he had proposed to grant for a simple armistice, declared the negotiations with the French government broken off. The allied powers added, through their representatives, that, faithful to the principles they had announced, they would never lay down arms until these principles had been recognized and admitted by the French government. The issue of these grand debates was thus referred to the chances of war—chances but little favorable to the man whose genius then strove against Europe in arms.

CHAPTER XXXI

Paris Taken by the Allies—Bonaparte Forced to Abdicate

THE campaign in which the important question was to be decided, Whether Napoleon should continue master of France? required from him a system of tactics different from all the warlike operations in which he had yet been engaged. He was now reduced to the defensive; and, instead of acting upon a plan established previously, his plans were constantly to be modified and rendered subordinate to the movements of an overwhelming superiority of numbers. He had quitted Paris on the 25th January, at which date Alexander, Francis, and the King of Prussia were assembled at Langres. Napoleon joined his guard at Vitry, and two days after quitting his capital put to rout the Prussian army then advancing by the Lorrain road, chasing it from St. Dizier. Two days after took place the battle of Brienne, in which, with fifteen thousand men, he kept in check for twelve hours eighty thousand Russians. This battle was brought on through a movement made by the Emperor on his right, in order to intervene between Paris and the grand Austro-Russian army, which had passed the Seine and Yonne at Montereau, and pushed forward upon Fontainebleau. What recollections and what thoughts must have agitated his mind on revisiting, as Emperor and King, and with an army lately so powerful, those scenes which, thirty-four years before, had witnessed the mimic combats of our boyhood! Then and there had he often said to me, "I will do these Frenchmen of thine all the mischief in my power." The desire, indeed, had been changed; but destiny had registered its fulfillment; for now had he brought into the bosom of *his* beautiful France the legions of armed Europe.

In two days after this engagement from seventy to eighty thousand men of the French and allied armies drew up against each other. There the chiefs of both incurred the greatest personal risks; for Napoleon had a horse killed under him, and at Blücher's side a Cossack was struck down by a shot. The operations of the Emperor's active warfare carried him, a few days after this great battle, to Troyes. There he remained but a brief space, and advanced toward Champ-Aubert, where ensued the battle which has immortalized that village. The Russians were beaten, and General Alsufieff, with two thousand men and thirty pieces of cannon, captured. This battle was fought on the 10th February; and really there would be no exaggeration in saying that at this period the French army had to sustain a battle every day, and frequently on several points at one and the same

time. Thus, on the 11th, the Prince of Wirtemberg entered
Sens, my native city, after a most obstinate resistance, while
General Bourmont vigorously repulsed the enemy before
Nogent, and at Montmerail, the Emperor defeated the
united corps of Generals Yorck and Sacken.

After the battle of Champ-Aubert the Emperor was so
elated by the success that at supper with Berthier, Marmont
and Alsufieff he said—"Courage, gentlemen! another such
victory and I am upon the Vistula." Observing that no
one replied, and thinking he read in the expression of the
marshals that they partook not in these hopes, he added
—"I see clearly, gentlemen, that you are all tired of war;
there is no longer any enthusiasm; the sacred fire seems
extinct within you." Then, rising from table and going
up to General Drouot, with the intention, by a marked
compliment, to hint a censure upon the marshals—"Is it
not true, general," asked he, clapping him on the shoulder,
"there wants to success only a hundred men such as you?"
Drouot replied, with as much spirit as appropriate modesty
—"Say one hundred thousand, sire!" This trait of Napoleon, which so completely paints the man, I had, a short
time afterward, from the two principal witnesses of this
moment of aberration.

Success, indeed, had returned, but only for a moment;
for how could it be otherwise? The loss of twenty men
was to us as great as of one hundred to the allies. Our
recruits could be raised with difficulty, while the allied reinforcements, stationed along the whole route from the centre
of Germany to the heart of France, arrived daily, and not
only covered the losses inflicted by French valor, guided
by the genius of Bonaparte, but unceasingly swelled the
hostile ranks. The whole of February was a series of battles—a succession of reverses and defeats nearly balanced.
The activity, the energies and the resources of the French
chief seemed inexhaustible. On the 10th, Marshal Blucher
forced a corps of the army to retreat, and on the morrow was
himself beaten at Vauchamp by the Duke de Ragusa. The

17th and 18th were favorable days; on the former the corps of Wittgenstein was completely defeated at Villeneuve, with great loss in men and material, and that of General Wrede at Nangis; and, on the latter, the Prince of Wirtemberg was obliged to evacuate Montereau after a severe conflict. It presented an afflicting spectacle thus to behold troops and leaders engaged against each other who, only two years before, had fought under the same standard. But Bonaparte would have it so by rendering his alliance an insupportable burden, and by constantly refusing to bend his ambition beneath the yoke of necessity.

Thus, wholly absorbed in war, Napoleon had little time to spare for the affairs of the interior. But already other disquieting events had occurred, in the arrival, at St. Jean de Luz, of the Duke d'Angouleme, nephew of Louis XVIII., in whose name he issued a proclamation to the French soldiers, while, on the 21st of the same month, the Count d'Artois made his entry into Vesoul. In the meantime hostilities continued on a vast line of operation, with an always increasing animosity. In vain did our soldiers cover themselves with glory in so many fights! Spite of their prodigies of valor, the masses thickened and bore down toward a centre. Thus is the eagle finally strangled by the very crowd of his puny enemies, though every stroke of his beak sends a dead raven circling downward through space. Gradually the war closed in upon Paris. Intelligence from the army, so eagerly expected, daily arrived earlier. While the cannon of the Invalids thundered forth the acclamations of victory, the distant roll of hostile artillery might be heard in the capital of France: so quickly came the changes in this war of extermination.

A little before the end of February the allies were in full retreat in different parts. Marmont had repulsed the attacks of Blucher, while Napoleon, occupied in pursuing the Austrians, had, by a skilful manœuvre, succeeded in dividing his forces, and throwing forward a part of them to oppose the army of Silesia, which menaced his rear. At the same

time Marshals Victor, Oudinot and Macdonald advanced
upon the route of the Aube and the Seine.   But the retreat
of the allies was not a flight.   Having experienced a reverse,
they retired beyond the Aube and waited for reinforcements,
which soon enabled them to resume the offensive.   Many
were those who, from these successes, looked for peace; they
hoped that the Emperor of Austria might be detached from
the coalition and would never consent that his daughter
should be driven from the throne of France.   They were
speedily undeceived by the ambassadors of England, Austria, Russia and Prussia signing, at Chaumont, on the 1st of
March, a league for twenty years, should that time be necessary, to force a peace by which France should guarantee the
independence and tranquillity of Europe.   Twenty years!—
thirty days sufficed.

Into these thirty days were crowded so many events that
a volume would be required to describe their history.
Troyes, from which they had been lately driven, was recovered by the allies.   And during these transactions the
Swedish army, commanded by the Prince Royal, arrived on
the frontiers of France.   Bernadotte, I know from a private
letter, kept saying to all who would listen that the allies
were firmly resolved to deprive Napoleon and his family of
power.   He spoke of the re-establishment of the Bourbons,
not as a condition which the allies would impose upon
France, but as a measure likely enough—thus leaving room
to return upon his words, according to circumstances and
the conference at Abo.   The Swedish contingent was no
great affair for the allies: they wished it to be said, in their
grand protestation, that Europe was armed against Napoleon.
But once more he astonished Europe, thus leagued against
him, by crushing the forces of Blucher on the 7th of March:
the contest, however, was obstinate, and cost the conqueror
dear.   Marshal Victor was grievously wounded, as were also
Generals Grouchy and Ferrière.   But a great moral reaction
was taking place in the inhabitants of Paris by the proximity
of warfare, the sight of the wounded, and of women, from

the palace to the cellar, occupied in preparing dressings. Hitherto, the glory of victory only had reached the capital. But the trophies of Champ-Aubert and Craonne had been accompanied by convoys of the wounded and the dying, who crowded the hospitals of Paris. Still the Emperor continued to dispute the ground foot by foot. But already had the Duke d'Angouleme entered Bourdeaux; it was known also what reception he had met with—more flattering, probably, than desired by those who had facilitated his return to France. The 21st of March (a day which fatality seemed to have marked out for great eras in the destiny of Napoleon) the second city in the empire—not Rome, but Lyons—was occupied by the Austrians under General Bubna.

The last days of March brought to Napoleon only a series of calamities. On the 23d the rear-guard of the French army suffered severe losses. Soon after Prince Schwartzenberg passed the Aube and marched upon Vitry and Chalons. Napoleon, reckoning upon the possibility of defending Paris, pounced with eager rapidity on the Austrian rear, and seeing the army execute a retrograde movement, mistook it for a retreat: but no such thing; the movement became an advance upon Paris, and at the same moment Blucher directed his march to meet Schwartzenberg. Thus Napoleon, who had intended to intercept their retreat, found himself cut off from Paris. All now depended upon the defence of the capital; or rather, by sacrificing Paris, the existence of the shade of the empire might perhaps be prolonged a few days.

On the 26th took place the conflict of Fère Champenoise, wherein valor could not long withstand numbers, and Marshals Marmont and Mortier were constrained to retire to Sezanne; and, on that day—I beg the reader to remark the date—Napoleon experienced a loss which, in his circumstances, was irreparable. During the combat of Fère Champenoise was captured by the allies a convoy of warlike stores, which consisted of an enormous quantity of arms, ammunition and equipments of all kinds, comprising almost the whole of the material that remained to us. This acquisition was deemed so important by the enemy that a bulletin and order of the day were printed announcing the success. A copy of this document fell into the hands of Marshal Macdonald, who rightly judged such intelligence should not be concealed from the Emperor, for he knew, as I have stated previously in these "Memoirs," that Napoleon always desired to be immediately informed of bad news. At this epoch, indeed, Napoleon was so unfortunate that all information, not authenticated, was concealed as long as possible; but of the veracity of the bulletin the marshal entertained no doubt; he, therefore, repaired in person to the imperial headquarters, where he found the Emperor preparing to recapture Vitry, then occupied by the Prussians. To dissuade him from this now useless attempt the marshal put into his hand the fatal bulletin. This was on the morning of the 27th. Napoleon read, but could not credit the intelligence. "No," said he to the marshal, "you are deceived; it cannot be true." Then, having inspected the bulletin with much attention, "See here," resumed he eagerly, "examine for yourself; to-day is the 27th, and the bulletin is dated the 29th. You must at once perceive that to be impossible; the bulletin is false!" The marshal, who paid more attention to the contents than to the date, was struck with astonishment, but, having shown the paper to Drouot, "Alas! marshal," said the general, "the information is but too true; there is only a mistake of the press—the 9 is a 6 reversed!" On what trifles do sometimes depend the mightiest events. A figure reversed sufficed to maintain Napoleon's dreams of empire!

Henceforth it was easy to perceive that all must be at an end. On the 28th, the allies passed the Marne at Tripot, and the next day at Meaux, where the divisions of Wrede and Sacken remained in position, in spite of the vigorous attack by which Marshal Mortier repulsed General Yorck at Claye. The remainder of the 29th was devoted by the allies to completing their preparations for attacking Paris on the morrow, and by the two Marshals, Marmont and Mortier, to sell dearly their entrance into the capital. They were unable to defend it with success; a capitulation saved the city. This was imputed as a crime to Marmont: such is the justice of men!

The grandees of the empire, and the ablest subjects of Napoleon, were divided, at this period, into two great classes, wholly different from each other. The first class was composed of those men who had been the companions in arms, and, in many instances, the patrons, of Napoleon. Theirs was a privileged set, whose members, though bowed beneath the same yoke which weighed upon all, and though serving with enthusiastic zeal the man who had lifted them from the crowd, did not, in their imagination, limit France to the imperial headquarters, nor forget that there had existed a home—a country—a France, in fine, before they gave her a master. They looked to the preservation of these as a measure separable from the existence of the empire. The other class, constituted of those whom I am inclined to term children of the empire, knew of nothing anterior to the present order of things. They saw only Napoleon and the empire. In ardent and adventurous youth they had been called from the school to the camp by the voice of him who seemed to have predestinated them to that glory, honor, and fortune which they courted above all things. Hence their devotedness to the person of a single man: their willingness to hazard all—compromise all—in order to prolong the political life of their Emperor. Fortunately, on the other hand, the constituents of the former class, those who had shed their blood on the fields fought prior even to the fame of General Bonaparte, or under his eye, and guided by his example, could not conceive that any single man, whatever might be his genius or his claims, ought to be preferred to France. These men dreaded nothing so much as the dangers of a civil war, and were ready to make every sacrifice for France. This distinction was not limited to the ranks of the army, but extended also to the high civil functionaries

of the state. The reader will bear this in mind, for it will
assist to explain the conduct of those of elevated rank during the events of the end of March, 1814.

It is impossible, without having witnessed their effects,
to conceive the intensity of those passions which, at this
period, agitated all minds in the capital, both for and against
Napoleon, before the name of the Bourbons had yet been
pronounced. In fact, these princes had no party. To the
new generation they were almost totally unknown; forgotten
by many; feared by those of the old conventionals by whom
they were still remembered, they possessed in reality only
the frail support of the drawing-rooms of the Faubourg St.
Germain, and of some remnant of the emigration. But as
the emigration could put forth only unavailing wishes in
favor of the ancient family of our kings, so it is very certain
that this class contributed very little to the return of the
Bourbons. One thing, however, is clearly demonstrated,
that the follies of the emigrants, and their absurd pretensions, alone rendered possible, in the following year, the
return of Bonaparte, and the second exile of Louis. In fact,
at the end of March, 1814, before the surrender of Paris,
there reigned in the public mind a longing for change; men
knew well what they would not have, but had not yet resolved on what to choose.

The departure of the Empress from Paris was not decided
upon till after considerable discussion. On the 28th of
March, the Council of Regency assembled in an extraordinary meeting, where Maria Louisa presided. Joseph strongly
advocated her departure, grounding his opinion on a letter
from the Emperor, which ordered that, if Paris should be
threatened, the Empress Regent and Council should retire
to Blois. The arch-chancellor (Cambacérès) supported the
same opinion, which was finally carried. It had been argued
in opposition that, by remaining in Paris, the Empress was
more likely to obtain favorable terms from the allies; or
even, like her grandmother, Maria Theresa, by presenting
herself with her son to the people, rouse the citizens to the

defence of the capital. This latter resolution doubtless was
the more advantageous to the interests of Napoleon; but,
even if acted upon, could only have retarded for a few days
an event which had now become inevitable. Still, it would
have been productive of great difficulties; but Joseph had
few resources in case of emergency; the arch-chancellor
desired to be gone, doubtless recollecting the comfortable
prediction uttered by Bonaparte in my hearing, "If the Bourbons return you will be hanged"; so the Empress and
Council, with the ordinary guards, set out for Blois.

The Prince of Benevento (Talleyrand), as member of the
Council of Regency, likewise received orders to quit Paris
on the 80th, but was prevented from passing the barrier.
I had called at his house and found him there with some
friends. At the time the prince was accused of himself contriving this agreeable restraint; I can as positively deny the
fact; at all events, his conduct showed prudent foresight.
From Talleyrand's I went to the Duke de Rovigo, in the
friendly intent of persuading him to remain, and to profit
by his situation to secure himself from inconvenience. But
he unhesitatingly refused—so exclusively had he attached
himself to the fortunes of the Emperor. I found him seated
before a large fire, burning all papers which might have
compromised those who had served the police. These
documents might have placed some obstacles in the way
of certain arrangements on the 1st of April.

At the moment when the Empress departed, I observed
many people looking out for a popular commotion and
change of government; but all remained tranquil. No
preparations were in progress for barricading the doors,
unpaving the streets, or pouring missiles and boiling water
from the roofs. A great number of the inhabitants, however, were thinking of defence—not to maintain the government of Napoleon, but from that irritation which belongs
to our national character. The Parisians were indignant at
the bare idea of beholding strangers masters of Paris, an
event unexampled since the reign of Charles VII. A thou-

sand different reports were in the meantime flying about, chiefly concerning Joseph, who, remaining in his capacity of Lieutenant-general of the empire, was said to be preparing to seize the supreme power. He had no energy for such an act; and, besides, he was no more wanted in Paris than he had lately been in Madrid.

Meanwhile the crisis approached. Marmont and Mortier, as mentioned, had fallen back upon Paris on the 29th, in order to defend the approaches. Throughout the night the watch and ward of the barriers, confided to the national guard, excluded all communication so completely that not a single stranger penetrated within the city. The two Polignacs, who had escaped from their confinement at Vincennes some time before, and were then at Alexander's headquarters, made vain attempts to get admittance. The allies, however, were informed of all that occurred in Paris; and I knew afterward that the departure of Maria Louisa hastened their resolution to bring the struggle to a close, by redoubling their efforts to enter the capital of France. On the evening of the 29th, Marmont took up a position at St. Mandé, with his right resting upon the Marne, while his left extended to Mortier's right, whose troops were collected under the heights of Montmartre.

The whole of the inhabitants of Paris were roused at daybreak on the 30th by the sound of cannon; in a short time the plain of St. Denis appeared covered with the allied army, whose columns poured into it from all points. The heroism of our troops could not withstand such numerical superiority; nevertheless, they made the allies pay dearly for their entrance into the capital. The national guard, under the orders of Marshal Moncey, and the pupils of the polytechnic school, transformed into artillerymen, behaved in a manner worthy of our veteran soldiers. The efforts of Marmont during that day would suffice to render immortal the name of any commander. His troops were reduced to between seven and eight thousand infantry and eight hundred horse: with this handful of brave men he maintained his ground for the space of twelve hours, against an army of one hundred and fifty thousand men, of whom, we are assured, fourteen thousand were killed or wounded. He was to be found in the thickest of the fight; a dozen men were bayoneted at his side, and his hat was shot through. But what could possibly be done against overwhelming numbers?

In this state of things the Duke of Ragusa informed Joseph of his situation, whose note, as follows, is important when connected·with subsequent events:

"If Marshals the Dukes of Ragusa and Treviso can hold out no longer, they are authorized to negotiate with Prince Schwartzenberg and the Emperor of Russia, who are in their front. JOSEPH.

"*Montmartre, the 30th March*, 1814,
    a quarter past midday.
"They will retire upon the Loire."

It was not till long after having received this formal authorization to treat that the French generals ceased their obstinate resistance against the allied army, since the suspension of hostilities did not take place till four in the afternoon. Joseph, as is well known, exactly at a quarter past twelve—that is, immediately after despatching the authority in question—made the best of his way for the road to Versailles, thence to proceed to Rambouillet. This precipitate flight astonished nobody except some few who did not know him; but several officers of his staff were sufficiently displeased at being made partners therein, as they at first imagined he was going to take up a new position in order to defend the bridge at Neuilly. In these circumstances, to save Paris, which could not be defended two hours longer, had become the only desirable measure. And when Marmont signed the suspension, which ended in the capitulation of the ensuing morning, he merited a civic crown rather than reproaches. I have still before my mind's eye that general's appearance on the evening of the 30th March, when he retired to his house in Paris from the field of battle. We were some twenty people, among whom appeared Perregaux and Lafitte, who received him in the green draw-ing-room, which, with its inmates at that moment, is now present to my recollection. When the marshal entered he was scarcely to be recognized; his beard showed a full week's growth, the greatcoat which covered his uniform hung in tatters, and from head to foot he was blackened with powder.

Here a discussion ensued on the necessity of signing the capitulation. This appeared to be the universal sentiment: the marshal will yet recollect that there arose but one cry around him—"You must save France!" The prefect of the department of the Seine, who was present at this meeting, well aware of what ought to be the sole duty of the chief magistrate of the capital, decidedly expressed his intention to repair in the course of the night to the headquarters of the allies at the head of the municipal body. I applauded highly this prudent resolution, and M. de Chabrol was fully alive to the immense responsibility that would be incurred if he did not exert every effort to save Paris from the horrors of pillage to which it would have been exposed by a protracted and vain resistance. Perregaux and Lafitte strongly expressed their opinion to the same effect; this opinion, too, they declared to be that of the public—of whose sentiments none could be better informed than these celebrated financiers—and that, in short, France was weary of the yoke of Bonaparte. This last proposition placed the question then to be discussed upon a much broader basis; now, not merely the capitulation of Paris but a change in the government was to be considered, and, for the first time, occurred the name of the Bourbons. I do not recollect who, of all present, upon hearing proposed the recall of the ancient dynasty, remarked upon the many difficulties opposed to a restoration without a return to the past; but I remember perfectly that M. Lafitte replied, in answer to this objection —"Gentlemen, we can have nothing to fear if we obtain a good constitution which shall guarantee the rights of all."

This prudent remark conciliated the majority of the assembly of the green drawing-room, and influenced not a little the conduct of the marshal.

Meanwhile this memorable conference was likely to be disturbed by an unexpected incident—the arrival of an aide-de-camp from the Emperor. Napoleon, having learned the movement of the allies upon Paris, had in all haste posted from the banks of the Marne to the road for Paris, by Fontainebleau, and already, at Froidmanteau, had despatched this envoy to the marshal. The language of this officer clearly showed that things were viewed very differently at headquarters and in Páris. He expressed his indignation at the bare idea of capitulation, and announced, with incredible assurance, the speedy arrival of Napoleon in Paris, which he still hoped to save from occupation. At the same time we were given to understand that Napoleon reckoned upon every species of defence being resorted to by an insurgent population. This address, and these proposals, I answered in terms of our own resolution, representing all such outrageous means of opposition as folly. The majority of those present seconded these opinions, and their reception was finally unanimous. At a later period the marshal said to me, speaking of the transactions of which I have now given a faithful recital—"I am blamed, my dear friend; but you were in my house on the 80th of March, and you there witnessed what were the sentiments of the choice of the population of Paris. I acted as I did only because I beheld assembled around me those who were entirely disinterested —men who had nothing to expect from the return of the Bourbons."

The capitulation of Paris saved France. It has been said, indeed, that, had the capital held out another day, the allies would have been ruined; that they had fired their last cartridge; and that the approach of Napoleon with his army would have rendered the plain of St. Denis their Caudine forks. These stories, wherewith to amuse children, and the fine discovery of the want of ammunition, were never

heard of till long after, while at the time it was evident to
all that Paris could not have held out for two hours longer.
A fearful conflict might doubtless have been maintained in
the streets, but burning and sacking would have been the
consequences; Napoleon would not the less have fallen,
leaving as a farewell gift to France a mountain of ashes
where had been her capital. On the contrary, what was
the immediate result of the capitulation? Peace obtained,
as if by enchantment. Europe was in arms against us; and
within forty-eight hours not a musket was fired. Napoleon
had everywhere exacted immense contributions; in 1814 not
a halfpenny of contribution was levied. The capitulation
of Paris, too, was unquestionably more honorable to France
than had been any one of these formerly signed by her enemies, when our victorious troops entered their capitals,
which had surrendered without resistance. The night
passed away in quietness; for, all being informed of the
suspension of arms after the 80th, men began to breathe
again. Still, the future was involved in vagueness and
doubt, but each, representing it according to his own wishes,
found a weight removed from his mind. One party entertained hopes of a regency which, under a different name,
might preserve the power for Bonaparte. This, above all
things, was to be avoided, if a durable peace were desired.
Affairs, however, in the first instance, promised not unfavorably for these views. But their opponents, those who supported a new or a more ancient order of things, were encouraged by the certainty that the Emperor Alexander had
determined against Bonaparte and all his family.

On the morning of the 31st, at daybreak, Paris presented
quite a novel spectacle. Scarcely had the French troops,
under Colonels Fabvier and Denys, marched from the city,
when from all its richest and most respectable quarters resounded shouts of "Down with Bonaparte! No more conscription! No more consolidated imposts!" With t'.ese
cries mingled that of "Long live the Bourbons!" But this
last was not so frequently repeated as the others, and in

general I observed that the populace heard and looked on
with a sort of indifference. I walked forth early to examine the state of things. Numerous groups were formed:
females were tearing their handkerchiefs and distributing
the fragments as symbols of the recovered lily: but I confess these manifestations exercised but small influence over
my mind. Some hours after, I met a cavalcade in the
square of Louis XV., traversing the streets, distributing
white cockades and shouting, "Long live the king! Long
live Louis XVIII.!" At the head of this train were several
of the ancient nobles, among whom I recognized Sosthenes
de la Rochefoucauld, Count de Froissard, the Duke de Luxembourg, the Duke de Crussol, Seymour, etc. In a little
time a pretty numerous crowd was thus collected, which
rushed tumultuously toward the Place Vendome. What
ensued there is well known; nor can the first excess of a
joy, legitimate in itself, excuse the insults offered to the
statue of a man whose misfortunes, merited or not, ought
to have been safe from such outrages. These insults, moreover, affected also the army of France, which yet acknowledged Napoleon, and irritated the partisans whom he still
numbered in Paris. It answered the purpose, however, of
one party to make these unmanly proceedings pass for an
expression of public sentiment, since Count Nesselrode had
demanded proofs that the Bourbons were supported by the
population of Paris before he would engage to second their
cause with his master.

A meeting, less public indeed, but scarcely less tumultuous, had meanwhile assembled in the house of Count Morfontaine, who, in consequence, presided. Here, after the
most violent and ridiculous motions, of which confusion rendered the discussion impossible, M. de la Rochefoucauld,
happily exercising his lungs so as to obtain a hearing where
all spoke and no one listened, proposed instantly to send
a deputation to the Emperor Alexander, who had his headquarters in the Hotel Talleyrand. Here I was present when
the deputation arrived, consisting of the proposer of the

measure, M. de Ferrand, Choiseul, and Chateaubriand, who
on that very day had become as it were the precursor of
the Restoration by his admirable pamphlet—"Bonaparte
and the Bourbons." He had indeed consented to join the
deputation, but nothing could induce him to speak. These
gentlemen were not introduced to Alexander, but had a conference with Nesselrode, who said, "I have just left the
Emperor: I guarantee his intentions: return and say Louis
XVIII. will reascend the throne of France." This happy
news, when announced, redoubled, if possible, the tumult
in the Hotel Morfontaine; nor is it to be conjectured when
or how it might have ended had not M. Talon proposed that
they should sally forth to make it public. I unite my grief
to theirs who lament the stigma brought on our national
glory; but I have no community of sentiment with those
who in all changes were ever found the suitors of fortune,
who, in shouting "Long live Alexander! Long live the
Bourbons! Down with Bonaparte!" meant only, "Long
live our places! Our pensions forever! God bless our
noble selves!"

I do not by this intend to blame the explosion of feeling
which met Alexander along the whole of the Boulevards,
when he entered as a conqueror into Paris. The French
beheld in him the hope of a happier future; they saw, indeed, an army of foreigners marching into their capital, but
each soldier wearing on his arm a white scarf, in token of
reconciliation and peace. Yet I would have had more
of decent sobriety: there is a certain dignity never to be
departed from and a national gravity which commands
respect: above all, I would have had forbearance toward
a fallen power. However this may be judged, the certain
truth is, that the allies, as they marched victorious into
Paris, were received with enthusiastic acclamations. Men
may approve or blame, but cannot deny, this fact. I observed all with close attention and with deeper feelings
than curiosity; for I remarked an expression of a sentiment
whose existence might have been long foreseen. Greatness

seemed to have unseated reason in the mind of Bonaparte.
Whoever carefully follows the series of facts during the last
four years of the empire will readily perceive that, from the
period of his alliance with the daughter of the Cæsars,
the administrative forms of the empire became daily more
severe and oppressive. In the intoxication of conquest or
the recklessness of reverse, one senatorial decree followed
another with a rapidity which almost decimated the population, incessantly hurrying more levies beyond the frontiers;
while to these most disproportionate requisitions was added
an unfeeling irony. St. Jean d'Angely dared to maintain
that the conscription favored population. I have already
mentioned the attempt of the legislative body, in 1813, to
emerge from its mute state and to give a lesson to him who
had never taken one. What was the consequence? The
gendarmes received orders to prevent the return of the
deputies to their House of Assembly. All these things were
remembered and tended to exasperate the spirits of men on
the 31st of March. The illusions also of an unparalleled
career were now daily suffering a rude dispersion; the glory
which had surrounded the imperial throne ceasing to dazzle,
allowed the eye to perceive that it was based on a mere
pageant. Master of France by the sword, Napoleon no
longer enjoyed right or claim when that sword was dimmed
and sheathed, since not one popular institution had identi-
fied with the nation the new dynasty which he had aspired
to found. The national admiration only, not attachment,
had followed him even in his best days. We love not where
we fear; and Napoleon had done nothing to merit the affections of France.

Having thus examined the aspect of Paris, and viewed
the march along the Boulevards, I hastened from the procession of the sovereigns to the hotel of M. de Talleyrand,
in order to be there before the Emperor Alexander, who
arrived about a quarter past one. Immediately after began
those political discussions upon which so many interests
were depending, and which continued till three o'clock. In

the existing state of things, only one of three arrangements
was practicable—1. To make peace with Napoleon under all
possible securities; 2. To establish a regency; 3. To recall
the Bourbons. As to Bernadotte, no one would have him;
not that objections rested against his personal character, but
because, on one hand, a cloud of rivals would have risen up
around him and civil war might have been the consequence;
and, on the other, his being a native Frenchman armed
against France was a circumstance of a nature strongly to
inflame the national susceptibilities. Still, though Alexander remained firm in his intention not ostensibly to
influence the government which France might select for
herself, he always inclined toward his former design in
favor of Bernadotte. As to Moreau, it is quite a gratuitous
supposition that the Czar ever intended to support him
in any view he might have entertained of placing himself
at the head of affairs in France. At all events, the cannon-
ball at Dresden had settled the question. The events which
he had that morning witnessed in his progress through the
capital had confirmed the Russian monarch in the determination he had formed since the campaign of Moscow, to overturn, should that ever be possible, the dynasty of Napoleon.
But, though the crisis had now arrived, Alexander, like
most of those opposed to Bonaparte, had resolved upon what
was to be put down, without having any fixed ideas of the
system to be established. I assisted at all the conferences.
When Alexander entered the saloon, the majority therein
assembled demanded the Bourbons. Meanwhile, he pronounced no decision; but, taking me apart to one of the
front windows, gave me to understand what that decision
would be by saying, "M. de Bourrienne, you have been
Napoleon's friend; so have I, and a sincere one too; but
peace is impossible with a man of such bad faith. *We must
have done with him.*"

These last words opened my eyes; and, in the discussion
that ensued upon the three forms above, and which Alexander himself had proposed, the Emperor plainly enacted

a part in pretending to doubt the possibility of restoring the Bourbons, in order to call forth more decidedly the opinions of those around him. M. de Talleyrand assured his imperial majesty that in case of this last resolution being definitely adopted, all the constituted authorities would act with as much regularity as circumstances permitted, and that he conceived himself empowered to pledge himself for the consent of the senate. He then left the Abbés Louis and Pradt (who, with General Desolles, had pronounced warmly in favor of the Bourbons) to explain their sentiments, and, I think, even recommended Alexander to interrogate them, as men interested solely in the welfare of France and thoroughly informed of public sentiment. There were present, besides us French and Alexander, the King of Prussia, Prince Schwartzenberg, M. de Nesselrode, M. Pozzo di Borgo, and the Prince de Lichtenstein. The Emperor kept standing or walking backward and forward with some appearance of agitation, then, elevating his voice, said to us, "Gentlemen, you know it was not I who commenced this war; you know that Napoleon came to attack me. We are not here thirsting for conquest or animated by the desire of vengeance. Neither I nor my allies are making a war of reprisal; and I should have been inconsolable had anything happened to your magnificent city, the miracle of art. We are not at war with France. We have but two opponents to combat—Napoleon and every enemy of French liberty. William, and you, Prince," added the Emperor, turning to the King of Prussia and Prince Schwartzenberg, the Austrian representative, "are not these also your sentiments?" Both assented; and Alexander repeated, in other terms, the same expressions of generosity, insisting particularly that he wished France to be perfectly free, and stating that, though their inclinations might be known, neither he nor his allies would exercise any influence as to the form of government. Upon this the Abbé de Pradt declared that we were all royalists, and that the whole of France thought with us. Paris, he went on to observe, had that morning proclaimed the same feelings in presence of their majesties, which sentiments would be expressed in a still more solemn manner when the people should no longer be chained down by fear. Besides, Paris was the head of France, and in all revolutionary movements the country had obeyed the impulse received from the metropolis. Alexander again enumerated the three propositions, speaking of maintaining Bonaparte on the throne—of the establishment of a regency —of Bernadotte—and of the restoration of the Bourbons. Upon this Talleyrand, who had shown himself throughout the most disposed to maintain Napoleon in power, by placing restrictions on the exercise of his authority, replied in the following words, too remarkable for me to forget—'Sire, there are but two possible alternatives—either Bonaparte or Louis XVIII. Bonaparte, if you can; but you cannot, for you are not alone. Whom would they give us in his place? A soldier! We will have no more soldiers. Did we wish one, we would retain him whom we have: he is the first soldier in the world. After him those who might be offered to us would not have ten men in their favor. I repeat, sire, whatever is not Louis XVIII. or Napoleon is an intrigue.''

These words produced upon the Emperor all the effect which could have been expected. The question was thus simplified; and as Alexander had resolved on the exclusion of Napoleon, pressed by us all, save Talleyrand, who still left the question undecided between the empire and monarchy, he declared that he would not treat with Napoleon, and being reminded that this applied only to the person of the Emperor, added, ''nor with any member of the Napoleon family.'' Thus, from the 31st of March, the Bourbons had in reality become sovereigns of France. A declaration was then drawn up, and signed by Alexander, ''That the allies would not treat with Napoleon; that they would respect the integrity of the ancient territories of France, as these had existed under her lawful kings; that they would recognize and guarantee the constitution which the French nation should adopt; and they invited the senate to name a Provisional Government to supply the immediate wants of administration and prepare a suitable constitution for the French people." This declaration was printed and placarded over all Paris within an hour. It produced a prodigious effect, and cut short all intrigues of a contrary tendency. In the evening I repaired again to the Russian headquarters, and about eleven o'clock at night Alexander said to me, "M. de Bourrienne, you must take upon you the office of postmaster-general." On instantly assuming my duties I found that not only had no preparations been made for a regular delivery next morning, but that the letter carriers had been dismissed. However, by laboring throughout the night, I reorganized the service, and on the morning of the 1st of April the delivery took place as usual—a circumstance of great importance to the cause of the Restoration. So passed the eventful 31st of March.

The 1st of April having been devoted to the organization of the Provisional Government, on the morning of the 2d the senate promulgated the following decree:

"I. Napoleon Bonaparte has forfeited the throne; and the right of succession established in his family is abolished.

"II. The French people and the army are released from their oath of fidelity to Napoleon Bonaparte.

"III. The present decree shall be transmitted by message to the Provisional Government of France, despatched afterward to all the departments, and to the armies, and proclaimed immediately in all the quarters of the capital."

Thus terminated the legal reign of Napoleon. It is worthy of remark that his act of abdication appeared in the "Moniteur" of the 12th of April, the day precisely on which _Monsieur_ (the Count d'Artois) made his entry into Paris as lieutenant-general of the kingdom for Louis XVIII., the day, too, on which was achieved, under the walls of Toulouse, the last grand deed in arms of the imperial army, when the French troops, commanded by Soult, made Wellington pay dearly for his entrance into the south of France.

CHAPTER XXXII

Return of the Bourbons—Bernadotte—Italy and Eugene—Hamburg Evacuated—
Napoleon's Farewell to his Soldiers—Adventures on the way to Elba

THE fall and abdication of Napoleon awakened in my mind two very opposite sentiments. While sincerely congratulating myself and my country on the termination of an oppressive government, I could not be insensible to the sufferings of Bonaparte, and never more than in these circumstances did I distinguish between the *man* and the *emperor*. Ah! had that man been so inclined—had he placed limits to his ambition—if his furious passion for European dominion had not dragged him into an abyss unfathomable —if he had consecrated to the happiness of France that superabundance of genius which he devoted to the enslaving of nations—if he had not cast beneath his feet the rights of Frenchmen, and constantly substituted his own arbitrary will for those rights—if, at least, after usurping power over the national liberties, he had devoted himself to the strengthening of internal order, he would unquestionably, in his own name, have kept a throne which so many victories and such mighty enterprises had clothed with splendor! If thus his name might have echoed with less of imposing sound to distant posterity, with how many blessings would that name have been saluted by contemporary generations! But the evil spirit of ambition within him overcame reason, and he accomplished his destiny. How profound the subjects for meditation in the fate of a man so accomplished and so strong! What a lesson is read in that fate to kings who hereafter dare, from his example, to believe in the possibility of contemning the rights of their people!

The Count d'Artois, as already noticed, had entered French territory on the 21st February, and seeing the favorable turn affairs were taking, repaired on the 16th March to

Nancy, where he awaited the issue of events. The allied sovereigns' encouraged the Provisional Government to request his presence in the capital, as a source of new vigor to the cause. The Abbé Montesquieu wrote; M. Rochefoucauld carried the letter; and on the 11th of April the prince reached the country house of Madame Charles de Damas, where he remained for the night. The news of his arrival spread like lightning, and every one prepared to solemnize his entrance into the ancient capital of his race. The national guard formed a double line from the barrier of Bondy to Notre Dame, for to the Cathedral, according to an ancient usage, little observed for twenty years, the procession was first to advance. In the meantime, the Provisional Government, with Talleyrand as president, went out to meet *Monsieur* beyond the barrier. In answer to a harangue by the former, the latter made the reply which, promising much, promptly became current in Paris—"Nothing is changed in France—there is only one Frenchman more." The prince then mounted on horseback and the *cortège* moved forward. I witnessed the whole from a particular station, more anxious to observe the aspect of the men and of the times than to be an actor. Near me stood an old knight of St. Louis, weeping for joy. The distant approach of the cavalcade was announced by the national air of "Henri IV.," long unheard in our streets. The open countenance of *Monsieur*, whom I had never seen before, delighted me, and seemed to inspire the confidence which it expressed. He was in the uniform of the national guard, and his staff appeared most brilliant, considering that no preparation had been made. I must, however, confess that the enthusiasm was confined to the cavalcade itself, or appeared elsewhere only among the upper classes. The people seemed to look on with more of curiosity and wonder than any other sentiment. I must here add, in the same spirit of truth, my expression of painful surprise on seeing a troop of Cossacks bringing up the rear: this was to be deemed the more inexplicable that General Sacken had informed me of Alexander's intention of permitting no foreign troops to appear. Admirable order, too, reigned throughout Paris, though seasons of change are commonly times of disturbance. This was owing to the excellent services of the national guard, and also chiefly to the strict discipline maintained, especially by General Sacken, in the allied army. Certainly, therefore, the *one Frenchman more* should, on that day, have been surrounded only by Frenchmen.

Two days previously had been witnessed a spectacle which, though infinitely less French, has been much talked of, namely, the religious ceremony according to the Greek Church, which the allied sovereigns and troops attended in the square of Louis XV. Almost in the centre of this place was erected an altar, of a square form and lofty proportions. Along the boulevard were posted, on opposite sides, the national guard and the allied army. All the avenues leading to the square were guarded so closely that no one, even on foot, could penetrate within the space. As I had a window in one of the public buildings overlooking the square at my disposal, I took my station there at eight in the morning, though my taste for pompous ceremonies was most assuredly not more pronounced than in times past. Here, after standing four hours, I had the pleasure, at midday, of seeing some half-dozen Greek priests with long beards enter the inclosure and solemnly advance to the altar. These were, of course, in full panoply, and looked quite as richly dight as high priests of the opera. After this first ceremony, another *entr'acte* of three-quarters of an hour had to be endured, when at length the infantry, followed by the cavalry, debouched, and in a few minutes the whole square appeared covered with uniforms. Last of all, the allied sovereigns made their entrance, followed by a brilliant staff. They alighted and advanced to the altar on foot. What struck me most was the profound silence among such an assemblage of men during the time of divine service; one would have imagined, from the motionless stillness of the symmetrical multitude, that he had under his eye an ably painted panorama rather than a mass of living men. For my own part, that which pleased me most in this ceremony, imposing as it might be, was to see it concluded. I may just mention, *en passant*, that I cannot think foreign uniforms at all equal to our own; we find in them something fantastic, and sometimes even grotesque. Besides, how is it possible for a soldier to have a military air when laced like a woman, and cut in two like a wasp?

After an interval of only two days from the arrival of a Bourbon, Paris witnessed another public entry—that of Francis II. This monarch was much disliked by the Parisians; in truth, he was the object of almost general reprobation. Even among those who, from her connection with Bonaparte, ardently wished the dethronement of the daughter, there were many who could not be reconciled to the conduct of the father toward the dynasty with which, in 1809, he had sought an alliance as his only safeguard. Misfortune has ever sacred claims in France, and Maria Louisa, now abandoned, had more friends than in the season of her greatest splendor. So judged the people instinctively. Each knew what it was to be a parent, and had the happiness not to know what it is to be a king. The entry of Francis, on the 15th, though surrounded with all the splendor of military procession, was a cold affair. The three sovereigns of Russia, Austria and Prussia met at the barrier on horseback, followed by the same troops as on their first entrance, and traversed Paris, but without the same acclamations. This new exhibition of the allied forces in the capital was in bad taste. A French prince resided in the Tuileries; and what a fortnight before had seemed an act of deliverance now appeared a display of arrogant pride.

Francis had not seen his daughter since she had left Vienna to unite hers with the fate of the master of the half of Europe. She, on her part, had, in her misfortunes, still looked to her father. Of this I have been assured by those who were well informed. While sending away Champagny on the mission noticed above, she said, to encourage him,

"Even should it be the intention of the allied sovereigns to dethrone the Emperor Napoleon, my father will not suffer it: twenty times did he repeat, when placing me on the throne of France, that there he would always support me; and my father is a man of honor." I know also that the Empress never ceased to regret having left Paris by the advice of the regency. On this point any blame could rest only upon Joseph and the blind obedience with which Napoleon had habituated his councillors to defer to his pleasure. But the destinies of Maria Louisa were accomplished. Deprived of all hope, she was preparing to quit Rambouillet—whither she had come from Orleans—and to return to Austria with her son, without having obtained permission to see Napoleon once more, as she had often entreated. Napoleon himself seems to have appreciated the painfulness attaching to such a farewell, otherwise he would have expressly stipulated a last interview as one of the conditions in the treaty of abdication. I learned, at the time, that the motive which prevented compliance with the wish of Maria Louisa, was an apprehension lest she should form some sudden resolution of accompanying Napoleon to the island of Elba; and the Emperor of Austria wished to get back his daughter.

At this moment it was not one of the least remarkable occurrences of these last times—so frightful in extraordinary events for the sovereigns of Europe—that the dethroned family and the princes returned from exile to succeed them were all present within a circuit of forty miles from the capital of France. A Bourbon was in the Tuileries—Napoleon at Fontainebleau—his wife and son at Rambouillet—the repudiated Empress only three leagues distant—the Emperors of Russia and Austria, with the King of Prussia, in Paris itself. All this appeared the more marvellous that, only two years before, it would have been pronounced impossible within any given time.

When Francis set out to visit his daughter at Rambouillet, it appeared also not a little extraordinary that Alexander should be of the party. The two Emperors, however, were

not quite together; Francis preceded by a short interval,
and consequently arrived first. The following particulars I
give on good authority: Maria Louisa received her father
with respect, and, at the same time, with affection; she
showed herself happy in meeting him again, but the tears
that streamed from her eyes were not all tears of joy. After
the first effusion of filial tenderness, she complained of the
condition to which she was reduced. Her father, much
moved, had yet no consolation to bestow, for her sorrows
were irremediable. Meanwhile time elapsed; Alexander
must be at hand, and the Emperor was forced to announce
the expected visitor. The first resolution of the ex-Empress
was a refusal, in which she long persisted, saying to her
father, "Will he make me also a prisoner before your eyes?
If he enter here by force, I shall retire to my chamber;
thither, I suppose, he will not dare to follow me in your
presence." Already the sound of Alexander's carriages
echoed through the courts of Rambouillet; as time pressed,
Francis became more urgent in his entreaties; his daughter
at last yielded; and the Emperor of Austria went himself to
his imperial ally, and conducted him into the saloon, where
deference to her father had detained Maria Louisa. That
deference, however, could not carry her the length of vouch-
safing a cordial reception to the man whom she regarded as
the author of all her misfortunes. She received with great
coldness the personal offers and protestations of the Emperor
of all the Russias, giving for answer that she had only one
wish to form—the liberty of returning to the bosom of her
family. Accordingly, a few days after this painful visit,
Maria Louisa, with her son, departed for Vienna; nor was
her resignation without dignity.

Of the illustrious personages at that period in Paris, I
had an interview with Blucher, on the 2d of April; to the
King of Prussia I was introduced some days after; and Bernadotte I saw frequently. "Sir," said Blucher, on entering
my room at the post-office, "I deemed it one of my first
duties in Paris to offer my thanks for your attentions at

Hamburg. I can assure you, had I known sooner of your being in Paris, the capitulation might have been obtained without bloodshed." I requested the marshal to explain. "Mon Dieu! had I been informed of your being here, I would have sent to beg you to come and see me; I would have given you a letter to the King of Prussia, who, I am sure, would have afforded you the means of procuring from the allies a suspension of arms before the environs of Paris had become the theatre of war." I represented the susceptibilities of national character, and the disgrace of delivering up the capital without a struggle. "But, bon Dieu! we would have proved to you that resistance could avail nothing; you had to do with masses."—"In my opinion, general, you are right; but, to the French, honor is everything."—"I grant you," said Blucher; "but have you not had enough of honor? You call us, too," added he, smiling, "notwithstanding our forbearance, northern barbarians!"—"Why, then, general," replied I in the same tone, "the present is an excellent opportunity to prove that the designation is a calumny." For this time nothing belied these good intentions; but things were changed in the following year, when I found Blucher—my Hamburg prisoner—in headquarters at St. Cloud, installed in the very study where I had so often worked with Napoleon, and wherein so many and vast schemes had been meditated!

At the private audience to which soon afterward I had the honor of being admitted by his Prussian Majesty, Berthier and Clarke were also presented. We had been some minutes in the saloon, when Frederick William entered from his closet. I remarked on his countenance some embarrassment and a certain air of severity, which made me think he had just been studying his part—as grand personages are wont to do on similar occasions. Berthier stood nearest and the King addressed him with nobleness and some emotion—"Marshal, I should have preferred receiving you as a peaceful traveller in Berlin to accepting this visit here; but war has its successes as well as reverses. Your troops are brave and ably commanded; but you could not resist numbers. Europe is armed against the Emperor: patience has its limits. Marshal, you have passed no little time making war in Germany; I have pleasure in saying to you that I shall never forget your conduct, your justice and moderation, in those seasons of misfortune." Berthier was not undeserving of this eulogium; for, though devoid of high talent, with a weak character and some follies, he was not a bad man. After receiving the salutations of Berthier, the King of Prussia turned toward Clarke, with symptoms of marked displeasure. "As for you, general, I cannot say the same of your conduct as of the marshal's. The inhabitants of Berlin will long remember your government. You abused victory strangely, and carried to extreme measures of rigor and vexation. If I have an advice to give you, it is, never to show your face in Prussia." It pained me much to hear the King thus address, before two witnesses, a man with whom, indeed, I had never sought to establish intimate relations, but with whom I had been in habits of intercourse on public affairs, and who, though weak by nature, and a flatterer through his weakness, was, as a private individual, an excellent person. Now for my portrait, thought I; for the King, who spoke these words in a strong and angry voice, turning away abruptly from Clarke, did not seem even to hear the few unintelligible words attempted in reply, and then accosted me: "Ah, M. de Bourrienne! [in a tone quite *piano*, as the Italians say], I am very glad to see you; and profit by this opportunity to repeat all I wrote from Königsberg. It is with pleasure I say to you, before these two gentlemen, that if all the French agents had thought and acted as you did, we should not probably have been here." I expressed my sense of so obliging a compliment by a profound reverence, and the King, having again saluted us, retired. Clarke was so overwhelmed by this reception from a crowned head that Berthier and myself, each taking an arm, were obliged absolutely to support him down the grand stair.

Bernadotte had come to Paris a few days after the arrival of the Count d'Artois. His situation was a disagreeable one, since, through the force of circumstances, the conference at Abo had become fruitless, and because certain writers did not spare to represent him as a traitor to his country. Opposite the hotel which he had retained at Paris for the habitation of the princess, his wife, cries might be heard—"Down with the traitor! down with the perjurer!" These threats, however, the effects of a spirit of petty revenge, evaporated in words; but, added to other things, they tended to disgust Bernadotte with Paris, notwithstanding the constant friendship manifested by Alexander, and he set out for Sweden in a few days. During the period of his brief sojourn I saw the Prince Royal daily, and, in testimony of his friendship, received one of the few orders of the Polar Star placed at his disposal by the Swedish government. At first he feebly denied all views on the supreme power in France; but subsequently, our confidential intercourse resuming its wonted character, he confirmed me positively in all then stated relative to the interview and promises of Alexander at Abo. I inquired also of Bernadotte what he thought of the designs attributed to Moreau, and whether he would have had him as competitor in aspiring to the dangerous honor of governing France. He assured me to the contrary; at least, that in all his conversations the Emperor of Russia had never mentioned Moreau save as one of whose military talents he was desirous to avail himself in the impending struggle. Bernadotte, too, expressed his surprise at the recall of the Bourbons, assuring me that he could never have supposed the French nation would yield so soon and so readily to receive them back. I, on my part, felt equal surprise that, with his experience, Bernadotte should have been simple enough to believe that the people go for something in the changes of governments.

Bernadotte returned also in 1815; but as I shall not again have occasion to speak of him, I may just state one fact, the authenticity of which I guarantee. When the Duke of Ca-

dore, as minister for foreign affairs, announced to Napoleon
the election of the Prince to the second grade of royalty in
Sweden, the Emperor remarked—"Ah, ha! so they have
fixed upon him? It is well—quite right: they could not
have made a better choice: I shall not stand in the way of
his good fortune. He must not go away empty-handed—
let him have two millions." An unforeseen circumstance,
however, quickly interrupted this good understanding. The
Crown Prince deemed his new title incompatible with that
of Ponte-Corvo; and Napoleon, who aspired to have all the
kings of Europe dignitaries of his crown, took this, in my
opinion, well-founded scruple in high dudgeon, and, calling
M. de Champagny—"What is all this about?" said he, with
irritation; "what does Bernadotte want? What is this fuss
about his being a Swede—always a Swede? How many are
there of these Swedes? I wish to have done with him and
to hear nothing more of them. M. de Champagny, you will
write to that effect." Two days afterward the Emperor
asked the minister if he had written? "Yes, sire."—"But
have you written fully, as I desired?"—"I believe so, sire."
—"Well, let us see the despatch." This was a demand
which he almost never made. "This is not the thing," said
he, sharply; "it is too mild! I said to you that I desired to
end the affair, and to be no more troubled with these two
or three millions of Swedes." There can be little doubt
that this intimation had some weight in determining Bernadotte's conduct from the campaign of Moscow to the battle
of Paris.

If we cast a parting glance on the wrecks of. the empire
abroad at the period, when its end had been accomplished
in France, we find Italy still occupied by an army of nearly
thirty thousand men, commanded by Eugene. Could Bonaparte have taken these brave and devoted followers across
the Alps, immediately after the fall of Paris, he might still
have effected a powerful diversion on the Austrian side.
But, on the 7th of April, Eugene, being certainly informed
of the irreparable disasters in France, signed, with Marshal

Bellegrade, the Austrian commander, a convention, which, ratified on the 10th, permitted the French troops to retire within the borders of old France. Before taking leave of an army which he had miraculously saved, still numbering twenty-one thousand infantry, and more than five thousand cavalry, Eugene addressed his soldiers in a farewell proclamation, dated from Mantua, where had been his headquarters since the month of February. (Mantua! how many recollections—glorious at once and painful—must that name have recalled. The fall of that town before the science of Bonaparte had been the first feat of arms which the youthful Beauharnais had witnessed; and now, in the same place, he was to bid adieu forever to the army of France, when, nearest to their imperial leader, he had become the second among its chiefs!) "Soldiers! lengthened misfortunes have weighed upon our country. France, seeking a remedy for her woes, *has returned beneath her ancient shield.* The feeling of all her sufferings is already appeased in the hope of a repose necessary after so much agitation. Soldiers! you are about to revisit your homes; it would have proved indeed gratifying to me to have conducted you thither. But, in separating from you, there remain for me other duties to fulfil toward the people of Italy." Upon this, the generals and officers under his command earnestly entreated Eugene, whom they all sincerely loved and esteemed, to lead them in person to the king. But the prince, either overrating his duties to the Italians, or cherishing some hopes that the son-in-law of Bavaria might secure an independent sovereignty beyond the Alps, resolved to await the decision of the allies in the kingdom where he had presided as viceroy. In fact, he attempted some correspondence with the senate of Milan, whose members he believed well disposed in his favor, to induce that body to solicit from the allies his continuance in the government of Italy. But the little inclination entertained for the family of Napoleon was far from being increased by the agent employed. Prina had incurred the hatred and contempt of the Milanese, who heard him only to testify their displeasure. In truth, the army had not made three marches from the headquarters at Mantua when a revolt broke out at Milan. The minister of finance, Prina, was assassinated, and nothing could have saved the viceroy from the same danger had he been in the capital; so highly exasperated were the Italians, always ready to show courage when there is no longer danger, and whose whole patriotism evaporates into being Austrians under a French yoke, and Frenchmen under the dominion of Austria. In this general effervescence, his friends considered the viceroy as fortunate in having been able, almost incognito, to join his father-in-law at Munich. At the same time, General Grenier, second in command, conducted the French army across the Alps. Thus, after nine years' existence, fell the kingdom of the Iron Crown.

In Germany we still retained two important points, Dantzic and Hamburg. In the former, my friend Rapp commanded. After sustaining a year's siege, he found himself constrained to open the gates and deliver up a city which he had defended to the last extremity, and yielded only when his post had become a heap of ashes. Rapp had stipulated that the garrison should be sent into France, and the Duke of Wirtemberg, who commanded the siege, had granted this condition; but the Emperor of Russia refusing the ratification, Rapp, now destitute of all means of defence, was made prisoner, and, with his men, marched off to Kiew. Of the siege of Hamburg I have already spoken. Early in April the Russian general, Beningsen, commanding before the place, informed of the Emperor's fall, hastened to notify the state of things to Davoust, in order to spare the further effusion of blood. The latter affected to discredit a report which cut short all his prospects of greatness, and even fired at the white flag hoisted in the allied lines as a signal that the Bourbons reigned. But, finally, having harangued his troops, told them of Napoleon's forfeiture, and caused them to mount the white cockade, he sent in his adhesion to the Provisional Government. The officers and men collected their *honorably* gathered wealth, converting it into diamonds and other commodities of small bulk and great value. In May, General Gerard arrived, with orders to take the command, and, toward the end of the same month, the inhabitants beheld, with inexpressible joy, the French troops march out of their city, though bearers of much of their property, and leaving to them the remembrance of a government which will be handed down with execration from one generation to another. Once beyond the walls, the various nations composing the garrison corps separated, according to the convention with Soult—French, Dutch, Italians and Poles pursuing their respective routes, never, probably, to be reunited under the same banner—a vain emblem of conquests and of glory that had forever passed away!

Meanwhile the fallen chief, who had been the soul of the mighty system whose last fragments were thus dissevered, remained still at Fontainebleau. But the period of departure was at hand. The 17th of April had been fixed as the day upon which he should set out on his journey for the Island of Elba. Napoleon, having agreed to the arrangements in this respect, demanded to be accompanied to the place of embarkation by a commissioner from each of the allied powers. Count Schuwaloff was sent on behalf of Alexander; Colonel Sir Neil Campbell represented England; General Köhler was chosen by Austria; and Count Waldenburg-Truchsess appeared for Prussia. These four commissioners arrived, for the first time, at Fontainebleau on the 16th, and next day had separately an audience with the Emperor, who still kept with him Generals Drouot and Bertrand.

Although in this audience the Emperor received with great coldness the commissioners, whose presence he had himself requested, considerable differences might be remarked in their respective receptions. Colonel Campbell experienced the most gracious treatment; and, as he still bore the traces of wounds, Napoleon asked in what actions he had fought and upon what occasions he had been decorated with the orders which he wore. Having afterward inquired concerning the place of his birth, and the colonel replying that he was a Scotsman, the Emperor congratulated him on being the countryman of Ossian, his favorite author, whose poems he praised highly, though (I know something of the matter) acquainted with them only through the medium of poor enough translations. In this first audience he said to the colonel, "I have cordially hated the English; I have made war against you by all possible means; but I esteem your nation. I am convinced there is more generosity in your government than in any other. I should like to make the passage from Toulon to Elba on board an English frigate." The Austrian and Russian commissioners were received with indifference, but without any marked displeasure. Not so the Prussian envoy. The two former Napoleon had kept about five minutes; the latter he dismissed in a harsh manner. "Are there Prussians in my escort?"—"No, sire."—"Why, then, give yourself the trouble of accompanying me?"—"Sire, it is no trouble but an honor."—"These are words of course. You can have no business here."—"Sire, it is impossible for me to omit discharging the honorable mission wherewith I have been intrusted by the king, my master." At these words Napoleon turned his back upon Baron Truchsess.

The commissioners supposed that Napoleon would start no difficulties, and depart without delay. But it was not so. Having required to see a copy of the route they were to follow, he objected to the arrangement, either through caprice or from a desire to prolong the time. It was singular that the course marked out was exactly that which he had himself proposed to take, from Toulon to Paris, on returning from Egypt; while the road he now pretended to prefer was the same for which, as the reader will recollect, he changed his original intention, and so caused Josephine to miss us. Again, by a coincidence not less remarkable, the route through Burgundy, as now traced by the allies, was that by which, in the following year, Napoleon marched tò Paris from his exile. But, to leave these curious, perhaps trivial, coincidences, the commissioners, unwilling to oppose Napoleon, whom they had orders to treat with every deference, yet without powers to agree to the change required, postponed the departure, wrote to their respective principals, and, on the night between the 18th and 19th, received authority to travel by such route as the Emperor might prefer, when the departure was finally fixed for the 20th of April.

On that day, by six in the morning, the carriages were in readiness, and the imperial guard drawn up in the grand court of the Palace of Fontainebleau, called the court of the "*White Horse.*" The whole population of the city and adjacent villages had assembled round the palace. Napoleon sent for General Kohler. "I have reflected," said the Emperor to the envoy, "upon what remains for me to do, and have come to the resolution not to depart. The allies are not faithful to their engagements; I can, therefore, recall my abdication, which was merely conditional. More than a thousand addresses were presented to me last night, conjuring me to resume the reins of government. I renounced all my rights to the crown only in order to spare France the horrors of a civil war, never having any other object in view than the glory and happiness of the country; but, aware now of the discontent inspired by the measures of the new government; seeing in what manner they have fulfilled the promises made to me—I can explain to my guard the reasons which have induced me to revoke my abdication, and we shall see if they can seduce from me the hearts of my veteran soldiers. It is true the number of troops upon whom I can reckon will not exceed thirty thousand men; but it will be an easy matter for me to raise them to one hundred and thirty thousand. Know, also, that I can, quite as easily, without compromising my honor, say to my guard that, considering only the repose and happiness of France, *I renounce all my rights*, and expect my soldiers, like myself, to support the will of the nation." These words, which I report from the general's own mouth, threw Kohler into great embarrassment. I remember also to have told him at the time that, had Bonaparte, at the commencement of the campaign of Paris, renounced all his rights and descended to the rank of a citizen, the immense masses of the allies must have sunk under the efforts of France. Kohler stated, also, that the Emperor complained of Maria Louisa not having been permitted to accompany him to Elba; but finally added, "Well! I shall remain faithful to my promise: but if new causes of complaint are given, I shall consider myself freed from all engagements."

Time, meanwhile, wore away. At eleven o'clock one of the Emperor's aides-de-camp, whose name I have forgotten, entered to say that the grand seneschal had desired to announce that all was ready for the departure. "Am I, then, reduced," said Napoleon, "to regulate my actions by the grand seneschal's watch? I shall set out when I choose: perhaps I shall not go at all: leave me." As all those points of imperial etiquette, which he so much loved, were retained, when it pleased him at length to leave his study in order to enter the saloon where the commissioners awaited his approach, the doors were thrown open and "The Emperor" announced. No sooner had the words been pronounced than he instantly drew back. However, his disappearance was but for a brief space; he entered the saloon, crossed the vestibule with hurried step, descended the stair, and, at midday precisely, stood at the head of his guards, as when reviewing them in the court of the Tuileries during the brilliant times of the Consulate and Empire. Then ensued a spectacle which was really touching—the parting of Napoleon and his soldiers. I enter not into details which are known to all. This address to his old companions in arms—his last in the court of Fontainebleau—which he delivered with a firm and sonorous voice, as in the days of his triumphs, belongs to history.

"Soldiers of my old guard, I bid you farewell. For twenty years I have ever found you in the path of honor and of glory. In these last times, as in those of our prosperity, you have not ceased to be models of bravery and fidelity. With men such as you, our cause was not lost—the contest had been interminable; but it must have become a civil war, and France would have been only the more unfortunate. I have sacrificed all my own interests to those of the country. I depart. Do you, my friends, continue to serve France. Her happiness was my sole thought; it will ever be the object of my prayers. Lament not my fate. If I have consented to survive myself, it is that I may once again be the instrument of your glory. I will give to history the great things which we have performed together. Adieu, my children! I long to press you all to my heart!" Having here desired the eagles to be advanced, Napoleon folded them in his arms and added, "I cannot embrace you all, but I do so in the person of your general. Soldiers, farewell! be always good and brave!"

After pronouncing, as the final adieu to his soldiers—"Farewell, my children! my best wishes shall ever accompany you; remember me!" Napoleon entered his carriage with Bertrand. The cavalcade drove off in the following order: General Drouot, in a close carriage with four seats; the imperial carriage; the commissioners of Austria, Russia, England and Prussia, each in a separate vehicle, and successively as mentioned; last came two carriages with the imperial household. Six other carriages, with the rest of the suite, followed by a different road, it having been proved by a report to me, as postmaster-general, that the horses otherwise necessary could not be found upon one road. During the whole of the first day nothing was heard along the whole of the route but shouts of "*Vive l'Empereur!*" and Napoleon, with ill-disguised irony, blamed the impertinence of the people toward their legitimate sovereigns. The guard accompanied him as far as Briaire. From this place he wished to set out during the night; but, notwithstanding my precautions, horses were wanting, and the journey was not resumed before midday of the 21st. A little before setting out he had another conversation with General Kohler, during which he said to him, among other things,

"Well! yesterday you heard my address to my soldiers; it pleased you, I understand; and you witnessed the effect it produced. Such is the manner in which they must be spoken to and treated; if Louis does not follow the same example, he will never make anything of the French soldiers."

While things continued to manifest the public opinion favorable to him, Napoleon conversed freely with the commissioners: but he always treated the Prussian envoy with least cordiality. All these particulars I know from subsequent conversations, and from daily reports transmitted to me at the time. He made no secret to Colonel Campbell of the motives whence this coldness proceeded, namely, that Prussia had shown the first example of desertion in the Russian campaign. At Briaire, the colonel having been invited to breakfast, the Emperor conversed with him on the Spanish war, and spoke in high praise of the English nation and the military talents of the Duke of Wellington. Yet, on the 21st, Napoleon must necessarily have been informed of the battle of Toulouse. In this conversation Napoleon broke out into reproaches against the senate, and expressed a desire that the funds which had been taken from him should be disbursed to the army.

In reference to this, I may introduce here some details on the imperial treasury. Napoleon, as I have mentioned, had amassed in the vaults of the left wing of the Tuileries a sum exceeding three hundred millions of francs. Of this more than forty millions were in gold. A great portion of this enormous sum disappeared during the campaign of France: great surprise was occasioned by the sudden circulation, in January, 1814, of a vast quantity of five-franc pieces, quite new, though with the date 1806. The Emperor had loaned from the imperial treasury sixty millions to the annuity fund, and forty millions to the consolidated duty fund; he had, besides, purchased a large share in the Bank of France. On the 31st of March there were found in the treasury only twenty-eight millions, of which ten were re-

claimed. In the confusion, too, the Provisional Government resumed what had been loaned; so that, in fact, the
administration, though debtor to the imperial treasury, constituted itself its creditor, and so balanced accounts. It was
of these transactions that Napoleon complained, and justly;
for whatever opinion might be entertained of the system
which thus, by forced means, hoarded up the greater proportion of the circulating medium of continental Europe;
or by whatever means the money might have been acquired;
it was now personal property, and in good faith not liable
to the law of reprisal—a savage code at the best. Even the
sums taken by the Empress to Blois were charged against
the treasury as fraudulent abductions. Those who acted
thus, in opposition to the faith of treaties, saw not at the
time that they were providing the only just pretext for
future disturbance.

On the 21st, Napoleon slept at Nevers, where he was
still received with acclamations by the people, who, as in
various other cities, mingled in their applause imprecations
against the commissioners of the allies. He set out again at
six next morning, but, beyond this, ceased the cheering
welcome; for, being no longer attended by the guard, which
Cossacks had now replaced, Napoleon had the mortification
of hearing *The Allies forever!* substituted for *The Emperor!*
At Lyons, however, which he entered in the night, and
where he merely changed horses, the favorite cheer arose
from a few scattered groups around the post-house.

Augereau, from first to last a republican, though made
Duke of Castiglione by Napoleon, had always been among
the malcontents. On the dethronement of the Emperor he
was one of a very considerable body who became royalists,
not from love to the Bourbons, but from hatred of Bonaparte. He commanded at this time in the south, and was
among the first to send in his adhesion to the Provisional
Government. Violent in all things, as uneducated men
always are, Augereau had allowed to be published, under
his name, a proclamation than which nothing could be more

rough or insulting, even to grossness, against the Emperor. Whether Napoleon was or was not informed of this proclamation, it is impossible to say; but this much is certain, that on the 24th, upon meeting Augereau at a short distance from Valence, he feigned to be ignorant of all, if not really so, and stopping his carriage, hastily alighted. Augereau did the same, and they embraced in presence of the commissioners, from one of whom I had these details. It was remarked that Napoleon took off his hat, while Augereau affectedly remained covered. "Where art thou going?" asked the Emperor, "to court?"—"No; at present I am on my way to Lyons."—"Thou hast behaved very badly toward me." Finding Napoleon used the familiar second person singular, Augereau assumed the same liberty, and they conversed as when both generals in Italy: "Of what hast thou to complain?" replied the latter; "hast not thy insatiable ambition brought us to the condition in which we are? Hast thou not sacrificed everything to it—even the welfare of France? 1 care no more [the term used had greater energy still] for the Bourbons than for thee: I think of my country alone." Such was Augereau's discourse, as he himself reported it to me. Upon this, Napoleon suddenly turned away from the marshal, took off his hat to him and returned to the carriage. The commissioners, and all those composing Napoleon's suite, were indignant at seeing Augereau remain in the road with his hands behind his back, keep a travelling cap on his head, and merely acknowledge the Emperor's courtesy by a disdainful wave of the hand. It should have been in the Tuileries (and there who more obsequious!) where this ought to have been the bearing of these haughty republicans: on the road to Elba such behavior was low-bred insolence.

At Valence, Napoleon beheld, for the first time, French soldiers with the white cockade in their caps: they belonged to Augereau's corps. At Orgon the air resounded with cries of "*Vive le Roi!*" Here the gayety, real or assumed, which Napoleon had shown throughout the whole of his journey, began to forsake him. Few cries of any kind had been heard for several stages, when, at the last post-house from Avignon, while fresh horses were getting ready, a person in a peasant's dress, but whose fine shoes and silk stockings strangely contrasted with such rude habiliments, and still more remarkable by his gold-branched spectacles, came up to the carriage. He had crossed the fields in all haste; and, getting upon the shoulders of another individual, leaned in at the window, as if endeavoring to recognize some one. He was reminded of his improper behavior by the Emperor's valet, and requested to retire; but paying no attention to this intimation, an attendant seated outside significantly showed a pistol, when he took the hint and moved off, apparently before his strange curiosity had been gratified.

Had Napoleon arrived at Avignon three hours later than he did, unquestionably it would have been all over with him; but the rioters were not astir at five in the morning, and the escort did not even change horses in the city. About an hour afterward the Emperor, tired of the carriage, alighted, and with Colonel Campbell and General Bertrand, walked up the nearest hill. His body servant, also on foot, was a few paces in advance, when he met a post-office courier who said—"These are the Emperor's carriages coming up there?"—"No, they are the equipages of the allies."—"I tell you they are the Emperor's. You must know I am an old soldier, and not so easily deceived. I served in the campaign of Egypt, and wish to save the life of my general. I have just passed through Orgon; the Emperor is there hung in effigy, and, should he be recognized, he is a dead man. The miscreants have put up a gallows, and suspended a figure dressed in a French uniform smeared with blood, and bearing this inscription on the breast: 'Thus shalt thou be one day.' I know not how it may fare with me for giving this information: but I care not—profit by it." The faithful courier then set off at a gallop. The valet took General Drouot aside and repeated what he had just learned. Drouot informed Bertrand, who

communicated the statement to the Emperor in presence of
the commissioners. These gentlemen, justly alarmed, held
a sort of consultation on the highway, and it was decided
that the Emperor should set out first. The valet-de-chambre
being asked what clothes he had in the carriage, produced
a long blue cloak and round hat. It was proposed to place
a white cockade in the latter, but to this Napoleon would
not consent. Thus disguised, he set out as a courier with
Amaudru, one of the lancers who escorted the carriage, and
once more eluded the good people of Orgon. When the
commissioners arrived they found the whole population of
the surrounding country assembled and shouting, "Down
with the Corsican! Down with the brigand!" The mayor
of Orgon, whom I had seen almost on his knees before General Bonaparte, on our return from Egypt, addressed Pelard,
one of Napoleon's valets-de-chambre—"Do you, sir, follow
that rascal?"—"No, I follow no rascal; I am attached at
present to the commissioners of the allied powers."—"Ah!
you do well; he is a great scoundrel. I would hang him
with my own hand. If you knew, sir, how we were cheated
by that thief. It was I who received him on his return from
Egypt. We wished, forsooth, to take out the horses and
draw his carriage; I would now avenge myself for the honors
which I rendered him on that occasion." The crowd increased visibly, vociferating with that fury by which the
inhabitants of the south manifest either their joy or hatred.
Some of the most infuriated wished to force the imperial
coachman to call out "*Vive le Roi!*" Upon his courageous
refusal more than one sabre was raised, when, fortunately,
the horses being harnessed, in an instant the postilions
started off at a gallop.

The commissioners would not stay to breakfast at Orgon,
but, paying for what had been ordered, they carried away
something to eat on the way. The equipages did not overtake the Emperor before reaching Calade, several stages in
advance, where he had arrived with his attendant about a
quarter of an hour previously. He was then standing by

the fire in the kitchen of the inn, chatting with the inn-
keeper's wife. At that moment she was asking him if the
tyrant would pass soon. "Ah! master," she went on, "it
is all nonsense talking; we have not done with him yet. I
am always for what I said before—we shall never get rid
of him till he be at the bottom of a well with stones over
him: I shall never be satisfied till I have him so pickled in
our yard. You see, sir, the Directory sent him to Egypt,
thinking to have done with him; but no! he came back
again; and back he will come now, you may be certain sure
of it, unless—" So far the good woman had her say, when,
having finished skimming her pot, on looking up she perceived that the only person who had not his hat in hand was
precisely the one to whom she had been thus speaking. She
stood in amazement; but her compunction for having spoken
in such terms of the Emperor to the Emperor himself banished all her wrath, which was speedily replaced by an
equal ebullition of kindness. There was no sort of attention or respect which she did not lavish upon everybody,
from Napoleon down to Amaudru. An express was instantly despatched to Aix for white ribbons to make cockades; she had all the carriages drawn within the courtyard,
and every entrance to the inn barricaded, and even disclosed
to the Emperor that it would not be prudent to pass through
Aix, where twenty thousand people were waiting to stone
him.

In the midst of all these disquieting transactions dinner
was served, and the Emperor seated himself at table. So
admirably did he maintain control over the agitation which
must necessarily have been internally experienced, that all
present at this strange entertainment who have spoken to
me on the subject declared that never had Napoleon played
the agreeable with greater success. The rich stores of memory and imagination which he displayed charmed every one;
and, as if throwing in the remark carelessly at the close,
he said—"I really begin to think the new government entertains a design upon my life: come, let us see how we can

foil the attempt?" Then, as if he had sought to exercise his ever active fancy, in which a thousand schemes were constantly crossing and succeeding each other, he fell upon contriving how they should avoid the threatened assassination at Aix. Again, for a moment, he would return to Lyons. Once on the borders of the Rhone, he would descend that river, take ship, and embark for Italy. These dreams occupied him but for a moment; stern necessity broke in upon his illusions, as some suppose it does upon our agency, and he prepared to continue his journey.

Meanwhile, many sinister faces were seen assembling about their present lodging, when the commissioners began seriously to consider what was to be done at Aix. While they deliberated about sending a messenger to the mayor of that city, a man from the crowd without, who would not give his name, requested to speak with the commissioners, and offered himself to be the bearer of their letter. This proposal was accepted, and a note written to the mayor, in which the commissioners stated that, if the gates of the town were not shut within an hour, they would pass, with two regiments of Uhlans, and six pieces of artillery, and fire upon all that should molest their passage. This menace produced its proper effect, and their unknown messenger returned with the assurance that the magistracy of Aix would be responsible for all consequences within their own jurisdiction. But urgent danger still threatened at Calade; the numbers outside the inn had greatly augmented during the seven or eight hours which the retinue had remained, and showed sufficiently to what excess they were ready to proceed if the entrances had not been carefully secured. The majority had five-franc pieces in their hands, bearing the head of the Emperor, whom, by this resemblance, they hoped to discover. At this moment Napoleon, who had not slept for two nights, was in a small apartment off the kitchen, and dozing on the shoulder of one of his valets. He was roused by the announcement that all were ready to start; but it had been previously understood that he should assume the cloak and bonnet of General Köhler's courier, and mount the box of the Austrian commissioner's carriage. The rightful owner of the habiliments happening to be almost twice the size of their temporary wearer, the Emperor, buried rather than concealed in his disguise, passed safely through two lines of *curious* observers, who looked in vain for the original of their five-franc pieces.

In a moment of despondency, at Calade, Napoleon said to those around him, "I renounce, now and forever, the world of politics. I will no longer take any part in whatever may happen. At Porto Ferrajo I can live peaceably; there I shall be happier than I have ever been. No! were this day the crown of Europe to be offered me, I would not accept. I will busy myself in study—with the sciences and mathematics. You have sufficient evidence what the people are— I have done well never to esteem mankind. My treatment of them has been better than they deserved. Yet France! —the French!—what ingratitude! I am disgusted with ambition; I have no longer a wish to reign!"

Napoleon having reached his own carriage in the manner just mentioned, the retinue drove off and passed round the walls of Aix—the gates being closed—without entering the city. The Emperor thus avoided the danger which had threatened, but did not escape altogether from the insults of the multitude. A part of the populace had got upon the walls and trees, whence a glimpse of the carriages could be descried, and his ears were again wounded with the cries, "Down with the tyrant! Down with Nic!" These ignoble vociferations were heard for the first quarter of a league from the town. About three miles from Aix were found horses and an escort of gendarmerie as far as the Castle of Luc.

At a little distance from Luc, in a country house belonging to M. Charles, a member of the legislative body, the Princess Pauline Borghese then resided. Informed of her brother's misfortunes, which she had hardly conceived it possible for him to survive, she resolved on accompanying him to Elba. Her presence was a source of great comfort amid the Emperor's tribulations; and she attended him to Frejus, in order there to embark in his company. At Frejus the Emperor found Colonel Campbell, who had quitted the escort on the road and had arranged for preparing in the harbor an English frigate, intended from the first to convey the Emperor. Notwithstanding the desire expressed by himself to that effect, Napoleon showed much reluctance to embark in the English vessel. At length, however, on the 28th of April, he set sail for Elba in that frigate, which now no longer bore Cæsar and his fortunes.

CHAPTER XXXIII

Louis XVIII. and his Ministers—Confusion at the News of Napoleon's Return —Escape of the King and Bourrienne—Madame de Staël

THE force of time is the most irresistible of all forces. We have seen it elevate and we have seen it overthrow the sovereign of half of Europe. Turn we now to his successors.

During the winter of 1813–14 some royalist proclamations made their appearance in Paris, and as they contained the germs of the charter, were carefully intercepted by the police. My family and myself devoted several hours each day to reproducing copies of these documents. But for some time the royalists could only cherish hopes. At length, as we have seen, Bordeaux received within its walls a son of France, and, on the 25th March, 1814, sent two of its citizens to invite within the same protection Louis XVIII. I know the King had resolved to accept this homage, and was preparing for his departure, on board a frigate, when the events of the 31st changed these dispositions. Leaving his retreat, he was received in London by the Prince Regent, on the 18th April, with all the ceremonial due to his rank. From the period of the Emperor of Russia's final declaration, an active correspondence had been maintained with the Provisional Government, and on the 24th of April,

Louis landed at Calais from the "Royal Sovereign," a
British man-of-war. The King slept at Amiens; next day,
at Compeigne, the Provisional Government, the ministers and marshals tendered the assurance of their respective homage and fidelity. Berthier spoke for the marshals
and the army. At Compeigne, too, the Emperor Alexander
met Louis XVIII., and the two monarchs dined together.

For my part, I did not go to Compeigne, the orders
which I had constantly to give not permitting me to be
absent, but was at St. Ouen on the 2d May, when the King
arrived. Here, when his majesty entered the saloon through
which he was to pass to dinner, M. Hué recognized me,
and apprised the King, who, advancing some steps toward
me, said, "Ah! M. de Bourrienne, I am most happy to see
you. I know the services you have rendered me, both in
Hamburg and in Paris. I have pleasure in expressing my
gratitude." We shall see. At St. Ouen, Louis XVIII.
promulgated the declaration which ushered in the charter.
Here, too, the Senate presented a draft of the "Constitution"; and to maintain, *in extremis*, its title of *Conservative*,
that body stipulated for the *conservation* of all its endow-
ments and pensions.

On the 3d of May Louis XVIII. made his entrance into
Paris, the Duchess d'Angouleme being in the same carriage.
There was not the same enthusiasm as when Monsieur entered. The people looked on in amazement. This coldness
became still more apparent a few days after, when he established the red corps, which Louis XVI. had abolished before
the Revolution. It was, moreover, deemed by all a most
strange proceeding to remit the direction of affairs to M.
de Blacas, who could know absolutely nothing of France.
This gentleman, too, affected an omnipotence quite ministerial. On the morning of the 11th May, I had gone to the
Tuileries to present my portfolio to the king, in virtue of
my privilege of being immediately under the sovereign.
M. de Blacas would needs receive my portfolio. I resisted,
and pleaded my right of immediate access to his Majesty:

he told me it was by order of the King. Of course my
papers were then resigned to him. I soon fell a victim
to the vengeance of a courtier. Two days after this affair
I had, as usual, repaired early to my room in the post-office,
and mechanically unfolded the "Moniteur," which lay upon
my desk. What did I read there? that Count Ferrand had
been appointed to the office of postmaster-general in my
stead. Without even an intimation! not a single line in
writing! no decree! no ordonnance! In very truth, I fell
a-rubbing my eyes, thinking it must surely be a dream.
Sic vos non vobis afterward recurred to me when, on account
of services and devotion to the cause of the Bourbons, I was
especially excepted from the deed of amnesty by Bonaparte.
On recollecting what had happened between Blacas and myself, I had no doubt whence the blow proceeded. The day
following that on which I had been thus expelled from office
appeared in the "Moniteur" the first ministry of Louis, thus
organized: Talleyrand, foreign affairs; Abbé Montesquieu,
home department; Abbé Louis, finance; General Dupont,
war; M. Malouet, admiralty; M. de Vitrolles, secretary of
state; M. de Blacas, master of the household, with a seat
in the council; and finally M. de Beugnot, for the police.
Of these eight, six had been recruited from the imbecility
of France. This was soon proved; from one end of the
kingdom to the other nothing was heard but complaints
against the measures of government. From every region
crowds upon crowds of courtiers were to be seen at the
Tuileries, mendicants for rewards, in virtue, it is to be
presumed, of the vows they had secretly put up for the
royal cause in the antechambers of the imperial court! The
Legion of Honor was absolutely put to the hammer; whoever could but contrive to show that he had worn an epau-
let, metamorphosed himself at once into colonel; and the
smallest sprig of the smallest gentility became sir count,
or my lord marquis, at least. The abuse of an institution
which had wrought prodigies was one of the greatest evils
of the first restoration.

Ridicule, meanwhile, had assailed the restoring the usages of the ancient régime under every shape. The satirist had here a wide field; for example, my successor, M. de Ferrand, was in the habit of saying, "Why, the charter may be a good sort of thing, but what possible dignity can it have when it was not registered by the parliament of Paris?" Really, I can yet scarcely think myself awake when reflecting on the miraculous incapacity of the people who managed our affairs after Talleyrand's removal to the congress at Vienna, whither he repaired in September. Everybody then would be and thought himself a statesman; and heaven knows what pranks the scholars played in absence of the master! The emigrants, as has been so aptly said, neither had forgotten nor had learned anything, and showed themselves with all the old pretensions and absurd vaunting. The greater part of these vain and silly personages might have served as counterparts of the character in one of Voltaire's novels, who goes about constantly exclaiming, in answer to everything, "*A man such as I!*"

From the month of December I had sure indications of an approaching catastrophe. Hortense, I knew, had been so busily intriguing at Plombières that Eugene, who intended to join his sister at the waters, hearing of, and not caring to be involved in these intrigues, had formed a different resolution, after his horses, carriages, and an aide-de-camp had already arrived. Friends, too, on both sides of the question, participated or enjoyed these apprehensions, while each added to my information. Proposals even were made directly to me of "titles, riches, honors, if I would range myself among the friends of an old friend." One of my intimations referred to a man afterward unfortunately but too conspicuous. "Yesterday," said my friend, one, too, entirely attached to the royal cause, "I met Charles de Labédoyère: you know how intimate we are. I remarked a strange agitation on his part. I asked him to dine with me, but he declined because we should not be alone, but begged me to dine with him to-day. We conversed long on the present posture of affairs, and you may be sure, as usual, did not agree. There is, however, a compact between us; we dispute—say a hundred ridiculous things, and still remain the same good friends as before. But what gives me real uneasiness is that, on parting this evening, Charles wrung my hand, saying, 'Courage, my friend—farewell! to-morrow I am off for Grenoble. Within a month you will hear of Charles de Labédoyère!' "

My conviction of an approaching crisis had become so strong that, in the month of January, I resolved to solicit an interview with M. de Blacas, certainly not with the intention of compromising any one, but to place the results of my information at the minister's disposal. Let me then be permitted a brief excursion into the region of absurdity; the reader will barely be able to conceive a union of such fatuity and self-conceit: M. de Blacas received me not. What was I in comparison with a *man such as he?* I enjoyed, however, the signal honor of seeing his secretary; and, if the circumstance merits remembrance, he was a churchman, by name Abbé Fleuriel. What a study for a comic poet! Abbé Fleuriel was the Adonis, the beau-ideal of self-satisfied impertinence! How vast a share he had of the dignity which befits the great secretary of a great minister; and how pretty, too, when he said, with the most careless grace, "My Lord the Count is not at home!" But three mouths such as his would have been required to add full volume to the words, "My Lord the Count," such inflation did he seem inclined to give them. My Lord the Count *was* at home; I knew it. But will it be believed?— the Abbé—the secretary, requested to be informed of my business with the minister! I turned my back upon the coxcomb, without deigning to reply, and left the place amazed to find the affairs of France confided to such hands. Devoted, however, to the cause of the Bourbons, and things appearing serious, I wrote on the same day to M. de Blacas. No answer. Two days after, although with regret, I wrote that I had something most important to communicate. No

answer. Unable to comprehend the cause of this inexplicable silence, I returned to the Pavilion of Flora, and besought the charming Abbé Fleuriel to explain, if so be he
might, the cause of his master's impertinent silence. "Sir,"
replied the sable penman, "I received both your letters; I
laid them before my Lord the Count; I do not know why
he has not replied to them. I can do nothing in the matter:
but my Lord the Count is so engaged! my Lord the Count
has so many affairs! my Lord the Count cannot attend to
all!"—"My Lord the Count will repent of it, perhaps," said
I. "Good-morning, sir." I may just conclude this affair
by stating that after the second restoration I again encountered the Abbé at the Tuileries. He expressed regret that
I had not been admitted by M. de Blacas; but, unwilling to
alter his tone, he had the assurance to repeat—"But really,
if you had known how he was engaged!"—"M. Abbé,"
said I, "there can be no doubt of the count's engagements.
We may judge of them from his works."

I had thus experience, in my own person, of the truth
of what had been reported to me of M. de Blacas. This
minister had succeeded Count d'Auvray, and enjoyed the
unlimited confidence of the king, centring the whole power
in his cabinet, and so monopolizing the royal favor that even
the most esteemed servants of Louis had first to apply to
M. de Blacas. As for him, upon any one giving salutary
advice, he would say, with imperturbable self-sufficiency,
"Who? that man? pshaw! he is an intriguer—a Bonapartist
—a visionary—an alarmist—a grumbler. I do not wish to
hear him mentioned." And the man with good advice was
fairly bowed out.

Seeing that nothing could be done with M. de Blacas,
I wrote to M. de Talleyrand, then at Vienna; and, as he
corresponded directly with the King, I make no doubt that
my communications reached his majesty through this channel. But time had been lost while events hurried on; and,
before Louis XVIII. had clearly learned his danger, it was
too late to take effectual precautions.

The circumstances of the return of Bonaparte are known to all, and may be read in various publications; I shall, therefore, forbear any recital of that inconceivable enterprise. As for myself, so soon as I was informed of the rapidity of his advance upon Lyons and the enthusiasm with which he was received by the army and the people, I prepared to set out for Belgium, there to await the close of this new drama. My arrangements were completed on the evening of the 13th of March, and I was on the point of commencing my journey when a special message from the Tuileries conveyed the King's pleasure that I should repair thither immediately. This order occasioned me no inconsiderable alarm, but I did not hesitate to obey. Being introduced, the King addressed me with great kindness, but in a tone very expressive of his meaning—"M. de Bourrienne, can we count upon you? I expect all from your zeal and fidelity."—"Your majesty shall have no cause to complain that I betray your confidence."—" 'Tis well; I am about to re-establish the prefecture of police, and appoint you prefect. Go, M. de Bourrienne, do for the best; I confide in you." It was singular enough that, on the 13th, while the King in Paris thus placed me in office, Bonaparte, at Lyons, signed a decree excluding Talleyrand, Marmont, myself, and ten others, from the general amnesty.

In the first moment I had listened only to my zeal for the royal cause, and accepted; but reflection on the responsibility and small chance of now being serviceable in my office, I confess, filled me with alarm. My apprehensions were not diminished on witnessing the proceedings of the council, which was held that night in the Tuileries in the apartments of M. de Blacas. The ignorance of our real position then manifested by the ministers surpasses all belief. These great men of the state, with all the means of power and knowledge in their hands—the telegraph, the post-office, money, the police and its innumerable agencies—absolutely knew nothing of Napoleon's march, and asked me to give them information. I could, of course, only report what I had collected on 'Change or picked up here and there during the last four-and-twenty hours. I did not conceal that all their precautions would be vain. This brought on the discussion how to dispose of the King? where was he to go? One proposed Bordeaux, another, La Vendée, a third, Normandy. At length, one high in authority gave his voice for Melun. "If it comes to blows," said I, "that is the most likely place for the engagement." I was answered that the appearance of the King in his carriage with eight horses would rouse a marvellous enthusiasm among the soldiers! "Do not think of resistance," said I; "not a soldier will draw a trigger. Defection among the troops is inevitable; they amuse themselves, and get drunk in their barracks with the money which, to purchase their fidelity, you have distributed among them within the last few days; but do you know what they say? I will tell you —'He is a good enough sort of person, Louis XVIII.; but, huzza! *the little corporal forever!*'"

On the first news of Bonaparte's landing, the King had sent an express for Marmont, then at Chatillon, whither he had gone to receive his mother's last sigh. The marshal had counselled Louis to remain in Paris, and to shut himself up with his household—about five thousand devoted and honorable men—in the Tuileries, capable of sustaining a siege. This design he supported by stating that the effect produced by the rapid advance of Napoleon from the Gulf of Juan would be more than counterbalanced on the public mind by the spectacle of an aged monarch defending himself in his palace. I was of a different opinion, and proposed Lille as the nearest and most secure, consequently, in the state of things, the best refuge. It was past midnight before the council broke up without coming to any determination, though, when the time came, Lille was selected for the King's retreat.

On being introduced into the royal cabinet, after the few words already noted, Louis asked what I thought of the situation of affairs? "Sire, I think Bonaparte will be here

in five or six days."—"How, sir?"—"Yes, sire; in five or
six days."—"But measures are taken, orders given, and the
marshals are faithful to me."—"Sire, I suspect no one's
fidelity; but I can assure your majesty, since Bonaparte has
disembarked, that he will be here in less than a week. I
know him, and your majesty does not know him so well as
I; but, sire, I dare to assure your majesty that he will not
be here six months: he will commit excesses which will be
his ruin."—"M. de Bourrienne, I augur more favorably
of events; but if misfortune decree that I must again leave
France, and if your second prediction be accomplished, you
may rely upon me." During this conversation the King
appeared calm and resigned, showing that philosophy which
springs from a peaceful conscience, tempered by adversity.

On the morrow I repaired again to the palace, and received an order to arrest five-and-twenty persons according
to a list given. I attempted to show the nullity and mischievous tendency of this step, but in vain; some abatement
was made in favor of twenty-three, who were to remain under
surveillance, but the first two were absolutely to be arrested
—namely, Fouché and Davoust. The King more than once
repeated—"I desire that you cause Fouché to be arrested."
—"Sire, I beseech your majesty to consider the effect."—
"It is my especial pleasure that you arrest Fouché; but
I am sure you will fail, for André could not succeed." I
dared not disobey an order so express; not a moment was
to be lost. Arrangements made, my agents presented themselves at the hotel of the Duke of Otranto. On exhibiting
their credentials—"How!" exclaimed Fouché, on glancing
it over, "this warrant is null—it is good for nothing; it purports to come from the prefect of police, and there is no such
functionary." In my opinion Fouché was right; for my
nomination having taken place during the night, the appointment had not yet been officially announced. On his
refusal to follow these my underlings, a party moved off to
the headquarters of the National Guard to obtain assistance.
Desolles, the commandant, repaired in his turn to the Tuil-

eries, to get fresh powers from the King. During these comings and goings, Fouché retained all his coolness; conversed with my agents, and, feigning to enter a closet, which opened upon a dark passage, left my unfortunate myrmidons bewildered in the midst of darkness, slipped away, gained the street, got into a hackney coach and drove off. So ends the famous history of Fouché's arrest. As to Davoust, he was my personal enemy; I therefore only placed him under surveillance.

These orders were given on the 15th; the same day I called upon M. de Blacas; and after some conversation on the best manner of securing the King's safety, asked him what previous information he had obtained of Bonaparte's departure from Elba. "The only thing which we knew positively," replied the minister, "was by an intercepted letter, written from the island of Elba, on the 6th of February, addressed to M. ——, resident in Grenoble; but I can show it you." He then took from the drawer of his writing-table the original letter, which I read. The writer thanked his correspondent for information which had been sent to the *inmate* of Elba. Afterward, the letter went on to state, that all was prepared for the departure; that the first favorable opportunity would be seized for that purpose, but before finally determining certain inquiries must be answered. Then followed questions upon a great many details —what regiments had been sent into the south—the place of their cantonment; whether the officers had been appointed, as agreed at Paris; if Labédoyère was at his post—concluding with a hope that the correspondent would leave nothing to desire in his replies on these important points. The communication was long, and struck me as containing all requisite information respecting the intended landing on the coast of Provence; on returning it, therefore, I could not help saying to M. de Blacas—"That letter, methinks, gave sufficient warning; what was done?"—"I immediately caused the letter to be copied, sent the copy to M. de André, that he might give the order to arrest the individual to whom it had been addressed." And this was all that had been done to counteract a conspiracy of this nature. The evil, however, was for the present irremediable; though I had no fear for the future: the momentary resurrection of the empire had, indeed, become inevitable, but only for a moment. My friends will bear witness that I constantly maintained Bonaparte would not remain six months in France. In recalling him men did not wish the individual whom they thus recalled; they acted not from love to his person; nor was it from faithfulness to the remembrance of the empire that a portion of France embraced its cause anew: it had become the general desire, at whatever price, to shake off those inane counsellors who conceived they might treat France as a country conquered by and for the emigrants; Frenchmen desired to rescue themselves from a government which seemed resolved on treading under foot all that is dear to France. In this state of things some hailed Bonaparte as a liberator, but the greater part regarded him merely as an instrument; to this latter class belonged, especially, the old republicans, united with whom were those of the new generation who had hitherto beheld liberty only in promises, and were blinded enough to believe that this idol of France would be restored by Napoleon.

But let us pass in brief review the circumstances and designs which had wrought this consummation, so far as respected the return of Napoleon. During the commencement of 1815 events in Italy, from the state of the rest of Europe, had not attracted much attention. These events, however, considered relatively to the gigantic plans long meditated by Napoleon, and now about to be attempted, were of vast importance. All was yet so complicated, and, in the congress, advanced so slowly, that a local occurrence might exercise an extensive influence over the general affairs of the Continent. In the month of February, when all arrangements were now completed for the departure from Elba, Murat requested permission from the court of Vienna to conduct, through its provinces of Upper Italy, an army destined for France.   On the 26th of the same month, Napoleon left his island prison.   These two facts have necessarily a close connection with each other.   Unquestionably, however extravagant, Murat never could have conceived it possible to obtain, by force, from the King of France, the recognition of his claim to the throne of Naples.   His occupying that kingdom had never been regarded save as a usurpation at the court of the Tuileries; and I know that the French plenipotentiaries at Vienna had special instructions to insist in congress on the restoration of the Two Sicilies to their ancient sovereign, as a consequence of the restoration of the crown of France.   I likewise know that this demand was strongly resisted on the part of Austria, whose government has never viewed, without extreme jealousy, three European thrones occupied by the single house of Bourbon.   Murat, therefore, was well aware of the part he might play in France, by there supporting the conspirators and the views of his brother-in-law.   Thus he daringly advanced to the banks of the Po, leaving his country and his capital exposed, and incurring by this movement the hostile resentment of both Austria and France.   It is incredible that he would have acted thus, unless previously assured of a powerful diversion and the assistance of Napoleon in his favor.   There is a possibility, indeed, that Murat contemplated securing himself in Italy, while the whole powers of Europe should be engaged anew with Napoleon; but both suppositions lead to the same conclusion—that he was a party to the enterprise of Bonaparte.   Murat, however, thus acting rather like an adventurer than a monarch, having failed in an attack against the bridge of Occhio-Bello, was constrained to retreat, and his ill-advised expedition ended by ruining the grand cause in which it was intended to co-operate.

· The plans and intentions of Napoleon, again, as conceived in the island of Elba, were as follows, and I guarantee the authenticity of the details now given:—Almost immediately after his arrival in Paris, he was to issue directions to his

most devoted marshals to defend, to the last extremity, the
entrances of the French territory and the approaches to
the capital by manœuvring within the triple line of fortresses which girdle the northeast frontier. Davoust was
set apart for the defence of Paris, while there was a stone
to defend; he was to arm the populace of the suburbs, and
to have, besides, twenty thousand of the National Guard at
his disposal. Napoleon, not knowing well the situation of
the allies, did not believe they could unite and march
against him so speedily as they did in the sequel. He
hoped to anticipate and counteract their dispositions by
causing Murat to march upon Milan, and by arming Italy.
The Po once passed, and Murat approaching the capital of
Italy, Napoleon, with the corps of Suchet, Brune, Grouchy,
and Masséna, aided by troops sent to Lyons, was to cross
the Alps and revolutionize Piedmont.   Having recruited
his army from among the insurgents, he was to join the
Neapolitans at Milan, there proclaim the independence of
Italy, united under a single chief, and afterward march at
the head of one hundred thousand men upon Vienna, through
the Julian Alps—a route by which victory had already
guided him in 1797. This was not all. Numerous emissaries, dispersed over Poland and Hungary, were there to
foment troubles, awaken thoughts of liberty and independence, in order to spread disquiet through Austria and
Russia; and we were to have beheld Europe freed, out of
revenge for not having allowed herself to be enslaved by
Napoleon. It would have been a solemn but singular spectacle; nor is the thought without grandeur that such a man,
in such a place, cherished these schemes.

As the means of success in these bold manœuvres and
mighty combinations, Napoleon had calculated upon assuming the initiative in military operations. For my part, never
had I beheld his geinus more fully developed than in this vast
conception—which was not matured in one day. This design, in fact, comprised the essence of all he had ever aspired
to accomplish—embraced all the great enterprises which he

had meditated, from the first of his fields to his latest hour
on the imperial throne. The final object alone was changed
—from empire to liberty; but success would, in all likelihood, have restored the original plan of selfish ambition.
According to this scheme his line of operation extended
over a basis of five hundred leagues, from Ostend, by the
Alps and Italy, to Vienna. He would thus have secured
immense resources of every kind, would not only have prevented the Emperor of Austria from marching troops against
France, but have probably constrained him to terminate a
war of which the hereditary estates supported the whole
burden. Such were the alluring prospects unfolded before
the imagination of Napoleon when he set foot upon the deck
of the vessel that bore him from the rocks of Elba to the
shores of France. But the reckless precipitation of Murat
roused Europe to an attitude of preparation, and the brilliant illusion faded like a dream.

Upon the attempted execution of this great enterprise,
it is unnecessary to enter; how troops, sent against their
ancient leader, served only to swell his triumphant escort,
is known to all the world; how his eagles flew from tower
to tower, has been repeated to satiety. These were the visible effects of the secret resolutions now for the first time
explained. I may mention one thing not generally known,
though it may be readily conceived—that after hearing of
the decree promulgated at Lyons, I little cared that he
should catch me at Paris. On the other hand, the duties
of office detained me, and I had resolved not to quit my
post before the royal family should be in safety. I need
not say with what distressful feelings, during March 19 and
20, I witnessed their departure, or how sad a spectacle is
the palace of a king at the moment when he is constrained
to leave it. After assuring myself that all was tranquil, and
that no danger existed so far as the princes were concerned,
I set out alone at four in the morning, taking the route for
Lille, so fully was I persuaded that the King had followed
the northern road. Nothing extraordinary marked my prog-

ress before reaching Fins. Here I found a great number of carriages stopped for want of the means of conveyance. I had entered more than once the public room and asked the postmaster for horses. "Wait your turn," very gruffly said the man in authority; then added, "Do you come from Paris?"—"I just passed through; I come from Sens."—"Anything new in Paris?"—"Nothing, so far as I know."—"An express has just passed; he will be there this evening."—"Who?"—"Pooh! You do not know? Bonaparte."—"No! Indeed?" I could not exactly tell what to make of his conversation, when the postmaster quitted the room rather mysteriously. Thus left to my own by no means pleasing cogitations, I had stuck myself up as if eagerly perusing a large proclamation in Russian and French, fixed against the wall. It was one I had procured, while post-master-general, from the Czar, protecting all post-horses from military requisition. "Sir," said the postmaster, who now entered, "you see there an order which saved me from beggary."—"You would not then surely do any injury to him who signed it?"—"God forbid!—I knew you from the first—you served me in a just matter, which had brought me to Paris when you were our head—I have this moment been out on your account; your chaise is at the corner of the garden with the only pair of horses remaining; my son is to act as postilion, and will not spare the spur." The postmaster was true to his word, for I observed the private signal of haste transmitted from one postilion to another, and by an hour after midnight of the 21st found myself before the gates of Lille. They were shut; but a wretched lodging was obtained in the suburbs, which I entered with a sense of happiness, surpassed only by the felicity of quitting it next morning.

On the 23d the King, who, after all, had adopted my opinion, arrived at Lille. As a consolation for my own mishap I found his majesty had scarcely fared better at the gate. I placed myself among those who waited his alighting at the hotel. No sooner did he perceive me than, extending his hand, the King said, "Follow me, M. de Bourrienne." I had the honor of sitting down to table with his majesty, but the breakfast was a melancholy one. The events of the time formed the subject of conversation, and all viewed them in a sombre light. Berthier, also present, partook largely in the general depression. I alone seemed to have any confidence, and ventured, as in the Tuileries, to predict "that most likely within three months the King would be on his return to his kingdom." Berthier continued biting his nails as usual, and his majesty, giving me plainly to understand, by his manner, that he put down my observation among the flatteries to which he was accustomed, replied—"Monsieur Bourrienne, when I am king, you shall be my prefect of police." We shall see. The kindly answer gratified without deceiving me. It soon appeared that Lille was no place for the King: the Napoleon fever had seized the troops in the garrison; even the guard showed evident symptoms of having caught the infection. Nor, it must be confessed, ought there to have been matter of surprise in the fact that the soldiers of the old army showed discontent, sacrificed as they were to constantly recurring arrivals of the ancient servants of a monarchy of which they recked not; nor that they hailed the return of him whom they had so often followed to victory and honor.

Yielding to the entreaties of his faithful friends, Louis, therefore, left Lille on the third day after his entrance; but the resolution was taken with regret, and not till Marshal Mortier, who commanded under the Duke of Orleans, and whose conduct under difficult circumstances merited the highest praise, had stated that he could no longer answer for his soldiers. The King removed to Ghent. In the preceding September he had named me chargé-d'affaires at Hamburg. On the point of departing beyond the soil of France the King conceived that my presence in the north of Germany would prove useful to his cause. I therefore set out immediately, and without reluctance, for a place where I had many friends. Though thus removed from the immediate theatre of events, I continued to be informed of all important transactions.

Bonaparte entered Paris on the 20th of March, at eight o'clock at night. Nothing could be more dismal than this entry. The darkness was increased by a thick fog. The streets were deserted, and on every countenance might be read an expression of vague alarm. The white standard, torn down in the morning from the Tuileries, had been replaced by the tricolored flag; but the former ensign still floated above most of the public buildings of Paris. Even throughout the day numbers of the military continued to display the white cockade. Not one appeared to greet Napoleon on his passage till he had arrived at the entrance to the Tuileries, where, in the vestibule and in the Pavilion of Flora, his intimate confidants had assembled, and conducted him to his apartments.

Two hours after my departure—that is, at six in the morning of the 20th—Madame Bourrienne also left Paris for a place of safety about twenty miles distant. At nine on the same morning an individual devoted to Bonaparte, with whom, however, I never had any intimate correspondence, sent an emissary to my house, requesting to see Madame de Bourrienne. My sister-in-law replied to the envoy and was strictly questioned respecting my absence. This envoy stated at the same time that, above all things, I ought to avoid following the King; and, if I returned quietly to Burgundy, the great personage whom I do not name, but whom the reader will perhaps divine, would answer for my pardon with the Emperor. Twelve hours after—when Bonaparte arrived—a lady also called upon my wife; my sister-in-law again went to meet her in the garden, without a light, that they might not be observed, and through a piercing cold, for the temperature seemed in unison with the transactions. She was accompanied by another lady, who, on the night preceding, had been at Fontainebleau to see Bonaparte and had been charged with a message for me to remain at my post as prefect of police and to fear nothing, as pardon was

certain.   On the morrow General Berton came to assure
Madame de Bourrienne of the same amicable relations and
to induce me, whom they supposed concealed in Paris, to
appear.   Though sensible to these instances of friendship, I
never for a moment regretted having left Paris.   At this
time, too, I obtained information which, afterward followed
up, enabled me to discover the real motive of Bonaparte's
hatred, namely, that he suspected me of a correspondence
with London.   This I found had arisen from a General Van
Driesen having mentioned my name in a letter to the King,
at Hartwell, as the person who, at Hamburg, had dictated to
him a draft of a royal proclamation, which I certainly did,
because, then a royalist at heart, I found he was likely to
ruin the cause by injudicious publications.   This had come
to the Emperor's ears—for he had agents about the King at
Hartwell whose station placed them above suspicion and
who thus knew the most secret matters transacted there.
The report, however, had been greatly exaggerated, and I
do not know, for certain, that he had now discovered his
mistake; but I am persuaded, had I remained in Paris, that
Napoleon would have given no serious evidence of his displeasure.   He was irritated, however, by my absence or supposed concealment, and six emissaries were sent to my house
to examine and seal my papers.   Their harsh investigations
gave great trouble to Madame de B. and my family.   They
even searched the pockets and ripped up the lining of my
old clothes for papers.   I was not the man, however, to be
so caught: before my departure I had taken precautions
which set my mind at rest; and they had their labor for
their pains.

But not only upon men able to bear the evils of flight
and exile did persecution fall; women, whom a system of
tricks, unworthy of the Emperor, had formerly condemned
to expatriation, had now to fear new severity.   The beautiful Madame de Chevreuse, who had been banished for having had the courage (then a rare quality, even among the
nobler sex) to say that she was not made to be the Queen

of Spain's jailer, died of a broken heart, in the arms of the Duchess de Luynes, her mother-in-law. The illustrious exile of Coppet, on the Emperor's return, was in a state of health little capable of bearing up against any sudden and violent emotion. This had been brought on by her flight from Coppet to Russia, immediately after the birth of her son, the issue of a private marriage with M. Rocca. Under these circumstances she saw no other means of safety but in renewed exile. This, indeed, was not a long one; but Madame de Staël never recovered from the effects occasioned by its anxieties and fatigues. The authoress of "Corinne" naturally recalls to my mind her most faithful friend, Madame Récamier, who was herself not secure against the severity of Napoleon. She did not, indeed, fly from Paris in 1815, though she had returned in 1814 only through the force of events, and without her exile having been revoked. That exile was pronounced in a singular way. Madame Récamier paid frequent visits to Madame de Staël at Coppet: irritated more and more by such intercourse, Napoleon ordered Fouché to intimate, on the last of these occasions, that Madame Récamier was perfectly mistress of her motions in going to Switzerland, but not so in returning to Paris. "Ah! sir," replied she, to the minister, "a great man may be pardoned the weakness of loving women, never that of fearing them": and Madame Récamier departed for Coppet.

CHAPTER XXXIV

The Hundred Days—Waterloo—Reinstatement of Louis XVIII.—Rapp and Napoleon—Bourrienne, Minister of State—Conclusion

TO RETURN to the epoch denominated the Hundred Days. It is worthy of remark that Bonaparte, on attaining the consulate, passed exactly a hundred days in the Luxembourg before his installation in the Tuileries. If I did not see Paris at this latter era, my correspondence sufficiently proved to me, and the information has since been confirmed by even the partisans of Bonaparte, that never since the excesses of the Revolution had the capital been so mournful and gloomy as during these three months of agony. None had confidence in the duration of this second reign. It quickly became the general opinion that Fouché, in supporting the cause of the usurper, was secretly betraying it. Throughout the whole mass of society fears of the future agitated men's minds, and discontent was at its height. The sight of the federates traversing the suburbs and Boulevards, shouting "Long live the Republic!" and "Death to the Royalists!"—their sanguinary songs—the revolutionary airs performed in the theatres—all threw a sort of stupor over the mind and an impatient anxiety as to the issue of these alarming events.

One circumstance which, at the commencement of the Hundred Days, tended most directly to open men's eyes, still dazzled by the reflected light of Napoleon's past glory, was the non-fulfilment of the boasting promises that the Empress and his son were to rejoin him immediately.

This clearly showed that he could not count upon a single ally; and it would have been blindness, indeed, notwithstanding the prodigious activity which reigned in the military preparations, to suppose that he could triumph over the whole of Europe, then evidently arming afresh against him. When the first news of Bonaparte's disembarkation was received at Vienna the congress had made but slender advances toward the final arrangement of affairs. The members of that high assembly considered themselves as laboring in the reconstruction of an enduring and desirable order of things, and proceeded with that wise caution and maturity of examination indispensable to the accomplishment of this object, especially after a period of agitation by which all interests had been more or less displaced. The plenipotentiaries, on hearing of the landing in the Gulf of Juan, signed a protocol of their conferences. This was supposed, but erroneously, to have been drawn up by M. de Talleyrand.

There had been another, which, chiefly through his instrumentality, operating by means of M. de Labrador, minister of Spain, had been rejected as too undecided. This first protocol, or declaration of the 5th May, being set aside, that of the 22d was adopted, which consisted in adhering to the Treaty of Paris. The following letters on these details were addressed to me by M. de Talleyrand:

"*Vienna, 19th April,* 1815.

"Every account that reaches me from the interior of France proves that Bonaparte is there in the greatest difficulty. All confirms that the immense majority of the nation is against him; that, in truth, he has no one on his side save the army; and that, even of the troops, the new levies are far from being devoted partisans. The southern provinces have not submitted to his authority. There the Duke d'Angouleme continues to maintain his position. His troops increase daily. He has advanced with them upon Lyons, and by my last news that city is declared in a state of siege. On the other hand, troops are advancing to the frontiers with the utmost celerity. Throughout, military operations are commencing with the greatest energy and activity. The Russian troops, which were upon the Vistula, have arrived in Bohemia four days sooner than was expected, and will reach the Rhine at the same time with the Austrian levies. Toward the middle of May, it is hoped, active operations will be begun, and the immensity of means assembled must completely remove all fear as to the issue of events. The King, of whom I had news yesterday, is still at Ghent, and well, full of courage and hope. The Duke d'Artois is at Brussels. The army of the Duke of Wellington, nearly eighty thousand strong, is concentrated near Mons. Great unanimity prevails between the Duke of Wellington and General Gneizenen, commanding the Russian troops. Murat conceiving that, while the allied powers were engaged against Bonaparte, he should find few obstacles in Italy, advanced to the Po, but has failed in his attack at Occhio-Bello, and retreated. Since then the Austrian troops, who are receiving daily reinforcements, have obtained some advantages over him on the side of Modena."

Another letter of 5th May, after blaming my long silence, continues thus:

"Since my last, you must have learned that the Duke
d'Angouleme has found it impossible to maintain his position in the south, as we had hoped. France, then, for the
moment is wholly under the yoke of Bonaparte. Hostilities
will not commence for some time, it being the design to
attack upon many points at once, and with great masses.
The most perfect unanimity prevails as to military measures
among the allied powers. The war against Murat continues
with a success that bids fair to render it of brief duration.
He has successively demanded two armistices, which have
been refused."

The following letter refers to the proceedings of the
congress, and is otherwise very important:

"M. DE BOURRIENNE—Bonaparte, subsequently to his
arrival in Paris, having first denied the authenticity of the
declaration of the 13th March, and afterward endeavored
to weaken its effect by different publications, some persons
here thought that it would be useful to publish a second.
The congress desired this question to be examined by a
commission, whose report was presented on the 12th current (May). That report, while it confirms the disposition
manifested by the powers in the declaration of the 18th
March, refutes the sophisms of Bonaparte, exposes his im-
postures, and concludes that his position with regard to
Europe being neither changed by the first success of his
enterprise, nor by the offer which he made to ratify the
Treaty of Paris, a second declaration is in no respect necessary. In the full verbal report hereupon published by the
plenipotentiaries it will be remarked that Europe is not represented as making war for the King and at his solicitation,
but that she declares war on her own account because her interest requires and her safety demands it. This is the exact
truth; and it is also the proceeding most suitable in reference
to the King and most favorable to his cause. Were they to
believe in France that the war is carried on solely for the
interest of the King, his subjects would behold in him the
author of the disasters which it will occasion. Such an
opinion could only have one effect—to alienate their feelings from his majesty and incline them to embrace the party
of Bonaparte. On the other hand, from the manner in which
the war is now represented, it is Bonaparte alone to whom

these evils can be attributed, a fact of which it is most important to convince all, especially in France.   Receive, etc.
"THE PRINCE DE TALLEYRAND."

Within less than a month after the reception of the above, these wise arrangements had decided the fate of the contest. During the interval I was kept informed of the military events as they took place; but these are known to all the world.   I shall make one or more extracts from a portion of my correspondence on less generally known topics.

"I have just learned," says my correspondent, the Marquis de Bonnay, "that Berthier has fallen from a window in the fourth story of the Castle of Bamberg.   There can be no doubt that he threw himself down.   You will ask me why? You will quote to me what he asseverated to you at Brussels, namely, his invariable attachment to the cause of the King.   But know we what he did afterward?   The German gazettes announced his being under observation; they related to us how he had attempted to enter France in disguise: are we sure that he had not compromised himself by some correspondence which had been seized?"

"I have the certainty," writes the marquis again, "that Fouché sent, as his secret agent, to Vienna, M. de M——, who made the following propositions, to which the subjoined answers were returned: 'Do not make war, and we will rid you of the *man*.'—'Well, begin by getting quit of him.'— 'Will you have the King of Rome or a regency?'—'Neither.' —'Will you have the Duke of Orleans?'—'No.'—'Well, if it must be Louis XVIII.—very well; but no nobles, no priesthood, and, above all, no Blacas.'—'Begin by getting rid of the *man* and his whole generation.'   I am much delighted to hear you say that the Duke of Orleans was sounded at Paris, and rejected all advances made to him. May God keep him in this good opinion.   I know not if you be aware that, last year, in passing through Paris for Sicily, his first visit was to Madame Genlis.   He remained with her till late at night, and then afterward told one, who informed me, that in recalling the past they had shed many tears together.

"Turkey has joined the universal crusade.   Bonaparte must needs be greatly touched by the love which Europe bears toward his person!—Thus far had I proceeded in my letter, when the arrival of an express informed me of the successful attack of the 16th, which appears, in fact, to have commenced on the 15th. I cannot conceive how the Duke of Wellington had allowed himself to be taken unawares. He set out from Brussels on the morning of the 16th June, to make a reconnoissance, and, if he had taken the right road, must have found them at it, not six leagues from his hotel. The Prince of Orange deserves much praise for having sustained the shock, and repulsed, *with great loss*, says the despatch, Bonaparte and his eighty thousand men. You will dispense with my tears for the Duke of Brunswick, who was good for anything only on the field of battle. After to-morrow I expect details. An officer who had left Paris on the 4th of June, and had trusted to his memory, not wishing to take with him any papers, gave to the Duke of Wellington all the details desirable on the force and distribution of the French army. A calculation, founded on inferences from this information, makes the troops of the line two hundred and seventy-seven thousand, and the national guard from one hundred to one hundred and fifty thousand. The infantry good and in fine order; the cavalry bad and naked; the light artillery better than could be expected; and, the best card in Bonaparte's hand, five hundred pieces of cannon. The fortified places in bad condition and imperfectly provisioned, except Lille; Valenciennes and Condé held by the national guard and by old soldiers who have renewed their service. Ah, sir! it is a great stroke to have overset the first enterprise of that man. A letter from M. de Staël, of date 2d May, states that Bonaparte cannot stand, and that France is divided between two parties: one for the republic, of which Benjamin Constant is the soul, the other for Monsieur the Duke of Orléans. This latter is the hope of all those who are too deeply engaged in late transactions ever to expect employment under the King."

My prediction was at length accomplished. The battle of Waterloo had thus opened the gates of France to Louis XVIII. The moment that information arrived of his having quitted Ghent to enter his kingdom, I also set out from Hamburg, making all possible haste, in the hope of reaching Paris in time to receive the King. On the 7th July I alighted at St. Denis, and, spite of intrigue, found an immense multitude eager to offer the homage of their congratulations. St. Denis, in fact, was so filled, that with the greatest difficulty I found a small apartment in a garret, by way of lodging. Having assumed my uniform of captain of the National Guard, I immediately repaired to the palace: the saloon was filled, and, in the crowd come to felicitate their sovereign, I found my own family, who, not knowing I had quitted Hamburg, were agreeably surprised. The Parisians were eager to salute their King, but stratagem was used to keep them at a distance. Paris was declared in a state of siege, and for four days Fouché contrived to remain master of the capital. At this time two things were attempted to be imposed upon Louis—the tricolor and Fouché: against the former he stood firm; but the nomination of that fatal man appeared inevitable.

On the 7th July the King was informed that Fouché alone could facilitate his entrance into Paris; that he alone had the keys; that he alone could direct public opinion. The value of these assertions could easily be estimated when it was found that the presence of the King became the first and sole bond of concord and unanimity. Every day might be seen groups of the better classes assembled under the windows of the King's apartments, giving themselves up to rejoicing and rendering to the royal family each day a holiday. The very appearance of joy and security displeased Fouché. His vile stipendiaries insinuated themselves amid these groups, threw corrosive liquids upon the ladies' dresses, committed indecencies, and mingled the seditious cry of " *Vive l'Empereur!* " with the loyal acclamations of " *Vive le Roi!* " By the aid of these miserable manœuvres Fouché triumphed and contrived to have it believed that he was the only man capable of preventing those disorders of which he was, in fact, the sole author. Fouché likewise obtained support from a very high quarter: Wellington was the influence which restored Fouché. Of the extent of that influence I felt well aware, though I did not at first believe it capable of supporting such an anomaly as Fouché, minister of the Bourbon. But I soon discovered my mis-

take. On the 8th of July, 1815, the principle of a privy
council, composed of the Bourbon princes and others afterward to be named, to surround the throne of Louis, was
determined; and subsequently his new treasury appointed
as follows: The Prince de Talleyrand, foreign affairs; Baron
Louis, finance; the Duke of Otranto (Fouché), police;
Baron Pasquier, chancellor; Marshal Gouvion St. Cyr,
war; Count de Jacourt, marine; Duke de Richelieu, master
of the household; Marshal Macdonald, to the satisfaction of
all, succeeded the Abbé de Pradt as chancellor of the Legion
of Honor. And my office, so frequently promised and under
circumstances so singular, was given to another—M. de Cazes
was made prefect of police. This I owed to the appointment
of Fouché; for how could I possibly serve under a minister
for whose arrest I had once issued a formal warrant?

Two days after these arrangements I called upon Blucher,
established, as I have already said, in the palace of St.
Cloud, in order to thank him for preserving my house from
pillage. After the usual compliments, "Who would have
predicted," said Blucher, "that, after having been your
prisoner, I should become the protector of your property?
You treated me well at Hamburg; I can now return the
favor at St. Cloud. God knows what may be the result of
all this; one thing is certain, that this time the allies will
enforce conditions which shall remove all fears of danger
for a long while to come. The Emperor Alexander is unwilling to make the French pay too dear for the evils they
have inflicted upon us. He attributes them to Napoleon;
but Napoleon cannot pay the expenses of the war—and pay
some one must. It might pass for once; but we will not be
brought back a second time at our own expense. Of one
thing I can, however, assure you, you will lose none of your
territory. The Emperor Alexander has several times repeated to the King, my master, in my presence, 'I honor
the nation; and I am resolved that the French shall retain
their ancient borders.' " Taking advantage of this communicative disposition, I made some remarks to Blucher on the

excesses committed by his troops. "What would you have me do? I cannot have an eye everywhere; but I assure you, for the future, on your recommendation, I shall cause to be punished severely all disorders that fall under my notice." Spite of these fine promises, however, his troops continued to give themselves up to the most revolting excesses. The Prussian troops have, consequently, left in the environs of Paris a remembrance as odious as that which is retained of Davoust's corps in Germany. Of this a singular instance fell under my own observation. In the spring of 1816 I was going to Chevreuse, and stopped to feed my horse at a village inn. I sat myself down on a seat near the door, beside the proprietor of the tavern. A large dog began a-growling, when his master, a respectable-looking old man, called out, "Will you be quiet, Blucher!"—"What a name," said I, "to give a dog!"—"Ah! sir, it is the name of a rascally ——, who did us much mischief last year. You see my house; there are the four walls, and that is all. The scoundrelly Prussians left me nothing. We were told they came for our good—but let them return! I am old, but have sons; we will track them at every turning of the woods, as we would so many wild boars." Still the dog kept growling —my host every now and then interrupted his discourse to call louder, "Quiet now, Blucher!" I looked in upon his house; it was, as he had said, denuded of everything, and tears filled the old man's eyes as he related his misfortunes.

Before his flight to Ghent the King had shown himself so condescending as to promise his signature to the marriage-contract of one of my daughters. The day appointed was precisely the fatal 19th of March; the signing, as may well be supposed, did not take place. In the month of July I renewed my request, and as my future son-in-law was only a lieutenant in the navy, the severe etiquette of the court required that the signature should be affixed at a petty levee; and it was even talked as if the new monarchy would be compromised by doing otherwise! The King, however, resolved to sign at a grand levee. The reader may laugh, but I frankly confess this little triumph afforded me no small pleasure.

Soon after this domestic incident the King named me councillor of state; and in August, having resolved on convoking a new Chamber of Deputies, appointed me to preside in the electoral college of my native department of the Yonne. Upon this nomination I called upon M. de Talleyrand to receive my instructions. The prince stated that, conformably to the intentions of the King, I must see the minister of police. "Absolutely," was my reply, "I cannot see Fouché; you know our relative positions."—"Go," said M. de Talleyrand, "go to him—you may be sure Fouché will say nothing of past occurrences."

My repugnance to this step is not to be described. I found Fouché, at nine in the morning, walking in his garden in the most complete deshabille. He was alone, and received me as an old and intimate friend whom he had not seen for a long while! This ought not to be matter of surprise—so well could he bend his hatred to the exigency of his position; he never once alluded to his arrest, and the reader may be assured such was not the subject upon which I wished to turn the conversation. I asked for instructions on the elections at Yonne. "On my word!" said Fouché; "I have none to give; get yourself elected if you can. Endeavor only to keep General Desfournaux at a distance; otherwise it is all the same to me."—"What is your objection, then, to Desfournaux?"—"The ministry dislike him." I was preparing to take leave—"You are in a great hurry," said Fouché; "stay a moment." He then turned the conversation upon the Bourbons in a way which I dare not mention: asked me how I could so easily resolve to support their cause? I replied, "That I wished to see France rescued from military despotism, and only aided in a restoration which I had long foreseen and ardently wished. I have the conviction," added I, "that Louis XVIII. will finally recognize the necessity of a constitutional government—the only one possible in France."—"Thus, you think the French unanimous in favor of the Restoration?"—"I believe the majority to be favorable."—"You know not, then, that a moral opposition to the government of the Bourbon dynasty manifested itself in all the departments from the very first months of their return? The old partisans of the republic and the agents of Bonaparte went about diffusing their opinions that the Bourbons would return with superstition and the emigration. I can show you a hundred reports to that effect. You know that whatever was attempted by the government for a whole year tended but too well to exhibit its real disposition. Has there ever been an opposition more direct against the interests and glory of a nation? and that relapse, so decided toward the past, did it not at the time impress every one with fearful apprehensions for the future? The royalists of 1815 have shown themselves exactly as they were in 1789. In all the important acts of 1814 a total oblivion was put upon the events that had intervened, and upon the march of progress. The egregious folly has been committed of wishing to force a people, enlightened by time, to forget its knowledge and to create for itself other truths. It was attempted by main force to cause a retrogression, and to put all to the hazard, that the present might decide upon all the past in favor of these antiquated notions. This inexplicable conduct gave us occasion to say that we had placed a counter revolution upon the throne. Again the same measures are in prospect; but I am here, and will oppose with my whole might. We must terminate the grand contest of the Revolution, which is not yet ended, after twenty-five years of overturnings and of lessons lost upon inexperience: the nobility and the clergy go for nothing everywhere, save in La Vendée. Not a sixth part of the French would place themselves under the ancient régime, and I pledge myself that not a fifth of the nation is frankly devoted to the legitimate authority. You pretend to be ignorant that, in 1814, the French declared themselves loudly for a foreign prince—for the Duke of Orléans—and for a regency: very well, there is not one foreign prince whom the constitutional party would not have preferred receiving at the hand of the Alliance, because, in such a case, the constitutionalists could have demanded, as the condition of submission, that the rights of the people should be upheld. I can assure you that, among the constitutional party, there would have been but one exclusion insisted upon—that of the family of our old kings. After this, surely, you would not rank one man of that party among the supporters of the Bourbons!"

Thunderstruck on hearing such language from the mouth of a minister of the crown, I answered Fouché—"I am, doubtless, far from approving of the system followed in 1814, and none blamed it more loudly than myself; but you will permit me to say that I cannot, with you, see those evils with which superstition and the emigration are about to deluge France. Unquestionably there will still be faults; there will be men incrusted with antiquated ideas, but time will, by degrees, remove these. On the contrary, I think there may be remarked a progressive feeling of attachment in favor of the dynasty of the Bourbons: the number of their partisans augments daily. Patience; there must be laggards in the march of civilization, as in the train of a victorious army. Illumination of the mind, like the light of day, must dawn gradually. There are no improvements which I do not desire, but I would not have them precipitate; and am therefore convinced that the Bourbons alone can, by little and little, establish true public liberty. You, I willingly grant, must be the better informed of the various tendencies of the public mind; but the agents who transmit to you these reports look with their own eyes upon the things of which they speak; and you know men too well not to be aware that they view matters through the prism of personal opinion. If all these reports on the state of France be correct, our situation would be deplorable; for from complaints the people will pass to menaces; from menaces to violence; attempts will be made to overthrow what at present exists; and there will infallibly result a civil war. From such a consummation may God preserve us!"

Fouché listened to me very attentively, mused for a moment, passing his long fingers across his pale forehead, and then replied—"I conceive you are in error; but the civil war will come: you may depend upon it that, in more than sixty departments, only a handful of royalists would oppose the mass of the people. The royalists would prevail in an eighth of the departments, and in the rest would be constrained to silence."—"But, if I understand Your Grace, you do not seem to think it possible that the Bourbons can remain?"—"I do not tell you my opinion," replied Fouché with an ironical smile; "but you may draw what conclusions you like from my words: that is to me a matter of absolute indifference."

I seized the moment to break off this most extraordinary interview, and, further, considered it as a sacred duty to lay the whole before the King. No Blacas any longer monopolizing access to the royal presence, I demanded and obtained a private interview with Louis; and, by aiding the prompt dismissal of Fouché, enjoyed the satisfaction of repairing at least one of the evils inflicted by the Duke of Wellington upon France. Fouché had, in fact, so completely betrayed the cause which he had previously pretended to serve, and Bonaparte knew this so well, that, during the Hundred Days, while they were discussing, in his presence, the King's ministry at Ghent, some one said, "But among all these I see no minister of police!"—"Eh, parbleu!" interrupted Bonaparte, "that's Fouché's place."

Soon after my interview with the King, I set off for the elections at Yonne, and had the honor of being returned representative for that department to the Chamber of Deputies. On revisiting Paris, I was profoundly affected to observe the government recur to measures of severity to punish errors which it had been better policy to attribute to the misfortune of the times. No consideration shall ever prevent me from giving tears to the memory of Ney, who, in my opinion, was the victim solely of certain foreign interferences. His death was conceived to be a means of dis-

abling France, and, for a length of time, incapacitating her
for undertaking anything, by enlisting against the royal
government the army of the Loire, who thus mourned
its best beloved chief, and one who had so often led on its
squadrons to victory. I have no positive proofs on the subject, but, in my opinion, the blood of Ney was the requital
of that gratitude which Fouché conceived he owed to the
foreign influence whereby he had been raised to the ministry. The reader will not have forgotten what Blucher said
to me of the determination to weaken France.

Toward the end of August I had the lively satisfaction
of meeting Rapp, whom I had not seen for a very long time.
Rapp was not of the number of those generals who betrayed
the King on the 20th of March. He told me he remained at
the head of his division at Ecouen, under the orders of the
Duke de Berri. "How did Napoleon receive you?" inquired I. "You know," answered he, "what sort of fellow
I am—a perfect ignoramus in politics: I waited till he sent
for me; I had taken my oath to serve the King; I acknowledged no other service, and would have fought against the
Emperor."—"Bah!"—"Yes, my good friend, and so I told
him."—"How! did you venture?"—"Without doubt: I
told him the revolution was a forced one. ''Sblood,' replied he, with somewhat of anger, 'I knew you were before
me; and, if we had come to blows, I would have sought
you out on the field of battle.'—'I would have shown you a
Medusa's head,' answered I.—'What! would you have fired
upon me?'—'Unquestionably,' said I.—'Ah! parbleu! that
is too much,' cried he; 'but your soldiers would not have
obeyed you; they retained all their affection for me.'—
'What could I do?' replied I: 'you had abdicated; you had
left France; you yourself had engaged us to serve the King,
and, afterward you return! And then, to speak frankly, I
augur no good of what has happened: wars, still more wars!
France has had more than enough of war already.' Upon
this," pursued Rapp, "he assured me he had other views;
that he wished no more war, but desired to govern in peace,

and to occupy himself exclusively with the happiness of his people. When I objected the hostility of foreign powers, he told me he had made alliances. He afterward spoke to me of the King—how I liked him. I answered that I had every reason to be satisfied. In the course of conversation, the Emperor extolled highly the conduct of the Duke of Orléans. Afterward, he related the occurrences of his passage from Elba and journey to Paris; complained of his being accused of ambition; and, as at this word I allowed a peculiar expression to escape, 'How! am I then ambitious? Look!' tapping his belly with both hands, 'can a man so fat as I be ambitious?' Then devil take me if I could help saying, 'Ah! sire; your majesty is surely quizzing me.' He pretended to speak very seriously; and, some minutes afterward, remarking my decorations, began to banter me on the Cross of St. Louis and of the Lily, which I still wore."

I conversed with Rapp about the enthusiasm said to have been shown on the route traversed by Napoleon, after his landing. "Why," said Rapp, "I was not there more than yourself; but all those who accompanied him have since confirmed the truth of the details as published; only, I think I remember to have heard Bertrand relate that, in one circumstance, he had some fears for the Emperor's life, had any assassin appeared. It was while approaching toward Paris from Fossard, where the Emperor had breakfasted. Napoleon's escort were so fatigued that they had fallen behind, so that he was left almost alone, when a squadron, then in garrison at Melun, came out to meet and escort him to Fontainebleau. On the whole route, from what I was told, he appears to have incurred no real danger."

We began afterward to talk of the existing state of affairs; and I asked my friend how he found himself situated; for the condition of the generals who had commanded divisions of the imperial army in the campaign of Waterloo was very different from what it had been in 1814. "I had resolved," said Rapp, "to live in retirement, to take no part in anything for the future, nor even to put on uniform.

I had thus never put my foot within the Court of the Tuileries since the King's return, when one morning, about eight days ago, riding out along the avenue of Neuilly, I observed one from a group of horsemen, on the opposite side, advance toward me. It was the Duke de Berri. I had merely time to say, 'Is it you, my lord?'—'Doubtless it is I, my dear general; and since you will not come to us, I must needs come to you; breakfast with me to-morrow morning.'—*Ma foi!*" continued Rapp, "what could I do? he said this with so much kindness that I could not refuse. On the morrow I went, and was so well received that I shall return; but I will never ask anything. If only these scoundrels of Russians and English—!"

The reader is aware of my nomination in August to be councillor of state; on the 19th of the following month I was appointed minister of state and member of the privy council. I shall be pardoned in concluding with a circumstance flattering to me on this latter occasion. The King had desired M. de Talleyrand, as president of the council of ministers, to present to his majesty a list of those persons who should compose his privy council. Having looked over this list, he said to the minister—"But, M. de Talleyrand, I do not see here two of our good friends, Bourrienne and Alexis de Noailles."—"Sire, I thought their nomination would appear to them much more flattering by coming directly from your majesty." The King then added my name to the list, and afterward that of Count Alexis de Noailles. Thus the two names are to be found in the original decree in the handwriting of Louis XVIII.

Here ends what I have to say of the extraordinary and often fantastic events whereof I have been a spectator, or wherein I have taken a part, during the course of an exceedingly agitated career, of which all that now remains to me is—the recollection.

THE END

Milton Keynes UK
Ingram Content Group UK Ltd.
UKHW020615050124
435507UK00005B/62